LICE FICER XAM

TH EDITION

Donald J. Schroeder, Ph.D.
Adjunct Professor,
John Jay College of Criminal Justice
Senior Instructor,
REMS Tutorial, Exam Preparation Specialists
Former Commanding Officer,
81st Police Precinct,
New York City Police Department

Frank A. Lombardo
Deputy Inspector (retired),
New York City Police Department
Adjunct Professor,
John Jay College of Criminal Justice,
Former Commanding Officer,
30th Police Precinct,
New York City Police Department

CONTENTS

Preface

Since the first edition of *How to Prepare for the Police Officer Examination* was published, tens of thousands of police candidates have used it to prepare for police officer examinations throughout the country. In addition we, along with others, have used this Barron's book exclusively and with great success in various courses given to help prepare candidates to take the entrance examination for both large and small police departments. Feedback from police candidates all over the country indicates that so much of the success they have experienced in taking police entrance examinations is directly attributable to this book. But you, the candidate, must understand that, while this book can be the vehicle that can help you earn your gun and shield, unless you make the required necessary effort to study and learn its contents, you are cheating yourself.

Just about every police department requires that a newly hired employee interested in working his or her way up the ladder must begin at the very bottom of the organization. We did just that and quickly ascended the civil service ranks of the New York City Police Department. This book contains many of the successful strategies we developed during our study for police examinations. However, we would like to share with you something else we learned that cannot be disputed: SUCCESS IN THE WORLD OF CIVIL SERVICE TESTS REQUIRES DEDICATION AND HARD WORK. If you are willing to pay that price, we are confident that this text can help you and you will be successful. Good Luck!

Donald J. Schroeder
Frank A. Lombardo

Acknowledgments

Our thanks to the New York City Police Department for permission to reprint the Patrol Guide material, the Legal Division bulletins, the Department forms, and the Operations orders used throughout this publication. Our thanks, also, to the New York City Department of Personnel for permission to reprint official New York City Police Department Examinations.

CHAPTER 1

About the Police Officer Examination

The Purpose of the Test

The type of examination that is administered throughout the country to select qualified men and women for careers in the police field has been greatly modified over the past few years. As a result of a Supreme Court decision a number of years ago, test writers are not permitted to use certain kinds of questions. For example, questions cannot be asked which require prior knowledge of the law, police procedures, or the duties and responsibilities of a police officer. You are not required to know what a police officer is to do under certain circumstances such as if he or she arrives at the scene of a robbery. That is the kind of knowledge you acquire after you are admitted to a police academy.

The procedures and questions used in this book were written after a continuous and careful analysis of recent major police officer examinations and all court cases dealing with police entrance level examinations. This chapter will serve to familiarize you with the contents of this manual so that you will be able to fully utilize it in preparing for the exam. By using this book properly, you will be prepared to take, and successfully complete, the most recent types of entry level police officer examinations.

What a Police Officer Does

You are planning to take the Police Officer Examination because you have decided to join the police force. Therefore, it seems only fitting to provide an overall view of the types of positions available and the compensation that can be expected.

As you probably already know, the basic mission of the police is to protect life and property, to find and arrest criminal offenders, to preserve the peace, to enforce laws, and to prevent and detect crime. The basic mission is the same for all police officers regardless of whether the department involved is a city, county, state or federal agency. The difference between police departments is one of degree of work and not kind of work. In other words, all police agencies perform the same kind of work and differ only in the amount of work they perform in each area of the basic mission. Also, in both large and small police departments, the activities of the police are divided into both "line" and "staff" duties. *Line duties* concern those jobs which directly deal with accomplishing the basic mission. *Staff duties* are jobs which help and support line duties.

TYPES OF POLICE POSITIONS

LINE POSITIONS

Patrol. In this position, uniformed police officers "patrol" through the community by foot, scooter, motorcycle, automobile, and sometimes by boat or plane. Responsible for a "beat," "post," or "sector," which is an assigned, fixed geographical area, the police officer spends much time answering a wide variety of calls for assistance from the public.

Traffic. An often difficult job, police officers working in uniform on traffic duty prevent vehicular accidents and congestion by issuing summonses, directing traffic, and investigating traffic accidents.

Detectives. Working in business attire, detectives, the investigators of the police department, are called to the scene after a major crime has been committed. They follow investigatory leads and attempt to identify and arrest persons responsible for past criminal acts.

Vice Enforcement. Usually involved in the enforcement of laws dealing with alcohol, prostitution, narcotics, gambling, and pornography, police in vice enforcement work in street clothes or disguise, and often act in a very demanding undercover role infiltrating criminal organizations.

Youth Work. Officers in youth work are involved in investigating crimes committed by and upon children. This work, performed either in uniform or plainclothes, calls for great sensitivity.

STAFF POSITIONS

Communications. These positions involve handling calls from the public, dispatching police to the scene of emergencies, inputting and retrieving crime data from computers, and maintaining surveillance equipment.

Criminal Identification. Police involved in this area must take fingerprints of victims or criminals, discover and retrieve fingerprints at the scenes of crimes, and search fingerprint files to identify criminals.

Forensic. Officers in this area use the sciences to identify the nature and origin of substances, such as blood, hair, semen, and other body fluids. They also interview witnesses, do ballistics work, induce hypnosis, and administer polygraph operations.

Support Services. Police officers perform a variety of support roles, ranging from that of ambulance attendant to auto mechanic. The scope and degree of support services depends on the size of the police department and the policies of that department.

THE WORK WEEK, SALARY, AND BENEFITS

Police work is not a 9 A.M. to 5 P.M., Monday to Friday occupation. A police officer could be assigned to work any day of the week at any hour. The work week is an average of 40 hours. While there may be some disadvantages of working "around the clock," it is in no way a humdrum existence.

What kind of salaries do police officers make? Many large departments begin their officers somewhere between $30,000 and $40,000 year, with increments to $55,000. Then promotions are available, often as a direct result of a civil service examination, which can bring a salary up to $100,000 annually.

But salaries are not the only benefit. There is usually early retirement; that is, retirement with a pension after 20 to 25 years of service. Also, there are liberal sick leave, paid uniforms, vacation allotments (in most departments), and job security.

The Steps to Becoming a Police Officer

First, visit your local Police Personnel Department, which does the testing and hiring of police employees and often publishes advertisements regarding hiring plans and examination dates. (In major cities, this department may be centralized.) You might, also, wish to either call or visit the recruiting section of your police department. Nevertheless remember to use the *non-emergency* police number if you decide to telephone.

You might also wish to call the Patrolmen's Benevolent Association, the local police union office, to find out when the next police officer test is scheduled. Other possibilities for obtaining job and testing information are to subscribe to the local civil service newspaper, or to ask a police officer.

The bottom line is—do not be afraid to ask. Police departments *want* good people. You are taking the time to prepare yourself for the examination and, therefore, have begun to qualify as one of the candidates that police departments would want.

Then, follow the next steps geared to getting an appointment.

The Steps **to** Appointment

1. File an *application.*
2. Take the *Police Officer Examination.*
3. If you are successful on the written examination, take the *physical* examination. This test includes lifting, running, jumping, and other kinds of physical activities that a police officer is required to do, but it is designed so as not to discriminate against women.*
4. Take the *medical exam.*
5. An *interview* often follows. This can include a battery of psychological tests.
6. Finally, a *background and character investigation* occurs.

After successfully completing these steps, your name is put on a list, and you will be notified as to when appointments will be made.

The Steps **After** Appointment

1. You will attend a *training school* for several months, sometimes referred to as a "Police Academy."
2. After the initial training, you will be assigned to a *police unit* for a probation period, during which you will be called a "probie" or "rookie." Most often, you will begin in a uniformed patrol assignment, the backbone of police work, to learn the basics. While on patrol, you will be evaluated for other types of assignments such as detective, youth work, etc. You then

*Many departments have now discontinued the physical examination before entrance to the department. They rely instead on a physical agility test administered after the official training period.

become eligible to take the civil service examination for promotion.

The police officer's job is both rewarding and satisfying. Pursue it. Make it your goal. Use this book to help you. Remember, all police officers were once in the same position you are in right now. They did it, and you can too.

How to Apply for the Test

The most important step in the application process is to obtain a copy of the "Job Announcement." It is available from the city, state or federal agency that is responsible for preparing and giving the examination.

Listed below are a series of items usually contained in the Job Announcement, along with helpful comments on each item. Remember that the comments are of a general nature and that requirements vary from one jurisdiction to another.

1. **FILING INFORMATION.** Most jurisdictions require applicants to file for the examination by filling out and submitting an application by a certain date. After you file, you are notified by mail where and when to appear for the examination. The Job Announcement tells you where to get an application form. However, sometimes "walk-in exams" are held which do not require prior filing.

2. **GENERAL REQUIREMENTS.** The typical requirements to take the examination and/or to become a police officer are as follows:

   Age: Because age requirements vary from jurisdiction to jurisdiction, this requirement should be checked with the department you are seeking to enter. However, the age range to take the exam is typically from 18 to 35, with candidates over 35 being eligible if they have served with the Armed Forces during certain time periods.

   Height Requirements: The height requirement is disappearing as a factor in determining eligibility. For example, the New York City Police Department does not have a height requirement.

   Citizenship: Most, if not all, departments require a person to be a citizen to be appointed to the job, but not to take the entrance examination.

   Eyesight: Eyesight requirements vary considerably from city to city, but the trend is toward more relaxed standards. Some departments use uncorrected standards, while others use a corrected standard (i.e. they allow you to wear glasses when taking the eye examination).

Physical Agility Test: Candidates are required to pass a physical agility test either before entry to the department or after their initial training period. Consult the Job Announcement or police recruiter for more details about your physical agility test.

Driver's License: This is usually a definite requirement to be appointed to the job, but not to take the test.

Fees: Very often, a nominal fee in the range of twenty-five dollars is required when you file to take the examination.

Education: The great majority of departments require either a high school diploma or a high school equivalency diploma to be appointed to the job, but not to take the examination. Some departments now require college credits. The individual department should be checked regarding its educational requirements.

When and Where the Examination Takes Place: Usually, police entrance examinations are held on Saturday mornings at local high schools. As mentioned above, candidates are usually notified by mail where and when to appear. This notification comes after the candidate has filed for the examination. Note that if the examination is scheduled for a Saturday, a "Sabbath Observers Examination" is held on a different day of the week in most jurisdictions for those who cannot take the examination on Saturday because of religious beliefs.

CHAPTER 2

How to Maximize Your Test Score

This chapter covers two very vital matters to scoring high on the Police Officer Examination. The first part of this chapter helps you develop good study habits; the second provides you with a specific strategy to deal with multiple-choice questions.

Because both of these items are so important, it would be best for you to periodically review this chapter as you study for the examination. At the very least, you should review this section prior to taking each of the full-length examinations included in this book.

Develop Good Study Habits

Many people incorrectly believe that the amount of time spent studying is the most important factor in test preparation. Nevertheless, efficient study habits are the key to successful test preparation. Of course, all else being equal, the amount of time you devote to your studies is a critical factor. But spending time reading is not necessarily studying. If you want to retain what you read, you must develop a system. For example, a person who devotes 60 minutes a day to uninterrupted study in a quiet, private area will generally retain more than someone who puts in twice that time by studying five or six times a day for 15 to 20 minutes at a time.

Ten Rules for Studying More Effectively

We have listed a number of rules for you to follow to increase study time efficiency. If you abide by these rules, you will get the most out of this book.

1. **MAKE SURE YOU UNDERSTAND THE MEANING OF EVERY WORD YOU READ.** Your ability to understand what you read is the most important skill needed to pass any test. Therefore, starting now, every time you see a word that you don't fully understand, make certain that you write it down and make note of where you saw it. Then, when you have a chance, look up the meaning of the word in the dictionary. When you think you know what the word means, go back to the reading material which contained the word, and make certain that you fully understand the meaning of the word.

   Keep a list of all words you don't know, and periodically review them. Also, try to use these words whenever you can in conversation. If you do this faithfully, you will quickly build an extensive vocabulary which will be helpful to you not only when you take the police officer examination, but for the rest of your life.

2. **STUDY UNINTERRUPTED FOR AT LEAST 30 MINUTES.** Unless you can study for at least an uninterrupted period of 30 minutes, you should not bother to study at all. It is essential that you concentrate for extended periods of time. Remember, the actual examination takes anywhere from 3 to 5 hours to complete, with the average being 3½ hours. You must concentrate just as hard in the third hour of the test as you did in the first hour. Therefore, as the examination approaches, study for more extended periods of time without interruption. And, when you take the practice examinations in Chapters 13 through 15, do a complete examination in one sitting, just as you must do at the actual examination.

3. **SIMULATE EXAMINATION CONDITIONS WHEN STUDYING.** Study under the same conditions as those of the examination, as much as possible. Eliminate as many outside interferences as you can. And if you are a smoker, refrain from smoking while studying since you will *not* be allowed to smoke in the classroom on the day of your examination!

4. **STUDY ALONE. IF POSSIBLE, ALSO FORM A STUDY GROUP TO MEET PERIODICALLY.** Studying alone is the best way to prepare for the police officer test. However, if possible, form a group of from three to five serious students and meet with them for 2 to 3 hours on a periodic basis, perhaps every other week. Prior to each meeting, the group should come prepared to discuss one area which will probably appear on the examination. In addition, everyone in the group should keep a list of items they are confused about; these items should be discussed at the study group meetings. Items that no one is certain of should be referred to an outside source, such as a teacher, parent, librarian, etc. Arguing in a study group defeats the purpose of the group, and must be avoided at all costs.

5. **MAKE SURE YOU UNDERSTAND THE ANSWERS TO EVERY QUESTION IN THIS BOOK.** Every answer is accompanied by an explanation. Whenever you get a question *wrong*, be sure that you understand why you missed it so you won't make the same mistake again. However, it is equally important to make certain that you have answered a question *correctly* for the right reason. Therefore, study the answer explanation to every question in this book as carefully as you study the question itself.

6. **ALWAYS FOLLOW THE RECOMMENDED TECHNIQUE FOR ANSWERING MULTIPLE-CHOICE QUESTIONS.** Later in this chapter we provide an invaluable technique for answering multiple-choice questions.

7. **ALWAYS TIME YOURSELF WHEN DOING PRACTICE QUESTIONS.** Running out of time on a multiple-choice examination is a tragic error that is easily avoided. Learn, through practice, to move to the next question after a reasonable period of time spent on any one question. Therefore, when you are doing practice questions, always time yourself—and always try to stay within the recommended time limits. The correct use of time during the actual examination is an integral part of the technique that will be explained later in this chapter.

8. **CONCENTRATE YOUR STUDY TIME IN THE AREAS OF YOUR GREATEST WEAKNESS.** The diagnostic examination in Chapter 3 will give you an idea of the most difficult question types for you. Though you should spend most of your time improving yourself in these areas, do not ignore the other types of questions.

9. **EXERCISE REGULARLY AND STAY IN GOOD PHYSICAL CONDITION.** Students who are in good physical con-

dition have an advantage over those who are not. It is a well-established principle that good physical health improves the ability of the mind to function smoothly and efficiently, especially when taking examinations of extended duration, such as the police officer examination.

10. **ESTABLISH A SCHEDULE FOR STUDYING, AND STICK TO IT.** Do not put off studying to those times when you have nothing else to do. Schedule your study time, and try not to let anything else interfere with that schedule. If you feel yourself weakening, review Chapter 1 and remind yourself of why you would like to become a police officer.

Strategies for Handling Multiple-Choice Questions

The remainder of this chapter outlines a very specific test-taking strategy valuable for a multiple-choice examination. Study the technique, practice it; then study it again until you have mastered it.

1. **READ THE DIRECTIONS.** Do *not* assume that you know what the directions are without reading them. Make sure you read and understand them. Note particularly whether there are differing directions from one section of the examination to another.

2. **MAKE SURE YOU HAVE THE COMPLETE EXAMINATION.** Check the examination page by page. Since examination booklets have numbered pages, simply make certain that you have all of the pages.

3. **TAKE A CLOSE LOOK AT THE ANSWER SHEET.** Some answer sheets are numbered vertically and some horizontally. The answer sheets on your practice examinations are typical of the one you will see on your exam. However, do *not* take anything for granted. Review the directions on the answer sheet carefully, and familiarize yourself with its format.

4. **BE CAREFUL WHEN MARKING YOUR ANSWERS.** Be sure to mark your answers in accordance with the directions on the answer sheet. Be extremely careful that:

   - you mark only one answer for each question,
   - you do not make extraneous markings on your answer sheet,

- you completely darken the allotted space for the answer you choose,
- you erase completely any answer that you wish to change.

5. **MAKE ABSOLUTELY CERTAIN YOU ARE MARKING THE ANSWER TO THE RIGHT QUESTION.** Many multiple-choice tests have been failed because of carelessness in this area. All it takes is one mistake. If you put down one answer in the wrong space, you will probably continue the mistake for a number of questions until you realize your error. We recommend that you use the following procedure when marking your answer sheet.

   - Select your answer, circle that choice on the test booklet, and ask yourself what question number you are working on.
   - If you select choice "C" as the answer for question eleven, circle choice "C" on the test booklet, and say to yourself, "C is the answer to question eleven."
   - Then find the space on your answer sheet for question eleven, and again say "C is the answer to question eleven" as you mark the answer.

   While this might seem rather elementary and repetitive, after a while it becomes automatic. If followed properly, it guarantees that you will not fail the examination because of a careless mistake.

6. **MAKE CERTAIN THAT YOU UNDERSTAND WHAT THE QUESTION IS ASKING.** Read the stem of the question (the part before the choices) very carefully to make certain that you know what the examiner is asking. In fact, it is wise to read it twice.

7. **ALWAYS READ ALL OF THE CHOICES BEFORE YOU SELECT AN ANSWER.** Don't make the mistake of falling into the trap that the best distractor, or wrong answer, comes before the correct choice! Read all choices!

8. **BE AWARE OF KEY WORDS THAT OFTEN TIP OFF THE CORRECT AND INCORRECT ANSWERS.**

   Absolute Words—*Usually a Wrong Choice*
   (They are generally too broad and difficult to defend)

never	always	only
none	all	any
nothing	everyone	
nobody	everybody	

Limiting Words—*Usually a Correct Choice*

usually	sometimes	many
generally	some	often
few	possible	
occasionally		

9. **NEVER MAKE A CHOICE BASED ON FREQUENCY OF PREVIOUS ANSWERS.** Some students pay attention to the pattern of answers when taking an exam. Always answer the question, without regard to what the previous choices have been.

10. **CROSS OUT CHOICES YOU KNOW ARE WRONG.** As you read through the choices, put an "X" through the letter designation of any choice you know is wrong. After reading through all of the choices, you only have to re-read the ones you did not cross out the first time. If you cross out all but one of the choices, the remaining choice should be the answer. Read the choice one more time to satisfy yourself, put a circle around its letter designation (if you still feel it is the best answer), and transpose it to the answer sheet. (See the procedure given above under Rule 5.) If you cross out all but two choices when you read through the first time, you only have to re-read the two remaining choices, and make a decision.

    Many times, the second time you read the remaining choices, the answer is clear. If that happens, cross out the wrong choice, circle the correct one, and transpose the answer to the answer sheet. If more than two choices are still not crossed out, re-read the stem of the question and make certain you understand the question. Then go through the choices again. (Keep in mind the key words mentioned in Rule 8 which may give you a hint of the correct answer.)

11. **SKIP OVER QUESTIONS THAT GIVE YOU TROUBLE.** The first time through the examination be certain not to dwell too long on any one question. Simply skip the question after putting a circle around the number in the test booklet (to keep your answers from getting out of sequence), and go to the next question. Do not guess at this point if you do not know the answer.

12. **RETURN TO THE QUESTIONS YOU SKIPPED AFTER YOU FINISH THE REST OF THE EXAMINATION.** Once you have answered all of the questions you were sure of on the entire examination, check the time remaining. If time permits (and it should if you follow our recommendations), return to each question you did not answer and re-read the stem and the choices that are not crossed out. It should be easy to find the questions you have not yet answered because,

as per the instructions in Rule 11, all of them will have their number designation circled on the test booklet. If the answer is still not clear and you are running out of time, then make "an educated guess" between those choices which you have not already eliminated. When making an "educated guess," follow the guidelines that are presented in Rule 15.

13. **NEVER LEAVE QUESTIONS UNANSWERED UNLESS THE INSTRUCTIONS INDICATE A PENALTY FOR WRONG ANSWERS.** In almost all police officer examinations, you do not lose credit for wrong answers. In this case, guess at any questions you are not sure of.

However, in rare instances, a penalty is assessed for wrong answers on multiple-choice examinations. Since this would have to be explained in the instructions, be sure to read them carefully. If this is the case on your examination, decide how strongly you feel about each individual question before answering each. Note that this almost never happens on entry-level police officer examinations.

14. **CHECK YOUR TIME PERIODICALLY.** It is very important for you to have a time management plan when you take your examination. For example, if the exam you are taking has 100 questions and has a time limit of 3½ hours, you will have no trouble at all with time if you average about 1½ minutes per question. In other words, *take about 15 minutes for every 10 questions.* Check yourself after every ten questions to make sure you are not taking too long. Never spend more than 2 minutes on any question. In that way, you will have plenty of time at the end of the examination to go back to the questions that you skipped over the first time through. (Always schedule your time to leave at least a half hour at the end of the examination to go back to the questions that you have skipped.) Of course, your time management plan has to be adjusted to reflect the number of questions given and the amount of time allowed on your examination.

15. **RULES FOR MAKING AN "EDUCATED GUESS."** Your chances of picking the correct answer to questions you are not sure of will be significantly increased if you use the following rules:

- Never consider answer choices that you have already eliminated. (See Rule 10.)
- Be aware of key words that give you clues as to which answer might be right or wrong. (See Rule 8.)
- If two choices have a conflicting meaning, one of them is probably the correct answer. And, if two choices are too

close in meaning, probably neither is correct. Consider the following question:

EXAMPLE.

John's complaint about the weather was that:

(A) It was too hot.
(B) It was too cold.
(C) It varied too much.
(D) It was unpredictable.

A B C D

In this example, choices C and D are so close together in meaning that neither is likely to be the correct answer. Choices A and B, on the other hand, are quite opposite each other, and one of them is most likely the correct answer.

- Many times, two choices are worded so that combined they encompass all of the possibilities. In these cases, one of them has to be the correct choice.

EXAMPLE.

Which of the following is the most accurate statement about John?

(A) John is guilty of murder.
(B) John is not guilty of murder.
(C) John is guilty of arson.
(D) John is guilty of assault.

A B C D

In this rather obvious example, John is either guilty of murder or he is not guilty of murder. The correct choice must be one or the other since together they encompass all of the possibilities.

Perhaps another example would help!

EXAMPLE.

How old is John?

(A) 7 years old or less
(B) 6 years old
(C) Over 7 years old
(D) 14 years old

A B C D

In this example, a correct answer has to be either choice A or C, because if John is not 7 years old or less, (choice A), then he must be over 7 years old, (choice C). Please note that even if he is 14 years old (choice D), choice C is still correct. His age must fit into either choice A or choice C.

- The answer choice that has significantly more or significantly fewer words in it is very often the correct choice.

- If all else fails, and you have to make an outright guess at more than one question, guess the same lettered choice for each such question. The odds are that you will pick up some valuable points.

16. **BE VERY RELUCTANT TO CHANGE ANSWERS.** Unless you have a very good reason, do not change an answer once you have chosen it. Studies have shown that all too often people change their answer from the right one to the wrong one.

The Test Format

The typical police entrance examination contains the following types of questions.

1. **MEMORY QUESTIONS.** In this question type, the candidate is given written material and/or pictorial material and is permitted a period of time, usually about five minutes, to commit to memory as much about it as he or she can. The material is then taken away and the candidate is asked a series of questions, usually ten to twenty, based on its contents.

2. **POLICE FORM QUESTIONS.** There are two kinds of questions asked concerning department forms, as follows:

    a. The candidate is given a written story about a police incident, a *blank police department form*, and a series of questions asking what information should be placed in various boxes on the form. The candidate must choose pertinent information from the story to answer the questions pertaining to the form.

    b. The candidate is given a *completed police department form* and is required to answer questions using the information already on the form.

3. **QUESTIONS ON UNDERSTANDING AND APPLYING POLICE DIRECTIVES, PROCEDURES, AND REGULATIONS.** In this question type, the candidate is given a series of police department procedures and is tested on his or her ability to understand the procedures and to apply them to typical police situations.

4. **READING COMPREHENSION QUESTIONS.** This question type tests the candidate's ability to understand

written material that is reflective of the kind of writing that a police officer must be able to read and understand.

5. **QUESTIONS ON UNDERSTANDING AND APPLYING LEGAL DEFINITIONS.** In this question type, the candidate is given a series of legal definitions and is tested on his or her ability to understand these definitions and to apply them to typical police situations.

6. **SENTENCE ORDERING QUESTIONS.** In this type of question, the candidate is presented with a series of sentences, usually five, and then tested to determine if he or she can arrange those sentences in the most logical sequence as if they were to appear in a police report.

7. **TRAFFIC MAP QUESTIONS.** In Traffic Map Questions, the candidate's ability to go from one location on a map to another is tested. These questions are based on the ability to follow directions while using a street map that contains such things as "one way streets" and "dead end streets."

8. **MATCHING SKETCHES QUESTIONS.** This is a type of question that is completely non-verbal. The candidate is shown a sketch of a person's face and then usually asked to select the same person from among a group of four other sketches. Sometimes the candidate is required to choose which of four sketches is NOT the same person as the original sketch.

9. **REPORT WRITING QUESTIONS.** In this type of question, the candidate is required to actually write a report or to examine written reports or written statements. The candidate is then asked to indicate if the reports have been written accurately and clearly or to select from several options the most correct way to express the same series of facts that have been presented in the stem of the question.

10. **DIRECTED PATROL QUESTIONS.** In this question type the candidate is given a number of facts about crime and/or other police related incidents. Based on this data, the candidate is then asked to select the optimum patrol areas and/or times to best deal with the crime or incident involved.

11. **WANTED POSTERS.** This is another type of question that tests the candidate's memory. The candidate is shown a series of about six wanted posters containing a likeness of the wanted person and written information about that person, including pedigree information and information about the crime or crimes for which he or she is wanted. The candidate

is given some time, usually five to ten minutes, to study the wanted posters; they are then taken away and the candidate is asked questions about the posters.

12. **FORMULA QUESTIONS.** In this type of question, the candidate is given information about what took place during a police officer's tour of duty. The candidate is then asked to express in a mathematical formula such things as the amount of time spent on certain functions during that tour of duty.

13. **FIND THE PERPETRATOR QUESTIONS.** In this question type, the candidate is given information about a person who has been arrested, such as his age, weight, height, clothing worn, hair style, etc. The candidate is then given a description of other suspects wanted for other crimes and asked which of the other suspects could be the arrested person.

14. **FREQUENCY OF INFORMATION QUESTIONS.** In Frequency of Information questions, the candidate is given information received from witnesses to a crime or police related incident and asked to choose which of the witnesses most likely gave the correct information.

15. **ARITHMETIC QUESTIONS.** Many departments ask questions that test a candidate's ability to perform the basic addition and subtraction skills needed by a police officer in the course of his or her day's work. In the typical arithmetic question, the candidate is given a listing of stolen property and required to select the choice that most accurately reflects the total value of the stolen property.

16. **APPLYING POLICE POLICY QUESTIONS.** In these question types, the candidate is given a statement about the policy of a police department and then tested to see whether he or she can apply that policy. These questions, which closely resemble reading comprehension type questions, require the candidate to exercise some degree of independent judgment. However, by carefully reading the introductory stem of the question (the part before the choices) and by following some simple rules, which we describe later in this text, most such judgment decisions become obvious.

Don't be concerned if your initial reading of the above information seems difficult for you. Each of the above question types are fully explained in this book, and for each question type we give you helpful hints and strategies to follow. You are also given many sample questions in each area, along with fully explained answers to each question.

How to Use This Book Effectively

To obtain maximum benefit from the use of this book, we recommend the following approach:

1. Learn the "Strategies for Handling Multiple-Choice Questions," which appear in this chapter.

2. Take the Diagnostic Examination. After completing this examination, fill out the diagnostic procedure chart that follows the examination. This will indicate your strengths and weaknesses. You can then devote most of your study time to correcting your weaknesses.

3. Study Chapters 4 through 12. As mentioned above, concentrate your study efforts in your weak areas, but make certain to cover each chapter. Be sure to follow the "Ten Rules for Studying More Effectively," which appear in this chapter. Also, make sure to employ the test-taking strategies mentioned earlier when doing the practice questions at the end of each chapter.

4. Take Practice Examination One. After you have finished this examination and have reviewed the explained answers, complete the diagnostic procedure chart that follows the examination. Then restudy the appropriate chapters in accordance with the directions on the bottom of the diagnostic chart.

5. Take Practice Examination Two. After you have finished this examination, follow the same procedure that you followed after finishing Practice Examination One.

6. Take Practice Examination Three. Once again, follow the same procedure you followed after Practice Examination One.

7. When the actual examination is two weeks away, read the final chapter of the book. Be sure to follow the recommended strategy contained in this chapter for the seven days immediately preceding the examination.

DIAGNOSE YOUR PROBLEM

Answer Sheet
Diagnostic Examination

Follow the instructions given in the test. Mark only your answers in the ovals below. WARNING: Be sure that the oval you fill is in the same row as the question you are answering. Use a No. 2 pencil (soft pencil).

BE SURE YOUR PENCIL MARKS ARE HEAVY AND BLACK. ERASE COMPLETELY ANY ANSWER YOU WISH TO CHANGE.

DO NOT make stray pencil dots, dashes or marks.

START HERE

1 Ⓐ Ⓑ Ⓒ Ⓓ	2 Ⓐ Ⓑ Ⓒ Ⓓ	3 Ⓐ Ⓑ Ⓒ Ⓓ	4 Ⓐ Ⓑ Ⓒ Ⓓ	5 Ⓐ Ⓑ Ⓒ Ⓓ	6 Ⓐ Ⓑ Ⓒ Ⓓ
7 Ⓐ Ⓑ Ⓒ Ⓓ	8 Ⓐ Ⓑ Ⓒ Ⓓ	9 Ⓐ Ⓑ Ⓒ Ⓓ	10 Ⓐ Ⓑ Ⓒ Ⓓ	11 Ⓐ Ⓑ Ⓒ Ⓓ	12 Ⓐ Ⓑ Ⓒ Ⓓ
13 Ⓐ Ⓑ Ⓒ Ⓓ	14 Ⓐ Ⓑ Ⓒ Ⓓ	15 Ⓐ Ⓑ Ⓒ Ⓓ	16 Ⓐ Ⓑ Ⓒ Ⓓ	17 Ⓐ Ⓑ Ⓒ Ⓓ	18 Ⓐ Ⓑ Ⓒ Ⓓ
19 Ⓐ Ⓑ Ⓒ Ⓓ	20 Ⓐ Ⓑ Ⓒ Ⓓ	21 Ⓐ Ⓑ Ⓒ Ⓓ	22 Ⓐ Ⓑ Ⓒ Ⓓ	23 Ⓐ Ⓑ Ⓒ Ⓓ	24 Ⓐ Ⓑ Ⓒ Ⓓ
25 Ⓐ Ⓑ Ⓒ Ⓓ	26 Ⓐ Ⓑ Ⓒ Ⓓ	27 Ⓐ Ⓑ Ⓒ Ⓓ	28 Ⓐ Ⓑ Ⓒ Ⓓ	29 Ⓐ Ⓑ Ⓒ Ⓓ	30 Ⓐ Ⓑ Ⓒ Ⓓ
31 Ⓐ Ⓑ Ⓒ Ⓓ	32 Ⓐ Ⓑ Ⓒ Ⓓ	33 Ⓐ Ⓑ Ⓒ Ⓓ	34 Ⓐ Ⓑ Ⓒ Ⓓ	35 Ⓐ Ⓑ Ⓒ Ⓓ	36 Ⓐ Ⓑ Ⓒ Ⓓ
37 Ⓐ Ⓑ Ⓒ Ⓓ	38 Ⓐ Ⓑ Ⓒ Ⓓ	39 Ⓐ Ⓑ Ⓒ Ⓓ	40 Ⓐ Ⓑ Ⓒ Ⓓ	41 Ⓐ Ⓑ Ⓒ Ⓓ	42 Ⓐ Ⓑ Ⓒ Ⓓ
43 Ⓐ Ⓑ Ⓒ Ⓓ	44 Ⓐ Ⓑ Ⓒ Ⓓ	45 Ⓐ Ⓑ Ⓒ Ⓓ	46 Ⓐ Ⓑ Ⓒ Ⓓ	47 Ⓐ Ⓑ Ⓒ Ⓓ	48 Ⓐ Ⓑ Ⓒ Ⓓ
49 Ⓐ Ⓑ Ⓒ Ⓓ	50 Ⓐ Ⓑ Ⓒ Ⓓ	51 Ⓐ Ⓑ Ⓒ Ⓓ	52 Ⓐ Ⓑ Ⓒ Ⓓ	53 Ⓐ Ⓑ Ⓒ Ⓓ	54 Ⓐ Ⓑ Ⓒ Ⓓ
55 Ⓐ Ⓑ Ⓒ Ⓓ	56 Ⓐ Ⓑ Ⓒ Ⓓ	57 Ⓐ Ⓑ Ⓒ Ⓓ	58 Ⓐ Ⓑ Ⓒ Ⓓ	59 Ⓐ Ⓑ Ⓒ Ⓓ	60 Ⓐ Ⓑ Ⓒ Ⓓ
61 Ⓐ Ⓑ Ⓒ Ⓓ	62 Ⓐ Ⓑ Ⓒ Ⓓ	63 Ⓐ Ⓑ Ⓒ Ⓓ	64 Ⓐ Ⓑ Ⓒ Ⓓ	65 Ⓐ Ⓑ Ⓒ Ⓓ	66 Ⓐ Ⓑ Ⓒ Ⓓ
67 Ⓐ Ⓑ Ⓒ Ⓓ	68 Ⓐ Ⓑ Ⓒ Ⓓ	69 Ⓐ Ⓑ Ⓒ Ⓓ	70 Ⓐ Ⓑ Ⓒ Ⓓ	71 Ⓐ Ⓑ Ⓒ Ⓓ	72 Ⓐ Ⓑ Ⓒ Ⓓ
73 Ⓐ Ⓑ Ⓒ Ⓓ	74 Ⓐ Ⓑ Ⓒ Ⓓ	75 Ⓐ Ⓑ Ⓒ Ⓓ	76 Ⓐ Ⓑ Ⓒ Ⓓ	77 Ⓐ Ⓑ Ⓒ Ⓓ	78 Ⓐ Ⓑ Ⓒ Ⓓ
79 Ⓐ Ⓑ Ⓒ Ⓓ	80 Ⓐ Ⓑ Ⓒ Ⓓ	81 Ⓐ Ⓑ Ⓒ Ⓓ	82 Ⓐ Ⓑ Ⓒ Ⓓ	83 Ⓐ Ⓑ Ⓒ Ⓓ	84 Ⓐ Ⓑ Ⓒ Ⓓ
85 Ⓐ Ⓑ Ⓒ Ⓓ	86 Ⓐ Ⓑ Ⓒ Ⓓ	87 Ⓐ Ⓑ Ⓒ Ⓓ	88 Ⓐ Ⓑ Ⓒ Ⓓ	89 Ⓐ Ⓑ Ⓒ Ⓓ	90 Ⓐ Ⓑ Ⓒ Ⓓ
91 Ⓐ Ⓑ Ⓒ Ⓓ	92 Ⓐ Ⓑ Ⓒ Ⓓ	93 Ⓐ Ⓑ Ⓒ Ⓓ	94 Ⓐ Ⓑ Ⓒ Ⓓ	95 Ⓐ Ⓑ Ⓒ Ⓓ	96 Ⓐ Ⓑ Ⓒ Ⓓ
97 Ⓐ Ⓑ Ⓒ Ⓓ	98 Ⓐ Ⓑ Ⓒ Ⓓ	99 Ⓐ Ⓑ Ⓒ Ⓓ	100 Ⓐ Ⓑ Ⓒ Ⓓ	101 Ⓐ Ⓑ Ⓒ Ⓓ	102 Ⓐ Ⓑ Ⓒ Ⓓ
103 Ⓐ Ⓑ Ⓒ Ⓓ	104 Ⓐ Ⓑ Ⓒ Ⓓ	105 Ⓐ Ⓑ Ⓒ Ⓓ	106 Ⓐ Ⓑ Ⓒ Ⓓ	107 Ⓐ Ⓑ Ⓒ Ⓓ	108 Ⓐ Ⓑ Ⓒ Ⓓ
109 Ⓐ Ⓑ Ⓒ Ⓓ	110 Ⓐ Ⓑ Ⓒ Ⓓ	111 Ⓐ Ⓑ Ⓒ Ⓓ	112 Ⓐ Ⓑ Ⓒ Ⓓ	113 Ⓐ Ⓑ Ⓒ Ⓓ	114 Ⓐ Ⓑ Ⓒ Ⓓ
115 Ⓐ Ⓑ Ⓒ Ⓓ	116 Ⓐ Ⓑ Ⓒ Ⓓ	117 Ⓐ Ⓑ Ⓒ Ⓓ	118 Ⓐ Ⓑ Ⓒ Ⓓ	119 Ⓐ Ⓑ Ⓒ Ⓓ	120 Ⓐ Ⓑ Ⓒ Ⓓ
121 Ⓐ Ⓑ Ⓒ Ⓓ	122 Ⓐ Ⓑ Ⓒ Ⓓ	123 Ⓐ Ⓑ Ⓒ Ⓓ	124 Ⓐ Ⓑ Ⓒ Ⓓ	125 Ⓐ Ⓑ Ⓒ Ⓓ	126 Ⓐ Ⓑ Ⓒ Ⓓ
127 Ⓐ Ⓑ Ⓒ Ⓓ	128 Ⓐ Ⓑ Ⓒ Ⓓ	129 Ⓐ Ⓑ Ⓒ Ⓓ	130 Ⓐ Ⓑ Ⓒ Ⓓ	131 Ⓐ Ⓑ Ⓒ Ⓓ	132 Ⓐ Ⓑ Ⓒ Ⓓ
133 Ⓐ Ⓑ Ⓒ Ⓓ	134 Ⓐ Ⓑ Ⓒ Ⓓ	135 Ⓐ Ⓑ Ⓒ Ⓓ	136 Ⓐ Ⓑ Ⓒ Ⓓ	137 Ⓐ Ⓑ Ⓒ Ⓓ	138 Ⓐ Ⓑ Ⓒ Ⓓ
139 Ⓐ Ⓑ Ⓒ Ⓓ	140 Ⓐ Ⓑ Ⓒ Ⓓ	141 Ⓐ Ⓑ Ⓒ Ⓓ	142 Ⓐ Ⓑ Ⓒ Ⓓ	143 Ⓐ Ⓑ Ⓒ Ⓓ	144 Ⓐ Ⓑ Ⓒ Ⓓ
145 Ⓐ Ⓑ Ⓒ Ⓓ	146 Ⓐ Ⓑ Ⓒ Ⓓ	147 Ⓐ Ⓑ Ⓒ Ⓓ	148 Ⓐ Ⓑ Ⓒ Ⓓ	149 Ⓐ Ⓑ Ⓒ Ⓓ	150 Ⓐ Ⓑ Ⓒ Ⓓ

CHAPTER 3

A Diagnostic Examination

There are 140 questions on this diagnostic examination, and you should finish the entire examination in 5 hours. For maximum benefit, it is strongly recommended that you take this examination in one sitting as if it were an actual test.

The answers to this examination and their explanations begin immediately following thc examination. By completing the chart in the section "Diagnostic Procedure," you can get an idea of which question types give you the most difficulty. You can then devote most of your time to those areas.

Before You Take the Examination

Before taking this examination, you should have read Chapters 1 and 2. Be certain that you employ the test-taking strategy recommended earlier while taking this examination.

Remember to read each question and related material carefully before choosing your answers. Select the choice you believe to be the most correct, and mark your answer on the Answer Sheet provided at the beginning of this chapter. (This Answer Sheet is similar to the one used on the actual examination). The Answer Key, Diagnostic Procedure, and Answer Explanations all appear at the end of this chapter.

NOTE: This diagnostic examination is more difficult than the typical official examination. It is divided into several sections to help you become familiar with various question types and for ease of diagnosing your results, since each section corresponds to a chapter in the book. However, the actual examination will probably *not* be divided into sections. For this reason, the three practice examinations appearing later in the book are not divided into sections. Also, please note that there are three ways to test memory: recalling what you read, recalling what you see, and wanted posters. In this diagnostic test we use "Recalling What You Read" to test your memory. Recalling what you see is tested and explained in the "Recalling What You See" chapter and in the practice tests; wanted posters are dealt with in the chapter entitled "Troublesome Question Types" and also in a practice test.

The Test

SECTION ONE— Remembering Written Material

MEMORY MATERIAL 10-MINUTE TIME LIMIT

***DIRECTIONS:* Answer questions 1 through 15 based on the following narrative. You are permitted 10 minutes to read the narrative and to commit to memory as much about it as you can. You are *not* permitted to make any written notes during the 10 minutes you are reading the story.**

At the end of the 10 minutes, you are to stop reading the material, turn the page, and answer the questions *without* referring to the written material.

You are a community relations police officer working in the 54th Police Precinct in Queens. Today is April 17 and you are performing a tour of duty from 1600 hours to 2400 hours. It is now 1730 hours, and you are attending a meeting at the offices of the local community board, which are located at 1548 Riverview Road. You have been directed by your commanding officer, Captain Richard Bartlett, to attend this meeting and to report to him concerning what took place. Also attending the meeting are Police Officer Robert Wallace, the Precinct's Crime Prevention Officer; and Detective Andrew Richardson, the Precinct's Highway Safety Officer.

The meeting is being held to discuss an outbreak of crime in the shopping district on Riverview Road between Andrews Avenue and Simpson Avenue (a stick-up team has been terrorizing this area) and an outbreak of serious motor vehicle accidents in the same neighborhood. The meeting is open to anyone in the community, but most people in attendance are members of two community groups, the local Merchant's Association and the Riverview Road Block Association. The principal spokespersons for these groups are Marjorie Jones from the Block Association and Jerome Jameson from the Merchant's Association; the chairperson, Ms. Maria Garcia, is district manager of the Riverview Community Board. Also in attendance is Mr. Harry Walker, assemblyman from the Riverview district.

The first topic discussed is the outbreak of robberies in the shopping district. Police Officer Wallace reports that Precinct statistics show that there have been eight holdups in the Riverview Road shopping district in the last three months although there may have been others that were not reported. Most of the stick-ups occurred in the evenings when the stores were ready to close. There are three members in the stick-up team, and good descriptions are available of two of them:

> Number One: Male, white, 19–22 years of age, 5′8″ to 5′10″, about 185 pounds. This suspect seems to be the leader of the team, as he does the talking during the commission of the crimes. He carries a 0.38 calibre revolver which is silver plated. He has pistol-whipped at least three victims.
>
> Number Two: Female, Hispanic, 17–19 years of age, 5′2″ to 5′4″, about 110 pounds, with long black hair. This suspect is usually armed with a 0.32 calibre silver-plated handgun.

No description is available of the third member of the team, as this person acts as the driver of the getaway car and has not been closely observed. The suspects never use the same car twice, but seem to favor high-powered automoblies.

The second topic discussed is the outbreak of serious automobile accidents in the Riverview Road area. Detective Richardson reports that there have been eleven accidents in the vicinity of Riverview Road in the last two months, and at least nine people have been injured. The principal victims are young pedestrians struck while crossing in the middle of the block from between parked cars. Ms. Jones disputed this information and stated that there have been at least nineteen accidents, with fifteen injured people. Ms. Garcia feels that the accidents are being caused by reckless driving habits of certain local young persons; namely, members of a gang called the Vampires.

After considerable discussion about the above issues, the meeting ends at about 1945 hours. You then return to the Precinct station house at 1845 Riverview Road and prepare a report of the results of the meeting. Before going to your office, you check in with Sergeant Robert Barker, your immediate supervisor.

DO NOT PROCEED UNTIL 10 MINUTES HAS ELAPSED.

TEST MATERIAL

$3\frac{1}{2}$ HOUR TIME LIMIT

1. The assemblyman who attended the meeting was:
(A) Walker.
(B) Jones.
(C) Richardson.
(D) Ryder.

2. According to Ms. Jones, the recent automobile accidents have resulted in at least:
(A) Nine injuries.
(B) Eleven injuries.
(C) Fifteen injuries.
(D) Nineteen injuries.

3. Which of the following is the most accurate statement about the stick-up team?
(A) The white male is the only member who is about 19 years of age.
(B) The Hispanic female is the only member who is about 19 years of age.
(C) The white male and the Hispanic female are the only members who are about 19 years of age.
(D) All three members could be about 19 years of age.

4. The Precinct's juvenile officer is:
(A) Bartlett.
(B) Wallace.
(C) Richardson.
(D) Unnamed.

5. The district manager of the local community board is:
(A) Garcia.
(B) Walker.
(C) Jones.
(D) Barker.

6. The number of stick-ups that have occurred in the Riverview Road shopping district in the last four months was reported as:
(A) At least nine.
(B) At least eleven.
(C) At least eight.
(D) At least nineteen.

7. The meeting took place at:
   (A) 1845 Riverview Road.
   (B) The Precinct station house.
   (C) 1548 Riverview Road.
   (D) The headquarters of the Riverview Block Association.

8. The date of the meeting was:
   (A) Not stated.
   (B) April 7.
   (C) September 6.
   (D) April 17.

9. Which of the following is the most accurate statement concerning the complaints made at the meeting?
   (A) The serious automobile accidents are being caused by a local youth gang called the Vampires.
   (B) Most of the people involved in the automobile accidents are senior citizens.
   (C) In the last three months, there have been at least eleven automobile accidents in the vicinity of Riverview Road.
   (D) The pedestrians involved in the automobile accidents were not in any way at fault.

10. Which of the following is an *inaccurate* statement concerning the suspects in the stick-up team?
   (A) The female Hispanic is known to always carry a 0.32 calibre silver-plated handgun.
   (B) The male white is known to carry a 0.38 calibre silver-plated revolver.
   (C) Very little is known about the suspect who drives the getaway car.
   (D) At least one member is known to have used violence during the stick-ups.

11. The address of the precinct station house is:
   (A) 1945 Riverside Road.
   (B) 1845 Riverview Road.
   (C) 1548 Riverview Road.
   (D) Not given.

12. According to the story, you are assigned to the:
   (A) 54th Precinct in Queens.
   (B) 45th Precinct in Queens.
   (C) 54th Precinct in Brooklyn.
   (D) 45th Precinct in Brooklyn.

13. The first topic discussed at the meeting was the:
(A) Automobile accidents in the Riverview Road area.
(B) Outbreak of robberies in the shopping district.
(C) Conflicting statistics concerning the automobile accidents.
(D) Need for additional police protection in the Riverview Road area.

14. Your immediate supervisor is:
(A) Captain Richard Bartlett.
(B) Sergeant Robert Barker.
(C) Sergeant Jerome Jameson.
(D) Not given.

15. The meeting ended at about:
(A) 1730 hours.
(B) 1945 hours.
(C) 2015 hours.
(D) 2400 hours.

GO ON TO NEXT PAGE

SECTION TWO—
Applying Police Directives

***DIRECTIONS:* Answer questions 16 through 25 *solely* on the basis of the following.**

Most police departments today utilize a combination of one- and two-person radio motor patrol (RMP). Until a short time ago, one-person patrol in an automobile was not used in many large urban areas. Much of the debate between proponents and adversaries of one-person patrol centers around safety. Those against one-person patrol maintain that it is dangerous to permit only one police officer to respond to emergency calls in an area with a high incidence of violence. (In most cases, unions representing the police officers are against one-person patrol.) Those in favor of one-person patrols argue that when potentially dangerous calls are received by the dispatcher, two one-person units can then be assigned to respond.

One facet of two-person motor patrol that is generally overlooked is the necessity to designate the responsibility of each officer assigned to the patrol car. Issues such as who should drive, who is responsible for making reports, and who is responsible for the condition of the vehicle must be spelled out. Listed below are the patrol duties and responsibilities of an officer assigned at the beginning of an eight-hour tour as the operator (driver) of a two-person radio motor patrol car. The operator's partner for the tour, the officer not initially assigned as the driver, is known as the recorder.

Patrol Duties and Responsibilities of a Radio Motor Patrol Operator

1. Exchange assignments each four hours with the recorder.

2. Operate the car for the entire tour when assigned as the driver of a superior officer.
   a. Monitor radio messages directed to an assigned area when the superior is out of car.

3. While on patrol, permit only members of the service performing related police duty to enter or ride in a radio motor patrol car.

4. Respond to messages of serious police emergency within five blocks of location, even if the message is directed to another car. Disregard sector, precinct and division boundaries.

5. Do not carry electric blasting caps in vehicles or transmit within 150 feet of any electric blasting operation.

6. Monitor the radio when the recorder is assigned to a school or church crossing.
   a. Pick up the recorder and respond to an assignment when directed by the radio dispatcher.
7. Leave the radio on and have the car ready for instant use when the car is being cleaned or supplied with fuel. The car is not to be put out of service.
8. Avoid remaining in areas where radio reception is poor.
9. Proceed to an emergency scene with due caution. (Do not use the siren unnecessarily; approach the scene of a reported crime quietly.)
10. Take RMP out of assigned sector when:
    a. directed by competent authority, or
    b. answering an emergency call, or
    c. servicing, repairing, or cleaning is required (with permission of the station house supervisor).
11. Patrol the assigned sector constantly.
12. Do not leave the car unattended unnecessarily. *Remove* the keys and *Lock* the car when answering a call. *Do not leave the portable radio in the car.*
13. Position the car at the scene of an emergency so as to avoid obstructing, or being blocked by, emergency apparatus.
14. Sign the return roll call at the end of the tour.
15. Perform the duties of the recorder when none is assigned.
16. Inspect the car when reporting for duty.
17. Make a Memo/Officer's Log entry of the findings, speedometer reading, and amount of gasoline in the tank, as registered by the indicator.
18. Notify the station house supervisor when a car requires repairs or parts replacement or accessories.
19. Operate the car in a manner to avoid injury to the person or damage to the property.
20. Drive at a slow rate of speed except under exceptional circumstances or extreme emergency.
21. Operate the RMP car only when assigned and when qualified by the Department to operate the vehicle to which assigned.

22. Take care of the car and all accessories, equipment, and tools assigned.

23. Cooperate with other operators of the same car to which assigned, in care and maintenance, particularly with reference to cleaning, washing and keeping the car in proper operating condition.

24. Whenever possible, make minor repairs to the car after placing the car out of service.

25. Deliver the car for regular preventive maintenance inspection.

26. Enter the appointment for preventive maintenance on the sticker affixed to the vehicle.

TURN TO NEXT PAGE

16. On April 4, Police Officer William Sweeney, Shield Number 234321, 36th Precinct, was assigned as the operator of RMP 3232, Sector Edward. His partner was Police Officer Mary O'Hara, Shield Number 543233, 36th Precinct. Her assignment is as recorder of RMP 3232. Both officers are performing a day tour, 0800 hours by 1600 hours. At 1130 hours, they came upon Police Officer John Barret who was assigned on foot to Patrol Post 18, which is part of Sector Edward. Officer Barret explained to Officer Sweeney that he had just started his meal hour and would appreciate a ride to the local restaurant. Officer Sweeney agreed, and gave Officer Barret a lift to a restaurant which was within the confines of RMP Sector Edward.

Based upon the above information, Officer Sweeney's decision to give Officer Barret a ride was:

(A) Proper, since at no time did Officer Sweeney have to take his RMP car out of his assigned sector.
(B) Improper, since Officer Barret was not performing a police duty.
(C) Proper, since Officer Sweeney left the radio on and did not take his unit out of service.
(D) Improper, since Officer Sweeney did not obtain the prior approval of his supervisor.

17. An RMP may *not* be taken out of an assigned sector:

(A) When done in accordance with directions by a competent authority.
(B) When done as a result of the operator's decision to have the RMP car cleaned.
(C) When answering an emergency call directed at an assigned unit.
(D) When responding to an emergency call four blocks outside the assigned sector even if the call was not directed to the assigned unit.

18. Which of the following is a correct statement about one-person patrol in a radio motor patrol car?
   (A) Nowadays, all police departments utilize a combination of one- and two-person patrol.
   (B) All police unions are against one-person patrols.
   (C) Until recently, one-person patrol was not used in large urban areas.
   (D) Proponents maintain that the safety hazards of one-person patrol can be neutralized by assignment policies that direct two units to potentially dangerous calls.

19. Police Officer Harold Robbens was assigned as the operator of RMP 5454 of the 56th Precinct. At 1345 hours his unit was directed by the radio dispatcher to respond to a "Robbery in Progress" call at a location about eight blocks from his present location. Officer Robbens switched on the RMP's emergency lights and siren and proceeded to the call, where he and his partner arrested three males for armed robbery.

   Based upon the above information, Officer Robbens' action in using the siren was:
   (A) Proper, since three arrests were made as a result of his using the siren.
   (B) Improper, since he was only eight blocks away from the crime scene when he got the call.
   (C) Proper, since he also employed the emergency lights.
   (D) Improper, since he is supposed to approach a crime scene quietly.

20. Police Officer James Carlin was assigned as the operator of RMP 6565 of the 57th Precinct. He was performing a tour of duty of 0001 by 0800 hours. At about 0245 hours the RMP car stalled as a result of a battery cable working loose. Officer Carlin put his unit out of service, notified his supervisor, and called the repair shop for an emergency roadside repair.

   Based upon the above information, Office Carlin's action in this situation was:

(A) Proper, since his car was disabled and unable to respond to emergency calls.
(B) Improper, since he is required to make minor repairs on his assigned vehicle.
(C) Proper, since at 0245 hours it is very difficult to find a neighborhood service station that is open.
(D) Improper, since he should not have put his unit out of service.

21. The crux of the argument about one-person patrol in a motorized unit is:
(A) Assignment policies.
(B) The safety of the police officers.
(C) The efficiency of one-person patrol units.
(D) The objections of the police unions.

22. It is not *always* a violation of department regulations to:
(A) Leave the keys in the RMP car when going on a call.
(B) Leave a portable radio in the RMP car when answering a call.
(C) Leave the RMP car unattended when answering a call.
(D) Leave the RMP car unlocked when going on a call.

23. Officer Ray Weeks is the operator of RMP 807. An *improperly* stated responsibility of the officer is to:
(A) Inspect the car when reporting for and going off duty.
(B) Perform the duties of the recorder when none is assigned.
(C) Patrol the assigned sector constantly.
(D) Sign the return roll call at the end of the tour.

24. Which of the following is an *incorrect* statement with regard to the duties and responsibilities of a radio motor patrol operator?

(A) All police officers assigned as operators of a two-person RMP car rotate after four hours and become recorders.

(B) An operator should never take his/her car out of service when the car is being supplied with fuel.

(C) An operator of an RMP car should operate the car in such a manner as to avoid damage to property.

(D) An operator of an RMP car should always proceed to an emergency call with due caution.

25. Which of the following is an *incorrectly* stated responsibility of a radio motor patrol operator?

(A) Never transmit a radio message within 150 feet of an electric blasting operation.

(B) Never remain in an area where the radio reception is poor.

(C) Never operate an RMP car unless assigned to do so.

(D) Never neglect to take care of assigned equipment.

TURN TO NEXT PAGE

DIRECTIONS: Answer questions 26 through 35 _solely_ on the basis of the information contained in the following procedures.

One of the most dangerous and sensitive tasks of a police officer is to safeguard a mentally ill person who is being removed to a hospital. The first thing that has to be remembered is that unless a person is voluntarily seeking medical assistance, the police cannot force such assistance on a person. There are only certain circumstances under which the police can remove a person to a hospital for psychiatric treatment. They are as follows:

a. when the person requests such assistance,
b. when a police officer observes an apparent mentally ill person who is conducting himself in a manner likely to result in serious physical harm to himself or others,
c. upon receipt of two (2) separate written statements from physicians who have examined the person concerned, or,
d. upon receipt of a court order.

When one of the above situations exists and a member of the service has to safeguard an apparent mentally ill person, the following procedures are to be followed.

1. Take the person concerned into custody, if he/she is not already in safekeeping.

2. Request an ambulance. If none is available, either bring the person to the station house and make a second request for an ambulance, or transport the person to the hospital if able to do so with reasonable restraint. In any event, follow these procedures:
   a. Use restraining equipment, including handcuffs, if the patient is violent or resists, or upon the direction of a physician examiner.
   b. If unable to transport with reasonable restraint, an ambulance attendant or doctor will request a special ambulance.
   c. When possible, a female patient being transported should be accompanied by another female or by an adult member of her immediate family.
   d. Remove property that is dangerous to life or will aid in escape.

3. Ride in the body of the ambulance with the patient.
   a. Two police officers will safeguard if more than one patient is being transported.

4. Safeguard the patient at the hospital until he/she is examined by a psychiatrist.
   a. When entering the psychiatric ward of the hospital, unload revolver.

5. Inform the psychiatrist of the circumstances which brought the patient into police custody.
   a. Inform the relieving police officer of circumstances if safeguarding extends beyond expiration of tour. The relieving police officer will inform the psychiatrist of details.

6. Enter details in the Activity Log and prepare an Aided Report.
   a. Indicate on Aided Report, the name of the psychiatrist to whom written statements concerning the patient were delivered, if appropriate.

7. Deliver the Aided Report to the station house officer.

NOTE: Prior to interviewing a patient confined to a facility of the Department of Hospitals, a member of the service must obtain permission from the hospital administrator, who will ascertain if the patient is mentally competent to give a statement.

TURN TO NEXT PAGE

26. Police Officer Cox, Shield 15432, 39th Precinct, is dispatched to 1010 Centre Avenue, Apartment 3B, to see a complainant. Upon arriving at the location, Officer Cox is met by John Adams, male, white, 54 years of age, who wants to have his wife removed to the hospital for psychiatric observation and treatment. Mr. Adams produces a note from two associate physicians who have examined Mrs. Adams and who have recommended hospitalization for further observation. Officer Cox then calls for an ambulance, and has Mrs. Adams removed to the hospital.

Based upon the above information, Officer Cox's actions were:

(A) Proper, since Mrs. Adams had been examined by two doctors.
(B) Improper, since Officer Cox did not observe Mrs. Adams acting in an insane manner.
(C) Proper, since Mrs. Adams volunteered to go to the hospital.
(D) Improper, since Mr. Adams produced only one doctor's note.

27. If there is no ambulance available to transport a violent mentally ill person to the hospital, a police officer should:

(A) Wait at the scene until an ambulance is available.
(B) Bring the person to the station house and make another request for an ambulance.
(C) Call the patrol supervisor to the scene and be guided by his directions.
(D) Request the special police ambulance that is available for this reason.

28. How many police officers are needed to transport four mentally ill patients?

(A) 1
(B) 2
(C) 3
(D) 4

29. Police Officer Mary Jones is assigned to transport a mentally ill person to the hospital. The patient is a mild-mannered teenage boy who is rather big for his age but quite docile. Officer Jones requests an ambulance and, upon its arrival, she handcuffs her patient and leads him off.

Based upon the previous information, Officer Jones acted:

(A) Properly, since the boy was big for his age.
(B) Improperly, since restraining equipment was not necessary in this case.
(C) Properly, since the officer had no partner to back her up.
(D) Improperly, since the boy was not crazy.

30. Under what circumstances must a police officer unload his or her revolver when transporting a mentally ill person to a hospital?

(A) Upon entering the ambulance
(B) Upon entering the hospital
(C) Upon entering certain parts of the hospital
(D) Never

31. Which of the following is the most accurate statement concerning the transportation of a female mental patient to a hospital?

(A) It requires a female police officer.
(B) It can be accomplished by one officer with no assistance.
(C) A third person must accompany the officer.
(D) A member of the immediate family must be present.

32. Police Officer James Poe is on his post on the Bowery when he is approached by a tourist who complains that the officer should obtain medical assistance for a nearby derelict who is bleeding from a head wound. Actually, the officer had just asked the derelict if he wanted medical assistance, and was told to mind his own business. The officer tells the tourist that he does not have the authority to summon an ambulance in this case.

Based upon the above information, the officer acted:

(A) Properly, since the police cannot force medical attention on a person.
(B) Improperly, since the officer is sworn to protect life and property.
(C) Properly, since the tourist has no right to interfere in this case.
(D) Improperly, since the police must tend to all sick or injured persons.

33. For the police, removing a mentally ill person to a hospital is a(an):

(A) Routine task.
(B) Dangerous and sensitive task.
(C) Undesirable task.
(D) Uncommon task.

34. There is a special ambulance available for transporting mentally ill persons to the hospital. This ambulance is used:

(A) When there are many persons to transport.
(B) When there are no police officers available to assist in the removal.
(C) When more than reasonable restraint is required to transport a patient.
(D) For patients with a history of extreme violence.

35. When the patient is being transported to the hospital in an ambulance, the assigned police officer should be:

(A) Following closely in his police car.
(B) In the front of the ambulance with the driver.
(C) In the body of the ambulance with the patient.
(D) Wherever he believes it is necessary to be.

GO ON TO NEXT PAGE

SECTION THREE— Reading Comprehension

***DIRECTIONS:* Answer questions 36 through 45 *solely* on the basis of the information contained in the following passage.**

Shortly after a taxicab driver, who had been robbed by a man wielding a sawed-off shotgun, identified a picture of Innis as being that of his assailant, a police officer saw Innis, who was unarmed at the time, on the street. The officer placed him under arrest and advised him of his rights under the Miranda decision, which is the landmark Supreme Court decision requiring the police to inform an arrested person of the constitutional rights to remain silent and to have an attorney. When other officers arrived, Innis was twice again advised of his Miranda rights. Innis said he understood his rights, and wanted to talk to a lawyer. He was then placed in a police car to be driven to a police station in the company of three officers who were instructed not to question him or to intimidate him in any way. While enroute to the station house, two of the officers engaged in conversation about the shotgun which was missing. One of the officers said, "There were a lot of handicapped children running around this area because a school for such children was located nearby and, God forbid, one of these children might find a weapon with shells and hurt themselves."

Innis, hearing this exchange, told the officers to turn around so he could show them where the gun was located. Upon returning to the scene of the arrest, where a search for the shotgun was in progress, Innis was re-advised of his Miranda rights. He said that he understood those rights, but that he wanted to get the gun out of the area because children were in the proximity of the school. He then led police to the shotgun.

The trial court denied Innis' motion to suppress the shotgun and the statements he made to the police connected to its discovery. The court ruled that he had voluntarily waived his Miranda rights and, thus, he was subsequently convicted. Nevertheless, the Rhode Island Supreme Court set aside the conviction, holding that Innis was entitled to a new trial, concluding that he had invoked his Miranda rights to counsel and that, contrary to Miranda's mandate that in the absence of counsel all custodial interrogation must cease, the police officers in the vehicle had "interrogated" Innis without a valid waiver of his right to counsel.

After the Rhode Island Supreme Court issued its decision, the state of Rhode Island appealed the case to the United States Supreme Court. The United States Supreme Court held that Innis had not been interrogated and, thus, the fact that he did not waive his right to counsel was not important.

The Miranda safeguards come into play whenever a person in custody is subjected to either express questioning or anything similar to express questioning. The term "interrogation" under Miranda refers not only to express questioning, but also to any words or actions on the part of the police (other than those normally attendant to arrest and custody, such as pedigree) that are reasonably likely to get an incriminating response from the suspect. (Note that "pedigree" refers to factual information regarding a person's name, age, date of birth, gender, and race.) Indeed, with respect to whether words or actions on the part of the police are likely to result in a person making an incriminating statement, it is less important whether the police intend to get the suspect to speak than whether the suspect believes the words or actions were meant to induce him to speak.

Clearly, when questions are directed to a suspect in custody (express questioning), that is "interrogation." However, when two or more officers talk to each other in a suspect's presence but do not direct their conversation to the suspect, and the suspect responds because of what the officers here said to each other, it is not always clear whether that is the same as questioning.

The key as far as police officers are concerned is whether they should have known when talking to each other that their conversation was reasonably likely to produce an incriminating statement from the suspect. If the officer intends to get a response, or hopes for a response, by his conversation with his fellow officer, then any statements made by the suspect who has not waived his rights or for some reason cannot waive his rights (e.g., lawyer not present), would not be admissible in evidence. This would constitute "interrogation" since it is equivalent of express questioning.

Even if a response is not intended but the officer is aware that the suspect is emotionally upset or would likely be touched by an appeal to his conscience (e.g., in this case the safety of handicapped children), then any conversation about the case would likely produce a response from the suspect and would be considered interrogation.

The Supreme Court of the United States indicated that there was no express questioning of Innis; the conversation between the two officers did not seek a response from Innis. It could not be said that the officers should have known that their conversation was reasonably likely to cause Innis to make an incriminating response.

GO ON TO NEXT PAGE

36. Throughout the entire story, how many times was Innis advised of his Miranda rights?
(A) Twice
(B) Three times
(C) Four times
(D) Five times

37. "Express questioning" is *not*:
(A) Interrogation.
(B) Actions by the police that are designed to make a person make an incriminating statement.
(C) Questions directed to a suspect in custody.
(D) The obtaining of a person's pedigree by the police.

38. Conversation by the police about a case involving a suspect who is present and emotionally upset, would:
(A) Not be considered an interrogation since no response is expected from the suspect.
(B) Not be considered interrogation unless the police intended to get a response from the suspect.
(C) Be considered an interrogation even if the police did not intend to get a response from the suspect.
(D) Be considered an interrogation since the courts have ruled that any conversation between the police and a suspect is interrogation.

39. Innis was arrested after:
(A) The victim spotted him in the street.
(B) He was picked out of a line up.
(C) His victim identified him from a photograph.
(D) He gave himself up.

40. Which of the following is a correct statement about the findings of the various courts in this case with respect to the suppression of the shotgun as evidence?
(A) The Supreme Court of Rhode Island agreed with the trial court.
(B) The United States Supreme Court agreed with the Rhode Island Supreme Court.
(C) The Supreme Court of the United States agreed with the trial court.
(D) None of the courts in the narrative agreed with each other.

41. With respect to whether words or actions on the part of the police are likely to result in a person making an incriminating statement, which is more important?

(A) The intention of the police
(B) The beliefs of the suspect
(C) The motives of the police
(D) The age of the suspect

42. The trial court based its decision on the fact that:

(A) Innis had not been interrogated.
(B) Innis had voluntarily waived his rights.
(C) Innis did not have a lawyer.
(D) Innis gave the information to the police of his own free will.

43. The United States Supreme Court based its findings on the position that:

(A) Innis had not been interrogated.
(B) Innis had waived his right to counsel.
(C) Innis was not emotionally upset when the incident occurred.
(D) Innis was asked if he wanted a lawyer.

44. When three officers have a conversation with each other in the presence of a suspect, but the officers do not direct the conversation to the suspect:

(A) It is considered questioning only if the suspect responds to the police.
(B) It is not considered questioning even if the suspect responds to the police.
(C) It is unclear whether it is questioning even if the suspect responds to the police.
(D) It is not considered questioning even if the suspect responds to the police as long as the suspect has been given his Miranda rights.

45. Which of the following is an *incorrect* statement concerning the findings of the United States Supreme Court in this case?

(A) No express questioning was involved.
(B) The officers should have known that their conversation was reasonably likely to cause Innis to make an incriminating response.
(C) Innis had not been interrogated.
(D) The term "interrogation" under Miranda refers to more than just express questioning.

GO ON TO NEXT PAGE

***DIRECTIONS:* Answer questions 46 through 50 *solely* on the basis of information contained in the following court case.**

Facts

Bartol was arrested by the Suffolk County Police Department for arson. He was arraigned on that charge, and was represented by counsel at the arraignment.

Seven days later, Bartol was again arrested by the Suffolk County Police Department, but this time, for homicide. The defendant's father was with him when he was arrested, but neither he nor the defendant told the police that the defendant had an attorney on the arson charge.

The homicide detectives knew Bartol was arrested for arson, but neither knew he had an attorney. They advised him of his rights, but no mention was made that he had an attorney on the arson charge. In response to his rights, Bartol said he did not want a lawyer, and that he would answer questions without a lawyer. He then made incriminating statements.

The trial court and the Appellate Division permitted the statements made to the homicide detectives to be used against Bartol. The Court of Appeals suppressed the statements.

Decision

The Court of Appeals has been progressively strengthening a defendant's right to counsel. This case adds to those rights which were previously granted by the court. The court feels that law enforcement personnel should be aware of the court's concern for, and protection of, a criminal defendant's right to the aid of counsel at every critical stage of proceedings against him.

Previous cases have held that knowledge by the police that a person is represented by a lawyer in an unrelated case prevents a waiver of counsel in his absence. It follows, naturally, that knowledge of an arrest should lead one to believe that a defendant may be represented by an attorney.

Accordingly, the Court of Appeals requires police officers, when they know the suspect has been recently arrested by someone in their department, to ask a suspect whether he has a lawyer. If the suspect is represented by a lawyer on a previous arrest case, he may not waive right to counsel unless his attorney is present.

TURN TO NEXT PAGE

46. The trend of the Court of Appeals has been to:
(A) Strengthen police powers.
(B) Agree with the lower courts.
(C) Strengthen a defendant's right to a lawyer.
(D) Weaken a defendant's right to counsel.

47. Which of the following is the most accurate statement concerning the opinions of the various courts in this case?
(A) The Appellate Division disagreed with the trial court.
(B) The Court of Appeals agreed with the Appellate Division.
(C) The trial court and the Appellate Court were in agreement.
(D) None of the courts involved were in agreement.

48. The original charge against Bartol was:
(A) Homicide.
(B) Arson.
(C) Burglary.
(D) Robbery.

49. The Court of Appeals feels that a defendant has a right to the aid of an attorney:
(A) Especially at arraignment.
(B) Especially at trial.
(C) Especially upon a rearrest.
(D) At every critical stage of proceedings.

50. According to the Court of Appeals, when can a suspect who has just been arrested and who is represented by a lawyer on a previous arrest case, waive his right to counsel on the new arrest case?
(A) Anytime
(B) Never
(C) Only when his attorney is present
(D) Only if he is pleading guilty

GO ON TO NEXT PAGE

***DIRECTIONS:* Answer questions 51 through 55 *solely* on the basis of information contained in the following court case.**

Facts

Sommers was descending the front steps of his house as police officers were about to execute a warrant to search the house for narcotics. The officers requested his assistance in gaining entry, and they detained him while they searched the premises. After finding narcotics in the basement and ascertaining that Sommers owned the house, he was arrested and searched. Heroin was found in his coat pocket. Sommers moved to suppress the heroin found on his person as the product of an illegal search in violation of the Fourth Amendment. The trial court granted the motion, and the State Appellate Court affirmed. The United States Supreme Court granted certiorari, and reversed.

Decision

The Court noted that the initial detention constituted a "seizure" within the meaning of the Fourth Amendment. Sommers was not free to leave the premises while the officers were searching his home. The issue was whether the pre-arrest detention ("seizure") was unreasonable since it was not supported by probable cause.

The Court restated the general rule that Fourth Amendment seizures are reasonable only if based on probable cause. However, the Court recognized that there are exceptions to the general rule for limited intrusions that may be justified by special law enforcement interests. (Examples within the exception include, but are not limited to, "stop-and-frisk" situations.) The Court stated:

> "These cases recognize that some seizures admittedly covered by the Fourth Amendment constitute such limited intrusions on the security of those detained and are justified by such substantial law enforcement interests that they may be made on less than probable cause, as long as police have an articulable basis for suspecting criminal activity."

In analyzing the character of the intrusion and its justification, the Court noted that the fact that the police had obtained a search warrant was of prime importance. Since the house search had been authorized, the limited detention of one of the residents at his premises, while it was being searched, was not unreasonable.

Conclusion

The rule of this case is that police officers, when executing search warrants of premises, may detain occupants therein while the search is being conducted. Should the search of the premises uncover contraband, the occupant in control of the premises can be arrested and charged with the possession of the contraband.

TURN TO NEXT PAGE

51. As a general rule, Fourth Amendment seizures are reasonable when:

(A) They are based on probable cause.

(B) They are made on the authority of a warrant.

(C) The safety of police officers is involved.

(D) They are accompanied by a search.

52. Who can be arrested if a house search pursuant to a warrant uncovers contraband?

(A) Only the owner of the house.

(B) Only the occupant in control of the house.

(C) Everyone present in the house.

(D) No one present in the house.

53. Which of the following is the most accurate statement concerning the opinions of the various courts involved in this case?

(A) The trial court was in agreement with the Appellate Court.

(B) The U.S. Supreme Court was in agreement with the Appellate Court.

(C) All of the courts involved were in agreement.

(D) None of the courts involved were in agreement.

54. According to the facts of this case, narcotics were found:

(A) Only in the basement of the house.

(B) Only in the defendant's coat pocket.

(C) In the basement and in the house owner's clothing.

(D) In at least three different locations.

55. A factor that the Supreme Court found to be of extreme significance in this case was that:

(A) Heroin was discovered.

(B) Sommers owned the house.

(C) There are exceptions to all judicial rules.

(D) The police had obtained a search warrant.

GO ON TO NEXT PAGE

SECTION FOUR—Police Department Forms

DIRECTIONS: **Answer questions 56 through 65 *solely* on the basis of the information recorded on the following "Overtime Report."**

RANK	SOCIAL SECURITY NO.		COMMAND
Police Officer	104-30-3356		39th Pct.
SHIELD	SURNAME	INITIAL(S)	SQD./CHT.
706	Pearson	T.R.	3

DATE ENTERED DEPT.	DATE PRESENT RANK
06/26/93	06/26/93

	FROM	TO	HRS.	MIN.
TIME ACTUALLY WORKED — DATE	4/1/XX	4/1/XX		
TIME	0800 hours	1900 hours	11	00
TIME SCHEDULED TO WORK — DATE	4/1/XX	4/1/XX		
TOUR NO. 1 — TIME	0800 hours	1600 hours	8	00

	HRS.	MIN.
OVERTIME PERFORMED	3	00
PLUS TRAVEL TIME (IF APPLICABLE)	N/A	
TOTAL OVERTIME	3	00
COMPENSATION OPTION: (INDICATE HRS. & MIN.) TIME	-	--
CASH	3	00

CMD./LOCATION WHERE DUTY PERFORMED 39 Pct.

INCIDENT TIME (Actual time of Occurrence) 1545 hours

REASON FOR LOST TIME: (Identify incident specifically)

Homicide Investigation

I hereby certify that this report is accurate:

Date	Rank/Signature of Requesting Member
4/2/XX	P.O. Thomas R. Pearson

SUPERVISORY OFFICER'S CERTIFICATION

MEMBER DIRECTED TO RETURN TO COMMAND?

☐ YES—Do not sign form. Advise member to submit at command.	☒ NO—Time dismissed: 1900 Hours (Forward form to member's C.O.)

Log Entry: Date	Time	Page No.
April 1, XXXX	1900 hours	107

Date	Rank/Signature of supervisor	Command
4/1/XX	Sgt. James Wilson	49 Pct.

INSTRUCTIONS: Submit one copy to stationhouse officer or supervisor at time of **FINAL** dismissal. Form must be certified by a supervisor and then forwarded to member's Commanding Officer without delay.

OVERTIME REPORT PD 138-064

Source of blank form: New York City Police Department

TURN TO NEXT PAGE

56. The rank and last name of the person requesting compensation is:
(A) Sergeant Wilson.
(B) Police Officer Thomas.
(C) Sergeant James.
(D) Police Officer Pearson.

57. The amount of overtime actually performed was:
(A) 11 hours.
(B) 8 hours.
(C) 3 hours.
(D) 1 hour.

58. The justification for the performance of overtime was a(an):
(A) Accident investigation.
(B) Court appearance.
(C) Homicide investigation.
(D) Robbery arrest.

59. The crime that caused the overtime was committed at:
(A) 1600 hours.
(B) 1545 hours.
(C) 1900 hours.
(D) An unknown time.

60. The requesting officer's scheduled tour of duty was:
(A) 0800 by 1600.
(B) 1600 by 2400.
(C) 0001 by 0800.
(D) Not stated.

61. When is this form to be delivered to the station house officer or supervisor?
(A) As soon as possible
(B) On the next scheduled work day
(C) Within three days of the overtime
(D) At time of final dismissal

62. Where was the overtime performed?
(A) In the 39th Precinct
(B) In the 49th Precinct
(C) In the Homicide Bureau
(D) Not stated

63. On what day did Officer Pearson obtain his present rank?
(A) On July 26.
(B) On May 26.
(C) On June 26.
(D) On the day that he entered the Department.

64. What happened to Officer Pearson at 1900 hours on the day he worked the overtime?
(A) He was sent back to his command.
(B) He was reassigned to another investigation.
(C) He was dismissed from further duty.
(D) He reported sick.

65. Officer Pearson will be compensated for this overtime by receiving:
(A) Compensatory time off.
(B) Extra cash.
(C) Time off or cash.
(D) A special award.

TURN TO NEXT PAGE

***DIRECTIONS:* Answers questions 66 through 75 *solely* on the basis of the following narrative and "Stop and Frisk Report." Some of the boxes on the form are numbered; some are not. The boxes are not necessarily consecutively numbered.**

On June 1, at about 2030 hours, Police Officer James Role, a male, black, 33 years of age, observed a male, white. This man was later identified as Thomas Loren, 27 years of age, residing at 6521 Courtland Avenue, the Bronx, New York City.

At 2015 hours on the same date, Officer Role had been notified by Sam Lopez, a male, Hispanic, 30 years of age, who is an owner of a store located at 240 Centre Street, New York, that a man wearing a red cap, a white shirt and Bermuda shorts had just robbed him at the corner of Centre and Canal Streets. Mr. Lopez said the thief, who was white and looked to be from 25 to 30 years old, had taken a white-handled pistol from his waistband and demanded money. Mr. Lopez gave him $130 in U.S. currency in a yellow envelope, and the robber fled the scene.

After observing the male, who acted suspiciously, for about five minutes, Officer Role approached him as he stood on the northeast corner of Centre Street and Worth Street. The male fit the description of the perpetrator in the robbery against Mr. Lopez. At 2035 hours, Officer Role, who was working alone, confronted the male and asked him to identify himself and give an explanation of his actions. After remarking, "Why are you hassling me?" he identified himself as Thomas Loren of 6521 Courtland Avenue. While questioning Mr. Loren, Officer Role noticed a bulge in the suspect's waistband. Believing his life to be in danger, Officer Role then frisked the outer garments of Mr. Loren, with particular attention to the bulge in his clothing at his waistline. The bulge felt like the handle of a pistol to the officer. The officer then lifted Mr. Loren's shirt and removed a white-handled pistol from his waistband. After ascertaining that Loren had no legal authority to carry a handgun, Officer Role placed him under arrest. A further search of the prisoner yielded a yellow envelope containing $130 in U.S. currency. Loren was charged with robbery and unlawful possession of a weapon.

Police Officer Role brought his prisoner to the Fourth Precinct, the precinct where the officer was assigned and where the incident occurred. He explained to Sergeant Hal Dian, Shield #426 of the Fourth Precinct, that he was on Post 26, as per his assignment, when he stopped, frisked, and arrested the prisoner. After hearing the story, Sergeant Dian said that the precinct serial number for the "Stop and Frisk Report" would be 621. Sergeant Dian further stated that the probability was that the stop required no force since the officer was in uniform when it occurred. The sergeant ascertained the officer's shield number to be 27, and signed the "Stop and Frisk Report" in the appropriate space. The arrest number was 1007.

TIME 1.	and DATE OF STOPPING 2.	PERIOD OF OBSERVATION PRIOR TO STOPPING 3.	LOCATION/KIND OF PUBLIC PLACE 4.	PCT. 5.	POST 6.	PCT. SER. NO. 7.

FACTORS WHICH CAUSED OFFICER TO REASONABLY SUSPECT PERSON STOPPED (Include information from third persons and their identity, if known)
8.

CRIME SUSPECTED 9.	How long was Person Stopped 10.	REMARKS BY PERSON STOPPED 11.

12. OFFICER IN UNIFORM ☐ YES ☐ NO | IF NO, HOW IDENTIFIED 13. ☐ SHIELD ☐ I.D. CARD ☐ BOTH | WAS FORCE USED 14. ☐ YES ☐ NO | IF YES, DESCRIBE 15.

16. WAS PERSON FRISKED ☐ YES ☐ NO | WAS SEARCH INSIDE CLOTHES MADE 17. ☐ YES ☐ NO | IF YES, DESCRIBE WHERE MADE AND BASIS FOR INSIDE SEARCH 18.

19. Was Weapon Found ☐ YES ☐ NO | IF YES, DESCRIBE 20. | Was Other Contraband Found 21. ☐ YES ☐ NO | IF YES, DESCRIBE 22.

NAME OF PERSON STOPPED (if given) 23. | and ADDRESS 24.

DESCRIPTION	SEX	COLOR	AGE	HEIGHT	WEIGHT	HAIR	EYES	BUILD	OTHER (Describe)
	25	26	27	28	29	30	31	32	33

IF PERSON STOPPED IS SUBSEQUENTLY ARRESTED, INCLUDE ADDITIONAL FACTORS WHICH LED TO ARREST
34.

CRIME CHARGED 35.	CONTRABAND FOUND IN POST-ARREST SEARCH 36.	COURT IN WHICH CASE PENDING 37.

RANK	SIGNATURE OF REPORTING OFFICER	SHIELD	COMMAND	RANK	SIGNATURE OF SUPERIOR OFFICER	COMMAND
38.	39.	40.	41.	42.	43.	44.

STOP AND FRISK REPORT

PD 344-151
(Formerly U.F. 250)

1st COPY · CENTRAL RECORDS DIVISION, CRIMINAL RECORDS SECTION — 2nd COPY · PRECINCT FILE — 3rd COPY · DETECTIVE DISTRICT

Source of blank form: New York City Police Department

TURN TO NEXT PAGE

66. Which of the following should be entered in Box 11?
(A) "What do you want?"
(B) "Leave me alone."
(C) "Why are you hassling me?"
(D) "I didn't do nothing!"

67. The correct entry for Box 12 is:
(A) Yes.
(B) No.
(C) Unknown.
(D) Not given.

68. The correct entry for Box 30 is:
(A) Brown.
(B) Black.
(C) Blond.
(D) Not known.

69. The proper entries for Boxes 5 and 6, respectively, are:
(A) 4 and 26.
(B) 26 and 4.
(C) 26 and 261.
(D) 26 and 27.

70. The signature of James Role should be placed in which box?
(A) 43
(B) 23
(C) 22
(D) 39

71. The sergeant's shield number should be entered in:
(A) Only one box on the form.
(B) Two boxes on the form.
(C) More than two boxes on the form.
(D) None of the boxes on the form.

72. The proper entries for Boxes 12, 16 and 17, respectively, are:
(A) Yes, no, no.
(B) No, yes, no.
(C) No, no, yes.
(D) Yes, yes, yes.

73. The answer to the question of whether force was used can be found in Box number:

(A) 7.
(B) 14.
(C) 18.
(D) 37.

74. Which of the following best indicates the proper entry for Box Number 3?

(A) 5 minutes
(B) 10 minutes
(C) 15 minutes
(D) 20 minutes

75. The correct information for Box 1 is:

(A) 2015 hours.
(B) 2020 hours.
(C) 2035 hours.
(D) 2030 hours.

TURN TO NEXT PAGE

SECTION FIVE—
Understanding Legal Definitions

***DIRECTIONS:* Answer questions 76 through 85 *solely* on the basis of the legal definitions given below. Do *not* answer the questions on any other knowledge of the statutes you might have. While the definitions are based on actual state penal laws, they might not be identical with the actual law or illustrative of recent court decisions. The definitions are not in any particular order and their sequence does not indicate rank order based on seriousness of the offense. You *may* refer to the definitions when answering questions.**

NOTE: The perpetrators in the following definitions are referred to as "he" solely for ease of examination; the pronoun "he" refers to either gender.

burglar's tools: A person commits this crime when he possesses an instrument which is commonly used in committing the crimes of burglary, larceny, or theft of services.

criminal possession of stolen property: A person criminally possesses stolen property when he is in possession of property not his own, when he believes the property is stolen, and when the property is actually stolen.

criminal possession of a weapon: A person criminally possesses a weapon when he possesses, with no legal right or license, a handgun, a sawed-off shotgun, a switchblade knife, or a blackjack. It does not matter if the handgun or shotgun is loaded or unloaded. For the purposes of this statute, a rifle is not included.

criminal impersonation: A person commits criminal impersonation when he pretends to be a police officer, a parole officer, a fireman, or any other public servant with the intent of having someone submit to his authority.

resisting arrest: A person is guilty of resisting arrest when he prevents, or attempts to prevent, a police officer from making an authorized arrest of any person.

adultery: A person commits adultery when he engages in sexual intercourse with another person, not his spouse, and either party has a living spouse.

felony murder: A person commits felony murder when during the commission of certain felonies, he causes the death of another person. The felonies referred to in this statute include burglary, arson, kidnapping, forcible rape, forcible sodomy, or robbery.

grand larceny: A person commits grand larceny when he takes property belonging to another person with the intent of keeping the property permanently for his own use, or for the use of someone other than the original owner; and the property is worth more than $1,000.

rape: A male person commits rape when he has sexual intercourse with a female by force and against her will; or, in any instance when the male is over 21 years of age and the female is less than 17 years of age. This law does not apply to persons who are legally married to each other.

sodomy: A person commits sodomy when he forces another person against that person's will to engage in oral or anal sex; or, when he is over 21 years of age and the other person is less than 17 years of age and they engage in oral or anal sex under any circumstances. However, this law does not apply to persons legally married to each other.

TURN TO NEXT PAGE

76. In order to be charged with the crime of burglar's tools a person must possess an instrument commonly used in the commission of all of the following crimes except:

(A) Burglary.
(B) Robbery.
(C) Larceny.
(D) Theft of services.

77. Mr. Smith likes to dress as a fireman to be able to get through police lines at the scene of fire emergencies. Only authorized persons are permitted past these lines. One day, at the scene of a big fire, Mr. Smith dresses like a fireman and the police allow him to pass through their lines. After a short time, during which he remains undetected, he becomes bored, leaves on his own, and goes home.

Based upon the above information, Mr. Smith has committed:

(A) Larceny of a fire uniform.
(B) Theft of services.
(C) Criminal impersonation.
(D) No crime.

78. John sees a police officer on foot legally arresting his friend for "driving while intoxicated." John knows that his friend, who is a truck driver, may lose his driver's license if he is arrested and later convicted. John, not wanting his friend to lose his license, jumps on the police officer, and tells his friend to run away.

Based upon the above information, John:

(A) Has not committed the crime of "resisting arrest" since it was his friend that was being arrested.
(B) Has committed the crime of "resisting arrest" even though he was not the subject of the arrest attempt.
(C) Has not committed the crime of "resisting arrest" since the arrest was not an authorized one.
(D) Has committed the crime of "resisting arrest" only if his friend does in fact run away and escape.

79. The crime of "criminal possession of stolen property" can be most properly charged:

(A) If the person in possession of the property believes it to be stolen, and it is actually stolen.

(B) If the person in possession of the property believes it to be stolen even if it is not.

(C) If the property is in fact stolen even though the person in possession of it does not believe it is.

(D) If the person in possession of the property is the person who actually stole the property.

80. Which of the following is the *least* correct statement concerning the above legal definitions?

(A) The crime of "criminal possession of a weapon" includes the illegal possession of a rifle.

(B) Causing the death of another during the commission of a robbery is a felony murder.

(C) An unmarried 22-year-old male having sexual intercourse with a 16-year-old female is committing the crime of rape.

(D) Taking another person's property and keeping it is grand larceny when the property is worth more than $1,000.

81. Mary meets John at a singles club. After dating for a period of time, Mary and John willingly have sexual intercourse. John is over 21 years of age, as is Mary. John is not married, and does not know that Mary is married.

Based upon the above information, select the most accurate statement.

(A) John is guilty of the crime of "adultery" but Mary is not.

(B) John and Mary are both guilty of the crime of "adultery."

(C) Only Mary is guilty of the crime of "adultery" since only she is married.

(D) John is guilty of no crime since he had no knowledge that Mary was married.

82. Which of the following is the most accurate statement concerning the crime of "sodomy"?

(A) The only way to commit sodomy by force is to compel another person to engage in oral sex.

(B) The only way to commit sodomy by force is to compel another person to engage in anal sex.

(C) Under certain circumstances, the crime of sodomy can be committed without using force.

(D) In order for the crime of sodomy to be committed, one of the parties involved must be less than 17 years of age.

83. Harry takes his friend's gold ring to wear on a date. He does not intend to keep the ring, which is valued at $1,600, but wants only to impress his date and then return the ring without his friend finding out.

Based upon the above information, Harry:

(A) Has committed grand larceny since the ring is valued at $1,600.

(B) Has not committed grand larceny since he does not intend to keep the ring.

(C) Has committed grand larceny since he does not have his friend's permission to use the ring.

(D) Has not committed grand larceny if he does, in fact, return the ring within 72 hours.

84. The police have discovered that Arthur has a sawed-off shotgun under his trench coat. Arthur can be charged with "criminal possession of a weapon":

(A) Only if he has ammunition on his person that fits the sawed-off shotgun.

(B) Only if the sawed-off shotgun is, in fact, loaded.

(C) Whether or not the sawed-off shotgun is loaded or unloaded.

(D) Whether or not he possesses it legally or illegally.

85. If the death of another is caused during the commission of certain felonies, the crime of felony murder is committed. These felonies include all of the following *except*:

(A) Burglary.
(B) Arson.
(C) Grand larceny.
(D) Robbery.

TURN TO NEXT PAGE

***DIRECTIONS:* Answer questions 86 through 89 *solely* on the basis of the following:**

criminal mischief A person commits criminal mischief when he/she intends to damage the property of another and, without any legal right to do so, does damage that person's property or the property of another. If the damage to the property exceeds $500, the crime is criminal mischief in the first degree, which is a Class E felony. If the damage to the property is $500 or less, the crime is criminal mischief in the second degree, which is a Class A misdemeanor. However, if the property belongs to a nonprofit organization of any kind, the crime is criminal mischief in the first degree regardless of the damage.

86. In order to commit the crime of criminal mischief, a person must:
(A) Damage property for no apparent reason.
(B) Recklessly cause another person's property to be damaged.
(C) Intentionally damage the property of another without a legal right to do so.
(D) Damage the property of a nonprofit organization.

87. What degree of criminal mischief is committed if a person intends to damage another person's car, which is worth $6,000 and, having no legal right to do so, does damage that other person's car?
(A) Criminal mischief in the first degree
(B) Criminal mischief in the second degree
(C) Either criminal mischief in the first degree or criminal mischief in the second degree
(D) The circumstances described do not amount to any crime

88. Henry Cabot is angry at his neighbor, John Smith. One night after Smith returned home from work, Cabot slashed all four tires on the car in which Smith drove home. Although Cabot thought the car belonged to Smith, the car actually belonged to the nonprofit organization that Smith works for. The tires were recently bought for $125 each.

Based upon the above information, Cabot has:
- **(A)** Committed criminal mischief in the second degree since the total value of the tires was $500.
- **(B)** Committed criminal mischief in the first degree since the car was owned by a nonprofit organization.
- **(C)** Not committed any crime since Cabot made a mistake and damaged a car that did not belong to Smith.
- **(D)** Not committed any crime because Cabot did not intend to damage the property of the nonprofit organization.

89. Which of the following elements do not have to be present for the crime of criminal mischief to be committed?
- **(A)** Damaged property
- **(B)** An intent to damage
- **(C)** Specific knowledge of the extent of damage
- **(D)** No legal right to damage

TURN TO NEXT PAGE

***DIRECTIONS:* Answer questions 90 through 97 *solely* on the basis of the following:**

burglary The crime of burglary has three degrees. A person commits the crime of burglary in the third degree, a Class E felony, when he/she unlawfully enters or remains in a building with the intent to commit a crime therein. A person commits burglary in the second degree when he/she unlawfully enters or remains in a building with the intent to commit a crime therein and, while doing so, either he/she or an accomplice is armed with a deadly weapon; burglary in the second degree is a Class C felony. A person commits burglary in the first degree when he/she unlawfully enters or remains in a dwelling at night while armed with a deadly weapon, with the intent to commit a crime therein; burglary in the first degree is a Class B felony.

For the purposes of this crime, the following definitions apply:

building: Any man-made structure where people usually congregate and/or do business.

deadly weapon: Any firearm, handgun, rifle, shotgun, or other device commonly classified as a gun; or any knife; or billy; or blackjack; or explosive.

dwelling: A building which is commonly used for the lodging of people overnight.

night: The period from sundown to sun-up.

Joe Jones is a derelict with no place to live. One night there is a television show that he wants very much to see, so he climbs into the window of his old girlfriend's house to watch it. He knows that his former girlfriend and her parents are on vacation. Halfway through the show, however, his ex-girlfriend's father returns home, finds Joe there, and calls the police.

90. Based upon the above information, Joe has:

(A) Committed burglary in the first degree since he unlawfully entered a dwelling at night.

(B) Committed burglary in the second degree since he unlawfully entered a building at night.

(C) Committed burglary in the third degree since he intentionally entered a building without the permission of the owner.

(D) Not committed burglary in any degree since he did not intend to commit a crime in the house.

91. For the purposes of the crime of burglary, which of the following is *not* considered to be a building?

(A) A ship used by a fishing club for fishing trips
(B) A tent used by an Indian club for weekly meetings
(C) A cave used by a nature club for camping
(D) A cabin used by a family for week-end hunting trips

92. Which of the following is the most accurate statement concerning nighttime as it relates to the crime of burglary?

(A) At 8:00 P.M. it would always be considered to be nighttime.
(B) At 7:00 A.M. it would always be considered to be daytime.
(C) Nightfall occurs at the same time on each day of the year.
(D) Nightfall does not occur at the same time on each day of the year.

TURN TO NEXT PAGE

***DIRECTIONS:* Answer questions 93 and 94 *solely* on the basis of the above definitions and the following story.**

Joe Jones and his friend, Harry Smith, plan to enter the home of Smith's boss and steal jewelry which Smith knows is kept in a special safe in the basement. They enter through the basement door at 3:00 A.M., while Smith's boss and his wife are asleep upstairs in their bedroom. Jones does not know it, but Smith is carrying a switchblade knife with him. They enter as planned, but cannot find the safe. They leave without taking any property.

93. Based upon the above information, Jones has:
(A) Committed a Class E felony.
(B) Committed a Class C felony.
(C) Committed a Class B felony.
(D) Not committed a burglary.

94. Based upon the above information, Smith has:
(A) Committed a Class E felony.
(B) Committed a Class C felony.
(C) Committed a Class B felony.
(D) Not committed a burglary.

95. Which of the following is *not* an element of burglary in the second degree?
(A) Possession of a deadly weapon
(B) The time of the commission of the crime
(C) The intent of the participants of the crime
(D) The type of structure in which the crime is committed

96. John Brown is shopping for a gift for his wife at Lacy's Department Store. It is very busy at the store, and there are many customers even though John had to wait at the door for the store to open. While shopping, John sees an expensive watch that he knows his wife would love to own, but that he cannot afford. He feels so badly that he impulsively puts it in his pocket and hurries out of the store through the front entrance. He is not apprehended.

Based upon the above information, John has:
(A) Committed burglary in the third degree.
(B) Committed burglary in the second degree.
(C) Committed burglary in the first degree.
(D) Not committed the crime of burglary.

97. Which of the following is the most accurate statement concerning the crime of burglary?

(A) The intent of the perpetrator is not an important element of the crime.

(B) A crime need not be committed inside the building for the crime of burglary to be committed.

(C) A deadly weapon has to be involved for the crime of burglary to be committed.

(D) A dwelling must be involved for the crime of burglary to be committed.

TURN TO NEXT PAGE

***DIRECTIONS:* Answer questions 98 through 100 *solely* on the basis of the following:**

robbery The crime of robbery has three degrees. A person commits robbery in the third degree when he/she takes the property of another person by the use, or threatened use, of immediate force against that person or any other person related to that person; robbery in the third degree is a Class D felony. A person commits robbery in the second degree when he/she commits the crime of robbery in the third degree and a person other than a participant in the commission of the crime receives a physical injury; robbery in the second degree is a Class C felony. A person commits robbery in the first degree when he/she commits the crime of robbery in the second degree and a person other than a participant in the commission of the crime receives a physical injury which requires hospitalization; robbery in the first degree is a Class B felony.

98. Joe Black stops Jack Brown in the street and demands his gold chain. Black tells Brown that unless he is given the chain he will kill Brown's girlfriend. Not wanting to endanger his girlfriend's life, Brown hands over his chain to Black.

Based upon the above information, Black has:
(A) Committed robbery in the third degree.
(B) Committed robbery in the second degree.
(C) Committed robbery in the first degree.
(D) Not committed the crime of robbery.

99. Which of the following has to occur before the crime of robbery can be committed?
(A) Force has to be used.
(B) Someone has to be injured.
(C) Property has to be taken.
(D) A weapon must be used.

100. Who has to be hospitalized for the crime of robbery in the first degree to be committed?
(A) Anybody
(B) A person whose property is taken
(C) A participant in the commission of the crime
(D) Anybody other than a participant in the crime

SECTION SIX—
Sentence Ordering Questions

DIRECTIONS: **Answer questions 101 through 105 *solely* on the basis of the following:**

Police Officer Rems is preparing a report for his supervisor concerning someone who has jumped from the roof of police headquarters. Officer Rems' report contains the following five sentences:

1. I went to the roof of headquarters, where I observed the person standing on the outer ledge of the building.
2. A security officer on the ground floor informed me that a man was up on the roof of the building.
3. At 3:30 P.M., the person jumped off the ledge and landed in the street below.
4. I received an order from my supervisor at 2:50 P.M. to investigate a report of a man in headquarters trying to commit suicide.
5. I did my best to convince the man not to jump.

101. The most logical order for the above sentences to appear in Officer Rem's report is:
(A) 1, 2, 4, 3, 5
(B) 3, 4, 1, 2, 5
(C) 5, 4, 1, 3, 2
(D) 4, 2, 1, 5, 3

102. The following five sentences are included in a report being submitted by Police Officer Rems concerning a burglary:
1. While on patrol, I was told by a passing motorist that a burglary was occurring in a store at 1400 Seventh Avenue.
2. I ordered, "Police, don't move."
3. As I silently entered the store undetected, I saw someone wearing a mask passing something through a window to another person standing outside the window.
4. When I arrived at 1400 Seventh Avenue, I noticed that someone had forced open the front door to the office.
5. When the burglars realized I was there, they both ran away.

The most logical order for the above sentences to appear in Officer Rems' report is:
(A) 4, 3, 1, 5, 2
(B) 1, 4, 3, 5, 2
(C) 1, 4, 3, 2, 5
(D) 4, 1, 3, 2, 5

103. A police officer is preparing a report concerning an incident involving lost property. His report contains the following five sentences:

1. Mr. Jones stated that he was walking up the stairs at Grand Central Terminal.
2. It wasn't until he was about to pay his subway fare that Mr. Jones realized his money was no longer in his pants pocket.
3. A man wearing a jogging suit assisted him to get up and also helped him brush himself off.
4. While on the stairs, Mr. Jones tripped over some debris and fell onto the landing.
5. Before Mr. Jones could thank the man, he was running down the stairs to the street.

The most logical order for the above sentences to appear in the police officer's report is:

(A) 1, 3, 5, 4, 2
(B) 1, 4, 3, 5, 2
(C) 4, 1, 2, 3, 5
(D) 4, 2, 1, 3, 5

104. Police Officer Rems is reviewing his report concerning a missing child. The report contains the following five sentences:

1. A distraught woman telephoned the precinct to report that her son, aged 11, had not returned from an errand.
2. She gave me a physical description of her son and told me he had gone into the local food store at about 8:30 P.M.
3. I directed the woman to give me a description of her son.
4. I visited the food store at 8:55 P.M. and asked the workers if they had seen a boy matching the description I had obtained.
5. One of the store workers told me that a boy fitting the description had been in the store a little while ago.

The most logical order for the above sentences to appear in Officer Rems' report is:

(A) 4, 3, 2, 5, 1
(B) 1, 3, 2, 4, 5
(C) 5, 4, 2, 3, 1
(D) 3, 4, 2, 1, 5

105. A police officer is writing a report concerning some summonses she issued. The following five sentences will be included in the report:

1. I stopped the driver of the auto and determined that he did not have a valid license to drive in New York State.
2. The summonses were issued for going through a stop sign and for being an unlicensed operator.

3. At 10:00 A.M. I saw a car traveling eastbound on Main Street go through a stop sign without stopping.
4. I was on precinct patrol on Main Street observing precinct conditions.
5. After informing the motorist of my observations, I told him I was going to issue him two summonses.

The most logical order for the above sentences to appear in the officer's report is:

(A) 4, 3, 1, 5, 2 **(C)** 5, 2, 4, 3, 1
(B) 4, 3, 5, 2, 1 **(D)** 1, 5, 2, 4, 3

Traffic Map Questions

DIRECTIONS: **Answer questions 106–108 based *solely* on the map that appears below.**

The traffic flow is shown by the arrows. One arrow indicates a one-way traffic flow in the direction the arrow is pointing. Two arrows indicates that a two-way flow of traffic is permissible. The correct answer can be obtained only by following the permissible flow of traffic.

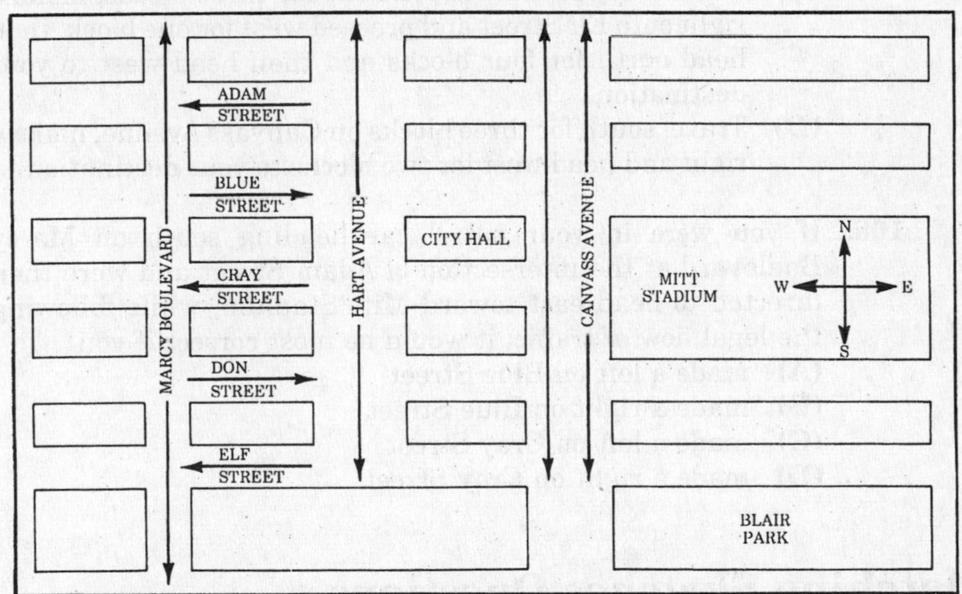

106. You are at the intersection of Adam Street and Marcy Boulevard in your police patrol car. You receive a call to respond to Blair Park. Which of the following is the most direct route for you to take in your police car, making sure to obey all traffic regulations?

(A) Head east on Adam Street to Canvass Avenue and then south on Canvass Avenue and continue for four blocks to your destination.

(B) Travel south on Marcy Boulevard to Don Street. Then head east for two blocks: turn right and continue to your destination.

(C) Head south on Marcy Boulevard for four blocks and then turn left and continue to your destination.

(D) Travel one block south to Blue Street, head east one block to Hart Avenue, make a left and go north one block, make a left and go one block, then make another left and head south on Marcy Boulevard to Don Street, go east for two blocks, make a right and continue to your destination.

107. You are at the intersection of Canvass Avenue and Blue Street. You receive an order to respond to the scene of an automobile accident involving only property damage at the intersection of Elf Street and Marcy Boulevard. Which one of the following is the most direct route for you to take in your police car, making sure to obey all traffic regulations?

(A) Head west on Blue Street, travel two blocks to Marcy Blvd., make a left and travel south for three blocks to Elf Street.

(B) Travel six blocks south on Canvass Avenue, then travel two blocks west on Elf Street to Marcy Blvd.

(C) Head south on Canvass Avenue for three blocks, make a right onto Elf Street and proceed west for one block, then head north for four blocks and then head west to your destination.

(D) Travel south for three blocks on Canvass Avenue, make a right and head west for two blocks to your destination.

108. If you were in your patrol car heading south on Marcy Boulevard at the intersection of Adam Street and were then directed to head east toward Mitt Stadium, while following the legal flow of traffic, it would be most correct if you

(A) made a left on Blue Street
(B) made a right on Blue Street
(C) made a left on Cray Street
(D) made a right on Cray Street

Matching Sketches Questions

***DIRECTIONS:* Answer questions 109–112 on the basis of the following sketches.**

The first face on top in the center of the page, is a sketch of an alleged criminal based on witnesses' descriptions at the scene of a crime. One of the four sketches below is the way the suspect looked after changing appearance. Assume that no surgery has been done on the suspect. Select the face that is most likely that of the suspect.

109.

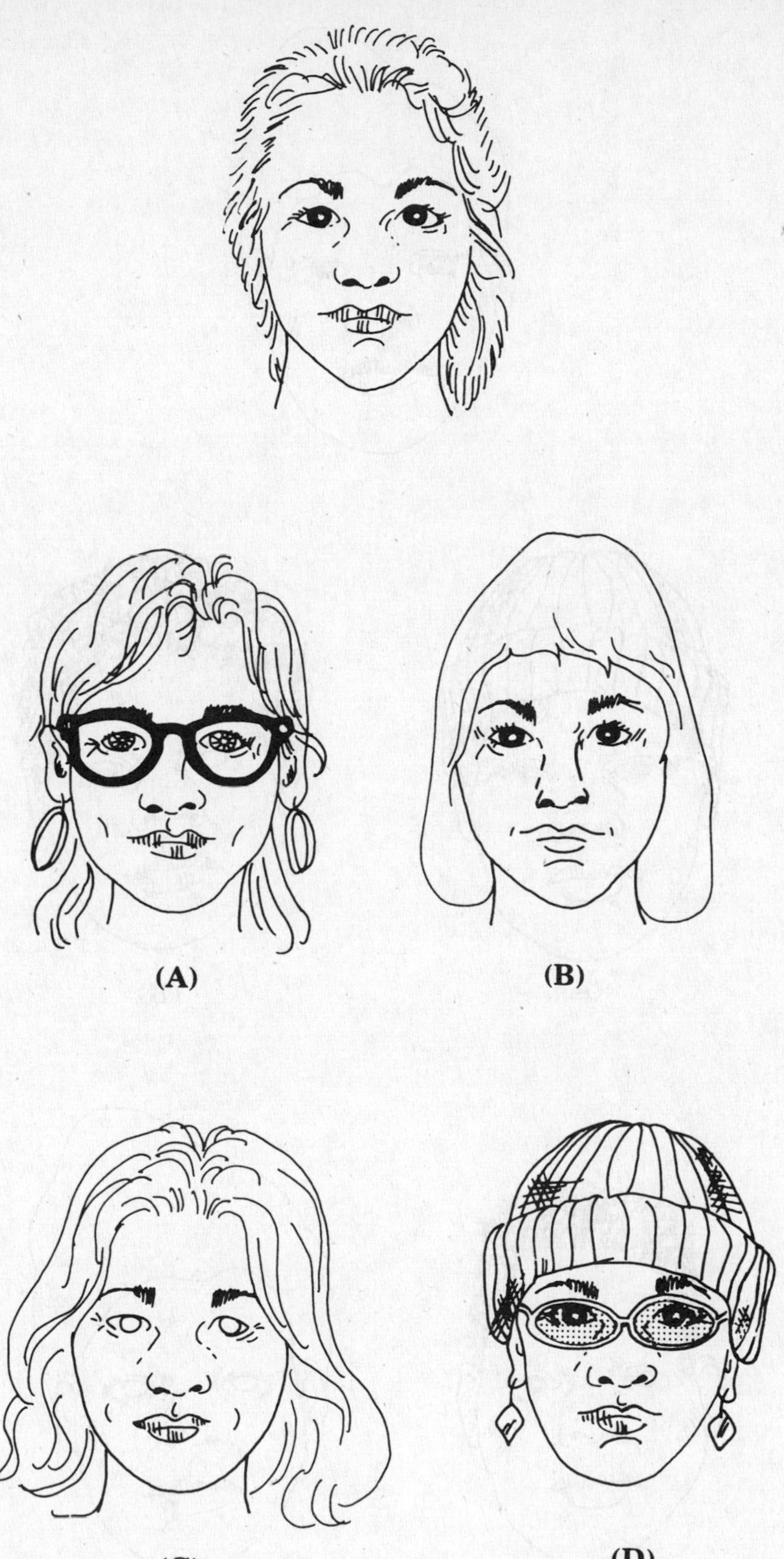

(A) (B)

(C) (D)

110.

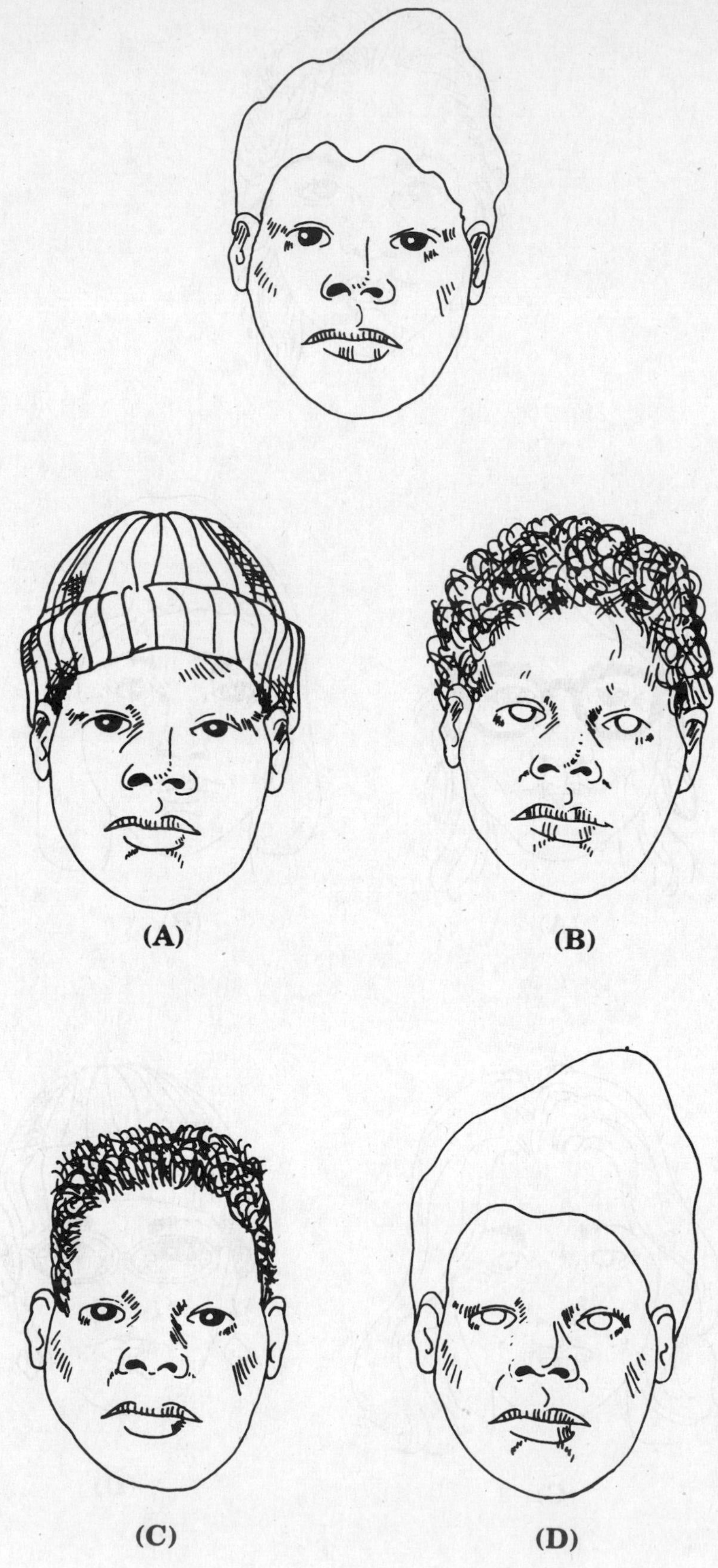

111.

(A)

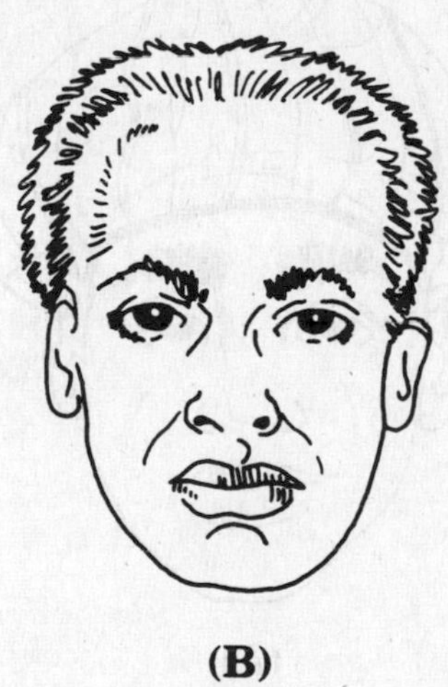

(B)

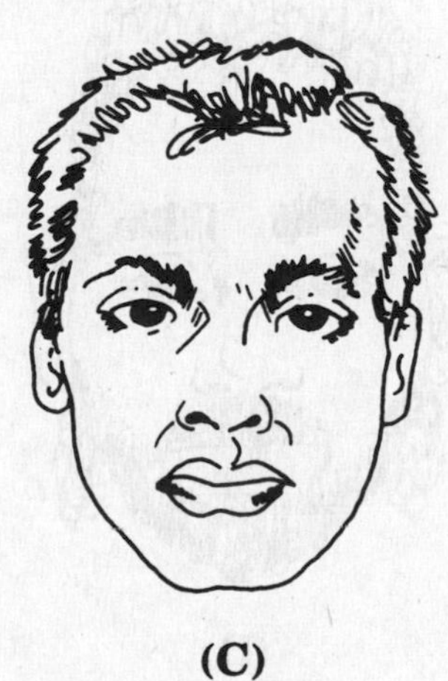

(C)

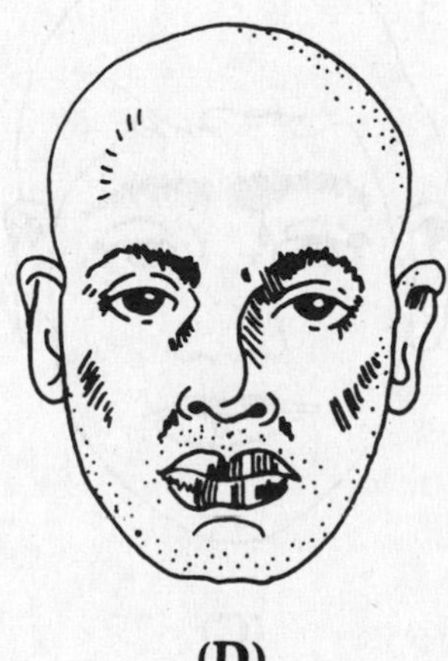

(D)

112.

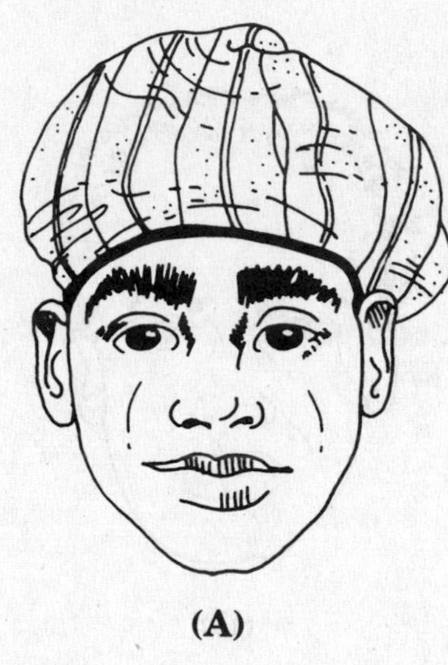

(A)

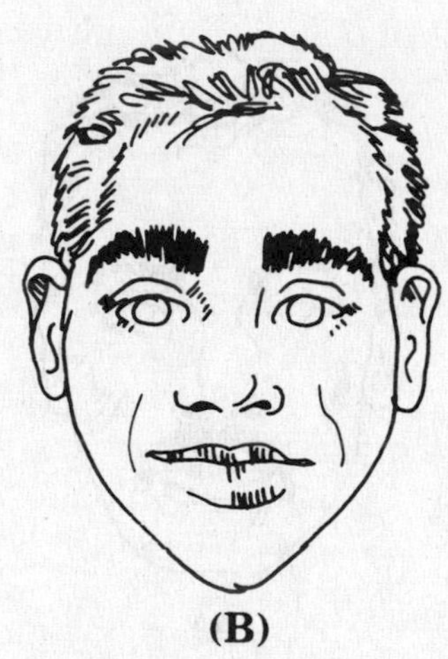

(B)

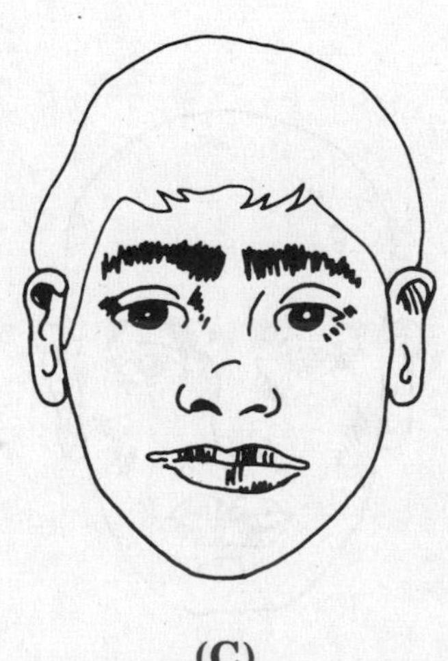

(C)

(D)

Report Writing Questions

113. The facts listed below were gathered by Police Officer Rems at the scene of a personal injury vehicle accident in which the driver left the scene of the accident without reporting:

Place of Occurrence:	Intersection of White Street and First Street
Time of Occurrence:	12:15 P.M.
Victim:	Roberta Black
Vehicle:	Green Ford, License Plate 828 APQ
Violation:	Leaving the Scene of an Accident

Officer Rems is required to submit a report on all vehicle accidents. Which onc of thc following expresses the above facts most clearly and accurately?

(A) A green Ford, License Plate 828 APQ, struck Roberta Black. It did leave the scene of an accident at 12:15 P.M. at the intersection of White Street and First Street.

(B) At 12:15 P.M., it was reported that Roberta Black was hit at the intersection of White Street and First Street. The green Ford, License Plate 828 APQ, left the scene.

(C) At 12:15 P.M. Roberta Black was crossing the intersection of White Street and First Street when she was hit by a green Ford, License Plate 828 APQ, which then left the scene.

(D) At the intersection of White Street and First Street, Roberta Black was the victim of a vehicle accident at 12:15 P.M. The vehicle then left the scene. It was a green Ford.

114. Police Officer Rems has brought an elderly male to Mt. Hope Hospital after finding him lying in an alley. At the hospital, Nurse Baker provided Officer Rems with the following facts:

Name of Patient:	Donald Jones
Address:	2596 West 79 Street
Age:	75 years old
Place of Occurrence:	Alley in rear of 31 Ace Street
Illness:	Cardiac problem

Officer Rems is completing a police report on the above incident. Which one of the following expresses the above facts most clearly and accurately?

(A) Mr. Donald Jones of 2596 West 79 Street, who is 75 years old, was found lying in an alley in the rear of 31 Ace Street and was brought to Mt. Hope Hospital, where it was determined he was suffering from a cardiac problem.

(B) Mr. Donald Jones suffers from a cardiac condition and was found lying in an alley. He is 75 years old. He lives at 2596 West 79 Street.

(C) Mr. Donald Jones, who suffers from a cardiac condition, collapsed on the street after suffering from a cardiac condition. He was brought to Mt. Hope Hospital suffering from a cardiac problem after having been found lying in an alley in the rear of 31 Ace Street. He is 75 years old and lives at 2596 West 79 Street.

(D) Mr. Donald Jones, lives at 2956 West 79 Street, has a cardiac condition, and is 75 years old. He was found lying in an alley in the rear of 31 Ace Street and was brought to Mt. Hope Hospital.

115. Police Officer Rems has responded to the scene of a burglary and obtained the following information:

Place of Occurrence: 982 Rose Street
Time of Occurrence: 3:15 A.M.
Witness: Mr. Lopez
Suspect: A male Hispanic, 5′10″, 160 pounds, wearing a brown jacket and army pants
Crime: Burglary of a jewelry store; three watches taken

Officer Rems is now completing the required report on this burglary. Which one of the following expresses the above information most clearly and accurately?

(A) At 3:15 A.M. Mr. Lopez reported that a male stole three watches while wearing a brown jacket and army pants in the store at 982 Rose Street. The Hispanic is 5′10″ and 160 pounds.

(B) A male Hispanic witnessed by Mr. Lopez was wearing a brown jacket and army pants. A premises at 982 Rose Street was victimized of three watches by a perpetrator weighing 160 pounds and 5′10″ at 3:15 A.M.

(C) Mr. Lopez reportedly observed a male Hispanic burglarize three watches from a store at 982 Rose Street. The suspect was described as being 5′10″, 160 pounds, wearing a brown jacket and army pants.

(D) Wearing army pants and a brown jacket, Mr. Lopez observed a burglary when he witnessed a Hispanic man steal three watches. At 3:15 A.M. he burglarized a store at 982 Rose Street. The suspect was 5′10″ and 160 pounds.

116. Police Officer Aponte has just completed an investigation of a sexual assault. She has obtained the following facts:

Place of Occurrence: Larry's Health Spa, 22 Main Street
Time of Occurrence: 7:35 P.M.
Time of Reporting: 8:30 P.M.
Victim: Sheila Jackson, customer at the Spa
Crime: Rape
Suspect: Male, white, armed with a knife

Officer Aponte is preparing the required report concerning this rape. Which one of the following paragraphs expresses the above information most clearly and accurately?

(A) At 8:30 P.M. a male, white, threatened Sheila Jackson with a knife at Larry's Health Spa at 22 Main Street which then led to Ms. Jackson being raped.

(B) At 8:30 P.M., Sheila Jackson reported that at about 7:35 P.M. a male, white, armed with a knife, entered Larry's Health Spa, located at 22 Main Street, and forced her to have sexual intercourse with him.

(C) Sheila Jackson, who works at Larry's Health Spa was raped by a male white who was armed with a knife. It happened at 7:35 P.M. and it was reported at 8:30 P.M.

(D) While working as a customer at Larry's Health Spa at 22 Main Street, Sheila Jackson was raped by a male with a knife at 7:35 P.M. and then reported it to the police at 8:30 P.M.

Directed Patrol Questions

***DIRECTIONS:* Answer question 117 *solely* on the basis of the following information:**

While reviewing crime statistics for his post, Police Officer Aponte, of the 113th Precinct, notices that most of the rapes occur between 2:00 A.M. and 4:00 A.M., purse snatches between 11:00 A.M. and 3:00 P.M., and robberies between 6:00 A.M. and 7:00 A.M. Most of the rapes seem to occur on Fridays, most of the purse snatches on Saturdays, and most of the robberies on Saturdays and Sundays.

117. Police Officer Aponte is instructed to work a steady tour that would allow her to concentrate on rapes and robberies within her patrol area. In order for her to do this, it would be most appropriate for Officer Aponte to work

(A) 2:00 A.M. to 10:00 A.M., Tuesday through Saturdays
(B) 4:00 A.M. to 12:00 P.M., Wednesday through Sunday
(C) Midnight to 8:00 A.M., Thursday through Monday
(D) 10:00 A.M. to 6:00 P.M., Monday through Friday

***DIRECTIONS:* Answer question 118 *solely* on the basis of the following information:**

Police Officer Rems works in the 33rd Precinct. She notices that most of the robberies on her beat are committed on Birch Street between Pleasant Street and Atlantic Street. All of the arsons are committed on North Street between Crown Street and Lake Street. All of the auto larcenies are committed on Fourth Avenue between Tipton Street and University Street. Most of the robberies occur on Fridays and Saturdays between 9:00 P.M. and 1:00 A.M. Most arsons occur on Sundays between 9:00 A.M. and 12 noon, and most of the auto larcenies on Sundays and Mondays between midnight and 3:00 A.M.

118. Officer Rems would most likely be able to reduce the number of auto larcenies by patrolling

(A) Birch Street on Fridays and Saturdays between 9:00 P.M. and 1:00 A.M.

(B) Atlantic Street on Sundays between 9:00 A.M. and 12 noon

(C) Crown Street on Thursdays between 10:00 A.M. and 2:00 P.M.
(D) Fourth Avenue on Sundays and Mondays between midnight and 3:00 A.M.

***DIRECTIONS:* Answer questions 119–120 *solely* on the basis of the following information:**

Police Officer Rems is informed by her patrol sergeant that her beat area has a high number of drug sales and a high number of homicides, assaults, robberies, and burlaries. The officer then determines that all the drug dealing takes place on Marvin Street, all the homicides take place on Edwin Street, all the assaults occur on Cherry Street, all the robberies take place on Beaver Street, and all the burglaries occur on Harvey Street. The drug dealing takes place between 2:00 A.M. and 3:00 A.M.; the homicides occur between 3:00 A.M. and 5:00 A.M.; the assaults happen between 1:00 A.M. and 3:00 A.M.; the robberies take place between 4:00 A.M. and 8:00 A.M.; and the burglaries occur between 5:00 A.M. and 7:00 A.M. The drug dealing takes place on Mondays, the homicides occur on Tuesdays, the assaults happen on Thursdays, the robberies are committed on Mondays, and the burglaries take place on Tuesdays.

119. Police Officer Rems would be most likely to reduce the amount of homicides which occur by patrolling
(A) Edwin Street on Tuesdays
(B) Beaver Street on Tuesdays
(C) Cherry Street on Wednesdays
(D) Marvin Street on Fridays

120. In order to deal with both assaults and robberies, Officer Rems should work from
(A) Monday to Friday
(B) Wednesday to Sunday
(C) Tuesday to Saturday
(D) Saturday to Wednesday

SECTION SEVEN—Formula Questions

121. Police Officer Rems worked a tour of duty from 8:00 A.M. to 4:00 P.M. on May 31st. From 8:00 A.M. until 11:30 A.M. he patrolled Post #4. From 11:30 A.M. until 1:00 P.M. he was assigned to school crossing #12. From 1:00 P.M. until 2:00 P.M. he was on his meal period. At 2:00 P.M. he resumed patrol on Post #4 until the end of his tour at 4:00 P.M. Which of the following is the most correct formula to use to determine how much time Officer Rems spent on patrol on Post #4?

(A) Time on meal minus 8
(B) 8 minus (time on meal plus time on school crossing)
(C) Time on school crossing plus time on meal minus time on patrol Post #4
(D) Time on Post #4—(time on school crossing plus time on meal)

122. The following is a list of property stolen during the commission of a burglary:

ITEM	*QUANTITY*	*VALUE*
Wristwatch	1	$250
Fur Jacket	2	$500 each
Television	2	$300 each

Which of the following is the most accurate manner to express the total value of the property taken?
(A) 2 × (250 + 500 + 300)
(B) (1) × (2) × (2) × (250 + 500 + 300)
(C) 250 + 2 × (500) + 2 × (300)
(D) 250 + 500 + 300

Find the Perp Questions

123. In the last three weeks, Police Officer Schroeder has received three complaints from elementary school officials concerning incidents involving children. In each case the perpetrator would expose himself to young girls. The description of the suspect in each incident is as follows:

Incident #1 (three weeks in the past)—male, white, 25–30, 6′4″, 190 pounds, straight black hair, short sleeved shirt, blue jeans, and white sneakers, tattoo on left hand.

Incident #2 (two weeks in the past)—male, white, 30–35, 6′2″, 185 pounds, straight black hair, tattoos on upper right arm and right hand, sweat shirt, jogging pants, and sneakers.

Incident #3 (one week in the past)—male, white, 27–31, 6′1″, 193 pounds, long straight blond hair, tattoo on right forearm, tank top, brown pants, and sneakers.

Yesterday, a fourth such incident occurred, but this time the perpetrator was arrested. The description of the prisoner is as follows:

Incident #4 (yesterday)—male, white, 28, 6′2″, 190 pounds, straight blond hair, tattoo on right thigh, right forearm, and left hand, long sleeved shirt, blue jeans, and sneakers.

Based on the description given above of the suspects in the first three incidents, the arrested person in the fourth incident should also be considered a suspect in
(A) Incident #1 and Incident #2, but not in Incident #3
(B) Incident #1 and Incident #3, but not in Incident #2

(C) Incident #2, but not in Incident #1 or Incident #3
(D) None of the three incidents

***DIRECTIONS:* Answer question 124 *solely* on the basis of the following information:**

During the month of May, three robberies occurred on successive days in the early morning hours near the downtown civic center area. The description of each of the three suspects is as follows:

Suspect #1: Male, black, early 40s, 5′5″, 140 pounds, black hair, large scar under right ear, brown jacket, brown pants, and army boots.

Suspect #2: Male, black, 40–45 years old, 5′5″, 180 pounds, dark hair, black pants, green jacket, and sneakers.

Suspect #3: Male, black, approximately 45 years old, 5′5″, 142 pounds, long black hair, green jacket and pants, sneakers.

In the first week of June, a fourth robbery occurred but this time the perpetrator is arrested. The description of the fourth suspect is as follows:

Suspect #4: Male, black, 40 to 45, 5′5″, 145 pounds, short curly black hair, scar on right side of neck, black pants, green jacket, and sneakers.

124. Based upon the above descriptions of the suspects in the first three robberies, the arrested person in the fourth robbery should also be considered a suspect in
(A) Robbery #1 and 2, but not in Robbery #3
(B) Robbery #1 and 3, but not in Robbery #2
(C) Robbery #2 and 3, but not in Robbery #1
(D) Robberies #1, #2, and #3.

***DIRECTIONS:* Answer question 125 based *solely* on the following information:**

Police Officer Lombardo received three reports of rapes in the month of June. The description of each of the three suspects is as follows:

Suspect #1: Male, Hispanic, 25–30 years old, 5′8″, 135 pounds, scar on left side of neck, blue short sleeved shirt, blue jeans, and sneakers.

Suspect #2: Male, Hispanic, late twenties, 5′9″, 140 pounds, 2″ scar on left side of neck, gold shirt, black pants, and black running shoes.

Suspect #3: Male, Hispanic, early twenties, 5′8″, 135–140 pounds, scar on neck, green shirt and pants, and sneakers.

Early in July, another rape occurs. However, in this instance the suspect was arrested. The description of the arrested suspect is as follows:

Suspect #4: Male, Hispanic, middle twenties, 5′2″, 145 pounds, scar on left side on neck, black shirt and pants, and sneakers.

125. Based on the description of the suspects in the first three rapes, the suspect in Rape #4 should also be considered a suspect in

(A) Rape #1, but not in Rapes #2 and #3
(B) Rape #3, but not in Rapes #1 and #2
(C) Rape #2, but not in Rapes #1 and #3
(D) None of the other three rapes.

DIRECTIONS: **Answer question 126 based *solely* on the following information:**

Police Office Aponte received three reports of muggings during the month of April. All of the muggings occurred in the same general area. The description of the suspect in each such report is as follows:

Report #1: Female, white, 25 years old, 5′8″, 165 pounds, long blond hair, blue turtleneck sweater, horn-rimmed glasses, brown slacks, and black shoes.

Report #2: Female, white, 25–30 years old, 5′7″, 160–165 pounds, blond hair, scar on neck, sunglasses, plaid dress, red shoes

Report #3: Female, white, early twenties, 5′8″, 170 pounds, long blond hair, green jacket and slacks, black shoes

During the first week of May, a fourth mugging occurred but this time the suspect was arrested. The report of this incident lists the description of the arrested suspect as follows:

Report #4: Female, white, 5′8″, 24 years old, 165 pounds, blond hair, scar on left side of neck, green sweater, green skirt, and green shoes.

126. Based on the above descriptions in the first three reports, the suspect in Report #4 should also be considered a suspect in

(A) Reports #1 and #2, but not in Report #3
(B) Reports #1 and #3, but not in Report #2
(C) Reports #2 and #3, but not in Report #1
(D) Reports #1, #2, and #3

Frequency of Information Questions

127. While patrolling his beat, Police Officer Brown comes across a past robbery. The officer interviews four witnesses who all saw the lone robber escape in a late model sedan type car. The following are license plate numbers that were reported by the four witnesses. Which one of these license plate numbers should the officer consider most likely to be the correct license plate?

(A) Pennsylvania Plate BDF-2890
(B) NY Plate BEF-2890
(C) NY Plate CEF-2890
(D) Pennsylvania Plate BEF-2790

128. Police Officer Rems responds to the scene of an accident in which one of the vehicles left the scene. Officer Rems interviews four witnesses to the accident. The following are descriptions given by each of the four witnesses of the vehicle that left the scene. Which one of these descriptions should Officer Rems consider most likely to be correct?

(A) Black Buick Riviera, NY Plate 3209 DBU
(B) Black Buick Riviera, NY Plate 3009 DBU
(C) Brown Buick Riviera, NY Plate 3209 DBU
(D) Black Buick Riviera, NY Plate 3209 DPU

129. A robbery has occurred. The perpetrators escaped in a late model sedan. The police find four witnesses, each of whom observed the license plate of the getaway car. Which of the following four license plate numbers obtained from the witnesses should the police consider most likely to be correct?

(A) ABE 123
(B) ACE 123
(C) ABD 123
(D) BBE 123

130. A mugging has occurred. Police Officer Rems obtains the following description of the mugger from each of four witnesses. Which of these descriptions should Officer Rems consider most likely to be correct?

(A) Male, white, 25 years old, 6′, 175 pounds, blue eyes
(B) Male, white, 30 years old, 6′4″, 175 pounds, blue eyes
(C) Male, white, 25 years old, 5′8″, 175 pounds, blue eyes
(D) Male, white, 30 years old, 6′, 150 pounds, blue eyes

131. A store was burglarized and the thieves used a late model truck to remove the property that was stolen. The following descriptions of the truck were obtained from four witnesses. Which of these descriptions should the police consider most likely to be correct?

(A) Black GMC Truck, Plate 123 DEF
(B) Black Dodge Truck, Plate 124 DEF
(C) Brown GMC Truck, Plate 123 DEF
(D) Black GMC Truck, Plate 123 BEF

132. A violent rape has occurred. The police locate four witnesses to this heinous crime. Each witness gives a description of the perpetrator. Which of the following four descriptions obtained from these witnesses should the police consider most likely to be correct?

(A) Male, Hispanic, 25 years old, 5′7″, 150 pounds, brown eyes
(B) Male, black, 25 years old, 5′7″, 150 pounds, brown eyes
(C) Male, white, 25 years old, 5′7″, 150 pounds, brown eyes
(D) Male, Hispanic, 25 years old, 5′7″, 150 pounds, blue eyes

Arithmetic Questions

133. At 4:45 P.M. on Tuesday, May 19th, Officer Rems responded to a burglary at an appliance store. The store owner reported that the following merchandise was stolen:

3 television sets, each valued at	$430.00
2 air conditioners, each valued at	$375.00
5 VCRs, each valued at	$325.00
1 answering machine, valued at	$75.00
3 FM radios, each valued at	$125.00

In addition to the above merchandise, the owner also reported that his cash register, valued at $900.000, was taken during the burglary. Officer Rems is required to prepare a report on this burglary. Which one of the following is the correct total value of the property stolen from the appliance store?

(A) $1330.00
(B) $2230.00
(C) $5015.00
(D) $4115.00

134. Police Officer Aponte of the 11th Precinct is approached by an irate citizen who explains to her that someone just broke into his parked auto and stole his alligator briefcase valued at $550.00. The citizen reported that the briefcase contained the following items:

A gold pen and pencil set, valued at	$400.00
A pocket calculator, valued at	$350.00
3 tickets to the Mets game, each valued at	$25.00

Sometime after making the report, the same irate citizen called the 11th Precinct and informed the police that the briefcase also contained $400.00 in cash. When preparing the required report on this incident, the police officer preparing the report would be most correct if she recorded the total value of the property and cash stolen as being

(A) $1775.00
(B) $1375.00
(C) $1700.00
(D) $1225.00

135. Police Officer Rems takes a report from a person who has just been robbed. The following is a list of the property taken during the robbery as reported to Officer Rems at the scene of the robbery:

Cash amounting to	$675.00
One man's YM watch valued at	$675.00
Two rings, each valued at	$450.00
One gold money clip valued at	$750.00

Later the same day, the victim in the above robbery called the station house and told the clerk that the actual value of the rings was $550.00 each. When preparing the required report on this incident, the police officer preparing the report would be most correct if he/she recorded the total value of the property and cash stolen as being

(A) $3000.00
(B) $3200.00
(C) $2550.00
(D) $2650.00

Applying Policy Questions

DIRECTIONS: **Answer questions 136–137 based *solely* on the following policy statement:**

Police Officer Rems is instructed to notify the station house when he observes a dangerous life-threatening situation.

136. Which one of the following should Officer Rems report to the station house?

(A) A truck with a horn that is stuck, parked in a lot
(B) A defective traffic signal light at a busy intersection
(C) A double-parked truck unloading vegetables on a quiet side street
(D) A car with a flat tire parked at the curb

137. Which one of the following should Officer Rems report to the station house?

(A) A missing manhole cover just off the curb near an elementary school
(B) A missing trash basket at a busy intersection
(C) A damaged parking meter in a shopping area
(D) An out of order public telephone in a business district

138. In order to prevent the sale of drugs from automobiles, it is the policy of the police department for police officers to observe parked vehicles on their posts if they have reason to suspect that the actions of the occupants of the vehicle are suspicious. Which one of the following situations should a police officer consider most suspicious?

(A) Two male adults sit in a parked vehicle close to a schoolyard during recess hours and are approached daily by various children.
(B) A van drops off a female in front of a school and then quickly leaves.
(C) A taxi driver is parked in the same spot for 30 minutes while reading a newspaper.
(D) Three teenagers sit in a parked auto near a busy park while listening to music from a radio.

139. According to police department policy, under certain circumstances, police officers are authorized to search a person who is suspected of being involved in criminal activity involving the use of a weapon. In accordance with that policy, which of the following persons would a police officer most likely be authorized to search?
(A) A person who is suspected by a store owner of engaging in unlicensed sales of jewelry
(B) A female who is identified by a man as someone who has recently committed an armed robbery
(C) A driver of a car who is stopped by a police officer for passing a stop sign
(D) An apparently homeless person who appears to be drunk and is staggering down the street

***DIRECTIONS:* Answer question 140 *solely* on the basis of the following police statement:**

140. "When an emergency occurs, a police officer may be required to immediately enter onto subway tracks."

It would be most appropriate for a police officer to immediately enter onto subway tracks in which one of the following situations?
(A) A female accidentally drops her pocketbook onto the tracks.
(B) A child throws his favorite toy onto the tracks.
(C) A passenger accidentally falls onto the tracks.
(D) A subway worker drops a bag of tokens onto the tracks.

END OF EXAMINATION

Answer Key, Diagnostic Procedure, and Explanations

Answer Keys

1.	A	15.	B	29.	B	43.	A	57.	C
2.	C	16.	B	30.	C	44.	C	58.	C
3.	D	17.	B	31.	B	45.	B	59.	B
4.	D	18.	D	32.	A	46.	C	60.	A
5.	A	19.	D	33.	B	47.	C	61.	D
6.	C	20.	B	34.	C	48.	B	62.	A
7.	C	21.	B	35.	C	49.	D	63.	D
8.	D	22.	C	36.	C	50.	C	64.	C
9.	C	23.	A	37.	D	51.	A	65.	B
10.	A	24.	A	38.	C	52.	B	66.	C
11.	B	25.	B	39.	C	53.	A	67.	A
12.	A	26.	D	40.	C	54.	C	68.	D
13.	B	27.	B	41.	B	55.	D	69.	A
14.	B	28.	B	42.	B	56.	D	70.	D

71.	D	85.	C	99.	C	113.	C	127.	B
72.	D	86.	C	100.	D	114.	A	128.	A
73.	B	87.	C	101.	D	115.	C	129.	A
74.	A	88.	B	102.	C	116.	B	130.	A
75.	C	89.	C	103.	B	117.	C	131.	A
76.	B	90.	D	104.	B	118.	D	132.	A
77.	C	91.	C	105.	A	119.	A	133.	C
78.	B	92.	D	106.	B	120.	A	134.	A
79.	A	93.	B	107.	D	121.	B	135.	B
80.	A	94.	C	108.	A	122.	C	136.	B
81.	B	95.	B	109.	D	123.	B	137.	A
82.	C	96.	D	110.	A	124.	B	138.	A
83.	B	97.	B	111.	D	125.	D	139.	B
84.	C	98.	D	112.	A	126.	D	140.	C

Diagnostic Procedure

Insert the number of correct answers you obtained in the blank space for each section of the examination. The scale in the next column indicates how you did.

SECTION NUMBER	QUESTION NUMBERS	AREA	YOUR NUMBER CORRECT	SCALE
one	1 to 15	memory		15 right—excellent 14 right—good 13 right—fair under 13 right—poor
two	16 to 35	applying police directives		19–20 right—excellent 18 right—good 17 right—fair under 17 right—poor
three	36 to 55	reading comprehension		19–20 right—excellent 18 right—good 17 right—fair under 17 right—poor
four	56 to 75	police department forms		19–20 right—excellent 18 right—good 17 right—fair under 17 right—poor
five	76 to 100	legal definitions		23–25 right—excellent 22 right—good 21 right—fair under 21 right—poor
six	101 to 120	sentence ordering traffic maps matching sketches report writing directed patrol		19–20 right—excellent 18 right—good 17 right—fair under 17 right—poor
seven	121 to 140	formula questions find the perp frequency of information arithmetic applying policy		19–20 right—excellent 18 right—good 17 right—fair under 17 right—poor

How to correct weaknesses:

1. If you are weak in Section One, concentrate on Chapters 5 and 6.
2. If you are weak in Section Two, concentrate on Chapter 8.
3. If you are weak in Section Three, concentrate on Chapter 4.
4. If you are weak in Section Four, concentrate on Chapter 7.
5. If you are weak in Section Five, concentrate on Chapter 9.
6. If you are weak in Section Six, concentrate on Chapters 10 and 12.
7. If you are weak in Section Seven, concentrate on Chapter 10.

NOTE: Consider yourself weak in a section if you receive other than an excellent rating in it.

Answer Explanations

SECTION ONE

1. **A** Mr. Harry Walker is named in the paragraph as being the assemblyman from the district. Notice that only last names are given. This makes it harder to remember.

2. **C** Remember that Ms. Jones disputed Detective Richardson's information.

3. **D** The written material specifically gives the age of the white male and the Hispanic female as around 19. Remember, however, that nothing is known about the third member of the team. Therefore, that member could also be about 19.

4. **D** No mention was made anywhere in the narrative about a juvenile officer.

5. **A** The district manager was specifically identified as Ms. Maria Garcia.

6. **C** While there is a good possibility that there have been more, at least eight stick-ups have been reported in the last three months.

7. **C** The address of the meeting was given in the paragraph. It is not a coincidence that the same numbers appear in choices A and C. It is meant to confuse you.

8. **D** Very early in the passage, the date of the story is given, the same date as the meeting.

9. **C** Choice C states that at least eleven accidents have occurred in the last three months. The material states that at least eleven accidents have occurred in the last two months. If at least eleven accidents happened in the last two months, then the same can be said of the last three months. If anything, the numbers of accidents in the last three months would be greater than the last two months. It could not be less.

10. **A** The material states that the female Hispanic is usually armed with a handgun. The choice states that she is always armed with a handgun.

11. **B** Notice the similarity of the numbers in the choices. Be aware that this is done on purpose. You must develop your own method to distinguish between the various numbers you will encounter in the story.

12. A If you only remembered the 54th Precinct, you had to guess as to whether it was in Queens or Brooklyn. Be careful to remember all of the significant details in the story.

13. B Any information that is labeled in the story as being the first, the last, the most important, the least important, etc., must be remembered.

14. B Don't get lazy at the end of the story. This information was contained in the last sentence.

15. B The chapters dealing with memory contain a detailed strategy for answering these questions. One important feature of the strategy is to be certain of the chronological sequence of events.

SECTION TWO

16. B Procedure 3 allows only other members who are performing related police duty to enter or ride in the car.

17. B Choice B is accurate as far as it goes, but it falls short of being complete. Permission of the station house supervisor is needed before this can be done.

18. D Answers A, B, and C all are too absolute. According to the paragraph, most, not all, departments use a combination of one- and two-person patrols; most, not all, unions are against one-person patrols; and until recently, one-person patrol was not used in many large urban areas.

19. D The fact that three arrests were made does not change the fact that procedure 9 specifically directs operators to approach a crime scene quietly. The reason for this rule is to minimize the danger of panic on the part of the criminals when they realize that the police are coming.

20. B Procedure 24 requires the operator to make minor repairs to the RMP car, and a battery cable is very easily tightened.

21. B The first paragraph stages that much of the debate between proponents and adversaries of one-person patrol centers around safety.

22. C Procedure 12 prohibits leaving the car unnecessarily unattended, but there are many times when it is necessary to leave the car unattended. At this time, the car has to be locked, the keys have to be removed, and portable radios have to be taken with the officers.

23. A The operator is not responsible for inspecting the car when going off duty; that is the responsibility of the oncoming operator.

24. A Procedure 1 calls for automatic rotation each four hours when two police officers are assigned to the car. Procedure 2 points out that when a police officer is the driver of a superior officer, he/she is to be the operator for the entire tour.

25. B Choice B is too strong. Procedure 8 states that an operator should *avoid* remaining in areas where radio reception is poor. There are times when this cannot be avoided.

26. D Subdivision c of the opening paragraph specifically requires two separate written statements. The story only mentioned one such statement. You must begin to realize that policing is a semi-military occupation, and it requires strict adherence to rules and regulations.

27. B This answer is contained in Procedure 2. The stem of the question indicated that the patient was violent. This rules out the police officer transporting the patient to the hospital without an ambulance.

28. B Procedure 3a indicates that two police officers are needed if more than one patient is being transported. Remember to answer only on the basis of the written material.

29. B As per Procedure 2a, handcuffs are not appropriate in this case.

30. C A police officer is required to unload his revolver when entering a psychiatric ward of a hospital.

31. B Procedure 2c states that, when possible, a number of provisions should be made when transporting a female patient. This does not mean that they have to occur. If necessary, a female patient can be transported by one officer with no assistance.

32. A This question outlines a common problem for the police. Most people do not realize that people in this country have the right to refuse medical assistance.

33. B This answer is specifically stated in the first sentence of the written material.

34. C This special ambulance is equipped with extra restraining devices to reduce the possibility of injuring the patient.

35. C The police officer stays with the patient in the body of the ambulance.

SECTION THREE

36. C Innis was advised of his rights once upon the initial arrest, twice again when other officers arrived, and a fourth time before he led the police to the shotgun.

37. D The narrative specifically mentions the obtaining of the suspect's pedigree as not being "express questioning."

38. C The key is whether the police are aware that the suspect is emotionally upset; the stem of the question indicates that the police know this.

39. C It is stated in the first paragraph that Innis was identified from a picture.

40. C The U.S. Supreme Court overruled the Rhode Island Supreme Court and agreed in its decision with the trial court that the evidence should not be suppressed.

41. B The more important factor is whether or not the suspect believes the words or actions of the police are meant to get him to speak.

42. B The trial court ruled that Innis had voluntarily waived his rights and was, subsequently, convicted.

43. A It was the finding of the U.S. Supreme Court that Innis had not been interrogated.

44. C The Supreme Court held that, under these circumstances, it is not always clear whether that is the same as questioning.

45. B On the contrary, the U.S. Supreme Court held that it cannot be said that the police should have known their conversation would probably make Innis respond with an incriminating statement.

46. C The paragraph states that the Court of Appeals has been progressively strengthening a defendant's right to counsel.

47. C The Trial Court and the Appellate Court allowed the statements to be used. The Court of Appeals disagreed and suppressed the statement.

48. B As is stated in the first sentence of the written material, arson was the original charge.

49. D Choices A, B, and C are included in Choice D since they all are critical times. Therefore, the more general Choice D is the answer, as is stated in the paragraph.

50. C This information is contained in the last sentence of the written material.

51. A In its decision, the court restated the general rule that Fourth Amendment seizures are reasonable only if based on probable cause.

52. B Note that it is the occupant in control of the premise who is liable for arrest. The person may or may not be the owner of the premise.

53. A In this case, the United States Supreme Court disagreed with the Trial Court and the Appellate Court and ruled against the defendant by allowing the heroin to be used as evidence.

54. C To answer this question, it was necessary to realize that heroin is classified as a narcotic.

55. D Being "of prime importance" and being "of extreme significance" are two ways of saying the same thing.

SECTION FOUR

56. D Choice A, Sergeant Wilson, is the supervisor. The other two choices are made up.

57. C Officer Pearson worked 11 hours on a day that he was supposed to work 8 hours; therefore, he worked 3 hours overtime.

58. C This is really the only possible logical choice. The other three choices are not mentioned on the form.

59. B This answer is given in the box that is captioned, "incident time."

60. A This answer is given in the box captioned by "time scheduled to work."

61. D This answer is written in bold print at the bottom of the form as part of the instructions.

62. A This information is contained in the middle of the form under the caption labeled "location where duty performed."

63. D Officer Pearson obtained his present rank on the same day that he entered the Department, which was June 26.

64. C According to the information contained in the part of the form filled out by Sergeant Wilson, Officer Pearson was dismissed from duty at 1900 hours.

65. B The form offers the officer an option to choose between compensatory time off or cash. Pearson chose cash.

66. C This is the only logical answer, as the other remarks do not appear anywhere in the story.

67. A The officer was described as being in uniform by the sergeant.

68. D No mention is made anywhere in the narrative of the color of the suspect's hair.

69. A Boxes 5 and 6 require the insertion of the precinct designation and the post number, which are 4 and 26, respectively.

70. D Box 43 calls for the signature of the superior officer; the other boxes are unrelated to signatures.

71. D There is no place on the form to enter the sergeant's shield number.

72. D The answer to all of the questions is "yes." The officer was in uniform, the suspect was frisked, and a search inside of the suspect's clothes was made.

73. B Box 14 specifically asks if force was used.

74. A The narrative clearly states that the officer observed the suspect for five minutes.

75. C The first observation was at 2030 hours. The period of observation was five minutes; therefore, the stop was made at 2035 hours.

SECTION FIVE

76. B Robbery is not one of the crimes enumerated in the law defining burglar's tools. Anytime a listing of crimes is included in a statute, pay particular attention. This is a favorite hunting ground for examiners.

77. C If the act is done with the intent of having someone submit to the pretended authority, it is the crime of criminal impersonation. Hence, choice C is correct.

78. B It is not significant that John is not being arrested. He merely has to prevent or attempt to prevent someone from legitimately being arrested. This is one of those crimes where the little word "or" is very important.

79. A In this case, a person has to believe that the property in his possession is stolen *and* the property must, in fact, be stolen property. Lacking either element leaves no crime. Once again, we see the importance of the little word "and."

80. A Illegally possessing a rifle might be some other offense, but for the purpose of "criminal possession of a weapon," it is specifically exempted.

81. B According to the given definition, only one person need be married for both to be guilty. Further, nothing in the statute indicates that knowledge of the other party's marriage is a required element of the crime.

82. C Choices A and B are wrong because this is an "or" situation. Oral sex and anal sex both can be elements of forceable sodomy. Choice D is wrong because, regardless of age, the crime can be committed if force is used. Choice C is correct because if the "actor" is over 21 and the other person is less than 17, then force is not required.

83. B The definition clearly states that the intent must be to keep the property permanently for someone's use, other than the owner's use.

84. C The statute states "whether loaded or not."

85. C Remember to pay particular attention to lists. In this case, grand larceny is not on the list.

86. C Choice C is the only choice that contains all of the necessary elements of the crime. Note that "intentionally" and "knowingly" have the same general meaning.

87. C The information in the stem of the question indicates how much the car is worth, but it does not tell you how much damage was done to the car. Hence, the crime is either criminal mischief in the first degree or criminal mischief in the second degree.

88. B Since the car was owned by a nonprofit organization, the crime becomes criminal mischief in the first degree regardless of the amount of damage done to the car.

89. C A person who commits this crime does not have to know how much damage he is doing for the crime to be committed.

90. D Joe's intent is given in the story as wanting to see a television show. Since this does not amount to an intent to commit a crime, no burglary is involved. In reality, the crime committed was a criminal trespass.

91. C Since a cave is not a man-made structure, it is not considered a building.

92. D Nighttime is defined as the period from sundown to sun-up. Since this time varies from season to season, the correct choice is D.

93. B Jones is guilty of burglary in the second degree because his accomplice Smith was armed with a deadly weapon. (Note that only the person who is actually armed with a deadly weapon can be charged in the first degree.)

94. C Since Smith was armed with a deadly weapon when he entered his boss's dwelling at nighttime, he is guilty of burglary in the first degree. This is a Class B felony.

95. B Burglary in the second degree can be committed at any time of the day or night.

96. D John did not commit burglary because he did not unlawfully enter the store or unlawfully remain in the store. The story makes it quite clear that he entered the store and left the store in the normal manner. In reality, John has committed larceny.

97. B All that is needed to commit the crime of burglary is an intent to commit a crime in the building. It does not matter if the intended crime is actually committed.

98. D Joe has not committed the crime of robbery for two reasons. He did not threaten a person related to Brown, nor is there any indication that he threatened the immediate use of force. In reality, the crime involved is extortion.

99. C Property must be taken for the crime to be committed. Force does not have to be used; it merely has to be threatened.

100. D The crime of robbery becomes first degree if, during the commission of the crime, someone other than a participant in its commission has to be hospitalized.

SECTION SIX

101. D Choices A, B, and C all suggest illogical first sentences. Only Choice D has a logical beginning.

102. C Sentence 1 has to come first since it starts the action; therefore, Choices A and D are wrong. Sentence 5 has to occur after sentence 2; therefore, Choice B is wrong.

103. B Sentence 1 must come before sentence 4. Therefore, Choices C and D are wrong. Sentence 4 must then come before sentence 3. Therefore, Choice A is wrong and the answer is Choice B.

104. B Choices A, C, and D are not correct because they all have an inappropriate beginning sentence. Only Choice B has a logical beginning.

105. A Choices C and D are wrong because they do not have a logical starting sentence. Choice B is wrong because sentence 1 is an inappropriate last sentence.

106. B Eliminate Choice A which directs you to head east on Adam Street, a westbound only street. Choice C is wrong since it suggests making a left onto Elf Street which is an eastbound only street. Choice D is wrong because, although it will get you to Blair Park, it is not as direct a route as Choice B, which is the answer.

107. D Choice A is wrong because it suggests travelling west on Blue Street, which is an eastbound only street. Choice B is wrong because it suggests travelling south six blocks on Canvass Avenue which would put you off the map. Choice C is wrong because following its direction would not get you to your destination. Choice D is the answer.

108. A Choice B is incorrect because making a right turn would be against the flow of traffic and have you heading west. Choice C is incorrect because making a left turn would have you going against the flow of traffic. Choice D is incorrect because making a right turn would have you heading west. Choice A is the correct answer.

109. D Choice A is wrong because the shape of the chin is different. Choice B can be eliminated because the shape of the nose is different. Choice C can be eliminated because the mouth is different.

110. A Choice B is wrong because of the shape of the chin. Choice C is wrong because the nose is different. Choice D is wrong because the eyes are different.

111. D The chin is different in Choice A. In Choice B the nose is different. In Choice C the mouth is different.

112. A In Choice B the chin is different. In Choice C the mouth is different. In Choice D the ears are different.

113. C Choice A does not clearly indicate that the accident occurred at the intersection of White and First streets. Choice B infers that the accident was reported at 12:15 P.M. instead of occurring at that time. Choice D left out the license plate number.

114. A Choice B is wrong because there is no mention of the hospital the patient was removed to. Choice C is wrong because it unnecessarily repeats the information about his cardiac problem. D is wrong because his address is not correctly indicated.

115. C Choice A incorrectly indicates the time of reporting is 3:15 A.M. Choice B is wrong because, among other things, it indicates that the store was the victim. Choice D is wrong since it appears that the witness was wearing army pants and a brown jacket.

116. B Choice A is wrong because the crime occurred at 7:35 P.M., and not at 8:30 P.M. Choice C is wrong because Sheila Jackson was a customer, not an employee. Choice D is wrong because it does not mention that the male was white.

117. C Aponte has to work on Fridays to deal with the rapes and Saturdays and Sundays to deal with the robberies. That eliminates Choices A and D. She has to work between 2 A.M. and 4 A.M. to deal with the rapes. That eliminates Choice B. Choice C is the answer.

118. D The auto larcenies are committed on Fourth Avenue on Sundays and Mondays between midnight and 3:00 A.M.

119. A According to the paragraph, all of the homicides occur on Edwin Street on Tuesdays.

120. A The assaults occur on Thursdays and the robberies take place on Mondays. Choice A is the only one that includes working on both of those days.

SECTION SEVEN

121. B Officer Rems worked for 8 hours, from 8:00 A.M. until 4:00 P.M. All 8 hours were spent on Post #4 except for (minus) his time on meal period and his time on school crossing.

122. C The total value of the property would be expressed by Choice C which indicates one wristwatch valued at $250, plus two fur jackets valued at $500 each, plus two televisions valued at $300 each.

123. B The suspect in Incident #2 had a tattoo on his upper right arm and right hand but the arrested perpetrator in Incident #4 was not described as having similar tattoos.

124. B Suspect #2 is too heavy to be the arrested person. Bear in mind that, as you will learn in a later chapter, the clothes the suspects are wearing play no part in the determination of the answer.

125. D All of the other three suspects are too tall to be the suspect in Rape #4.

126. D Based on gender, race, age, height, weight and scars of suspect #4, she could also be the suspect in each of the other three reports.

127. B Choice C is wrong because three witnesses suggested the first letter of the plate was a "B". Choice A is wrong because three witnesses suggested the second letter of the plate was an "E". Choice D is wrong because three witnesses suggested that the second number of the plate was an "8."

128. A Choice C is wrong because three witnesses said the car was black. Choice B is wrong because three witnesses said the second number in the plate was "2." Choice D is wrong because three witnesses said the second letter in the plate was "B."

129. A Choice B is wrong because three witnesses gave the second letter of the plate as "B." Choice C is wrong because three witnesses gave the third letter of the plate as "E." Choice D is wrong because three witnesses gave the first letter of the plate as "A."

130. A Two witnesses said the height was 6′, witness B said 6′4″ and witness C said 5′8″. Therefore, Choices B and C are wrong. Choice D is wrong because three witnesses gave the weight as 175 pounds.

131. A Choice C is wrong because three witness said the truck was black. Choice B is wrong because three witnesses said the truck was a GMC. Choice D is wrong because three witnesses said the first letter in the plate was "D."

132. A Choices B and C are eliminated because two witnesses said the rapist was Hispanic. Choice D is wrong because three witnesses said the rapist had brown eyes.

133. C Choice A is the total value of one of each of the stolen items, not counting the cash register. Choice B is the total value of one of each of the stolen items including the cash register. Choice D is the total value of all of the property stolen except for the cash register.

134. A Choice B does not include the cash. Choice C does not include the price of all three baseball tickets. Choice D does not include the value of the briefcase.

135. B Choice A does not take into consideration the amended value of the rings. Choice D takes into consideration the amended value of only one of the rings. The amount reported in Choice C reflects the original value of only one of the rings.

136. B Of the four choices, the only life-threatening situation is in Choice B.

137. A Remember, the most dangerous situation is one that is dangerous to life. Choice A is the only such situation described in the choices.

138. A Choice B does not involve a "parked" vehicle. Choice C and Choice D are common sights and can easily be justified. There does not, however, seem to be a plausible, legitimate reason for the situation described in Choice A.

139. B Unlicensed selling, passing a stop sign, and being drunk, as described in Choices A, C, and D are not criminal activities involving the use of a weapon. However, armed robbery as described in Choice B, is a criminal activity.

140. C The cardinal rule is that life is more important than property. Choice C is the only life-threatening situation.

CORRECT YOUR WEAKNESSES

CHAPTER 4

Understanding What You Read

This chapter is one of the most important because so much of your success on the examination depends on how well you understand written material. In addition, other sections of the test also require good reading comprehension ability; namely, those sections in Chapter 5 "Recalling What You Read," Chapter 7 "Handling Police Department Forms," Chapter 8 "Understanding and Applying Police Directives, Procedures, and Regulations," and Chapter 9, "Understanding Legal Definitions."

Therefore, spend as much time as you can with this chapter. Reading ability can be improved through diligent practice in the same way as any similar skill. In this chapter, you will find general hints for improving your overall skills, as well as specific instructions for answering reading comprehension questions.

How to Concentrate

How often do you "read" something by looking at the words without concentrating on their meaning. This is the biggest roadblock to overcome if you want to become a good reader. Actually, letting your mind wander is not bad for light reading. However, for the kind of reading that is essential to master almost any examination, you *must* learn how to totally concentrate on the material. One way to accomplish this is to continuously ask yourself questions about what you are reading. Another way is to use your imagination and create mental impressions about what you are reading. Above all, don't let your mind wander!

A simple way to practice concentration is to read a passage of any kind, and to write down the key points you remember. Then return to the passage and see how well you did. You will become more proficient with practice. Remember, the key is: *concentrate*.

Increase Your Vocabulary

Concentration will not help if a reading passage contains a significant number of words that you don't understand. Therefore, follow these suggestions to increase your vocabulary:

1. When you read a word you don't fully understand, make a note of it along with a reminder of where you read it. Keep a special notebook for this purpose.

2. Look up the meaning of the word in the dictionary as soon as possible.

3. Return to the material where you read the word, and make sure you understand its meaning.

4. Try to use these words in your everyday conversation.

5. Keep a separate list of these words, and review them periodically until you are certain you have mastered them.

6. Ask a friend or another student to test you on the meaning of the words.

Strategies for Handling Reading Comprehension

1. **READ THE DIRECTIONS.** Today's police examinations contain *general directions* at the beginning of the examination, along with *specific directions* preceding each different question type. *Be sure to read all instructions carefully before doing the questions.*

   Note that the most important instruction given for reading comprehension questions is to answer the questions based *solely* on the information in the paragraph. Never introduce knowledge you possess into a reading comprehension question.

2. **SCAN THE CONTENTS OF THE PASSAGE.** Get an idea of the general subject matter of the passage by skimming it. A good rule is to read the first sentence of each paragraph and the entire last paragraph. But do it quickly, just to get an idea of what is contained in the passage.

3. **READ THE STEM OF EACH QUESTION PERTAINING TO THE PASSAGE.** After scanning the passage, read the stem of each question pertaining to it. The *stem* of the question contains the information that precedes the choices. Get an understanding of what is to be tested in the passage. (Also, scan some of the choices, but do this quickly.) By knowing what you are to be tested on, you can make the best use of your reading time.

4. **READ THE PASSAGE CAREFULLY.** Now you know what the passage is about, and what type of information you need to answer the questions. Next, read the passage *very carefully*. This is the time when it is necessary to concentrate exclusively on the material in the passage. While you are reading these materials, note the key facts and mark them according to strategy 5.

5. **UNDERLINE OR CIRCLE KEY WORDS OR PHRASES. WRITE KEY FACTS IN THE MARGIN.** Unless the directions prohibit doing so, all good multiple choice test takers use their pencil to underline key items in the reading passage and to write notations in the margin.

   Regarding *key words or phrases*. Underscore or circle:

   - Transitional words that signal a change in thought, as:

     therefore in conclusion
     however yet

   - Absolute words that are all encompassing, as:

     all
     never

     (See the complete list in Chapter 2.)

   - Limiting words, as:

     generally
     sometimes

     (See the complete list in Chapter 2.)

Regarding *key facts*. Place an asterisk in the margin next to important information, and write short notes to yourself with arrows to the portion of the passage to which you are referring. Important information includes:

- Items covered in the questions,
- Time of occurrence,
- Complainant's name,
- Type of crime,
- Statements of key people,
  —victim,
  —witness,
  —officer.

Remember, the purpose is to help you understand the passage and retrieve information quickly.

6. **ASK YOURSELF QUESTIONS WHILE READING THE PASSAGE.** Your ability to understand the passage is increased significantly when you pause occasionally and ask yourself questions about what you are reading, such as:

- What is the main idea of the entire passage?
- What is the main purpose of each paragraph within the passage?
- What was the crime?
- When did the crime happen?
- Who committed the crime?
- Who was the victim?

7. **DEVELOP A MENTAL PICTURE OF WHAT YOU ARE READING.** Many people find that the best way to understand and enjoy a novel is to project themselves into the story, and to try to re-live the characters' experiences. Good test takers should use this technique when doing reading comprehension questions. Use your imagination and develop a mental picture or impression of what you are reading. Practice this when you do your everyday reading, i.e., newspapers, magazines, etc., and see how this helps you retain what you read.

8. **ANSWER THE QUESTIONS.** When answering the multiple-choice questions, use the strategy outlined in Chapter 2. However, remember that the answer is contained somewhere in the reading passage and review the passage quickly to verify your answer or to refresh your memory if you cannot select an answer. Writing key notes in the margin of the test booklet should help you because it is a technique that will enable you to find quickly the portion of the passage that you want to reexamine.

Practice Exercises

GROUP ONE—20 Minute Time Limit

***DIRECTIONS:* Answer questions 1 through 10 *solely* on the basis of information contained in the following passage.**

One of the most successful innovations in police administration in the last fifty years has been the civilianization of police departments. There are a number of tasks in and about a police station which must be performed, but which do not involve law enforcement duties and responsibilities. Therefore, it is not necessary to require a sworn police officer to perform these tasks. Yet, traditionally, very few police departments had civilians working side by side with their police officers. The officers would perform all the required tasks regardless of the nature of the work involved. As a result, police officers performed such duties as answering incoming telephone calls, dispensing gas, driving the patrolwagon, typing and filing reports, and even keeping the station house clean. Mounting fiscal problems for municipal governments have generally provided the impetus to replace police officers performing non-enforcement duties with civilians. The primary advantages of civilianization are two-fold. Civilians can be hired to do the same work as the police officers but at a lower cost, and more police officers can be assigned to enforcement duties. In addition, having civilians working in police stations makes it less stressful for some members of the community to visit the police station.

Listed below, as examples of the kinds of work performed by civilian members of the police departments, are the typical duties and responsibilities of three civilian titles: the Gasoline Dispenser, the Patrolwagon Operator, and the Attendant.

<u>Gasoline Dispenser</u>

1. Possess a Certificate of Fitness from Fire Department.
2. Supply gasoline and oil to department vehicles and authorized private vehicles.

3. Have operator of vehicle sign the receipt for gas, oil, grease and anti-freeze.

4. See that no one smokes or carries lighted substance in premises where gas is dispensed.

5. Display "No Smoking" signs.

6. Have buckets filled with sand available.

7. Sprinkle sand to absorb spilled gasoline, oil, or grease.

8. Make certain that the ignition is turned off when gasoline is dispensed into fuel tanks.

9. Measure the contents of the station house gasoline tank before and after the delivery of gasoline, and make the appropriate entry in the "Gas, oil, grease and anti-freeze" book.

10. Make certain that fire extinguishers in the premises are full and serviceable.

11. Notify the station house supervisor when gas storage tanks are half full.

12. Perform other duties as directed by station house supervisor.

13. Keep gasoline pumps locked when not present.

14. Keep garage area neat and clean.

<u>Patrolwagon Operator</u>

1. Report to station house supervisor at beginning of tour and, when relieved, at end of tour.

2. Keep the patrolwagon and equipment in clean, serviceable condition.

3. Maintain the Patrolwagon Record in a plain Number 2 book. Enter

   - name,
   - time reporting for duty,
   - time leaving and returning from meal,
   - time relieved.

4. Make entry of time leaving precinct, stops made, and time of return to garage.

5. Keep the garage and abutting driveways, areaways, and sidewalks clean and free from snow and ice.
6. Report necessary repairs to the commanding officer.
7. Report to station house supervisor on leaving and returning from calls and meal.
8. Remain within hearing of the signal for services, and render police assistance as special duty permits.
9. Call the Communications Division from all stops on way to court or other destination, upon arrival at destination, and prior to departure.
10. Perform duty in proper uniform.
11. Deliver Division mail.
12. Inspect all RMP cars on reserve at station house, and obtain gas and oil for those in need of same.
13. Bring RMP cars to authorized car wash.
14. Pick up department supplies and equipment.

<u>Attendant</u>

1. Have charge of the male prisoners and be responsible for their safekeeping while confined.
2. Inspect prisoners in cells and report their physical condition and wants to the station house supervisor immediately after reporting for duty and every 30 minutes thereafter.
3. Visit female detention cells or the quarters of a female officer assigned to matron duty as follows:
   a. when accompanied by female officer and then, only with permission of officer in command of the station house, or
   b. in daily cleaning of female cells, or
   c. in an emergency.
4. Keep station house and abutting areaways, yards, and sidewalks clean and sanitary.
5. Prevent rubbish or dust from accumulating in any part of the station house.
6. Report necessary repairs to the commanding officer.

7. Wash male and female cells thoroughly, and test emergency alarms in the cell block each day immediately after prisoners have been taken to court.

8. Operate heating plant.

9. Keep cells supplied with paper cups, toilet paper, and paper towels.

10. Perform other duties as directed by station house supervisor.

11. Make necessary entries on prison roster.

---

1. Which of the following is *not* a stated advantage of civilianization?
   (A) It results in lower overall operating costs.
   (B) Civilians perform non-enforcement work such as typing more efficiently than most police officers.
   (C) The presence of civilian workers in the station house makes it easier for citizens to visit the station house.
   (D) Civilianization results in more police officers being assigned to enforcement duties.

A B C D
1 | | | | | | | |

2. Which of the following is stated in the passage as having provided the momentum for civilianization to take hold?
   (A) More police officers are needed on the street.
   (B) Good police-community relations are important.
   (C) Crime rates, particularly in the area of violent crimes are rising.
   (D) Budgetary concerns for local governments are increasing.

A B C D
2 | | | | | | | |

3. Which of the following is the most accurate statement concerning *civilianization*?
   (A) Civilianization represents the only successful innovation in police administration in the last fifty years.
   (B) History shows that no police departments used civilian employees until recent years.
   (C) All tasks in and about the typical station house can be performed equally as well by civilians.
   (D) Not all police officers perform enforcement type work.

A B C D
3 | | | | | | | |

4. Which of the following workers routinely leave the precinct station house and surrounding area as part of their assigned duties?
(A) Gas Dispensers
(B) Patrolwagon Operators
(C) Attendants
(D) Patrolwagon Operators and Attendants

4 A B C D

5. Which of the following workers are required to perform other tasks as directed by the station house supervisor?
(A) Only the Gasoline Dispensers
(B) Only the Patrolwagon Operators
(C) Only the Attendants
(D) Only the Gasoline Dispensers and the Attendants

5 A B C D

6. Attendants are authorized to visit the quarters of a female officer assigned to matron duty in each of the following instances *except*:
(A) As part of the daily cleaning of the female cells.
(B) In an emergency situation.
(C) When accompanied by a female officer.
(D) When directed by the station house supervisor.

6 A B C D

7. Which of the following duties is performed once each day?
(A) The Gasoline Dispenser reports when the gas storage tanks are half full.
(B) The female cells are cleaned by the Attendant.
(C) Entries are made in the Patrolwagon Record Book by the Patrolwagon Operator.
(D) Gasoline and oil are supplied to department vehicles by the Gasoline Dispenser.

7 A B C D

8. Which of the following workers are required to be in uniform while working?
(A) Patrolwagon Operators
(B) Attendants
(C) Gasoline Dispensers
(D) Patrolwagon Operators, Attendants, and Gasoline Dispensers

8 A B C D

9. Which of the following is an *inaccurate* statement concerning the typical duties of civilian workers in police departments? 9 A B C D

(A) The Patrolwagon Operator must inspect all RMP cars in use and obtain gas and oil for those in need of same.

(B) The Gasoline Dispenser must keep the gasoline pumps locked when he/she is not present.

(C) The Gasoline Dispenser must see that no one smokes or carries a lighted substance in premises where gas is dispensed.

(D) The Attendant must prevent rubbish or dust from accumulating.

10. Which of the following workers are required to make some type of entries in department records or forms? 10 A B C D

(A) Only the Gasoline Dispenser

(B) Only the Patrolwagon Operator

(C) Only the Attendant

(D) The Gasoline Dispenser, the Patrolwagon Operator, and the Attendant

GROUP TWO—15 Minute Time Limit

***DIRECTIONS:* Answer questions 11 through 18 *solely* on the basis of information contained in the following passage.**

On November 10, defendant Myers and three other people were traveling north on the New York State Thruway when their car was stopped by a New York State trooper for speeding. Approaching the vehicle, the officer smelled marijuana coming from within the vehicle and observed an envelope on the floor of the vehicle which he recognized as a type commonly used in selling marijuana. The officer then ordered the occupants out of the vehicle, frisked each one, removed the envelope from the floor, and determined that it contained a small amount of marijuana.

After the marijuana was found, Myers and the three other people standing outside the car were placed under arrest for the illegal possession of marijuana. The officer reentered the vehicle, searched portions of it likely to conceal drugs, and searched the pockets of five jackets lying on the back seat. He opened the zippered pocket of one of the jackets and discovered a small amount of cocaine. The officer placed an additional charge against Myers for illegally possessing cocaine. All four prisoners were then removed to the State Police Headquarters where they were interrogated for twenty minutes.

Myers and his three accomplices engaged in plea bargaining with respect to the charges concerning possession of marijuana, but Myers elected to go to trial with respect to the charge concerning possession of cocaine. Myers was convicted by Trial Court, and a unanimous Appellate Division Court affirmed, holding that the warrantless search of the jacket was lawful as incident to the defendant's arrest.

Myers appealed to the Court of Appeals. In arriving at its decision, the Court of Appeals discussed the right of privacy and the area that might be searched when an arrest is made. The Court held that when a person is placed under arrest, there is always a danger that he/she may seek to use a weapon to effect an escape or to destroy or conceal evidence of a crime or other contraband. Accordingly, it would be reasonable (pursuant to the Fourth Amendment) for the arresting officer to conduct a prompt warrantless search of the arrestee's person and the area within his/her immediate control in order for the officer to protect himself and others and to prevent loss of evidence. The area within the arrestee's immediate control would mean any area from which he/she might reach a weapon or evidence that could be destroyed.

Both the Trial Court and the Appellate Division Court concluded that as a factual matter, the jacket was *not* within the exclusive control of the police *nor* were the arrestees effectively neutralized. The Court of Appeals disagreed, holding that once the defendant Myers was arrested and removed from the vehicle, he was incapable, as were his confederates, of reentering the vehicle to attempt to obtain a weapon or destroy evidence.

11. The Court of Appeals held that it is reasonable for the arresting officer to search the person of an arrestee and the area under the arrestee's immediate control. The Court defined *immediate control* as being:

(A) The area within reach of the arrested person's arms.
(B) The entire area inside the car, but not including the inside of jacket pockets.
(C) Any area from which the arrested person might gain a weapon.
(D) Any area from which the arrested person might gain evidence.

11 A B C D

12. Which of the following can accurately be concluded from the information in the above narrative?

(A) Myers is a male.
(B) The jacket with the cocaine belonged to Myers.
(C) Myers was questioned alone for twenty minutes.
(D) None of the defendants was sentenced to prison.

12 A B C D

13. Which of the following courts ruled in favor of Myers?
(A) The Trial Court
(B) The Appellate Division Court
(C) The Court of Appeals
(D) The Trial Court, the Appellate Division Court, and the Court of Appeals

A B C D
13 | | | | | | | |

14. According to the narrative, which of the following statements is most accurate concerning actual ownership of the cocaine?
(A) Myers was the owner of the cocaine.
(B) One of Myers' three accomplices owned the cocaine.
(C) Someone other than Myers and his three accomplices owned the cocaine.
(D) It is impossible to state who owned the cocaine from the information given in the narrative.

A B C D
14 | | | | | | | |

15. Which of the following is the *least* accurate statement concerning Myers and the three accomplices?
(A) All four were arrested for possession of marijuana.
(B) All four engaged in plea bargaining.
(C) All four were arrested for the possession of cocaine.
(D) All four were questioned at New York State Police Headquarters.

A B C D
15 | | | | | | | |

16. The Court of Appeals based its findings primarily upon which of the following?
(A) The officer smelled marijuana upon approaching the stopped car.
(B) None of the defendants could have reentered the vehicle after they were arrested.
(C) The officer acted in an unreasonable manner with respect to the Fourth Amendment.
(D) The jacket in which the cocaine was found was discovered in the car that Myers was driving.

A B C D
16 | | | | | | | |

17. As used in the above narrative, the word *incident* means:
(A) Occurrence.
(B) In connection with.
(C) Unusual happening.
(D) A minor event.

A B C D
17 | | | | | | | |

18. Pursuant to the Fourth Amendment, the Court of Appeals held that searches of arrested persons are reasonable if they are made for any of the following reasons *except*:

(A) To strengthen the case of the arresting officer.
(B) To prevent the arrested person from using a weapon.
(C) To stop the arrested person from destroying evidence.
(D) To prevent the arrested person from effectuating an escape.

18 A B C D

GROUP THREE—25 Minute Time Limit

***DIRECTIONS:* Answer questions 19 through 33 *solely* on the basis of information contained in the following passage.**

One of the most important police functions is to render aid to people in need of assistance. In police parlance, taking action to help someone is considered handling an "aided case." The official police definition of an "aided case" is "any occurrence coming to the attention of a member of the service which requires that a person, other than a prisoner, receives medical aid or assistance. Included are such occurrences as rendering aid to sick or injured persons; assisting people who are lost; dealing with the mentally ill; and caring for abandoned, destitute, abused, or neglected children."

The most sensitive "aided cases" are those which involve dead human beings. The pain and suffering of relatives and friends of a deceased person can be eased by a thoughtful police officer acting in a professional manner. Nevertheless, the officer cannot dismiss the possibility of foul play. For these reasons, the New York City Police Department has developed very precise guidelines for its police officers to follow to ensure that notifications to concerned authorities and relatives are properly made and recorded, that evidence is properly preserved in the appropriate cases, and that proper disposition is made of the body.

When a member of the police department arrives at the scene of an apparently dead human being, he/she must do the following:

1. Request, through the radio dispatcher, that an ambulance and a patrol supervisor respond.
2. Exclude unauthorized persons from the scene.
3. Obtain names of witnesses and detain them at the scene if circumstances indicate a suspicious death.
4. Screen the area from public view, if possible.

5. Cover the body with waterproof covering if publicly exposed.

6. Ascertain the facts and notify the station house officer as soon as possible.

7. Request that the aided person be removed to the hospital or that a hospital doctor be dispatched if a pronouncement of death by an ambulance attendant is questioned by anyone.

After the station house officer is notified by the police officer at the scene of the facts involved in the case, the station house officer must notify the following:

1. The precinct detectives.

2. The Harbor Unit, if the aided is removed from navigable waters by other than a member of the Harbor Unit.

3. The Crime Scene Unit, if the death is an apparent homicide, suicide, or in any way suspicious.

4. The Communications Division, if the death is suspicious.

5. The medical examiner. When notifying the medical examiner (M.E.), the station house officer must obtain the M.E. case number, for entry on the Aided Report. If the medical examiner fails to respond on the scene within one hour, a follow-up notification shall be made.

The police officer at the scene must remain with the body until the medical examiner makes his decision as to the disposition of the body, and the decision is effectuated. During this time, the officer at the scene has a number of definite responsibilities, as follows:

1. To prevent anyone from disturbing the body of its effects *except*:
   a. the ambulance attendant and doctor after they are cautioned not to disturb evidence,
   b. the medical examiner or an assistant medical examiner,
   c. the district attorney or the assistant district attorney,
   d. a member of the Detective Bureau, the Crime Scene Unit, or the precinct detective squad.

2. To prepare the Identification Tag and attach it to the body. In accordance with department policy, this tag is to be placed on dead human bodies, parts of bodies, and human fetuses that are to be delivered to the morgue; and unconscious persons at the scene of an accident. The lower half of the Identification Tag serves as a receipt for the body when it is removed to the morgue, and for the body and the death certificate if released to a funeral director or other authorized person.

3. To prepare an Aided Report after the body is removed in accordance with the directions of the medical examiner, and to include in the report:
   a. the name and badge number of the morgue vehicle operator removing the body; or,
   b. the name and address of the undertaker authorized to remove the body, as well as the name, address, and relationship of the person authorizing such removal; or,
   c. the name, address, and relationship of the person to whom the body was released.

In all cases involving the death of a human being, the police department is responsible for notifying, if possible, a member of the immediate family of the deceased. This notification is to be made tactfully and, preferably, in person. Efforts should be made to have a friend or a neighbor present when making such notification.

The patrol supervisor who responds to the scene also has very definite responsibilities, as follows:

1. To ascertain that the precinct detectives have been notified.

2. To ascertain that the Crime Scene Unit has been notified, when appropriate.

3. To supervise, if appropriate, a search of the body and premises in the presence of witnesses if the deceased resided alone or died at a location other than his/her residence.

4. To direct the member of the service who searched the body to safeguard the property.

In homicide cases, the station house officer must make arrangements for the officer who discovered the body to report to the morgue at 9:00 A.M. the following day to identify the body to two (2) medical examiners. If the officer who was first on the scene is not available, the station house officer shall direct another member who can identify the body as the body observed at the scene, to report to the morgue on the following day.

---

19. A member of the service would be correct to attach an Identification Tag in all of the following cases *except*:
   (A) On a human fetus that is to be delivered to the morgue.
   (B) On any unconscious person who is being sent to the hospital.
   (C) On a dead human body.
   (D) On a part of a body.

19 A B C D

20. All of the following are correctly stated responsibilities of the patrol supervisor at the scene of a dead human body case *except*:

(A) To determine if the Crime Scene Unit has been notified, if required.
(B) To supervise a search of the dead body, in appropriate cases.
(C) To notify the precinct detectives.
(D) To direct the member making the search to safeguard the property, in cases where searches have been performed.

A B C D
20 | | | | | | | |

21. All of the following are authorized to disturb the body or its effects *except*:

(A) Any member of the service.
(B) An ambulance attendant.
(C) An assistant medical examiner.
(D) An assistant district attorney.

A B C D
21 | | | | | | | |

22. Who is responsible for the preparation of the Aided Report concerning a dead human body case?

(A) The station house officer
(B) The patrol supervisor
(C) The officer at the scene
(D) The detective assigned to the case

A B C D
22 | | | | | | | |

23. The station house officer is responsible for assigning an officer to be at the morgue the following day to identify the body as being the one at the scene whenever:

(A) The body was delivered to the morgue.
(B) The death was classified as suspicious.
(C) The case is a homicide.
(D) The deceased lived alone.

A B C D
23 | | | | | | | |

24. Which of the following is the most accurate statement concerning the notification of a member of the immediate family of the deceased?

(A) The notification must always be made in person.
(B) A friend or a neighbor must be present when the notification is made.
(C) The notification has to be made.
(D) The notification must always be made tactfully.

A B C D
24 | | | | | | | |

25. In cases where a death certificate is issued, the correct way for the police to account for its disposition is to:

(A) Obtain a receipt for it on the lower half of the Identification Tag.
(B) Include the pertinent information in the Aided Report.
(C) Obtain a written statement from the person authorized to take the body.
(D) Hold the station house officer responsible for recording the necessary information.

A B C D
25 |||| ||||

26. Which of the following is the most accurate statement concerning the search of a dead human body?

(A) A search of the body must always be made.
(B) The patrol supervisor is responsible for making the search.
(C) The search must be made in the presence of witnesses.
(D) The property found during the search can be released only to a member of the immediate family.

A B C D
26 |||| ||||

27. An "aided case" would *not* be classified by the police as:

(A) Helping a lost child to get home.
(B) Sending an abused child to a children's shelter.
(C) Dispatching a prisoner to the hospital for medical assistance.
(D) Delivering a mentally retarded person to a mental institution.

A B C D
27 |||| ||||

28. In cases involving dead human bodies, the station house officer must always notify the:

(A) Harbor Unit.
(B) The Medical Examiner.
(C) The Communications Division.
(D) The Crime Scene Unit.

A B C D
28 |||| ||||

29. Of the following, the most sensitive "aided case" is:

(A) One involving a lost three-year-old child.
(B) One involving a dead human being.
(C) One involving a prisoner.
(D) One involving an abused two-year-old baby.

A B C D
29 |||| ||||

30. Which of the following is the *least* accurate statement concerning dead human body cases?

(A) The police department has very strict guidelines for police officers to follow in these cases.

(B) In some cases, the police officer on the scene must consider the possibility of foul play.

(C) The proper disposition of the body is a responsibility of the police.

(D) These cases often involve pain and suffering.

A B C D
30 | | | | | | | |

31. It is *always* a responsibility of the member of the service arriving at the scene of a case involving an apparently dead human body to:

(A) Screen the body from public view.

(B) Cover the body with a waterproof covering.

(C) Detain witnesses at the scene.

(D) Request that a patrol supervisor respond to the scene.

A B C D
31 | | | | | | | |

32. Who is responsible for determining if a death is suspicious?

(A) The precinct detective

(B) The patrol supervisor

(C) The member at the scene

(D) The station house officer

A B C D
32 | | | | | | | |

33. Who is responsible for obtaining the M.E. case number for the Aided Report?

(A) The station house officer

(B) The patrol supervisor

(C) The member on the scene

(D) The precinct detective

A B C D
33 | | | | | | | |

Answer Key and Explanations

Answer Key

1. B	10. D	19. B	28. B
2. D	11. C	20. C	29. B
3. D	12. A	21. A	30. B
4. B	13. C	22. C	31. D
5. D	14. D	23. C	32. C
6. C	15. C	24. D	33. A
7. B	16. B	25. A	
8. A	17. B	26. C	
9. A	18. A	27. C	

Answer Explanations

GROUP ONE

GENERAL COMMENT: The type of question which utilizes more than one list is generally used to test the ability to make comparisons. When reading the lists, mark any similarities. And, if you followed the rules given earlier in the chapter, you would have first read the stems of the questions and have known that comparisons among the lists would be asked. Your job should have been easier if you noted the similarities with your pencil as you were reading. If you did not do this, return to the paragraph and ask yourself what you could have written in the margin of the booklet to make answering the questions easier.

1. **B** This is one of those questions which tempts you to use common sense to answer it. Choice B seems like a logical answer. However, it was *not* mentioned in the passage. It cannot, therefore, be a *stated* advantage of civilianization.

2. **D** The paragraph states that "mounting fiscal problems for municipal governments provided the impetus" (momentum) for civilianization.

3. **D** The paragraph states that police officers type, file, and perform other non-enforcement type work.

   Note the existence of *absolute words* in each of the wrong choices.

   Choice A—the word "only."
   Choice B—the word "no."
   Choice C—the word "all."

4. B Items 4, 7, 11, 13, and 14 under Patrolwagon Operator indicate duties which involve leaving the station house area. There are no such indications for the other two titles.

5. D Item 12 under Gasoline Dispenser, and item 10 under Attendant state this requirement.

6. C Item 3 under Attendant's duties explains when the Attendant can visit female detention cells *or* the quarters of a female officer. Choice C is accurate as far as it goes, but it is incomplete. In addition to being accompanied by a female officer, the Attendant *also* needs the permission of the officer in charge. This is a favorite trick of examiners. The examiners like to give you a statement that is accurate, but incomplete. Be careful about this. Choice D is also an appropriate instance as indicated by item number 10.

7. B Note that this was the only duty in all of the lists which was prefaced with the word "daily." Perhaps you should have circled that word when you originally read the paragraph. If you did that, you are becoming a very good test taker.

8. A Task 10 under the Patrolwagon Operator's duties specifically states, "perform duty in proper uniform." Even if you believe the other two workers wear uniforms, you can answer these questions based only on the written material.

9. A Choice A is very similar to the Patrolwagon Operator's Task 12. Note, however, that there is a significant difference that is easily overlooked. The actual responsibility is to inspect all RMP cars on *reserve* at the station house, and Choice A mentions all RMP cars in use. Bear in mind that examiners very often will make a small change in an otherwise good statement.

10. D All three lists include the responsibility to make entries in department records.

GROUP TWO

GENERAL COMMENT: This passage was taken almost verbatim from a New York City Police Department Legal Division bulletin. This is the type of writing you will encounter when you become a police officer.

11. C Choosing between choice C and choice D is the difficult part of this question. However, in the paragraph, evidence is qualified, by limiting it to evidence that can be destroyed. There is a difference between evidence, and evidence that can be destroyed. Get used to this kind of qualified statement because examiners often qualify statements to make them incorrect.

12. A Myers is never specifically designated in the paragraph as a male, but in a number of instances the author of the paragraph uses the masculine form of pronouns when referring to Myers. In the final sentence it states when referring to Myers that "*he* was incapable, as were *his* confederates, of reentering the vehicle."

13. C The Trial Court and the Appellate Court ruled against Myers when they held that the search was constitutional. The Court of Appeals reversed both courts by holding that the evidence was unconstitutionally obtained.

14. D Be careful of this one. Because Myers was arrested for the possession of the cocaine, you might conclude that he owns the cocaine. However, it is never stated anywhere in the paragraph who actually owned the cocaine. In all probability, Myers was the owner of the car; this would explain why he got arrested when the drugs were found in the jacket pocket in the back seat of the car. At any case, you can rely only on what is written, and the passage does not give any clues as to the ownership of the cocaine.

15. C Only Myers was arrested for the possession of the cocaine.

16. B See the last sentence of the passage. Please note that students of constitutional law would argue that choice C is factual, but it is not based on what is written. Therefore, it cannot be the answer.

17. B A search incident to an arrest is a search that occurs in connection with an arrest. If you did not know this word, you could have answered the question anyway. Simply substitute the wording of each choice for the word "incident" in the passage. "In connection with" is the only phrase that makes sense when it is inserted into the passage in place of "incident."

18. A This should have been an easy one. No mention is made anywhere about strengthening the case of the arresting officer.

GROUP THREE

GENERAL COMMENT: Most of this material comes directly from the rules and regulations of the New York City Police Department. When you see a relatively short passage having 15 questions, almost every portion of the passage will probably be involved in the questioning. In these cases, take a little extra time to read and understand the passage.

19. B Only unconscious persons at the scene of an accident will be tagged. This is done to avoid identity mistakes when it is highly likely that more than one unconscious person will be sent to the hospital.

20. C The station house officer is responsible for notifications. The patrol supervisor must ascertain (make certain) that the notifications have been made.

21. **A** The only members of the police service that are permitted to disturb the body are detectives or Crime Scene Unit members.

22. **A** If you missed this one, you are merely being careless. It states in the passage that the number at the scene is responsible for preparing an Aided Report.

23. **C** If you picked choice B, you probably did not read all of the choices. A homicide is, of course, a suspicious death. However, in the paragraph it is specifically stated that this procedure applies only to homicide cases.

24. **C** The notification must be made in person, if possible. This is another example of how an examiner qualifies a statement to test your attention to detail. In reality, there are times when no notification can be made, in person or otherwise, because the dead person cannot be identified. However, whenever a notification can be made, it must be made tactfully.

25. **A** Choices B, C, and D all sound logical. However, only choice A is mentioned in the passage.

26. **C** A search does not always have to be made. When one is made, it must always be done in the presence of witnesses. In reality, the witnesses must be civilians, not members of the police department.

27. **C** An aided case is defined as involving a person other than a prisoner. When prisoners receive assistance, it is recorded on the arrest record.

28. **B** The medical examiner and the precinct detectives are always notified. The other notifications are made under specific circumstances.

29. **B** No matter how sensitive you think the other choices are, the passage specifically designates choice B as the most sensitive.

30. **B** The police officer must always consider the possibility of foul play in the case of a dead human being. Or, as it states in the passage, the officer cannot dismiss the possibility of foul play. Therefore, the phrase "in some cases" makes choice B the least accurate statement.

31. **D** Choices A, B, and C are all responsibilities under certain circumstances. For example, note choice A—screen area from public view. The question indicates this must *always* be done, while the passage indicates to do it *if possible*.

32. **C** The third item, outlining the responsibilities of the member of the police service at the scene, makes that officer the person to make this determination.

33. **A** This is another easy one that is stated in the passage.

CHAPTER 5

Recalling What You Read

In the previous chapter, we provided strategies for handling reading *comprehension*. In this chapter, we will go one step further. Now you will learn to *remember* what you read.

When you handled reading comprehension questions, you were encouraged to write in the margins next to the passages and to refer to the written materials, when necessary. That section of the test permits you to do this.

Nevertheless, when you handle reading recall questions, you should *not* take notes while reading the material and you should *not* refer to the written material after the reading time is finished. This section of the test does not allow this. (At the test, in fact, the reading passage is collected before the questions are started.) The materials below indicate typical instructions you would receive before beginning reading recall questions.

<u>Test Procedure for Reading Recall</u>

1. You will be given a "Memory Booklet" at the start of the examination, in addition to the regular examination booklet, and you will be told not to open either booklet until instructed to do so. The memory items will be based on written material (which is covered in this chapter), pictorial material (which is covered in the next chapter), or, a combination of the two. The rest of this chapter will deal exclusively with memory items that are based on written material.

The written material will contain a story about a police-related incident. Common topics are street demonstrations, emergencies, automobile accidents, and crimes in progress.

2. You are given a specified time period, usually 10 to 20 minutes, to read the story and to remember the key details involved. *You are told not to take notes while reading the story*.

3. After the allotted reading time, you will be told to close the booklet, and it will be taken from you. Many times it is returned at the conclusion of the examination.

Strategies for Recalling Written Material

These questions are not as difficult as you may think since the story is never a complicated one to understand. Perhaps more than any other test area, this area can be improved upon significantly by practice. So, if you work hard and follow the guidelines listed below, you will be able to do very well on this part of your examination.

1. **DON'T READ THE STORY; BECOME PART OF IT!** When you are reading the story, you must clear your mind of everything except what you are reading. *You must concentrate.* The kind of intense concentration that is needed is best achieved by "putting yourself into the story." Create a mental picture of what is happening.

2. **RELATE THE UNKNOWN TO THE KNOWN.** You will find it easier to put yourself into the story if you create mental images involving persons, places, and things that you know and are familiar with. For example, if the story is about a subway station, try to imagine it as a subway station you use.

3. **DON'T TRY TO MEMORIZE THE ENTIRE NARRATIVE.** Some students attempt to memorize the story verbatim. For most of us, this is an impossible task. The trick is to identify the key facts in the story and to remember them. Later, we will provide you with a list of the kind of information you should remember. And don't be concerned if the story seems incomplete; it will not necessarily have a conclusion. All the examiner is interested in is giving you enough information to test your memory.

4. **DON'T STOP CONCENTRATING WHEN THE BOOKLETS ARE COLLECTED.** The time between the closing of the memory booklets and the answering of the questions is

the most critical. Be sure that you maintain your concentration during this time. Most inexperienced test takers forget what they read during these few minutes.

5. **WRITE DOWN EVERYTHING YOU RECALL FROM THE STORY AS SOON AS YOU ARE PERMITTED.** After the Memory Booklet is collected, there will be a delay before you are allowed to open the actual test booklet and begin taking the examination. This is the time during which you must continue to concentrate. However, once the signal is given to begin the examination, quickly write on your test booklet all of the details you can remember or simply make a quick sketch of the scene. Only after you have written down all you can remember, should you start taking the memory questions. This will be the first group of questions in the test.

6. **USE ASSOCIATIONS TO HELP YOU REMEMBER.** Rote memory will not suffice in most cases; you must make associations to help you remember. The type of association you make will vary tremendously from individual to individual, depending upon background, interests, and imagination. This is where practice will help you the most. The technique involves associating or relating what you are trying to remember to something you already know or that you find easy to remember. As an example of how this works, listed below are some facts that you might want to remember about a story and some suggested associations to help you remember them.

FACTS	POSSIBLE ASSOCIATIONS
The murderer is 23 years old.	The murderer is the same age as you (or someone you know well.)
Altogether 10 police officers were assigned to the riot.	There were just enough police officers (10) to have a full court basketball game.
The Dodge received considerable damage in the accident.	The Dodge got Dented and Damaged.
A 1997 Ford with license plate No. BAS 971	Two of the numbers in the year match with two numbers in the license plates (97).
One member of the gang was 24 and the other was 42.	The reverse of one gang member's age equals the other's age.
The young boy was wearing a blue coat.	The Boy was in Blue.

The examples should help you understand how to use associations to aid memory. Bear in mind, however, that your degree of success with this technique depends upon practice. Incidentally, you do not need police material to practice. Your daily newspaper will do just fine. Study a news story for about ten minutes, put the paper down, and then see how many details you can remember.

7. **CONSTANTLY ASK YOURSELF QUESTIONS ABOUT THE STORY AS YOU ARE READING IT.** This will help you remember details, especially if you try to anticipate the questions you might be asked. Note that you can be certain of being asked to compare items. If there is more than one car, victim, perpetrator, or whatever, you will be asked to differentiate between them. For example, which car got damaged, which victim got shot? The next section will provide more hints as to what the examiner might ask.

How to Focus on the Key Facts

Every police recruit who trains at the police academy is taught how to capture the key facts in a story in order to write an accurate report. More often than not, they are taught to use the code word, "NEOTWY." This code word is derived from taking the last letter from each of the six key items that must be contained in any thorough report of a police incident:

The Key Facts

whe	N
wher	E
wh	O
wha	T
ho	W
wh	Y

If you answer these questions, you have a complete report; and you will, therefore, be able to answer any test questions based on that story. Basically, read a story slowly and carefully the first time. Make sure to create a mental image of what you are reading. Follow the seven suggestions listed above. Then zero in on remembering the answers to the six key questions. To help you, we will now list the most common kinds of information to be found in each of the six categories.

1. **WHEN.** Times and dates are ripe for the examiners. Remember, there can be a number of times involved in a police incident. The most common are:

- time of occurrence,
- time of reporting,
- time of arrest.

The best way to remember them is in chronological order. Keep asking yourself, "When did that happen?" When dealing with times, do not neglect the dates. Don't assume everything is happening on the same date.

2. **WHERE.** Critical elements in any police incident are:

- where incidents happen,
- where evidence is located.

If the story mentions directions such as north, east, south, or west, be alert because this is a very fruitful question area. If more than one incident occurs in the story, make sure you can relate each incident to its location.

3. **WHO.** There are a number of who's in every police story, including:

- perpetrators,
- victims,
- witnesses,
- accomplices.

If physical descriptions, clothing descriptions, and distinguishing characteristics such as beards, buzz cuts, glasses, etc., are included, you can be certain you will be tested on that information. If there are cars in the story with license plate numbers, it's a sure bet that you will see a question or two about that, also.

4. **WHAT.** Key questions are:

- what happened?
- what did the perpetrators do?
- what did the police do?
- what was the crime scene (or scene of the police incident) like?

5. **HOW.** The most common questions are:

- how many?
- how were things accomplished?

Whether a weapon was used, along with the weapon's description, is a crucial "how" question.

6. **WHY.** "Motive" is the primary "why" question. Why people do things is of utmost importance.

Practice Exercises

Following are five groups of questions with ten questions in each group. When taking these questions, it is imperative that you do not refer to the written material once the allotted time has elapsed. Remember that the time limit relates only to the reading of the material and not to the answering of the questions. The questions are to be answered within the $3\frac{1}{2}$ hours allowed for the completion of the entire test. However, be guided by the general rule to allot $1\frac{1}{2}$ minutes for each question, and never more than 2 minutes.

NOTE: Rember that in the actual examination, the written material will be collected. (The memory questions will probably be the first on the examination.)

GROUP ONE—25 Minute Time Limit

DIRECTIONS:* The following story is about an occurrence involving police officers. You are allowed 10 minutes to read it and commit to memory as much about it as you can. You are *not* allowed to make any written notes during the time you are reading. *At the end of 10 minutes you are to stop reading the material, and answer the questions without referring to the written material.

MEMORY STORY—10 MINUTE TIME LIMIT

You are one of forty police officers working the day tour in the Third Precinct, which is located at Main Street and Spruce Avenue. The date is April 11, and it is now 7:30 A.M. You start work at 8:00 A.M., and you are assigned to traffic duty at the intersection of Main Street and Elm Avenue. Two other police officers are assigned to traffic duty on Main Street. At about 10:00 A.M. a motorcade will be traveling east on Main Street, bringing the mayor to an important town hall meeting at Theodore Roosevelt High School at Main Street and Oak Avenue.

Main Street is an east- and westbound four-lane, two-way thoroughfare. Heading from west to east, Elm Avenue, then Ash Avenue, and then Oak Avenue all intersect Main Street. There is a traffic signal controlling the intersection at Main and Elm Avenue; a stop sign at the intersection of Main and Ash Avenue, where Officer Brown is assigned; and a traffic signal at Main and Oak Avenue, where Officer Jones is assigned. Elm Avenue and Oak Avenue are two-way streets, and Ash Avenue is a one-way street for traffic traveling north.

At roll call training prior to leaving the station house, Sergeant Wright informs everyone that two groups are opposed to the mayor and might try to prevent him from appearing at the high school as scheduled. One group, which calls itself the Extremists, holds radical beliefs and has used violence in the past to further its cause. The other group, a nonviolent association known as the Pacifists, has used sit-ins and group-chaining to achieve its goals in the past.

The Extremists are known to travel in a blue Ford station wagon, bearing license plate number ACG 368. The Pacifists use two automobiles. One is a red Plymouth sedan, registration number ACW 228; the other is a green Dodge pick-up truck, with plate number ACP 445.

At 9:10 A.M., an accident occurs at the intersection of Main Street and Ash Avenue. A Nissan, registration number TCU 333, proceeded in the wrong direction on Ash Avenue, entered the intersection at Main Street, and struck an unidentified pedestrian who was crossing Ash Avenue from east to west on the north side of Main Street. Officer Brown called an ambulance for the pedestrian, and issued a summons to the driver of the Nissan for going the wrong way on a one-way street. The pedestrian, who was described as male, white, 35 to 40 years of age, about 5′10″, was removed to Franklyn Roosevelt Hospital, and admitted for treatment of internal injuries. The intersection of Main and Ash was cleared by 9:45 A.M.

At 10:10 A.M., the Mayoral motorcade proceeded down Main Street to its destination without incident. The meeting lasted about two hours and by 12:30 P.M. the mayor had left the confines of the Third Precinct.

DO NOT PROCEED UNTIL 10 MINUTES HAS ELAPSED

QUESTIONS—15 MINUTE TIME LIMIT

DIRECTIONS: **Answer questions 1 to 10 *solely* on the basis of the Memory Story.**

1. Officer Jones was assigned to:
(A) Main Street and Elm Avenue.
(B) Main Street and Ash Avenue.
(C) Main Street and Oak Avenue.
(D) Main Street and Spruce Avenue.

1 A B C D

2. The time of the accident with the pedestrian was:
(A) 9:00 A.M.
(B) 9:10 A.M.
(C) 9:45 A.M.
(D) 10:10 A.M.

2 A B C D

3. The car which struck the pedestrian was traveling:
(A) north.
(B) south.
(C) east.
(D) west.

3 A B C D

4. Which intersection are you assigned to?
(A) Main and Spruce
(B) Main and Elm
(C) Main and Ash
(D) Main and Oak

4 A B C D

5. Which direction did the Mayor's motorcade travel on Main Street when going to the high school?
(A) north
(B) south
(C) east
(D) west

5 A B C D

6. The plate number of the car involved in the accident was:
(A) TCU 333.
(B) ACG 368.
(C) ACW 228.
(D) ACP 445.

6 A B C D

7. The Extremists are known to travel in a:
(A) Nissan.
(B) Plymouth.
(C) Dodge.
(D) Ford.

7 A B C D

8. The name of the hospital where the pedestrian was sent is the: **8** A B C D

(A) Theodore Roosevelt Hospital.
(B) Manhattan General Hospital.
(C) Franklyn Roosevelt Hospital.
(D) Main Street Hospital.

9. Which intersection is controlled by a stop sign? **9** A B C D

(A) Main and Spruce
(B) Main and Elm
(C) Main and Ash
(D) Main and Oak

10. The Sergeant who conducted roll call training was: **10** A B C D

(A) Sergeant Jones.
(B) Sergeant Wright.
(C) Sergeant Brown.
(D) Sergeant Spruce.

GROUP TWO—25 Minute Time Limit

DIRECTIONS:* The following story is about an occurrence involving police officers. You are allowed 10 minutes to read it and commit to memory as much about it as you can. You are *not* allowed to make any written notes during the time you are reading. *At the end of 10 minutes you are to stop reading the material, and answer the questions without referring to the written material.

MEMORY STORY—10 MINUTE TIME LIMIT

You are one of twenty-eight police officers assigned to strike duty during the day shift on September 18. The complement of officers will be divided into four equal groups, and each group will be supervised by a sergeant.

The scene of the strike is Metropolis Hospital, a large private hospital occupying a one-square block area in the downtown section of Brooklyn. The hospital is bordered by Green Boulevard on the north, Second Avenue on the east, Tulip Road on the south, and Third Avenue on the west. There is an entrance for visitors on Third Avenue and Tulip Road. Hospital personnel generally use the entrance on Second Avenue, which is not accessible to the public. The west side of Second Avenue is a restricted parking area reserved for doctors. The emergency entrance is located on Green Boulevard, a two-way thoroughfare.

The strike is now in its eighteenth day, and tempers are running high. Two unions are involved. The National Association of Hospital Workers, which represents the non-medical workers, is the more influential of the two unions and, also, the more militant. The other union, the Association of Professional Hospital Workers, represents the paraprofessional workers. While all of the non-medical workers are respecting the picket lines and are staying away from work, only sixty percent of the one hundred paraprofessionals are respecting it. This increases the potential for violence, especially when the working paraprofessional crosses the picket line while going to and from work.

This morning at roll call training, you were told that intelligence reports indicate that the National Association of Hospital Workers has brought in three infamous union strong arm thugs to prevent the non-strikers from going to work. The three have already been spotted at the intersection of Green Boulevard and Second Avenue, close to the special entrance for hospital personnel. The following descriptions have been obtained:

a. Strong Arm Person One: Male, black, 25 to 30 years old, between 5′9″ and 5′11″, wearing a brown army jacket, black pants, combat boots, and a black-and-orange knit hat.

b. Strong Arm Person Two: Female, Hispanic, 20 to 25 years old, 5′4″, wearing dungarees and a black leather jacket, white sneakers, and a brown felt hat.

c. Strong Arm Person Three: Male, white, 40 to 45 years old, about 6′, sandy-colored hair, wearing black pants, a gold baseball jacket, a black-and-gold baseball cap, and glasses.

Your unit, supervised by Sergeant Richter, is assigned to the visitor's entrance on Tulip Road. The unit that is expecting the most trouble is the one on Second Avenue, supervised by Sergeant Morris.

DO NOT PROCEED UNTIL 10 MINUTES HAS ELAPSED

QUESTIONS—15 MINUTE TIME LIMIT

***DIRECTIONS:* Answer questions 11 to 20 *solely* on the basis of the Memory Story.**

11. How many police officers are assigned to each of the four units on strike duty? 11 A B C D
- **(A)** 7
- **(B)** 8
- **(C)** 14
- **(D)** 10

12. On what day did the strike start? 12 A B C D
- **(A)** September 18
- **(B)** September 10
- **(C)** September 1
- **(D)** September 28

13. The emergency entrance to the hospital is located on: 13 A B C D
- **(A)** Third Avenue.
- **(B)** Tulip Road.
- **(C)** Green Boulevard.
- **(D)** Second Avenue.

14. The name of the supervisor of the Second Avenue unit is: 14 A B C D
- **(A)** Sergeant Morris.
- **(B)** Sergeant Richter.
- **(C)** Sergeant Willis.
- **(D)** Sergeant Brown.

15. The name of the hospital is: 15 A B C D
- **(A)** Brooklyn Hospital.
- **(B)** Downtown Hospital.
- **(C)** Metropolis Hospital.
- **(D)** Tulip Hospital.

16. The black strong arm person was wearing: 16 A B C D
- **(A)** combat boots.
- **(B)** a baseball cap.
- **(C)** a leather jacket.
- **(D)** glasses.

17. The strong arm person who was wearing sneakers was: 17 A B C D
- **(A)** the white female.
- **(B)** the Hispanic male.
- **(C)** the black male.
- **(D)** the Hispanic female.

18. According to the descriptions, which strong arm person is the oldest?

18 A B C D

(A) the white female.

(B) the white male.

(C) the black female.

(D) the Hispanic male.

19. How many of the paraprofessionals employed at the hospital are reporting to work?

19 A B C D

(A) 60

(B) 40

(C) 100

(D) Unknown

20. The parking area reserved for doctors is located on:

20 A B C D

(A) Second Avenue.

(B) Third Avenue.

(C) Tulip Road.

(D) Green Boulevard.

GROUP THREE—25 Minute Time Limit

DIRECTIONS:* The following story is about an occurrence involving police officers. You are allowed 10 minutes to read it and commit to memory as much about it as you can. You are *not* allowed to make any written notes during the time you are reading. *At the end of 10 minutes you are to stop reading the material, and answer the questions without referring to the written material.

MEMORY STORY—10 MINUTE TIME LIMIT

You are a police officer performing an evening tour of duty on December 18. You are working alone on foot patrol, and your assignment is Post 18. The geographical boundary of your three-block post is as follows: Both sides of Dryer Avenue, from the north building line of King Street to the south building line of Harbor Street. Included on your post is Market Street, one block north of King Street; and Clinton Street, one block south of Harbor Street. The street numbers on your post run from 122 Dryer, at the southern tip of your post on the corner of King Street, to 151 Dryer, at the northern tip of your post at the corner of Harbor Street. Odd number street addresses are on the western side of Dryer Avenue; even number addresses are on the eastern side of Dryer.

There are four stores on your post that have been the scenes of crimes in the last three months. The National Jewelry Company Store, located at 122 Dryer, was robbed on December 2; the Nitecap Bar and Grill, located at 136 Dryer, was burglarized on October 11; Sullivan's Liquor Store, located at 137 Dryer, was held up on September 19; and the Acme Check Cashing Store, located at 145 Dryer, was the scene of a homicide on November 30.

The owner of the National Jewelry Company is Ms. Jean Garcia of 23-27 Ditmars Avenue in Queens. She frequently complains that she does not get enough police protection. Your supervisor, Sergeant John Cantwell, has instructed you to make sure that she sees you on patrol. You have also received word that your commanding officer, Captain William Sweeney, wants you to be in front of her store at 9:00 P.M. when she closes for the night.

The owner of the Nitecap Bar and Grill is Mr. Harold Robinson of 2811 Mariot Avenue in the Bronx. His major concern is that his silent robbery alarm is not working, and he has requested that you give his store extra attention until it is repaired. The alarm has been broken since December 8.

Mr. James Sullivan, the proprietor of Sullivan's Liquor Store, is currently in the hospital recuperating from a heart attack. His son-in-law, William Blake, is running the store in his absence. Mr. Blake's complaint is the vagrants loitering in front of the store.

The owner of the Acme Check Cashing establishment is Mr. Robert Myers of 1611 Jerome Road in Yonkers. He is quite concerned that the thieves who committed the murder in his store might return. He feels this way because on the night of the killing, one of the three perpetrators told him they would be back.

During your tour of duty, you make certain that each store owner is aware of your presence. Nothing eventful happens and at midnight you return to the station house at 96 Dryer Avenue, having completed your evening's work.

DO NOT PROCEED UNTIL 10 MINUTES HAS ELAPSED

QUESTIONS—15 MINUTE TIME LIMIT

***DIRECTIONS:* Answer questions 21 to 30 *solely* on the basis of the Memory Story.**

21. On which side of Dryer Avenue is the National Jewelry Company Store located? 21 A B C D
(A) north
(B) south
(C) east
(D) west

22. Your commanding officer is: 22 A B C D
(A) Captain Cantwell.
(B) Captain Sweeney.
(C) Captain Blake.
(D) Captain Myers.

23. The silent alarm at the Nitecap Bar and Grill has been broken since: 23 A B C D
(A) November 30.
(B) December 2.
(C) December 8.
(D) December 18.

24. The owner of the Acme Check Cashing Store is: 24 A B C D
(A) Mr. Robinson.
(B) Mr. Myers.
(C) Ms. Garcia.
(D) Mr. Sullivan.

25. Mr. Sullivan's home address is: 25 A B C D
(A) 1611 Jerome Avenue.
(B) 2811 Mariot Avenue.
(C) 23-27 Ditmars Avenue.
(D) Not given.

26. The precinct station house is located: 26 A B C D
(A) east of your post on Dryer Avenue.
(B) west of your post on Dryer Avenue.
(C) north of your post on Dryer Avenue.
(D) south of your post on Dryer Avenue.

27. Which establishment was the scene of the recent homicide? 27 A B C D
(A) Sullivan's Liquor Store
(B) Nitecap Bar and Grill
(C) Acme Check Cashing Store
(D) National Jewelry Company

28. You are assigned to Post number:

(A) 18.
(B) 12.
(C) 22.
(D) 30.

28 A B C D

29. The address of the Acme Check Cashing Store is:

(A) 122 Dryer.
(B) 137 Dryer.
(C) 136 Dryer.
(D) 145 Dryer.

29 A B C D

30. Clinton Street is located:

(A) one block north of Harbor Street.
(B) one block south of Market Street.
(C) one block north of King Street.
(D) one block south of Harbor Street.

30 A B C D

Answer Key and Explanations

Answer Key

1.	C	10.	B	19.	B	28.	A
2.	B	11.	A	20.	A	29.	D
3.	B	12.	C	21.	C	30.	D
4.	B	13.	C	22.	B		
5.	C	14.	A	23.	C		
6.	A	15.	C	24.	B		
7.	D	16.	A	25.	D		
8.	C	17.	D	26.	D		
9.	C	18.	B	27.	C		

Answer Explanations

GROUP ONE

GENERAL COMMENT: Before answering the questions, write down as much of the story as you can remember. However, also use quick drawings or sketches wherever possible. In this case, it would have been ideal to make a quick sketch of the streets involved:

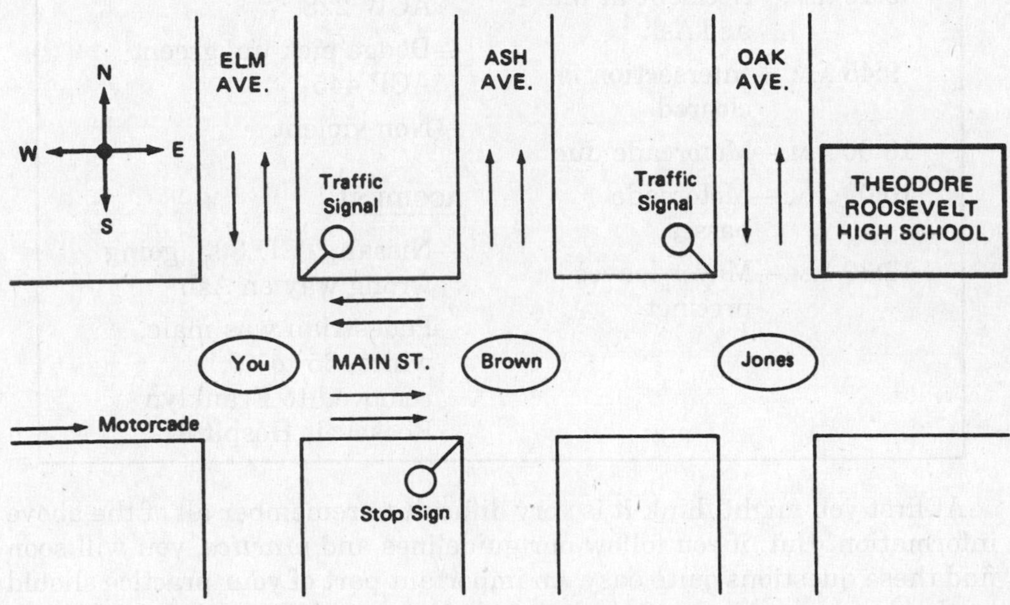

A number of important facts about this drawing must be kept in mind.

- **a.** The sketch does not contain all of the information. Some of it must be written down independently of the sketch.
- **b.** In many cases, you will have to make certain assumptions in order to make the drawing. In this instance, the story does not contain information about the relative width and length of the streets. However, if the story had given information about their relative size, it would *have* to be drawn accordingly.
- **c.** Making the above drawing is quite easy if you created a mental picture of the scene as you read the story. It would be especially easy if you related the street in your mind to an east-west street you are familiar with. Remember, put yourself into the story.
- **d.** If compass directions are given, *always* start your sketch with an indication of where north, east, south, and west are located. The remainder of the information in this story could be very easily captured by grouping details in column form, as follows:

TIME		EXTREMISTS
7:30 A.M.	—Story begins at station house at Main and Spruce	—Blue Ford station wagon, ACG 368
8:00 A.M.	—Start work instruction by Sergeant Wright	—Radical and violent
9:10 A.M.	—Accident at Main and Ash	**PACIFISTS**
9:45 A.M.	—Intersection is cleared	—Red Plymouth sedan, ACW 228
10:00 A.M.	—Motorcade due	—Dodge pick-up, green, ACP 445
10:00 A.M.	—Motorcade passes	—Non-violent
12:30 P.M.	—Mayor leaves precinct	**ACCIDENT**
		—Nissan, TCU 333, going wrong way on Ash
		—Pedestrian was male, white, 35 to 40, removed to Franklyn Roosevelt Hospital

At first you might think it is very difficult to remember all of the above information. But, if you follow our guidelines and *practice*, you will soon find these questions quite easy. An important part of your practice should be the development of associations to help you remember. Remember, we said that the associations you use will be a product of your own imagination and background. To give you a further idea of what we mean, however, we have listed some associations you might make in this story to help you remember key facts:

FACTS	POSSIBLE ASSOCIATIONS
The Sergeant who gave the instruction was Sergeant Wright.	People who give instructions are always *right* (Wright).
The motorcade was heading east.	This is known as an alphabetical association. The last letter of motorcade is the same as the first letter of east.
The accident occurred on Ash Avenue.	Another alphabetical association. The first letter of Ash and accident is A.
The plate number of the car in the accident is TCU 333.	Every other plate number in the story begins with the letter A.
Main Street is a four-lane thoroughfare.	There are four letters in the word *main*.
The station house in on Spruce Avenue.	This is another alphabetical association.

A word of caution is now in order. Don't think that you can use associations for everything. You must also develop rote memory. The more you practice, however, the more proficient you will become at developing associations.

---

1. **C** A quick look at the sketch provides this information.

2. **B** Specific times will be asked if they are part of the story. The *only* way to remember them is in chronological sequence.

3. **B** This information is not given directly. Two pieces of information must be connected to arrive at the answer. The car in the accident was going the wrong way on Ash Avenue, and Ash Avenue is a one-way northbound street. Therefore, the car was heading south at the time of the accident.

4. **B** As listed on the drawing, you are assigned to Main and Elm.

5. **C** The mayor's motorcade was traveling east on Main Street.

6. **A** The plate number of the accident car was the only one in the story that did not begin with an A, and the 333 part of the number is easily remembered.

7. **D** The Extremists travel in a Ford. This could have been remembered by an alphabetical association. E, as in the first letter of Extremists, comes right before F, as in the first letter of Ford.

8. C Note that both the high school and the hospital was named after a Roosevelt. If you see something similar on your test, you can be certain that it will be asked as a question. Once again, an alphabetical association could have been used. T, as in the first letter of Theodore, comes right after S, as in the first letter of school.

9. C The stop sign is at Main and Ash.

10. B This item in the story lends itself to an easy association. The Sergeant who instructs everyone is always *right*, or Sergeant *Wright*.

GROUP TWO

GENERAL COMMENT: This story lends itself ideally to a sketch:

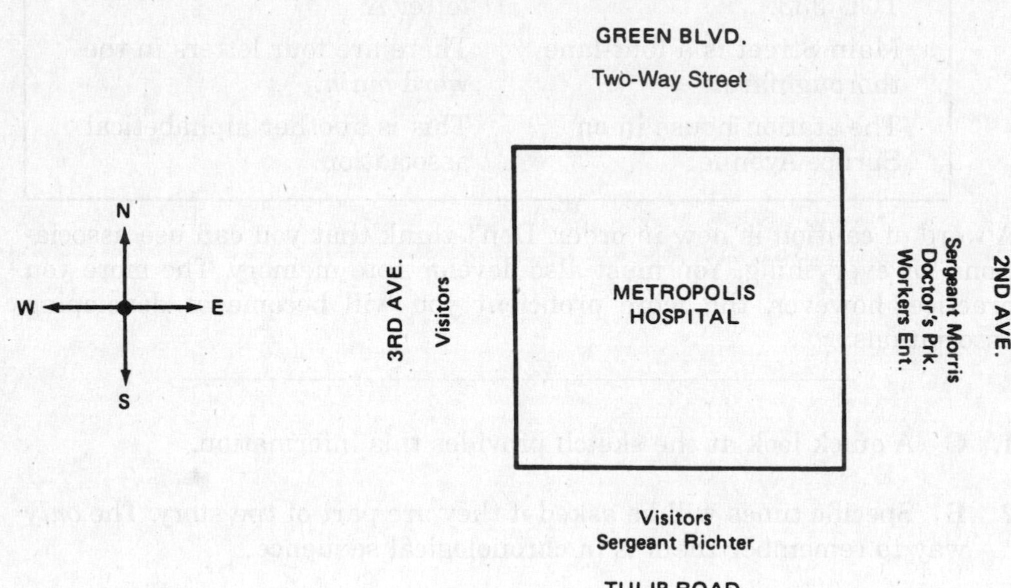

In addition, the information you want to capture in column form could be organized as follows:

POLICE DETAIL	STRIKE INFORMATION	STRONG ARM INFORMATION
—28 officers —4 equal groups —1 sgt. per unit —day shift —September 18	—18 days old —Nat'l Assoc. of Hosp. Workers (influential and militant) —Assoc. of Prof. Hosp. Workers (paraprofessionals —60% striking)	—seen at Green and Second. —Person 1: male, black, 25 to 30, 5′9″ to 5′11″, brown jacket, black pants, combat boots, knit hat. —Person 2: female, Hispanic, 20 to 25, 5′4″, dungarees and black leather jacket, white sneakers, and brown felt hat. —Person 3: male, white, 40 to 45, 6′, sandy hair, black pants, gold baseball jacket, baseball cap, glasses.

There are two very important items you must master.

1. Learn to use your own set of abbreviations when writing down information. Not only does this save time, but, more importantly, it allows you to capture the information before you forget it. (Abbreviations are used sparingly here so that you can easily understand the material presented.)

2. There is no one way to organize the information. You must develop your own method, and learn to master it.

Some associations you might use for this story are listed below. However, you should be doing well at making your own associations by this time.

FACTS	POSSIBLE ASSOCIATIONS
Green Boulevard is on the north.	This is an alphabetical association, using the last letter of green and the first letter of north.
Your supervisor is Sergeant Richter.	This is another alphabetical association.
The emergency entrance is on Green Boulevard.	Emergency vehicles need a lot of green lights to get to the hospital.
Tulip Road is on the south.	This is a different kind of alphabetical association, using the progression of the alphabet. T, as in Tulip, comes right after S, as in south.

11. A Whenever you see numbers in the passage, you should be aware of the possibility of questions concerning those numbers. In this case, you have 28 police officers divided into 4 equal groups, with 7 in each group (28 divided by 4 equals 7).

12. C This question requires you to use information from two parts of the story; it is now September 18, and the strike is in its 18th day.

13. C The emergency entrance is on Green Boulevard. See our suggested association in the above table.

14. A The supervisor is Sergeant Morris.

15. C Don't overlook something as basic as names. Sometimes you get so involved in remembering descriptions, that you tend to disregard other basic facts.

16. A Note that the other three choices pertain to strong arm persons two and three. Get used to this. Examiners will frequently use this technique. If the other three choices were not from the story, the question would be much easier.

17. D The Hispanic *female* was wearing the sneakers. If you picked choice B, you were careless. You were probably looking for the Hispanic, and did not even see choice D. Remember, read all of the choices.

18. B The white male is the oldest strong arm person. Be careful of jumping at choices. If you picked choice A because you saw the word "white," you were careless. Read all of the choices.

19. B If you missed this question, you were careless. Sixty percent of the 100, or 60, are staying *away* from work. That means that 40 are reporting *for* work, which is what was asked in the stem of the question.

20. A The doctors' parking lot is on Second Avenue.

GROUP THREE

GENERAL COMMENT: This story lends itself almost completely to capturing all of the information in a quick sketch:

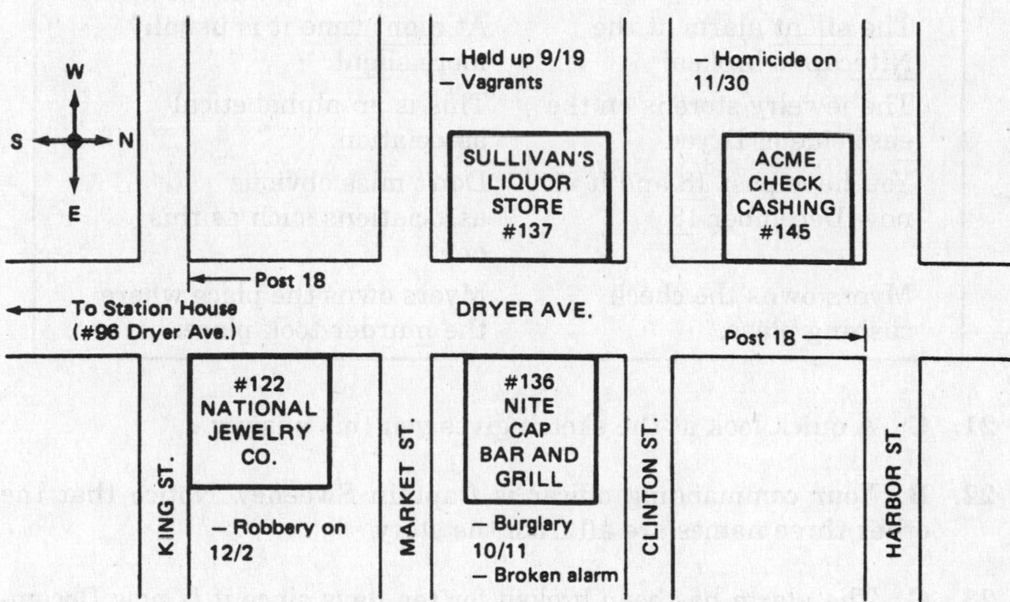

Remember, if you wait until after the material is removed from you to think about what the sketch should look like, you will be in trouble. As you read the story, you *must* make a mental picture of it. In this case, Dryer Avenue could very well be Broadway in Manhattan, which is a major street that runs north and south, with lower addresses towards the south.

Also, by now you should have been able to develop a number of associations to remember the details of this story. How do your associations shape up with these suggested ones?

FACTS	POSSIBLE ASSOCIATIONS
The homicide took place in the check cashing store.	In New York City, it's murder trying to get a check cashed.
Harold Robinson owns the Nitecap Bar and Grill.	Jackie Robinson played a lot of night games.
Street numbers run from low on the south to high on the north.	The suggested picture would give you this association.
The liquor store is located opposite the Bar and Grill.	Both establishments sell alcohol.
The silent alarm at the Nitecap is broken.	At night time it is usually more silent.
The jewelry store is on the east side of Dryer.	This is an alphabetical association.
You have post 18 and it is now December 18.	Don't miss obvious associations such as this one.
Myers owns the check cashing place.	Myers owns the place where the murder took place.

21. C A quick look at the sketch gives you this answer.

22. B Your commanding officer is Captain Sweeney. Notice that the other three names are all from the story.

23. C The alarm has been broken for ten days since it is now December 18 and it broke on December 8. It has been broken for ten. Don't overlook the value of rhymes for associations.

24. B Myers owns the check cashing place where the murder took place.

25. D Sullivan's address is not given in the story. You must become sensitive to this kind of question. Addresses were given for all of the owners except Sullivan. This should have been obvious to you when you read the story.

26. D This information had to be inferred from the story. You know that the station house is located at 96 Dryer Avenue. You also know that the lower numbers on Dryer Avenue are located to the south. Therefore, the station house is south of your post.

27. C The murder took place at Myers store where it's murder to cash a check.

28. A Today is the 18th, and your post is 18.

29. D The check cashing place is located at 1<u>45</u> Dryer. Maybe the murder was committed with a <u>45</u>. With time, you can quickly develop associations for everything.

30. D Clinton Street is located one block south of Harbor Street. If De Witt Clinton once rode a steamboat, a wild association would be that Clinton's steamboat sailed south out of the harbor. It doesn't matter how far-out an association is as long as it helps you to remember.

CHAPTER 6

Recalling What You See

In Chapter 5, we provided you with test strategies to handle questions that test your ability to *remember what you read*. In this chapter, you will learn to handle questions that test your ability to *remember what you see*.

In this question-type, you are given a picture or sketch, or some other non-written material; and you are permitted to study it for a specified time period, usually 5 minutes. You are then asked a series of questions based on what you observed. You are *not* permitted to make notes while studying the material, and you *cannot* refer to it when answering the question. (At the test, in fact, the pictorial material is collected before the questions are started.)

Strategies for Recalling Pictorial Details

The picture you are given to study is never very complicated. Therefore, all you need to become proficient at answering these questions based on the picture is a *strategy*, *concentration*, and *practice*. The concentration must develop. The practice can be done every time you look at a picture. The strategy is as follows:

1. **DEVELOP A STANDARDIZED METHOD OF STUDYING THE MATERIAL.** If you want to remember pictorial details, you must look at the picture in an organized fashion. You cannot stare at it with the mistaken idea that your mind is recording all the details. You must be methodical, and you must practice your method.

2. **ANSWER BASIC QUESTIONS.** You should start your observation of the picture by answering these questions:

When?

- Is there any indication in the picture of when it was taken?
- Is there a clock anywhere?
- Is there a calendar with a date on it?
- Is it day or night?

Where?

- Is there any indication in the picture of where it was taken?
- Is it indoors or outdoors?
- Is there a street sign or an address?
- What are the placement of items in relation to one another?
(This is a key item. For example, if there is a gun in the picture, what other object is near it?)

Who?

If there are people in the picture, you will be asked questions about them, such as:

- What do they look like?
- What are they wearing?
- Is there anything unusual about any of them?
- What items are placed near the person or persons?
(This is a key item because the examiners almost have to refer to the people in the picture in relation to what they are near. For example, if you see a picture with two people and one is standing near a fire hydrant, while the other

is close to a double-parked car, the examiner might ask you what the person was wearing who was standing by the fire hydrant.)

What?

- What is happening in the picture?
- Is there a crime in progress?
- Has someone been injured?
- Is there some other emergency?

Why?

- Is there anything unusual in the picture? (For example, if a door is open, ask yourself *why*; if someone is running, ask yourself *why*.)

3. **OBSERVE ALL READABLE MATTER.** If there is information in the picture that can be read, then you can be sure that you will be asked about it. Therefore, look for these most common "readables":

- Clocks,
- Street signs,
- Addresses,
- Store signs,
- Automobile license plates.

4. **SEARCH FOR ODDITIES.** The following are some of the unusual things to look for:

- Is a door open when it should not be?
- Is a window broken?
- Is a gun or other weapon placed anywhere in the picture?
- Is something out of place in a scene, such as a chair placed on a bed, a car on a sidewalk?

5. **COUNT ALL OBJECTS.** Make a quick count of all major objects, as:

- Cars,
- People,
- Animals,
- Bicycles.

6. **USE ASSOCIATIONS TO REMEMBER.** In the last chapter we spoke a great deal about the use of associations to help you remember things. This applies equally to the questions covered in this chapter. Don't rely exclusively on rote memory to remember all of the items in the picture. Develop associations!

7. **DO NOT BREAK YOUR CONCENTRATION.** Do not stop concentrating. If you go through Steps 2 through 5 once, repeat them in the *same order*. If you get through them twice and still have time, repeat them again in the *same order*. You should get fast enough that you always go through the material at least twice.

8. **DON'T STOP CONCENTRATING WHEN THE BOOKLETS ARE COLLECTED.** The time between the closing of the memory booklets and the answering of the questions is the most critical time of all. It is imperative that you maintain your concentration during this time. This is the time when most inexperienced test takers forget what they observed.

9. **WRITE DOWN EVERYTHING YOU RECALL FROM THE STORY AS SOON AS YOU ARE PERMITTED.** After the memory booklet is collected, there will be a delay before you are permitted to open the actual test booklets and begin taking the examination. Be sure you continue to concentrate. However, once the signal is given to begin the examination, write on your test booklet all that you can remember from the picture. Write the information in the *same order* that you followed when observing the picture (Steps 2 through 5). You are then ready to do the questions.

Practice Exercises

Following are three groups of questions with ten questions in each group. When taking these questions, do *not* refer to the pictorial material once the allotted time of 5 minutes has elapsed. Remember that the time limit relates only to looking at the material and not to answering the questions. The questions are to be answered within the 3½ hours usually allowed for the completion of the test. However, be guided by the general rule to allot 1½ minutes to answer each question, and never more than 2 minutes.

NOTE: Remember that in the actual examination, the written material will be collected. (The memory questions will probably be the first on the examination.)

GROUP ONE—20 Minute Time Limit

DIRECTIONS: **Questions 1 through 10 are based *solely* on the following picture. You are to study this picture for 5 minutes and commit to memory as much about it as you can. You are *not* allowed to make written notes during the 5 minutes you are studying the picture. *At the end of 5 minutes you are to stop looking at the picture, and answer the questions without referring to it.***

MEMORY PICTURE—5 MINUTE TIME LIMIT

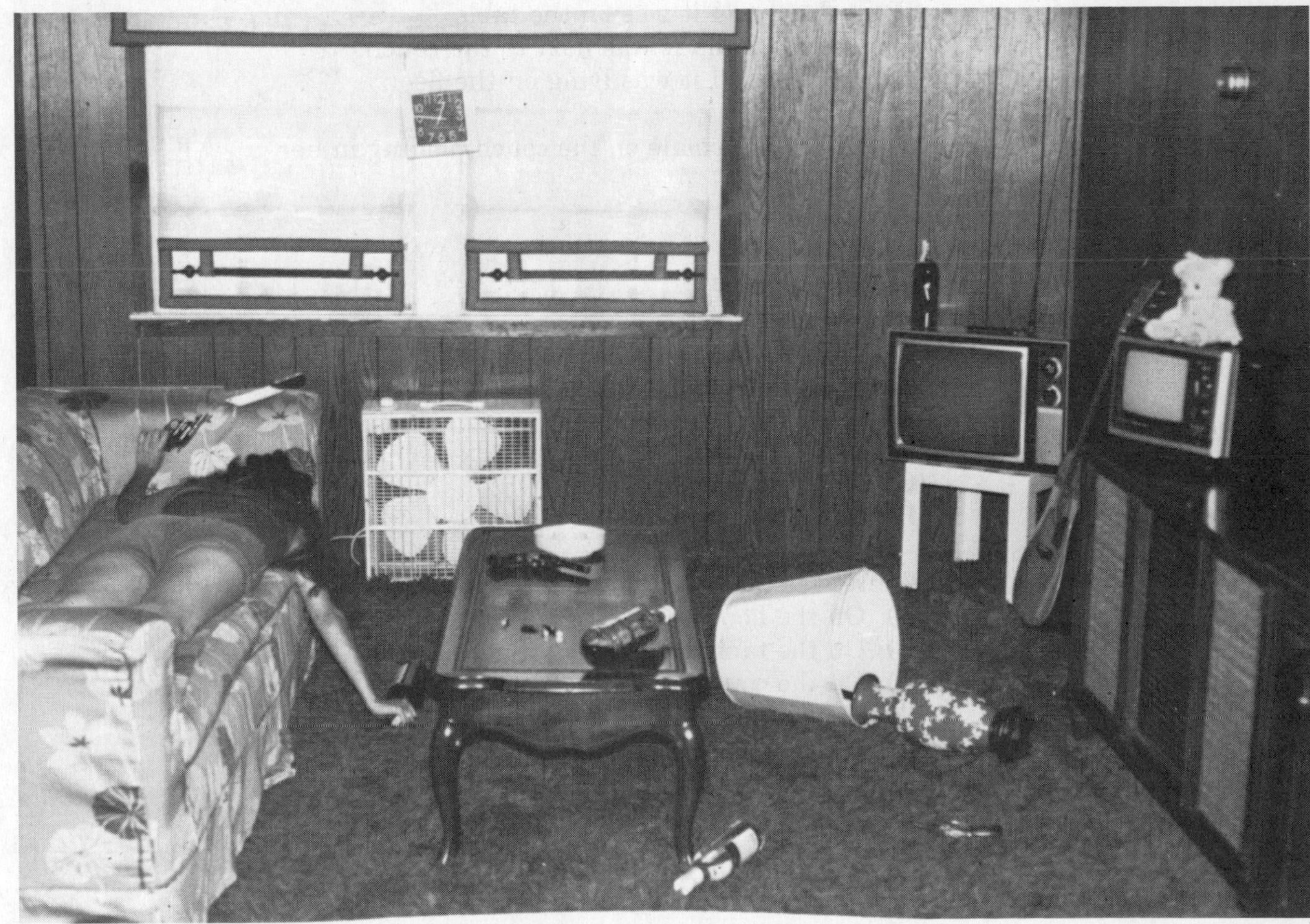

DO NOT PROCEED UNTIL 5 MINUTES HAS ELAPSED

QUESTIONS—15 MINUTE TIME LIMIT

1. How many television sets were in the scene? A B C D 1
   (A) None
   (B) 1
   (C) 2
   (D) 3

2. What time was shown on the clock when the picture was taken? A B C D 2
   (A) 12:47 P.M.
   (B) 9:05 P.M.
   (C) Either 12:47 A.M. or 12:47 P.M.
   (D) There was no clock

3. The female on the couch was wearing: A B C D 3
   (A) A dress.
   (B) Slacks.
   (C) A bathrobe.
   (D) Shorts.

4. The musical instrument in the picture was: A B C D 4
   (A) A guitar, and it was next to a television.
   (B) A flute, and it was on the table.
   (C) A guitar, and it was next to the couch.
   (D) A flute, and it was lying on the floor.

5. What was the female on the couch holding in her left hand? A B C D 5
   (A) A knife
   (B) A gun
   (C) A meat cleaver
   (D) Nothing

6. Where was the lamp? A B C D 6
   (A) On the table
   (B) On the couch
   (C) On the floor
   (D) There was no lamp

7. Where was the meat cleaver? A B C D 7
   (A) On the floor
   (B) On the table
   (C) On the couch
   (D) There was no meat cleaver

8. What was on the table right next to the ashtray? A B C D
(A) A bottle
(B) A gun
(C) A knife
(D) Nothing

9. How many bottles were in the picture? A B C D
(A) None
(B) 1
(C) 2
(D) 4

10. Whcrc was thc fan? A B C D
(A) In the window
(B) On the floor
(C) On a table
(D) There was no fan

GROUP TWO—20 Minute Time Limit

DIRECTIONS: Questions 11 through 20 are based _solely_ on the following picture. You are to study this picture for 5 minutes and commit to memory as much about it as you can. You are _not_ allowed to make written notes during the 5 minutes you are studying the picture. _At the end of 5 minutes you are to stop looking at the picture, and answer the questions without referring to it._

MEMORY PICTURE—5 MINUTE TIME LIMIT

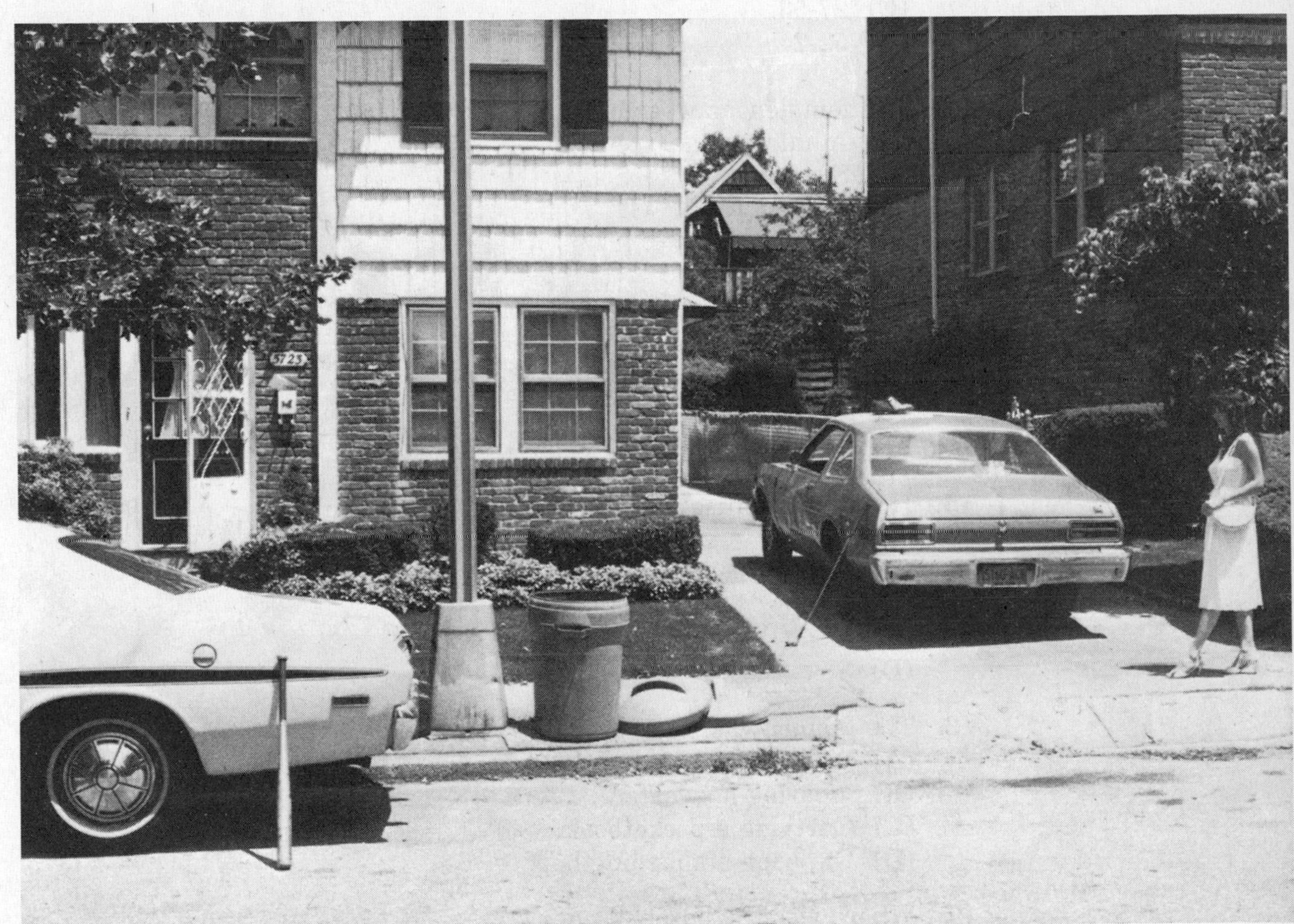

DO NOT PROCEED UNTIL 5 MINUTES HAS ELAPSED

QUESTIONS—15 MINUTE TIME LIMIT

11. The refuse container in the scene was: A B C D 11
(A) In the street.
(B) Uncovered.
(C) Filled with refuse.
(D) There was no refuse container.

12. The address of the house in the picture was: A B C D 12
(A) 23-57.
(B) 57-23.
(C) 27-53.
(D) 52-27.

13. The female was wearing: A B C D 13
(A) A hat.
(B) Slacks.
(C) A dress.
(D) Shorts.

14. The storm door of the house was: A B C D 14
(A) Open.
(B) Closed.
(C) Broken.
(D) There was no storm door.

15. How many refuse container tops were lying on the sidewalk? A B C D 15
(A) None
(B) 1
(C) 2
(D) 3

16. The female was: A B C D 16
(A) Wearing gloves.
(B) Wearing a sweater.
(C) Carrying a pocketbook.
(D) Carrying a shopping bag.

17. Where was the baseball bat? A B C D 17
(A) Lying in the street
(B) Leaning against the house
(C) Leaning against a car
(D) There was no baseball bat

18. The car in the driveway: A B C D 18
(A) Had a flat tire.
(B) Was a station wagon.
(C) Had a shoe on its roof.
(D) Had its front end pointing towards the street.

19. Where was the golf club?
(A) Leaning against the lamppost
(B) Leaning against a car
(C) Leaning against the house
(D) Leaning against the refuse container

A B C D
19 || || || ||

20. How many cars were in the picture?
(A) None
(B) 1
(C) 2
(D) 3

A B C D
20 || || || ||

GROUP THREE—20 Minute Time Limit

***DIRECTIONS:* Questions 21 through 30 are based *solely* on the following picture. You are to study this picture for 5 minutes and commit to memory as much about it as you can. You are *not* allowed to make written notes during the 5 minutes you are studying the picture. *At the end of 5 minutes you are to stop looking at the picture, and answer the questions without referring to it*.**

MEMORY PICTURE—5 MINUTE TIME LIMIT

DO NOT PROCEED UNTIL 5 MINUTES HAS ELAPSED

QUESTIONS—15 MINUTE TIME LIMIT

21. How much money is being given away according to the "Summer Giveaway" poster in the picture?
(A) $50,000
(B) $100,000
(C) $500,000
(D) $750,000

A B C D
21 | | | | | | | |

22. What type of greeting card was on the counter?
(A) Wedding
(B) Birthday
(C) Easter
(D) Passover

A B C D
22 | | | | | | | |

23. Assuming it is after noon, what time was on the clock when the picture was taken?
(A) 1:40 P.M.
(B) 4:05 P.M.
(C) 1:40 A.M.
(D) There was no clock

A B C D
23 | | | | | | | |

24. According to the sign on the front of the counter, what is the name of this store?
(A) Irv's Greeting Card Store
(B) Sam's Smoke Shoppe
(C) Edie's Card Shop
(D) Larry's Gift Emporium

A B C D
24 | | | | | | | |

25. According to the sign hanging behind the counter, what was being given away at no cost?
(A) A gift boxed rose
(B) A pipe
(C) A carton of cigarettes
(D) Fifty dollars

A B C D
25 | | | | | | | |

26. Where was the hat?
(A) On the cash register
(B) On the counter
(C) On the floor
(D) There was no hat

A B C D
26 | | | | | | | |

27. According to the sign hanging behind the counter, winnings will be paid by check only, in amounts over:
(A) $25.
(B) $50.
(C) $100.
(D) $500.

A B C D
27 | | | | | | | |

28. Which brand of cigarettes was not advertised over the cigarette rack behind the counter?
(A) Winston
(B) Viceroy
(C) Salem
(D) Camel

28 A B C D

29. What kind of pipes were being advertised in the sign behind the counter?
(A) Corn cob
(B) Import
(C) American
(D) Italian

29 A B C D

30. According to the sign on the front of the counter, the store most likely stocked:
(A) Shoes.
(B) Fresh fruit.
(C) Wedding party favors.
(D) Decorative flags.

30 A B C D

Answer Key and Explanations

Answer Key

1. C	6 C	11. B	16. C	21. D	26. B
2. C	7. C	12. B	17. C	22. B	27. B
3. D	8. B	13. C	18. C	23. D	28. B
4. A	9. D	14. A	19. B	24. C	29. B
5. B	10. B	15. C	20. C	25. A	30. C

Answer Explanations

GROUP ONE

1. C There are two television sets in the picture, both in the right corner of the room.

2. C The clock shows about 12:47. However, there is no way of knowing if it is A.M. or P.M. If you jumped at choice A, you must remember to read and consider all of the choices.

3. D What people wear is an item that is always asked.

4. A Remember, a very important "where" item is where things are in relation to each other.

5. B Above everything, be aware of the exact location of all weapons in a scene.

6. C Take note of all unusual items in a scene, such as a lamp on the floor.

7. C A meat cleaver on a couch is certainly unusual enough to remember. Don't forget using associations. This one was a natural. The cleaver is on the couch.

8. B As previously noted, be aware of the position of all weapons.

9. D Remember to count items.

10. B What an association! The fan was on the floor.

GROUP TWO

11. B The refuse container should have aroused your curiosity since there was only one although there were two tops. Also, it was uncovered.

12. **B** Addresses will always be asked. Don't overlook them.

13. **C** Another vital area is what people are wearing. You will always see questions on this.

14. **A** Open doors are something that would always be of interest to an officer on patrol.

15. **C** Although there was only one container, there were two tops.

16. **C** When there is only one person in the picture, it is not unusual to see more than one question about that person. In this case, the female is carrying a pocketbook. Remember, unless the picture is in color (and that is unlikely on an examination), you will not be asked about colors.

17. **C** Remember to look for unusual things in the picture. If you find them, you can be fairly certain that you will be asked about them.

18. **C** If you were not sure what was on the car roof in the driveway, you could have arrived at the correct answer by eliminating the other choices. However, you had to know something was on the roof.

19. **B** The golf club was leaning against the car in the driveway.

20. **C** Although only half of the car in the street was included in the picture, the answer is two cars. You had no choice indicating one and one-half. You had to choose choice C.

GROUP THREE

GENERAL COMMENT: This is a difficult memory item since there are no people in the picture, and it is difficult to focus on items. In this situation, follow your organized approach very carefully and pay particular attention to the "readables." However, don't try to read items that are not legible.

21. **D** This should have been easy.

22. **B** Even if you were not sure it was a greeting card, you should have gotten this one.

23. **D** This was a tricky one. There was no clock in the picture.

24. **C** The sign says, "Everything is coming up roses at Edie's Card Shop."

25. **A** This should have been easy since that sign was almost in the center of the picture.

26. **B** This was an "oddity" item that you should have noticed quite readily.

27. **B** This information is included in the sign that begins with the word "ATTENTION." This should have attracted your attention.

28. **B** You should read all of the "readables" that can be read. Don't waste time trying to read illegible items. The examiner knows what can and cannot be read.

29. **B** This is stated in bold print in the upper-left portion of the picture.

30. **C** Wedding party favors were advertised in a sign on the front of the counter.

CHAPTER 7

Handling Police Department Forms

One of the most important tasks of a police officer is the accurate completion of police department forms. This is true for a number of reasons:

1. Police department forms are often offered as evidence in official hearings and trials. They must be able to withstand the scrutiny of the defendant's attorney and the judge before being officially accepted as evidence.

2. Manpower and other resource deployment within the department depend primarily on data gathered from department forms.

3. The rights of citizens many times depend upon accurate police reporting.

It is also important for police officers to extract information accurately from already completed department forms. There are a number of reasons for this:

1. Many investigators depend heavily on information contained in previously completed crime reports.

2. Missing person cases are often solved by reviewing police forms against hospital admissions forms.

3. Recovered stolen or lost property is often returned to its owner because of information contained in various police reports.

The Two Question Types

Since it is necessary for police officers to handle raw data accurately, whether for its insertion on departmental forms or its extraction from forms and reports, questions testing this skill have been included on the Police Officer Examination. Therefore, you must become familiar with the following two question types.

USING INFORMATION TO FILL OUT FORMS AND REPORTS

In this type of question, you will be given a *blank* police department form; a story describing a police incident such as a robbery, an automobile accident, an assault, or a missing persons report; and a series of questions asking what information should be placed in various boxes on the form. You must choose pertinent information from the story to answer the questions pertaining to the form.

Most boxes on the form are numbered or lettered, so that the question can be easily understood. Typical questions might be:

1. What information should be entered in Box 31 of the form?

2. What information should be entered in Boxes A, B, C of the form?

If the boxes on the form are not numbered or lettered, then the question might be asked like this:

1. Whose name should be placed in the box on the form entitled "Complainant"?

EXTRACTING INFORMATION FROM COMPLETED DEPARTMENT FORMS AND REPORTS

In this less complex question type, you will be given a *completed* department form and will be required to correctly answer questions using the information already on the form. In other words, you are reconstructing the story.

Information Commonly Found on Police Department Forms

Listed below are the kinds of information usually required on most department forms. Understanding certain distinctions about this information will be helpful when answering either of the above question types. Don't let the apparent complexity of this material bother you. You will be given ample practice questions to prepare thoroughly for these items.

"WHEN" INCIDENTS OCCURRED

Most police reports require information about:

- when an incident occurred,
- when the incident was discovered,
- when the police were notified,
- when the official report was made.

You can see from the above that a typical police incident could have many different dates and times involved. A favorite technique of examination writers is to mix up times when relating the facts of an incident. The earlier times of the incident may be given last while the times of official reporting are given first. Therefore, you should be very careful when answering questions about "when."

"WHERE" INCIDENTS OCCURRED

Many times there is more than one location involved in a police incident.

> *EXAMPLE.*
> An automobile accident involves a moving automobile, two parked cars, and a pedestrian. It ends in a police chase and another accident when the car being chased crashes into a tree.

In this case, there could be four different accident locations involved, as follows:

- Where the moving car struck the first parked car.
- Where the moving car struck the second parked car.

- Where the moving car struck the pedestrian.
- Where the accident occurred when the car being chased struck the tree.

In the same example, there could be a number of *other locations* involved which would have to be recorded by the officer:

- To what hospital was the pedestrian taken?
- Where were all three of the damaged cars taken?
- Where was the driver of the moving car taken?

These examples should make you aware that you must take the utmost care in distinguishing the various locations involved in a police incident.

"WHO" WAS INVOLVED IN THE INCIDENT

To answer questions about "who was involved," it is quite helpful to be familiar with the police terms as indicated below. For example, in a crime report, you would always have to know:

- Who is the complainant?
- Who is the victim?
- Who is the perpetrator or alleged perpetrator?
- Who is the witness?
- Who is the arresting officer?
- Who is the reporting officer?

When answering these questions, you have to be alert to sort the various people who are involved, and you must be familiar with the above terms.

"WHAT PROPERTY" WAS INVOLVED

All property coming into police custody must be accurately described and safeguarded. In most cases, a value is placed on the property. Serial numbers and other methods of positive identification must be recorded. General descriptions are *not* appropriate.

“WHAT ACTUALLY HAPPENED, AND HOW” DID IT HAPPEN

It is important to realize that unless a police officer personally witnessed an incident, he or she cannot be sure of exactly what took place. It is the officer’s job to reconstruct the story from the statements of the parties concerned and from his observations of the scene. The officer’s report must separate fact from allegation. This point can be made clear by the following correct and incorrect ways to record information:

EXAMPLE:
Mr. Henry Smith told Officer Green that Mr. John Jones hit him in the face.

Wrong
John Jones hit Henry Smith in the face.

Right
Henry Smith states that he was hit in the face by John Jones.

EXAMPLE.
Officer Green responded to an auto accident. Mr. John Jones told Officer Green that he lost control of his car after his right front tire had a blowout.

Wrong
The auto driven by John Jones went out of control as a result of a blowout of the right front tire.

Right
John Jones states that he lost control of his auto after his right front tire had a blowout.

EXAMPLE:
Officer Green was directing traffic when he observed two motorists having a dispute on the street. Officer Green saw one of the motorists, later identified as John Adams, kick the second motorist, later identified as James Polk, in the groin.

Wrong
James Polk states that he was kicked in the groin by John Adams.

Right
Officer Green states that he observed John Adams kick James Polk in the groin.

Many years ago, a television series depicted a detective as seeking “just the facts.” While there was some humor in portraying the stereotyped officer, the message was accurate. Deal in facts, not assumptions.

Strategies for Handling Forms

Listed below is a suggested strategy for you to follow to increase your speed and accuracy with questions about department forms.

FOR BOTH TYPES OF QUESTIONS

1. *Understand the basic purpose of the form.* For example, is the purpose to record a crime, to report an accident? The purpose can generally be determined simply by reading the title of the form.

2. *Determine what type of question it is.* Basically, determine whether you must fill in information on a form with the help of a story, or whether you must just extract information from a form.

FILLING OUT NEW FORMS AND REPORTS

1. *Briefly review the blank report form, and determine its purpose.*

2. *Quickly read the stem or lead-in of the questions* (i.e., the part before the choices) to determine the information needed to answer the questions.

3. *Read the story through carefully, asking yourself questions* to make sure you are understanding what you are reading. Total concentration is vital at this time. Try to understand clearly such things as:

   - Who is the complainant?
   - Who is the victim?
   - Who is (are) the perpetrator(s)?
   - Where did the incident take place?
   - What actually happened?
   - Who are the witnesses?
   - When did the various incidents take place?

4. *Answer the questions*, using the general test-taking strategies presented in Chapter 2, and referring to the narrative and form whenever necessary.

EXTRACTING INFORMATION FROM FORMS AND REPORTS

1. *Quickly read the stem or lead-in of each question* to determine what information is needed to answer the questions.

2. *Review carefully the completed report form*, and determine its purpose. As you review the form, ask yourself questions to make sure you are understanding the information. Total concentration is needed.

3. *Answer the questions*, using the general test-taking strategies presented in Chapter 2 and referring to the completed form.

COMMON MISTAKES TO AVOID

1. *Do NOT read information into the incident that is not given.* Don't assume anything. The answers to these questions are contained in the information supplied to you.

2. *Do NOT confuse standard time with military time.* Many times the caption on the report calls specifically for military time to be used. However, you are not required to determine military time from standard time unless you are instructed how to make the conversion as in the "Group Four Questions" in the chapter dealing with applying police directives. Just remember that standard or civilian time uses A.M. and P.M., while military time is given in terms of hours, i.e., 3:00 A.M. is 0300 hours.

3. *Do NOT assume that the boxes on the forms are consecutively numbered.* Many times this will not be the case.

4. *Do NOT become confused by various dates and times.*

5. *Do NOT confuse the various locations.*

6. *Be careful NOT to interchange descriptions of perpetrators.*

7. *Do NOT confuse the identities of the police officers involved.* Remember, there could be a difference between the responding officer, the arresting officer, and the reporting officer.

8. *Remember that the victim does NOT have to be the person reporting the crime.*

9. *Remember that the answers to some questions might be "unknown" or "not known."* Once again, don't assume.

10. *Always check all of the choices* before deciding.

Practice Exercises

You are now ready to do some practice questions. Always try to answer the questions in the allotted time. After completing a group of questions, make sure you thoroughly review the explanation for each answer before going to the next set of questions. This includes reviewing the explanation for all questions: those you answered correctly and incorrectly. This is done to ensure that you always arrive at the correct choice for the right reasons. Remember, now is the time to make mistakes. If you understand why you made a mistake, you should not make the same mistake on the examination when it really counts.

GROUP ONE—25 Minute Time Limit

***DIRECTIONS:* Answer questions 1 through 15 *solely* on the basis of the following narrative and Complaint Report Form. Some of the boxes on the complaint form are numbered, some are not. The boxes are not necessarily consecutively numbered.**

On January 5, Police Officers Donald James, Shield Number 111, Tax Registry Number 999999, and James Steel, Shield Number 222, Tax Registry Number 888888, were assigned to Sector A, 29th Precinct, tour 0800 hours to 1600 hours, in radio motor patrol car number 990. At about 1409 hours, they were dispatched to 207 E. 158th Street for a past burglary. A "911" Operator, Police Communications Technician Brown, had received a call at 1407 hours from a Mrs. Goldberg that her house had been "robbed" and that she had been "cleaned out."

Arriving at the location at 1415 hours, Police Officers James and Steel were met by Mrs. Wilson, a white, 30-year-old female, who resides at 209 E. 158th Street. She stated that at 12 noon (1200 hours), she saw two men leaving the Goldberg's residence carrying several pillow cases. The men entered a gray station wagon with a broken headlight and went east on 158th Street.

The officers then went to the Goldberg's residence. Mrs. Edna Goldberg, a female, white, 47 years old, told the officers what she discovered upon coming home from work. She works as a mail clerk at the U.S. Post Office located at E. 157th Street and the Grand Concourse. "This morning," she told them, "I went to work at 5 A.M. (0500 hours) and finished at 1 P.M.

(1300 hours)." After shopping at the local supermarket, she arrived home at 2 P.M. (1400 hours). She tried to enter the front of her house, but the key would not fit. She then went around to the back of the house and saw that the window of her rear porch door had been broken. Concerned, she went across the street and asked Mr. Silverman, an off-duty corrections officer, who resides at 208 E. 158th Street, to come into the house with her. Mr. Silverman is a male, black, 33 years of age, who is employed as a New York State corrections officer, Shield Number 456. His telephone number is 569-7768.

Both Officer Silverman and Mrs. Goldberg entered the house through the rear porch door and discovered that someone had broken into the house and had taken a stereo, some jewelry, and a sum of cash. It was then that Mrs. Goldberg called 911.

After hearing Mrs. Goldberg's story, Officer James went to re-interview Mrs. Wilson. Officer Steel obtained more details from Mrs. Goldberg as to what property was missing since he would be the reporting officer in this case.

Mrs. Wilson told Officer James that one of the two males was about six feet tall, weighed about 160 pounds, and had a small mustache. He was wearing a blue baseball-type hat and jeans. She could remember nothing else about him except that he was a male, white, and about 25 to 30 years old.

Mrs. Wilson described the second male as black, about 5′5″ tall, and weighing about 140 pounds. She was sure of his size because her husband, Thomas Wilson, was just about the same size. She could not describe the second male's clothing, but felt that he was about the same age as the other male. Mrs. Wilson said that her home telephone number was being changed but that her work number is 352-5092.

Officer Steel ascertained from Mrs. Goldberg that she could be reached at home at 532-2798 and at work at 776-4200. She reported the following items as missing:

a. 1-Webco Disco Tune Stereo—value $400. Serial #1827 EAG.
b. 1-Bulota Watch—value $100.—Woman's Lafem Model, 18K Gold. No serial number available.
c. 1-DeWitt Clinton High School Ring—value $50. 1951-Yellow metal with the initials "RG" on the inside.
d. 1-18K Gold chain—value $200. 24 inches in length.
e. 1-Loral hand calculator—value $40. Serial #492672B.
f. $240. in assorted bills in U.S. Currency.

The officers completed their interviews, and Officer Steel prepared the complaint form. It was filed in the 29th Precinct, assigned Complaint Number 106, at 1520 hours. The crime was classified as a burglary.

NOTE: See the Complaint Form on following page; the questions follow.

Jurisdiction & Reporting Agency Codes: 00-NYPD, 01-Transit, 02-Housing, 03-Port Authority, 04-Triborough Bridge and Tunnel Authority, 05-Marine & Aviation 06-Long Island Railroad, 07-Amtrak, 08-Conrail, 09-Staten Island Rapid Transit, 11-N.Y. State, 12-N.Y. State Parks, 13-U.S. Park Police

Complaint Report

PD 313-152A

Additional Copies For | 1 Jurisdiction | 3 | 9 Pct of Report | 12 Complaint No. | File No. | 22 Perp. 1

1 Military Time and Date of This Report | Time (13) | 17 Date | Occurrence on or From | 23 Time | 27. Date | Day of Week | Occurrence Through | Time | Date | 33 | Perp. 2

Offense(s) If Any (14) | P.L. Section | If fire related, was structure: Occupied / Vacant | If burglary, was entry forced: Yes / No / Attempt (15) | ibe weapon: Used / Possessed

Victim

2 Last Name, First, MI | Address, include City, State, Zip (16) | Apt. No. | 23 Perp. 1

Home Telephone (17) | Business Telephone (18) | Actions of Victim Prior to Robbery, Larceny or Sex Crimes | Aided/Acc No. | Perp. 2

34 Victim's Sex: 1-Male, 2-Female, 3-Corporation, 4-State | 9 | 35 AGE | 99 | 37 Victim's Race: 1-White, 2-Black, 3-Amer. Ind., 4-Asiatic, 5-Hisp./White, 6-Hisp./Black | 9 | 38 Can Identify? 0-If No, IF YES ANSWER BELOW Victim states perp. is: 1-Spouse, 2-Common Law, 3-Child, 4-Parent, 5-Other Relation, 6-Friend, 7-Stranger, 8-Other | 9 | 39 How Comp. Recv'd: 1-Radio, 2-Walk-in, 3-Phone, 4-Written, 5-Pick up | Will View Photo? YES / NO / UNKNOWN | Will Prosecute? YES / NO / UNKNOWN

3 Date of Birth

Reportee

Last Name, First, MI | Address, include City, State, Zip | Apt. | 24 Perp. 1

4 Home Telephone | Business Telephone | Position/Relationship | Date of Birth | Witness: Yes / No | Perp. 2

Type of Location (Specific) | 40 | Address/Location of Occurrence | 41 Sec/Post | 0 | 44 Visible by Patrol: 1 Yes 2 No

45 | 48 | 49 | 50 | 51 | 52 | 53 Pct of Arrest | 56 Arrest No.'s | 61 Rep. Ag'cy Code | PDU Case No. | 25

5 Evidence | Voucher No. | Case Status: Open / Closed | Unit Referred to | Log No.

Perp. 1 | Perp. 2

Vehicle

Plate: Lost / Stolen | License No. | State | Exp | Type | No. Of Plates | Vin No. | 26 Perp. 1

Year | Make | Model | Style | Color | Value | Ins. Code | Policy No. | Larceny of Motor Vehicle Only: P-Parking Lot, Q-Public Garage, J-Street, M-Other | Perp. 2

6 Voucher No. | Veh. used in Crime: Yes / No | Veh. reported Stolen: Yes / No | Alarm No. | Pct | Time | Date

Perp. 1 | Perp. 2 | 27 Perp. 1 | Perp. 2

Property Information Lost / Stolen

Quantity | Article | Description-Brand, Model, Serial No

Property Summary

Item	64	66 Value Stolen	72 Value Recovered
Motor Vehicle Stolen-Recv'd	01		
M.V. Recv'd By Or For Other Auth.	02		
Currency	04		
Jewelry	05		
Furs, Clothing	06		
Firearms	07		
Office Equip.	08		
TV's-Radio's Cameras	09		
Household Goods	10		
Consumables	11		
Misc.	13		

7 Perp. 1 | Perp. 2 | 28

8 Perp. 1 | Perp. 2 | 29 Perp. 1 | Perp. 2

Involved Person No. 1

9 Perp. 1 | Wanted | Arrested | Witness | Name - Last, First, MI | Address, include City, State, Zip, Apt.

Perp. 2 | Res. Pct. | Wanted Person Alarm | Arrest No. | NYSIIS No. | Sex | Race (19)

Age | Date of Birth | Nickname, First Name, Alias | Eyeglasses: Yes / No | Height FT IN | Weight | 30 Perp. 1 | Perp. 2

Involved Person No. 2

10 Perp. 1 | Wanted | Arrested | Witness | Name - Last, First, MI | Address, include City, State, Zip, Apt.

Perp. 2 | Res. Pct. | Wanted Person Alarm | Arrest No. | NYSIIS No. | Sex | Race (20) | 31 Perp. 1

Age | Date of Birth | Nickname, First Name, Alias | Eyeglasses: Yes / No | Height FT IN | Weight | Perp. 2

11 Perp. 1

Details: List Additional Victims & Involved Persons - Reconstruct Occurrence Including Method of Entry & Escape - Include Unique or Unusual Actions

Latent Fingerprint Response Team - To Respond: Yes / No | Complaint Report Prepared By | Title | Command

Reporting/Investigating Officer's Rank, Signature | Name Printed | Tax Registry No. (21) | Command

Supervisor Approving | Tax Registry No. | Command

Perp. 1 | Perp. 2 (14) | Perp. 1 | Perp. 2 (15) | Perp. 1 | Perp. 2 (16) | Perp. 1 | Perp. 2 (17) | Perp. 1 | Perp. 2 (18) | Perp. 1 | Perp. 2 (19) | Perp. 1 | Perp. 2 (20) | Perp. 1 | Perp. 2 (21)

Source of blank form: New York City Police Department

1. Which one of the following should be entered in Box 9?
   - (A) 26th Precinct
   - (B) 29th Precinct
   - (C) 92nd Precinct
   - (D) 62nd Precinct

A B C D
1 || || || ||

2. Which one of the following should be entered in Box 13?
   - (A) 1520 hours
   - (B) 1400 hours
   - (C) 3:20 P.M.
   - (D) 1415 hours

A B C D
2 || || || ||

3. What date should be entered in Box 27?
   - (A) June 5
   - (B) January 15
   - (C) June 15
   - (D) January 5

A B C D
3 || || || ||

4. Which offense should be entered in Box 14?
   - (A) Robbery
   - (B) Grand larceny
   - (C) Criminal possession of stolen property
   - (D) Burglary

A B C D
4 || || || ||

5. Which of the following should be checked in Box 15?
   - (A) Yes
   - (B) No
   - (C) Attempt
   - (D) Cannot be determined

A B C D
5 || || || ||

6. Which address should be entered in Box 16?
   - (A) 209 E. 158th Street
   - (B) 208 E. 158th Street
   - (C) 206 E. 158th Street
   - (D) 207 E. 158th Street

A B C D
6 || || || ||

7. Which telephone number should be entered in Box 17?
   - (A) 776-4200
   - (B) 532-2798
   - (C) 352-5092
   - (D) 569-7768

A B C D
7 || || || ||

8. Which telephone number should be entered in Box 18?
(A) 776-4200
(B) 532-2798
(C) 352-5092
(D) 467-8132

A B C D
8 || || || ||

9. Where should Mrs. Goldberg's age be entered?
(A) Box 35
(B) Box 38
(C) Box 34
(D) Box 39

A B C D
9 || || || ||

10. The victim's race should be entered in:
(A) Box 37.
(B) Box 38.
(C) Box 53.
(D) Box 56.

A B C D
10 || || || ||

11. The value of the jewelry to be entered in Box 66 next to the jewelry caption is:
(A) $390.
(B) $1,030.
(C) $350.
(D) $240.

A B C D
11 || || || ||

12. The value of the currency to be entered in Box 66 next to the currency caption is:
(A) $790.
(B) $1,030.
(C) $450.
(D) $240.

A B C D
12 || || || ||

13. The correct entry for Box 19 is:
(A) White.
(B) Black.
(C) Hispanic/Latino.
(D) Asian.

A B C D
13 || || || ||

14. The correct entry for Box 20 is:
(A) White.
(B) Black.
(C) Hispanic/Latino.
(D) Asian.

A B C D
14 || || || ||

15. The correct entry for Box 21 is:
(A) 999999.
(B) 111.
(C) 222.
(D) 888888.

A B C D
15 || || || ||

GROUP TWO—15 Minute Time Limit

DIRECTIONS: **Answer questions 16 through 25 *solely* on the basis of the information recorded on the following Aided Report.**

FRONT

Date of Occur.	Surname	First Name and Initial	Sex	Color	Age	Pct.
Feb.6	KENDALL	William	M	B	11	49

Time of Occur.	Address	Apt./	Aided No.
1830 hrs	14-27 Amsterdam Ave.	2E	107

Place of Occurrence: Front of 451 W. 151 Street (Playground)

Check One: ☐ Abandoned Destitute Neglected ☐ Dead ☐ Injured ☒ Sick ☐ Lost ☐ Abused Child ☐ Mentally Ill — Nature of Illness or Injury: Unconscious

Removed To	Admission No.	Responding Attendant	Treated by (Name)
☐ Home Columbia ☒ Hospital ☐ Morgue	438	CARTER	Dr. NAHRA

Children or Dependent Adults Uncared For	If Yes, indicate their disposition on reverse side under "Details"	Log Entries	Pct.	Complaint No.	M.P.S. No.
☐ Yes ☒ No		☒ Yes ☐ No	49	N/A	N/A

NOTIFICATIONS: (Enter name, address and relationship of friend or relative notified. If aided is unidentified, list who at M.P.S. was notified. In either case, list date and time of notification.)

Mother Florence Kendall present at scene.

Comm. Div. Notified	Time	Date	Received By	Sent By
☐ Yes ☒ No				

City Involved ☐ Yes ☒ No. If yes, prepare form Accident Report - City Involved (PD 301-155) — To Dept. or Agency — ☐ Arrest ☐ Summons No.

DUPLICATE REPORTS FORWARDED TO: ☐ Harbor Unit ☐ Emer. Svc. Unit ☐ Youth Aid Unit No.

AIDED REPORT PD 304-152

BACK

DETAILS: (Include descriptions of lost, abandoned, abused, neglected, destitute child, unidentified person. When CPR is administered, include length of time CPR performed and results obtained.)

Aided, William Kendall, fell to the pavement on the street in front of 451 W. 151 Street, a playground.

Aided's mother Florence was present and notified. Mother's address is the same as the aided's address. Telephone number 860-0900.

ADDITIONAL REPORTS PREPARED: NONE

NAME AND ADDRESS OF WITNESSES (If none, so state)

Bernard Judge - Postal Employee
453 W. 145 Street - tel. 683-1498

	Rank	Name (Print or Type)	Shield No.	Com'd.	Signature
REPORTED BY	P.O.	John REILLY	1420	49Pct	J. Reilly

	Rank	Signature of Reviewing Officer	Pct.	Aided No.
REVIEWED BY	Sgt.	Howard Smith	49Pct	107

Source of blank form: New York City Police Department

16. The aided case reported in the above Aided Report occurred at:
(A) 1800 hours.
(B) 1600 hours.
(C) 0830 hours.
(D) 1830 hours.

16 A B C D

17. The aided person's name is:
(A) William Kendall.
(B) John Reilly.
(C) Howard Groth.
(D) Bernard Judge.

17 A B C D

18. The aided number for this case is:
(A) 49.
(B) 1420.
(C) 107.
(D) 438.

18 A B C D

19. Concerning this aided case, CPR:
(A) Was administered at the scene.
(B) Was administered at the hospital.
(C) May or may not have been administered.
(D) Was not administered.

19 A B C D

20. The aided was removed to:
(A) Home.
(B) Columbia Hospital.
(C) Harlem Hospital.
(D) Lebanon Hospital.

20 A B C D

21. The aided's home telephone number is:
(A) 683-1498.
(B) 860-9000.
(C) 860-0900.
(D) 683-1948.

21 A B C D

22. The admission number for this case was:
(A) 49.
(B) 1420.
(C) 107.
(D) 438.

22 A B C D

23. The witness was a:
(A) Police officer.
(B) Park attendant.
(C) Postal employee.
(D) Friend.

23 A B C D

24. This aided case was reviewed by:
(A) Sergeant Judge.
(B) Sergeant Groth.
(C) Police Officer Reilly.
(D) Police Officer Kendall.

A B C D
24 | | | | | | | |

25. This aided case was reported by:
(A) Mr. Judge.
(B) Mrs. Kendall.
(C) Sergeant Groth.
(D) Police Officer Reilly.

A B C D
25 | | | | | | | |

GROUP THREE—20 Minute Time Limit

***DIRECTIONS:* Answer questions 26 through 40 *solely* on the basis of the following narrative and Crime Incident Data Sheet. Note that the boxes on the form are consecutively numbered on the outer edge of the form.**

On February 6, at 0930 hours, a female, white, 36 years of age, whose true identity is known to the department, was opening the Togs Boutique, 6555 Madison Avenue, where she is employed as the manager. Shortly afterwards, the subject female saw an old station wagon pull up in front of the boutique and a male got out. The male, white, about 30 years of age, entered the store.

Once inside he asked the female if she was alone. She became concerned. The male then showed her a gold colored badge with the word, "Detective" on it. He said he was investigating a narcotics complaint and that she might be of some help. He asked if they might talk in the rear of the store away from the front window so that no one would "spot them together." The female said there was an office area in the rear of the store where they might talk. Once in the office area, the male, who identified himself as Detective Kelly and spoke in a northern European/Irish accent, took out a silver handgun, forced the female to disrobe, and demanded that she have sexual intercourse with him. After consummating an act of rape, the male struck the female victim with the silver handgun and fled.

Shortly thereafter, the police were summoned and the female victim described the male perpetrator to them as follows:

> He was a male, white, about 30 years old. He was wearing a waist-length jacket, a ski cap, and loafer-type shoes. He had on designer jeans. His hair was brown and partly balding. He kind of looked like a cop because his hair was short. His eyes were blue and, if it were not for his moustache, his medium complexion would not make him particularly noticeable. He had a bad body odor and a birthmark on his neck.

Sergeant O'Connell took her complaint, and said there had been a rash of crimes where a male fitting the description she had given was impersonating a detective and raping female victims.

NOTE: Read the form on the following pages carefully; the questions follow.

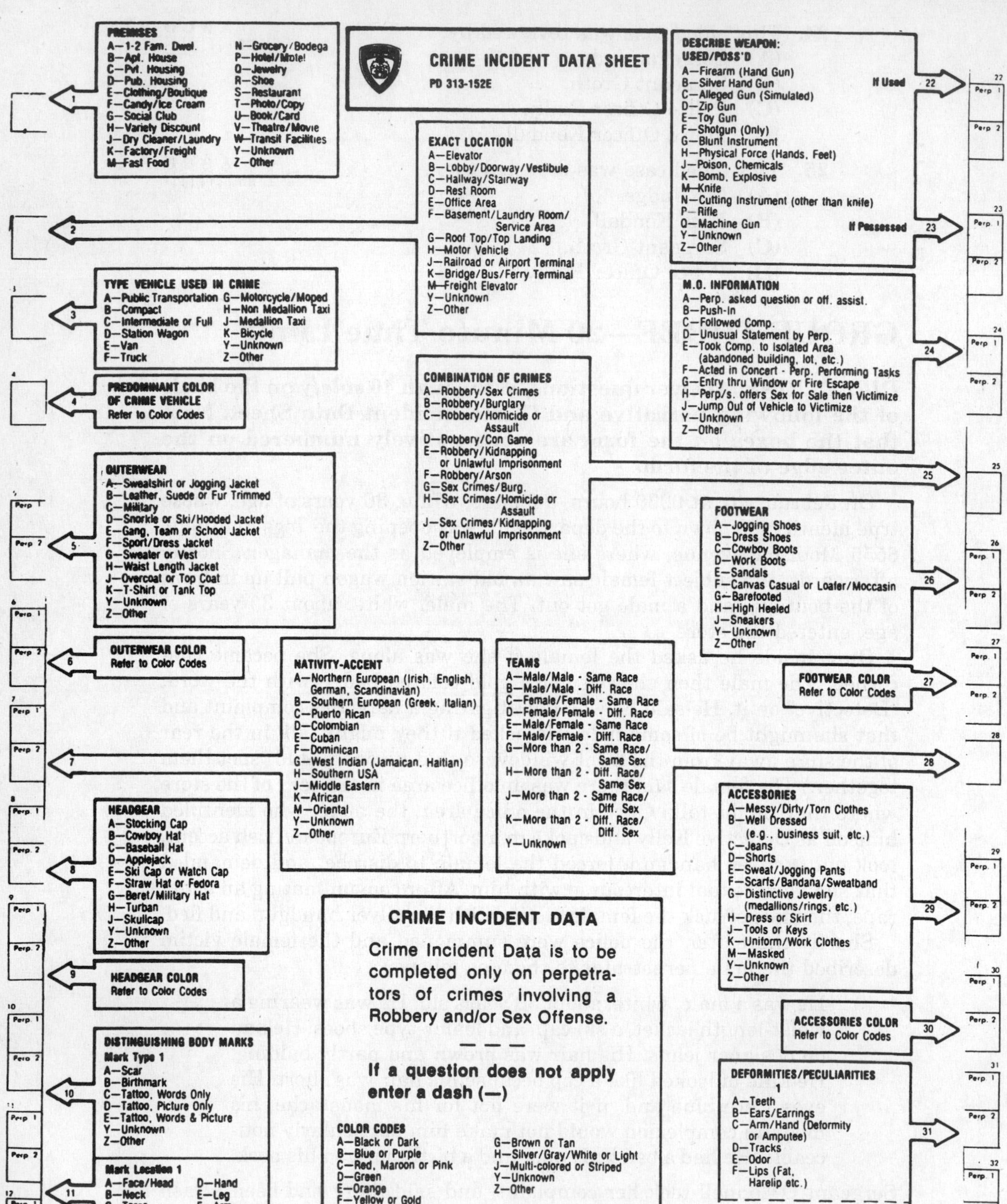

CRIME INCIDENT DATA SHEET
PD 313-152E

PREMISES
A—1-2 Fam. Dwel.
B—Apt. House
C—Pvt. Housing
D—Pub. Housing
E—Clothing/Boutique
F—Candy/Ice Cream
G—Social Club
H—Variety Discount
J—Dry Cleaner/Laundry
K—Factory/Freight
M—Fast Food
N—Grocery/Bodega
P—Hotel/Motel
Q—Jewelry
R—Shoe
S—Restaurant
T—Photo/Copy
U—Book/Card
V—Theatre/Movie
W—Transit Facilities
Y—Unknown
Z—Other

EXACT LOCATION
A—Elevator
B—Lobby/Doorway/Vestibule
C—Hallway/Stairway
D—Rest Room
E—Office Area
F—Basement/Laundry Room/Service Area
G—Roof Top/Top Landing
H—Motor Vehicle
J—Railroad or Airport Terminal
K—Bridge/Bus/Ferry Terminal
M—Freight Elevator
Y—Unknown
Z—Other

DESCRIBE WEAPON: USED/POSS'D
A—Firearm (Hand Gun)
B—Silver Hand Gun
C—Alleged Gun (Simulated)
D—Zip Gun
E—Toy Gun
F—Shotgun (Only)
G—Blunt Instrument
H—Physical Force (Hands, Feet)
J—Poison, Chemicals
K—Bomb, Explosive
M—Knife
N—Cutting Instrument (other than knife)
P—Rifle
Q—Machine Gun
Y—Unknown
Z—Other
If Used 22
If Possessed 23

TYPE VEHICLE USED IN CRIME
A—Public Transportation
B—Compact
C—Intermediate or Full
D—Station Wagon
E—Van
F—Truck
G—Motorcycle/Moped
H—Non Medallion Taxi
J—Medallion Taxi
K—Bicycle
Y—Unknown
Z—Other

M.O. INFORMATION
A—Perp. asked question or off. assist.
B—Push-In
C—Followed Comp.
D—Unusual Statement by Perp.
E—Took Comp. to Isolated Area (abandoned building, lot, etc.)
F—Acted in Concert - Perp. Performing Tasks
G—Entry thru Window or Fire Escape
H—Perp/s. offers Sex for Sale then Victimize
J—Jump Out of Vehicle to Victimize
Y—Unknown
Z—Other

PREDOMINANT COLOR OF CRIME VEHICLE
Refer to Color Codes

COMBINATION OF CRIMES
A—Robbery/Sex Crimes
B—Robbery/Burglary
C—Robbery/Homicide or Assault
D—Robbery/Con Game
E—Robbery/Kidnapping or Unlawful Imprisonment
F—Robbery/Arson
G—Sex Crimes/Burg.
H—Sex Crimes/Homicide or Assault
J—Sex Crimes/Kidnapping or Unlawful Imprisonment
Z—Other

OUTERWEAR
A—Sweatshirt or Jogging Jacket
B—Leather, Suede or Fur Trimmed
C—Military
D—Snorkle or Ski/Hooded Jacket
E—Gang, Team or School Jacket
F—Sport/Dress Jacket
G—Sweater or Vest
H—Waist Length Jacket
J—Overcoat or Top Coat
K—T-Shirt or Tank Top
Y—Unknown
Z—Other

FOOTWEAR
A—Jogging Shoes
B—Dress Shoes
C—Cowboy Boots
D—Work Boots
E—Sandals
F—Canvas Casual or Loafer/Moccasin
G—Barefooted
H—High Heeled
J—Sneakers
Y—Unknown
Z—Other

OUTERWEAR COLOR
Refer to Color Codes

NATIVITY-ACCENT
A—Northern European (Irish, English, German, Scandinavian)
B—Southern European (Greek, Italian)
C—Puerto Rican
D—Colombian
E—Cuban
F—Dominican
G—West Indian (Jamaican, Haitian)
H—Southern USA
J—Middle Eastern
K—African
M—Oriental
Y—Unknown
Z—Other

TEAMS
A—Male/Male - Same Race
B—Male/Male - Diff. Race
C—Female/Female - Same Race
D—Female/Female - Diff. Race
E—Male/Female - Same Race
F—Male/Female - Diff. Race
G—More than 2 - Same Race/Same Sex
H—More than 2 - Diff. Race/Same Sex
J—More than 2 - Same Race/Diff. Sex
K—More than 2 - Diff. Race/Diff. Sex
Y—Unknown

FOOTWEAR COLOR
Refer to Color Codes

HEADGEAR
A—Stocking Cap
B—Cowboy Hat
C—Baseball Hat
D—Applejack
E—Ski Cap or Watch Cap
F—Straw Hat or Fedora
G—Beret/Military Hat
H—Turban
J—Skullcap
Y—Unknown
Z—Other

ACCESSORIES
A—Messy/Dirty/Torn Clothes
B—Well Dressed (e.g., business suit, etc.)
C—Jeans
D—Shorts
E—Sweat/Jogging Pants
F—Scarfs/Bandana/Sweatband
G—Distinctive Jewelry (medallions/rings, etc.)
H—Dress or Skirt
J—Tools or Keys
K—Uniform/Work Clothes
M—Masked
Y—Unknown
Z—Other

CRIME INCIDENT DATA
Crime Incident Data is to be completed only on perpetrators of crimes involving a Robbery and/or Sex Offense.

If a question does not apply enter a dash (—)

HEADGEAR COLOR
Refer to Color Codes

ACCESSORIES COLOR
Refer to Color Codes

DISTINGUISHING BODY MARKS
Mark Type 1
A—Scar
B—Birthmark
C—Tattoo, Words Only
D—Tattoo, Picture Only
E—Tattoo, Words & Picture
Y—Unknown
Z—Other

DEFORMITIES/PECULIARITIES
1
A—Teeth
B—Ears/Earrings
C—Arm/Hand (Deformity or Amputee)
D—Tracks
E—Odor
F—Lips (Fat, Harelip etc.)

Mark Location 1
A—Face/Head
B—Neck
C—Torso
D—Hand
E—Leg
F—Arm

COLOR CODES
A—Black or Dark
B—Blue or Purple
C—Red, Maroon or Pink
D—Green
E—Orange
F—Yellow or Gold
G—Brown or Tan
H—Silver/Gray/White or Light
J—Multi-colored or Striped
Y—Unknown
Z—Other

CRIME INCIDENT DATA SHEET (cont'd)

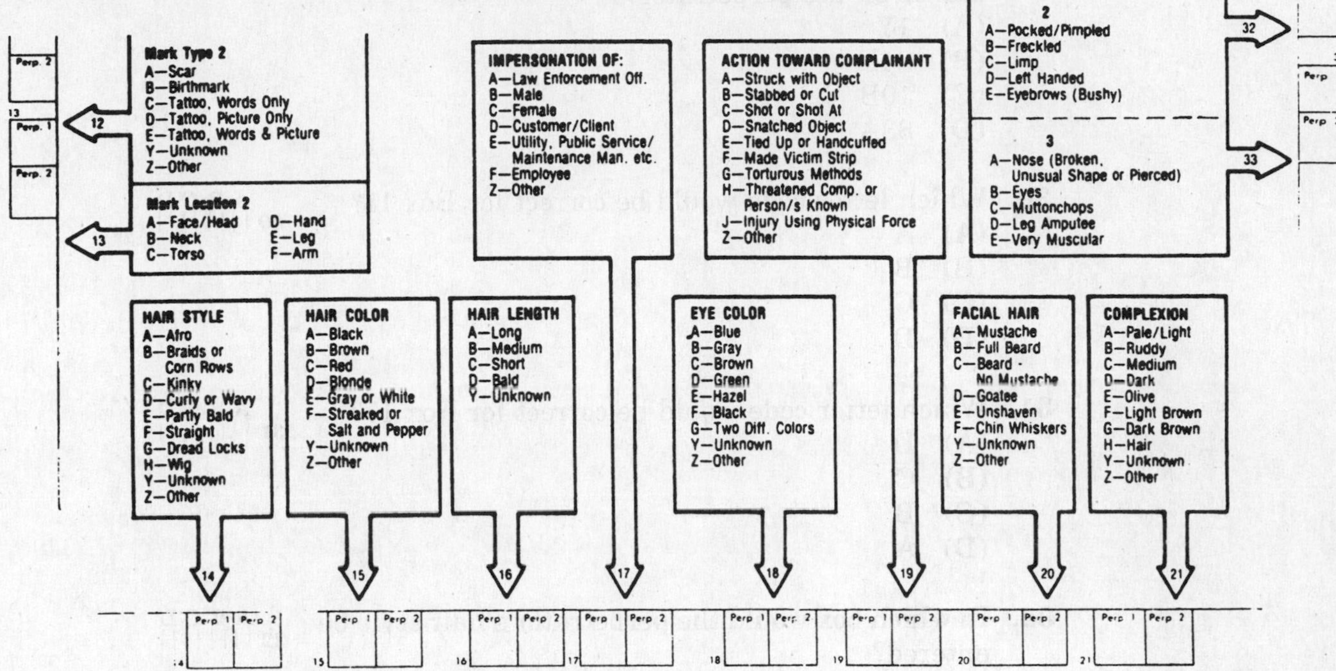

Perp. 2
13 Perp. 1
Perp. 2

12
Mark Type 2
A—Scar
B—Birthmark
C—Tattoo, Words Only
D—Tattoo, Picture Only
E—Tattoo, Words & Picture
Y—Unknown
Z—Other

13
Mark Location 2
A—Face/Head
B—Neck
C—Torso
D—Hand
E—Leg
F—Arm

IMPERSONATION OF:
A—Law Enforcement Off.
B—Male
C—Female
D—Customer/Client
E—Utility, Public Service/ Maintenance Man. etc.
F—Employee
Z—Other

ACTION TOWARD COMPLAINANT
A—Struck with Object
B—Stabbed or Cut
C—Shot or Shot At
D—Snatched Object
E—Tied Up or Handcuffed
F—Made Victim Strip
G—Torturous Methods
H—Threatened Comp. or Person/s Known
J—Injury Using Physical Force
Z—Other

2
A—Pocked/Pimpled
B—Freckled
C—Limp
D—Left Handed
E—Eyebrows (Bushy)
32

3
A—Nose (Broken, Unusual Shape or Pierced)
B—Eyes
C—Muttonchops
D—Leg Amputee
E—Very Muscular
33

33 Perp. 1
Perp. 2

HAIR STYLE
A—Afro
B—Braids or Corn Rows
C—Kinky
D—Curly or Wavy
E—Partly Bald
F—Straight
G—Dread Locks
H—Wig
Y—Unknown
Z—Other

HAIR COLOR
A—Black
B—Brown
C—Red
D—Blonde
E—Gray or White
F—Streaked or Salt and Pepper
Y—Unknown
Z—Other

HAIR LENGTH
A—Long
B—Medium
C—Short
D—Bald
Y—Unknown

EYE COLOR
A—Blue
B—Gray
C—Brown
D—Green
E—Hazel
F—Black
G—Two Diff. Colors
Y—Unknown
Z—Other

FACIAL HAIR
A—Mustache
B—Full Beard
C—Beard - No Mustache
D—Goatee
E—Unshaven
F—Chin Whiskers
Y—Unknown
Z—Other

COMPLEXION
A—Pale/Light
B—Ruddy
C—Medium
D—Dark
E—Olive
F—Light Brown
G—Dark Brown
H—Hair
Y—Unknown
Z—Other

	Perp 1	Perp 2
14		
15		
16		
17		
18		
19		
20		
21		

Source of blank form: New York City Police Department

26. Which of the following letter codes for place of occurrence is most appropriate for Box 1?

(A) W
(B) M
(C) E
(D) B

26 A B C D

27. The exact location of the rape would be entered in Box number:

(A) 2.
(B) 9.
(C) 25.
(D) 30.

27 A B C D

28. The most appropriate code for Box 26 is best shown by choice:

(A) B.
(B) A.
(C) E.
(D) F.

28 A B C D

29. Which box and letter code would reflect the body marks on the perpetrator?
(A) 1Y
(B) 24H
(C) 10B
(D) 33A

29 A B C D

30. Which letter code would be correct for Box 11?
(A) A
(B) B
(C) C
(D) D

30 A B C D

31. Which letter code would be correct for Box 17?
(A) D
(B) C
(C) B
(D) A

31 A B C D

32. In which box would the perpetrator's hair style be entered?
(A) 14
(B) 15
(C) 16
(D) None

32 A B C D

33. The correct letter code for Box 7 is:
(A) G.
(B) D.
(C) B.
(D) A.

33 A B C D

34. Which is an accurate matching of box numbers and letter designations?
(A) Box 15-F
(B) Box 15-D
(C) Box 16-C
(D) Box 16-A

34 A B C D

35. Which box would record the fact that the victim was struck by the perpetrator?
(A) 24
(B) 19
(C) 8
(D) 4

35 A B C D

36. In which box should the fact be entered that the perpetrator displayed a silver handgun?

(A) 28
(B) 32
(C) 22
(D) 5

36 A B C D

37. According to the narrative, the proper letter code for Box 18 would be:

(A) G.
(B) F.
(C) A.
(D) B.

37 A B C D

38. What would be the proper letter code for Box 8?

(A) H
(B) E
(C) C
(D) J

38 A B C D

39. The perpetrator was described as wearing a waist-length jacket. In which box should this information be recorded?

(A) 5
(B) 6
(C) 7
(D) 8

39 A B C D

40. The victim stated that the perpetrator was wearing jeans. In which box should this fact be recorded?

(A) 5
(B) 25
(C) 8
(D) 29

40 A B C D

Answer Key and Explanations

Answer Key

1.	B	11.	C	21.	C	31.	D
2.	A	12.	D	22.	D	32.	A
3.	D	13.	A	23.	C	33.	D
4.	D	14.	B	24.	B	34.	C
5.	A	15.	D	25.	D	35.	B
6.	D	16.	D	26.	C	36.	C
7.	B	17.	A	27.	A	37.	C
8.	A	18.	C	28.	D	38.	B
9.	A	19.	D	29.	C	39.	A
10.	A	20.	B	30.	B	40.	D

Answer Explanations

GROUP ONE

GENERAL COMMENT: If you followed the suggested strategy, you would have first determined that the form is a "Complaint Form" used to record details about crimes committed, and that it is a fill-in form.

1. **B** The 29th Precinct is indicated as the precinct receiving the report. An easy question. However, read carefully and do not confuse 29 with 92.

2. **A** The report calls for military time, and the narrative clearly states when the report was filed at the precinct. Choice B is when Mrs. Goldberg arrived home. Choice D is the officers' arrival time.

3. **D** Note the difference between choices B and D. Care in recording data is extremely important.

4. **D** A civilian may claim to have been the victim of one type of crime, but it is the professional police officer who classifies the crime based on the facts he/she uncovers.

5. **A** The complainant, Mrs. Goldberg, discovered a broken window in the rear porch. It definitely indicated a forced entry.

6. **D** Do not confuse Mrs. Goldberg's address with her neighbors'. Mrs. Goldberg was the victim.

7. **B** Box 17 calls for the home telephone number of the victim; it has nothing to do with the neighbor or witness.

8. A Box 18 calls for the business telephone of the victim, not that of the witness.

9. A Box 35 is the caption allotted for the victim's age.

10. A Box 37 deals with the victim's race.

11. C The amount of $350. is the total value of the jewelry taken. Choice A, $390., is the value of the jewelry plus the calculator. Choice B is the value of all the property taken. Choice D is the value of the currency taken.

12. D The amount $240. is the value of the currency taken. See explanation 11 given above.

13. A The first perpetrator was described by the witness, Mrs. Wilson, as being white.

14. B The second perpetrator was described by the witness, Mrs. Wilson, as being black.

15. D The reporting officer was Police Officer Steel. His Tax Registry Number is 888888. Do not confuse that number with the officer's Shield Number or his partner's Shield Number.

GROUP TWO

GENERAL COMMENT: Now that you have taken both kinds of "Form Question Types," you should again review the material at the beginning of this chapter. Also, when doing extraction questions, your initial review of the form should be more thorough than your initial review of fill-in questions. This is so because in extraction questions, you have no narrative story to deal with. All the information you need in order to answer the questions is contained in the prepared form.

16. D The time of occurrence is 1830 hours. No other time is given on the form.

17. A Kendall is the victim. The other three names appear on the form but in different capacities.

18. C Notice that all of the numbers in the incorrect choices are contained in the story. The number 49 is the precinct designation, 1420 is Officer Reilly's shield number, and 438 is the hospital's admission number.

19. D Under "DETAILS" on the back of the Aided Report, the small print indicates that if CPR is administered, certain information must be given. Since no mention is made of CPR in the report, CPR was not administered.

20. B The aided went to Columbia Hospital. If he had gone home, that caption would have been checked on the report.

21. C The aided, who was 11 years old, has the same address as his mother with whom he resides. Therefore, his telephone number is the same as his mother's telephone number.

22. D See the explanation for question number 18 above.

23. C Mr. Judge was identified as a postal employee under the witness caption.

24. B Choices A and D are fabrications. Choice C, Police Officer Reilly, is the reporting officer.

25. D Police Officer Reilly's name appears next to the caption "reported by."

GROUP THREE

26. C The "premises" refers to the place of occurrence. Remember, our previously mentioned strategy emphasizing that where things happen is very important in police work. In this case, it is a boutique.

27. A The box dealing with the exact location of the crime is Box 2.

28. D Box 26 deals with type of footwear. The narrative states that the perpetrator was wearing loafers.

29. C Choice D makes reference to Box 33, which has to do with the body, but choice C more readily refers to body marks.

30. B The narrative clearly states that the birthmark is on the neck.

31. D By going to Box 17 and examining the choices in the question, you should immediately recall that the perpetrator impersonated a detective.

32. A If you examined the form before answering the question, you should have remembered that "hair style" was one of the boxes and have gone directly to choice A, which indicates hair style.

33. D The narrative clearly states that the perpetrator had a northern European/Irish accent.

34. C This type of question requires a review of each of the choices to eliminate the wrong ones, as well as to select the right one.

35. B Use the same method in arriving at this answer as in question 34 above.

36. C This answer is stated clearly. He "took out a silver handgun."

37. C This was specifically stated in the victim's description of the perpetrator.

38. B This was stated in the victim's description.

39. A It would be best for this question to go to each box offered in the choices and to make sure which one deals with a waist-length jacket.

40. D Use the same procedure as that used for answering question 39 above.

CHAPTER 8

Understanding And Applying Police Directives, Procedures, and Regulations

The questions you will learn about in this chapter are closely related to the general reading comprehension questions discussed earlier, but they usually go one step further. While the ability to understand what you read is essential, you must also demonstrate your ability to *apply what you read to practical police-related situations*.

A close examination of a police officer's job reveals a need not only to read and understand written material, but also to apply that written material in new unsupervised situations. For example, a procedure might be implemented to provide for tighter control of evidence found at the scene of a crime. A police officer will be told of the new procedure, will read about it, and might even take a copy of the new procedure on patrol. When the officer first follows the procedure, he/she must apply it to the *particular* situation that exists *at that time*. Situations can be very different, and the application of the procedure might also have to differ. Therefore, the questions in this chapter are designed to test your ability to apply written material in a variety of realistic police situations.

The Three Question Types

There are three question formats that test your ability to understand the written material involved and that require you to make judgments or decisions based on the contents of the writing. Listed below are explanations of each item type:

1. **"UNDERSTANDING" PROCEDURES.** In this item type you are given a police department procedure. Then, based solely on the information in that procedure, you will be asked to do such things as: identify accurate or inaccurate statements, choose the best example of the procedure, etc.

   EXAMPLE 1
   Police officers are prohibited from firing warning shots under any circumstances. Police officers are also not permitted to shoot at a moving vehicle unless the vehicle being shot at is being used in an assault attempt.

   Based solely upon the information in the reading selection above, which one of the following statements is most accurate?
   (A) When their lives are threatened, police are authorized to fire warning shots.
   (B) Police officers are never allowed to shoot at moving vehicles.
   (C) Police officers can shoot at moving vehicles only if a police officer's life is threatened.
   (D) Police officers can sometimes shoot at a moving vehicle.

   Answer D

2. **"UNDERSTANDING" NARRATIVE SITUATIONS.** In this item type you are given a short narrative about a police incident and are then asked to choose a correct or incorrect statement about the narrative.

   EXAMPLE 2
   At about 3:30 P.M. on a weekday in June, an explosion took place in a private home in Elmhurst, Queens. Two police officers responded about ten minutes after the incident occurred, and observed two teenagers running away from the scene. Five people were seriously injured in the explosion, and one eventually died.

   Based upon the information above, which of the following is a correct statement?

(A) The explosion took place on a Tuesday.
(B) A total of six people were injured in the explosion.
(C) The police responded at about 3:40 P.M.
(D) Teenagers were responsible for setting the explosion.

Answer C

NOTE: The two question types demonstrated above could very easily be categorized as straight reading comprehension items, covered in an earlier chapter. Nonetheless, we are including them in this chapter for two reasons: (1) we want you to be as familiar as possible with all types of question formats, and (2) we feel that the application question format explained below is best understood by reviewing the above formats first.

3. **"APPLYING" PROCEDURES TO SITUATIONS.** In this item type you are given a police procedure and a narrative describing a police situation. You are then asked to choose the correct (or incorrect) course of action for a police officer to follow, based upon your understanding of the procedure involved and how it should apply to the situation described. Or, you may be asked what the officer should do next.

EXAMPLE 3

In police terms a vehicle accident is one which occurs on a public highway; or on a street between building lines involving a vehicle including a parked vehicle, attended or unattended; or vehicles on private property to which the public has access.

On January 25, Officer Jones responds to the parking lot of the Bronxville Shopping Center. Upon arrival at the scene, Officer Jones observes over a hundred automobiles belonging to people who are shopping at the various stores in the shopping center. The officer further observes one parked vehicle as it rolls down a slight incline in the parking lot and strikes another parked vehicle, causing minor damage to both vehicles. The officer determines that a vehicle accident has occurred and follows the applicable procedures.

Based *solely* upon the information above, Officer Jones' determination was:

(A) Proper, since the accident occurred on a street between building lines.
(B) Improper, since neither car was attended at the time of the accident.
(C) Proper, since the accident occurred on private property which is open to public access.
(D) Improper, since the accident did not occur on a public highway.

Answer C

Strategies to Help You "Understand" Procedures and Narrative Situations

The strategy outlined for answering these questions is similar to the strategy suggested previously for answering general reading comprehension questions since both item types are similar.

1. **SCAN THE POLICE PROCEDURE OR NARRATIVE.** Get a quick idea of the substance of the procedure or narrative involved.

2. **SCAN THE STEM OF THE QUESTION, OR QUESTIONS, INVOLVED.** Most often, you will be asked one question per procedure or narrative, but sometimes more than one question will be asked about the same procedure or narrative. After scanning the written material, scan the stem of the question, or questions, pertaining to that material. The objective of this scanning is to get an idea on what areas of the written material you are being questioned. Also, quickly scan some of the choices for each question.

3. **READ THE POLICE PROCEDURE, OR NARRATIVE, CAREFULLY.** You now have a general idea of what the paragraph is about and on what area you will be questioned. Your task now is to read the paragraph carefully, remembering to concentrate as deeply as possible. Don't forget to use your pencil to underline or circle key words or sentences. (Review the material in the reading comprehension chapter for a complete discussion of the use of your pencil when doing reading questions.)

4. **QUESTION YOURSELF WHILE READING; DEVELOP A MENTAL PICTURE OF WHAT YOU ARE READING.** Pause when reading to ask yourself questions. This will ensure that you are reading with the proper degree of concentration. You will also understand the written material more, especially if it is a narrative, if you try to create a mental picture of what you are reading.

5. **ANSWER THE QUESTIONS.** Using the strategy outlined in Chapter 2, answer the questions. Remember that it is advisable to return to the procedure to verify the answers you select. Also keep in mind that the answers are to be based *solely* on the information contained within the written material.

EXAMPLE—HOW TO USE THIS STRATEGY

Using Example 1 to demonstrate, we will take you step-by-step through the recommended strategy.

Step one—scan the material A quick reading of this procedure informs you that the passage concerns itself with the circumstances under which police officers can and cannot fire their weapons.

Step two—scan the stem and some choices A quick reading of the stem and some of the choices informs you that you will be asked to select an accurate statement as to when police officers are authorized to fire their weapons.

Step three—read the material carefully A careful reading of the paragraph will reveal that warning shots can never be fired, and that shooting at moving vehicles is prohibited unless someone is being assaulted by that vehicle.

Step four—question yourself and develop a mental picture An example of a question you might ask yourself is: "Can a police officer ever fire a warning shot?" Of course, the answer is "NO!" Words that you might underline are: "under any circumstances" and "unless." Also, this is an ideal passage for creating a mental image. Can't you see yourself as part of this story?

Step five—answer the question Choice A is incorrect because the police can never fire warning shots. Note that the examiner makes it very tempting to select this answer. After all, common sense indicates that officers should be able to fire a warning shot when lives are threatened. Nonetheless, the paragraph is quite clear; the choice is wrong and you should put an "X" through the letter "A," indicating that it is incorrect.
Choice B is wrong because, under certain circumstances, police officers are allowed to fire at moving vehicles. Note the key word "never" in this choice. Put an "X" through choice B.
Choice C is another tempting selection. However, note the key word "only." The paragraph indicates that a moving vehicle can be shot at when "someone" is being assaulted. The choice limits "someone" to a "police officer." It is therefore incorrect, and the letter "C" should be crossed out.
Choice D is correct as stated. Verify it in the procedure, circle the letter "D," and transpose it carefully on to your answer sheet.

Strategies to Help You "Apply" Procedures to Situations

This question type has both police procedure (or policy) and a narrative describing some specific situation. These questions test your ability to understand the procedure or policy and apply it to an actual situation. Your approach to these questions should be as follows.

1. **SCAN THE PROCEDURE (OR POLICY).** Be sure you understand the procedure being described: its intent, to whom it applies, and when to apply it. If a sequence of steps is involved (as is often the case), make sure you are aware of it. Try to visualize the procedure. Use your pencil to emphasize key words and thoughts.

2. **SCAN THE NARRATIVE.** Get a quick idea of the situation described in the narrative. The major objective of this initial scanning is to see how the narrative relates to the procedure.

3. **SCAN THE QUESTION(S).** Scan the stem of the question, or questions, involved and the choices, just to get an idea of what you will be asked. This helps you focus on the pertinent material when re-reading the procedure and narrative.

   NOTE: Don't waste time on Steps 1 through 3. All that is required is that you get a good idea of the procedure, a quick idea of the details of the narrative, and an awareness of the focus of the questions.

4. **RE-READ THE PROCEDURES.** If you have used your pencil effectively in the first reading, the re-reading should be easy. This time, however, be alert for information relating to the questions.

5. **READ THE NARRATIVE.** This time concentrate on the narrative. Use your pencil, ask yourself questions, and "put yourself into the story." You already know what the procedures are and the focus of the questions, so you should be able to direct your attention to the most important parts of the story.

6. **ANSWER THE QUESTION(S).** Refer to the written material when answering the questions. However, you can save much time if you used your pencil effectively when initially reading the material. You should be able to refer immediately to the important parts of the procedure and the narrative. Remember to use the strategy that has been outlined for you earlier while answering the questions.

EXAMPLE—HOW TO USE THIS STRATEGY

Using Example 3 to demonstrate, we will take you step-by-step through the recommended strategy.

Step one—scan the procedure or policy Remember, however, when dealing with procedures and policies, it is important to fully understand the distinction between the word "or" and the word "and," as follows:

- "Or" connotes the meaning that either of two alternatives is acceptable. If a vehicle accident occurs on a public highway *or* on a street between building lines, then either location is a possible site for a vehicle accident.
- "And" connotes the meaning that more than one alternative is necessary. If a vehicle accident requires the element of a public highway or a street between building lines *and* the involvement of a vehicle, then you need both elements before you have a vehicle accident. In other words, if you are driving your vehicle on private property and run into a tree, it is *not* a vehicle accident since the element of a public highway or street is missing.

Therefore, according to the procedural statement in the above example question, a vehicle accident is one which requires more than one element. When reading these types of procedures, always underline the words "and" and "or" to draw your attention to them.

Step two—scan the narrative A scanning of the narrative in the sample question reveals that the situation involves a parked car rolling into another parked car in private parking lot, where over a hundred cars are parked; and that the officer has determined that the incident is a vehicle accident. With that in mind, you now proceed to Step 3.

Step three—scan the question Reading the question makes it obvious that you must focus on whether Officer Jones acted properly or improperly in classifying the incident as a vehicle accident. Note that you must also provide a justification for your answer, for you must decide why you believe he acted properly or improperly.

Step four—re-read the procedural statement This should be done quickly since you have already scanned the statement once and have highlighted the important parts with your pencil.

Step five—read the narrative, question yourself, put yourself into the story This time when you read the story, you know what you are looking for. Is the incident a vehicle accident in accordance with the official definition? Why? Does it matter if there is no driver in either car? Does the accident occur on private property and, if so, does the public have access to the private property? These are the questions you should ask yourself.

Step six—answer the question In this type of question the first item to answer is whether Officer Jones acted properly or improperly. Was it a vehicle accident, or not? The answer is that it was a vehicle accident since it occurred in a private parking lot which is open to the public, and it involved a vehicle. Having made this determination, cross out choices B and D as being wrong. Since the accident did not occur on a street between building lines, choice A is also incorrect, so cross it out. This leaves you with choice C. Make a quick review of the written material to verify your answer, circle choice C as the correct answer, and transpose it carefully to your answer sheet.

Practice Exercises

GROUP ONE—20 Minute Time Limit

***DIRECTIONS:* Following are practice questions. Each question in this group is to be answered *solely* on the basis of the information in the passage preceding it.**

Answer question 1 through 3 based *solely* on the following:

There is a specific procedure that must be followed to report damage to a department property other than department vehicles. The member of the service who discovers the damaged property must make an entry in his memo book and report the information to the station house clerk. The clerk then prepares an original and three copies of a report on official letterhead, which must include the following information:

a. Date and time of occurrence,
b. Details,
c. Department property involved,
d. Damage to other property,
e. Owner of other property,
f. Action taken by discovering officer,
g. Witnesses,
h. Brief description of injury, if any.

The ranking officer in command of the precinct of occurrence must investigate the facts and endorse the report.

The station house supervisor then files the original of the report and forwards the three copies to the appropriate unit, as follows:

PROPERTY INVOLVED	TO
a. Booths, buildings	Building Maintenance Section
b. Horses	Mounted District
c. Aircraft, launches	Emergency Service District
d. Telephone signal boxes, illuminated telephone signs	Communications Division
e. Any other property	Deputy Commissioner Administration

1. Which of the following statements about reporting damaged department property is true? 1 A B C D

(A) All damaged department property must be reported on official letterhead.

(B) The member of the service who discovers the damaged property must prepare an original and three copies of a report.

(C) The station house supervisor must endorse the reports and forward them as required.

(D) The ranking officer in command of the precinct of occurrence must investigate the facts.

2. The reports involving damaged department property other than vehicles must always include all of the following *except*: 2 A B C D

(A) A brief description of injuries, if any.

(B) The time of occurrence.

(C) A description of the department property involved.

(D) The name of the owner of property damaged other than department property.

3. An incident involving damage to a department aircraft must be reported to the: 3 A B C D

(A) Mounted District.

(B) Emergency Service District.

(C) Deputy Commissioner Administration.

(D) Communications Division.

4. At about 9:20 P.M., June 25, a three-car accident occurred on the Grand Central Parkway, in Queens. One of the cars in the accident caught on fire after the collision, and the driver and both passengers were severely burned. The driver that caused the accident escaped injury when she was thrown from her car and landed safely on the grass 4 A B C D alongside of the parkway. Nothing is known about the four occupants of the third car since that vehicle left the scene of the accident without stopping.

Based upon the information above, which of the following is a correct statement?

(A) A total of three people were injured in the accident.
(B) Only one car was damaged in the accident.
(C) There were three people in the car that caught on fire.
(D) The police did not respond to the accident.

5. On July 15, shortly after midnight, three armed men and one unarmed female held up Joe's Bar and Grill located at 30-85 61st Road, in Astoria, Brooklyn. The female had bright red hair and extremely long fingernails that were painted green. One of the males stuttered when he talked, and wore a stocking over his head. The second male walked with a limp and wore a black baseball jacket with gold trim. The third male wore a Halloween-type mask and carried a stiletto and handgun. No shots were fired during the robbery, but on the way out of the premise, the male with the stiletto accidentally stabbed the female perpetrator in the right leg.

A B C D
5 | | | | | | | |

Based upon the above information, the most useful item in apprehending the perpetrators is that:

(A) One of the males in the group stuttered.
(B) The second male walked with a limp.
(C) The female was stabbed in the right leg.
(D) The female had long fingernails and bright red hair.

Answer questions 6 through 8 *solely* on the basis of the following:

To assist members of the service, the following procedure should be used upon observing a person commit an offense punishable by a summons:

1. Inform the violator of the offense committed.

2. Request the violator to show proof of identity and residence.
   a. In traffic cases, examine the driver's license, the vehicle registration and, when appropriate, the insurance identification card for New York State registered vehicles.
   b. Take the violator to the station house for investigation if doubt exists concerning identity.

3. Issue summonses in numerical order.

4. Use a ballpoint pen to legibly print information in block letters.

5. Enter all available information required by captions on the summons.

6. Enter only one offense on each summons.

7. Use a separate summons for each additional offense.

   NOTE: If the violator commits multiple offenses arising out of a single traffic incident and one offense is returnable to criminal court, make all related summonses returnable to criminal court.

8. Give the violator the part of Universal Summons designated for the agency to which it is returnable.

9. Enter information concerning the summons on the Certification of Summonses Served form.

10. Enter complete details in the Memo/Patrol Officer's Log.

11. Deliver the remaining three parts of the Universal Summons intact, to the precinct of occurrence at the end of tour, or as directed by the commanding officer.

12. Place the summons in the appropriate receptacle at the desk according to the returnable agency.

---

6. On April 11, at 1:55 A.M., Police Officer Maria Ruiz observed a Ford, bearing New Jersey Plate AWD 242, proceed through a red light at the intersection of Green Avenue and 48th Street in the borough of Queens. One block later, the same Ford made an illegal U-turn, and sped off at a rate of speed far in excess of the legal limit. Officer Ruiz pursued the vehicle in her police car and forced it to the side about four blocks from the place of the illegal U-turn. The officer examined the driver's license of the operator of the Ford, and asked to see the vehicle registration and insurance identification card covering the vehicle. Officer Ruiz became suspicious because the description on the driver's license did not match that of the operator of the car, so she brought the violator to the station house for purposes of identification.

6 A B C D

All of the following actions of Officer Ruiz were in accordance with the department procedure *except* that of:

(A) Asking to see the vehicle registration.
(B) Asking to see the insurance identification card.
(C) Bringing the violator to the station house.
(D) Examining the driver's license of the operator of the car.

7. Police Officer Harry Smith works out of the Grand Central Parkway Precinct in the Bronx. His assignment is to patrol the limited access highways within the confines of the 92nd, 95th, 97th, and 99th Precincts. On June 4, he observed a vehicle entering the highway in the 95th Precinct by going the wrong way on the exit ramp. Officer Smith gave chase to the subject vehicle. The chase route included streets within the 95th and 97th Precincts, with the violating vehicle finally being apprehended in the 99th Precinct. Officer Smith issued the operator a summons for traveling the wrong way on a one-way street. Then he resumed patrol.

A B C D
7 | | | | | | | |

At the end of his tour, Officer Smith should deliver the three parts of the Universal Summons to:

(A) The Grand Central Parkway Precinct.
(B) The 99th Precinct.
(C) Any of the precincts involved except the 92nd Precinct.
(D) The 95th Precinct.

8. While on routine patrol, Officer Brown observed a late model sedan commit three traffic offenses punishable by summonses, as well as one violation for which a summons returnable in criminal court can be issued. Officer Brown apprehended the driver of the vehicle and cited the driver for all of the offenses that he observed.

A B C D
8 | | | | | | | |

Based upon the above information, which of the following is a correct statement?

(A) Officer Brown has to issue two summonses: one for the traffic offenses, and one for the offense returnable in criminal court.
(B) All of the offenses can be entered on one summons which can be made returnable in criminal court.

(C) Four summonses must be issued: three retunable to traffic court, and one returnable to criminal court.

(D) Four summonses must be issued, and they all must be made returnable to criminal court.

Answer questions 9 and 10 based *solely* on the following:

An arrest is defined as taking a person into custody to answer for an offense. A pick-up arrest is an arrest for an offense or delinquency not previously reported. Upon arresting a person for an offense, the following procedure must be followed by the arresting officer and by the station house supervisor:

Arresting Officer

1. Inform the individual being arrested of your authority.

2. Advise the prisoner of the cause of the arrest except when:
   a. Arrested in the actual commission of an offense, or
   b. Pursued immediately after an escape.

3. Handcuff the prisoner when circumstances require.

4. Search the prisoner for weapons, evidence, or contraband.

5. Advise the prisoner of his/her rights before questioning.

6. Take the prisoner to the station house of the precinct of arrest.
   a. Request a patrolwagon, if necessary,
   b. Safeguard apparatus operated by the prisoner before removing him/her to the station house.

7. Bring the prisoner before the station house supervisor and inform him/her of the charge.

Station House Supervisor

8. Direct the arresting officer to make a thorough search of the prisoner in your presence. However,
   a. Female prisoners are to be searched by a female police officer in all possible privacy.

9. Have the following property removed from the prisoner which is:
   a. Unlawfully carried,
   b. Required as evidence,
   c. Lawfully carried, but would be dangerous to life or would aid in escape,

d. Can be used to damage or deface property.
e. Personal, except clothing, if prisoner is intoxicated or unconscious.

---

9. Sergeant John Jones was assigned as the station house supervisor on the night of May 31, when Officer Mary Black brought in a male prisoner whom she arrested for armed robbery. Sergeant Jones directed Officer Black to search the prisoner. As a result of the search, Sergeant Jones ordered that the gun used in the robbery and all of the prisoner's personal property be removed from him.

9 A B C D

Based upon the above information, which of the following statements is correct?

(A) Sergeant Jones was in error when he removed the prisoner's personal property.
(B) Police Officer Black was not the right sex to search the prisoner.
(C) In this case, Sergeant Jones was wrong in directing a search.
(D) This case can be classified as a pick-up arrest.

10. On Friday evening, June 22, at 9:45 P.M., Officer Green observed a lone male attempting to burglarize the supermarket on the corner of 74th and Keyster Road, which is within the confines of the 47th Precinct. Officer Green approached the suspect and identified himself as a police officer. A struggle ensued during which the criminal was knocked unconscious. Moments later, the prisoner regained consciousness but was extremely weak and groggy. The officer brought the prisoner into the 47th Precinct station house without hancuffing him.

10 A B C D

Based upon the above information, which of the following statements about the actions of Officer Green is correct?

(A) The officer was wrong because he did not advise the prisoner of his rights.
(B) The officer should have handcuffed the prisoner before bringing him into the station house.
(C) The officer should have searched the prisoner before bringing him into the station house.
(D) The officer should have advised the prisoner of the cause of arrest.

GROUP TWO—15 Minute Time Limit

***DIRECTIONS:* Following are practice questions. Each question in this group is to be answered *solely* on the basis of the information in the passage preceding it.**

11. Early in the morning of October 22, three customers were having breakfast at John's Diner when two masked gunmen entered and announced a stickup. While one gunman kept everyone under armed surveillance, the other removed $148 from the cash register and $500 from John. All four customers were searched, with the thieves removing a total of $355 from them. As the perpetrators were leaving, a well-dressed couple entered the diner. The two robbers then removed $200 from them, as well as two watches worth $450 each and a diamond ring valued at $2,500.

A B C D
11 | | | | | | | |

Based upon the information above, which of the following is a true statement?

(A) The total value of the cash and property lost in the holdup was $4,153.

(B) The value of the property lost in the holdup was $2,950.

(C) The value of the cash and property lost by the well-dressed couple was $3,600.

(D) The total amount of cash lost in the holdup was $1,003.

Answer questions 12 through 16 based *solely* on the following:

According to the New York State Criminal Procedure Law, the police must take the fingerprints of certain arrested persons. The purpose of taking fingerprints in these cases is to establish positive identification and to provide the arraignment court with prior criminal records.

Arresting officers are to take the fingerprints of all arrested persons charged with:

a. A felony, or
b. A misdemeanor defined in the Penal Law, or
c. A misdemeanor defined outside the Penal Law which would constitute a felony if the arrested person had a previous conviction for a crime, or
d. Loitering, as defined in the Penal Law.

Arresting officers shall also fingerprint all arrested persons:

a. Whose identity cannot be ascertained, or
b. Who arouse reasonable suspicion that the identification given is not accurate, or

c. Who arouse reasonable suspicion that they are being sought by law enforcement officials for the commission of some other offense.

NOTE: Whenever fingerprints are required, photographs and palmprints may also be taken.

12. One of the purposes of taking fingerprints is to:
(A) Provide the grand jury with prior criminal records.
(B) Verify positive identification of arrested persons.
(C) Obtain information for the purpose of setting bail.
(D) Supply the judge at arraignment with prior criminal records.

12 A B C D

13. The mandate for the police to take the fingerprints of certain arrested persons comes from:
(A) The courts.
(B) The Penal Law.
(C) The Criminal Procedure Law.
(D) Police rules and regulations.

13 A B C D

14. Based upon the above information, which of the following is the most accurate statement?
(A) The person arrested for a felony must be photographed.
(B) The decision to photograph arrested persons depends solely on the seriousness of the offense.
(C) Every person who is fingerprinted must also be palm printed.
(D) Whether an arrested person is photographed sometimes depends on the suspicions of the arresting officer.

14 A B C D

15. On May 31st, Officer Ann Jones arrested a male, white, for a misdemeanor defined outside of the Penal Law. The officer brought her prisoner to the 116th Precinct for the purpose of identification and booking. The prisoner identified himself as Henry Adams and presented a driver's license, an automobile registration, and a number of credit cards to substantiate his identity. Nothing unusual was uncovered during the questioning of her prisoner, but Officer Jones had a hunch that the prisoner was being sought by the Federal Bureau of Investigation. Therefore, she arranged to have him fingerprinted and photographed.

15 A B C D

Based upon the above, Officer Jones' decision to have her prisoner fingerprinted and photographed was:

(A) Proper, since the prisoner was arrested for a misdemeanor.

(B) Improper, since a hunch does not constitute reasonable suspicion.

(C) Proper, since the charge might become a felony.

(D) Improper, since persons arrested for misdemeanors are never photographed.

16. Taking a person's palmprints:

(A) Is prohibited.

(B) Is done every time a person is fingerprinted.

(C) Can be done only if a person is also fingerprinted.

(D) Is always accompanied by the taking of photographs.

A B C D
16 | | | | | | | |

Answer questions 17 through 20 based *solely* on the following:

The patrol precinct is the hub of all police department patrol operations. According to the management principle of "unity of command," everyone in the precinct should know how they fit into the overall organization and to whom they report. For these reasons, it is important for everyone who works in a precinct to understand its organization. An organization chart for a police precinct is shown below.

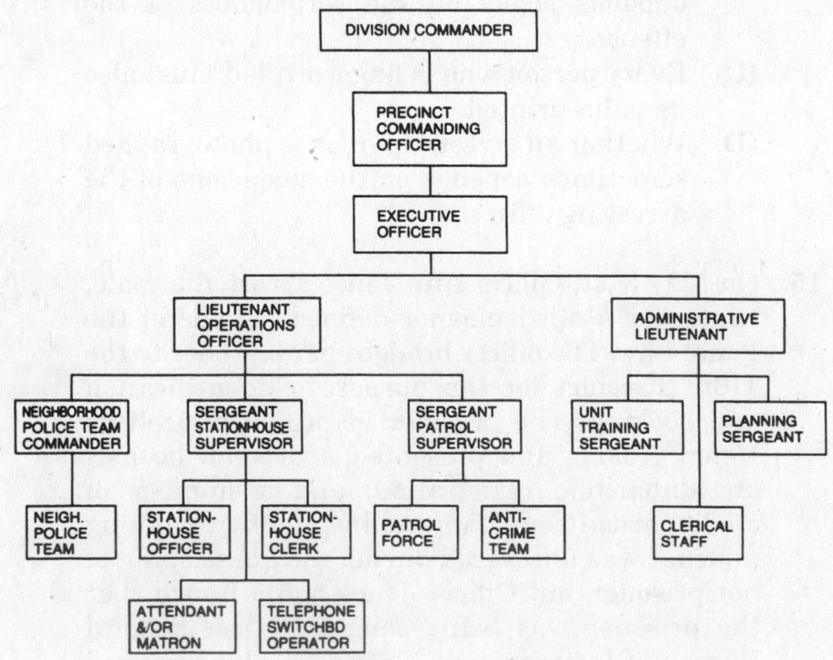

Source: New York City Police Department

17. Based upon the above information, the station house officer reports directly to the:

(A) Station house supervisor.
(B) Operations officer.
(C) Executive officer.
(D) Station house clerk.

17 A B C D

18. Based upon the above information, the clerical staff is under the supervision of the:

(A) Unit training sergeant.
(B) Planning sergeant.
(C) Administrative lieutenant.
(D) Operations officer.

18 A B C D

19. Based upon the above information, how many people report directly to the Executive Officer?

(A) 1
(B) 2
(C) 3
(D) 4

19 A B C D

20. Listed below is a partial assignment roster for the 117th Precinct.

NAME	ASSIGNMENT
Maria Grossman	Telephone switchboard operator
Sergeant David Murphy	Patrol supervisor
Captain Wayne Talleir	Precinct commanding officer
Lieutenant Robert McWilliams	Operations officer
Sergeant Robert Crass	Unit training sergeant
Detective Mike Corcoran	Anti-crime team
Police Officer John Roe	Patrol force
Roscoe Myers	Attendant

Based upon the above information, which of the following is an *incorrect* statement?

(A) Roscoe Myers reports to the station house supervisor.
(B) Sergeant Murphy reports to Lieutenant McWilliams.
(C) Detective Corcoran reports to Sergeant Crass.
(D) Police Officer Roe reports to Sergeant Murphy.

20 A B C D

GROUP THREE—15 Minute Time Limit

***DIRECTIONS:* Following are practice questions. Each question in this group is to be answered *solely* on the basis of the information in the passage preceding it.**

Answer questions 21 through 27 based *solely* on the following:

Police departments are semi-military organizations and require strict adherence to a code of conduct. All sworn members of the department must be disciplined if they engage in prohibited conduct. Listed below are specific examples of prohibited conduct for sworn members of police departments.

1. Consuming intoxicants while in uniform.
2. Entering a premise that serves intoxicants, except for a meal or in the performance of duty.
3. Carrying a package, umbrella, cane, etc., while in uniform, except in the performance of duty.
4. Recommending the use of any particular business, professional, or commercial services to any person except when transacting personal affairs.
5. Steering business, professional, or commercial persons to a prospective client who might require services, except when transacting personal affairs.
6. Consenting to payment by anyone to regain lost or stolen property, or advising such payment.
7. Riding in any vehicle other than a department vehicle to which assigned while in uniform, except when authorized or in an emergency (sergeants and police officers only).
8. Using department logo unless specifically authorized by the police commissioner.
9. Divulging or discussing official department business.
10. Engaging in conduct prejudicial to good order, efficiency, or discipline of the department.
11. Making a recommendation for, or concerning, any person or premises to any government agency in connection with the issuance, revocation, or suspension of any license or permit, except when required in the performance of duty.

12. Campaigning for a candidate for public office or being a member of a political club.

13. Being a candidate for election or serving as a member of a school board, if the school district is located within the city limits.

14. Accepting an additional position of "public trust or civil emolument" without retiring or resigning his position in the police department, except as specifically provided in Section 443, of the City Charter, concerning leave of absence without pay.

15. Smoking in public view while in uniform.

16. Occupying a seat in a public conveyance while in uniform, to the exclusion of a paying passenger.

17. Using a personal card describing police business, address, telephone number, or title except as authorized by the Department Manual.

18. Rendering any service for private interest which interferes with the proper performance of duty.

---

21. Based upon the above information, which of the following is a true statement? 21 A B C D
    (A) A police officer cannot consume intoxicating beverages while on duty.
    (B) A police officer in uniform cannot enter a premise which serves intoxicating beverages.
    (C) A police officer in uniform cannot consume alcohol, even when on meal in a licensed premise.
    (D) A police officer can never consume alcohol to the point where he becomes intoxicated.

22. Based upon the above information, which of the following actions is prohibited at all times? 22 A B C D
    (A) Divulging official department business
    (B) Smoking in uniform
    (C) Using the department logo
    (D) Using a personal card

23. Based upon the above information, which of the following is *not* always a prohibited action for a police officer? 23 A B C D
    (A) Being a member of a political club
    (B) Serving as a member of a school board
    (C) Campaigning for a candidate for public office
    (D) Encouraging friends to vote for the incumbent mayor in the mayoral election

24. Sergeant Henry Adams is a twenty-year veteran of the police department, and works in the department's legal bureau. A member of his family has just been arrested and has asked Sergeant Adams to recommend a lawyer to represent him in court. Sergeant Adams gives him the name and telephone number of a highly respected defense attorney.

24 A B C D

Based upon the above information, Sergeant Adams acted:

(A) Properly, since he was dealing with a member of his family.

(B) Improperly, since department regulations specifically prohibit the making of such recommendations.

(C) Properly, since Sergeant Adams is assigned to the legal bureau.

(D) Improperly, since it is a very definite conflict of interest for Sergeant Adams, considering his assignment to the legal bureau.

25. Detective Harry Mulligan works in the Robbery Squad in the 15th Precinct. He is working in plain clothes on a day tour, and has just received a notification to report immediately to the criminal court at 100 Centre Street concerning an arrest he recently made. Considering the traffic pattern, Detective Mulligan decides to take the subway to the court. When he enters the train, there are a number of empty seats, so he sits down and begins to review his notes on the arrest involved. As the train continues its way downtown, it fills up and paying passengers are now standing in the aisles. However, since Detective Mulligan wants to be prepared when he arrives at court, he continues to remain seated and to review his notes.

25 A B C D

Based upon the above information, Detective Mulligan's decision to remain seated was:

(A) Justified, since he has an obligation to be prepared when he arrives at the court.

(B) Not justified, since he is prohibited from occupying a seat to the exclusion of a paying customer.

(C) Justified, since he is not in uniform.

(D) Not justified, since Detective Mulligan is riding the train at no cost to himself.

26. Police Officer Randolph Smith is working a day tour out of the 31st Precinct in the Bronx. He is assigned to Post 33, which is four blocks long and is in the middle of a very busy shopping area. Officer Smith, who is a chain smoker, constantly smokes while performing his patrol duties.

26 A B C D

Based upon the above information, which of the following is an accurate statement concerning Officer Smith's actions?

(A) He is in violation of department regulations since he is smoking on patrol.
(B) He is not in violation of department regulations since he is not in public view.
(C) He may be in violation of department regulations, depending upon whether he is in uniform.
(D) He may be in violation of department regulations, depending upon whether he is in public view.

27. Police Officer Mary Smith is at home on her vacation. She receives a phone call from her brother, who tells her that his apartment was recently burglarized and his stamp collection was stolen. He further explains that he now has an opportunity to get his stamp collection back by making a payment to a party representing the burglars. Officer Smith advises her brother to make the payment to get his property back since it is highly unlikely that the police will get it back for him.

27 A B C D

Based upon the above information, Officer Smith acted:

(A) Properly, since she was not on duty when she gave her brother the advice.
(B) Improperly, since department regulations prohibit this type of conduct in all situations.
(C) Properly, since she was advising her brother in the course of conducting her own personal affairs, which are not the concern of the department.
(D) Improperly, since there is always a chance that the police will get the property back for her brother.

28. On September 13, Officers John Smith and Mary Jones went to the home of Derrick Walker and arrested him for raping a 14-year-old school child on May 19. The officers were in possession of an arrest warrant for Walker. The warrant was issued on June 3, after a grand jury investigation determined there was reasonable cause to believe that Walker had committed the crime. The rape was originally reported by the parents of the young girl on May 25.

A B C D
28 | | | | | | | |

Based upon the above information, which of the following is *not* a true statement?

(A) About seven months elapsed from the time of the commission of the rape to the arrest of the suspect.
(B) The grand jury considered the case before the arrest was made.
(C) The arrest was made on the authority of a warrant.
(D) There were three witnesses to the commission of the crime.

Answer questions 29 through 30 based *solely* on the following:

In order to make a legal arrest, a police officer has to have reasonable grounds to believe that the person being arrested has committed a crime. In order to obtain a conviction, the people must prove beyond a reasonable doubt that the accused person has committed the crime with which he/she is being charged. In order to stop and question a person in a public place, a police officer has to have reasonable suspicion that the person being stopped has committed a crime. In a civil action, a case is won by the party who has the most evidence on his or her side.

29. Harry Jones has just been convicted of murder. This means that:

A B C D
29 | | | | | | | |

(A) There were reasonable grounds to suspect that Jones had committed the murder.
(B) There were reasonable grounds to believe that Jones had committed the murder.
(C) There was proof beyond a reasonable doubt that Jones had committed the murder.
(D) Most of the evidence pointed to the probability that Jones had committed the murder.

30. A person involved in a civil suit who has 51% of the evidence on her side:

A B C D
30 | | | | | | | |

(A) Must win the suit.
(B) Might win the suit.
(C) Will probably win the suit.
(D) Will lose the suit.

GROUP FOUR—15 Minute Time Limit

***DIRECTIONS:* Following are practice questions. Each question in this group is to be answered *solely* on the basis of the information in the passage preceding it.**

Answer questions 31 through 37 based *solely* on the following:

Most police departments throughout the country use the military method of telling time. The major advantage of the military method of determining time is that it uses a twenty-four hour clock, which means that it is not necessary to distinguish between A.M. and P.M. Under the standard (or civilian) method of telling time, which uses a twelve-hour clock, the same numbers appear in the time twice a day and are distinguished by adding either A.M. or P.M. For example, under the civilian method, it is eleven o'clock twice during each day, in the morning when it is 11 A.M. and at night when it is 11 P.M. Since the military method utilizes a twenty-four-hour clock, the same numbers never appear in the time more than once a day. For example, at 11:00 A.M. in the civilian method, it is 1100 hours in the military method; and at 11:00 P.M., it is 2300 hours. Noon in the military method is represented by 1200 hours, and midnight is represented by 2400 hours. The time between midnight and noon is fairly easy to remember in the military system since it is similar to the civilian method. For example, when it is 3:00 A.M. civilian time it is 0300 hours military time; when it is 4:30 A.M. it is 0430 hours. It is the time after noon that becomes a little difficult to determine under the military system. The rule to follow is to add 12 hours to the civilian time to determine the military time during the second half of the day. For example, when it is 2:25 P.M. in civilian time it is 1425 hours in military time (2:25 hours plus 12 hours because it is P.M.).

31. Based upon the above information, the major advantage of using military time is that:

31 A B C D

(A) It is less confusing.
(B) It is more accurate.
(C) The same numbers never appear in the time more than once a day.
(D) It is a better way to distinguish between A.M. and P.M.

32. Based upon the above information, which of the following is a true statement?

32 A B C D

(A) Civilian time is less accurate than military time.
(B) All police departments in the country use military time.
(C) Military time was devised by the United States Army.
(D) Military time uses a twenty-four-hour clock.

33. Based upon the above information, the military time equivalent of 3:28 P.M. is: 33 A B C D

(A) 0328 hours.
(B) 1528 hours.
(C) 1828 hours.
(D) 2028 hours.

34. Based upon the above information, at 35 minutes after noon, it is: 34 A B C D

(A) 12:35 A.M. and 0035 hours.
(B) 12:35 P.M. and 0035 hours.
(C) 12:35 A.M. and 1235 hours.
(D) 12:35 P.M. and 1235 hours.

35. Based upon the above information, the correct military time when it is 4:45 P.M. civilian time is: 35 A B C D

(A) 0445 hours.
(B) 0045 hours.
(C) 1445 hours.
(D) 1645 hours.

36. Based upon the above information, when it is 20 minutes after midnight, it is: 36 A B C D

(A) 0020 hours and 12:20 A.M.
(B) 2420 hours and 12:20 A.M.
(C) 1220 hours and 12:20 A.M.
(D) 2020 hours and 12:20 A.M.

37. Based upon the above information, which of the following is a true statement concerning the initials A.M.? 37 A B C D

(A) They stand for "after midnight."
(B) They stand for "ante meridiem."
(C) They stand for "après minuit."
(D) It is not known.

Answer questions 38 through 40 based *solely* on the above paragraph and the following information:

On August 3, at fifty minutes after midnight, an explosion took place in front of the Transylvania Embassy in Brooklyn. One hour and ten minutes prior to the explosion, a bearded man was observed loitering in front of the embassy. Fifty-five minutes after the explosion a telephone call was received at police headquarters stating that the explosion was the responsibility of the Anti-Vampire League. At 1:45 P.M. on the same day, a rock was thrown through the embassy window injuring two diplomats. Fifty minutes prior to the rock-throwing incident, the same bearded man was observed in front of the embassy. At 8:35 P.M., the bearded man was arrested by Police Officer Maureen Williams when he once again returned to the embassy.

38. At what time was the bearded man first observed in the vicinity of the Transylvania Embassy?

(A) 0050 hours
(B) 2340 hours
(C) 0210 hours
(D) 0010 hours

38 A B C D

39. At what time was the telephone call made to police headquarters, claiming responsibility for the explosion?

(A) 0135 hours
(B) 0055 hours
(C) 0435 hours
(D) 0145 hours

39 A B C D

40. At what time was the bearded man arrested?

(A) 2035 hours
(B) 0835 hours
(C) 1435 hours
(D) 1345 hours

40 A B C D

GROUP FIVE—20 Minute Time Limit

DIRECTIONS: **Following are practice questions. Each question in this group is to be answered *solely* on the basis of the information in the passage preceding it.**

Answer questions 41 through 43 based *solely* on the following information:

When a police officer issues a summons, he or she has to be aware of the agency that has jurisdiction over the offense for which the summons was issued. Listed below are various agencies which have jurisdiction over the most common summonsable offenses:

OFFENSES PROCESSED	AGENCY
Stopping, standing, and parking offenses.	N.Y.C. Transportation Administration, Parking Violations Bureau
Traffic infractions (other than Stopping, Standing, and Parking), and: a. Unlicensed operator, b. Unregistered vehicle, c. No insurance identification card.	N.Y.S. Department of Motor Vehicles Administrative Adjudication Bureau

OFFENSES PROCESSED	AGENCY
Pedestrian offenses and traffic misdemeanors except unlicensed operator, unregistered vehicle, and no insurance identification card.	N.Y.C. Criminal Court, Part 5
Garages and parking lots	N.Y.C. Criminal Court, Part 6
All other summonsable offenses	N.Y.C. Criminal Court, Part 7

41. Based upon the above information, a summons that would *not* be processed in N.Y.C. Criminal Court, Part 7, is:

41 A B C D

(A) Uncovered garbage can.
(B) Parking by a fire hydrant.
(C) Unleashed dog.
(D) Littering.

42. A summons for unregistered vehicles comes under the jurisdiction of the:

42 A B C D

(A) N.Y.S. Department of Motor Vehicles, Administrative Adjudication Bureau.
(B) N.Y.C. Criminal Court, Part 5.
(C) N.Y.C. Transportation Administration, Parking Violations Bureau.
(D) N.Y.C. Criminal Court, Part 6.

43. Offenses involving garages and parking lots come under the jurisdiction of the:

43 A B C D

(A) N.Y.S. Criminal Court, Part 6.
(B) N.Y.C. Criminal Court, Part 7.
(C) N.Y.S. Criminal Court, Part 5.
(D) N.Y.C. Criminal Court, Part 6.

Answer questions 44 through 50 based *solely* on the following information:

Certain summons cases require the police officer issuing the summons to follow special procedures, as follows:

SITUATION	PROCEDURE
U.S. Mail Trucks	1. Serve summons for moving traffic violations only. 2. Report all traffic offenses to commanding officer, giving: operator's name, time and place of occurrence, whether summons was served.
NOTE: Government vehicles do not require registration plates.	
Violation of the Administrative Code relating to Bingo, occurring when a representative of the State Lottery Control Commission is present.	1. Obtain name and title of representative. 2. Request representative to appear in court to sign corroborating affidavit. 3. Report facts, including representative's name and title, to commanding officer.
Violation of Administrative Code Criminal and Civil Penalty	1. Serve summons. 2. Prepare Administrative Code Violation Notice (PD372-151).
Premises licensed by State Liquor Authority	Report any summons served on premises to station house supervisor. Report facts to commanding officer.
Sale of alcoholic beverages during prohibited hours	1. Check time by radio, telephone, or other official media. 2. Seize beverage as evidence. 3. Secure other evidence such as proof of sale, identity of persons served, identity and job title of persons on premises, number of persons entering during prohibited hours. 4. Deliver evidence to crime laboratory for analysis. 5. Report facts to commanding officer.

SITUATION	PROCEDURE
Violation of Noise Control Code	1. Serve summons. 2. Prepare Administrative Code Violation Notice (PD372-151).
Purchase of alcoholic beverages by fraudulent proof of age	If violator is over 16 years of age, make summons returnable to Part 7 of Criminal Court (under 16—juvenile report). Report facts to commanding officer.
Public Service Commission Certificate—Violation of Section 61, subdivision 14, Public Service Law	Make summons returnable to Criminal Court, Part 7. Report facts to commanding officer.
Garages and Parking Lots	Offenses returnable to Part 6, Criminal Court, except Richmond, Part 1. Report facts to commanding officer.
Speeding	Circle speed when 25 MPH or more over speed limit.
Unleashed dog in park	Serve summons for violation of Health Code (Section 161.05).
Summons served by Highway Patrol District member for offense not personally observed	Draw line through statement on summons that reads: "I personally observed the commission of the offense charged above."
Traffic offense observed, unable to serve summons	Report circumstances to commanding officer, who may direct applying for court summons.
Missing Meter Number	Determine number from numbers of adjoining meters.
Overtime Parking	Enter time of observation.

44. Based upon the above information, when is a "Garages and Parking Lots" summons returnable in Part 1 of the Criminal Court?

44 A B C D

(A) Never
(B) When it is issued in Richmond
(C) When it is so directed by the commanding officer
(D) All of the time

45. Based upon the above information, Section 161.05 of the Health Code deals with: 45 A B C D
(A) Missing parking meter numbers.
(B) Unleashed dogs in a park.
(C) Noise control.
(D) Overtime parking.

46. Based upon the above information, when is a summons issued for "Purchase of alcoholic beverages by fraudulent proof of age" returnable to Part 7 of the Criminal Court? 46 A B C D
(A) All of the time
(B) Never
(C) When the violator is under 16 years of age
(D) When the violator is over 16 years of age

47. Based upon the above information, which of the following is the most accurate statement? 47 A B C D
(A) When a speeding summons is issued for speeds of 25 MPH or more, the speed is circled on the summons.
(B) In cases of missing meter numbers, the officer is to get the meter number involved from the numbers of adjoining meters.
(C) Any summons case involving alcoholic beverages requires the seizing of the alcoholic beverage as evidence.
(D) Summonses are not served for violations of the Noise Control Code.

48. While on routine patrol on August 23, Officer Carole Jones observed a U.S. mail truck without license plates or a valid inspection stamp proceed through a red light at the intersection of 31st Road and Broadway in the Borough of Richmond. Officer Jones pulled the vehicle over to the side of the road and issued the driver two summonses: one for going through the red light, the other for driving a vehicle without license plates. 48 A B C D

Based upon the above information, the officer's action was:
(A) Proper, since the summonses issued were for moving violations only.
(B) Improper, since the driver of a U.S. mail truck is immune from summonses.
(C) Proper, since the driver of a U.S. mail truck is eligible to receive moving and parking summonses.
(D) Improper, since U.S. mail trucks are not required to have registration plates.

49. On July 15, Police Office Clarence Williams observed a Dodge, registration number SWE 337, traveling well over the speed limit in a school zone posted for 35 miles per hour. Officer Williams was on foot patrol so he could not pursue the vehicle to serve a summons. Instead, Officer Williams went directly to court and applied for a court summons.

A B C D
49 | | | | | | | |

Based upon the above information, Officer Williams acted:

(A) Properly, since the violation was such a serious one.
(B) Improperly, since there is no provision for such a procedure to be followed.
(C) Properly, since the safety of so many children was endangered.
(D) Improperly, since Officer Williams should have first reported to his commanding officer.

50. Based upon the above information, which of the following instances does *not* require a notification to an officer's commanding officer?

A B C D
50 | | | | | | | |

(A) A situation involving illegal sale of alcoholic beverages.
(B) A situation involving a summons served in a parking lot.
(C) A situation involving purchase of alcoholic beverages by fraudulent proof of age.
(D) A situation involving a summons served in a premise licensed by the State Liquor Authority.

Answer Key and Explanations

Answer Key

1. D	10. C	19. B	28. A	37. D	46. D
2. D	11. C	20. C	29. C	38. B	47. B
3. B	12. D	21. C	30. A	39. D	48. D
4. C	13. C	22. A	31. C	40. A	49. D
5. C	14. D	23. B	32. D	41. B	50. A
6. B	15. B	24. A	33. B	42. A	
7. D	16. C	25. C	34. D	43. D	
8. D	17. A	26. C	35. D	44. B	
9. A	18. C	27. B	36. A	45. B	

Answer Explanations

GROUP ONE

1. **D** Choice A is wrong because this procedure does not apply to department vehicles. Choice B is wrong because the clerk prepares the report from information supplied by the police officer. Choice C is wrong because it is the ranking officer who conducts the investigation who also endorses the report.

2. **D** If you missed this question you probably overlooked the word "always" in the stem of the question. The name of the owner of other property damaged can be included in the report only if there is, in fact, other property involved. If department property is damaged, it does not necessarily mean that other property will always be involved. Be careful of the word "always"; it is a very strong word.

3. **B** This should have been easy for you. Remember, however, that you will see questions like this on the examination, and that your enemy is carelessness. Whenever you are dealing with lists, make certain that you take the time to read them accurately.

4. **C** This is an example of a question that tests your ability to understand a police narrative. A key element in the stem is that one of the cars left the scene and that nothing is known about that car. That is why choices A and B are not the answer; we do not know if the third car was damaged or if anyone in it was injured. Choice D is not the answer because there is nothing in the passage that confirms it as the answer. Remember, the answer is to be based on the information in the stem of the question. Choice C is correct. According to the passage, the driver and *both* passengers of the car that caught on fire were severely burned. This means that there were three people in that car.

5. **C** The key to the correct answer is the fact that the stutter, the limp, and the red hair and long fingernails could all be contrived. Criminals will, many times, deliberately alter their appearance and physical characteristics to conceal their true identity. However, the fact that the female was stabbed is factual.

6. **B** Procedure 2a specifically states that insurance identification cards are required only for cars with New York State plates. This car had New Jersey plates.

7. **D** Procedure 11 states that summonses have to be delivered to the precinct of occurrence, which, according to the information in the narrative, was the 95th Precinct.

8. **D** According to the note after procedure 7, if one summons goes to criminal court, they all go to criminal court. Also, a summons must be used for each offense.

9. **A** Choice A is the answer because a prisoner's personal property is removed only if the prisoner is intoxicated or unconscious (procedure 9e). Choice D is not the correct answer because there is not enough information in the narrative to determine if it was a pick-up arrest. It might have been, but it is not certain.

10. **C** Procedure 4 clearly states that the prisoner is to be searched before being taken to the station house. Choice A is not the right answer because the prisoner does not have to be given his rights unless questioning is going to take place (procedure 5). Nor was the cause of arrest to be given since the suspect was caught in the act.

GROUP TWO

11. **C** If you picked Choice A, you probably missed the fact that the two watches were worth $450 each, or a total of $900. It is probable that you will be asked to do simple arithmetic on the examination, so be ready.

12. **D** If you picked Choice B, you probably confused the meaning of the words "establish" and "verify."

13. **C** This answer is contained in the first paragraph. If you are not sure of the meaning of the word "mandate," make sure you look it up and then repeat the question. Remember to constantly work to improve your vocabulary.

14. **D** Photographs can be taken any time the authority exists to take fingerprints. Fingerprints can be taken when the officer reasonably suspects that the prisoner is sought by other law enforcement officials.

15. **B** This question illustrates an important point. To answer this question properly, the student must realize that a hunch is different from "reasonable suspicion." Police officers have to make this distinction every day. Once again, the value of good vocabulary surfaces.

16. **C** Palmprints may be taken only if a person is fingerprinted. It is optional as long as the authority for fingerprinting does, in fact, exist.

17. **A** Reading an organization chart is simple once you understand how it is done. You should visualize arrows going out of the top of each box and into the bottom of a higher box. The box that the arrow leads to is the next in line in the chain of command. In this case, the line out of the top of the station house officer's box leads to the bottom of the station house supervisor's box.

18. **C** The line leaving the top of the clerical staff box leads directly into the bottom of the administrative lieutenant's box.

19. **B** The operations officer and the administrative lieutenant report directly to the executive officer.

20. **C** Detective Corcoran is on the anti-crime team, and he reports to the patrol supervisor, who is Sergeant Murphy. If you picked choice A, you probably thought you were looking for a correct statement. Remember, read all of the choices before settling on an answer. In this case, you would see right away that there is more than one correct statement, and you would have realized that you were looking for an incorrect statement.

GROUP THREE

21. **C** Procedure 1 prohibits consuming intoxicants while in uniform, with no exceptions. A uniformed officer can enter a premise which serves intoxicants to have a meal, but he/she cannot drink intoxicants while so doing. However, a police officer on duty in plain clothes can drink intoxicants. Choice D is not found in the regulations.

22. **A** Choices B, C, and D can be done under special circumstances.

23. **B** If the school board is not located in New York City, the officer can be a member of it. The other three choices are prohibited at all times to all officers.

24. **A** Procedure 4 specifically states that recommending a professional service is permitted if done while transacting personal affairs.

25. **C** Procedure 16 limits this prohibition to those members in uniform. Detective Mulligan works in plain clothes.

26. **C** The information in the question clearly establishes that he is on patrol in a very busy area, but does not say whether he is in uniform.

27. **B** Procedure 6 makes no exceptions to the rule that advising this type of payment is prohibited.

28. **A** Choice D may or may not be true, but your answer must be based on the information in the paragraph. Thus Choice A is the answer.

29. **C** A conviction requires proof beyond a reasonable doubt.

30. **A** In a civil action, the "case is won by the party who has the most evidence on her side." Fifty-one percent of the evidence has to be the "most" since there is only 49% left.

GROUP FOUR

31. **C** Choices A and B may be correct, but it doesn't say so in the paragraph.

32. **D** Military time runs from 0001 hours at one minute after midnight to 2400 hours at midnight on the next night.

33. **B** P.M. time after the 1200 hour is determined by adding 12 to the civilian time. Choice A represents the military equivalent of 3:28 A.M.

34. **D** Choice A is the equivalent of 35 minutes after midnight.

35. **D** Add 12 hours to 4:45 and you get 1645 hours.

36. **A** Choice B might be tempting, but military time uses a 24-hour clock. After 2400 hours, which is midnight, the time reverts to zero and starts over.

37. **D** No mention is made in the paragraph of the meaning of these initials.

38. **B** This question requires you to use information in two places in the paragraph to get the right answer. The explosion took place at 0050 hours (50 minutes after midnight). The bearded man was first seen one hour and ten minutes prior to that, which is 2340 hours.

39. **D** The explosion took place at 0050 hours, and 55 minutes later the telephone call was made. Fifty-five minutes after 0050 hours is 0145 hours.

40. **A** The bearded man was arrested at 8:35 P.M., which is 2035 hours.

GROUP FIVE

41. **B** Parking violations go to the Parking Violations Bureau, as indicated in the written material. The other three choices are not mentioned in the material and are not the answer.

42. **A** This is simply a matter of correctly interpreting the chart.

43. **D** If you picked choice A, you were careless. You were looking for N.Y.C., Part 6, and settled for N.Y.S., Part 6.

44. **B** Usually these summonses are forwarded to Part 6, except in Richmond, where they go to Part 1.

45. **B** This is simply a matter of locating the reference to 161.05 of the Health Code and associating it with unleashed dogs in the park.

46. **D** This is specifically stated in the procedures.

47. **B** If you picked choice A, you misread the information. The speed is circled when it is 25MPH or more *over* the speed limit.

48. **D** According to the note, government vehicles (U.S. mail trucks included) do not require registration plates.

49. **D** Officer Williams is required to confer with his commanding officer before going to court for a summons.

50. **A** Only prohibited hour sales require notification to a commanding officer.

CHAPTER 9

Understanding Legal Definitions

In this chapter you will be taught to deal with questions concerning legal definitions. The definitions used on the examination are based on state law. However, the exact wording of the law is not used. The test writers amend the laws to make it easier to write questions and to make the laws more understandable for you. Thus, you must learn to forget anything you might already know about the law. As in all similar examination questions, answer *only* on the basis of the given information.

Two Key Words

Students of the law know that two little words, "and" plus "or," are the most important words in the law. Many laws have more than one element that must exist simultaneously before a crime is committed. Some laws have a number of elements, and the existence of any one of them results in the commission of a crime. The most common way to show these distinctions is with the words "and" and "or." To understand this principle better, consider the following examples:

a. The crime of burglary is committed when a person illegally enters a building, *and* illegally removes property from therein.
b. The crime of burglary is committed when a person illegally enters a building, *or* illegally removes property from a building.

In the first example (example A), two things (or elements) have to happen before the crime of burglary is committed. A person has to illegally enter a building plus he has to illegally remove some property from that building. Doing one element, either illegally entering or illegally removing property, may be some other crime, but based on the wording of example A, it is not burglary.

In the second example (example B), only one of the two elements has to happen for the crime of burglary to be committed. If a person illegally enters a building he has committed burglary even if he does not steal property.

Be careful, therefore, when you see these two little words in the legal definitions on your examination, and make sure that you understand the difference either word can make in the meaning of a law.

The Two Question Types

The two types of questions you are likely to encounter in this area are very similar to the question categories you learned about in the chapter on police procedures and directives. They are as follows:

DIRECT UNDERSTANDING OF A LEGAL DEFINITION

In this question type, you will be given a legal definition or a series of legal definitions. Then, based *solely* on the information contained in that definition, you will be asked to identify accurate or inaccurate statements, or choose the best application of the legal definition involved. A simple example of this type of question is as follows:

EXAMPLE.
The crime of grand larceny occurs when a person takes permanent possession of the property of another without proper authorization, and the value of the property exceeds $1,000.

Based solely on the above information, which of the following is a correct statement concerning the crime of grand larceny?

(A) Stealing a fifty-dollar radio could be grand larceny.
(B) Taking temporary possession of property could be grand larceny.
(C) The value of the property taken is a key element in the crime of grand larceny.
(D) Grand larceny is a felony.

Answer C

APPLYING A NARRATIVE TO A LEGAL DEFINITION

In this question type, you are given a legal definition or a series of legal definitions, as well as a narrative which usually describes some form of criminal misconduct. You are then asked to apply the details of the narrative to the legal definition and to choose a correct (or incorrect) answer. An example of this type of question is as follows:

EXAMPLE.
The crime of grand larceny occurs when a person takes permanent possession of the property of another without proper authorization, and the value of the property exceeds $1,000.

On June 18, Charles Young went to the home of his college classmate, Bob Smith. Young had a heavy date that evening and intended to borrow Smith's new motorcycle, valued at $4,280. Finding no one home at Smith's house, Young used a master key and took his classmate's motorcycle without permission. Five hours later, Young returned the motorcycle but was forced to leave it in a different parking spot from where he took it. Shortly thereafter, Smith went to use the motorcycle and discovered it missing from where he had parked it. He called the police and reported it stolen.

Based solely on the above information, Young:

(A) Committed the crime of grand larceny since the motorcycle was valued at more than $1,000.
(B) Did not commit the crime of grand larceny since he did not take permanent possession of the motorcycle.
(C) Committed the crime of grand larceny since he did not have permission to take the motorcycle.
(D) Did not commit the crime of grand larceny since he was acquainted with the owner of the motorcycle.

Answer B

Strategies for Handling Legal Definitions

In this section we will offer a recommended strategy to follow when answering questions in each of the two categories described above.

HOW TO UNDERSTAND A LEGAL DEFINITION

1. **SCAN THE LEGAL DEFINITION.** Quickly read the legal definition (or definitions) while looking for and underlining key words and elements.

2. **READ THE QUESTION.** Read the stem of each question. Sometimes you will get one definition and one question. Other times you will get a series of definitions and a series of questions. The questions are always based *solely* on those definitions. The purpose of reading the stems quickly is to allow you to focus in on the pertinent sections of the definitions when you re-read them. Also, scan some of the choices for the same reason.

3. **READ THE LEGAL DEFINITION CAREFULLY.** You now have an idea of what is contained in the definitions and the questions. Your next task is to read the definition carefully, and concentrate. Also remember to ask yourself questions while reading. Remember to use your pencil to highlight important words or phrases in the definitions. You can also write in the margin next to the information you recognize as being pertinent, based on your initial reading of the questions.

4. **ANSWER THE QUESTION(S).** Remember, you look at the definitions to verify your answer and this is easily done if you've used your pencil effectively, as explained in item 3 above.

HOW TO APPLY A NARRATIVE TO A LEGAL DEFINITION

As previously discussed, these questions contain one or more legal definitions, followed by one or more narratives, and then the actual choices. Your approach to these questions should be as follows:

1. **SCAN THE LEGAL DEFINITION(S).** Get a good idea of the laws being described. Make sure you recognize the key words and various elements that are involved in each defined crime. Visualize the crime taking place, and use your pencil to emphasize the key words and thoughts.

2. **SCAN THE NARRATIVE(S).** Get a quick idea of the situation described in the narrative. The major objective of this initial scanning is to see how the narrative relates to the definitions.

3. **SCAN THE QUESTION(S).** Read the stem of each question involved and scan the choices to get an idea of what you will be asked. This will help you focus in on pertinent material when re-reading the definitions and narratives.

   NOTE: Don't waste too much time on Steps 1 through 3. All that is required is that you get a good idea of the definition, a quick idea of the details of the narrative, and an awareness of the focus of the questions.

4. **RE-READ THE DEFINITION(S).** If you use your pencil effectively in the first reading, this re-reading should be easy. This time, however, be especially alert for information relating to the questions.

5. **READ THE NARRATIVE.** Use your pencil, ask yourself questions, and "put yourself into the story." You already know what the definitions contain and what the questions ask, so direct your attention to the most important parts of the story.

6. **ANSWER THE QUESTION(S).** Refer to the written material when answering the questions. However, you can save time if you have used your pencil effectively in the steps above. Also, remember to use the test-taking strategies outlined in an earlier chapter while answering the questions.

Practice Exercises

GROUP ONE—25 Minute Time Limit

***DIRECTIONS:* Answer questions 1 through 15 based *solely* on the content of the legal definitions given. Do not use any other knowledge of the law that you may have. You may refer to the definitions when answering the questions.**

NOTE: The perpetrators in the following definitions are referred to as "he" solely for ease of examination. However, the pronoun "he" refers to either gender.

arson A person commits arson when he intentionally damages a motor vehicle or a building by causing an explosion or otherwise starting a fire. If the building is worth more than $10,000, or the motor vehicle is worth more than $7,500, it is second degree arson, which is a Class D felony. If the building or motor vehicle is occupied at the time of the fire, it is first degree arson, which is a Class B felony. All other arsons are third degree arson, which is a Class E felony.

assault A person commits assault when he intends to cause a physical injury to another person, and he commits an act which causes physical injury to that person or any other person. This is simple assault, which is a misdemeanor. If the assault results in serious physical injury, or if a deadly weapon is used to commit the assault, or if more than one person commits the assault, it is a felonious assault, which is a Class D felony. However, if an assault is committed in self-defense, no crime has been committed.

criminal mischief A person commits criminal mischief when he intends to damage the property of another and, without any legal right to do so, does damage to that person's property. If the property is worth more than $250, it is a Class E felony and constitutes criminal mischief in the first degree. If the property is worth $250 or less, it is criminal mischief in the second degree, which is a misdemeanor.

petit larceny A person commits petit larceny when he takes property belonging to another person without that person's consent, with the intent to keep the property for his own or someone else's use, and the property is worth $250 or less. Petit larceny is a misdemeanor.

robbery A person commits robbery when he takes the property of another person by the use or threatened use of force against that person or another person. The force used must be to prevent or overcome resistance to the taking of the property. Robbery is a felony in all degrees.

adultery A person commits adultery when he engages in sexual intercourse with another person and either he or the other person has a living spouse at that time. Adultery is a misdemeanor.

bribe receiving A public servant commits bribe receiving when he asks for, or accepts, a benefit on the understanding that his official actions will thereby be influenced. Bribe receiving is a Class E felony.

burglar's tools A person commits the crime of burglar's tools when he possesses an instrument which is commonly used in the commission of burglary, larceny, or theft of services. Burglar's tools is a misdemeanor.

consensual sodomy A person commits the crime of consensual sodomy when he engages in oral or anal sex with another person who is not his spouse at the time. Consensual sodomy is a misdemeanor.

criminal contempt A person commits criminal contempt when he refuses to be sworn in before a grand jury or a court, or he refuses to answer the legal questions of a grand jury or a court. Criminal contempt is a misdemeanor.

criminal impersonation A person commits criminal impersonation when he pretends to be a police officer, a parole officer, a fireman, or any other public servant, with the intent of having someone submit to his authority. Criminal impersonation is a misdemeanor.

burglary in the first degree A person commits burglary in the first degree when he knowingly enters or remains unlawfully in a dwelling with intent to commit a crime therein, and while effecting the entry, or while inside the dwelling, or in the immediate flight from the dwelling, he or another participant in the crime is armed with explosives or a deadly weapon, or uses a dangerous instrument, or causes injury to someone who is not a participant in the crime. Burglary in the first degree is a Class B felony.

1. Hugh Bett sets fire to his own farmhouse in order to collect the fire insurance. The house is worth $8,500.

Based upon the above information, Hugh Bett has committed:

(A) Arson in the third degree.
(B) Arson in the second degree.
(C) Arson in the first degree.
(D) No crime since he owns the farmhouse.

1 A B C D

2. Tom, who is armed with a deadly weapon, finds the front door of a private residence open. He enters, looking for money, and takes $150 in United States currency from a bedroom nightstand.

Based upon the above information, Tom should:

(A) Not be charged with burglary in the first degree because he did not injure anyone.
(B) Be charged with burglary in the first degree, which is a Class C felony.
(C) Not be charged with burglary in the first degree since he did not threaten anyone with a weapon.
(D) Be charged with burglary in the first degree since it was a dwelling, and he was armed with a deadly weapon.

2 A B C D

3. Which of the following is the most accurate statement concerning the crime of assault?

(A) Assault is always a felony.
(B) To commit the crime of assault, you must injure the party whom you intended to assault.
(C) Felonious assault can occur even though no serious physical injury results.
(D) Simple assault is a Class E felony.

3 A B C D

4. Larkin has an ongoing feud with his neighbor, Phillips. Whatever Larkin buys for his home, Phillips immediately purchases for his home. One day, Larkin took a rake worth $20, which he believed was Phillip's property, and damaged it.

4 A B C D

The rake actually belonged to Larkin, as Mrs. Larkin had lent it to the Phillips family earlier.

Based upon the above information, Larkin is guilty of:

(A) A misdemeanor.
(B) A felony.
(C) A felony or a misdemeanor, depending upon the amount of damage.
(D) No crime.

5. Roe sells Jones an automobile for $3,000. Jones begins to boast that Roe was stupid for selling the automobile so cheaply. Roe sees the car parked in the street one night and sets fire to it, not knowing that an old derelict is sleeping in the back seat.

A B C D
5 | | | | | | | |

Based upon the above information, Roe committed:

(A) A Class E felony.
(B) Either a Class E felony or a Class D felony, depending upon the true market value of the automobile.
(C) A Class B felony.
(D) A misdemeanor.

6. Smith and West are told by their cousin, Green, that John Harper has been spreading rumors about them. In fact, Harper does not even know Smith and West. One evening, Smith and West attack Harper on his way home from work. Harper is trained in self-defense and fights back fiercely. Although Harper receives a minor injury in the fight, Smith and West have to go to the hospital for treatment of their injuries.

A B C D
6 | | | | | | | |

Based upon the above information, which of the following is the most accurate statement:

(A) Smith, West, and Harper are not guilty of a crime since it is a personal matter.
(B) Smith, West, and Green are all guilty of a felony.
(C) Smith and West are guilty of a Class D felony.
(D) Harper is guilty of simple assault.

7. Which of the following is an *inaccurate* statement concerning the crime of criminal mischief?

(A) Damage to property must always take place for the crime to be committed.
(B) Criminal mischief is sometimes a misdemeanor.
(C) The difference between first degree and second degree is the value of the damaged property.
(D) Under certain circumstances, criminal mischief can be a Class D felony.

A B C D
7 | | | | | | | |

8. Which of the following crimes is always a felony?

(A) Theft of property worth $225.
(B) Arson of an automobile worth $200.
(C) Intentional damage to another person's property valued at $245.
(D) Assault of a seventeen-year-old female by an adult.

A B C D
8 | | | | | | | |

9. Which of the following is the most *inaccurate* statement concerning the crime of robbery?

(A) The property of another must be taken for the crime to be completed.
(B) A person who commits robbery is always guilty of a felony.
(C) Force must be used against the person whose property is involved for the crime to be committed.
(D) The threat of force is sufficient to commit the crime of robbery.

A B C D
9 | | | | | | | |

10. Harvey is a traveling salesman. While on the road, he falls in love with Ellen, who is not married. Harvey tells Ellen he is not married although in fact he is. He romances Ellen and one night invites her to his motel room. They begin to embrace when suddenly Harvey's wife calls on the phone. Very upset, Ellen leaves and returns to her home.

Based upon the above information, which of the following is the most accurate statement?

(A) Harvey committed adultery since he was married.
(B) Harvey and Ellen both committed adultery.
(C) Harvey and Ellen would have been guilty of a felony if they had engaged in sexual intercourse.
(D) Neither Harvey nor Ellen has committed a crime.

A B C D
10 | | | | | | | |

11. Police Officer Barry finds Moe in possession of an instrument which is commonly used in committing the crime of larceny. Moe should be charged with:

(A) Attempted petit larceny.
(B) Petit larceny.
(C) Burglar's tools.
(D) No crime since there was no indication of intent to use the instrument illegally.

11 A B C D

12. Former City Councilman Lively has been subpoenaed before a grand jury to answer questions about his activities when in office. Lively answers the subpoena, but refuses to be sworn in.

Based upon the above information, which of the following is the most accurate statement?

(A) Lively has a right to refuse to be sworn in since he is no longer in public office.
(B) Lively could be guilty of a misdemeanor.
(C) If Lively refuses to answer the questions of the grand jury, he will commit a felony.
(D) Lively is not committing any crime since the grand jury is acting in an illegal manner.

12 A B C D

13. Feeble is a corrupt city water inspector. Over the years, he has received bribes in excess of $10,000. He accepts the bribes in exchange for his promise that his official actions will be influenced. In fact, he never alters his official actions for anyone.

Based upon the above information, Feeble could, if discovered:

(A) Not be charged with any crime since he never altered his official actions.
(B) Be charged with a misdemeanor for accepting the bribes.
(C) Not be charged with any crime because he is not a public servant.
(D) Be charged with a Class E felony based solely on his promise to alter his official actions.

13 A B C D

14. Ralph Sparks is a fireman. However, he always wanted to be a police officer. One day, Ralph put on a borrowed police uniform and directed traffic at an intersection close to his home. While he was directing traffic, he did a good job despite a heavy flow of trucks and buses. However, after an hour or so Ralph got tired and returned home.

14 A B C D

Based upon the above information, Ralph has:

(A) Committed criminal impersonation because it was his intent to have the motorists submit to his authority.

(B) Not committed criminal impersonation since he is a public servant in his own right.

(C) Committed criminal impersonation since the uniform he used was a borrowed one.

(D) Not committed criminal impersonation since he did a good job of directing traffic.

15. Which of the following is the *least* accurate statement concerning consensual sodomy? 15 A B C D

(A) Consensual sodomy can be committed between persons of the same gender.

(B) Consensual sodomy is a misdemeanor.

(C) Consensual sodomy can be committed even if the two people involved are willing participants.

(D) Married persons cannot be charged with consensual sodomy.

GROUP TWO—15 Minute Time Limit

***DIRECTIONS:* Answer questions 16 through 25 based *solely* on the content of the legal definitions given. Do not use any other knowledge of the law that you may have. You may refer to the definitions when answering the questions.**

NOTE: The perpetrators in the following definitions are referred to as "he" solely for ease of examination. However, the pronoun "he" refers to either gender.

criminal trespass A person is guilty of criminal trespass when he knowingly enters or remains unlawfully in a building.

criminally negligent homicide A person commits criminally negligent homicide when he causes the death of another person by engaging in negligent behavior which he failed to perceive as a risk to other person(s).

consensual sodomy A person commits the crime of consensual sodomy when he engages in oral or anal sex with another person who is not his spouse. Consensual sodomy is a misdemeanor.

criminal contempt A person commits criminal contempt when he refuses to be sworn in before a grand jury or a court, or when he refuses to answer the legal questions of a grand jury or a court.

bribe receiving A public servant commits bribe receiving when he asks for, or accepts, a benefit on the understanding that his official actions will thereby be influenced.

aggravated harassment A person commits aggravated harassment when he intends to annoy or alarm another person, and he makes a telephone call to that person with no legitimate purpose of communication. It does not matter whether a conversation takes place.

murder A person commits murder when, with the intent to cause the death of another person, he does cause the death of that person.

burglary A person commits burglary when he knowingly enters or remains unlawfully in a building or a dwelling with the intent to commit a crime therein. A dwelling is a building wherein someone usually lodges overnight.

bribery A person commits bribery when he offers or gives some benefit to a public servant so that the public servant's official actions will be influenced.

manslaughter A person commits manslaughter when, with the intent to cause physical injury to another person, he causes that person's death.

16. Ms. Jones, who is 19 years of age, is upset with her physics professor, Mr. Allen. She obtains his home phone number and calls him late at night to annoy him.

16 A B C D

Based upon the above information, Ms. Jones has:

(A) Committed aggravated harassment since she called him at his home.
(B) Not committed aggravated harassment since she was under 21 years of age at the time.
(C) Committed aggravated harassment since her intent was to annoy him.
(D) Not committed aggravated harassment since no conversation took place.

17. Which of the following is the most accurate statement concerning the crime of burglary?

17 A B C D

(A) A burglary can only take place in a dwelling.
(B) Unlawful intent must exist for the crime of burglary to be committed.
(C) A person must steal property for the crime of burglary to be committed.
(D) A dwelling is any place where a person sleeps overnight.

18. Young Rick and Ted hide in a rest room in Madison Square Garden. They remain there long past the time paying customers are authorized to be in the arena. When they think it is safe, they come out and play a one-on-one basketball game on the garden floor. After the game, they go home. A B C D 18 | | | | | | | |

Based upon the above information, Rick and Ted have:

(A) Committed no crime since they did not have an unlawful intent.
(B) Committed burglary since they unlawfully remained in a building.
(C) Committed no crime since their actions went undetected.
(D) Committed criminal trespass even though they had no unlawful intent.

19. Which of the following is the *least* accurate statement concerning the crime of bribery? A B C D 19 | | | | | | | |

(A) The actual giving of a benefit is not necessary for the crime to be committed.
(B) An intent to influence the public servant's actions is necessary for the crime to be committed.
(C) Money must be offered or given to a public servant before the crime can be committed.
(D) It is not necessary for a public servant to take official action on behalf of the bribe giver for the crime of bribery to be committed.

20. Harry wants a well in his backyard, so he proceeds to dig a deep hole outside the rear entrance to his home. When darkness falls, he covers the hole with a canvas. Later that evening, Harry's five-year-old son goes into the backyard, and falls into the hole, which now has a considerable amount of water in it. As a result, the little boy dies. A B C D 20 | | | | | | | |

Based upon the above information, Harry has committed:

(A) No crime since the boy who died was his son.
(B) Murder since he caused the death of the little boy.
(C) Manslaughter since he did not intend to cause the boy's death even though it happened.
(D) Criminally negligent homicide since he should have perceived that his risky actions could cause someone's death.

21. Which of the following is the most accurate statement concerning the crime of bribe receiving?

21 A B C D

(A) The public servant must actually ask for the benefit for the crime to be committed.
(B) The public servant must actually accept a benefit for the crime to be committed.
(C) The public servant's official acts must, in fact, be influenced for the crime to be committed.
(D) A public servant must, in fact, be involved for the crime to be committed.

22. Joe Doe, who is a well-known racketeer, would be guilty of the crime of criminal contempt in all of the following instances *except*:

22 A B C D

(A) Refusing to answer the legal questions of a court.
(B) Refusing to be sworn in before a grand jury.
(C) Refusing to be sworn in before a court.
(D) Refusing to answer any questions of a grand jury.

23. Which of the following is the *least* accurate statement concerning the crime of consensual sodomy?

23 A B C D

(A) Force is not an element of consensual sodomy.
(B) Gender is not an element of consensual sodomy.
(C) A married person cannot commit the crime of consensual sodomy.
(D) Consensual sodomy is a misdemeanor.

24. Ruth wants to seriously injure Ann. One day Ruth throws acid in Ann's face. Ann is then rushed to the hospital, where she dies several days later as a result of the acid-throwing incident.

24 A B C D

Based upon the above information, Ruth:

(A) Has committed the crime of aggravated harassment since she caused serious physical injury to Ann.
(B) Has committed criminally negligent homicide since she failed to perceive the risk involved in her actions.
(C) Has committed the crime of manslaughter since with the intent to cause physical injury to Ann she caused her death.
(D) Has committed murder since her actions caused Ann's death.

25. Which of the following is the *least* accurate statement concerning the crime of murder?

(A) An intent to kill must be present for the crime to be committed.
(B) The intended victim must die for the crime to be committed.
(C) A weapon need not be involved for the crime to be committed.
(D) It need not be the intended victim who dies for the crime to be committed.

25 A B C D

GROUP THREE—15 Minute Time Limit

***DIRECTIONS:* Answer questions 26 through 35 based *solely* on the content of the legal definitions given. Do not use any other knowledge of the law that you may have. You may refer to the definitions when answering the questions.**

NOTE: The perpetrators in the following definitions are referred to as "he" solely for ease of examination. However, the pronoun "he" refers to either gender.

menacing A person commits the crime of menacing when, through physical threat, he intentionally places, or attempts to place, another person in fear of immediate physical injury.

reckless endangerment in the second degree A person commits this crime when he recklessly engages in conduct which creates a substantial risk of serious physical injury to another person. It is a misdemeanor.

reckless endangerment in the first degree A person commits this crime when, under circumstances indicating a grave indifference for human life, he engages in conduct which creates a grave risk of death to another person. It is a Class D felony.

reckless endangerment of property A person is guilty of this crime when he recklessly engages in conduct which creates a substantial risk of damage to the property of another. It is a misdemeanor.

promoting a suicide attempt A person is guilty of this crime when he intentionally causes, or aids, another person in attempting suicide. It is a Class E felony. However, if the person attempting suicide does, in fact, die as a result of the suicide attempt, then the person rendering the aid is guilty of murder.

theft of services A person is guilty of this crime when he fails to pay for subway, bus, or other transportation service. It is a misdemeanor.

sexual abuse A person commits this crime when he subjects another to sexual contact, without the latter's consent. This crime cannot be committed by persons married to each other. It is a misdemeanor.

rape A male commits this crime when he has sexual intercourse with a female by force and against her will, or in any instance when the male is over 21 years of age and the female is less than 17 years of age. This law does not apply to persons who are legally married to each other. It is a Class B felony.

sodomy A person commits sodomy when he forces another person against that person's will to engage in oral or anal sex; or, in any instance when he is over 21 years of age and the other person is less than 17 years of age. This law does not apply to persons who are legally married to each other. It is a Class B felony.

burglar's tools A person commits this crime when he possesses an instrument which is commonly used in the commission of the crimes of burglary, larceny, or theft of services. It is a misdemeanor.

assault A person assaults another person when he intends to cause a physical injury to another person, and he does commit an act which causes physical injury to that person or any other person.

jostling A person commits jostling when, in a public place, he intentionally places his hand near the pocket or handbag of another person, or unnecessarily crowds another person, while an accomplice places his hand near another person's pocket or handbag. It is a misdemeanor.

criminal mischief A person commits criminal mischief when he intends to damage another person's property and, without any legal right to do so, he does damage that person's property.

26. Howard approaches Felix and tells him that he is going to get even for what Felix has said about him. Howard then produces a baseball bat and intentionally waves it at Felix. Howard then tells Felix that he is going to knock his brains out. Felix laughs and walks away unharmed, leaving Howard standing there waving his bat.

26 A B C D

Based upon the above information, Howard has:

(A) Committed an assault since he intended to cause injury to Felix.

(B) Committed reckless endangerment in the second degree since he recklessly created a risk of serious physical injury to Felix.

(C) Committed menacing since he intentionally attempted to place Felix in fear of immediate physical injury.

(D) Committed no crime since Felix walked away unharmed.

27. Larry comes home one night and finds his wife very despondent. She confides in him that she is contemplating suicide. He tells her that if she wishes, he will provide her with sleeping tablets to do the job. She agrees. The next day she takes a large dose of sleeping tablets which Larry has supplied. Her intent is to kill herself, but some friends intervene, and she is rushed to the hospital and is saved. 27 A B C D

Based upon the above information, Larry is:
(A) Not guilty of any crime.
(B) Guilty of assault.
(C) Guilty of menacing.
(D) Guilty of promoting a suicide attempt.

28. Hal places his hand on the buttocks of a 19-year-old boy on a crowded subway. The boy is quite annoyed and quickly gets off at the next stop. 28 A B C D

Based upon the above information, Hal is guilty of:
(A) Jostling.
(B) Sodomy.
(C) Sexual abuse.
(D) No crime.

29. Which of the following acts does *not* constitute the crime of burglar's tools? 29 A B C D
(A) Possessing a slug to be used in place of a token to get on the subway.
(B) Possessing a "jimmy" used to gain entry to a building to commit a burglary
(C) Possessing a handgun to be used in a robbery
(D) Possessing a false-bottom box to be used to commit larceny from retail stores

30. Chris is fed up with his mother-in-law, who is very elderly and has been somewhat depressed lately. She tells him that if she could get the courage, she would kill herself. Chris opens the window and tells her, "Go ahead, it's easy." She then goes to the window and leaps to her death. 30 A B C D

Based on the above information, Chris has committed:
(A) Reckless endangerment in the first degree.
(B) Promoting a suicide attempt.
(C) Assault.
(D) Murder.

31. After school one day, Tom, Dick, and Jerry, three high school students, decide to jump over the subway turnstile to get on the train without paying. They just want to do it for fun and mean no harm to anyone. However, they are apprehended by the Transit Police.

Based upon the above information, they have committed:

(A) Criminal mischief.
(B) Jostling.
(C) Burglar's tools.
(D) Theft of services.

A B C D
31 || || || ||

32. Police Officer Gordon sees a man with a sledge hammer beating on the hood of a very expensive car. He approaches the man and asks him what he is doing. The man says that he has had an argument with his wife and is venting his frustration by beating on his own car, which he proves he owns. Officer Gordon then places the man under arrest for the crime of criminal mischief.

Based upon the above information, the officer's actions were:

(A) Correct since the man was causing damage to a very expensive automobile.
(B) Incorrect since the damage had already been done to the car.
(C) Correct since the incident took place in a public place.
(D) Incorrect since you cannot commit criminal mischief to your own property.

A B C D
32 || || || ||

33. Which of the following is the most accurate statement concerning the crime of reckless endangerment?

(A) It is always a felony.
(B) It is always a misdemeanor.
(C) Someone must always be injured for the crime to be committed.
(D) The difference in the degrees of the crime revolves around the seriousness of the risk created.

A B C D
33 || || || ||

34. Tom has just started a new job and does not want to be late on his first day. As he approaches the subway turnstile, he notices that he has forgotten his tokens. There is a very long line at the token booth and a train is just pulling into the station. Tom jumps over the turnstile and gets on the

A B C D
34 || || || ||

train. He makes himself a promise that he will send the Transit Authority the fare in the mail.

Based on the above information, Tom has committed:

(A) A violation.
(B) A misdemeanor.
(C) A felony.
(D) No crime.

35. Which of the following is the most accurate statement concerning the crime of rape?

(A) Gender is an element of the crime of rape.
(B) A female less than 17 years of age must be involved.
(C) The crime of rape cannot be committed if the female involved is a willing participant.
(D) The element of force must be present.

35 A B C D

Answer Key and Explanations

Answer Key

1. A	**7. D**	**13. D**	**19. C**	**25. D**	**31. D**
2. D	**8. B**	**14. A**	**20. D**	**26. C**	**32. D**
3. C	**9. C**	**15. D**	**21. D**	**27. D**	**33. D**
4. D	**10. D**	**16. C**	**22. D**	**28. C**	**34. B**
5. C	**11. C**	**17. B**	**23. C**	**29. C**	**35. A**
6. C	**12. B**	**18. D**	**24. C**	**30. D**	

Answer Explanations

GROUP ONE

1. A The farmhouse is worth $8,500. Thus, it is arson in the third degree. Do not confuse the value of motor vehicles with the value of buildings.

2. D Tom unlawfully entered a dwelling and was armed with a deadly weapon. Therefore, Choice D is correct. There is no need to threaten or injure anyone if the perpetrator is armed with a deadly weapon. It is burglary in the first degree.

3. C There is more than one way that an assault can become a felony. Even though no serious physical injury is involved, felonious assault can occur if more than one person commits the assault.

4. D To commit criminal mischief, you must damage someone's property other than your own.

5. C Setting fire to an automobile with a person in it is arson in the first degree regardless of the value of the automobile or the lack of knowledge that it was occupied.

6. C According to the definitions, when more than one person assaults another person, it is a felonious assault. Harper is entitled to defend himself.

7. D Criminal mischief in the first degree is a Class E felony. It goes no higher.

8. B Arson is always a felony. Depending upon the circumstances, the other three crimes could be felonies or misdemeanors.

9. **C** The use of force in robbery can be directed at the person who owns the property or at any other person.

10. **D** Since no sexual intercourse took place, no crime was committed.

11. **C** According to the definitions, mere possession is enough to be charged with the crime. This is one instance where outside knowledge of the law could harm you, since in reality more than mere possession is needed to commit this crime.

12. **B** The crime involved is criminal contempt, and it is a misdemeanor. The definition for that crime mentions nothing about being a public official.

13. **D** No change of official action is needed to commit this crime. Simply receiving the benefit with an understanding that official acts will be influenced is sufficient.

14. **A** Ralph made all of the motorists submit to his authority while he was directing traffic. Thus, Ralph committed criminal impersonation.

15. **D** Married persons can commit consensual sodomy by engaging in it with other than their legal spouses.

GROUP TWO

16. **C** To commit aggravated harassment, you do not have to converse with the person you are calling. The key element of the crime is the intent to annoy or alarm.

17. **B** The other three choices are wrong. A burglary can take place in a building; property does not have to be stolen; and a dwelling is a "building," not "any place."

18. **D** Rick and Ted unlawfully remained in a building, which makes them guilty of criminal trespass.

19. **C** Money is just one form of a benefit. Therefore, the giving or offering of money is not a necessary element of bribery.

20. **D** Harry should have perceived the risk he created by his actions. It was not manslaughter because Harry did not intend to injure anyone; he was merely negligent.

21. **D** A public servant must be involved in bribe receiving, but he need not actually ask for a bribe or actually receive it.

22. D The word "any" makes this choice wrong. The only questions that have to be answered are legal questions.

23. C Married persons cannot commit this crime with their own spouses, but they could commit it with other people.

24. C Manslaughter occurs when someone intends to injure another person, but instead causes that person's death.

25. D For the crime of murder to be committed, the person who dies must be the person whom the murderer intended to kill.

GROUP THREE

26. C Howard acted intentionally. Therefore, it was not a reckless endangerment. The critical factor was Howard's intent.

27. D The suicide attempt need not be successful for Larry to be guilty of a crime. The fact that he intentionally aided another person to attempt suicide is sufficient. In fact, if Larry's wife had died, he would be guilty of murder.

28. C The key to this answer is that the teenage boy did not give his consent.

29. C Robbery is not one of the crimes specifically named in the definition of burglar's tools.

30. D Chris helped his mother-in-law commit suicide. Therefore, Chris committed murder.

31. D The crime is committed when a person fails to pay the fare. Intent is not an issue in this crime.

32. D According to the definitions, a person cannot commit criminal mischief on his own property.

33. D The difference in these two crimes is a difference in the risk created. In one case, it is a risk of serious physical injury; in the other, it is a grave risk of death.

34. B Tom committed theft of services, which is a misdemeanor.

35. A According to the definitions provided, rape is one crime where gender is an element of the crime. In this definition, rape is committed by males against females.

CHAPTER 10

Troublesome Question Types

Since this book was first published, the authors have been monitoring the entrance examinations given by major police departments. We have noted that, although the types of questions outlined in the original edition of this book have, in fact, been used on most such examinations, there are some variations of the original types of questions that seem to give candidates difficulty. This chapter provides a strategy to deal with such questions.

Troublesome Types of Questions

1. **SENTENCE ORDERING QUESTIONS.** In this type of question, the candidate is given a series of sentences, usually five, and then tested to determine if he or she can arrange those sentences in the most logical sequence.
2. **TRAFFIC MAP QUESTIONS.** This question type tests the candidate's ability to go from one location on a map to another location. Questions are based on the ability to follow directions while using a map that contains such things as one way streets and dead end streets.

3. **"MATCHING SKETCHES" QUESTIONS.** This is a strictly non-verbal type question in which the candidate is shown a sketch of a person's face and then usually asked to select the same person from among a group of four other sketches. Sometimes you are asked to choose which one of four sketches is *not* the same person as the original sketch.

4. **"DIRECTED PATROL" QUESTIONS.** In this question type the candidate is given a number of facts about crimes and/or other police incidents. The candidate is then asked to select, based on the data provided, the optimum patrol areas and times to best prevent recurrence of the crime or incident involved.

5. **ARITHMETIC QUESTIONS.** Many departments have gone back to asking questions that test a candidate's ability to perform the basic addition and subtraction skills needed by a police officer in the course of his or her day's work. In one common version of the typical arithmetic question, the candidate is given a listing of lost or stolen property and required to select the choice that most accurately reflects the total value of the stolen property.

6. **"FREQUENCY OF INFORMATION" QUESTIONS.** In this question type, the candidate is given information from a number of different sources, usually four, and asked to determine which information is most likely to be accurate. For example, the candidate might be given four different license plate numbers that are quite similar, and asked to select the plate number that is most likely to be accurate. In essence, this question type tests the candidate's ability to apply the law of probability.

7. **"FIND THE PERPETRATOR" QUESTIONS.** Here the candidate is given a description of a criminal suspect who is in custody as well as descriptions of suspects in other crimes. Typically, the description includes such things as the suspect's age, height, weight, scars, clothing worn, and hair style. The idea is to test the candidate's ability to determine whether the suspect in custody could possibly be the suspect in the other crimes.

8. **"APPLYING POLICE POLICY" QUESTIONS.** Here the candidate is given a statement about the policy of a police department and then tested to see whether he/she can apply that policy. These questions, which bear some resemblance to reading comprehension questions, are somewhat different in that they require the candidate to exercise judgment similar to that of a police officer during his/her tour of duty.

9. **"FORMULA" QUESTIONS.** These questions are designed to measure the candidate's ability to determine the correct method to make certain calculations, such as how much of a police officer's tour is spent performing a specific function. It is different from **Arithmetic Questions** in that the candidate is not asked to do the actual calculation, rather, to select the correct method or formula to make this calculation.

10. **"WANTED POSTER" QUESTIONS.** These questions are a variation of a method used by examiners to test a candidate's memory. The candidate is shown a group of "wanted posters," usually six different suspects, and allowed to view the posters for a short time, about five minutes. The posters themselves usually contain a sketch of the wanted person, and some written information about that person. As is the case with all memory type questions, the posters are then taken away and the candidate must answer questions about the information from the posters.

Please note that all of these item types are asked in a multiple-choice format. The remainder of this chapter will discuss strategies involved in answering each of these ten question types and will give practice exercises for each type.

Sentence Ordering Questions

This question type is just another way to test your ability to understand what you read. Typically you are given a series of numbered facts concerning an incident about which you, as a police officer, might have to make a report. Your task is to arrange the numbered sentences (facts) in logical order as if you were writing a report about the incident. Most of the time all you have to do is arrange the details in chronological (time) sequence. Once in a while there is no clear time order. In that case, the details should be arranged in logical reporting order.

RECOMMENDED STRATEGY

Many candidates answer these questions by first determining what they believe should be the correct order of all of the sentences and then comparing their sequence with the proposed answers to find the correct choice. This is an acceptable strategy for some, but given the large number of items like this on examinations, such a strategy is time consuming and tiring. We recommend the following strategy for answering these questions:

1. Bear in mind that the correct order is already listed for you as one of the choices. Since this is so, *use the suggested choices as a guide for arriving at the right answer.*

2. Concentrate initially on the first and last sentence in the ordering arrangement of each suggested choice from "A" to "D." It is always easiest to figure out what happened first in an incident and what happened last. Many times this is as far as you will have to go because you will eliminate all of the incorrect choices simply because they contain the wrong first and/or last sentence. If this sounds complicated, you will see as we go through some examples that it is really quite simple.

   - Begin with what comes first. Look at the choices from "A" through "D" and eliminate those which clearly have inappropriate sentences coming first. In about ten to twenty percent of the time this is all you will have to do. In other words, you will be able to answer the question, not by ordering the entire five sentences, but merely by deciding which sentence comes first. In any case, you will almost always be able to eliminate one or two choices with this first step.

   - Next, go through the same process to eliminate those choices with obviously wrong last sentences. In about fifty percent of the time, after this step, you will have arrived at the correct choice.

3. Look at the second sentence. If you have come to this step, that means that you have two (or more) choices with the same suggested first and last sentences. Therefore, you should now compare the second sentences. Select as your answer the choice which offers a second sentence that most logically follows the first. After this step you will almost always have arrived at the answer. Once in a while, however, you will have two choices with the same first, last, and second sentences. In those cases, go on to the final step as outlined below. We should mention, however, that selecting the correct second sentence is often quite easy and is sometimes a quicker indication of the answer than identifying which sentence should come last. Thus, if you are not sure about the last sentence, determine which is the second sentence, and, in all probability, your decision will be made much easier.

4. Compare sentences three and four. As a review, if you have come this far, it means you have at least two choices with the same first, second, and last sentences. The difference at this point has to come from the ordering of sentences three and four.

HELPFUL HINT: Learn to take advantage of the words "the" and "a" or "an." They are articles that are used with nouns. However, the first time the noun is mentioned in the report the article "a" or "an" is used. The next time the same noun is used, the article "the" is used. For example:

CORRECT ORDER	INCORRECT ORDER
1. A car has been stolen.	1. The car has been stolen.
2. The car belongs to John.	2. A car belongs to John.

This hint can help you many times. However, the sentences you are given may sometimes reflect a portion of the middle of a report so this rule does not always hold. Just the same, most of the time it can be relied on.

EXAMPLES AND EXPLANATIONS

AN EXAMPLE OF THE FIRST SENTENCE PROVIDING THE ANSWER

Police Officer Jones is completing an incident report concerning his rescue of a female being held hostage by an estranged lover. His report will contain the following five sentences:

1. I saw a male holding a .38 caliber revolver to a woman's head but he did not see me.
2. I then broke a door down and gained access to the house.
3. As I approached the house on foot, a gunshot rang out and I heard a scream.
4. A decoy auto brought me as close as possible to the house where a female was being held hostage.
5. I ordered the man to drop his weapon, and he released the woman and was taken into custody.

The most logical order for the above sentences to appear in the report is . . .

(A) 1,3,2,4,5 **(C)** 3,2,1,4,5
(B) 4,3,2,1,5 **(D)** 5,1,2,3,4

Answer Explanation:

According to the choices, which you will recall you should use as your guide, the following sentences come first:

Choice A—Sentence one comes first
Choice B—Sentence four comes first
Choice C—Sentence three comes first

Choice D—Sentence five comes first

NOTE: Sentence two *cannot possibly* come first since it is not listed as one of the choices.

This is one of those questions where all you have to do is to decide which sentence comes first and you arrive at the answer. This is so because each of the four choices lists a different first sentence. Upon reading sentences 1,3,4, and 5, it should be obvious to you that sentence 4 starts the actions and logically comes first. Before the action in the other sentences can occur, the officer has to be close to the house. Therefore, sentence 4 comes first and the correct answer is choice "B." And, remember, you arrived at the correct answer simply by choosing the first sentence, and not by ordering all five into the correct sequence. In this case you save time and effort.

AN EXAMPLE OF THE LAST SENTENCE PROVIDING THE ANSWER

In the above example, the first sentence gave you the answer. Now let's look at a more common question type, one in which the last sentence provides the key to answering the question:

Police Officer Schroeder responded to the scene of a burglary committed at the home of a local politician, Henry Club. Officer Schroeder's report of the incident will contain the following five sentences:

1. When Mr. Club attempted to stop the burglar by grabbing him, he was pushed to the floor.
2. The burglar had apparently gained access to the premises by forcing open the 3rd floor bedroom window.
3. Mr. Club sustained a head injury in the scuffle and the burglar left the home via the front entrance.
4. Finding nothing in the dresser, the burglar proceeded downstairs to the first floor where he was confronted by Mr. Club, who was reading in the library.
5. Once inside he searched the bedroom dresser.

The most logical order for the above sentences to appear in the report is:

(A) 5,4,1,2,3 **(C)** 2,4,5,3,1
(B) 2,5,4,1,3 **(D)** 3,2,1,5,4

Answer Explanation:

Following our strategy, we can quickly eliminate choices "A" and "D" because sentences 5 (choice "A") and 3 (choice "D") could not logically come first in the report. This leaves us with choices "B" and "C," both of which start with sentence 2, which makes sense because all of the action takes place after the burglar gained access to the premises. The next step we take is to look at the last sentence. If sentence 3 logically occurs last, then choice "C" is the answer. Please note how easy it is to make this decision. In sentence 3 the burglar left the premises. In sentence 1 the burglar was still in Mr. Club's home. The answer has to be choice "B." And, remember that you arrived at the answer without ordering all of the sentences.

AN EXAMPLE OF A QUESTION WHERE THE MIDDLE SENTENCES PROVIDE THE ANSWER

Now let's take a look at a question which requires you to look to the middle sentences to arrive at an answer. Remember, when this happens you should first check out sentence 2, and only go to sentences 3 and 4 if it is necessary. As mentioned above, however, sentence 2 is quite often the tipoff to the correct answer.

Police Officer Green is completing an entry in her memo book. The entry contains the following five sentences:

1. Mr. Aponte gave me a complete description of the robber.
2. Ray Aponte, owner of the Royal Coach Taxi Company, called to report he had just been robbed.
3. I then notified all vehicles on patrol to look for a black male in his early twenties wearing red pants and a blue shirt.
4. I arrived at the scene after being notified by the precinct that a robbery had just occurred at the Royal Coach Taxi Company.
5. Fifteen minutes later, a man fitting the description was arrested by a police officer on patrol six blocks from the taxi company.

The most logical order for the above sentences to appear in the memo book is . . .

(A) 2,1,4,3,5 **(C)** 2,4,1,3,5
(B) 2,4,3,1,5 **(D)** 2,4,1,5,3

Answer Explanation:

The first sentence listed offers no help since it is 2 in each of the four choices. A comparison of the last sentence just enables us to eliminate choice "D" since sentence 3 cannot possibly occur last. A comparison of the second sentences in choices "A," "B," and "C" allows us to eliminate choice "A" since the officer has to be on the scene before Aponte can give her a description of the robber. The only thing left to do is to compare the third and fourth sentences in choices "B" and "C." If sentence 3 should logically come before sentence 1, then choice "B" is the answer. And, if sentence 1 comes before sentence 3, then choice "C" is the answer. A comparison of sentences 1 and 3 clearly shows sentence 1 comes before sentence 3 since the description cannot be broadcast until the officer obtains it from the complainant. Choice "C" is the answer.

PRACTICE QUESTIONS

1. A certain police officer is completing a report about her response to a crime in progress. The report includes the following five sentences:

1. The officers saw two armed men run out of the liquor store and into a waiting car.
2. Police Officers Connor and Colella received the call and responded to the liquor store.
3. The robbers gave up without a struggle.
4. Connor and Colella blocked the getaway car with their patrol car.
5. A call came into the precinct reporting a robbery in progress at Goldberg's liquor store.

The most logical order for the above sentences to appear in the report is . . .

(A) 5,2,1,4,3 **(C)** 5,1,4,2,3
(B) 2,5,1,3,4 **(D)** 1,5,1,3,4

2. Police Officer Ellington is writing a report concerning a dispute in a tavern. The report will contain the following five sentences:

1. Jimmy Cleary, the bartender, ordered the two males out of the tavern.
2. Two men dressed in business suits entered the 14th Ave Tavern at 6:30 PM.
3. The two men refused to leave and started to beat up Cleary.
4. A customer in the tavern saw me on patrol and yelled to me to come and help Cleary.
5. The two men became very intoxicated and boisterous within a short while.

The most logical order for the above sentences to appear in the report is . . .

(A) 2,1,5,3,4 **(C)** 3,1,2,5,4
(B) 2,3,4,5,1 **(D)** 2,5,1,3,4

3. Police Officer Jane Lopez is writing a report concerning the discharge of a firearm. The report will contain the following five sentences:

1. The man fell to the ground when hit in the stomach with three bullets from the .22 caliber gun.
2. Hill's .22 caliber gun was seized and he was given a summons for not having a pistol permit.
3. James Hill, the owner of the Fidler's Tavern, shot a man who attempted to rob him.
4. Police Officer Goldberg responded and asked Hill for his pistol permit, which he could not produce.
5. Hill phoned the police to report he had just shot a man who had attempted to rob him.

The most logical order for the above sentences to appear in the report is . . .

(A) 3,1,5,4,2 **(C)** 3,1,5,2,4
(B) 1,3,5,4,2 **(D)** 1,3,2,5,4

4. A detective is preparing a report concerning a homicide. The report will contain the following five sentences:

4 A B C D

1. Police Officers Jones and Brown responded to the scene.
2. I received the assignment to investigate the murder in Bronx Park from Detective Charles Chan.
3. Jones notified the Detective Bureau after questioning Mason.
4. An unknown male, apparently murdered, was discovered in Bronx Park by Horace Mason, a park employee.
5. Jones and Brown questioned Mason.

The most logical order for the above sentences to appear in the report is . . .

(A) 1,4,5,3,2 **(C)** 4,1,5,3,2
(B) 4,1,5,2,3 **(D)** 4,5,1,3,2

5. Police Officer Randers is writing a report concerning the arrest of a youthful offender. The report will contain the following five sentences:

5 A B C D

1. Randers telephoned Ray's parents from the station house to inform them of their son's arrest.
2. The store owner resisted and Ray then shot him and ran from the store.
3. Ray was transported directly to the station house by Officer Randers.

4. James Ray, a juvenile, walked into a drug store and announced a holdup.
5. Police Officer Randers, while on patrol, arrested Ray a block from the drug store.

The most logical order for the sentences to appear in the report is . . .

(A) 4,5,2,1,3 (C) 2,4,5,3,1
(B) 4,2,5,3,1 (D) 5,4,2,1,3

Traffic Map Questions

Map questions are designed to test your ability to apply directions. If you follow our recommended strategy you should do very well with them. The format for these questions is very simple. You are given a street map which usually contains the following features:

- An indication of the main compass points, i.e., North, East, South, and West. Sometimes only one main point is given, i.e., North. In that case you should fill in the other three points.
- A legend which tells you the location of certain buildings or other places of interest on the map.
- A number of named, one-way and two-way streets. The idea behind the typical map question is that you are told you are at a certain location and then asked to select from several alternatives the best way to go from that location to another location on the map. You are usually told to obey traffic regulations. Sometimes, however, you are told to go from one location to another without regard to traffic regulations as you might do in an emergency situation.

RECOMMENDED STRATEGY

1. Read the directions carefully. Make certain you know exactly what the ground rules are.
2. Look for any legend and codes that accompany the map and be certain you understand them.
3. Find the compass points on the map. Fill in all four of the compass points if you are only given one of the points. You must know the relationship between north, east, south, and west. It is a relationship that never changes while answering the questions that follow. Note that it is not always necessary to know where the compass points are located since the questions sometimes do not require this information. Most of the time, however, the location of north, east, south, and west is critical.

4. Using your fingers as a guide, take a quick trip through the map while taking notice of one-way streets, two-way streets, dead ends, detours, excavations, and other items of importance.
5. Remember that most questions will require you to obey all traffic regulations but that some might state that there is an emergency and tell you to disregard traffic regulations and simply find the quickest route between one point and another.
6. There are no shortcuts to answering these questions; you must consider all choices in order to eliminate the incorrect choices. We recommend that you use your pencil and lightly trace on the map the route suggested by each choice. After determining the answer to one question, erase completely all pencil marks before starting on the next question.
7. When you eliminate a choice because it suggests you travel the wrong way on a one-way street, mark that incorrect direction of travel in the margin of the test booklet. Afterwards, you will be able to automatically eliminate any choice that contains the incorrect direction of travel. For example, if the map shows Elm Avenue as a one-way northbound street, and a choice suggests traveling south on Elm Avenue, that choice is wrong. If you make note of the incorrect direction as we have suggested, e.g., write "south on Elm Avenue" in the margin, you can automatically eliminate any further choices in that question or any other question from the same map which suggest that you travel "south on Elm Avenue."
8. Bear in mind that there is often more than one legal route from one point to another among the choices. When this occurs you should select the most direct route as the answer. This is one more very important reason why you must consider all choices before selecting an answer.
9. Always imagine yourself in the driver's seat of the vehicle as you travel around the map. In this way, when you are told to turn right, you will, in fact, make a right turn. This is especially important when the vehicle is traveling downward on the map. Remember, a right or left turn MUST be made from the perspective of the person driving the automobile.
10. Remember, for the most part, that when the question tells you to obey all traffic regulations, you must make sure you do not go the wrong way on a one-way street.

PRACTICE QUESTIONS

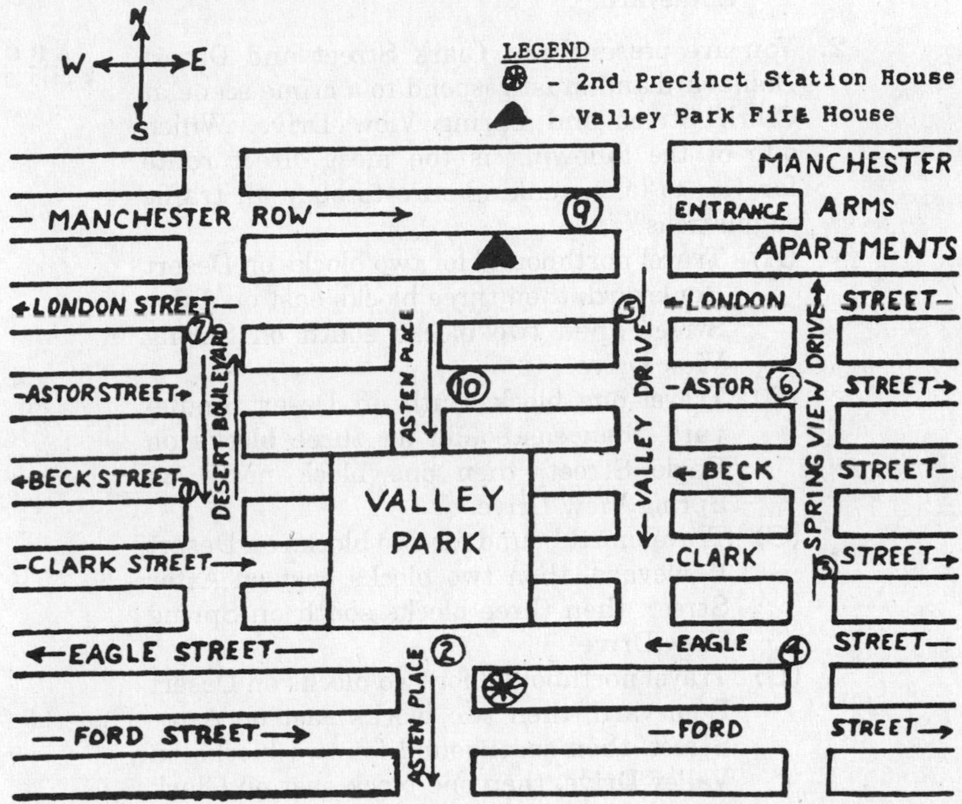

DIRECTIONS: Answer questions 1 through 5 solely on the basis of the map shown above. The flow of traffic is indicated by the arrows. You must follow the flow of traffic.

1. You are located at Astor Street and Spring View Drive. You receive a report of a robbery in progress at the intersection of Beck Street and Desert Boulevard. Which of the following is the most direct route for you to take in your patrol car, making sure to obey all of the traffic regulations?

   1 A B C D

   (A) Travel one block north on Spring View Drive, then travel three blocks west on London Street, then two blocks south on Desert Boulevard.

   (B) Travel westbound for three blocks on Astor Street, then one block south on Desert Boulevard.

   (C) Travel south for one block on Spring View Drive, then travel three blocks west on Beck Street.

(D) Travel south for three blocks on Spring View Drive, then three blocks west on Eagle Street, then two blocks north on Desert Boulevard.

2. You are presently at Clark Street and Desert Boulevard and must respond to a crime scene at Clark Street and Spring View Drive. Which one of the following is the most direct route for you to take, making sure to obey all traffic regulations?

2 A B C D

(A) Travel northbound for two blocks on Desert Boulevard, then three blocks east on Astor Street, then two blocks south on Spring View Drive.

(B) Travel one block south on Desert Boulevard, then eastbound for three blocks on Eagle Street, then one block north on Spring View Drive.

(C) Travel northbound for two blocks on Desert Boulevard, then two blocks east on Astor Street, then three blocks south on Spring View Drive.

(D) Travel northbound for two blocks on Desert Boulevard, then two blocks east on Astor Street, then southbound for two blocks on Valley Drive, then one block east on Clark Street.

3. You are located at the entrance to the Manchester Arms Apartments on Manchester Row. You get a call to respond to the intersection of Spring View Drive and Eagle Street. Which one of the following is the most direct route for you to take, making sure to obey all traffic regulations?

3 A B C D

(A) Travel southbound for five blocks on Valley Drive, then for one block eastbound on Eagle Street.

(B) Travel southbound for two blocks on Valley Drive, then eastbound for one block on Astor Street, then southbound for three blocks on Spring View Drive.

(C) Travel southbound for five blocks on Valley Drive, then westbound for one block on Eagle Street, then one block south on Asten Place, then one block east on Ford Street, then one block north on Spring View Drive.

(D) Travel southbound for one block on Valley Drive, then two blocks westbound on London Street, then four blocks south on Desert Boulevard, then three blocks east on Eagle Street.

4. You are located in front of the 2nd Precinct Station House on Eagle Street and are directed to respond to the Valley Park Fire House on Manchester Row. It is an emergency situation and you must get there as soon as possible without regard for traffic regulations. Which of the following is the most direct route for you to take? 4 A B C D

(A) Travel eastbound on Eagle Street to Valley Drive, then travel for five blocks southbound on Valley Drive, then turn left into Manchester Row.

(B) Travel west on Eagle Street to Desert Boulevard, then north for four blocks to Manchester Row, then turn right into Manchester Row.

(C) Travel east for two blocks to Spring View Drive, then north for four blocks to London Street, then west on London Street for three blocks to Desert Boulevard, then north for one block to Manchester Row, then turn east into Manchester Row.

(D) Travel east on Eagle Street to Valley Drive, then five blocks north on Valley Drive, then turn west into Manchester Row.

5. If you are located at point 7 on the map and travel southbound for one block, then turn left and travel two blocks, then turn south and travel two blocks, then turn east and travel one block, you will be closest to point . . . 5 A B C D

(A) 2 **(B)** 3 **(C)** 4 **(D)** 6

Matching Sketches Questions

Usually in this type of question, you will be given a photo or a sketch of one face and then asked to pick out the same or matching face from three or four other faces. In some instances you might be asked to pick out the sketch that is different from the given sketch.

RECOMMENDED STRATEGY

1. Read the instructions very carefully. Also note that this strategy of reading the instructions carefully applies to every type of question you do. You will not arrive at the right answer consistently if you do not know the ground rules established by the examiner. In "match-

ing sketches" questions the instructions usually indicate that you are to assume that no surgery has been done to change *permanent* facial features.

2. Concentrate and compare those parts of a person's face which cannot be changed. Don't pay any attention to those features which can easily be changed by a disguise.

3. Always compare items such as eyes, ears, mouth, nose, and the shape of the jaw. Do *not* be concerned with things that are easily changed without surgery such as eyeglasses (which can be taken off or replaced by contact lenses) or hair (which can be grown or cut off).

4. Remember that the examiner will try to confuse you by showing you a sketch of a person with a scar and then showing you a sketch of a person with hair or clothing covering the area where the scar should be located. This does not mean that the scar is not there. Make decisions in these cases based on other features.

5. Remember that while faces can become a little fatter, thinner, or older, the bone structure does not change.

6. Also remember that for the sake of these questions, facial lines do not change *without surgery*. Therefore, the face you choose as the matching face must have the same facial lines as the subject face or else there must be hair or clothing covering the area where the facial lines are located. When comparing sketches, check that the number and curvature of facial lines are the same.

7. Don't overlook the shape of the chin. It does not change.

8. Do not make a decision based on the overall appearance of the person. Eliminate choices for the specific reasons we have mentioned. And, as in all question types, always consider *all* of the choices.

PRACTICE QUESTIONS

DIRECTIONS: Answer questions 1 through 5 on the basis of the following sketches. The first face, the one appearing on the left of the dotted line, is a sketch of a wanted person. One of the four sketches on the right of the dotted line is the way the wanted person looked after changing appearance. You are to assume that no surgery has been performed on the wanted person. Select the face that is most likely that of the suspect.

1.
(A)
(B)
(C)
(D)
A B C D
1
2.
(A)
(B)
(C)
(D)
A B C D
2
3.
(A)
(B)
(C)
(D)
A B C D
3

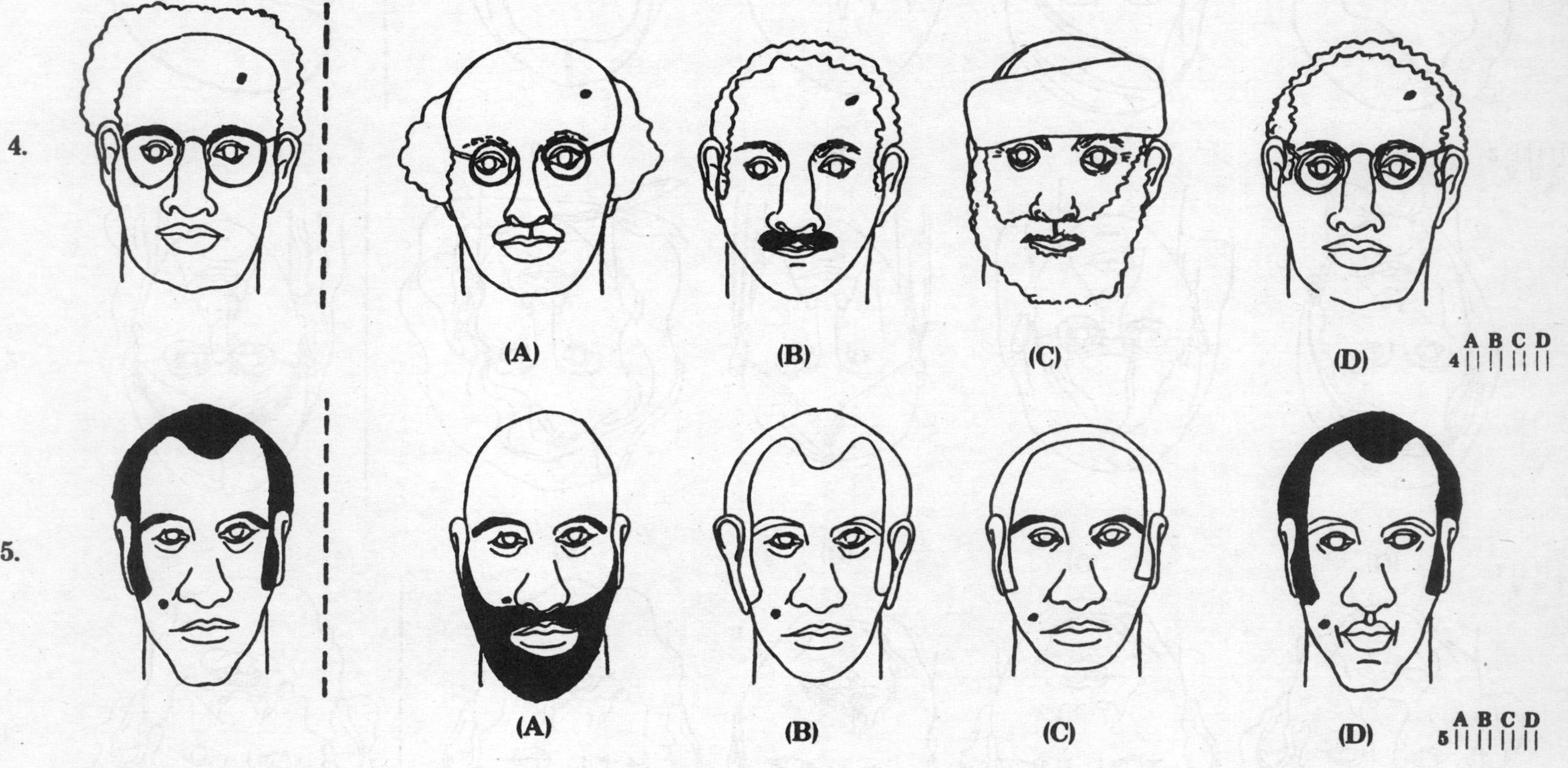
4.
(A)
(B)
(C)
(D)
4 A B C D
5.
(A)
(B)
(C)
(D)
5 A B C D

Directed Patrol Questions

In this question type, the candidate is given a number of facts about crimes and/or other police related incidents. Based on the data provided, the candidate is then asked to select the best areas and times to patrol in order to reduce the occurrence of these crimes and/or incidents.

RECOMMENDED STRATEGY

1. Do *not* try to determine independently what the best place and times of patrol should be. As with so many other question types, the strategy involves examining the choices since the correct place and times of patrol must be contained in one of them.

2. The first choices you should eliminate are the ones which simply do *not* deal with the specific problem you are trying to reduce. For example, if you want to reduce robberies, you would eliminate any choice which suggests you patrol at a place where there is no reported robbery activity. This will become clearer to you as you do the practice questions.

3. After step 2 above, you will be left with choices which in fact deal with the problem you are trying to reduce. Usually, you can eliminate two choices using step 2 above and you are then left with two choices that actually address the condition. You then make your answer selection based on which remaining choice offers you the best opportunity to reduce the crime or deal with the incident involved. As an example, if you are attempting to reduce burglaries, and in a recent time period three burglaries were committed on Clark Street and five burglaries were committed on Main Street, then your best chance to reduce burglaries would occur if you patrolled on Main Street.

FIVE PRACTICE QUESTIONS

DIRECTIONS: Answer questions 1 through 4 based on the following information:

Report #	Date	Day	Offense	Time	Location
0001	3/3	Saturday	Rape	3:00AM	105 Elm Street
0005	3/7	Tuesday	Trespass	4:20PM	415 Oak Street
0009	3/7	Tuesday	Homicide	9:00AM	321 Pine Street
0014	3/9	Thursday	Homicide	12:10AM	203 Elm Street
0019	3/11	Saturday	Trespass	4:00AM	300 Elm Street
0023	3/11	Saturday	Rape	6:00PM	439 Oak Street
0028	3/11	Saturday	Trespass	3:45AM	567 Main Street
0036	3/12	Sunday	Rape	4:00PM	400 Oak Street
0043	3/16	Thursday	Rape	7:00PM	387 Oak Street
0051	3/18	Saturday	Trespass	1:15AM	145 Elm Street
0065	3/21	Tuesday	Homicide	7:00AM	345 Pine Street
0069	3/22	Wednesday	Homicide	1:45AM	187 Elm Street
0074	3/22	Wednesday	Trespass	5:00AM	535 Oak Street
0081	3/25	Saturday	Trespass	7:00AM	095 Elm Street
0083	3/26	Sunday	Rape	1:00AM	310 Pine Street
0089	3/31	Saturday	Rape	4:00PM	349 Pine Street

1. A Police Officer would most likely be able to reduce the number of trespasses by patrolling . . .

A B C D
1 || || || ||

(A) Elm Street between 4:00PM and midnight on Tuesdays
(B) Oak Street between 1:00PM and 9:00PM on Mondays
(C) Elm Street between midnight and 8:00AM on Saturdays
(D) Oak Street between midnight and 8:00AM on Tuesdays

2. A Police Officer would most likely be able to reduce the number of rapes by patrolling . . .

A B C D
2 || || || ||

(A) Pine Street between 4:00PM and midnight, Wednesday through Sunday
(B) Oak Street between 3:00PM and 11:00PM, Tuesday through Saturday
(C) Oak Street between 4:00PM and midnight, Wednesday through Sunday
(D) Pine Street between 1:00PM and 9:00PM, Tuesday through Saturday

3. A Police Officer would be most likely to reduce the number of homicides by patrolling . . .

(A) Elm Street between 11:00PM and 7:00AM, Tuesday through Saturday
(B) Pine Street between midnight and 8:00AM, Tuesday through Saturday
(C) Oak Street between noon and 8:00PM, Monday through Friday
(D) Main Street between midnight and 8:00AM, Wednesday through Sunday

3 A B C D

4. A Police Officer who works on Elm Street, Oak Street, Pine Street, and Main Street should know that for the month of March the combined total of rapes, trespasses, and homicides was greatest on . . .

(A) Elm Street
(B) Pine Street
(C) Oak Street
(D) Main Street

4 A B C D

5. Police Officer Aponte observes that all of the cocaine sales in her sector take place on Bryant Avenue; all the heroin sales occur on James Street between Bryant Avenue and Williams Street; and all of the "crack" sales happen on Apple Avenue between Harris Street and Jewel Avenue. Most of the heroin sales take place between 7:00PM and midnight. Most of the "crack" sales occur between 6:00PM and 10:00PM and between 10:00AM and 2:00PM. Most of the cocaine sales take place between 4:00PM and 10:00PM. Most of the "crack" sales happen on Tuesdays, most of the heroin sales take place on Wednesdays and Fridays, and most of the cocaine sales take place on Fridays and Saturdays. Officer Aponte would be most likely to reduce the number of heroin sales by patrolling . . .

(A) Bryant Avenue on Wednesday and Friday from 4:00PM to 10:00PM
(B) James Street on Wednesday and Thursday from 8:00PM to midnight
(C) James Street on Wednesday and Friday from 7:00PM to 11:00PM
(D) Apple Avenue on Tuesday from 6:00PM to 10:00PM

5 A B C D

Thus far in this chapter, each of the preceding five troublesome types of questions has been identified and explained, with practice questions presented immediately after each type.

For the remaining five troublesome types of questions, each type will again first be identified and explained, but questions on these five types will be presented together in the format of a timed mini-quiz. This allows you, the student, to answer some of these troublesome types of questions under exam-like conditions.

Arithmetic Questions

The first issue that must be addressed concerning **Arithmetic Questions** is the degree of difficulty of the mathematics involved. When we hold courses to prepare candidates to take a police officer examination, as we always do when a major New York City entrance test is being held, we ask the candidates to do the following three math questions:

a. Multiply 750 times 3, and
b. Add 650 plus 450 plus 360, and
c. Subtract 120 from 1180.

The point we try to make when we do this is that the actual mathematical skills required to answer the type of arithmetic questions that appear on many police officer entrance examinations is quite elementary. Still, many candidates do poorly on these questions even though they have the needed math skills. This is because, as is so often the case, there are certain "gimmicks" the test writers use to make the questions more difficult. Before we go any further, let us consider a typical math question.

SAMPLE QUESTION

Q. Police Officer Rems responded to 233 Major Street to investigate a past burglary. Officer Rems arrived at the scene and interviewed Mrs. Joan Bates who stated that her apartment had been broken into and $220.00 in cash had been stolen, along with the following property:

1 ring valued at	$415.00
1 television set valued at	$400.00
coin collection valued at	$410.00
3 cameras, each valued at	$175.00

After Officer Rems returned to the station house, she received a telephone call from Mrs. Bates, who informed her that another coin collection worth $300.00 was also stolen.

Officer Rems is preparing a report on the burglary. Which of the following is the correct total value of the missing property and cash?

(A) $2270.00
(B) $1920.00
(C) $2050.00
(D) $1970.00

The correct answer to the above question is Choice A. It was determined by making the following calculation:

1.	The value of the cash	=	$220.00
2.	plus the value of the ring	=	415.00
3.	plus the value of TV set	=	400.00
4.	plus the value of the first coin collection	=	410.00
5.	plus the value of 3 cameras worth $175 each	=	525.00
6.	plus the value of the second coin collection	=	300.00
	Total value	=	$2,270.00

RECOMMENDED STRATEGY

By using the above sample question, we can now show you the strategy to follow when answering **Arithmetic Questions**. Note, however, that understanding the strategy to follow requires an understanding of the three most common "gimmicks" used in these question types:

1. **An attempt is often made to "hide" the numbers needed to make the necessary calculation.** For example, a quick look at the sample question could lead a careless candidate to believe that all the question requires him/her to do is to add the numbers in the list that the question contains. However, a careful reading of the question reveals that there are numbers in the first and third paragraphs that also must be added to determine the correct total value of cash and property stolen, i.e., the $220.00 in cash in paragraph one and the $300.00 value of the second coin collection in paragraph three. The first rule in our strategy, therefore, is: *Make certain you have included all of the necessary values or numbers in your calculations.*
2. **The use of the word "each."** Careless candidates often overlook the importance of the word "each" when doing these types of questions. For example, in the question above, the value of one camera is given in the listing of values. However, since that is the value of "each" camera, it is necessary to multiply $175.00 by 3 in order to obtain the correct total value of the cameras that were stolen. The second strategy rule, therefore, is: *Make sure you include in your calculations the total value of items stolen when several items of equal value were stolen and you are given the value of one of these items.*
3. **The use of misleading answer choices.** This is the most common "gimmick" used when writing Arithmetic Questions. The wrong choices are very often some wrong combination of the numbers actually given in the question. So, if you fall for one of the "gimmicks" and arrive at a total value that is wrong, you will very often see that wrong value listed as a choice. For example,

   Choice B includes only the value of 1 camera, and
   Choice C leaves out the cash from paragraph one, and
   Choice D omits the value of the second coin collection.

Therefore, the third strategy rule is stated in the negative, as follows: *Do not assume you are correct just because your answer appears as one of the choices*. Or, stated in the positive: *Always check to make certain the numbers you use in your calculations are accurate and complete*.

Frequency of Information Questions

As explained on page 255, **Frequency of Information Questions** test a candidate's ability to apply the law of probability. They can be asked in many ways, but the concept is always the same. The candidate is given pieces of information, usually four, and asked to select which one is "most likely" to be correct. (This is the same as saying which one is probably correct.) Note: The candidate is not asked to select the one that is correct. Rather, he/she is asked to select the one that is "probably correct." For ease of understanding, consider the following basic example:

A BASIC EXAMPLE

Answer the question below based *solely* on the following information:

A robbery has just taken place. Four witnesses are located. The witnesses offer the following descriptions of the robber.

Witness #1 says the robber was a white male
Witness #2 says the robber was a white male
Witness #3 says the robber was a white male
Witness #4 says the robber was a black male

Q. Which of the following descriptions of the robber is most likely to be correct?

(A) a white male
(B) a black male

Naturally, the correct choice is A. If this example seems extremely simple to you, you are correct. But this is the concept that will ALWAYS lead to the right answer. Majority rules. Since 3 of 4 witnesses said the robber was a white male, he probably is a white male. Now let's look at another basic example:

A SECOND BASIC EXAMPLE

Answer the question below based *solely* on the following information.

A robbery has just taken place. Four witnesses are located. The witnesses offer the following descriptions of the robber.

Witness #1 says the robber was a white male
Witness #2 says the robber was a white male
Witness #3 says the robber was an Hispanic male
Witness #4 says the robber was a black male

Q. Which of the following descriptions of the robber is most likely to be correct?

(A) a white male
(B) a black male
(C) an Hispanic male

In this example, the answer is still A. Two witnesses said the robber was a white male, one said he was a black male, and one said he was an Hispanic male. Therefore, it is most likely that the robber was a white male. Now, let's look at a third basic example.

A THIRD BASIC EXAMPLE

Answer the question below based *solely* on the following information.

A robbery has just taken place. Four witnesses are located. The witnesses offer the following descriptions of the robber.

Witness #1 says the robber was a white male
Witness #2 says the robber was a white male
Witness #3 says the robber was a black male
Witness #4 says the robber was a black male

Q. Which of the following descriptions of the robber is most likely to be correct?

(A) a white male
(B) a black male
(C) Cannot be determined

In this example the answer is Choice C. Since two witnesses said the robber was white, and two witnesses said the robber was black, the likelihood of the robber being white or black cannot be determined since there is no plurality opinion. Or, said another way, you cannot make a decision on a piece of information based on a tie; you need, at the very least, a plurality before a decision can be made.

RECOMMENDED STRATEGY

When handling a **Frequency of Information Question**, use the following rules to select the correct answer:

1. Compare each piece of information in all 4 choices and use a process of elimination based on the rule that the piece of information that is most frequently mentioned is most likely to be the correct piece of information. It's like holding an election: The piece of information that receives the most votes is the winner.

2. Don't eliminate a choice based on a tie.
3. Circle the piece of information that eliminates a choice and put an **X** through the letter of that choice. BUT continue to use the information in that choice after you have eliminated it.

Here is an example:

Answer the sample question based *solely* on the basis of the following information:

Police Officers must sometimes rely on eyewitness accounts of incidents, even though eyewitnesses may make mistakes with regard to some details.

Q. Police Officer Rems responds to the scene of a hit-and-run car accident. He locates four witnesses. The following are license plate numbers that were given to the officer by the witnesses of the car that left the scene. Which one of these plate numbers should Officer Rems consider most likely to be correct?

(A) JKL 456
(B) KKL 456
(C) JKK 456
(D) JKL 556

Answer and Explanation

The answer to the question is Choice A. Here is the step-by-step process you should have followed to arrive at this answer.

1. Remember, arrive at the answer to **Frequency of Information Questions** by holding an election. Each witness votes for each piece of information. The candidate's job is merely to count the votes.
2. In the sample question, three candidates voted that the first letter in the plate was a "J." Therefore, Choice B is eliminated. Note, however, that even though Choice B has been eliminated, it will still be used to determine the answer. In other words, it still can vote on the remaining pieces of information.
3. All four witnesses voted that the second piece of information in the plate was the letter "K" so no choice can be eliminated by the second piece of information.
4. Three witnesses voted that the third piece of information in the plate was the letter "L." Therefore, Choice C can be eliminated since it suggests that the letter "K" is the third piece of information.
5. Three witnesses voted that the fourth piece of information in the plate was the number 4. Therefore, Choice D can be eliminated and the answer is the remaining Choice A, the description that contained the greatest number of common characters.

Find the Perpetrator Questions

As described previously, **Find the Perpetrator Questions** usually involves a format in which three suspects in a series of recent similar crimes are described. Then, a description is given of a fourth suspect who has been arrested and is in custody. The job of the candidate is to determine whether the suspect under arrest should be considered a suspect in any of the other crimes. The idea is to compare the descriptions of the three perpetrators of the unsolved crimes with the description of the suspect in custody to see if the suspect in custody could have committed any of the unsolved crimes. Here is a sample:

Answer the sample question based *solely* on the following information:

During the month of November there have been three murders in the 11th Precinct where Police Officer Schroeder works. Officer Schroeder is responsible for investigating these murders. The description of each of the three murder suspects is as follows:

Murder #1: Male, white, 40 years old, 6′4″, 220 pounds, short black hair, black pants, brown shirt, black jacket, construction boots, moustache, scar on face

Murder #2: Male, white, 25 years old, 6′3″, 170 pounds, short Afro, gray pants, brown sweatshirt, brown boots, moustache, beard

Murder #3: Male, white, 35 years old, 6′0″, 225 pounds, black hair, gray pants, brown sweatshirt, brown shoes, moustache, long sideburns

On December 3, Police Officer Schroeder arrested a suspect for the murder of a store owner. The description of the arrested suspect is as follows:

Murder #4: Male, white, about 38 years old, 6′5″, 225 pounds, short hair, gray pants, brown sweatshirt, brown construction boots, moustache, 2″ scar above right eye.

Q. Based on the above description of the suspects in the three previous murders, Officer Schroeder should tell his supervisor that the suspect in the last murder should also be considered a suspect in

(A) Murder #1, but not Murder #2 or #3
(B) Murder #3, but not Murder #1 or #2
(C) Murders #1 and #2, but not Murder #3
(D) Murders #2 and #3, but not Murder #1

Answer Explanation and Strategy

The answer to the sample question is Choice A. The following is a suggested strategy to arrive at the correct answer. Compare the description of the suspect in custody with each of the other three suspects, making the comparisons one piece of information at a time. For example, in the sample question, first compare the gender of the arrested person, which is male, with the gender of each of the other suspects. Based on this comparison, the suspects are either kept in consideration or eliminated. Once a suspect is eliminated, it is no longer necessary to make any further comparisons with that suspect. When making your comparisons, you are to be guided by the following rules:

1. Don't consider any part of the description that could change in a very short time, such as hair, clothes, and glasses. These things DO NOT PLAY ANY PART IN THE DETERMINATION OF THE ANSWER. Or, said another way, they are *not* to be compared.
2. *Do* compare and *do* eliminate suspects based on the following criteria:
   - **Gender**—the arrested person and the suspect must be of the same gender to be considered the same person;
   - **Race**—the arrested person and the suspect must be of the same race to be considered the same person;
   - **Age**—the arrested person's age should be within five years of the wanted suspect's age to be considered the same person as the wanted suspect. Therefore, if the arrested person is 40, and the wanted suspect is 35, they could be the same person. Or, if the wanted suspect's age is given as between 35 and 40, then the arrested person could be anywhere from 30 to 35, 35 to 40, or 40 to 45 and still be considered the same person as the wanted suspect;
   - **Height**—the arrested person's height should be within two inches of the wanted suspect's height to be considered the same person;
   - **Weight**—the arrested person's weight must be within ten pounds of the suspect's weight to be considered the same person;
   - **Scars and tattoos**—this is the trickiest of all of the criteria. Remember, the only suspect who is in custody is the arrested person. Therefore, the arrested person is the only one who should have a complete listing of all scars and tattoos, since the non-apprehended suspect might have a scar or a tattoo that was not observed by the witnesses. For example, clothing could have been covering the scar or tattoo. But the arrested person is very carefully scrutinized by the police and any scars or tattoos will be detected. Therefore, if the suspect is described as having a scar or tattoo, then the arrested person must also have a similar scar or tattoo. But, the opposite is not true.

RECOMMENDED STRATEGY

In the sample question, the correct answer is determined by:

a. Recognizing that the arrested person and the suspects are all white males, so no elimination is made based on these two criteria.

b. Recognizing that the age of the arrested person is more than five years greater than Suspect #2. Therefore, Suspect #2 is eliminated since he cannot be the same person as the arrested person.

c. Recognizing that there is more than a 2-inch difference between the height of the arrested person and Suspect #3. Therefore, Suspect #3 is eliminated since he cannot be the same person as the arrested person.

d. Recognizing that the arrested person and Suspect #1 both have scars on their face so they could be the same person.

e. Recognizing that the clothing worn and facial hair have no bearing on the determination of the answer.

Therefore, the arrested person could be Suspect #1, but not Suspects #2 or #3. Thus, the answer is Choice A.

Applying Police Policy Questions

In these question types, the candidate is given a statement about the policy of a police department and then tested to see whether he/she can apply that policy. As mentioned previously, these questions are the only ones that require the candidate to exercise independent judgment. However, by following two simple rules, most such judgment decisions become obvious. The rules are as follows:

"Life threatening situations are more serious than situations in which property may be damaged or public inconvenience may be caused," and

"Situations which may cause widespread death or injury are more important than situations in which a single person is involved."

While these rules will not provide the answer to all "police policy" questions, they will lead to the answer in many of them.

When writing these questions, the exam writers almost have to go back to the same concepts again and again. In our opinion, it is this fact that makes these questions so easy. Once the candidate understands the **repeating theme** of these questions, they become quite easy to answer correctly. These **repeating themes** can best be understood once the candidate obtains a feel for them. For this reason we offer the following listing of priorities that have appeared on previous exams:

- A more serious emergency situation occurs when a person falls onto the subway tracks than when property falls onto the tracks.
- Smoke from an apartment window creates a more dangerous condition than a car's anti-theft alarm going off.
- An asbestos fire under a train in a tunnel is a more pressing reason to evacuate an area than a train delay.
- When a blind man is crossing the street against a red light, it is better to stop all traffic than to call out to the blind man to stop.
- A large amount of oil spilled on a busy street is more of a hazardous condition than cars double parked on a one-way street.
- Bricks falling from a tall building create a more dangerous situation than an intoxicated male sleeping on the sidewalk.

It should be obvious from the above listing that the **repeating theme** of these questions is that life is more important than property. This will become increasingly apparent as you do the practice questions.

A SAMPLE QUESTION

The following question is typical of the way **Applying Police Policy Questions** are written:

Answer this sample question based *solely* on the following information:
Police officers have to report dangerous conditions immediately to the desk officer at the station house of the precinct of occurrence.

Q. Which of the following situations would require an immediate notification to the desk officer of the precinct of occurrence?

(A) An intoxicated male is lying in the doorway of a church
(B) An abandoned car on a side street has no wheels
(C) A teenager is playing in a garbage strewn vacant lot
(D) An odor of gas is detected in the basement of a residential building.

Answer and Explanation

The answer to the sample question is D. While it could be argued that Choices A and D could be classified as a dangerous condition involving death or injury, Choice D has the potential to create a widespread tragedy involving many people.

A SECOND SAMPLE QUESTION

Q. Police officers are often responsible for calling for an ambulance for seriously injured people. In which of the following situations would it be most appropriate for a police officer to call for an ambulance?

(A) An intoxicated person claims he is having trouble maintaining his balance

(B) A pregnant female complains of feeling nauseated
(C) A teenage boy falls while roller blading and bruises his leg
(D) A construction worker is knocked unconscious when he falls from a building.

Answer and Explanation

The correct answer is Choice D. We used this sample question to illustrate that sometimes the candidate has to exercise common sense and determine which was a serious injury. A person who is knocked unconscious in a fall is easily categorized as a serious injury. None of the other examples fits the category.

Formula Questions

What we call **Formula Questions** are very closely related to **Arithmetic Questions**. The difference between the two is that in **Arithmetic Questions** the candidate must do the calculation involved and arrive at a specific answer. In contrast to this, **Formula Questions** require the candidate to show what calculations must be made to arrive at a specific answer to an arithmetic problem.

RECOMMENDED STRATEGY

Our strategy is based on the fact that:

- There is only one correct formula among the choices, and
- The actual arithmetic answer to the question is usually readily available.

Based on these two facts, we recommend that the candidate first solve the arithmetic problem involved. Then, knowing the correct answer, the candidate simply calculates the answer yielded by each of the formulas in the choices. As soon as one of the formulas in the question yields the actual arithmetic answer, the correct choice has been identified and no further calculations are required.

SAMPLE FORMULA QUESTION

Q. At 16:45 on Tuesday, May 19th, Officer Rems responded to a reported burglary at an appliance store. The store owner reported that the following merchandise was stolen:

2 television sets, each valued at	$430.00
2 air conditioners, each valued at	$375.00
5 VCRs, each valued at	$325.00

Officer Rems is required to prepare a report on this burglary. Which one of the following is the correct formula for Officer Rems to follow to determine the total value of the stolen merchandise?

(A) 2 × (value of the television sets) + 2 × (value of the air conditioners) + 5 × (value of the VCRs)

(B) 9 × (value of the television sets + value of the air conditioners + value of the VCRs)

(C) 2 × 2 × (value of the television sets + value of the air conditioners) + 5 × (value of the VCRs)

(D) (value of the television sets) + (value of the air conditioners) + (value of the VCRs) × 2 + 2 + 5

Answer to Sample Question and Explanation of Strategy

According to our proposed strategy, the first step is to calculate the actual numerical answer to the problem posed in the stem of the question. In the above sample question the total value of the stolen property can be easily calculated, as follows:

2 times $430 (value of TV sets)	=	$860.00
plus 2 times $375 (value of air conditioners)	=	+$750.00
plus 5 times $325 (value of VCRs)	=	+$1625.00
equals the total value of the stolen property	=	$3235.00

Now, knowing that the total value of the stolen property is $3235.00, the next step is to calculate the results of each suggested formula. As soon as you locate the formula that yields an answer of $3235.00 you have your answer and you do not have to go any further.

The verbal equivalent of the formula in Choice A is, "the total value of the stolen merchandise is equal to twice the value of a television set, plus twice the value of an air conditioner, plus five times the value of a VCR." By inserting the values given in the stem of the question, this formula yields an answer of $3,235.00. Since we already know that this is the actual total value involved, it is not necessary to go any further as the answer is Choice A.

ONE FINAL NOTE ABOUT FORMULA QUESTIONS

Should you run across a **Formula Question** that does not have actual values or numbers in the question, our strategy can still work. In these cases you simply assign very simple values and do everything else the same.

For example, in the above sample question, if the various appliances did not have actual values, you simply assign such values. And, to make things easy, assign simple values. You could assume that each of the stolen appliances was worth $10.00. We will give you some practice at this in the practice questions.

Wanted Poster Questions

As mentioned earlier, **Wanted Poster Questions** are classified as **Memory Questions**. The wanted poster consists of a photo or sketch of the wanted person, information about that person, and information about the crime he is suspected of committing. Typically, the candidate is given a number of wanted posters, about six of them, and also given a period of time, usually about five minutes, to study these posters. The wanted posters are then taken away and the candidate is asked a series of questions about them. The number of questions asked rarely exceeds more than two for each poster. So, if you were given six wanted posters, you could usually expect a maximum of twelve questions.

THE FORMAT OF THE QUESTIONS

There are two basic ways that **Wanted Poster Questions** are asked, as follows:

1. You could be asked questions about the various wanted persons and the choices could be written. For example, suppose one of the wanted persons with the name of James White had a scar over his right eye, and this particular person was wanted for robbing a blind peddler. The question might be worded as follows:

Q. The name of the robbery suspect who has a scar over his right eye is:

(A) James White
(B) John Brown
(C) Charles Green
(D) Joseph Black

2. Or you could be asked questions about the various wanted persons and the answer choices could be sketches of the suspects. In this version of the question type, the question might be as follows: "Which of the following is wanted for robbery of a blind peddler?" and the choices could merely be four of the six sketches you previously studied. Based on the above, it should be clear that you have to remember what each suspect looks like and you also have to remember specific information about each poster.

MEMORY BY ASSOCIATION RULE

In two earlier chapters of this book, we explained the concept of **memory by association**. This concept is applicable to wanted posters also. Unless you have a gifted memory, and most of us don't, you should not rely on brute memory to retain the information you will need to answer **Wanted Poster Questions**. Instead, you should rely on associations to help you retain the information needed to answer all types of memory questions, including **Wanted Poster Questions**. Therefore, we suggest very strongly that you review those portions of this book's earlier chapters dealing with **memory by association**, and that you use that information when you are answering **Wanted Poster Questions**.

THE CONTRAST RULE

This is a rule that is extremely helpful when answering **Wanted Poster Questions**. Simply stated, the rule is that exam writers will quite often require the candidate to remember the differences between posters, and not the similarities. Or, put another way, if you want to do well on these questions, you must remember facts which show differences or dissimilarities among the various wanted posters. For example,

- **a.** If all of the persons are wanted for robbery, except one who is wanted for murder, you will probably be asked, "Who is wanted for murder?"
- **b.** If only one of the persons on the posters has a scar, you will probably be asked about the person with that scar.
- **c.** If only one of the persons on the posters is violent and dangerous, you will probably be asked which wanted person should be considered dangerous and approached with great caution.
- **d.** If all of the persons in the posters are male except for one female, you will probably be asked about the female.
- **e.** If one of the persons is described as being usually armed with a gun and dangerous, you will probably be asked which person usually carries a gun.

The point is this: The exam writers build contrast into the **Wanted Poster Questions** so they will have a framework upon which they can ask questions. If you understand this and pay particular attention to any such contrasts, you will be rewarded with correct answers.

MULTIPLE ASSOCIATIONS

Wanted Poster Questions lend themselves to multiple associations. For example, suppose you get a question about a man named Michael Grant who is wanted for murder. You might remember that "**Michael** is a **Murderer**." Now suppose that Michael lives in Manhattan and has a moustache. Then you might remember that "**Michael** is a **Murderer** who has a **Moustache** and lives in **Manhattan**." Obviously this illustration is self-serving; however, it is offered as an example of how to approach this type of question. You must associate items on each poster with the name and sketch of the person on the poster, and you must stay aware of the contrast rule. And, finally, overall, you must develop your ability to remember by association.

A SAMPLE QUESTION

Assume that the wanted poster below is one of several that you have been given to study within an allotted time period. (For purposes of this example, take one minute.) Then, after you have studied the wanted poster with its accompanying information, try to answer the sample question. Remember, you cannot refer back to the actual poster when answering the question. You must answer the question based on what you recall from the poster.

WANTED FOR RAPE AND ROBBERY

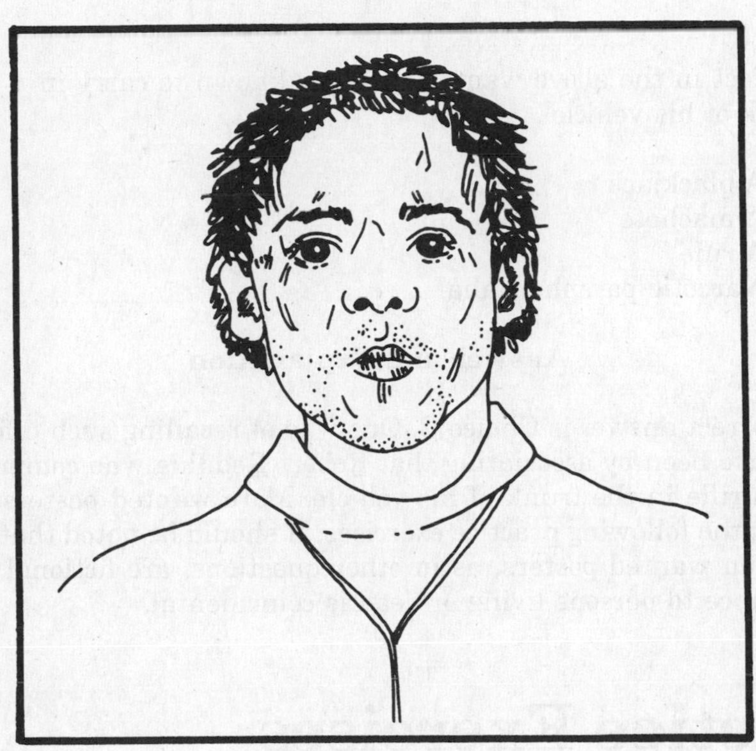

Robert Redding

Age:	29
Race:	White
Height:	72″
Weight:	180 pounds
Eyes:	Hazel
Hair:	Dark brown
Scars:	None
Tattoos:	The word "Mary" on his right wrist

Subject is wanted in connection with the rape and robbery of a 22-year-old female. He was last seen leaving the scene of the crime in late model dark sedan. The subject is currently on parole after serving 36 months of an eight-year sentence for rape. He is known to carry a rifle in the trunk of his vehicle. He may be employed as a construction laborer.

QUESTION

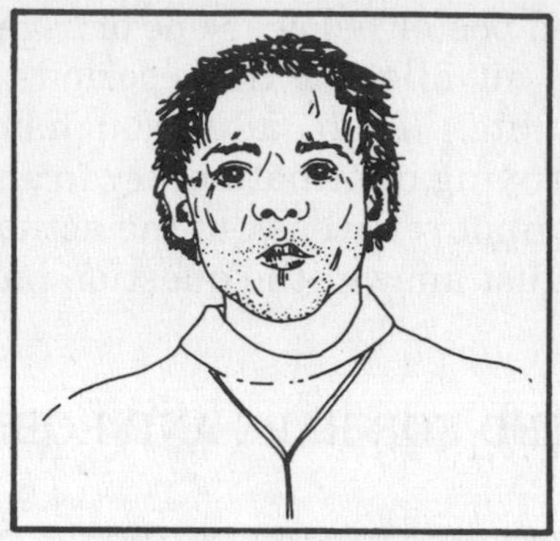

The subject in the above wanted poster is known to carry in the trunk of his vehicle . . .

(A) A blackjack
(B) A machete
(C) A rifle
(D) Narcotic paraphernalia

Answer and Explanation

The correct answer is Choice C. One way of recalling such information might have been by associating that Robert Redding who commits rapes carries a rifle in the trunk of his vehicle. More wanted posters are presented in the following practice exercises. It should be noted that subjects depicted in wanted posters, as in other questions, are fictional and any resemblance to persons living or dead is coincidental.

Practice Exercises

TIME ALLOWED—35 MINUTES FOR THE FIRST 17 QUESTIONS

***DIRECTIONS:* Answer question 1 based *solely* on the following information:**

Three rapes occurred in the 81st Precinct during the month of April. The reported description of each of the suspects is as follows:

Rape #1: Male, white, about 25 years old, short brown hair, gray pants, white tank top shirt, black shoes, scar above right eye and across right cheek, earring in left ear.

Rape #2: Male, white, early 40's, black hair, gray pants, white shirt, black shoes, black leather jacket, wearing sunglasses.

Rape #3: Male, white, 21 years old, black hair, blue dungarees, white sneakers, black leather vest, white T-shirt, tattoo on left arm, earring in right ear.

On April 21, Officer Rems arrested a suspect during an attempted rape. The description of the suspect is as follows:

Rape #4: Male, white, 20 years old, short black hair, blue jeans, white sneakers, white T-shirt, tattoo of a ghost on left arm, earring in left ear.

1. Based on the descriptions of the suspects in the first three rapes, Officer Rems should consider the suspect in the fourth rape as a suspect in

(A) Rape #1, but not Rape #2 or #3.
(B) Rape #3, but not Rape #1 or #2.
(C) Rape #1 and Rape #3, but not Rape #2.
(D) Rape #1 and Rape #2, but not Rape #3.

1 A B C D

DIRECTIONS: Answer question 2 *solely* on the basis of the following information:

While on patrol in January, Police Officer Harris received several reports from people who were robbed as they exited the Georgia Street subway station. The description of each suspect is as follows:

Robbery #1: Male, black, early 20's, 5′10″, 180 pounds, dark hair, moustache, blue jeans, black jacket, running shoes.

Robbery #2: Male, black, 25 to 30, 5′9″, 165 pounds, dark hair, dark moustache, glasses, black jeans, green sweatshirt, running shoes.

Robbery #3: Male, black, 40 to 45 years old, 5′8″, 150 pounds, dark hair, clean shaven, blue jeans, black jacket, black cap, sneakers.

On February 6, of the same year, a woman was robbed by a male who was loitering near the Georgia Street subway station. Police Officer Harris witnessed the robbery and apprehended the suspect. The description of the suspect is as follows:

Robbery #4: Male, black, 20 to 25 years old, 5′10″, 175 pounds, dark hair, moustache, blue jeans, black jacket, black cap, sneakers.

2. Based on the above description of the suspects in the first three robberies, Officer Harris should consider the suspect in the fourth robbery as a suspect in

2 A B C D

(A) Robbery #1, but not Robbery #2 or #3.
(B) Robbery #1 and Robbery #2, but not Robbery #3.
(C) Robbery #2 and Robbery #3, but not Robbery #1.
(D) Robbery #1, Robbery #2, and Robbery #3.

DIRECTIONS: **Answer question 3 based *solely* on the following information:**

There has been a recent rash of muggings within the confines of the 81st Precinct where Officer Rems works. The following are the descriptions of three of the suspects in these muggings, all of which occurred in the first three weeks of June.

Mugging #1: Male, white, 25 to 30, 5′10″, 180 pounds, scar on forehead, blue pants and shirt, horn-rimmed glasses, and sneakers.

Mugging #2: Male, white, 25, 5′8″, 175 pounds, scar on face, black shirt, full face beard, and running shoes.

Mugging #3: Male, white, early 30s, 5′9″, 185 pounds, moustache, scar above right eye, green pants and shirt, and army boots.

On July 4th of the same year, Officer Rems arrested a suspect in a mugging. The description of this arrested person is as follows:

Mugging #4: Male, white, 30, 5′9″, 180 pounds, clean shaven, scar over right eye, brown pants, black shirt, sunglasses, and sneakers.

3. Based on the above description of the suspects in the first three muggings, Officer Rems should consider the suspect arrested in the fourth mugging in

(A) Muggings #1 and #2, but not Mugging #3
(B) Muggings #1 and #3, but not Mugging #2
(C) Muggings #2 and #3, but not Mugging #1
(D) Muggings #1, #2, and #3

3 A B C D

4. Mrs. Levy was the victim of a hit-and-run accident. When Police Officer Bailes arrived at the scene, he interviewed four witnesses who saw a black car strike the victim and leave the scene. The following are license plate numbers provided by the four witnesses. Which one of these numbers should Officer Bailes consider most likely to be correct?

(A) P-82324
(B) P-82342
(C) F-83224
(D) F-62323

4 A B C D

5. Officer Rems responds to the scene of a bank robbery. He identifies four witnesses who all saw the robbers escape in their getaway car. The following are descriptions of the getaway car provided by each of the four witnesses. Which of these descriptions should Officer Rems consider most likely to be correct?

(A) Black Ford, two door sedan, dent on left fender, New York plate
(B) Black Buick, two door sedan, dent on right fender, New York plate
(C) Black Ford, four door sedan, dent on left fender, New York plate
(D) Brown Chevy, two door sedan, dent on left fender, New York plate

5 A B C D

6. Police Officer Aponte is hailed by a woman who states she has just had her purse snatched from her as she was walking down the street. Four witnesses saw the incident and offered descriptions of the perpetrator. Which of the following descriptions should Officer Aponte consider most likely to be accurate?

(A) Male, white, 25, 5′8″, 175 pounds, green pants, white shirt
(B) Male, white, 30, 5′8″, 175 pounds, green pants, white shirt
(C) Male, white, 30, 5′10″, 175 pounds, green pants, white shirt
(D) Male, white, 30, 5′8″, 180 pounds, green pants, white shirt

6 A B C D

7. A robbery has just occurred. Four witnesses have been located. They offer descriptions of the robber. Which of the following descriptions should the police consider most likely to be correct?

(A) Female, Hispanic, 5′4″, 140 pounds, armed with a gun
(B) Female, black, 5′4″, 140 pounds, armed with a gun
(C) Female, Hispanic, 5′4″, 150 pounds, armed with a knife
(D) Female, Hispanic, 5′6″, 140 pounds, armed with a gun

7 A B C D

8. Police Officer Lombardo responded to 233 Major Street to investigate a past burglary. Officer Lombardo arrived at the scene and interviewed Mrs. Joan Bates. Mrs. Bates stated that her apartment had been broken into and the following items were missing:

1 ring valued at	$415.00
Cash	$220.00
coin collection valued at	$410.00
3 cameras, each valued at	$175.00

8 A B C D

Officer Lombardo is preparing a report on the burglary. Which one of the following is the total value of the missing property and cash?

(A) $1,220.00
(B) $1,395.00
(C) $1,570.00
(D) $1,615.00

9. Officer Rems takes a report about a burglary. The victim states that $550.00 in cash was taken in addition to the following property:

1 television set, valued at	$675.00
4 paintings, each valued at	$400.00
2 radios, each valued at	$100.00

Some time after Officer Rems took the report, the victim contacted the officer and stated that a microwave oven valued at $600.00 was also taken in the burglary. Officer Rems is preparing a report on the burglary. Which one of the following is the total value of the missing property and cash?

(A) $3625.00
(B) $3075.00
(C) $3025.00
(D) $3525.00

A B C D
9 | | | |

10. While on patrol, Police Officer Schroeder comes upon a male who states that he had just been robbed. The victim states that the following property was stolen from him:

1 gold chain, valued at	$950.00
1 wristwatch, valued at	$1250.00
2 rings, each valued at	$750.00
U.S. currency in the amount of	$550.00

In addition to the above property, the robbery victim tells Officer Schroeder that the robber also took his alligator briefcase valued at $900.00.

Officer Schroeder is preparing a report on the robbery. Which one of the following is the total value of the missing property and cash?

(A) $4250.00
(B) $4400.00
(C) $5150.00
(D) $5450.00

A B C D
10 | | | |

11. Police Officer Rems is assigned to a special post near a school between the hours of 9:00 AM and 5:00 PM on weekdays only. Part of his assignment is to report unusual activities that may indicate drug activity. Which of the following most likely indicates possible drug activity?

(A) Many students from the school go into an arcade during lunch breaks and after school.

A B C D
11 | | | |

(B) Many construction workers buy hot dogs from a vendor between 10:00 AM and 2:00 PM.
(C) Many people go into a local grocery store and leave without any apparent packages.
(D) Many younger students go into a local candy store after school.

12. It is the policy of the police department to respond to fire scenes that are especially dangerous. In which one of the following situations would it be most necessary for the police to respond?
(A) Homeless persons have started a fire in a metal can in an attempt to keep warm on a cold night.
(B) Some teenagers in a park have started a small fire to roast marshmallows.
(C) A bolt of lightning has ignited some twigs near the shore of a lake.
(D) A discarded cigarette has started an oil fire in a gas station near a residential building.

12 A B C D

13. Police officers are trained to call for backup assistance when the situation warrants such assistance. In which of the following situations would it be most necessary for a police officer to request backup assistance?
(A) Two older women are engaged in a shouting match.
(B) An intoxicated man is blocking the sidewalk.
(C) Two men are threatening each other with bottles.
(D) Teenagers are being noisy in a local park.

13 A B C D

14. It is the policy of the police department to reduce the potential for subway booth holdups by paying attention to suspicious activity around these booths. Which of the following activity is most likely to portray suspicious activity around a token booth?
(A) A female youth is talking to the clerk in the booth while the clerk is counting money.
(B) A male adult is consulting a subway map on the side of a token booth.
(C) A young adult is standing on the subway stairs signaling to his friend who is standing by the booth looking back and forth.
(D) Two preteen youths are wrestling near a token booth.

14 A B C D

15. While on patrol, Police Officer Kegler comes upon a male who states that he was just the victim of a robbery. The victim states that the following property was stolen from him:

15 A B C D

1 gold bracelet, valued at $850.00
1 wristwatch, valued at $1250.00
3 rings, each valued at $650.00

Officer Kegler is preparing a report on the robbery. Which of the following is the correct arithmetic formula for the officer to use to determine the total value of the property stolen in the robbery?

(A) $850 + 1250 + 650$
(B) $(850 + 1250) + (3 \times 650)$
(C) $3 \times (850 + 1250 + 650)$
(D) $(650 + 1250 + 850) + 3 \times (650)$

16. Officer Aponte takes a report about a burglary. The victim states that $800.00 in cash was taken in addition to the following property: A B C D 16

1 VCR, valued at $775.00
4 radios, each valued at $400.00
3 lamps, each valued at $100.00

Some time after Officer Aponte took the report, the victim contacted the officer and stated that a painting valued at $600.00 had also been taken in the burglary. Officer Aponte is preparing a report on the burglary. Which one of the following formulas most correctly represents the total value of the missing property and cash?

(A) $(800) + (775) + (4 \times 400) + 3 \times (100)$
(B) $(800) + (775) + 4 \times (400 + 100) + 600$
(C) $(800) + (775) + (3 \times 500) + 600$
(D) $(800) + (775) + (4 \times 400) + 3 \times (100) + 600$

17. The following information concerns the eight-hour working tour of Police Officer Rems as it appeared in the officer's notebook on August 31st of a certain year. A B C D 17

4:00 PM:	On patrol on Post #11
7:00 PM:	Present at school board meeting
8:00 PM:	On meal at station house
9:00 PM:	Relieved telephone switchboard operator at station house
10:00 PM:	Off telephone switchboard; assigned to process a prisoner at the station house.
10:30 PM:	Left station house and transported prisoner to court
10:45 PM:	Present with prisoner at court
12:00 AM:	Prisoner arraigned; scheduled tour ended.

Which of the following is the most correct arithmetic formula to determine the amount of hours Officer Rems spent in the station house during his tour?

(A) $8 - (1 + 1 + \frac{1}{2})$
(B) $8 - 3$
(C) $1 + 1 + .30 - 8$
(D) $8 - (3 + 1 + 1\frac{1}{2})$

DIRECTIONS: For the next three questions take five minutes to first examine the four wanted posters with the information that accompanies each poster. Then take another five minutes to answer questions 18–20 without referring back to the wanted posters.

WANTED FOR MURDER

Sean Kraft

Age:	19
Race:	White
Height:	66″
Weight:	140 pounds
Eyes:	Blue
Hair:	Reddish Brown
Scars:	Pockmarked Face
Tattoos:	None

Subject is wanted in connection with the stabbing death of his mother, a 42-year-old female, during an argument over his choice of colleges. He was last seen in the vicinity of Killigan's Bar where he was employed as a part-time porter. The subject is enrolled in John's County Community College.

WANTED FOR GRAND LARCENY (CONFIDENCE GAMES)

Miriam Leon

Age:	49
Race:	Hispanic
Height:	63″
Weight:	135 pounds
Eyes:	Brown
Hair:	Dark Brown
Scars:	Three Inch Appendix Scar
Tattoos:	The name "Poppy" on her right inner thigh

Subject is wanted in connection with the theft of $42,000.00 during a confidence game swindle of an eighty-year-old male. Believed to be operating with a white male (no further description) in the vicinity of banks. Subject is known to this department and may be using the name "Elizabeth Spockbotch" and posing as a stock broker.

WANTED FOR GRAND LARCENY (EXTORTION)

Neil Bailes

Age:	39
Race:	White
Height:	73″
Weight:	185 pounds
Eyes:	Brown
Hair:	Light Brown (May be dyed)
Scars:	none
Tattoos:	The name "Vivian" on his left bicep

Subject is wanted in connection with the organized extortion of merchants in the fish markets. Believed to be a strong arm for several organized crime families, he is armed and is to be considered extremely violent. Subject is known to this department and may be using the name "Nick Bianco" while posing as an undercover law enforcement agent. Bailes is currently wanted by the federal authorities for questioning in connection with the poisoning death of U.S. Congressman Teddy Minogue.

WANTED FOR SEXUAL ABUSE (CHILD UNDER 10)

Fred J. Kelger

Age:	43
Race:	Black
Height:	73″
Weight:	225 pounds
Eyes:	Brown
Hair:	Brown (severely receding); may be wearing hairpiece as shown in above sketch
Scars:	None
Tattoos:	The name "Jimmy" on his chest

Subject has been indicted for the sexual abuse of two nine-year-old boys. Believed to be the organizer of a nationwide group seeking to legalize child pornography, subject may be working as an insurance adjuster in the southeastern U.S.

NOTE: Do not refer back to the posters when answering questions 18–20.

18. Which of the subjects illustrated in the following wanted posters is to be considered extremely dangerous?

18 A B C D

(A)

(C)

(B)

(D)

19. Which of the subjects illustrated in the following posters is being sought for the crime of sexual abuse?

19 A B C D

(A)

(C)

(B)

(D)

20. The subject illustrated in the wanted poster directly above is believed to be operating

A B C D
20 || || || ||

- **(A)** in the vicinity of senior citizens' homes
- **(B)** with another female named Spockbotch
- **(C)** with a male described as heavy set
- **(D)** in the vicinity of banks

Answer Key and Explanations

Answer Key

Sentence Ordering	Traffic Map	Matching Sketches
1. A	1. A	1. C
2. D	2. D	2. A
3. A	3. C	3. D
4. C	4. D	4. D
5. B	5. B	5. A

Directed Patrol

1. C
2. C
3. A
4. A
5. C

Answer Explanations

SENTENCE ORDERING

1. A Remember, the key to our strategy is to use the suggested answers as your guide. In this question it should be obvious that sentence 5 belongs first. Therefore, you can eliminate choices B and D. Since both of the remaining choices, A and C, end with sentence 3, you must go to the middle sentences. And, remember, when that occurs you should first look at the second sentence. If sentence 2 comes directly after 5, then choice A is the answer. Since the officers would have to respond to the liquor store before they could see the two armed men, sentence 2 must come after sentence 5 and choice A must be the answer.

2. D Sentence 2 belongs first since it starts the action. Sentence 4 signals the end of the action and must come last. This leaves us with choices A and D. In both of these choices, the fourth sentence is sentence 3. Therefore, the answer once again keys on the second sentence. Since it follows that the men would have to get intoxicated and boisterous before the bartender ordered them out of the bar, sentence 5 must come second so choice D is the answer.

3. A This is one of those questions which is decided by the last sentence. It is obvious that sentence 3 belongs first since it begins the action, so choices B and D can be eliminated. Remember to mark an "X" through them on the test booklet. Sentence 2 closes the action so it should conclude the report. Therefore, choice A is the answer. Note that it was not necessary to order the middle sentences.

4. C Sentence 4 belongs first since it begins the action. Sentence 2 belongs last since it indicates how the detective (see the question stem) got involved. Also helpful is recognizing that sentence 1 must come before sentence 5 because the officers have to be on the scene before they can question Mason.

5. B Sentence 4 belongs first since it starts the action. Note the use of the full name of the juvenile in sentence 4. In sentences 1, 2, 3, and 5, the juvenile is referred to only as Ray. This is another sign that sentence 4 comes first. The first time a person's name is used in a report, the entire name is usually used. Thereafter, that person may be referred to by his first or last name. Sentence 1 belongs last since it takes place after the arrest and at the station house. Choice B is the only choice with sentence 4 first and sentence 1 last. There is no need to look at the middle sentences.

TRAFFIC MAP QUESTIONS

1. A In this question, choice B is wrong because it requires traveling westbound on Astor Street, a one-way eastbound street. Choices C and D are wrong because they both require going south on Spring View Drive, a one-way northbound street.

2. D Choice B is wrong since you can't go east on Eagle Street. Choices A and C are wrong because you cannot go south on Spring View Drive. Note that in the above question (#1), two choices were wrong (C and D) because they required going south on Spring View Drive. If you had noted that going south on Spring View Drive is prohibited, you would have answered this question that much faster.

3. C Choices A and D require going the wrong way on Eagle Street. Choice B requires going the wrong way on Spring View Drive (for the third question in a row). Choice C must be the answer.

4. D In this question you are looking for the most direct route without regard for traffic directions. Choice A is wrong because traveling south for five blocks on Valley Drive would take you off the map. Choice B is wrong because Manchester Row is five blocks (not four) away from Eagle Street. Choice C would get you there but it is a longer route than the one outlined in the correct choice, which is Choice D.

5. B Simply trace the route with your pencil and you will wind up on Spring View Drive and Clark Street, which is location 3. Don't forget to erase the trace marks before you start the next question. Also, understand that when you travel south ("down" the map) from point 7 and turn left, you wind up going in an eastbound direction. If you don't consider left and right turns from the perspective of the person driving the car, you will not travel in the correct direction if the turn is being made while the vehicle is traveling "down" the map.

MATCHING SKETCHES

1. C In choice A the eyes are wrong. In choice B the ears are wrong. In choice D the nose is wrong.

2. A In choice B the eyes are wrong. In choices C and D the nose is wrong.

3. D In choices A and B the lips are wrong. In choice C the chin is wrong.

4. D In choice A the nose is wrong. In choice B the chin is wrong. In choice C the nose and eyes are wrong.

5. A In choice B the ears are wrong. In choice C the chin is wrong. In choice D the mouth is wrong. Note that for all of these questions we arrived at the answer by considering eyes, ears, nose, mouth, chin, and lips. We did not consider eyeglasses, hair, hats, or beards. That is the key to answering these questions correctly.

DIRECTED PATROL QUESTIONS

1. C There were three trespasses reported on Elm Street on Saturdays between midnight and 8:00AM. Only two trespasses were reported as occurring on Oak Street.

2. C Of the six reported rapes, three of them occurred on Oak Street between 4:00PM and midnight on either Thursday, Saturday, or Sunday.

3. A Choices C and D are wrong since there were no reported homicides on Oak or Main Street. Choice A is correct since there were two homicides on Elm Street between 11:00PM and 7:00AM from Tuesday through Saturday. The homicide on Pine Street on Tuesday the 7th occurred at 9:00AM, which is not included in choice B.

4. A Of the 16 reported crimes, 6 of them took place on Elm Street.

5. C According to the stem of the question, most of the heroin sales take place between 7:00PM and midnight, on Wednesdays and Fridays on James Street.

Answer Key
Timed Mini-Quiz

1. B	6. B	11. C	16. D
2. B	7. A	12. D	17. D
3. D	8. C	13. C	18. C
4. A	9. A	14. C	19. A
5. A	10. C	15. B	20. D

Answer Explanations

TIMED MINI-QUIZ

1. B All four suspects are male, white, so no elimination can be made on those criteria. Suspect #2 is too old to be the arrested suspect, so Suspect #2 is eliminated. The arrested person, who is in custody, is not described as having a scar on his face as Suspect #1 has. Therefore, Suspect #1 is eliminated. Both Suspect #3 and the arrested suspect have a tattoo on the left arm, and #3 is the only one of the three suspects who could also be the arrested person.

2. B Suspect #3 is too old to be the apprehended person. There is no reason to eliminate Suspects #1 or #2.

3. D There is no reason to eliminate any of the three suspects as they are all within the allowable limits with respect to gender, race, age, weight, height, and facial scars.

4. A Choice D is eliminated since three witnesses say the first number on the plate is 8. Choice C is wrong because three witnesses say the second number on the plate is 2. Choice B is wrong because three witnesses say the next to last number on the plate is 2.

5. A Choice D is eliminated since three witnesses said the car was black. Choice B is wrong because two witnesses said the car was a Ford, while only one said it was a Buick and one said it was a Chevy. Choice C is wrong because three witnesses said the car was a two door sedan.

6. B Choice A is eliminated since three witnesses said the age of the perpetrator was 30. Choice C is wrong because three witnesses said the perpetrator was 5′8″. Choice D is wrong because three witnesses said the perpetrator was 175 pounds. (Note that in **Frequency of Information Questions**, unlike the **Find the Perp Questions**, there is no need to consider ranges of age or measurements. If a witness identifies a robber as being 25 years old, the candidate should not consider the age to have a range of 5 years either way as was recommended to correctly answer the **Find the Perp Questions**.)

7. A Choice B is eliminated since three witnesses say the robber was Hispanic. Choice C is wrong because three witnesses say the robber weighed 140 pounds. Choice D is wrong because three witnesses say the robber was 5′4″.

8. C Choice A is the total considering only one of three cameras. Choices B and D are simply made up.

9. A Choice B ignores the value of the cash in the first paragraph. Choice C overlooks the value of the microwave. Choice D only includes 1 radio.

10. C Choice A ignores the value of the briefcase. Choice B only includes the value of one ring. Choice D is made up.

11. C The key is that the people leave the grocery store without packages. The other three situations are not unusual.

12. D Remember, the more potential for injury, the more the situation is judged to be dangerous. In this case, the residential building is in danger, and that makes Choice D the answer.

13. C Choice C describes a potential life-threatening situation.

14. C Both the youth on the stairs and the youth at the token booth are displaying suspicious conduct.

15. B The verbal equivalent of the formula in Choice B is 850 plus 1250 plus three times 650. This is the correct formula. However, if you were unsure, you could have determined the total value, which is $4050.00. Then, you could have solved the formula in Choice A and arrived at $2750.00, which would eliminate Choice A. However, the formula in Choice B yields an answer of $4050.00, which is the correct total value. Therefore, B is the answer and you do not have to go any further.

16. D The verbal equivalent of Choice D is 800, plus 775, plus 4 times 400, plus 3 times 100, plus 600. The formula in Choice A is correct as far as it goes but it leaves out the value of the painting.

17. D Be careful of this one. Choice A gives the amount of time NOT spent in the station house. The verbal equivalent of Choice D is eight hours minus the sum of, *three* hours on patrol plus *one* hour at the school board meeting, plus *one and one half* hours transporting and processing the prisoner at court.

18. C Bailes was the only subject (note the contrast rule) who was mentioned to be extremely violent.

19. A Association might have helped you remember that Kelger, who is wanted for Sexual abuse, is in the Southeastern U.S.

20. D Miriam Leon was the only female in the wanted posters so you can expect a question on her (the contrast rule). Association might have helped you by remembering that she operates with a Buddy in the vicinity of Banks.

CHAPTER 11 The Oral Interview

In an earlier chapter you were told that oral interviews are often a part of the process used in selecting police officers. Therefore, candidates who are seeking employment with a police department that uses the oral interview as a formal component of its entry-level selection process must attach great importance to the information presented in this chapter. We believe the information in this chapter is of importance to you even if the department you are interested in does not have a formal oral interview component, because the qualities measured in a formal oral interview are always evaluated. If they are not specifically evaluated in a structured oral interview, then they are evaluated as part of the probationary period. Said another way, police departments know the profile of their ideal candidate. They know what they want their officers to be like and how they want them to behave. In some cases, they use a formal process to determine if you fit that profile. In other cases, they make this determination in other, less direct ways. But they always make that determination before granting you full civil service tenure. Your job is to find out the kind of person they want you to be, and then, insofar as it is possible, to be that person.

The Importance of Truthfulness

Sometimes candidates, in their desire to obtain employment as a police officer, will present false factual information about their background to investigators. This is a grievous and irreversible error. You must understand that the factual information about yourself that you supply will be checked. If a subsequent determination is made that you misrepresented your background in an attempt to deceive, you will be rejected. In many cases, the rejection is made even if the information you misrepresented is not cause for automatic disqualification. The bottom line is this: Be truthful and accurate about your background. You will not be judged solely on any one fact but on the total of all of the facts.

Understanding the Process

Your chances of success on an oral interview are increased if you have a good working knowledge of the oral interview process. Please understand that we cannot describe for you the exact process as it exists in each jurisdiction. There are simply too many variations of the process. There are certain concepts, however, that are the same regardless of the exact process, and it is these concepts that you should understand.

WHY ARE ORAL INTERVIEWS NEEDED?

The first thing you should understand is the reason oral interviews are needed. There are certain attitudes and abilities that a police officer must have that cannot be measured by a written examination. For example, during an oral interview, an evaluator can measure your communication abilities. In addition, your attidude, which means your approach toward police work, can also be observed during an oral interview. These attitudes and abilities are not as effectively measured on a written test.

ARE ORAL INTERVIEWS PART OF ALL SELECTION MODELS?

No! Some jurisdictions do not include an oral component in their selection process. In most cases when they are not used, the reason is economics. Oral interviews are costly; therefore, they are not used in some jurisdictions, especially in larger ones where hundreds—even thousands—of prospective candidates would have to be interviewed. On the other hand, some jurisdictions rely heavily on oral interviews and not on written tests.

WHO ARE THE PANELISTS ON THE ORAL BOARD?

To begin with, most oral interviews are usually conducted by a panel of three people, although you might see anywhere from one to five panelists. In almost all cases you can expect to have someone on the board who has a police background, and someone from the local personnel agency. Quite often an attempt is made to have community representation on the board, and in some instances the services of a psychologist are used. If you are furnished ahead of time with information about the composition of the board, you should display this knowledge during the interview since it will probably help you score better. For example, if you know the names of the board members, use them during the interview.

ARE THE QUESTIONS YOU ARE ASKED STANDARDIZED?

Yes! There are mandatory questions that must be asked of each candidate. Think of the interview as being quite structured. Panelists do not ask different questions of candidates based on how the interview goes; they ask each candidate the same basic questions. These questions must, of course, be legal. For example, questions about marital status, religious affiliation, or political beliefs would be illegal. Questions must also be job related. For this reason, you should secure a copy of the job description (also known as a position description) for the police officer title in the jurisdiction where you are applying. This description is very often included as part of the job announcement (sometimes called the test announcement) that is published when the police test is scheduled. The job description is important to you with respect to the oral interview because it tells you those typical tasks of a police officer that are emphasized in the jurisdiction where you are applying. The persons responsible for formulating the questions asked during the oral interview almost always use the job description to develop interview questions. It is, therefore, relatively safe for you to assume that some of the questions during your oral interview will be related to those tasks that are included in the job description.

HOW ARE ORAL INTERVIEWS SCORED?

Each board member is an evaluator and is trained in the scoring process. From the start of the interview until its conclusion you will probably see board members making notes as you speak. What they are doing is recording positive or negative comments about you in accordance with the guidelines that were established during their training. Immediately after each interview, the panelists independently arrive at a numerical rating within an agreed upon range, e.g., from one to ten, with, for example, one being the lowest rating and ten being the highest. Then, after each board member has arrived at a score for the interview, a group discussion is held to guard against the possibility that one of the members missed some very important negative or positive information. While consensus among the raters is not required, quite often the ratings have to fall within a certain range of each other.

IS THE SCORING PROCESS SUBJECTIVE OR OBJECTIVE?

From the preceding discussion it is now quite apparent to you that the scoring of oral interviews is a subjective process. Unlike a written multiple-choice examination, there is not just one correct answer to each question asked during an oral interview. Although evaluators are trained to be as objective as possible, to overlook the fact that the process is subjective is a big mistake. Therefore, you should not answer questions from your perspective of what the ideal police officer should be. Rather, your goal should be to convince the board members that you will be the kind of police officer they think is ideal. And you can rest assured that they are very traditional in their beliefs. They have a fixed idea of how a police officer should behave and how a police officer should present himself/herself. This includes appearance. This is why it is a good idea to find out in advance whatever you can about the composition of the board. This will be discussed in more detail later.

WOULD IT BE HELPFUL TO SEE A SAMPLE RATING FORM?

Yes. Reviewing a sample rating form allows a candidate to see at a glance the attitudes and skills that are typically measured during an oral interview for the position of police officer. A sample oral interview rating form is shown below. Remember, however, when you review this form that it is only a sample of what a rating form typically looks like. It is meant to give you a general idea of what the form used in your jurisdiction might be.

POLICE OFFICER CANDIDATE
ORAL INTERVIEW RATING FORM

1. APPEARANCE AND BEARING — SCORE ___
   Has appropriate general appearance, poise, confidence, level of enthusiasm.

2. COMMUNICATION SKILLS — SCORE ___
   Speaks with clarity of expression, good tone of voice, uses body language, has ability to listen.

3. JUDGMENT — SCORE ___
   Statements are logical, reasonable, and supported by facts.

4. UNDERSTANDING OF POSITION SCORE ____
Shows a good grasp of the duties and responsibilities of a police officer.

5. ATTITUDE SCORE ____
Displays a service attitude and a desire to serve the community.

6. SELF-ASSURANCE SCORE ____
Recognizes the essence of questions and responds with confidence.

7. INTERPERSONAL SKILLS SCORE ____
Indicates an understanding of the point of view of others; shows a level of tolerance for those with different values.

8. PERSONAL INTEGRITY SCORE ____
Answers show a high level of personal integrity.

9. OBJECTIVITY SCORE ____
Displays the ability to keep subjective feelings out of the decision-making process.

10. EMPATHY SCORE ____
Displays concern for those victimized by events beyond their control.

Advance Preparation—The Key to Success

In those departments that use a formal oral interview as part of their selection process, you will often be told by those conducting the examination that you cannot prepare for it. In some jurisdictions you will be told to simply appear at the appointed time and to be yourself. This is bad advice. The truth is that there are a number of steps you can take ahead of time that can greatly increase your chances of being selected. These steps follow:

1. **STUDY THE JOB ANNOUNCEMENT.** The police officer job announcement for your jurisdiction usually contains statements concerning the knowledge, skills, and abilities required for the job. It also contains examples of the typical tasks per-

formed by police officers in that jurisdiction. The oral board members are very often given the job announcement as the source for the questions they develop for the interview. It, therefore, contains many clues as to the types of questions you will be asked and the responses you should give. Study this announcement, anticipate questions from it, and frame tentative answers.

2. **REVIEW YOUR JOB APPLICATION.** You may very well be asked questions during your interview about information you included on your job application. You should be quite familiar with that information so that you will be able to answer promptly and coherently when asked about it. Also consider the possibility that you could be asked to elaborate on some portion of the job application at the interview. You should, therefore, be prepared to do so.

3. **LEARN ABOUT THE DEPARTMENT INVOLVED.** Make an effort to gain knowledge about the department you want to join. Know the salary, fringe benefits, retirement policy, and promotional opportunities. Also try to gain an understanding of the current critical issues the department is trying to deal with. As explained below, this information should be discussed during the interview if it becomes relevant to the interview, and it should.

4. **TAKE PART IN VOLUNTEER PROGRAMS.** Almost every police department uses civilian volunteers to supplement the work of its paid members. Insofar as possible, you should participate in such a volunteer program. Examples are internships arranged through educational programs, ride-along programs, and auxiliary police programs.

5. **ENROLL IN A CRIMINAL JUSTICE PROGRAM.** If you have the opportunity, you should enroll in a criminal justice program at an accredited college or university. This would not only help you at the interview, but by doing so you would be taking the first step toward getting promoted after you are appointed.

6. **SPEAK TO SOMEONE WHO SUCCESSFULLY COMPLETED THE PROCESS.** Find relatives or friends who are members of the department and discuss the process with them. Unless they are prohibited from doing so, and that is unlikely, they can give you a lot of insight and valuable information about the interview. Although the specific questions asked from test to test usually differ, the structure of the interview usually remains fixed. Find out the type of questions that are asked and then prepare yourself to answer them as discussed below.

7. **WORK ON YOUR METHOD OF ANSWERING QUESTIONS.** It is a mistake to believe that having the correct response to a question is the only thing that matters. Of course, accuracy is important, but your method of answering questions is also of great importance. Your answer must reflect organized thought. Where appropriate, introduce your answer, give your answer, and then conclude your answer. In other words, employ a format that includes an introduction, a body, and a conclusion. In addition, using the above sample rating form as your guide:
   a. Present a good appearance.
   b. Show enthusiasm.
   c. Speak loudly enough to be heard, but remember to modulate your tone of voice. Candidates who speak in a monotone lose points.
   d. Use appropriate hand gestures to make a point. Don't sit with your arms crossed or with your hands folded in front of you.
   e. Maintain eye contact with the board members.
   f. Display empathy for crime victims and other unfortunate people, such as the homeless.
   g. Have tolerance for the lifestyles of others.

8. **PREPARE TO MAKE A GOOD PERSONAL APPEARANCE.** Your personal appearance at your interview is of critical importance. Board members expect you to dress in conservative business attire. Any departure from that mode of dress can hurt your chances. Remember, appearance is the first thing noticed about you when you enter the interview room, and first impressions are extremely important. If you do not own conservative business attire, borrow it, rent it, or buy it, and then be sure to wear it.

9. **LEARN SOME SUGGESTED RESPONSES.** Below we have listed some interview responses. Practice working these responses, rephrased in your own words, into the interview. Couple these responses with information gleaned from the job announcement, your job application, your volunteer efforts, your college experience, and your police officer contacts in answering general questions you might be asked. Then, ask a friend to help you and do some dry runs. With your friend acting as the interviewer, practice answering a series of general questions. To facilitate this, we have included below a list of general questions often asked during interviews of police officer candidates. We strongly urge that you videotape these dry run interviews, then listen to your answers, observe your body language, and strive to improve on the content of your answers as well as your method of delivery.

SUGGESTED RESPONSES

Remember, learn to use only those responses that apply to your situation.

a. I have a relative (or friend) who has been a police officer for quite a long time and over the years I have discussed police work a lot with him (or her). These discussions led me to admire the work being done by police officers and to want to be one myself.

b. My interest in police work led me to do volunteer work with the police department, and/or to enroll in a college-level criminal justice program, and that experience served to increase my interest in becoming a police officer.

c. Perhaps more so than any other public servant, police officers should be extremely honest and have ethical standards that are beyond reproach. I feel this way because police officers are armed and they are entrusted with a great deal of authority, which gives them an even greater responsibility to the community they serve.

d. Police officers should be mature individuals who possess a great deal of common sense. I feel this way because I realize that it is impossible for a police department to have a standard procedure for every situation encountered in the street. And, when exercising common sense, police officers should always be guided by the truism that their job is to serve the community.

e. If I am fortunate enough to earn the job of being a police officer, I will treat people just as I would like my family to be treated by the police, and I will be guided by the rule that it is never appropriate to be anything except courteous and respectful to those whom I deal with in an official capacity.

f. All my life I have enjoyed helping other people. It makes me feel good. And, what better way is there to help people than working as a police officer?

g. Police officers should be able to communicate well. This certainly includes listening. A police officer who doesn't take the time to listen carefully to what others are telling him is not doing his job properly.

h. Police officers must be extremely tolerant of the viewpoints of others. They must understand that just because a person is different from them, that doesn't mean they are not entitled to the same level of police service any officer would want given to his family or friends.

i. If I was forced to choose, I would have to say that having high ethical standards is the most important characteristic a police officer should possess.

j. In my opinion, a police officer should use force only as an absolute last resort, when it is absolutely necessary to protect someone. And, even then, the amount of force used should be the minimum necessary to deal with the situation at hand.

k. The protection of life is clearly the most important responsibility, and it takes precedence over all other matters.
l. Concerning the need to be honest, a police officer should not accept anything from a merchant without paying for it, even a free cup of coffee.
m. I occasionally drink alcoholic beverages at social functions, but I would not, under any circumstances, use illegal drugs. Nor would I attend any function where illegal drugs were being used.
n. When a police officer is off duty, he or she must remain mindful of the fact that he or she is still a police officer. For this reason, a police officer's off-duty conduct must be beyond reproach.
o. If someone offered me money to violate my oath of office, I would follow the policy of my department. If the policy was to make an immediate arrest, I would not hesitate to do so.
p. If I had knowledge that another police officer was involved in a criminal activity, such as taking a bribe, I would follow the policy of my department in that situation. If the policy was to make an immediate arrest, I would not hesitate to do so. In my opinion, it is doubly wrong for a police officer to commit a crime, and I simply would not tolerate it.
q. If a well-known celebrity or politician committed a criminal act and I was aware of it, I would handle that person in the same manner as I would handle any other person in the same situation. It is wrong to give preferential treatment to anyone for any reason.
r. There is no question that I am interested in the salary, pension, and other fringe benefits that go with the job of a police officer, but my interest in being a police officer involves more than just these material considerations. I want a job that will give me a feeling that I am contributing to the betterment of society, and that, more than anything else, is why I want to be a police officer.

A LIST OF GENERAL QUESTIONS

The following is a list of general questions that are often used during oral interviews for the police officer's job.

a. Tell us about your background and life experience.
b. Why do you want to be a police officer?
c. Are you prepared to be a police officer?
d. Why would you make a good police officer?
e. What is it about the police officer's job that appeals to you?
f. What kind of person should a police officer be?
g. What would you do if you were offered a bribe?
h. What would you do if a friend of yours committed a crime and you knew about it?
i. How do you feel about alcohol and drugs?
j. How should a police officer conduct himself while off duty?

Interview Day

You have done everything possible to prepare yourself for your interview. You have learned a lot and it is now time for all of your effort to pay off. It would be a tragedy if all that work was wasted because of a foolish mistake you made on the day of your interview. Listed below are our recommendations to prevent that from happening.

1. **DRESS APPROPRIATELY.** We already discussed the importance of appearance, but it is important enough to mention once again. Don't dress to be stylish. Dress the way the board members think you should be dressed; they want you to dress neatly and conservatively. Also, be sure to bring notes with you to use as last-minute reminders of your interview room strategy. Review them just before the interview.

2. **PLAN TO ARRIVE EARLY.** You absolutely must arrive on time for your interview. Arriving late, or even at the last minute, is a big mistake. Punctuality is the hallmark of a reliable police officer. Make sure you know the route you are going to take and how much travel time is involved in the trip to the interview site. If you are using public transportation, make sure you know the bus or train schedules for the day you are being interviewed. Remember that in other than peak rush hour times, there are fewer buses and trains running. If you are traveling by car, make sure you are aware of the traffic patterns involved at the time of your trip, and make sure you know ahead of time where you will park upon arrival. For all of the above reasons, we recommend that you make a practice run one week ahead of the day of your interview at the exact time you will be making the trip on interview day. All of this may seem excessive, but there have been many instances where people lost their opportunity because they did not take the necessary precautions against arriving late for their interview. If it turns out that you have to wait to have your interview, take time to review your interview room strategy.

3. **MAINTAIN A PROFESSIONAL DEMEANOR FROM START TO FINISH.** Be courteous and dignified from the time you walk into the interview site to the time you leave. Don't make the mistake of believing that you will be judged solely during the interview. Quite often the impression you make upon arrival and while you are waiting for your interview can help you or hurt you. Remember that first impressions are quite often lasting impressions.

4. **HOW TO START THE INTERVIEW.** When you are finally called into the interview room, here is what you can expect.

You will see the board members, and they will probably be sitting down. Don't sit down until you are invited to do so. Be sure to thank whoever extends that invitation to you. You may or may not be introduced to the board members. If you are introduced, listen carefully to their names. If, during the interview, you refer to board members by their names you will enhance your chances. Expect to see a recording device on the desk, and note pads and other papers.

5. **LISTEN.** While this may seem to be a basic recommendation, it is the most important recommendation for you to follow while you are being interviewed. Don't anticipate the question. Listen attentively and make sure you understand the question before you answer.

6. **BE GUIDED BY THE FOLLOWING SUGGESTIONS:**

   - Sit up straight.
   - Maintain eye contact with the board members.
   - Use simple but complete sentences while responding.
   - Maintain an appropriate volume of speech.
   - Inflect your voice when appropriate.
   - Appropriately use hand gestures to emphasize important points.
   - Use only words you can pronounce and fully understand.
   - Be confident but not cocky.
   - Don't display nervous mannerisms.
   - Don't fold your arms in front of you.
   - Don't make jokes.
   - Don't ever interrupt a board member.
   - Think for a moment before responding.
   - Don't be overly repetitious.

7. **THANK EVERYONE PRESENT AT THE END OF THE INTERVIEW**

A Final Word

This chapter has given you an overview of what to expect in a typical oral interview for the police officer position. We have explained concepts to follow to achieve your optimal score. But you must remain flexible on the day of the interview. Apply those concepts that are appropriate to your interview as it unfolds. Don't get flustered if the interview involves a format you are not expecting. Stay cool. Regardless of the format, if you come across as possessing the attributes we have discussed in this chapter, you should do well. Good Luck.

CHAPTER 12

Report Writing

Police officer entrance examinations often include components designed to test the candidate's potential to be a successful report writer and/or to test the candidate's verbal abilities. This chapter covers the most common ways this potential is tested. We will begin with some general information about reports, then we will discuss report-writing exercises, and we will conclude with a section showing how report-writing questions can be asked in a multiple-choice format. Knowledge of the information in this chapter can help candidates with police examinations when:

1. multiple-choice questions about reports and report writing are asked, or

2. candidates are given a series of facts about an incident and asked to write a report about the incident as part of the testing process, or

3. the subject of reports and report writing is brought up during an oral interview.

General Information About Reports

Report writing is one of the most important duties of police officers, but it is also one of the least popular duties of police officers. It is an important duty because the effectiveness of police work is often influenced by written reports. This is especially true in large police departments when face-to-face communication among all officers is not feasible. Clearly written reports often lead to the capture of wanted criminals, and also result in various improvements in the work of the police agency involved.

For this reason, police departments prefer to hire those candidates who demonstrate the potential to become a good report writer.

DEFINITION OF A POLICE REPORT

A good working definition of a police report is that it is a verbal or written account of a police incident or a matter under investigation, or it is an official statement of fact. This account may be lengthy or brief; it may be simple or complex. It must, however, contain two indispensable elements:

1. It must be accurate. Accuracy is the most important quality of a police report.
2. It must communicate what its sender intends it to communicate.

In addition to these two essential elements, reports should also be concise, clear, and complete.

Report-Writing Guidelines

Good reports are the product of a good fact-finding effort. Poor reports are the result of poor investigations. This is why note taking, which we will discuss later, and interviewing are so vital to the preparation of good reports. A good police report is prepared, whenever possible, in chronological order. The properly prepared police report should also always answer six questions, known in police circles as the NEOTWY questions.

THE NEOTWY QUESTIONS

When a police officer is involved in a fact-finding effort of any kind, it is very important that all pertinent information be obtained. If the officer obtains the complete answers to the following questions, it is generally agreed that all the needed information has been obtained:

w h e N
w he r E
w h O
w h a T
h o W
w h Y

Please note that the last letters of these essential six questions end in the well-known and often-used acronym NEOTWY. If the answers to all of the NEOTWY questions are obtained, the officer involved has obtained the needed information. This is not as easy as it sounds, however, because there are so many variations of each one of the six NEOTWY questions. It is up to the investigating officer to cover all of the variations involving a particular incident. In other words, the many variations of these six essential questions must be tailored to the specifics in each case.

1. **The WHEN Question**. There are many "when" questions in almost any police incident.

   EXAMPLES:
   - When did it happen?
   - When was it discovered?
   - When were the police notified?
   - When was anything unusual observed?

When inserting the answers to the "when" questions in a report, you must remember to put them in chronological order.

2. **The WHERE Question.**

   EXAMPLES:
   - Where did it happen?
   - Where were you when it happened?
   - Where is the suspect now?
   - Where was the forced entry into the building made?
   - Where was the victim taken?

3. **The WHO Question.** The "who" question is perhaps the most controversial, primarily for two reasons.

   1. The average person is relatively unskilled at describing others. It is not unusual to obtain such varying descriptions of the same suspect from two different witnesses, so much so that one would swear the witnesses weren't describing the same person.

   2. Persons who seem to be too anxious to answer the "who" question might have ulterior motives. For example, in traffic cases, a friend of one of those involved might attempt to pose as a neutral witness and convince the officer "who" caused the accident.

EXAMPLES:

- Who was at fault?
- Who is the suspect?
- Who is the victim?
- Who had a motive?
- Who was present?

4. **The WHAT Question.**

EXAMPLES:

- What happened?
- What evidence was recovered?
- What type of weapon was involved?
- What was the license plate number?

5. **The HOW Question.** The "how" question is very important because it is the modus operandi question. Criminals tend to commit their crimes in the same way, and this is known as their method of operation, or modus operandi. In some cases a modus operandi is so unique that it is like a criminal's signature at the scene of the crime. In fact, many police departments have computerized the "how" of all major crimes and the modus operandi of known criminals. If the "how" of a particular crime matches the modus operandi of a known criminal, a very important investigative lead is uncovered. But if the original police report is not properly prepared, this cannot occur.

EXAMPLES:

- How did the criminal enter the building?
- How did the criminal act at the time of the incident?
- How did the criminal leave the scene?

6. **The WHY Question.** The "why" question is the motive question. In criminal investigations, motive is a very important factor in the investigation. Why someone would commit a particular crime is a question that often leads to the perpetrator.

EXAMPLES:

- Why was the crime committed?
- Why didn't the complainant report the incident sooner?

- Why would someone want to hurt you?
- Why would someone know the victim had cash on hand?

Report Preparation

A good report writer is systematic. The following is a recommended procedure to follow if you are given a series of facts on a police officer entry test and asked to write a report about those facts.

1. **UNDERSTAND THE PURPOSE OF THE REPORT.** Before you do anything else, you *must* understand the purpose of the report as it is explained to you in the test directions. You have to pay attention to such things as whom the report is going to and what specifically must be put in the report.

   For example, you could be given a series of facts about police problems in a number of various locations and then asked to write a report about police problems in a specific location. In that case, you would have to sort through all the material to identify the relevant material. You would lose points if you included information in the report that is not responsive to the test's specific directions.

2. **UNDERSTAND THE AMOUNT OF TIME ALLOWED.** Time management when you are writing a report on a test is a critical issue. You must make certain that you do not run out of time. If you are given sufficient time, it is best if you first write a draft of your report, but in many cases you do not have enough time to do that. We always recommend to candidates that they write a final copy first. If time permits, that copy can be rewritten. The best way to handle the time issue is through practice. If you know that you have to write a report as part of the test process, then you should do a lot of advance practice. Get a good sense ahead of time for how much time it takes you to write reports of different lengths. Remember never to write more than the directions state. If you are told to write a three-page report, you should NOT exceed three pages or you may lose points.

3. **MAKE A BRIEF OUTLINE.** The outline should, if possible, be chronological, and the order of the material must make good sense to the writer, namely you, or else the finished product will not make sense to the reader. Don't waste too much time on the outline. Just make it a good guide for you to follow to make sure you don't leave anything out.

4. **WRITE YOUR REPORT.** When writing the report, be guided by the following:
    a. The first paragraph should include an explanation of what the report contains and why it was written.
    b. Use simple, concise sentences. Do NOT use run-on sentences.
    c. Deal with only one issue per paragraph. Do not violate this rule. A report with a series of short, easy-to-read paragraphs is always worth more points on the test than one with fewer and lengthier paragraphs.
    d. Use only words you understand and that you can spell. Don't try to impress the examiner with an extensive vocabulary. Being clearly understood is the goal, and you DO NOT earn points solely because of the use of big words.
    e. Make sure of the accuracy of your facts. You must be careful to accurately transpose the material from the facts you are given to your report.
    f. Make sure to use the facts given you to support any conclusions or recommendations you make.

The Best Preparation

It should be noted that most police department entrance examinations, especially those for large departments such as in New York City, do not include the actual writing of a report. Instead, many of them use a multiple-choice format to test report-writing skills. The most common ways of testing report-writing skills in a multiple-choice format are covered in the next section of this chapter. However, many police departments use a report-writing exercise as part of some form of personal interview prior to appointment.

The best way to deal with the many report-writing possibilities is to learn ahead of time from the testing agency what type of test you will be given and the general content matter of the test. If you are going to be required to actually write a report as part of the testing process, you will be so informed. Learning about the details of a pending entrance examination is something we addressed in an earlier chapter that should be stressed again here. The more you can find out about the test ahead of time, the more focused your preparation effort can be. Preparing for every possible format and question type is foolish when the testing agency will give you information about the test format ahead of time. It is true, unfortunately, that some agencies release very little advance information about their entrance tests, but most police agencies today supply a significant amount of advance information about the format and content matter of their entrance examinations.

Evaluating a Written Report Using a Multiple-Choice Format

In this part of a police entry examination dealing with report writing, the examiner will seek to have you, the candidate, do one or a combination of two things:

1. Examine written reports or written statements and indicate by answering multiple-choice questions if the reports have been written accurately and clearly.

2. Within a multiple-choice question format, select from several options the most correct way to express the same series of facts that are given to you as part of the stem of the question.

For ease of explanation, the questions that require candidates to examine written reports or written statements and indicate by answering multiple-choice questions whether such written reports or written statements have been written accurately and clearly shall be referred to as Type A questions.

The questions that require a candidate to select from several options the most correct way to express the same series of facts that have been previously presented to the candidate shall be referred to as Type B questions.

Type A Questions— Evaluating Police Reports

RECOMMENDED STRATEGY

1. Before attempting to answer Type A questions, review the following about word usage. These distinctions are often used by examiners when testing report writing through the use of Type A questions.
   a. Accept/Except
      Accept means to take what is offered.
         I accept the nomination.
      Except means to exclude.
         All the officers except Officer Don were part of the group.
   b. Adapt/Adopt
      Adapt means to fit or adjust as needed.
         The new officer adapted to precinct life.

Adopt means to take as one's own.

Because of his prior conviction for child abuse, John could not legally adopt a child.

c. Affect/Effect

Affect as an action word or a verb means to influence something.

The new rules will affect all the members of the club.

Effect as an action word or a verb means to produce a result.

The new arrest procedures will effect the needed changes.

d. Agree with/Agree to

A person *agrees with* a person.

Officer Mays agrees with Officer Doors.

A person *agrees to* a plan.

The officers agree to a cut in salary.

An item or thing may *agree with* a person.

Milk agrees with me.

e. All ready/Already

All ready means totally prepared.

The officers are all ready to execute the search warrant.

Already means occurring before a specific time period.

It is already too late for the captain to postpone the raid.

f. All together/Altogether

All together means in a group.

The arrested perpetrator and his accomplices will be all together for the trial.

Altogether means totally or wholly.

It is altogether too risky to exchange hostages.

g. Among/Between

Between is used when referring to two persons or two things.

He was shot between his eyes.

Among is used when referring to more than two people or more than two things.

She stood out among the five suspects.

h. Beside/Besides

Beside means next to or at the side of.

The bomb-sniffing dog stood beside the officer.

Besides means in addition to.

No one visited the scene besides the detective.

i. Continual/Continuous

Continual means something that is repeated, often in a pattern.

The cuckoo bird figure of the clock appeared once each hour on a continual basis.

Continuous means without interruption.

The ticking of the clock was continuous.

j. Emigrate/Immigrate

Emigrate means to leave a country.

He was arrested as he tried to emigrate from the country without a visa.

Immigrate means to enter a country.

As soon as he immigrated into the country, he was arrested as an escaped convict.

k. Good/Well

Good is an adjective and as such usually modifies or describes names of persons, places, or things.

Because the officer had a good attendance record, she was excused for the holidays and had a good time.

Well is an adverb and as such usually modifies or describes action words or verbs or adjectives or other adverbs.

Because he reads well, he also writes well.

l. I/Me

I should be used when the intent is to describe the doer of an action.

I wanted to be a police officer as soon as I learned about the job.

Me should be used when the intent is to describe the receiver of an action.

After chasing me through the backyard, the officer arrested me.

m. Imply/Infer

Imply means to suggest or hint.

The host tried to imply to his guests that he was tired.

Infer means to conclude by reasoning.

If you yawn and look at the clock, a guest will infer that you are tired.

n. In/Into

In means a location, place, or situation.

The suspect sat in the interrogation room.

Into means movement toward a place.

The suspect sank into the chair.

o. Its/It's

Its means possession.

The station house has maintained its stark appearance.

It's means it is.

It's too dangerous to try to shoot at the fleeing felon.

p. Later/latter

Later means that something is more late in time.

Officers May and Cane were both late, but Officer May arrived later.

Latter means the second of two things that were mentioned.

The 35th and 37th are both tough precincts to work in, but I prefer the latter.

q. Lay/Lie

Lay means to put something down or place something somewhere.

Lay your weapons on the floor.

Lie means to recline.

I like to lie in the sun.

NOTE: The problem with *lay* and *lie* arises when different time frames are involved with the use of these two words.

EXAMPLE

Concerning the word *lie*, meaning to recline:

In the present tense

To Lie or lie: I lie down when I'm sleepy.

In the past tense

Lay: I lay down last night.

Using the past participle with words like *have* or *has*:

Lain: When tired, I have lain down on the bed.

Concerning the word *lay*, meaning to put or place something down

In the present tense

To lay or lay: Lay down your guns right now.

In the past tense

Laid: The robbers laid down their weapons.

Using the past participle with words like *have* or *has*:

Laid: The suspect has agreed and has laid down his gun.

r. Learn/Teach

Learn means to get knowledge.

I learn something every time I speak to my dad.

Teach means to give knowledge.

My Dad teaches me something every time he speaks to me.

s. Moral/Morale

Moral means good or virtuous conduct.

Giving the money back was a very moral act.

Morale means spirit or the mood of someone or of an organization.

The morale among the several hundred officers was high.

t. Practical/Practicable

Practical means useful, workable, sensible, not theoretical.

Keeping a spare set of keys to the police van is a practical idea.

Practicable means that something is possible or feasible. It is capable of being put into practice.

The plan to round up the suspects was practicable.

u. Their/They're/There

Their shows possession relating to the word *they*.

They ate in their radio car.

They're means "they are."

They're very happy.

There means a location.

The police officers never searched there.

v. To/Too/Two

To means in a certain direction.

Detective Cane went to the laboratory.

Too means also or more than.

Don wanted to go, too, but it was too hot.

Two is a number.

There are two officers in each radio motor patrol car.

w. Which/Who

Which is used to refer to one or more of a group, generally in a question.

Which rope was used by the inmate?

Who is used to refer to people.

The inmate who escaped last week was captured by the police.

x. Whose/Who's

Whose shows possession relating to the word *who*.

The police officer could not identify whose shoes were thrown from the rooftop.

Who's means "who is."

Who's using all the soap powder?

y. Your/You're

Your shows possession relating to the word *you*.

You had better drop your weapon.

You're means "you are."

You're surrounded.

2. Remember, if a verbal usage error is found in a choice, mark that choice as not correct and go on to the next choice. Once an error is found in a choice, you need not continue to examine that choice.

3. Circle the part of a choice that contains incorrect word usage. This is important so that when reviewing the examination, it will quickly become evident why the choice was believed to not be the correct one.

4. Examine all the choices and use a process we refer to as *deselection*. This means that it is not enough to believe that a certain choice contains no verbal usage errors; rather, such belief should be corroborated by finding the verbal usage errors in the other remaining choices.

Practice Exercises

When answering the following practice questions, try to answer them in the time allotted. After answering all the questions in a group, turn to the answers and check your work. Also make sure to review the answer explanations to help you understand why your choice of answers is correct or incorrect.

Type A Questions—20 Minute Time Limit

***DIRECTIONS:* In each of questions 1 through 10 you will be given four choices. Three of the choices—A, B, and C—contain a written statement. You are to evaluate the statement in each choice and select the statement that is most accurately and clearly written. If all or none of the three written statements is accurately and clearly written, you are to select choice D.**

1. According to the above directions, evaluate the following statements.
(A) A change in assignments always effects the officers.
(B) The police officer was able to adapt to the transfer.
(C) Let's keep it among us two.
(D) All or none is accurate.

1 A B C D

2. According to the above directions, evaluate the following statements.
(A) It's all ready too late to register for the class.
(B) The actions of the police officer were all together inappropriate.
(C) Who's book is that?
(D) All or none is accurate.

2 A B C D

3. According to the above directions, evaluate the following statements.
(A) The rookie police officer did not run the machine very good.
(B) The captain pointed at him and I.
(C) After questioning the suspect, I was able to infer he was innocent.
(D) All or none is accurate.

3 A B C D

4. According to the above directions, evaluate the following statements.
(A) The police officer had emigrated to the United States from Ireland.
(B) The prisoner wanted to immigrate from the United States back to his homeland after serving his sentence.

4 A B C D

(C) The police officer implied to the captain that he did not want a transfer to the youth division.
(D) All or none is accurate.

5. According to the above directions, evaluate the following statements.
(A) Its a different world in prison.
(B) The commanding officer is actually a very moral man.
(C) Apples and oranges are delicious but I prefer the later.
(D) All or none is accurate.

6. According to the above directions, evaluate the following statements.
(A) That is to hard.
(B) Whose using the soap?
(C) There are two officers in the police van.
(D) All or none is accurate.

7. According to the above directions, evaluate the following statements.
(A) They're getting away.
(B) There is room in the muster room.
(C) They went to get their car.
(D) All or none is accurate.

8. According to the above directions, evaluate the following statements.
(A) It's a long trip to the pistol range.
(B) Who's pistol is this?
(C) All the inmates excepted the apology from Don.
(D) All or none is accurate.

9. According to the above directions, evaluate the following statements.
(A) The heroin-sniffing dog lost it's way.
(B) Your a good sport.
(C) Morale is high among the scores of officers.
(D) All or none is accurate.

10. According to the above directions, evaluate the following statements.
(A) Keeping a list of expenses is very practicable.
(B) We are lucky that the escape was stopped because there plan was very practical.
(C) I like to lie on my sofa.
(D) All or none is accurate.

Type B Questions—Expressing Police Information

In this question type you are given a series of facts about a police incident and asked to select the choice which most *accurately* and *clearly* presents these facts in paragraph form. The kind of information you are given usually includes information about the names of people, such as victims, witnesses, and suspects, and their addresses, as well as information about when the incident occurred, where it occurred, and a brief description of what happened.

RECOMMENDED STRATEGY

1. Bear in mind that the correct answer is the one that is accurate and clear. Accuracy is checked by making sure your selected answer correctly presents the information supplied. Clarity is determined by a logical presentation of the information in the most correct grammatical form. In other words, the correct answer is the one that contains correct information and is written in the most logical and grammatically correct from.

2. Consider each choice one at a time. The first consideration should be the accuracy of the information since that is the easiest to check. The types of inaccuracies you will encounter are as follows:
   - Names will be incorrectly used, i.e., the victim's name will be used when referring to the suspect or the witness.
   - Descriptions will be switched.
   - Not enough information will be expressed by a choice, such as the time when events occurred.
   - Addresses will be inaccurately expressed in some of the choices.

3. After checking for accuracy in a choice, look for sentences that are inappropriately structured. The types of errors you will encounter are as follows:
   - Repetition. The correct answer will not unnecessarily repeat information.
   - Capitalization. Sometimes a sentence will be started without a capital letter.
   - Misplaced modifiers and confusing pronouns. A misplaced modifier makes the sentence sound silly. For example, "after being fingerprinted, the officer put the prisoner in

the cell." You should see that in that sentence it is not clear who was fingerprinted—the officer or the prisoner. Or, "The grocer pushed the customer. He was not very happy." In those sentences it is not clear who is "not very happy."

- Grammatical errors or errors in sentence construction.

4. When checking for clarity, consider the following hints:
   - Most properly worded paragraphs in police reports are written in chronological (time) order. What happened first should come first in the paragraph.
   - The first time a person is named in the paragraph, he/she should be identified. For example, "John Smith, the owner of the liquor store," or, "Eileen Brown, the witness in the case." Subsequently, the person may be referred to as "he" or "she".
   - The paragraph should very rarely start with a pronoun, unless it is the pronoun "I" referring to the writer of the paragraph.
   - Very often, the correct choice will start with someone's name or a statement of the time of occurrence.

PRACTICE QUESTIONS

1. While on patrol, Police Officer Johnson responds to a case of a lost child. The following information relating to this case was obtained by the officer:

   1 A B C D

   Name of lost child: Joan Larkin
   Age: 9 years old
   School: PS 194
   Information provided by:
   Teacher Mary Brown
   Disposition of case: Child is all right. She was picked up by her mother.

   Officer Johnson is completing a report on this incident. Which one of the following expresses the above information *most clearly* and *accurately*?

   (A) Because she was with her mother when I arrived at the school the little girl was not lost according to the teacher Joan Larkin. She was with her mother and not lost.
   (B) I arrived at PS 194 and spoke with Mary Brown, the teacher of Joan Larkin. She informed me that the lost child, Joan Larkin, age nine, was not really lost as she was picked up by her mother.

(C) The little girl was with her mother. Joan Larkin was not really lost according to her teacher, Mary Brown of PS 194.

(D) Nine year old Joan Larkin was lost. Teacher Mary Brown said that she was with her mother and was fine.

2. At about 11:30 AM Police Officer Bailes responds to a report of a burglary. The officer obtains the following information about the case:

2 A B C D

Time of occurrence: 11:25 AM
Place of occurrence: John's Shoe Store
1000 Main Street
Victim: John Rogers, owner of John's Shoe Store
Amount stolen: $1000.00
Suspects: 4 male whites

Officer Bailes is completing a report on the burglary. Which one of the following expresses the above information *most clearly* and *accurately?*

(A) John Rogers, the owner of John's Shoe Store, located at 1000 Main Street, at 11:30 AM reported that at 11:25 AM 4 white males burglarized his shoe store of $1000.00.

(B) At 11:30 AM, John Rogers, shoe store owner, reported that John's Shoe Store, located at 1000 Main Street was burglarized of $1000.00 by four white males.

(C) John Rogers reported that at 11:25 AM about $1000.00 had been stolen from John's Shoe Store by four white males at 1000 Main Street.

(D) At 11:30 AM it was reported by the shoe store owner that John Rogers had been burglarized of $1000.00 about five minutes ago.

3. While on patrol, Officer Bill Byrnes was at the scene of a shooting and obtained the following information:

3 A B C D

Place of occurrence: 88 Jones Avenue, inside the theatre
Suspect: Mr. George Burns, owner of the Bronx Theatre
Victim: Michael Benton, theatre customer
Crime: Felonious Assault
Police action taken: Suspect arrested

Officer Byrnes is preparing a report on the shooting. Which one of the following expresses the above information *most clearly* and *accurately?*

(A) Michael Benton was present at the Bronx Theatre when George Burns and Benton got into a shooting. It occurred at 88 Jones Avenue. An arrest was made for Felonious Assault.

(B) George Burns and Michael Benton were involved in a shooting inside the theatre at 88 Jones Avenue for which Burns, the theatre manager was arrested for Felonious Assault.

(C) Michael Benton, a patron at the Bronx Theatre, located at 88 Jones Avenue, was shot by Mr. George Burns, the theatre owner. Mr. Burns was arrested for Felonious Assault.

(D) George Burns, the owner of the Bronx Theatre, and Michael Benton, a theatre customer, were involved in a shooting at the theatre. One arrest was made for Felonious Assault.

4. The following information concerning a reported theft was obtained at the scene of the crime by Officer Bradley:

4 A B C D

Time of occurrence: Between 5:00 PM and 6:00 PM
Place of occurrence: In front of 123 Main Street
Victim: Sean Grennan
Crime: Grand Larceny Auto
Type of Car: Buick Riviera

Officer Bradley is completing a report on the incident. Which one of the following expresses the above information *most clearly* and *accurately*.

(A) Reported stolen between 5:00 PM and 6:00 PM was a Buick Riviera from in front of 123 Main Street. Its owner is Sean Grennan.

(B) Sean Grennan reported that between the hours of 5:00 PM and 6:00 PM his Buick Riviera was stolen from in front of 123 Main Street.

(C) Between 5:00 PM and 6:00 PM it was reported by Sean Grennan that someone stole his car in front of 123 Main Street.

(D) In front of 123 Main Street, it was reported by the car's owner, a Buick Riviera, that the car was stolen between 5:00 PM and 6:00 PM.

5. While on subway patrol, Police Officer Harris is notified on the radio to respond to the southbound platform to investigate a reported crime. The following information relating to the crime was obtained by Officer Harris:

Time of occurrence: 12 Noon
Place of occurrence: Southbound GG Train
Victim: Joan Murphy
Witness: Joe Connors
Crime: Pocketbook Snatch

Officer Harris is completing a report on this incident. Which one of the following expresses the above information *most clearly* and *accurately?*

(A) Joan Murphy informed me that her pocketbook was taken aboard a southbound GG train at 12 Noon. Joe Connors witnessed the crime.
(B) Joan Murphy and Joe Connors were on the southbound GG train when her pocketbook was snatched at 12 Noon.
(C) Joe Connors, while traveling on the southbound GG train witnessed someone taking Joan Murphy's pocketbook at 12 Noon on the GG train going south.
(D) There was a purse snatching incident on the GG train in which Joan Murphy's pocketbook was taken as witnessed by Joe Connors.

A B C D
5 | | | | | | | |

6. At the scene of a murder, the following information is gathered by Officer Sparkles:

Location:	Men's room of Dew Drop Bar
Victim:	Jay Turns, proprietor of the Dew Drop Bar
Perpetrator:	Hank Green, porter of the Dew Drop Bar
Crime:	Murder in the second degree
Weapon:	A 10″ kitchen knife
Additional details:	The victim was stabbed in the chest after arguing with the perpetrator over back wages.

The officer is preparing a report on the incident. Which one of the following expresses the above information *most clearly* and *accurately*?

(A) In the men's room of the Dew Drop Bar, a 10″ kitchen knife was used to murder Jay Turns, the proprietor of the bar, in the chest.

A B C D
6 | | | | | | | |

Hank Green, porter of the Dew Drop Bar, was arrested and charged with Murder in the 2nd Degree.

(B) In the men's room of the Dew Drop Bar, a 10″ kitchen knife murdered Jay Turns, the proprietor of the bar, who was stabbed in the chest. Hank Green, porter of the Dew Drop Bar, was arrested and charged with Murder in the 2nd Degree.

(C) After a dispute over back wages, in the men's room of the Dew Drop Bar, Jay Turns, the proprietor of the bar, was killed by a 10″ kitchen knife. Hank Green, porter of the Dew Drop Bar, was arrested and charged with Murder in the 2nd Degree.

(D) In the men's room of the Dew Drop Bar, Hank Green, porter of the Dew Drop Bar, used a 10″ kitchen knife to stab Jay Turns, the proprietor of the bar, in the chest, after a dispute over back wages. Mr. Green was charged with Murder in the 2nd Degree.

7. Police Officer Brooks responds to the emergency room at Holly Hospital where nurses have summoned him to investigate the circumstances surrounding gunshot wounds sustained by an unidentified male. At the hospital the following facts were supplied to Officer Brooks by hospital authorities at 11:00 P.M., this date:

7 A B C D

Time of occurrence:	10:20 P.M., this date
Place of occurrence:	In the rear yard of 756 Melrose Avenue
Patient's name:	Pat Forest
Description:	Male, white, 45 years old
Diagnosis:	Two .38 caliber bullet wounds to the right hand

The officer is preparing a report on the incident. Which one of the following expresses the above information *most clearly* and *accurately*?

(A) I found out at 11:00 P.M. that Mr. Pat Forest of 756 Melrose Avenue, a male, white, 45 years old, received two .38 caliber bullet wounds to his right hand at 10:20 P.M. this date while in the rear yard of 756 Melrose Avenue. He was treated at Holly Hospital.

(B) I responded to Holly Hospital at 11:00 P.M. and was informed by hospital authorities that at 10:20 P.M. this date, while in the rear yard of 756 Melrose Avenue, Mr. Pat Forest, a male, white, 45 years old, received two .38 caliber bullet wounds to his right hand.

(C) Mr. Pat Forest, a male, white, 45 years old, received two .38 caliber bullet wounds to his right hand. I responded to Holly Hospital and was informed by hospital authorities that the incident occurred at 11:00 P.M. this date, in the rear yard of 756 Melrose Avenue.

(D) I responded to Holly Hospital at 11:00 P.M. I was informed by hospital authorities that at 10:20 P.M. this date, Mr. Pat Forest, a male, white, 45 years old, was shot. Mr. Forest received two .38 caliber bullet wounds to his right hand. While he was in the rear yard of 756 Melrose Avenue, he was shot in the right hand.

8. Officer Marks is called by a female victim to the scene of a past sexual assault. The officer has obtained the following facts: **8** A B C D

Victim:	April Barker, owner of Barker Liquor Store
Place of occurrence:	Barker Liquor Store, 81 Doom Place
Perpetrator:	Male, black, armed with a pistol
Time of occurrence:	8:00 P.M., November 12, this year
Crime:	Sodomy in the first degree
Time of reporting:	8:30 P.M., November 21, this year

The officer is preparing a report on the incident. Which one of the following expresses the above information *most clearly* and *accurately*?

(A) At 8:30 P.M., on November 21, this year, April Barker, the owner of the Barker Liquor Store, 81 Doom Place, reports being the victim of Sodomy in the first Degree in the Barker Liquor Store. The offense was committed at 8:00 P.M. on November 12, this year by a male, black, armed with a pistol.

(B) At 8:00 P.M., November 12, this year, April Barker, owner of the Barker Liquor Store was the victim of Sodomy in the first Degree committed by a male, black, armed with a pistol. The offense took place at the Barker Liquor Store, 81 Doom Place. At 8:30 P.M., the incident was reported.

(C) An offense was committed at 8:00 P.M. on November 12, this year by a male, black, armed with a pistol. At 8:30 P.M., on November 21, this year, April Barker, the owner of the Barker Liquor Store, 81 Doom Place, reports being the victim of the offense in the Barker Liquor Store.

(D) At 8:30 P.M., on November 21, this year, April Barker, the owner of the Barker Liquor Store, 81 Doom Place, reports being sodomized in the Barker Liquor Store. At 8:00 P.M. on November 12, this year, a male, black, was armed with a pistol.

9. Police Officer Brown finds an unconscious female on a public sidewalk. The officer brings the female to Glory Hospital where the following information is uncovered:

9 A B C D

Name of aided:	Willow Marsh
Address:	3805 Park Place
Age:	37 years old
Place of occurrence:	Front of 887 Grand Avenue
Diagnosis:	Heat exhaustion

The officer is preparing a report on the incident. Which one of the following expresses the above information *most clearly* and *accurately*?

(A) Ms. Willow Marsh of 3805 Park Place, suffered from heat exhaustion and was discovered unconscious in front of 887 Grand Avenue. She is 37 years old.

(B) Ms. Willow Marsh of 3850 Park Place became unconscious in front of 887 Grand Avenue and was brought to Glory Hospital, where it was diagnosed that she is suffering from heat exhaustion. She is 37 years old.

(C) Ms. Willow Marsh of 3805 Park Place, who is 37 years old, was discovered unconscious in front of 887 Grand Avenue and was brought to Glory Hospital, where it was diagnosed that she was suffering from heat exhaustion.

(D) A 37-year-old female was found to be suffering from heat exhaustion. Ms. Willow Marsh of 3805 Park Place, who is 37 years old, was discovered unconscious in front of 887 Grand Avenue and was brought to Glory Hospital, where it was diagnosed that she is suffering from heat exhaustion.

10. While on desk duty in the station house, Police Officer Bowler receives a report from a complainant of an arson of an automobile. The following information is obtained by the officer concerning the incident:

10 A B C D

Place of occurrence:	Corner of Rock and York Avenues
Automobile:	A black Plymouth sedan
Suspect:	Female Hispanic
Complainant:	Pedro Ruiz, owner of the vehicle
Crime suspected:	Arson
Substance used:	A mixture of diesel fuel and gasoline

The officer is preparing a report on the incident. Which one of the following expresses the above information *most clearly* and *accurately*?

(A) On the corner of Rock and York Avenue, Pedro Ruiz reported that his black Plymouth sedan was damaged by arson by a mixture of diesel fuel and gasoline used by a female Hispanic.

(B) Using a mixture of diesel fuel and gasoline at the corner of Rock and York Avenues, Pedro Ruiz reported that his black Plymouth sedan was damaged by arson by a female Hispanic.

(C) At the corner of Rock and York Avenues, a female Hispanic, who used a mixture of diesel fuel and gasoline, damaged a black Plymouth sedan by arson, reported Pedro Ruiz.

(D) Pedro Ruiz reported that his black Plymouth sedan was damaged by arson at the corner of Rock and York Avenues by a female Hispanic using a mixture of diesel fuel and gasoline. The vehicle belongs to Ruiz.

Answer Key and Explanations

Answer Key

Type A Questions

1. B	**2. D**	**3. C**	**4. C**	**5. B**
6. C	**7. D**	**8. A**	**9. C**	**10. C**

Type B Questions

1. B	**2. A**	**3. C**	**4. B**	**5. A**
6. D	**7. B**	**8. A**	**9. C**	**10. D**

Answer Explanations

TYPE A QUESTIONS

1. **B** *Affects* means to influence and should have been used in Choice A. Choice C is incorrect because *between* should be used when two people are involved.

2. **D** Choice A is incorrect because *already* should have been used to indicate before a specific time. Choice B is incorrect because *altogether*, meaning totally, should have been used, and Choice C is incorrect since *Whose* should have been used to show possession. The answer is D because none of the three written statements is accurately and clearly written.

3. **C** Choice A is incorrect because it should use *very well*, not very good. Choice B is incorrect because it should have stated "at him and me." When not sure if *I* or *me* should be used with another pronoun or noun, remove the first pronoun or noun, in this case *him*, and substitute *I* or *me*. You will quickly see how awkward it would be to say, "The captain pointed at I." Therefore, *me* should have been used.

4. **C** The word *emigrate* means to leave the country you are in presently, whereas the word *immigrate* means to enter a country. That is just the opposite of what was stated in Choices A and B. *Imply* means to hint, so Choice C is correct.

5. **B** Choice A is incorrect: *It's* should have been used. Choice C is incorrect since *later* deals with time and *latter* means the second of two things that were mentioned.

6. **C** Choice A incorrectly uses the word *to*; the word *too* should have been used to indicate "more than." Choice B uses the word *whose* incorrectly; it should be *who's*.

7. **D** All are correct.

8. **A** Choice B should use *whose*, not *who's*. Choice C should use *accepted*, not *excepted*.

9. **C** Choice A should state "*its* way." Choice B should state "*You're* a good sport." Choice C is correct.

10. **C** Choice A should state "very *practical*" to indicate it was sensible, and Choice B should use *their* to indicate possession.

TYPE B QUESTIONS

1. **B** Choice A is repetitive so it is incorrect. Choice C is incorrect because it first speaks of *the little girl* and then gives her name in the second sentence. Choice D is incorrect because it is incomplete in that it fails to give the name of the school.

2. **A** Choice B is inaccurate in that the time of occurrence is omitted. Choice C is incorrect because it is incomplete in that it fails to identify Rogers as the owner of the store. Choice D is incorrect since it makes it sound like the store owner and John Rogers are two different people.

3. **C** Choice A is incorrect because it does not clearly indicate who shot whom. Choice B is incorrect for the same reason plus it fails to say who Michael Benton is (he is a customer at the theatre). Choice D is incorrect because it is not clearly written, i.e., it doesn't stipulate who was arrested.

4. **B** Choice A is incorrect because it fails to make clear whether the report was made between 5:00 PM and 6:00 PM or if the car was stolen during that time. Choice C is incorrect for the same reason. Choice D is incorrect because it sounds like a Buick is the owner of the car.

5. **A** Choice B is incomplete because it does not clearly indicate that Joe Connors is a witness. Choice C is repetitive in that it mentions more than once the fact that the train was going south. Choice D is incomplete in that it fails to mention the direction the train was traveling and the time of occurrence of the crime.

6. **D** Choices A and B are incorrect since they do not mention the dispute over wages, nor do they clearly state who used the knife. At times a choice may be incorrect for more than one reason. Choice C

is incorrect since it does not mention where the fatal injury was inflicted, namely to the chest.

7. **B** Choice A is incorrect since it indicates that Mr. Forest resides at 756 Melrose Avenue. Nothing in the information given substantiates that. Do not assume. Choice C is incorrect since it indicates that the time of occurrence is 11:00 P.M. That is the time of reporting. Choice D is incorrect since it unnecessarily repeats that the subject was shot.

8. **A** Choice B is incorrect since it does not indicate that the offense was reported on a different date than the day it occurred. Choice C is incorrect since it does not indicate what the offense is. Choice D is incorrect since it merely indicates a male, black, was armed with a pistol, but it does not state who is the perpetrator of the sodomy.

9. **C** Choice A is incorrect since no mention is made of the hospital where the diagnosis took place. Choice B is incorrect since her address is incorrectly given. Remember, care must be taken to pay attention to details such as addresses. Choice D is incorrect since it repeats Ms. Marsh's condition.

10. **D** Choice A is incorrect since it seems as if the place of occurrence is where the offense was reported. Choice B is incorrect since it appears that the complainant, Ruiz, was using a mixture of diesel fuel and gasoline. Choice C is incorrect since it does not indicate that the vehicle belongs to Ruiz.

TEST YOURSELF

Answer Sheet
Practice Examination One

Follow the instructions given in the test. Mark only your answers in the ovals below. WARNING: Be sure that the oval you fill is in the same row as the question you are answering. Use a No. 2 pencil (soft pencil).

BE SURE YOUR PENCIL MARKS ARE HEAVY AND BLACK. ERASE COMPLETELY ANY ANSWER YOU WISH TO CHANGE.

DO NOT make stray pencil dots, dashes or marks.

START HERE

1 Ⓐ Ⓑ Ⓒ Ⓓ	2 Ⓐ Ⓑ Ⓒ Ⓓ	3 Ⓐ Ⓑ Ⓒ Ⓓ	4 Ⓐ Ⓑ Ⓒ Ⓓ	5 Ⓐ Ⓑ Ⓒ Ⓓ	6 Ⓐ Ⓑ Ⓒ Ⓓ
7 Ⓐ Ⓑ Ⓒ Ⓓ	8 Ⓐ Ⓑ Ⓒ Ⓓ	9 Ⓐ Ⓑ Ⓒ Ⓓ	10 Ⓐ Ⓑ Ⓒ Ⓓ	11 Ⓐ Ⓑ Ⓒ Ⓓ	12 Ⓐ Ⓑ Ⓒ Ⓓ
13 Ⓐ Ⓑ Ⓒ Ⓓ	14 Ⓐ Ⓑ Ⓒ Ⓓ	15 Ⓐ Ⓑ Ⓒ Ⓓ	16 Ⓐ Ⓑ Ⓒ Ⓓ	17 Ⓐ Ⓑ Ⓒ Ⓓ	18 Ⓐ Ⓑ Ⓒ Ⓓ
19 Ⓐ Ⓑ Ⓒ Ⓓ	20 Ⓐ Ⓑ Ⓒ Ⓓ	21 Ⓐ Ⓑ Ⓒ Ⓓ	22 Ⓐ Ⓑ Ⓒ Ⓓ	23 Ⓐ Ⓑ Ⓒ Ⓓ	24 Ⓐ Ⓑ Ⓒ Ⓓ
25 Ⓐ Ⓑ Ⓒ Ⓓ	26 Ⓐ Ⓑ Ⓒ Ⓓ	27 Ⓐ Ⓑ Ⓒ Ⓓ	28 Ⓐ Ⓑ Ⓒ Ⓓ	29 Ⓐ Ⓑ Ⓒ Ⓓ	30 Ⓐ Ⓑ Ⓒ Ⓓ
31 Ⓐ Ⓑ Ⓒ Ⓓ	32 Ⓐ Ⓑ Ⓒ Ⓓ	33 Ⓐ Ⓑ Ⓒ Ⓓ	34 Ⓐ Ⓑ Ⓒ Ⓓ	35 Ⓐ Ⓑ Ⓒ Ⓓ	36 Ⓐ Ⓑ Ⓒ Ⓓ
37 Ⓐ Ⓑ Ⓒ Ⓓ	38 Ⓐ Ⓑ Ⓒ Ⓓ	39 Ⓐ Ⓑ Ⓒ Ⓓ	40 Ⓐ Ⓑ Ⓒ Ⓓ	41 Ⓐ Ⓑ Ⓒ Ⓓ	42 Ⓐ Ⓑ Ⓒ Ⓓ
43 Ⓐ Ⓑ Ⓒ Ⓓ	44 Ⓐ Ⓑ Ⓒ Ⓓ	45 Ⓐ Ⓑ Ⓒ Ⓓ	46 Ⓐ Ⓑ Ⓒ Ⓓ	47 Ⓐ Ⓑ Ⓒ Ⓓ	48 Ⓐ Ⓑ Ⓒ Ⓓ
49 Ⓐ Ⓑ Ⓒ Ⓓ	50 Ⓐ Ⓑ Ⓒ Ⓓ	51 Ⓐ Ⓑ Ⓒ Ⓓ	52 Ⓐ Ⓑ Ⓒ Ⓓ	53 Ⓐ Ⓑ Ⓒ Ⓓ	54 Ⓐ Ⓑ Ⓒ Ⓓ
55 Ⓐ Ⓑ Ⓒ Ⓓ	56 Ⓐ Ⓑ Ⓒ Ⓓ	57 Ⓐ Ⓑ Ⓒ Ⓓ	58 Ⓐ Ⓑ Ⓒ Ⓓ	59 Ⓐ Ⓑ Ⓒ Ⓓ	60 Ⓐ Ⓑ Ⓒ Ⓓ
61 Ⓐ Ⓑ Ⓒ Ⓓ	62 Ⓐ Ⓑ Ⓒ Ⓓ	63 Ⓐ Ⓑ Ⓒ Ⓓ	64 Ⓐ Ⓑ Ⓒ Ⓓ	65 Ⓐ Ⓑ Ⓒ Ⓓ	66 Ⓐ Ⓑ Ⓒ Ⓓ
67 Ⓐ Ⓑ Ⓒ Ⓓ	68 Ⓐ Ⓑ Ⓒ Ⓓ	69 Ⓐ Ⓑ Ⓒ Ⓓ	70 Ⓐ Ⓑ Ⓒ Ⓓ	71 Ⓐ Ⓑ Ⓒ Ⓓ	72 Ⓐ Ⓑ Ⓒ Ⓓ
73 Ⓐ Ⓑ Ⓒ Ⓓ	74 Ⓐ Ⓑ Ⓒ Ⓓ	75 Ⓐ Ⓑ Ⓒ Ⓓ	76 Ⓐ Ⓑ Ⓒ Ⓓ	77 Ⓐ Ⓑ Ⓒ Ⓓ	78 Ⓐ Ⓑ Ⓒ Ⓓ
79 Ⓐ Ⓑ Ⓒ Ⓓ	80 Ⓐ Ⓑ Ⓒ Ⓓ	81 Ⓐ Ⓑ Ⓒ Ⓓ	82 Ⓐ Ⓑ Ⓒ Ⓓ	83 Ⓐ Ⓑ Ⓒ Ⓓ	84 Ⓐ Ⓑ Ⓒ Ⓓ
85 Ⓐ Ⓑ Ⓒ Ⓓ	86 Ⓐ Ⓑ Ⓒ Ⓓ	87 Ⓐ Ⓑ Ⓒ Ⓓ	88 Ⓐ Ⓑ Ⓒ Ⓓ	89 Ⓐ Ⓑ Ⓒ Ⓓ	90 Ⓐ Ⓑ Ⓒ Ⓓ
91 Ⓐ Ⓑ Ⓒ Ⓓ	92 Ⓐ Ⓑ Ⓒ Ⓓ	93 Ⓐ Ⓑ Ⓒ Ⓓ	94 Ⓐ Ⓑ Ⓒ Ⓓ	95 Ⓐ Ⓑ Ⓒ Ⓓ	96 Ⓐ Ⓑ Ⓒ Ⓓ
97 Ⓐ Ⓑ Ⓒ Ⓓ	98 Ⓐ Ⓑ Ⓒ Ⓓ	99 Ⓐ Ⓑ Ⓒ Ⓓ	100 Ⓐ Ⓑ Ⓒ Ⓓ	101 Ⓐ Ⓑ Ⓒ Ⓓ	102 Ⓐ Ⓑ Ⓒ Ⓓ
103 Ⓐ Ⓑ Ⓒ Ⓓ	104 Ⓐ Ⓑ Ⓒ Ⓓ	105 Ⓐ Ⓑ Ⓒ Ⓓ	106 Ⓐ Ⓑ Ⓒ Ⓓ	107 Ⓐ Ⓑ Ⓒ Ⓓ	108 Ⓐ Ⓑ Ⓒ Ⓓ
109 Ⓐ Ⓑ Ⓒ Ⓓ	110 Ⓐ Ⓑ Ⓒ Ⓓ	111 Ⓐ Ⓑ Ⓒ Ⓓ	112 Ⓐ Ⓑ Ⓒ Ⓓ	113 Ⓐ Ⓑ Ⓒ Ⓓ	114 Ⓐ Ⓑ Ⓒ Ⓓ
115 Ⓐ Ⓑ Ⓒ Ⓓ	116 Ⓐ Ⓑ Ⓒ Ⓓ	117 Ⓐ Ⓑ Ⓒ Ⓓ	118 Ⓐ Ⓑ Ⓒ Ⓓ	119 Ⓐ Ⓑ Ⓒ Ⓓ	120 Ⓐ Ⓑ Ⓒ Ⓓ
121 Ⓐ Ⓑ Ⓒ Ⓓ	122 Ⓐ Ⓑ Ⓒ Ⓓ	123 Ⓐ Ⓑ Ⓒ Ⓓ	124 Ⓐ Ⓑ Ⓒ Ⓓ	125 Ⓐ Ⓑ Ⓒ Ⓓ	126 Ⓐ Ⓑ Ⓒ Ⓓ
127 Ⓐ Ⓑ Ⓒ Ⓓ	128 Ⓐ Ⓑ Ⓒ Ⓓ	129 Ⓐ Ⓑ Ⓒ Ⓓ	130 Ⓐ Ⓑ Ⓒ Ⓓ	131 Ⓐ Ⓑ Ⓒ Ⓓ	132 Ⓐ Ⓑ Ⓒ Ⓓ
133 Ⓐ Ⓑ Ⓒ Ⓓ	134 Ⓐ Ⓑ Ⓒ Ⓓ	135 Ⓐ Ⓑ Ⓒ Ⓓ	136 Ⓐ Ⓑ Ⓒ Ⓓ	137 Ⓐ Ⓑ Ⓒ Ⓓ	138 Ⓐ Ⓑ Ⓒ Ⓓ
139 Ⓐ Ⓑ Ⓒ Ⓓ	140 Ⓐ Ⓑ Ⓒ Ⓓ	141 Ⓐ Ⓑ Ⓒ Ⓓ	142 Ⓐ Ⓑ Ⓒ Ⓓ	143 Ⓐ Ⓑ Ⓒ Ⓓ	144 Ⓐ Ⓑ Ⓒ Ⓓ
145 Ⓐ Ⓑ Ⓒ Ⓓ	146 Ⓐ Ⓑ Ⓒ Ⓓ	147 Ⓐ Ⓑ Ⓒ Ⓓ	148 Ⓐ Ⓑ Ⓒ Ⓓ	149 Ⓐ Ⓑ Ⓒ Ⓓ	150 Ⓐ Ⓑ Ⓒ Ⓓ

CHAPTER 13 Practice Examination One

This chapter includes the first of three practice examinations you will be taking. This examination is an original examination prepared to conform with the actual police officer examination as closely as possible. *When you have finished taking all three examinations, you will see that you are prepared to take most major police officer examinations, including those for Transit and Housing Police Officer*.

Be sure to take Practice Examination One in one sitting. You will then become accustomed to concentrating for a period of 4 hours, which is the length of time allowed for the examination. Be sure to review the test-taking stragtegy outlined in Chapter 2 before taking this practice examination.

Before You Take the Examination

When you begin this examination, look first at the material marked "Memory Material," which begins on the following page. After reading the material for the time specified, continue to the "Test Material" and do not look back at the material marked "Memory Material." Then continue with the rest of the test.

Remember to read each question and related material carefully before choosing your answers. Select the choice you believe to be the most correct, and mark your answer on the Answer Sheet provided at the beginning of this chapter. The Answer Key, Diagnostic Procedure, and Answer Explanations appear at the end of this chapter. (Be sure to gauge your time, allotting no more than $1^1/_2$ to 2 minutes per question.)

The Test

MEMORY MATERIAL 10-MINUTE TIME LIMIT

***DIRECTIONS:* Answer questions 1 through 15 based on the following narrative. You are allowed 10 minutes to read the narrative and commit to memory as much about it as you can. You are *not* permitted to make any written notes during the 10 minutes you are reading the story.**

At the end of 10 minutes you are to stop reading the material, turn the page, and answer the questions *without* referring to the written material.

You are Police Officer John Madden, Shield #3232 of the 64th Precinct in Queens. You are assigned for today, May 19, as the operator of RMP 3220, Sector Edward of the 64th Precinct. The tour you are working is 1600 by 2400 hours, and your partner is Police Officer Martin Balsam, Shield #3331, also of the 64th Precinct. Your immediate supervisor is Sergeant Donald Black, Shield #113. The time is now 1720 hours.

A radio call from the dispatcher has just been directed to your unit. You are to respond to the Interboro Highway, eastbound, near Metropolitan Street. There has just been a three-car accident at that location, and personal injury is involved. Two ambulances have also been dispatched to the scene.

You attempt to enter the highway at the eastbound entrance at Grant Street, which is just west of Metropolitan Street, but the traffic has become impassable. You notify Sergeant Black of the traffic jam on the highway. He instructs you to respond to the accident scene by entering the highway westbound at York Avenue, which is just east of the accident, and approaching the accident from the westbound side of the highway. The sergeant also directs Sector Frank of the 64th Precinct to respond to the eastbound exit at Grant Street to detour traffic off the highway. Further, he directs the dispatcher to inform the responding ambulances to approach the accident by using the westbound lane of the highway.

Upon arrival at the accident location approximately ten minutes after you have received the call, you determine that additional assistance is needed for traffic control. You inform Sergeant Black, and he directs the dispatcher to send Sector George to assist you. Sector George arrives approximately five minutes later and proceeds to direct traffic around the disabled vehicles from the accident. In the meantime, you and your partner determine that there are four injured persons: the driver and only passenger of vehicle number one, the driver of vehicle number two, and a passenger from vehicle number three. You then gather the following information:

1. *Vehicle One:* A blue late-model Datsun, two-door sedan, New York State Registration #16 BFN, owned and operated by Jerry Goodman of 1543 Eastern Avenue of the Bronx.

2. *Vehicle Two:* A black, late-model Ford, four-door sedan, New York State Registration #85 SWE, owned and operated by Harvey Richter of 54-31 Metropolitan Street, Queens.

3. *Vehicle Three:* A green, late-model Plymouth, four-door sedan, New Jersey Registration #445 FGF, owned and operated by James Kirk of 3241 Jersey Avenue, Newark, New Jersey.

Moments later the two ambulances arrive: one from Bayside Hospital, the other from Malba Hospital. The two injured parties from vehicle number one are put in the Bayside Hospital ambulance; and the other two injured parties are placed in the Malba Hospital ambulance.

According to accounts obtained from uninjured participants in the accident and from two impartial eyewitnesses, the accident occurred when vehicle number one made an unsafe lane change, causing vehicle number two to brake hard to avoid hitting vehicle number one in the rear. Vehicle number three then slammed vehicle number two in the rear, which caused vehicle number two to pile into the rear of vehicle number one.

DO NOT PROCEED UNTIL 10 MINUTES HAVE ELAPSED

TEST MATERIAL

4 HOUR TIME LIMIT

1. Your partner's shield number is:
(A) 3232.
(B) 3220.
(C) 3331.
(D) 3241.

2. Your supervisor's name is:
(A) Black.
(B) Goodman.
(C) Madden.
(D) Balsam.

3. You arrived at the scene of the accident at approximately:
(A) 1720 hours.
(B) 1730 hours.
(C) 1800 hours.
(D) Not given.

4. Which unit did your supervisor assign to respond to the Grant Street exit of the highway?
(A) 64th Precinct Sector George
(B) 64th Precinct Sector Edward
(C) 64th Precinct Sector Frank
(D) 64th Precinct Sector Henry

5. What unit was dispatched to the accident scene to assist with traffic control?
(A) 64th Precinct Sector George
(B) 64th Precinct Sector Edward
(C) 64th Precinct Sector Frank
(D) 64th Precinct Sector Henry

6. Which driver was uninjured in the accident?
(A) Vehicle number one
(B) Vehicle number two
(C) Vehicle number three
(D) None

7. Which of the vehicles was registered in New Jersey?
(A) Vehicle number one
(B) Vehicle number two
(C) Vehicle number three
(D) None

8. Your partner's name is:
   (A) Black.
   (B) Goodman.
   (C) Madden.
   (D) Balsam.

9. York Avenue is located:
   (A) West of Metropolitan Street.
   (B) East of Grant Street.
   (C) North of the Interboro Highway.
   (D) South of the accident location.

10. Who lives at 54-31 Metropolitan Street in Queens?
   (A) Goodman
   (B) Richter
   (C) Kirk
   (D) Madden

11. The date of the accident was:
   (A) April 4
   (B) May 19
   (C) April 19
   (D) May 4

12. Which vehicle caused the accident?
   (A) Vehicle number one
   (B) Vehicle number two
   (C) Vehicle number three
   (D) Information not included

13. What was the registration number of vehicle number one?
   (A) 16 BFN
   (B) 85 SWE
   (C) 445 FGF
   (D) Not given

14. The driver of vehicle number three was:
   (A) Goodman.
   (B) Richter.
   (C) Kirk.
   (D) Madden.

15. The injured passenger from vehicle number three was placed in the ambulance from:
   (A) Whitestone Hospital.
   (B) Malba Hospital.
   (C) Bayside Hospital.
   (D) Metropolitan Hospital.

TURN TO NEXT PAGE

DIRECTIONS: *Questions 16 through 25 are based* ***solely*** **on the following picture. You are to study this picture for 5 minutes and commit to memory as much about it as you can. You are *not* allowed to make written notes during the five minutes you are studying the picture, and you cannot refer to the picture while answering the questions.**

Do not look at the questions until after you have studied the picture for the 5 minutes permitted.

Note: Do *not* include this 5-minute period in the 4-hour time limit for completing the examination.

DO NOT PROCEED UNTIL 5 MINUTES HAVE ELAPSED

TURN TO NEXT PAGE

16. What street number is indicated on the lamppost?
    (A) 151st Place
    (B) 15th Street
    (C) 51st Road
    (D) None

17. The female on the sidewalk is:
    (A) Pushing a shopping cart.
    (B) Carrying a shopping bag.
    (C) Carrying packages in her arms.
    (D) A professional cook.

18. Where is the lawn mower in the scene?
    (A) On the lawn
    (B) On the sidewalk
    (C) On the stoop
    (D) There is none

19. The house faces a:
    (A) One way street.
    (B) Dead end street.
    (C) Major thoroughfare.
    (D) Play street.

20. The female in the dress is located:
    (A) In the garage.
    (B) On the stoop.
    (C) Next to the stoop.
    (D) In the driveway.

21. The first three numbers of the license plate on the car parked to the left of the lamppost are:
    (A) 252.
    (B) 461.
    (C) 191.
    (D) 822.

22. The female on the sidewalk is:
    (A) Wearing a dress.
    (B) Wearing dark glasses.
    (C) Wearing a coat.
    (D) Wearing a jacket.

23. The female in the dress is carrying:
    (A) A pocketbook.
    (B) A pail.
    (C) A package.
    (D) A broom.

24. The garage door in the picture was:

(A) Open.
(B) Closed.
(C) Broken.
(D) Half open.

25. The refuse container was located:

(A) In the garage.
(B) In the driveway.
(C) On the sidewalk.
(D) There was none.

TURN TO NEXT PAGE

***DIRECTIONS:* Answer questions 26 through 35 *solely* on the basis of the following narrative and Civilian Complaint Report. Some of the boxes on the form are numbered and others are not. The boxes are not necessarily consecutively numbered.**

On Wednesday July 8, at about 2230 hours, Mr. Manny Rodriquez, of 8207 First Avenue, Manhattan, Apartment 25, telephone number 262-4511, came to the Third Precinct station house to make a civilian complaint. The details are as follows:

At about 2200 hours, July 8, Mr. Rodriquez was walking south on Broadway at the intersection of Chambers Street. He had just finished work at the Gleem Computer Company of 280 Broadway, telephone number 374-0001, where he is employed as a key punch operator. He was on his way to the subway when he met a co-worker, Lydia James. Suddenly a uniformed police officer on foot patrol approached him. The officer took Mr. Rodriquez into City Hall Park and searched him. Ms. James, who lives at 322 Archer Street, Staten Island, telephone number 743-3304, witnessed the incident. She, however, became frightened and ran away.

According to the complainant, he was searched and then told by the police officer that he looked like a trouble maker and that the officer knew how to control "his kind." The officer then pushed Mr. Rodriquez and told him to "beat it."

Mr. Rodriquez was very upset and returned to his place of employment. There he met John Colon, his office supervisor. Mr. Colon told Mr. Rodriquez that he should report the incident to the precinct. Mr. Rodriquez agreed, but did not think he could do it because he did not speak English very well. Mr. Colon, who lives at 46-02 Bellow Street, Queens, telephone number 820-0603, said he would go to the precinct with Mr. Rodriquez and help explain the details.

They went to the Third Precinct station house and Mr. Rodriquez, with Mr. Colon's help, restated what had taken place. Sergeant Howe had them prepare a Civilian Complaint Form and asked if Mr. Rodriquez could describe the police officer. He said he could. He said the officer was white, about five feet eight inches, with a shield number of 770. That was all he could remember.

At 2245 hours, Sergeant Howe called the complaint into the Civilian Complaint Review Board and spoke to Police Officer Wilson. The Civilian Complaint Review Board (C.C.R.B.) serial number of 2046 was assigned by Officer Wilson, whose shield number is 84. The sergeant thanked them for bringing the matter to his attention and said that the matter would be further investigated. Mr. Rodriquez and Mr. Colon left the station house at 2300 hours.

GO TO NEXT PAGE

50M - 702620 (77)

CITY OF NEW YORK

CIVILIAN COMPLAINT REPORT — POLICE DEPARTMENT — P.D. 313-154

(FOR POLICE DEPARTMENT USE ONLY) — JURISDICTION: ☐ C.I. ☐ C.C.R.B.

TIME 1	and DATE REPORTED 2	COMMAND OR LOCATION WHERE RECEIVED 3	C.C.R.B. (NAME) NTFD: 4	SERIAL NUMBER 5 C.C.R.B. C.I.
HOW COMPLAINT MADE 6 ☐ PERSON ☐ MAIL ☐ PHONE	CCRB NOTIFIED 7 TIME 8 DATE	COMPLAINT RECEIVED TIME DATE	EXACT TIME COMPLAINANT APPEARED/TELEPHONED	

INDICATE ANY ADDITIONAL FORMS PREPARED OR ENTRIES MADE IN DEPARTMENT RECORDS WITH DATES (EXCEPT BLOTTER ENTRY)

COMPLAINANT'S SURNAME 9	FIRST	ADDRESS 10	APT/FLOOR	TELEPHONE NO. 11
NAME OF PERSON WITH WHOM RESIDING 12	TELEPHONE NO.	ADDRESS WHERE RESIDING IF NOT A NEW YORK CITY RESIDENT		HOW LONG WILL YOU RESIDE IN NEW YORK CITY?
EMPLOYER'S NAME 13	BUSINESS ADDRESS 14	YOUR OCCUPATION 15		TELEPHONE NO. 16
REPRESENTATIVE/INTERPRETER/PERSON ASSISTING 17		ADDRESS 33	APT/FLOOR	TELEPHONE NO.

NAME OF POLICE DEPARTMENT MEMBER COMPLAINED OF (If unknown, provide description of officer and type of duty performed, e.g., foot, auto, detective, etc.)	SHIELD NO.	COMMAND
18	19	20

TIME 21	and DATE OF OCCURRENCE 22	LOCATION 23

NAME OF WITNESS 24	ADDRESS 25	APT/FLOOR	RELATIONSHIP 26	TELEPHONE NO. 27

DETAILS OF COMPLAINT (In your own handwriting, give a brief story of what happened. Use reverse side of form if more space is required.)

28

RANK 29	Signature of Member of Force Receiving Complaint 30	Signature of Person Assisting Complainant 31	Signature of Complainant 32

INSTRUCTIONS FOR COMPLAINANT: Prepare this report in your own handwriting. You will immediately receive a typewritten copy as your receipt. The Chairman, Civilian Complaint Review Board or an investigating officer will communicate with you in writing in the near future relative to the investigation of your complaint and will arrange to schedule any necessary investigative interview at a time and date convenient to you.

Source of blank form: New York City Police Department

TURN TO NEXT PAGE

26. The Gleem Computer Company should be entered in Box number:

(A) 17.
(B) 15.
(C) 13.
(D) 9.

27. The correct entry for Box 11 is:

(A) 743-3304.
(B) 374-0001.
(C) 820-0603.
(D) 262-4511.

28. Mr. Colon's address should be entered in Box number:

(A) 10.
(B) 14.
(C) 25.
(D) 33.

29. The word "co-worker" would best be entered in Box number:

(A) 24.
(B) 26.
(C) 20.
(D) 12.

30. The most accurate entry for Box 1 is:

(A) 2200.
(B) 2230.
(C) 2245.
(D) 2300.

31. Police Officer Wilson's name should be entered in Box number:

(A) 30.
(B) 9.
(C) 31.
(D) 4.

32. The correct entry for Box 5 is:

(A) 770.
(B) 84.
(C) 2046.
(D) 2300.

33. Which of the following persons is *not* required to sign the form?
(A) Sergeant Howe
(B) Mr. Colon
(C) Ms. James
(D) Mr. Rodriquez

34. Which of the following should *not* be entered in Box 18?
(A) Uniformed police officer
(B) On foot
(C) A male, white
(D) Five feet, eight inches

35. City Hall Park should be entered in Box number:
(A) 23.
(B) 25.
(C) 3.
(D) 22.

TURN TO NEXT PAGE

DIRECTIONS: **Answer questions 36 through 45 *solely* on the basis of information recorded on the following Property Clerk's Invoice.**

THE CITY OF NEW YORK

PROPERTY CLERK'S INVOICE **POLICE DEPARTMENT** Pr. Clk. 1 (Rev. 4-67) P.D. 521-141 100M-328059 (73)

THIS PROPERTY IS: ☒ Required as EVIDENCE ☐ *DECEDENT'S PROPERTY ☐ FOUND PROPERTY ☐ OTHER

(See instructions on reverse side)

Date: January 26 XXXX

Officer Assigned	Rank	Shield No.	Command
Gleason, John	Police Officer	82	38th Precinct

Prisoner's Name	Address
Murray, Fred	38 Pleasant Plaza Brooklyn, NY

Date of Arrest	Arrest No.	Charge	U.F. 61 No.
Jan.26, XXXX	48	Burglary	479

	Name	Address	Apt. No.
Finder of Property	not applicable	-------	
Owner's Name (See instruction 3)	not applicable	-------	
Complainant's Name	Murphy, Jane	367-22 12th Avenue, Queens	2H

ITEM NO.	QUANTITY	ARTICLE	**CASH VALUE U.S. Currency only	(For Property Clerk's Use Only) DISPOSITION and DATE
1	1	19 inch portable t.v.	$ 200 00	
2	2	gold earrings	$ 100 00	
3	1	N.Y.S. college ring	$ 75 00	
		TOTAL	$ 375 00	LOCATION WHERE PROPERTY STORED: Manhattan property clerk

REMARKS; (See instructions on rear of form)

Rank	Signature of Desk Officer	Shield No.	PRECINCT	VOUCHER NO.	YEAR
Sergeant	Henry Blake	28	38	83	XX
Rank	Signature	Shield No. PROPERTY CLERK		PROPERTY CLERK'S VOUCHER NO.	

Source of blank form: New York City Police Department

GO TO NEXT PAGE

36. What is the complainant's address?
(A) 38 Pleasant Plaza, Brooklyn
(B) 367-22 12th Avenue, Queens
(C) 29-02 Sedgewick Avenue, Bronx
(D) Not given

37. What is the name of the desk officer?
(A) Fred Murray
(B) John Gleason
(C) Jane Murphy
(D) Henry Blake

38. What is the assigned officer's shield number?
(A) 28
(B) 38
(C) 82
(D) 83

39. Fred Murray is:
(A) The officer assigned.
(B) The property clerk.
(C) The prisoner.
(D) The complainant.

40. Is the television set a color, or black and white, set?
(A) Color
(B) Black and white
(C) No television set is mentioned
(D) It cannot be determined

41. The date of the arrest is:
(A) The same as the date of the preparation of the form.
(B) June 26.
(C) The day before the preparation of the form.
(D) Not given.

42. The crime charged is:
(A) Robbery.
(B) Larceny.
(C) Burglary.
(D) Assault.

43. The command of the assigned police officer is:
(A) 82nd Precinct.
(B) 38th Precinct.
(C) 28th Precinct.
(D) 83rd Precinct.

44. What is the voucher number?

(A) 84
(B) 83
(C) 82
(D) 38

45. How many college rings were stolen?

(A) One
(B) Two
(C) Three
(D) None

GO TO NEXT PAGE

***DIRECTIONS:* Answer questions 46 through 52 *solely* on the basis of the following information.**

The police handling of family disputes has received an increasing amount of attention in recent years. Quite often, such situations involve complex decisions because of the potential for physical danger both to the police officer and the parties involved in the dispute.

In the past, when some police officers responded to scenes of family disputes, they invariably referred the people involved to Family Court without arresting anyone. Such handling was considered "the practical way" to handle these situations because, in a matter of days, hours or even minutes, the antagonists would resolve their differences and reconcile. This prompted the people involved to feel that the police had not discharged their duties properly. Indeed, a lawsuit was instituted on behalf of some wives who felt that the police should have arrested their husbands instead of attempting to mediate the problem or refer it to court. In some instances the Department agreed that an arrest should have been made and, accordingly, the Department policy in this Bulletin was developed.

Department Policy

The victim of a criminal act which occurs in the home or involves another family member has the right to demand that police take appropriate action. This action may include an arrest. The fact that the persons involved are related should not matter. Accordingly, the following two situations demonstrate departmental policy with respect to the role of the police officer at the scene of a dispute involving a husband and a wife.

A. THE POLICE ARE SUMMONED TO A LOCATION, AND A SPOUSE (HUSBAND OR WIFE) OR SOMEONE ELSE HAS AN ORDER OF PROTECTION ISSUED PURSUANT TO THE FAMILY COURT ACT.

When the police arrive at the scene of a dispute where one of the parties alleges that he or she has an Order of Protection, they should ask for a copy of that Order. A police officer has a right to see the Order of Protection before making a decision as to how to proceed. The Order will indicate the type of conduct prohibited and its date of expiration. If the person to whom the order was issued (the Petitioner) asks the officer to arrest the offender (the Respondent) for violations of the Order, that Respondent *must* be taken into custody if there is probable cause to believe that the Order has been violated. The fact that the people involved are husband and wife *may not* be a factor in determining the existence of probable cause.

If the person who violated the Order is absent when the police arrive, normal procedures should be followed.

An Order of Protection may prohibit conduct which is not ordinarily criminal in itself. For instance, an Order may demand that the spouse not appear in an intoxicated condition before the children; not be present in a specific location; or not use abusive language in front of his or her spouse, children, etc. Arrests will be made in such situations even though the conduct is not criminal.

If an Order of Protection has been violated and the petitioner-victim does *not* want the respondent arrested, the officer should make an appropriate entry in his/her log book and ask the victim to sign it. If the victim refuses, the officer should write the words, "refused signature" in lieu of the person's signature. Such an entry will serve to protect the police officer in the event of future legal action against the officer, the Police Department, or the City of New York since such an entry will permanently record the reason that no arrest was made.

B. THE POLICE RESPOND TO A SITUATION IN WHICH ONE SPOUSE ALLEGES THAT THE OTHER SPOUSE PUSHED, SHOVED, KICKED, STRUCK, OR OTHERWISE PHYSICALLY ABUSED HIM OR HER.

If the dispute involves some type of physical abuse, such as pushing, shoving, kicking, or punching; but there is no physical injury, the offense involved is harassment. Harassment is a violation, but must have occurred in the presence of an officer for an arrest to be made legally.

In cases of this nature, the complaining party should be referred to Family Court for an Order of Protection, or to the Summons Part of the Criminal Court of the City of New York.

BY DIRECTION OF THE POLICE COMMISSIONER
DISTRIBUTED TO ALL COMMANDS

GO TO NEXT PAGE

46. In the past, "the practical way" to handle family disputes was considered:

(A) Arresting everyone concerned.
(B) Disregarding violations of law.
(C) Informal mediation since the antagonists would soon resolve their differences.
(D) Referring those involved to Family Court without arresting anyone.

47. On December 11, Officer Paula Parker responds to the home of Mrs. Virginia Blake. Mrs. Blake possesses a valid Order of Protection to prohibit her husband, Otto Blake, from being in her residence. Mr. Blake is in the house and has possession of a deed for the house which indicates that he is co-owner. Mrs. Blake wants her husband arrested. Mr. Blake is now quite willing to leave and never return. Officer Parker, after considering the above facts, arrests Otto Blake.

Based upon the above information, Officer Parker's action in this case was:

(A) Proper, since the Order of Protection was violated and Mrs. Blake wants an arrest made.
(B) Improper, since Otto Blake is a co-owner of the house.
(C) Proper, since Otto Blake is known by the officer to beat his wife.
(D) Improper, since Otto Blake's conduct is not criminal.

48. Family disputes often involve complex decisions because they have the potential for:

(A) Future legal action against the police officer and the City of New York.
(B) Physical danger to the police and the parties involved.
(C) A continuing drain on police resources.
(D) A drain on the resources of the courts.

49. At 0930 hours, on August 19, Officer Rudolph Martin is dispatched to 2914 Powell Street in the Borough of Brooklyn. This address is Mr. and Mrs. James Wilson's residence. Upon arrival, Officer Martin is told by James Wilson that while trying to sleep the previous night, he was repeatedly shoved off the bed by his wife, Edna Wilson. Although he did not receive physical injury, he wanted his wife arrested for physical abuse.

Based upon the above information, Officer Martin should:

(A) Arrest Edna Wilson since she has no legal right to abuse her husband.
(B) Refer James Wilson to Family Court or Criminal Court.
(C) Personally mediate the case.
(D) Call his supervisor to the scene for assistance.

50. The department policy concerning the proper handling of disputes involving husbands and wives was developed as a result of:

(A) A lawsuit.
(B) A recently enacted statute.
(C) A court decision.
(D) Political pressure.

51. On January 13, Police Officer John Dackson of the 39th Precinct responded to a call at the apartment of Julia Simpson. Julia Simpson wanted her husband, Harry Simpson, who was sleeping on her couch, arrested for violating an Order of Protection which she obtained from Family Court Judge Adams on January 7. Officer Dackson requested to see the Order of Protection, and Mrs. Simpson refused to show it to him. Based on Mrs. Simpson's refusal to show the order, the officer refused to arrest Henry Simpson.

Based upon the previous information, Officer Dackson's actions were:

(A) Proper, since all civilians must obey the police.
(B) Improper, since Mrs. Simpson states that she has the Order of Protection.
(C) Proper, since Officer Dackson has a right to see the Order of Protection.
(D) Improper, since Mr. Simpson was present in the house at the time.

52. If an Order of Protection has been violated and the victim who possesses the order does not want the respondent arrested, the officer should:

(A) Arrest the respondent anyway.
(B) Talk the victim into changing his/her mind.
(C) Take no further action and resume patrol.
(D) Make an appropriate log entry and ask the victim to sign it.

GO TO NEXT PAGE

***DIRECTIONS:* Answer questions 53 through 55 *solely* on the basis of information contained in the following Operations Order.**

TO ALL COMMANDS
SUBJECT: FIREARMS SAFETY STATIONS IN DEPARTMENT FACILITIES

1. Firearms Safety Stations are being installed in all patrol precincts, highway unit facilities, and Central Booking locations so that uniformed members of the service may be provided with a secure location to safely unload or otherwise handle and/or inspect firearms which come into their possession (evidence, found property, etc.). Safety stations have already been installed in those commands that have been designated as one-officer RMP precincts.

2. A poster, similar to the one depicting procedures for the safe handling of a shotgun, will be distributed to commands concerned in the near future. This poster, depicting the correct way to unload a handgun safely, should be permanently posted near the safety station.

3. Commanding officers of precincts, units, or facilities concerned will survey their command to determine the appropriate location for a safety station. Consideration will be given to safety factors, i.e., to persons present or in the vicinity, and to the necessary supervision of the unloading process.

4. The correct use of safety stations should prevent personal injury and/or property damage which could result from an accidental discharge.

5. If all reasonable safety precautions have been followed and a firearm accidentally discharges within a safety station during the loading, unloading, or examination process, but *no* personal injury or property damage results, a Firearms Discharge/Assault Report *will not* be prepared. However, a brief report will be forwarded to the Firearms and Tactics Section, Outdoor Range.

BY DIRECTION OF THE POLICE COMMISSIONER
DISTRIBUTION
All Commands

TURN TO NEXT PAGE

53. The implementation of this new procedure will be accompanied by the distribution of a poster. This poster will illustrate:

(A) The safe loading and unloading of handguns.
(B) The safe method of unloading a handgun.
(C) The safe method of handling handguns.
(D) The safe handling of a shotgun.

54. Who is responsible for choosing the location of a Firearms Safety Station within each department facility?

(A) The Firearms and Tactics Section
(B) The facility's safety officer
(C) The commanding officer concerned
(D) The commanding officer of the outdoor range

55. One of the anticipated benefits of safety stations is:

(A) The prevention of accidental firearms discharges in departmental facilities.
(B) The prevention of property damage from accidental firearms discharge.
(C) The reduction of personal injuries throughout the station house.
(D) A private place for officers to load and unload weapons.

GO TO NEXT PAGE

***DIRECTIONS:* Answer questions 56 through 59 *solely* on the basis of the following information.**

Police departments have used Scooter Patrol quite successfully for over twenty years. The scooter is an ideal vehicle to use for enforcing parking regulations and for patrolling beach areas and municipal parks. Listed below are the typical regulations for police officers assigned to motor scooters:

1. Operate scooter at a slow, safe rate of speed.

2. Operate scooter with headlight switched on at all times.

3. Report to station house by signal box each hour, or more frequently during emergencies, as directed by commanding officer.

4. Do not use scooter to pursue motor vehicles; they are not assigned to expressways or parkways.

5. Check road conditions of the entire post and make a Memo/Patrolman's Log entry immediately after arrival on post.

6. Request reassignment when the original assignment is hazardous due to spillout from trucks, construction, or other poor road surface conditions.

7. Do not perform scooter duty when:
a. rain, snow, sleet, heavy fog, or any precipitation cause ground to become slippery,
b. patches of snow or ice remain from a previous storm,
c. high winds interfere with the control of the scooter,
d. temperature falls below 32 degrees Fahrenheit.

8. Receive refresher training in motor scooter operation when:
a. involved in a scooter accident.
b. scooter duty has been performed for a one (1) year period without attending a refresher training course.

9. Monitor a portable radio.

10. Wear a helmet and goggles.

TURN TO NEXT PAGE

56. Scooter patrol is not used when the temperature falls below:
(A) 20°F.
(B) 32°F.
(C) 40°F.
(D) 60°F.

57. Scooter patrol is quite useful in all of the following situations except:
(A) Enforcing parking regulations.
(B) Following routine parkway duties.
(C) Patrolling beach area.
(D) Patrolling municipal parks.

58. Which of the following is the least accurate statement concerning the regulations of a scooter officer?
(A) He must wear a helmet.
(B) He must operate at a slow rate of speed except in an emergency.
(C) He must be retrained after every one-year period of scooter duty.
(D) He must wear goggles.

59. A scooter officer:
(A) Can operate in high winds.
(B) Can pursue motor vehicles.
(C) Can operate in the rain.
(D) Can carry a portable radio.

GO TO NEXT PAGE

***DIRECTIONS:* Answer questions 60 through 66 *solely* on the basis of information contained in the following Operations Order.**

TO ALL COMMANDS
SUBJECT: CONFLICT RESOLUTION DISPUTE CENTERS—MANHATTAN AND BRONX COMMANDS

1. The Institute for Mediation and Conflict Resolution (IMCR) Dispute Center, located at 435 West 144th Street, Manhattan, provides a police officer in a Manhattan or Bronx command with an option to have a dispute mediated rather than to issue a summons or effect an arrest when dealing with an interpersonal dispute.

2. Cases that qualify for IMCR mediation are disputes between family members, tenants, acquaintances, common law relationships, neighbors, friends, and co-workers. IMCR Center personnel also mediate referrals involving strangers, particularly where a form of restitution can be awarded. Under the mediation resolution procedure, the following misdemeanors and/or violations are amenable to mediation referral:

A. Assault—3rd Degree
B. Menacing
C. Reckless Endangerment—2nd Degree
D. Reckless Endangerment of Property
E. Misapplication of Property
F. Criminal Mischief—4th Degree
G. Aggravated Harassment
H. Harassment
I. Disorderly Conduct
J. Trespass
K. Criminal Trespass—2nd and 3rd Degree
L. Custodial Interference—2nd Degree

3. In non-arrest cases referred to IMCR, uniformed members of the service will direct the complainant to the appropriate geographical IMCR office, where a "Request to Appear" application may be prepared as part of the mediation process. The locations of IMCR Centers, and their area of jurisdiction, are as follows:

a. *MANHATTAN*—Complainants residing *south* of 110th Street (street numbers lower than 110) in Manhattan, will be referred to the IMCR Dispute Center Office 346 Broadway, New York, New York, (1st Floor).
Complainants residing *north* of 110th Street (street number of 110 or higher) in Manhattan, will be referred to the IMCR Dispute Center Office, 425 West 144th Street, New York, New York, (4th Floor).

b. *BRONX*—Complainants residing within Bronx commands will be referred to the IMCR Dispute Center Office located in Room M-4, Bronx Criminal Court Building, 216 East 161st Street, Bronx, New York.

4. IMCR screens each complaint application to determine if the case is amenable to mediation. If a case is not amenable to mediation, IMCR personnel will refer a complainant to the Office of Court Administration for further action.

BY DIRECTION OF THE POLICE COMMISSIONER

DISTRIBUTION
All Commands

GO TO NEXT PAGE

60. Which of the following misdemeanors or violations is not amenable to mediation referral?
(A) Any disorderly conduct charge
(B) Any menacing charge
(C) Any assault charge
(D) Any harassment charge

61. Police Officer Charles Brown, shield #666, is working a day tour in the 89th Precinct in Brooklyn. His assignment is patrol post 16. At 1030 hours, he comes upon a dispute in the street between two friends. The dispute centers around an act of Disorderly Conduct. With the consent of both parties, Officer Brown elects to refer the dispute to the Institute for Mediation and Conflict Resolution.

Based upon the above information, Officer Brown's action in this case was:
(A) Proper, since the dispute centered around an act of Disorderly Conduct.
(B) Improper, since Officer Brown is working in a Brooklyn command.
(C) Proper, since the parties in the dispute are friends.
(D) Improper, since the procedure does not apply to disputes in the street.

62. If IMCR personnel decide that a dispute is not amenable to mediation, a complainant is referred to:
(A) The police.
(B) The Office of Court Administration.
(C) The district attorney's office.
(D) The appropriate criminal court.

63. The decision on whether to refer a dispute to the Institute for Mediation and Conflict Resolution is made by:
(A) The parties to the dispute.
(B) The party in the dispute against whom the misdemeanor or violation was committed.
(C) Both parties in the dispute, as well as the police officer.
(D) The police officer.

64. This new conflict resolution procedure was introduced in the Police Department by:
(A) The Institute for Mediation and Conflict Resolution.
(B) The Manhattan and Bronx Criminal Courts.
(C) The police commissioner.
(D) Not stated.

65. Police Officer Margaret Dwyer, shield #816, is performing an evening tour of duty out of the 96th Precinct in Manhattan. At approximately 1915 hours, she is dispatched to 2312 87th Street, apartment 3F. Upon arrival she encounters a common law husband and wife having a dispute concerning a possible trespass into the apartment by the husband. Since both parties thought it was a good idea, Officer Dwyer exercised her option and referred the dispute to the IMCR Dispute Center Office at 425 West 144th Street, New York (4th Floor).

Based upon the above information, Officer Dwyer's action in this case was:
(A) Proper, since the Center accepts cases involving common law relationships.
(B) Improper, since the case is not amenable for mediation.
(C) Proper, since both parties thought it was a good idea.
(D) Improper, since the officer referred the disputants to the wrong location.

66. What police department commands received copies of this order?
(A) All Commands
(B) All Manhattan and Bronx Commands
(C) All Patrol Commands
(D) Not stated

GO TO NEXT PAGE

DIRECTIONS: **Answer questions 67 through 76 *solely* on the basis of information recorded in the following "Desk Appearance Ticket Investigation."**

DESK APPEARANCE TICKET INVESTIGATION PD 360-091

Precinct	Precinct Control Number	Date of Report
12	431	April 20, XX XX

STATEMENT TO BE READ TO DEFENDANT: The crime with which you are charged may be processed in one of two ways: First, you may be detained until your court appearance and then possibly be held in bail. Second, by furnishing certain information concerning your background, employment and family, you may be found eligible for the issuance of a desk appearance ticket, in which case you may leave here today and return to court on your own on a specified date within the next three weeks. None of the questions you will be asked concern the crime with which you are charged. If you agree to be interviewed, you authorize the Police Department to verify the information by calling persons named by you as references.

ACKNOWLEDGEMENT OF DEFENDANT: I hereby consent to interview and verification of the information given. Signature of Defendant: *Doris A. White*

Date of Arrest	Time	Location of Arrest	Within Precinct No.
4/20/XX	1000	411 5th Ave	12

ARRESTING OFFICER	Rank/Title	Name	Tax Registry No.	Shield No.	Command / Agency / Phone
	Ptl.	Charles F. Brown	731428	1234	12 Pct P.D. 637-1212

Charge	Arrest No.
Petit Larceny 155.25 PL	2534

SECTION 1 — IDENTIFICATION AND RESIDENCE

Defendant's Surname	First Name and Initial	Date of Birth	Female / Male	Single / Married
White,	Doris A.	12/7/41	Female ☑ Male ☐	Single ☐ Married ☑

Address (Number and Street)	City or Post Office	State	How Long At Current Address	How Long At Previous Address
246 Green Ave.	N.Y.	N.Y.	2 yrs	5 yrs

Apt. No.	Telephone No.	Proof of Identity (Driver's Lic., Auto Reg., I.D. Card, etc. - Indicate Type and Serial Numbers)
6	XL 9-9000	WØ3462 56285 162349-41

SEC. 1 SCORE	Residence Over 1 Year:	Present Residence—Six Months or Present and Prior—One Year:	Present Residence—Four Months or Present and Prior—Six Months:	Present and Prior—Under Six Months:	SCORE: 3 Points
	3 Points ☑	2 Points ☐	1 Point ☐	0 Points ☐	Verified ☑ Interview ☐

SECTION 2 — FAMILY TIES

Lives With (Name)	Relationship	If Married, Name of Defendant's Spouse	Number of Children
William White	Husband	same	1

If Separated, Spouse's Address; OR If Minor Not Living At Home, Parent's Address	Number, Street, Borough, Apt. No.	Telephone No.

Relatives In The N.Y.C. Area That Defendant Keeps In Close Contact With:

Name	Address	Telephone No.	Relationship	How Often Seen
Mildred Gold	240 E. 42nd. St. Manh.	YK 2-1234	Mother	weekly

SEC. 2 SCORE	Lives With Family And Has Regular Contact With Other Family Members	Lives Alone But Has Regular Contact With Other Relatives	Lives With Family But Has No Other Family Contacts	Lives Alone Or With Non-family Person And Has No Contact With Relatives	SCORE: 3 Points
	3 Points ☑	1 Point ☐	2 Points ☐	0 Points ☐	Verified ☑ Interview ☐

SECTION 3 — EMPLOYMENT

Currently Employed By	Name of Company	Address	Telephone No.
	N.Y. Telephone Co.	18 River St. Bronx	KG 5-4321

How Long	If Under 1 Year, How Long At Previous Job	Type of Work	Name of Immediate Supervisor
5 mo.	3 yrs	Telephone Operator	Alex G. Bell

If Housewife Or Minor	Husband's or Parent's Occupation	Business Address	Telephone No.

Score Housewife Or Minor On Husband's Or Parent's Occupation

SEC. 3 SCORE	Current Job Over One Year	Current Job Over Six Months	Present Job Between 4-6 Months or Supported By Family Or Present and Prior Job—Six Months.	Unemployed Or Not Otherwise Supported	SCORE: 1 Points
	3 Points ☐	2 Points ☐	1 Point ☑	0 Points ☐	Verified ☐ Interview ☑

SECTION 4 — PRIOR ARRESTS AND CONVICTIONS

Have You Ever Been Arrested Before	How Many Times	On What Charges
Yes ☑ No ☐	1	Pros. 230.00 PL

Investigating Officer Must Conduct Name Check By Telephoning The Identification Section And, In The Case Of A Minor, The Youth Records Section.

Results Of Name Check — Det./Ptl./(Trainee) (Ident. Sect.)/Youth Records: Silver

SEC. 4 SCORE	No Previous Convictions	One Misdemeanor Or Violation Conviction	Two Misd. Or Viol. Convictions Or One Felony Conviction	Three Misd. Or Viol. Convictions Or Two Felony Convictions	Four Or More Misd. Or Viol. Convictions Or Three Or More Felony Convictions	SCORE: 1 Points
	2 Points ☐	1 Point ☑	0 Points ☐	Minus(−) 1 Point ☐	Minus(−) 2 Points ☐	Verified ☑ Interview ☐

Source of blank form: New York City Police Department

TURN TO NEXT PAGE

67. The arresting officer's last name is:
(A) Silver.
(B) Brown.
(C) Gold.
(D) White.

68. The charge is:
(A) Prostitution 230.00 PL.
(B) Burglary 140. PL.
(C) Petit Larceny 155.25 PL.
(D) Assault 125.05 PL.

69. The defendant lives with her:
(A) Mother.
(B) Brother.
(C) Sister.
(D) Spouse.

70. The defendant is employed by:
(A) A telephone company.
(B) A computer company.
(C) A driving school.
(D) A beauty parlor.

71. The defendant's home telephone number is:
(A) KG5-4321.
(B) XL9-9000.
(C) 637-1212.
(D) 731-4280.

72. The defendant has lived at:
(A) 240 E. 42nd Street for 3 years.
(B) 18 River Street for 1 year.
(C) 246 Green Street for 2 years.
(D) 1840 Apple Street for 5 years.

73. The arrest number for this case is:
(A) 431.
(B) 2354.
(C) 341.
(D) 2534.

74. The date of this arrest is:
(A) April 2.
(B) April 12.
(C) April 20.
(D) Not stated.

75. The arresting officer's shield number is:

(A) 731428.
(B) 3241.
(C) 371824.
(D) 1234.

76. The name of the defendant's immediate supervisor at her place of employment is:

(A) Bell.
(B) Gold.
(C) White.
(D) Silver.

TURN TO NEXT PAGE

***DIRECTIONS:* Answer questions 77 through 80 *solely* on the basis of following Operations Order.**

TO ALL COMMANDS
SUBJECT: ENERGY CONSERVATION PREVENTIVE MAINTENANCE PROGRAM

1. In an effort to conserve energy and yet maintain comfortable working conditions and improve department facilities, deficiencies in building maintenance and/or cleaning (particularly those affecting air conditioning and energy waste) should be reported so that repairs may be made.

2. Therefore, all commanding officers will conduct a physical inspection of facilities under their respective jurisdictions. The inspection should focus on conditions which directly affect the department's energy costs, such as, but not limited to:

a. an imbalance in the heating/cooling system in new buildings,
b. faulty or broken thermostats,
c. broken windows and/or doors, particularly those leading from air conditioned to non-air conditioned spaces,
d. faulty lights,
e. blockage of air vents supplying cooled air,
f. display of educational posters relative to federal energy regulations concerning temperature,
g. condition of window air conditioner filters.

3. In addition, commanding officers concerned are requested to instruct subordinate personnel to conform to the following energy conservation guidelines:

a. use air conditioning equipment *only* when outside temperature exceeds 80 degrees Fahrenheit,
b. adjust window air conditioner settings at *no less than* 78 degrees Fahrenheit, and set thermostats midway between the warm and cool settings,
c. do not set window air conditioners on constant run position,
d. ensure that pre-season filter maintenance is performed on window air conditioners and that fresh air louvers are kept in "*closed*" position on hot days,
e. do not turn on air conditioners prior to 1000 hours in commands not operating on a 24-hour basis. These air conditioners should be shut off at least one-half hour prior to closing time,
f. keep blinds and shades closed to prevent air conditioned space from being exposed to sunlight,
g. inspect windows and interior doors leading from air conditioned to non-air conditioned rooms, to prevent loss of cooled air when air conditioners are operating,

h. *do not permit unauthorized personnel* to tamper with central air conditioner settings. These settings are preset by Building Maintenance Section personnel.

BY DIRECTION OF THE POLICE COMMISSIONER

DISTRIBUTION
All Commands

TURN TO NEXT PAGE

77. Deficiencies in building maintenance and/or cleaning should be reported for all of the following reasons *except*:

(A) To increase employee morale.
(B) To conserve energy.
(C) To improve the appearance of department facilities.
(D) To maintain comfortable working conditions.

78. Police Officer James Jones is working a day tour in an office in police headquarters. While the office has central air conditioning, the air conditioning does not seem to be working properly. It is 92°F. outside, and Officer Jones and his fellow workers are sweltering. Although Jones is not sure what to do, he sees nothing wrong with trying to adjust the central air conditioner settings.

Based upon the above information, Officer Jones' decision to adjust the settings is:

(A) Proper, since it is above 78°F. outside.
(B) Improper, since he is not authorized to adjust the central air conditioner settings.
(C) Proper, since his fellow workers are also involved.
(D) Improper, since the outside temperature is not warm enough.

79. At 0900 hours on August 14, Police Officer Mary Smith reported for work at the 89th Precinct. It is already 76°F. outside, and the temperature is predicted to rise to the high eighties. Officer Smith turns on her window air conditioner and sets the thermostat midway between the warm and cool settings.

Based upon the above information, Officer Smith's actions were:

(A) Proper, since she set the thermostat correctly.
(B) Improper, since she is not authorized to touch the air conditioner setting.
(C) Proper, since it is so hot outside.
(D) Improper, since it is only 76°F. outside.

80. A physical inspection is required to detect any conditions which affect:

(A) The police officers' morale.
(B) The department's energy costs.
(C) Conservation guidelines.
(D) Physical safety.

TURN TO NEXT PAGE

***DIRECTIONS:* Answer questions 81 through 90 *solely* on the basis of the legal definitions given below. Do *not* base your answers on any other knowledge of the law you may have. You may refer to the definitions when answering the questions.**

crime Either a misdemeanor or a felony.

misdemeanor An offense for which a person can be sentenced to imprisonment for periods of time from 16 days to one year.

felony An offense for which a person can be sentenced to imprisonment for more than one year. Felonies are classified as either A, B, C, D, or E. An A felony is more serious than a B felony, and so on.

violation An offense for which a sentence of imprisonment of no more than 15 days can be given.

offense An act which is prohibited by the Penal Law. Offenses are felonies, misdemeanors, or violations.

physical injury An impairment of a physical condition, or a condition causing substantial pain.

serious physical injury A physical injury which involves a substantial risk of death, a protracted disfigurement, or an impairment of an organ.

deadly weapon Any loaded gun, capable of firing a shot which can cause death or serious physical injury; or a switchblade knife, billy, blackjack, or metal knuckles.

dangerous instrument Any article or substance (including a vehicle) which, depending upon circumstances, is capable of causing death or serious physical injury.

GO TO NEXT PAGE

81. The most severe punishment is given for a:
(A) Felony.
(B) Violation.
(C) Misdemeanor.
(D) Felony or violation, depending upon the age of the perpetrator.

82. A deadly weapon is:
(A) Any gun capable of firing a shot which can cause death.
(B) A billy.
(C) A vehicle.
(D) A hunting knife.

83. John has been convicted of a felony. He would receive the greatest punishment available if he were convicted of:
(A) An "E" felony.
(B) A "C" felony.
(C) An "A" felony.
(D) A "D" felony.

84. A crime is:
(A) Always a felony.
(B) Always a misdemeanor.
(C) Either a misdemeanor or a felony.
(D) Neither a misdemeanor nor a felony.

85. One thing that a felony, misdemeanor, and violation have in common is that they:
(A) Are crimes.
(B) Have a maximum punishment stated in their respective definitions.
(C) Require the prosecutor to set the maximum sentence.
(D) Are offenses.

86. Which of the following is a false statement?
(A) Every serious physical injury involves a physical injury.
(B) If substantial pain occurs, a physical injury has taken place.
(C) Every physical injury involves a serious physical injury.
(D) If there is an impairment of a physical condition, a physical injury has occurred.

87. Which of the following statements is most accurate?

(A) The use of a deadly weapon always causes physical injury.

(B) The use of a dangerous instrument always causes physical injury.

(C) The use of a dangerous instrument always causes serious physical injury.

(D) The use of a deadly weapon may cause no injury.

88. All of the following could be considered a deadly weapon *except*:

(A) A switchblade knife.

(B) A billy.

(C) A hammer.

(D) Metal knuckles.

89. Consider the following statements and select the *least* inaccurate statement:

(A) Under certain circumstances, a bottle of soda could be a deadly weapon.

(B) Under certain circumstances, an ax would be a dangerous instrument; but it could never be a deadly weapon.

(C) A blackjack is a deadly weapon but could never be a dangerous instrument.

(D) Any article could be either a dangerous instrument or a deadly weapon depending upon the circumstances under which it is used.

90. If Joe Jones was convicted of an offense and sentenced to 10 days imprisonment, he was convicted of a:

(A) Violation.

(B) Misdemeanor.

(C) Felony.

(D) Cannot be determined.

GO TO NEXT PAGE

DIRECTIONS: **Answer questions 91 and 92 *solely* on the basis of the following.**

burglary in the second degree A person is guilty of this crime when he knowingly enters or remains unlawfully in a building with intent to commit a crime therein. He is also guilty of this crime when, in effecting the entry or while inside the building or while in immediate flight, he or another participant is armed with explosives or a deadly weapon, or uses a dangerous instrument, or causes physical injury to someone who is not a participant. (A dwelling is considered a building wherein a person usually lodges overnight.) Burglary in the second degree is a Class C felony.

On July 10, at 10 A.M., Spencer Marlond and Bob Kew climb in the open bedroom window of Jane Adams' residence. Ms. Adams is in the bathroom taking a shower when the two men enter looking for valuables. She does not hear them enter. Marlond and Kew quickly go through her dresser drawers and remove a gold locket worth $280. They also remove $221 in U.S. currency. Kew has previously been convicted of burglary twice, and has vowed that he will never go to jail again. Kew has a switchblade knife in his jacket pocket and is ready to use it. Marlond has no knowledge of Kew's past criminal record, nor that Kew is carrying a deadly weapon. The two men leave through Ms. Adams' front door; they escape without being observed.

91. Based upon the above information, which of the following is the most accurate statement?

(A) Both men are guilty of burglary in the second degree since the total value of the property taken is more than $500.

(B) Kew is guilty of burglary in the second degree since he is carrying the switchblade knife; but Marlond, who knew nothing of the weapon, is not.

(C) Kew and Marlond would be guilty of burglary in the second degree only if Kew used the switchblade knife against Adams.

(D) If the two men had been discovered after entering the bedroom and had fled without taking property, they would still be charged with burglary in the second degree.

92. Based on the preceding definition and narrative, which of the following statements is false?

(A) No crime was committed because Ms. Adams left her windows open.

(B) The fact that the crime occurred at 10 A.M. has no bearing on the charge.

(C) If Ms. Adams had not been home, the scene of the crime would still be considered a "dwelling."

(D) Kew's prior record has no bearing on the charge.

***DIRECTIONS:* Answer question 93 *solely* on the basis of the following information.**

A private person may use deadly physical force to defend himself or another person against the imminent use of deadly physical force. Deadly physical force is the kind of force which produces death or the kind of injury which may cause death.

93. Peter and Paul are walking through Central Park. Tom, a former employee of Paul's, sees them and tells them to stop. He is angry with Paul, and tells Paul that he wants his job back. Tom further tells Paul that if he does not get his job back the next day, he is going to kill him. Peter intercedes and tells Tom to calm down. Tom says he has no quarrel with him, but if he (Peter) wants to get involved, he will kill them both the next day. Peter and Paul then leap on Tom and begin to beat him. Tom dies as a result of the beating.

Based upon the above information, Peter and Paul were:

(A) Justified, since Tom had threatened them with death.
(B) Not justified, since Paul had a right only to defend himself; Peter should not have interfered.
(C) Justified, since a person may defend himself or another person against deadly physical force.
(D) Not justified, since Tom had not threatened the imminent use of deadly physical force.

***DIRECTIONS:* Answer questions 94 and 95 *solely* on the basis of the following information.**

A private person may use deadly physical force to arrest a person who has committed robbery, forcible rape, forcible sodomy and who is in immediate flight therefrom.

94. Maryann is asleep in her apartment. A male picks the lock of her door, enters, wakes her, and rapes her at knifepoint. The male escapes, and Maryann does not report the crime to the police. Instead she applies for, and receives, a pistol permit. Several months later, she sees the male who raped her. She confronts him and tries to make a citizen's arrest. When he tries to run away, Maryann kills him with her licensed handgun.

Based upon the above information, were Maryann's actions justified?

(A) Yes, since the male was the person who forcibly raped her.

(B) No, since she did not originally report the rape to the police.

(C) Yes, since the gun she used was licensed.

(D) No, since the male was not in immediate flight from the rape.

95. John is returning home from a hunting trip. He is legally carrying a rifle. He hears a noise in an alley, and sees a man running from it. He goes into the alley and encounters an old woman who tells him that a man just attempted to rob her with a knife. The old woman then points down the street and says, "That's him." John wants to arrest the man so he loads the rifle, fires one shot, and kills the man.

Based upon the above information, were John's actions justified?

(A) Yes, since John legally possessed the rifle.

(B) No, since a private person is not authorized to use deadly physical force to arrest for an attempted robbery.

(C) Yes, since the old woman would have been robbed if it had not been for John.

(D) No, since John should have first fired a warning shot into the air.

TURN TO NEXT PAGE

***DIRECTIONS:* Answer questions 96 and 97 *solely* on the basis of the following.**

Robbery in the first degree occurs when a person forcibly takes the property of another person and, while committing the crime or in immediate flight therefrom, he or another participant causes serious physical injury to someone who is not a participant, or is armed with a deadly weapon, or uses a dangerous instrument against someone who is not a participant. Robbery in the first degree is a Class B felony.

96. Harold enters a supermarket and tells the manager to open the safe and give him the money. Harold is armed with a 0.38 caliber revolver, which is a deadly weapon. He fires one shot into the ceiling, takes the money from the manager, and escapes in an automobile driven by a female accomplice.

Based upon the above information, which of the following is the most accurate statement?

(A) Harold committed robbery in the first degree since he had an accomplice with him in the robbery.
(B) Harold committed robbery in the first degree since he used an automobile to escape.
(C) Harold committed robbery in the first degree since he was armed with a deadly weapon.
(D) Harold committed robbery in the first degree since he damaged property in the course of the robbery.

97. Which of the following is the *least* accurate statement concerning the crime of robbery in the first degree?

(A) Property must be taken for the crime to be committed.
(B) Someone must be injured for the crime to be committed.
(C) Robbery in the first degree is a Class B felony.
(D) A person does not need an accomplice to commit robbery in the first degree.

GO TO NEXT PAGE

***DIRECTIONS:* Answer questions 98 through 100 *solely* on the basis of the following.**

The two powers that the police have that set them apart from ordinary citizens is the power of arrest and the authority to use legal force. Since the authority to use legal force leaves much potential for abuse, the necessity to have strict guidelines regulating the use of the police revolver is very pressing. The following guidelines are typical of those that exist in most police departments today. They are not meant to restrict a police officer in the performance of his/her lawful duty, but are intended to reduce shooting incidents and, consequently, protect life and property. In every case, department policy requires only the minimum amount of force be used consistent with the accomplishment of the mission.

In addition to Penal Law restrictions on the use of deadly physical force, police officers will adhere to the following guidelines concerning the use of firearms:

1. Use all means before using firearm when effecting arrest to prevent or terminate a felony, or when defending self or others.

2. Do not fire warning shots.

3. Do not discharge firearm to summon assistance, except when safety is endangered.

4. Do not discharge firearm from or at a moving vehicle unless occupants are using deadly physical force against officer or another by means other than a vehicle.

5. Do not discharge firearm at dogs or other animals unless there is no other way to bring the animal under control.

6. Do not discharge firearm if innocent persons may be endangered.

---

98. The above guidelines are meant to:
(A) Restrict an officer's performance.
(B) Protect life and property.
(C) Eliminate the need to discharge firearms.
(D) Prevent all abuses from occurring.

99. In addition to the above guidelines, other restrictions on the use of firearms can be found in:
(A) The Code of Criminal Procedure.
(B) The City Charter.
(C) The Penal Law.
(D) The Administrative Law.

100. Police officers are always forbidden to:

(A) Discharge firearms to summon assistance.
(B) Fire warning shots.
(C) Fire shots from a moving vehicle.
(D) Fire shots at animals.

101. Police Officer Booker arrives at the scene of a robbery at the Apex Bank where an eyewitness relates the following information to the officer.

<u>Suspect</u>

Gender:	Female
Race:	White
Height:	5′10″
Weight:	140 lbs. to 150 lbs.
Hair:	Brown
Clothing:	Tan jacket, white slacks
Weapon:	.32 caliber pistol

Officer Booker is completing a report on the incident. Which one of the following expresses the above information most clearly and accurately?

(A) A white female weighing 140–150 pounds robbed the Apex Bank. She was a female who was white with a tan jacket and white slacks and was 5′10″ tall. She had a .32 caliber pistol.
(B) A white female weighing 140–150 pounds robbed the Apex Bank with a .38 caliber pistol. She was 5′10″ tall and had brown hair and wore a tan jacket and white slacks.
(C) A white female, 5′10″ tall, weighing 140–150 pounds, robbed the Apex Bank. She was armed with a .32 caliber pistol, had brown hair, and wore a tan jacket and white pants.
(D) A white female, 5′10″ tall, weighing 140–150 pounds, robbed the Apex Bank. She had brown hair and was wearing a tan jacket, white pants, and a .32 caliber pistol.

102. Police Officer Rays is sent to investigate vandalism to the side of a private home. As a result of interviewing the owner and complainant, Mr. Rems, at 10:30 A.M., the officer obtains the following information:

Place of occurrence:	207 West 258 Street
Time of occurrence:	9:30 A.M.
Time of reporting:	10:30 A.M.
Crime:	Criminal Mischief
Exact damage:	Grease sprayed on the walls of the house.
Only witness:	Mae Bells of 209 West 258 Street
Suspect:	A male Hispanic between 19 and 20 years old

Officer Rays is preparing a report on the incident. Which one of the following expresses the above information most clearly and accurately?

(A) At 10:30 A.M. a male Hispanic between 19 and 20 years old was seen by a witness, Mae Bells of 209 West 258 Street, committing the crime of Criminal Mischief by spraying grease on the walls of a house at 207 West 258 Street, owned by the complainant, Mr. Rems.

(B) At 9:30 A.M. a male Hispanic between 19 and 20 years old was seen by a witness, Mae Bells of 207 West 258 Street, committing the crime of Criminal Mischief by spraying grease on the walls of a house at 209 West 258 Street, owned by the complainant, Mr. Rems.

(C) At 10:30 A.M. the complainant, Mr. Rems, reported that a male Hispanic between 19 and 20 years old was seen by a witness, Mae Bells of 209 West 258 Street. The crime of Criminal Mischief was committed by spraying grease on the walls of a house at 207 West 258 Street.

(D) At 10:30 A.M. the complainant, Mr. Rems, reported that a male Hispanic between 19 and 20 years old was seen by a witness, Mae Bells of 209 West 258 Street, committing the crime of Criminal Mischief by spraying grease on the walls of a house at 207 West 258 Street.

103. The radio dispatcher directs Officer Banks to respond to investigate a missing person from the Lily Nursing Home. The following information is obtained by the officer:

Name of missing person:	Don Grime, resident of nursing home
Age:	75 years old
Height:	6′
Weight:	200 lbs.
Information provided by:	Ms. Green, Nursing Supervisor
Results of case:	Subject was found by custodial staff in the basement gym of the nursing home ten minutes after the officer arrived.

The officer is preparing a report on the incident. Which one of the following expresses the above information most clearly and accurately?

(A) I responded to the Lily Nursing Home and determined that Don Grime, a resident of the nursing home, was missing. He was found in the basement gym by the custodial staff and was 75 years old and was weighing 200 pounds and is 6′ tall. The information was provided by Ms. Green, the Nursing Supervisor.

(B) I responded to the Lily Nursing Home and was informed by Ms. Green, the Nursing Supervisor, that Don Grime, a resident of the nursing home, 75 years old, 200 pounds, and 6′ tall, was missing. He was found by the custodial staff in the basement gym ten minutes after I arrived.

(C) Ten minutes after I arrived at the Lily Nursing Home, I was informed by Ms. Green, the Nursing Supervisor, that Don Grime, a resident of the nursing home, 75 years old, 200 pounds, and 6′ tall, was missing. He was found in the basement gym by the custodial staff.

(D) Ten minutes after I arrived at the Lily Nursing Home, Don Grime, a resident of the nursing home, 75 years old, 200 pounds, and 6′ tall, was found to be missing. I was informed by Ms. Green, the Nursing Supervisor, that he was found in the basement gym by the custodial staff.

104. At 8:30 P.M., Officer Knight responds to a past larceny of an auto. Officer Knight obtains the following information regarding the incident:

Time of occurrence: 8:00 P.M.
Place of occurrence: Intersection of Taylor Ave. & Market St.
Complainant and witness: Frank Parks
Owner of vehicle: June Parks
Vehicle description: Blue Ford Pickup Truck
Perpetrators: Two white males

The officer is preparing a report on the incident. Which one of the following expresses the above information most clearly and accurately?

(A) At 8:00 P.M., a blue Ford pickup truck was stolen at the intersection of Taylor Avenue and Market Street. At 8:30 P.M., June Parks, the owner of the vehicle who witnessed the crime, reported to me that two white males stole the vehicle.

(B) At 8:30 P.M., a blue Ford pickup truck was stolen at the intersection of Taylor Avenue and Market Street. Frank Parks, who witnessed the crime, reported to me that two white males stole the vehicle.

(C) At 8:00 P.M., a blue Ford pickup truck was stolen by two white males. At 8:30 P.M. at the intersection of Taylor Avenue and Market Street, Frank Parks, the owner of the vehicle, reported the crime to me.

(D) At 8:30 P.M., Frank Parks reported to me that he witnessed at 8:00 P.M. two white males stealing a blue Ford pickup truck. The vehicle, which is owned by June Parks, was stolen at the intersection of Taylor Avenue and Market Street.

105. Officer Rivers comes upon an assault in progress. The details of the incident are as follows:

Time of occurrence: 9:30 P.M.
Location: In front of 899 3rd Avenue
Victim: Frank Baron
Suspects: The Melford Guys Street Gang
Weapons: Chains and bats

Additional information: Victim was treated and released at Sunrise Hospital

The officer is preparing a report on the incident. Which one of the following expresses the above information most clearly and accurately?

(A) At 9:30 P.M., in front of 899 3rd Avenue, Frank Baron was assaulted by chains and bats. He was released after being treated at Sunrise Hospital. Suspected in the assault are members of the Melford Guys Street Gang.

(B) At 9:30 P.M., members of the Melford Guys Street Gang were in front of 899 3rd Avenue, when chains and bats struck Frank Baron. He was released after being treated at Sunrise Hospital.

(C) Frank Baron was released after being treated at Sunrise Hospital at 9:30 P.M. He had been assaulted in front of 899 3rd Avenue, by members of the Melford Guys Street Gang, who used chains and bats to assault him.

(D) Frank Baron was released after being treated at 899 3rd Avenue, Sunrise Hospital. He had been assaulted at 9:30 P.M. by members of the Melford Guys Street Gang, who used chains and bats to commit the assault.

***DIRECTIONS:* In each of questions 106 through 110 you will be given four choices. Each of the choices A, B, and C contains a written statement. You are to evaluate the statement in each choice and select the statement that is most accurately and clearly written. If all or none of the three written statements is accurately and clearly written, you are to select choice D.**

106. According to the directions, evaluate the following statements.

(A) It is impossible to reach you and I.
(B) Put you're gun into the holster.
(C) It's a shame she was convicted.
(D) All or none of the choices is accurate.

107. According to the directions, evaluate the following statements.

(A) Yesterday, all the robbers lay down their weapons and surrendered.
(B) Last night, all the students laid down in front of the campus administration building to protest the firing of a teacher.
(C) We should learn the prisoners a lesson.
(D) All or none of the choices is accurate.

108. According to the directions, evaluate the following statements.

(A) After being searched, the detective put the prisoner into the cell.
(B) After the inmate was searched, he went in the cell.
(C) The precinct's basketball team has good morale.
(D) All or none of the choices is accurate.

109. According to the directions, evaluate the following statements.

(A) The precinct commanding officer praised Jim and me.
(B) That is too dangerous for the rookie officers.
(C) There is no way out of the bank other than the front door.
(D) All or none of the choices is accurate.

110. According to the directions, evaluate the following statements.

(A) They were sure of their facts.

(B) The front of the embassy was a stationery post.

(C) Someone wrote a threatening note to the police commissioner on department stationary.

(D) All or none of the choices is accurate.

111. Police Officer Drake is taking a report of the burglary of an appliance store. The proprietor of the store states that the following property is missing:

1 Sony 19-inch television, valued at $290.00
3 G.E. microwaves, each valued at $299.00
1 Smart personal computer valued at $2,295.00

Officer Drake is preparing a report on the robbery. Which of the following is the correct arithmetic formula for the officer to use to determine the total value of the property stolen?

(A) $290.00 + $299.00 + $2,295.00

(B) (3 × $290.00) + $299.00 + $2,295.00

(C) $290.00 + (3 × $299.00) + $2,295.00

(D) $290.00 + $299.00 + $2,295.00 + (3 × $299.00)

112. If *r* equals the rate of speed traveled at, and *t* equals the time traveled, then multiplying $r \times t$ will equal the distance, or *d*, actually traveled. Therefore, if an officer knows how far he must travel, which is the distance represented by *d*, and also knows how fast he will travel, which is the rate of speed represented by *r*, then which of the following formulas will most likely indicate how long the trip will take, which is *t* or the time traveled?

(A) $t = \frac{t}{r \times d}$

(B) $t = \frac{d}{r}$

(C) $t = \frac{r}{d}$

(D) $t = r \times d$

113. The following information appeared on a roll call concerning a certain police officer's assignment for an eight-hour tour of duty.

8:00 A.M. to 9:30 A.M.	Traffic Court
9:30 A.M. to 12:30 A.M.	Patrol Foot Post #3
12:30 A.M. to 1:30 A.M.	Meal Hour at the Station House
1:30 A.M. to 2:00 A.M.	Relieve the Clerk at the Station House
2:00 A.M. to 4:00 A.M.	Patrol Radar Speed Control Duty

Which of the following is the most correct arithmetic formula to determine the amount of time the officer spent on assignments other than patrol.

(A) 8 – 1 + 1/2 – 1 – 1/2
(B) 8 – 3 + (2)
(C) 8 – (1 1/2 + 1 + 1/2)
(D) 8 – (3 + 2)

DIRECTIONS: **Answer questions 114–115 based *solely* on the following information.**

In the 39th Precinct a gambling raid has been conducted resulting in the arrest of seven prisoners. Each of the prisoners was found to be in possession of money in bill and coin form. The money was removed from each prisoner and was put into individual envelopes bearing the name of the prisoner from whom the money was removed. The individual sums were $92.77, $9.25, $52.72, $6.73, $14.41, $12.38, and $12.22.

114. The total of all the monies found on the prisoners is:

(A) Under $200.
(B) Between $200 and $205.
(C) Between $206 and $210.
(D) Over $210.

115. One of the prisoners arrested in the gambling raid is able to make bail and is released from the station house. The money belonging to the prisoner being bailed out amounts to $12.38. In addition, a further search of one of the remaining prisoners reveals an additional $18.36. What is now the total amount of all the monies found on the prisoners?

(A) Under $200
(B) Between $200 and $205
(C) Between $206 and $210
(D) Over $210

DIRECTIONS: **Before answering questions 116–120, take 5 minutes to examine the following four wanted posters with the information that accompanies each poster.**

Chuckie Gifford

Age:	**28**	**Race:**	**White**
Height:	**5' 9"**	**Weight:**	**225 pounds**
Eyes:	**Blue**	**Hair:**	**Brown**
Scars:	**None**	**Tattoos:**	**None**

Subject, who was serving a 5-year sentence for extortion, is a lifelong con artist who preys on older women. Often represents himself as a law enforcement officer.

WANTED — ESCAPED PRISONER

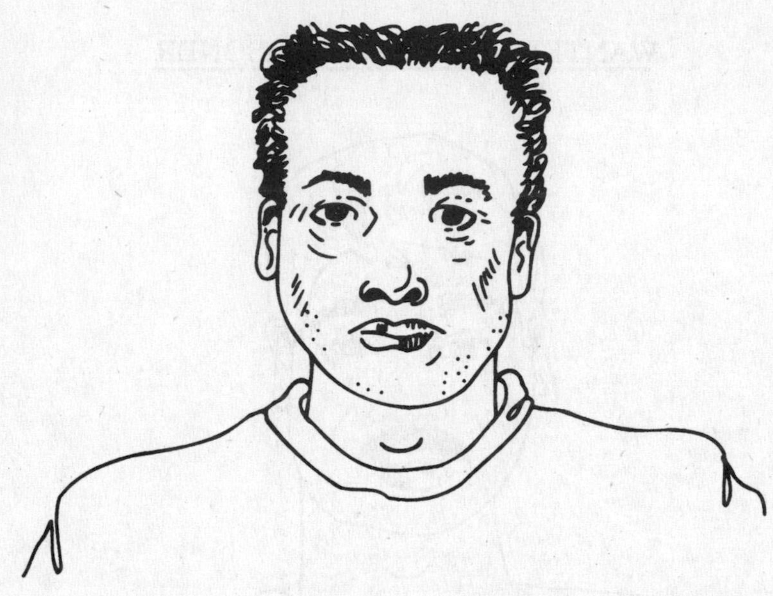

Samuel Youngblood

Age:	32	Race:	White
Height:	5' 9"	Weight:	200 pounds
Eyes:	Brown	Hair:	Bald
Scars:	None	Tattoos:	None

Subject, who was serving a life sentence for rape and child abuse, often wears a hairpiece as shown in above poster. Often loiters in the vicinity of schools in search of victims.

WANTED — ESCAPED PRISONER

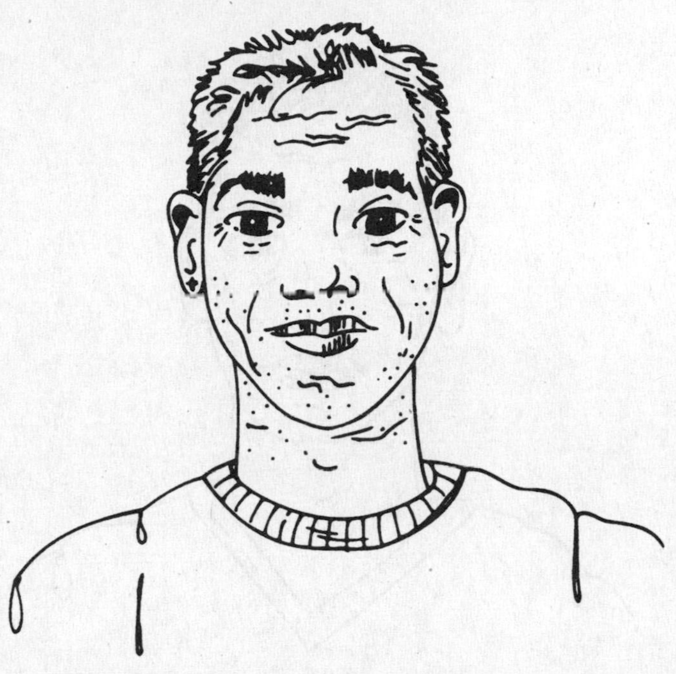

Jack Hunt

Age:	62	Race:	White
Height:	5' 10"	Weight:	210 pounds
Eyes:	Blue	Hair:	Brown
Scars:	None	Tattoos:	None

Subject, who was serving a 10-year sentence for tax evasion, often uses the alias Ben Hogan. He is a chronic drug user.

WANTED — ESCAPED PRISONER

James Short

Age:	45	Race:	White
Height:	5' 9"	Weight:	160 pounds
Eyes:	Brown	Hair:	Brown
Scars:	None	Tattoos:	None

Subject, who was serving a 20-year sentence for armed robbery, is considered armed and dangerous. His weapon of preference is a sawed-off shotgun, which he almost always carries on his person. Speaks five languages, including Chinese and Spanish.

DO NOT PROCEED UNTIL 5 MINUTES HAVE ELAPSED

TURN TO NEXT PAGE

DIRECTIONS: **Answer questions 116–120 *solely* on the basis of the wanted posters on the preceding pages. Do NOT refer back to the posters when answering these questions.**

116. Which of the escaped inmates illustrated in the following posters often loiters in the vicinity of schools?

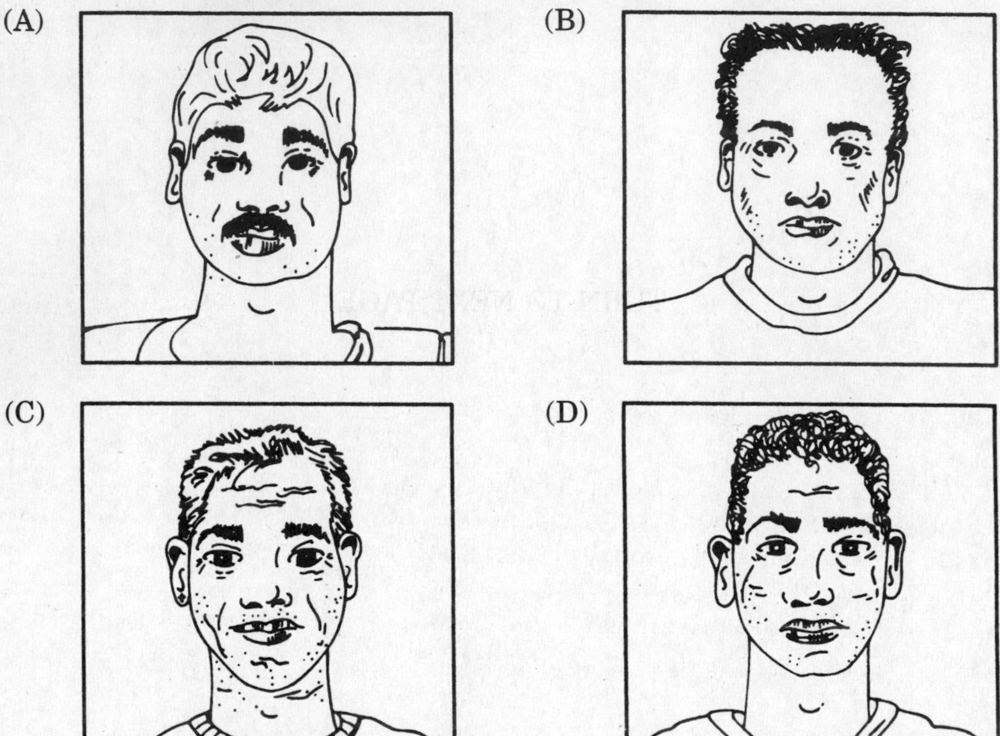

(A) (B) (C) (D)

117. Which of the escaped inmates illustrated in the following posters often carries a sawed-off shotgun?

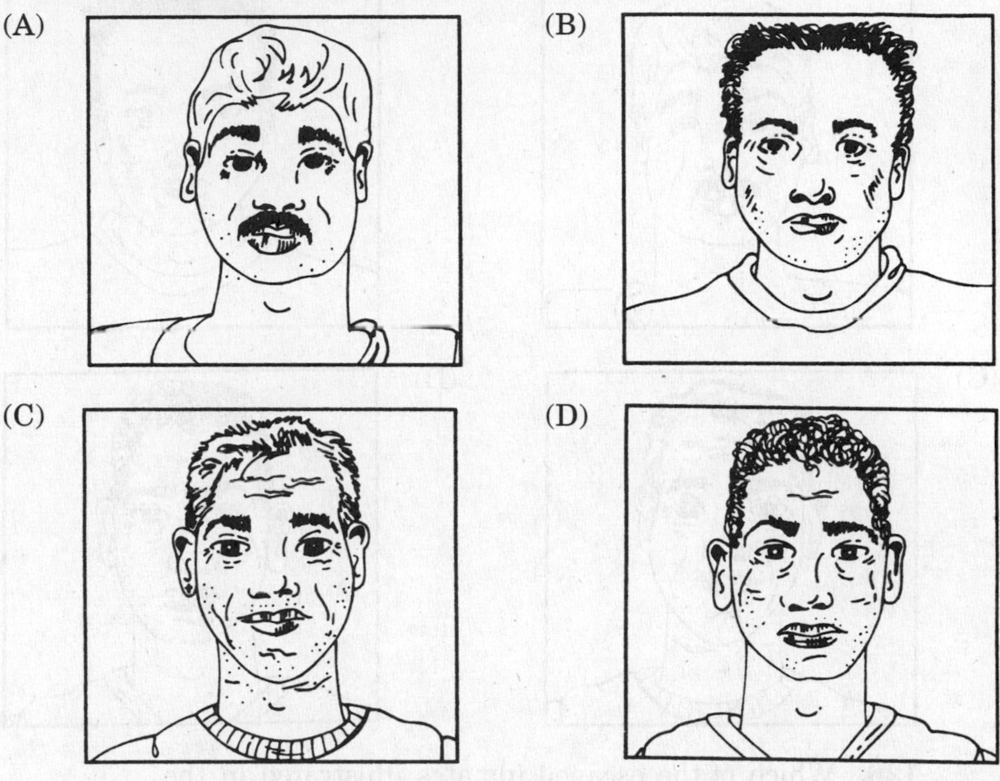

118. Which of the escaped inmates illustrated in the following posters uses the alias Ben Hogan?

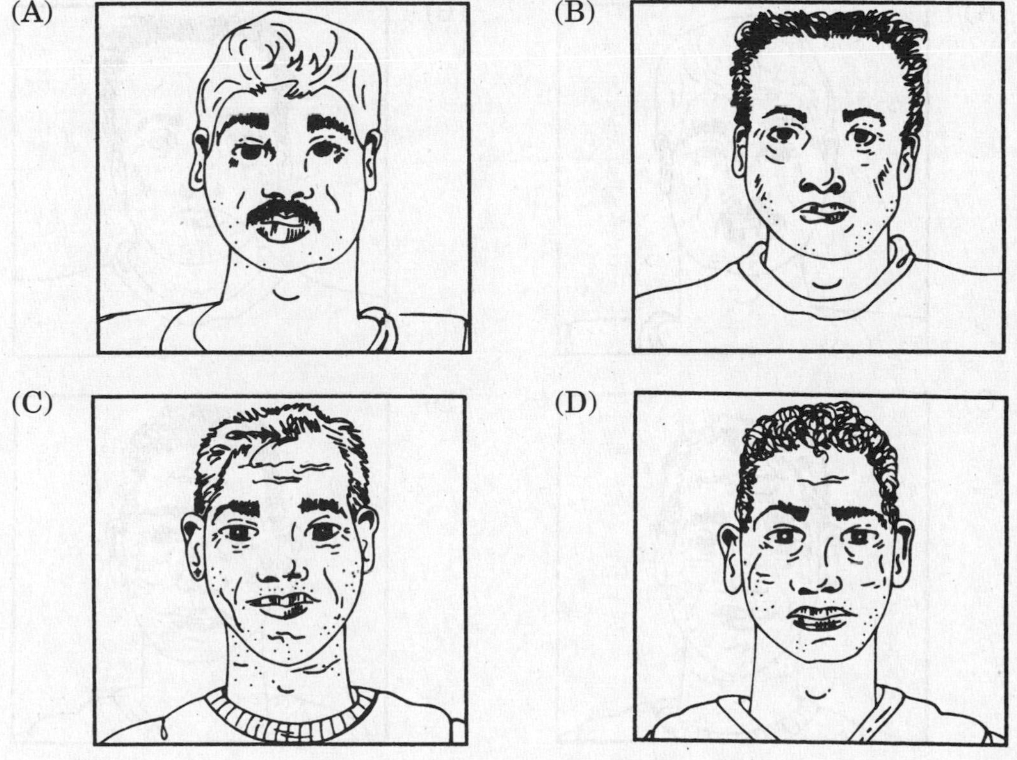

119. Which of the escaped inmates illustrated in the following posters often wears a hairpiece?

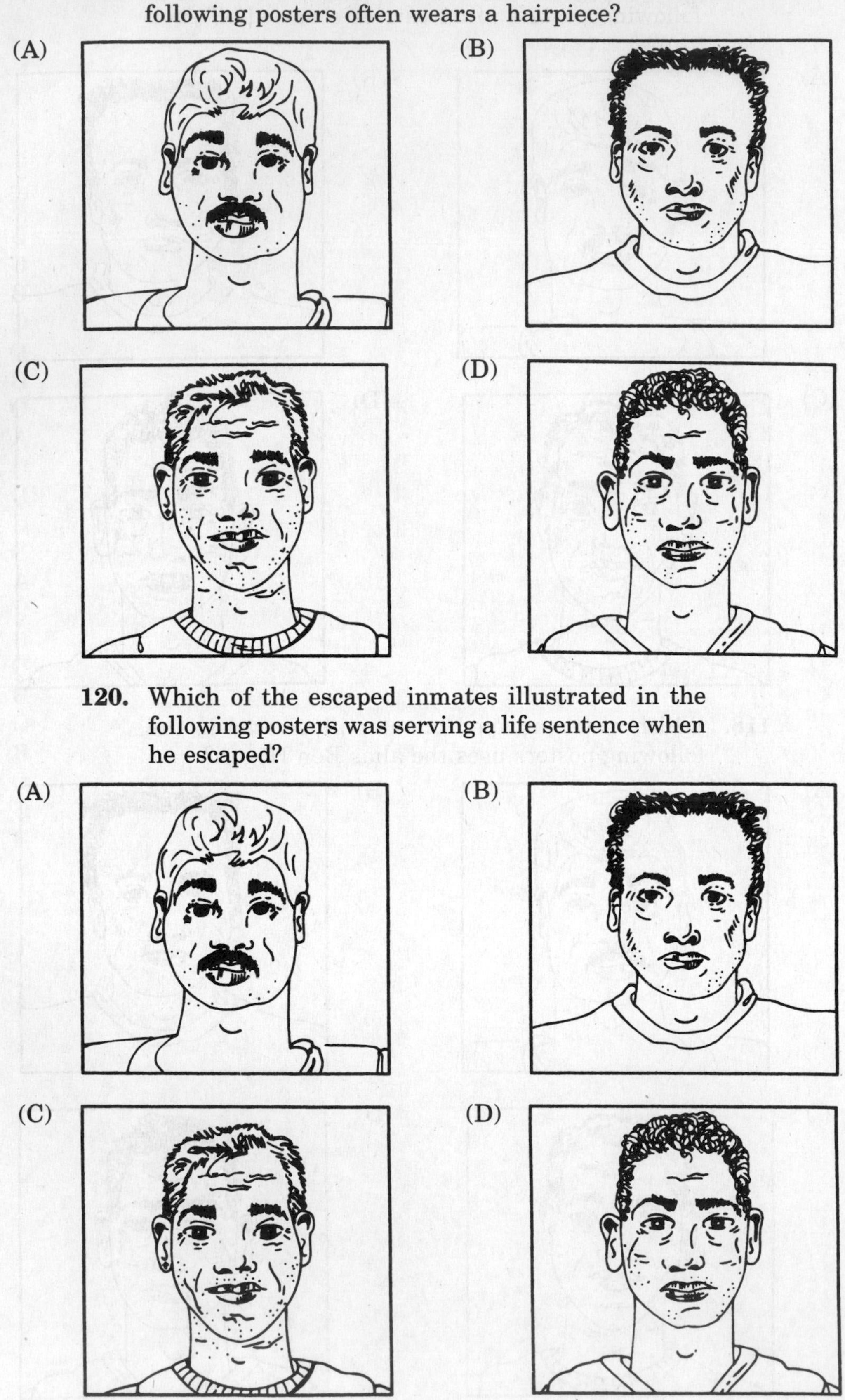

120. Which of the escaped inmates illustrated in the following posters was serving a life sentence when he escaped?

Answer Key, Diagnostic Procedure, and Explanations

Answer Key

1. C	25. C	49. B	73. D	97. B
2. A	26. C	50. A	74. C	98. B
3. B	27. D	51. C	75. D	99. C
4. C	28. D	52. D	76. A	100. B
5. A	29. B	53. B	77. A	101. C
6. C	30. B	54. C	78. B	102. D
7. C	31. D	55. B	79. D	103. B
8. D	32. C	56. B	80. B	104. D
9. B	33. C	57. B	81. A	105. A
10. B	34. C	58. B	82. B	106. C
11. D	35. A	59. D	83. C	107. D
12. A	36. B	60. C	84. C	108. C
13. A	37. D	61. B	85. D	109. D
14. C	38. C	62. B	86. C	110. A
15. B	39. C	63. D	87. D	111. C
16. A	40. D	64. C	88. C	112. B
17. A	41. A	65. D	89. B	113. D
18. C	42. C	66. A	90. A	114. B
19. B	43. B	67. B	91. D	115. C
20. C	44. B	68. C	92. A	116. B
21. C	45. A	69. D	93. D	117. D
22. B	46. D	70. A	94. D	118. C
23. B	47. A	71. B	95. B	119. B
24. A	48. B	72. C	96. C	120. B

Diagnostic Procedure

Insert the number of correct answers you obtained in the blank space for each section of the examination. The scale in the next column indicates how you did. The information at the bottom indicates how to correct your weaknesses.

SECTION	QUESTION NUMBERS	AREA	YOUR NUMBER CORRECT	SCALE
1	1–25	Memory		24 or 25 right—excellent 22 or 23 right—good 20 or 21 right—fair under 20 right—poor
2	56–59 77–80	Applying Police Directives		8 right—excellent 7 right—good 6 right—fair under 6 right—poor
3	46–55 60–66	Reading Comprehension		17 right—excellent 15 or 16 right—good 13 or 14 right—fair under 14 right—poor
4	26–45 67–76	Police Department Forms		39 or 30 right—excellent 27 or 28 right—good 25 or 26 right—fair under 25 right—poor
5	81–100	Legal Definitions		20 right—excellent 18 or 19 right—good 16 or 17 right—fair under 16 right—poor
6	101–110	Report Writing		10 right—excellent 8 or 9 right—good 7 right—fair under 7 right—poor
7	111–115	Arithmetic/ Formula Questions		5 right—excellent 4 right—good under 4 right—poor
8	116–120	Wanted Posters		5 right—excellent 4 right—good under 4 right—poor

1. If you are weak in Section One, then concentrate on Chapters 5 and 6.
2. If you are weak in Section Two, then concentrate on Chapter 8.
3. If you are weak in Section Three, then concentrate on Chapter 4.
4. If you are weak in Section Four, then concentrate on Chapter 7.
5. If you are weak in Section Five, then concentrate on Chapter 9.
6. If you are weak in Section Six, then concentrate on Chapter 12.
7. If you are weak in Section Seven, then concentrate on Chapter 10.
8. If you are weak in Section Eight, then concentrate on Chapter 10.

NOTE: Consider yourself weak in a section if you receive other than an excellent rating in it.

Answer Explanations

GENERAL COMMENT FOR QUESTIONS 1 THROUGH 15: If ever a memory story lent itself to a quick sketch, this one did. A quick mental sketch of an east-west highway with the various entrances and exits would have saved you a lot of problems.

1. C There were four numbers in the story—3232, 3220, 3331, and 3241—which were very similar. If you see this on your examination, you can be sure it will be a question area. By now, you should be able to predict a lot of the questions while reading the story.

2. A Sergeant Black is your supervisor. If you remembered this by association, you are doing very well. If you did not use an association, can you think of one now that you could have used?

3. B Remember times chronologically. Your unit got the job at 1720 hours, and you arrived at the scene 10 minutes after you received the call. Therefore, you arrived at the scene at 1730 hours.

4. C Sector Frank went to Grant Street. This was a ripe area for an alphabetical association. Sector Frank went to Grant Street.

5. A Sector George went to help you at the accident location. If you remembered that Frank went to Grant Street, it would be easy to remember that George went to the accident.

6. C The driver of the New Jersey car was the only driver who did not go to the hospital.

7. C Vehicle number three, with Kirk driving, was registered in New Jersey. This is another area where you should have anticipated a question. Exceptions are *prime* question areas.

8. D Your partner was Balsam and your supervisor was Black. This is an obvious association.

9. B A quick sketch would have made this one easy.

10. B Richter lives right by the accident.

11. D Sometimes the month and date are remembered, but the year is not. Be careful and concentrate.

12. A The key to this answer was the word "unsafe." The operator of vehicle number one, Goodman, made a bad mistake.

13. A The registration number of vehicle number one started with the number one.

14. **C** Kirk was an exception in a few ways. Kirk's vehicle was not registered in New York, and he was the only driver who was uninjured.

15. **B** An easy association. The two people from vehicle number one (the first) were placed in the Bayside Ambulance; the other two went into the Malba ambulance. The letter B is one of the first in the alphabet.

16. **A** This is an item you must focus in on when observing a street scene.

17. **A** At this point you are aware of the need to remember what people in the picture are wearing and doing.

18. **C** This is an "oddity" question. It should have caught your attention.

19. **B** The street sign on the picture clearly indicates that 151st Place is a dead end street.

20. **C** Remember, where people or things are in relation to each other is always a prime question area.

21. **C** Since the numbers are not that easy to read, the choices were quite varied.

22. **B** Choices C and D are too close to each other in meaning for either one of them to be the correct choice. Even if you were not sure if she was wearing a dress, she most certainly was wearing dark glasses.

23. **B** An easy question. Since she is in a dress, you should have thought it odd that she was carrying a pail.

24. **A** Concerning Choice C, you have no way of knowing if it were broken. Remember, don't read into the picture and don't make assumptions not based on facts.

25. **C** In this question you should assume that the object on the sidewalk is a refuse container since it is based on fact; a container that looks like a refuse container is on the sidewalk.

26. **C** Choice A refers to the person assisting the complainant. Choice B refers to the complainant's occupation. Choice D refers to the complainant's name.

27. **D** Choice A is the witness's telephone number. Choice B is the Gleem Computer Company's telephone number. Choice C is Mr. Colon's telephone number.

28. D This is Mr. Colon's address; he is the person assisting the complainant. Note that the boxes are out of sequence. You were advised of this possibility in the instructions. You should have read them carefully.

29. B The witness, Ms. Lydia James, was identified as the complainant's co-worker.

30. B The narrative opens indicating that at 2230 hours, Mr. Rodriquez, the complainant, was at the Third Precinct to make a complaint. Choice A is the time of the incident with the police officer. Choice C is the time that the complaint is called in by Sergeant Howe to the Civilian Complaint Review Board. Choice D is the time Mr. Rodriquez and Mr. Colon leave the Third Precinct station house.

31. D Choice A refers to Sergeant Howe's signature. Choice B refers to Mr. Rodriquez's name. Choice C refers to Mr. Colon's signature.

32. C Choice A is the shield number of the officer who was complained about. Choice B is the shield number of the C.C.R.B. police officer. Choice D is the time Mr. Colon and Mr. Rodriquez left the Third Precinct station house.

33. C Boxes 30, 31, and 32 call for the only signatures on the form. A witness is not required to sign the form.

34. C Mr. Rodriquez indicates that the officer is in uniform, on foot, white, and five feet eight inches tall. He does not indicate that the officer is a male. Don't assume! Base your answers on the form and the narrative.

35. A Choice B refers to Ms. James's address. Choice C refers to the command where the complaint is received, the Third Precinct. Choice D refers to the date of occurrence.

36. B Choice A is the prisoner's address. Choice C is fabricated. Choice D is obviously incorrect. The complainant's address is Choice B.

37. D Choice A—Fred Murray is the prisoner. Choice B—John Gleason is the assigned officer. Choice C—Jane Murphy is the complainant.

38. C Choice A is the desk officer's shield number. Choice B is the precinct number. Choice D is the voucher number.

39. C Choice A—the officer is John Gleason. Choice B—no property clerk name is given. Choice D—the complainant is Jane Murphy.

40. D Don't read into a question. If the information is not given, so be it.

41. **A** Remember that dates are always ripe areas for questions.

42. **C** The only crime mentioned is burglary.

43. **B** Officer Gleason's command is the 38th Precinct.

44. **B** The voucher number is 83. Do not confuse numbers which are similar but which appear in other captions.

45. **A** The college ring was the third item on the voucher, but was only one in number.

46. **D** This answer is contained in the second paragraph, where the answer is given just as stated in Choice D. Do not be tempted by Choice C just because it contains some exact wording from the paragraph.

47. **A** It does not matter if Otto's conduct was not criminal so long as he violated the terms of the order, which he did. It also does not matter that he was co-owner of the house. The judge knew that and issued the order anyway.

48. **B** Once again, don't let Choice A lead you astray because it uses words from another part of the paragraph. This answer is stated in the very first paragraph.

49. **B** This situation is covered in Situation B. There is no physical injury, and the offense did not occur in the presence of the officer. Therefore, referral is the correct course of action.

50. **A** The last two sentences of paragraph two point out that the present policy resulted from an agreement prompted by a lawsuit.

51. **C** Any police officer has a right to see the Order of Protection before making a decision, as is stated in the first paragraph of Situation A.

52. **D** This answer appears in the last paragraph of the Situation A explanation.

53. **B** The safe way to handle shotguns is illustrated in an existing poster. The new poster depicts the proper way to unload a handgun safely.

54. **C** Commanding officers concerned are directed to survey these commands to determine the appropriate location for a safety station.

55. **B** The prevention of personal injury and/or property damage resulting from accidental handgun discharges should result from the use of safety stations.

56. B This is an easy one. The temperature 32°F. is the only temperature mentioned in the entire examination.

57. B Procedure 4 forbids the assignment of scooters to expressways and parkways.

58. B There is no exception to the slow speed rule. Scooters are not meant to be used at high speeds, even in emergency situations.

59. D The first three choices are in violation of the procedures. Choice D is okay; see Procedure 9.

60. C The assault category is limited to assault third degree. The reason for this is that any other assault is a felony.

61. B The procedure applies only to officers in the Bronx or Manhattan Commands.

62. B See Paragraph 4 of the Order.

63. D It is stated in the first paragraph that this procedure provides a police officer with an option. It is, therefore, his decision to make.

64. C This is indicated on the bottom left portion of the Order. Remember to read everything.

65. D For people who live below 110th Street, the proper referral is 346 Broadway.

66. A As with question 64, the answer to this question is in the lower left portion of the order. Also note that the Order is addressed to "All Commands."

67. B Silver is an Identification Section Employee. Gold is the defendant's mother. White is the defendant.

68. C The charge is listed under the arresting officer's name on the top of the form. Choice A is listed as a previous charge against Ms. White.

69. D This information is contained in Section 2 of the form, where it indicates that Ms. White lives with her husband, William.

70. A Under Section 3, it indicates that Ms. White is currently employed by the New York Telephone Company.

71. B This information is contained in Section 1 of the forms.

72. C This information comes from two different areas of the form, both of which are under Section 1.

73. D This information appears next to the charge at the top of the form. Note the similarity between Choices B and D. Be careful when dealing with numbers.

74. C If you picked Choice A, you probably did not read all of the choices. When dealing with dates, be careful of the year.

75. D This information is contained on the top of the form next to the officer's command.

76. A This information is contained in Section 3.

77. A While increasing employee morale sounds logical, it is not in the written material. Therefore, it is wrong.

78. B Paragraph 3h states that only authorized personnel can adjust central air conditioner settings.

79. D Later in the day, if the temperature goes over 80 degrees F. as predicted, Officer Smith can use her window air conditioner. At the time in the story, she is not yet authorized to turn it on.

80. B This is stated in the second paragraph.

81. A A person can be sentenced to more than one year for committing a felony.

82. B A billy is specifically enumerated as a deadly weapon. As for Choice A, the gun has to be loaded to be a deadly weapon.

83. C An A felony is the most serious of all crimes.

84. C A crime is either a misdemeanor or a felony.

85. D Offenses are defined as either felonies, misdemeanors, or violations. A violation is not a crime.

86. C There are many instances when a physical injury does not amount to a serious physical injury.

87. D The use of a deadly weapon does not have to result in an injury. For example, I could shoot at you and miss.

88. C All of the other three choices are specifically enumerated as deadly weapons. Hammers are not mentioned.

89. B When you are looking for the least inaccurate statement, you are looking for a true statement, which in this case, is Choice B. According to the definitions, almost anything could be a dangerous instrument; but only those items specifically enumerated could be deadly weapons.

90. A The maximum penalty for a violation is fifteen days. Penalties for misdemeanors start at sixteen days.

91. D The taking of property is not an element of the crime of burglary in the second degree. Concerning Choice B, it is not necessary for Marlond to know that his accomplice is carrying a deadly weapon.

92. A The fact that the window was open does not affect the fact that both men unlawfully entered the apartment.

93. D The word imminent means immediate. Tom was going to kill Peter and Paul on the next day. Therefore, Tom was not threatening imminent use of deadly physical force.

94. D According to the definition, the perpetrator has to be in immediate flight from the crime. In this case, Maryann killed the perpetrator months after the crime was committed.

95. B It clearly states in the narrative that it was an attempted robbery. The right to use deadly physical force is only present if the robbery was actually committed.

96. C One of the elements of robbery in the first degree is for the perpetrator to be armed with a deadly weapon, as Harold was in this case.

97. B It is not necessary for an injury to occur for the crime of robbery in the first degree to be committed.

98. B This will be accomplished by reducing shooting incidents.

99. C The guidelines given are in addition to the restrictions in the Penal Law.

100. B Warning shots are prohibited in all instances.

101. C Choice A is incorrect since it unnecessarily repeats that the suspect is white. Choice B is incorrect since it incorrectly states the weapon was a .38 caliber pistol; it was a .32 caliber pistol. Choice D is incorrect since it states the suspect was wearing a .32 caliber pistol. Remember the instructions mandate that the correct choice clearly and accurately express the information given.

102. D Choice A is incorrect since the time of occurrence was 9:30 A.M.; 10:30 A.M. was the time of reporting. Choice B is incorrect since the addresses of the witness and place of occurrence were switched. Choice C is incorrect since it does not clearly indicate that the male Hispanic is a suspect.

103. B Choice A is incorrect since it makes it appear that Don Grime no longer is 75 years old and no longer weighs 200 pounds. Choice C is incorrect since it incorrectly indicates that Officer Banks did not receive any information until the officer has been at the location for ten minutes. Choice D is incorrect since it states that Mr. Grime was not missing until the officer was at the nursing home for ten minutes.

104. D Choice A is incorrect since it states that the owner, who is June Parks, witnessed the incident. The incident was witnessed by Fred Parks. Choice B is incorrect since it indicates that the incident occurred at 8:30 P.M. It occurred at 8:00 P.M. Choice C is incorrect since it states that Frank Parks is the owner of the vehicle.

105. A Choice B is incorrect since it does not indicate who used the chains and bats. Choice C is incorrect since it indicates that Frank Baron was released from the hospital at 9:30 P.M. That was the time of assault. Choice D is incorrect since it gives the address of the hospital as 899 3rd Avenue.

106. C Choice A is incorrect because it should state "impossible to reach you and me." Remember that if you have difficulty evaluating this type of statement, just remove the first pronoun, in this case *you*, and then read the statement to yourself. In this case it would then read "impossible to reach I," which you can easily see is incorrect. Choice B is incorrect because it should indicate *your* to show possession.

107. D Choice A should state "laid their weapons down," since it is intended to indicate a placing of something in the past. Choice B is incorrect because reclining in the past should be stated as "all the students lay down." Choice C should use *teach*, to indicate giving knowledge. All the choices are incorrect.

108. C Choice A is unclear because it cannot be determined who was searched, the prisoner or the detective. It should have stated, "After the prisoner was searched." The use of *in* instead of *into* makes choice B incorrect. Choice C is correct.

109. D All the statements are correctly presented.

110. A *Stationary* means placed in a fixed position, whereas *stationery* means writing supplies, such as envelopes and writing paper. Choices B and C are therefore incorrect. Choice A is stated correctly.

111. C The total value of the property is $3,482.00, which is what using the formula given in choice C yields.

112. B To answer this question use numbers that are fairly easy to work with and substitute them into each formula. For example if an officer wishes to travel 100 miles, the distance d, and wishes to travel at 50 miles per hour, the rate of speed r, the time t it will take is obviously 2 hours or $\frac{100}{50} = 2$. This is what is expressed in choice C, where we have $t = \frac{d}{r}$.

113. D The officer spent 5 hours of the 8-hour tour of duty on patrol assignments. Therefore, the officer spent a total of 3 hours on assignments other than patrol. The calculations recommended by choice D are correct, since 3 hours on a foot post plus 2 hours on radar patrol equals 5 hours, and when that is subtracted from 8 hours, the total hours of the tour, it yields 3 hours.

114. B The sum of all the monies comes to $200.48. When adding numbers with decimals it is key to correctly align the numbers being added by using their decimal points.

115. C From the previous question, it is known that the sum of all the monies comes to $200.48. Now subtract $12.38, which is being returned to a bailed out prisoner, and then add back $18.36, which had been found due to a further search of one of the prisoners in custody and the amount is now a total of $206.46.

116. B Hopefully, you haven't fogotten to use associations to deal with memory questions. It doesn't matter what specific type of memory question you are given—the association technique is always applicable. In this question the word *young* in the inmate's name would be a good way to remember that he loiters near schools (where young people attend).

117. D Sawed-off shotguns are shorter than regular shotguns. This inmate's name is Short. A perfect association.

118. C An alphabetical association suits this question just fine. Jack Hunt uses the alias Ben Hogan.

119. B Once again the *young* in this inmate's name could have helped you remember the information needed to answer the question (e.g., young people don't often wear hairpieces).

120. B Youngblood was serving a life sentence. An association like Youngblood will get old in prison would have been perfect for this association.

Practice Examination Two Answer Sheet

ANSWER SHEET

THE CITY OF NEW YORK
DEPARTMENT OF PERSONNEL

T.P. NO.

DO NOT WRITE IN THIS BOX

DO NOT WRITE IN THIS BOX

YOUR SOCIAL SECURITY NO.

EXAM NO.

H J K L M N P R S T

EXAM TITLE	TODAY'S DATE	
SCHOOL OR BUILDING	ROOM NO.	SEAT NO.

PRINT WITH SOFT PENCIL ONLY. Print, with pencil, your SOCIAL SECURITY NO. and the EXAM. NO. in the boxes at the tops of the columns. ONE NUMBER IN A BOX. In each column, darken (with pencil) the oval containing the number in the box at the top of the column. Only ONE OVAL in a COLUMN should be darkened. Then, using your pencil, print in the: Exam. Title, School or Building, Room No., Seat No., and Today's Date.

Follow the instructions given in the question booklet. Mark nothing but your answers in the ovals below.
SAMPLE QUESTION: When we add 5 and 3 we get: (A) 11 (B) 9 (C) 8 (D) 2. Since the answer is 8, your answer should be marked like this: A B ● D
WARNING: Be sure that the oval you fill is in the row numbered the same as the question you are answering. Use a No. 2 pencil (soft pencil).
BE SURE YOUR PENCIL MARKS ARE HEAVY AND BLACK. ERASE COMPLETELY ANY ANSWER YOU WISH TO CHANGE.
DO NOT make stray pencil dots, dashes or marks ANYPLACE on this SHEET.

START HERE

1 A B C D	2 A B C D	3 A B C D	4 A B C D	5 A B C D	6 A B C D
7 A B C D	8 A B C D	9 A B C D	10 A B C D	11 A B C D	12 A B C D
13 A B C D	14 A B C D	15 A B C D	16 A B C D	17 A B C D	18 A B C D
19 A B C D	20 A B C D	21 A B C D	22 A B C D	23 A B C D	24 A B C D
25 A B C D	26 A B C D	27 A B C D	28 A B C D	29 A B C D	30 A B C D
31 A B C D	32 A B C D	33 A B C D	34 A B C D	35 A B C D	36 A B C D
37 A B C D	38 A B C D	39 A B C D	40 A B C D	41 A B C D	42 A B C D
43 A B C D	44 A B C D	45 A B C D	46 A B C D	47 A B C D	48 A B C D
49 A B C D	50 A B C D	51 A B C D	52 A B C D	53 A B C D	54 A B C D
55 A B C D	56 A B C D	57 A B C D	58 A B C D	59 A B C D	60 A B C D
61 A B C D	62 A B C D	63 A B C D	64 A B C D	65 A B C D	66 A B C D
67 A B C D	68 A B C D	69 A B C D	70 A B C D	71 A B C D	72 A B C D
73 A B C D	74 A B C D	75 A B C D	76 A B C D	77 A B C D	78 A B C D
79 A B C D	80 A B C D	81 A B C D	82 A B C D	83 A B C D	84 A B C D
85 A B C D	86 A B C D	87 A B C D	88 A B C D	89 A B C D	90 A B C D
91 A B C D	92 A B C D	93 A B C D	94 A B C D	95 A B C D	96 A B C D
97 A B C D	98 A B C D	99 A B C D	100 A B C D	101 A B C D	102 A B C D
103 A B C D	104 A B C D	105 A B C D	106 A B C D	107 A B C D	108 A B C D
109 A B C D	110 A B C D	111 A B C D	112 A B C D	113 A B C D	114 A B C D
115 A B C D	116 A B C D	117 A B C D	118 A B C D	119 A B C D	120 A B C D
121 A B C D	122 A B C D	123 A B C D	124 A B C D	125 A B C D	126 A B C D
127 A B C D	128 A B C D	129 A B C D	130 A B C D	131 A B C D	132 A B C D
133 A B C D	134 A B C D	135 A B C D	136 A B C D	137 A B C D	138 A B C D
139 A B C D	140 A B C D	141 A B C D	142 A B C D	143 A B C D	144 A B C D
145 A B C D	146 A B C D	147 A B C D	148 A B C D	149 A B C D	150 A B C D

CONFIDENTIAL QUESTIONNAIRE: **Completion of this information is voluntary.** The Department of Personnel, pursuant to guidelines issued by the United States Equal Employment Opportunity Commission and provisions of the State Human Rights Law, requests that all candidates complete the section below. We request your cooperation in completing this Questionnaire section accurately. Answers to these questions will be used to conduct studies to identify and resolve possible problems in recruitment and testing for the purpose of insuring equal opportunity for employment in the Civil Service. Please darken one oval for each of the five items below.

ANSWER QUESTION 2 ON THE BASIS OF THE FOLLOWING INFORMATION: CHOOSING ONLY ONE GENERAL CATEGORY.
BLACK: African descent, Jamaican, Trinidadian, West Indian.
WHITE: Caucasian or white whose ancestors came from Europe or Western Asia, including Pakistan or East India.
SPANISH SURNAMED: Mexican, Puerto Rican, Cuban, Latin American, or Spanish descent.
AMERICAN INDIAN: American Indian or member of an Indian tribe.
ASIAN AMERICAN: Japanese, Chinese, Korean, or Filipino descent.
OTHER: Aleut, Eskimo, Malayan, Thai, or other not covered by above categories.

1. SEX — MALE / FEMALE

2. To which one of the following groups do you belong? — BLACK / WHITE / SPANISH SURNAMED / AMERICAN INDIAN / ASIAN AMERICAN / OTHER

3. MARK HIGHEST diploma or degree received. — HIGH SCHOOL DIPLOMA / ASSOCIATE DEGREE / BACCALAUREATE DEGREE / MASTERS DEGREE / DOCTORS DEGREE

4. If no diploma above, mark highest grade completed. — 6 / 7 / 8 / 9 / 10 / 11 / 12

5. If a diploma but no degree received, mark number of years of college completed. — 1 / 2 / 3 / 4

Misc. 1088N (3-81)

CHAPTER 14

Practice Examination Two

This chapter includes the second of three practice examinations that you will be taking. The first was an original test; this one was an official one administered by the New York City Police Department. *When you have finished taking all three examinations, you will see that you are prepared to take most major police officer examinations, including those for Transit and Housing Police Officer administered in many cities.*

Be sure to take Practice Examination Two in one sitting. You will then become accustomed to concentrating for a period of $4\frac{1}{2}$ hours, which is the length of time allowed for the examination. Be sure to review the test-taking strategy outlined in Chapter 2 before taking this practice examination.

Before You Take the Examination

When you begin this examination, look first at the material marked "Memory Booklet," which begins on page 431. After reading the material for the time specified, continue to the "Test Booklet" and do not look back at the material marked "Memory Booklet." Then continue with the rest of the test.

Remember to read each question and related material carefully before choosing your answers. Select the choice you believe to be the most correct, and mark your answer on the Answer Sheet provided at the beginning of this chapter. The Answer Key, Diagnostic Procedure, and Answer Explanations appear at the end of this chapter. (Be sure to gauge your time, averaging 1½ to 2 minutes per question.)

Note that we have included a copy of the official Instruction Booklet on pages 425 to 430 so that you can become familiar with normal test procedures. We have not attempted to include all accompanying forms, as test instructions do change occasionally.

City of New York
Department of Personnel

Soc. Sec. No. ______
Seat No. ______
Room No. ______
School ______

EXAMINATION NO. 4061
POLICE OFFICER SERIES

Written Test: 70th Percentile Required, Weight 100

December 15, 1984

TEST INSTRUCTIONS FOR CANDIDATES—READ NOW

GENERAL INFORMATION Read these TEST INSTRUCTIONS FOR CANDIDATES and fill out the information requested at the top of this booklet. Following are explanations of the information requested.

The Soc. Sec. No. is your Social Security Number as shown on your admission card which you brought with you today. If your Social Security Number is not correct on your admission card, you must draw a line through the incorrect number, and write your correct Social Security Number on the card. Use your correct Social Security Number on the fingerprint card and the Answer Sheet. Be sure to fill out the pink correction form (DP-148) if your Social Security Number is incorrect, so that the correction can be taken care of after the test.

Your Seat No. is the number shown on the sheet of scrap paper on your desk.

Your Room No. and School are written on the blackboard.

THE FORMS: YOU MUST NOW FILL OUT YOUR FINGERPRINT CARD AND ANSWER SHEET AS EXPLAINED BELOW. Use pencil only.

Fingerprint Card: Print in pencil all information requested including your Social Security Number. Your fingerprints will be taken approximately 15 minutes after the seventh signal.

Answer Sheet: Print in pencil all the information requested on the Answer Sheet including your Social Security No., and the Exam. No. 4061 in the boxes at the top of the columns, ONE NUMBER IN A BOX. In each column, blacken (with pencil) the oval containing the number in the box at the top of the column; only ONE OVAL in a COLUMN should be blackened. Then, using your pencil, print the Exam. Title, School or Building, Room No., Seat No., and Today's Date in the appropriate spaces.

After filling in this information at the top of the Answer Sheet, please read the Confidential Questionnaire at the bottom of the Answer Sheet, and answer the questions accurately.

TEST INSTRUCTIONS (Continued)

After answering the Confidential Questionnaire, please complete the following survey questions.

TUTORIAL SURVEY The New York City Department of Personnel requests your assistance in providing information on candidate participation in tutorial programs which have been designed to prepare candidates for the Police Officer Series Examination. The information you provide will not affect your score in any manner. Please blacken items 141 through 143 on your Answer Sheet as follows:

I. If you DID NOT participate in any tutorial program, blacken Item Number 141, option A.

II. If you participated in a tutorial program conducted by the New York City Police Department, blacken Item Number 141, option B.

III. If you participated in a tutorial program conducted by someone other than the New York City Police Department, for example, a college-sponsored program or a privately operated program, blacken Item Number 141, option C.

IV. If you participated in BOTH the New York City Police Department program and any other tutorial program, blacken Item Number 141, option D.

V. (a) If you participated in any tutorial program and attended ONE session, blacken Item Number 142, option A.

(b) If you attended TWO sessions, blacken Item Number 142, option B.

(c) If you attended THREE sessions, blacken Item Number 142, option C.

(d) If you attended FOUR sessions, blacken Item Number 142, option D.

(e) If you attended FIVE sessions, blacken Item Number 143, option A.

(f) If you attended SIX sessions, blacken Item Number 143, option B.

(g) If you attended MORE THAN SIX sessions, blacken Item Number 143, option C.

TEST INSTRUCTIONS (Continued)

LANGUAGE SURVEY The eligible list resulting from this examination may be selectively certified to fill vacancies which require a working knowledge of Spanish, Cantonese, or another language.

Only those candidates who possess the minimum requirements and are placed on the eligible list may be permitted to take a language proficiency test. Results of the language proficiency test will have no bearing on list standing.

In order to take a qualifying oral test to demonstrate your ability to speak and understand Spanish, blacken Item Number 148, option A.

In order to take a qualifying oral test to demonstrate your ability to speak and understand Cantonese, blacken Item Number 149, option A.

If you are interested in taking a qualifying oral test to demonstrate your ability to speak and understand any other language, blacken Item Number 150, option A.

RECRUITMENT SURVEY Please read the Recruitment Survey, and place your answers on the form attached to the questionnaire.

EIGHT SIGNALS WILL BE USED DURING THIS TEST. Following is an explanation of these signals.

FIRST SIGNAL:	Memory Booklet is distributed. DO NOT OPEN THE BOOKLET.
SECOND SIGNAL:	OPEN MEMORY BOOKLET. You will be given five minutes to try to remember as many details about the first scene as you can. You may not write or make any notes during this time. DO NOT TURN TO ANY OTHER PAGE DURING THIS TIME.
THIRD SIGNAL:	TURN TO THE NEXT PAGE. DO NOT TURN TO ANY OTHER PAGE DURING THIS TIME.
FOURTH SIGNAL:	TURN TO THE NEXT PAGE. Answer the seven questions on the Answer Sheet. You will have five minutes to complete this section. DO NOT TURN TO ANY OTHER PAGE DURING THIS TIME. You may wish to record your answers next to each question on the page.

TEST INSTRUCTIONS (Continued)

FIFTH SIGNAL: TURN TO THE NEXT SCENE. You will be given five minutes to try to remember as many details about the second scene as you can. You may not write or make any notes during this time. DO NOT TURN TO ANY OTHER PAGE DURING THIS TIME.

SIXTH SIGNAL: CLOSE THE MEMORY BOOKLET. It will be collected by the monitor. The Test Booklet will then be distributed. You may not write or make any notes during this time. DO NOT OPEN THE TEST BOOKLET.

SEVENTH SIGNAL: OPEN THE TEST BOOKLET and begin work. Finish the Memory questions first and then go on to the other questions. This test consists of 140 questions. After you finish the Memory questions check to make sure that the Test Booklet goes up to and includes question 140, and is not defective. You will have $4\frac{1}{2}$ hours from this signal to complete all the questions. YOU WILL BE FINGER-PRINTED DURING THIS PERIOD.

EIGHTH SIGNAL: END OF TEST. STOP ALL WORK. If you finish before this signal and wish to leave, raise you hand.

ANYONE DISOBEYING ANY OF THESE INSTRUCTIONS MAY BE DISQUALIFIED—THAT IS, YOU MAY RECEIVE A SCORE OF ZERO FOR THE ENTIRE TEST!

DIRECTIONS FOR ANSWERING QUESTIONS: Answer all the questions on the Answer Sheet before the Eighth Signal is given. ONLY YOUR ANSWER SHEET WILL BE MARKED. For future reference, you should also record your answers in your Test Booklet before the end of the test and in your Memory Booklet before the Fifth Signal. Use a soft pencil (No. 2) to mark your answers. If you want to change an answer, erase it and then mark your new answer. Do not make stray pencil dots, dashes or marks any place on the Answer Sheet. DO NOT fold, roll or tear the Answer Sheet.

Here is a sample of how to mark your answers:

TEST INSTRUCTIONS (Continued)

SAMPLE O: When we add 5 and 3, we get

(A) 11 (B) 9 (C) 8 (D) 2

Since the answer is 8, your Answer Sheet is marked like this:

SAMPLE O: (A) (B) ● (D)

WARNING: You are not allowed to copy answers from anyone, or to use books or notes. It is against the law to take the test for somebody else or to let somebody else take the test for you. There is to be NO SMOKING anywhere in the building.

LEAVING: After the test starts, candidates may not leave the building until after they are fingerprinted. No one may come in after 11:30 A.M. During the test, you may not leave the room unless accompanied by a monitor. If you want to drop out of the test and not have your answers marked, write "I withdraw" on your Answer Sheet and sign your name.

MEDICAL AND PHYSICAL STANDARDS: Eligibles must meet the medical and physical fitness standards to be established and posted on the Department of Personnel Bulletin Board at 49 Thomas Street, New York, N.Y., 10013. Candidates must pass a qualifying physical fitness test and a qualifying medical test. Eligibles will be rejected for any medical, psychiatric, or physical impairment which impairs their ability to perform the duties of Police Officer. Periodic reexaminations of employees in these titles will be required in accordance with Executive Order No. 31, dated October 10, 1966.

There are no height requirements.

Medical evidence to allow participation in the physical fitness test may be required, and the Department of Personnel reserves the right to exclude from the physical fitness test any eligibles who, upon examination of such evidence, are apparently medically unfit. Eligibles will take the physical fitness test at their own risk of injury, although every effort will be made to safeguard them.

CHARACTER: Proof of good character will be an absolute prerequisite to appointment.

TEST INSTRUCTIONS (Continued)

The following are among the factors which would ordinarily be cause for disqualification: (a) conviction for an offense, the nature of which indicates lack of good moral character or disposition toward violence or disorder; (b) repeated convictions for offenses, where such convictions indicate a disrespect for the law; (c) repeated discharges from employment, where such discharges indicate poor performance or inability to adjust to discipline. In accordance with provisions of the law, persons convicted of a felony or receiving a dishonorable discharge from the Armed Forces are not eligible for appointment to this position. Persons convicted of petit larceny may be declared ineligible for appointment.

INVESTIGATION: At the time of appointment and at the time of investigation, candidates must present all the official documents and proof required to qualify. At the time of investigation, candidates will be required to present proof of date of birth by transcript of record from the Bureau of Vital Statistics or other satisfactory evidence. Proof of military service and similar documents may be required. Failure to present required documents, including proof of educational or license requirements, will result in disqualification for appointment or a direction to terminate services.

Any willful misstatement will be cause for disqualification.

Take This Booklet With You.

Certificate of Attendance
Department of Personnel
December 15, 1984

Soc. Sec. No.____________
Room No.____________
Seat No.____________
School____________

This is to certify that ________________ took the examination for Police Officer Series, Exam No. 4061 on this date. The candidate was summoned for 10:30 A.M. and released by ________.

____
Room Monitor

DEPARTMENT OF PERSONNEL

Social Security No.____________
Room No.____________
Seat No.____________
School____________

Memory Booklet

POLICE OFFICER SERIES

December 15, 1984

EXAMINATION NO. 4061

DO NOT OPEN THIS BOOKLET UNTIL THE SECOND SIGNAL IS GIVEN!

Write your Social Security Number, Room Number, Seat Number and School in the appropriate spaces at the top of this page.

You must follow the instructions found on pages two and three of the TEST INSTRUCTION BOOKLET.

ANYONE DISOBEYING ANY OF THE INSTRUCTIONS FOUND IN THE TEST INSTRUCTION BOOKLET MAY BE DISQUALIFIED—RECEIVE A ZERO ON THE ENTIRE TEST.

This booklet contains TWO different scenes. For each scene try to remember as many details as you can. You should pay equal attention both to objects and to people shown in the scenes.

DO NOT WRITE OR MAKE ANY NOTES WHILE STUDYING EITHER OF THE SCENES.

DO NOT OPEN THIS BOOKLET UNTIL THE SECOND SIGNAL IS GIVEN!

The New York City Department of Personnel makes no commitment, and no implication is to be drawn, as to the content, style, or format of any future examination for the position of Police Officer.

SMOKE
LUCKY'S
SCHOOL of Dance
BOB'S FURNITURE
PAT'S CLEANERS
PETS
PETS
SHOES
ANN ST.
79
BARBER
89
99
ConEd
EAT AT JOE'S
FORD
512
MEN WORKING
TOOLS
TRUCK IV893

SCENE 1

HAIR DESIGN
ONE FLIGHT UP
STORAGE WAREHOUSE 102
BLOOM'S factory outlet
ONE WAY
NO PARKING
261
1598732
12 58 9
72
NUTS 1.50 lb.
FORD
MAT'S
160 BROADWAY
MAT-1
POISON
POISON
POISON

Answer questions 1 through 7 solely on the basis of sketch number 1.

1. What is the license plate number of the truck parked in front of Bloom's Factory Outlet?

   (A) 512-Aut (B) MAT-1 (C) PAT-1 (D) MIDAS-1.

2. What is the address of the pet shop outlet?

   (A) 79 Ann Street
   (B) 89 Ann Street
   (C) 99 Ann Street
   (D) 109 Ann Street.

3. The person with the sign is

   (A) walking toward the woman with the dog
   (B) walking toward the truck partially parked in the warehouse
   (C) walking toward the woman with the carriage
   (D) walking toward the train.

4. There is a picture of a man's face

   (A) on the train
   (B) on the nut cart
   (C) in the window of the pet store
   (D) on the truck in front of Bloom's Factory Outlet.

5. The Con Ed man is

   (A) driving the truck
   (B) talking to the man crossing the street
   (C) carrying boxes
   (D) handling a hose near a manhole.

6. What school is located above the Barber Shop?

   (A) A dance school
   (B) A typing school
   (C) A boxing school
   (D) A karate school.

7. How many people are in the scene?

   (A) 6 (B) 7 (C) 8 (D) 9.

DEPARTMENT OF PERSONNEL

Social Security No.________________
Room No.________________
Seat No.________________

Test Booklet POLICE OFFICER SERIES

December 15, 1984 EXAMINATION NO. 4061

Written Test: Weight 100

Time Allowed: $4\frac{1}{2}$ Hours

DO NOT OPEN THIS BOOKLET UNTIL THE SEVENTH SIGNAL IS GIVEN!

Record your answers on the official Answer Sheet before the last signal. If you wish, you may also record your answers in the Test Booklet, before the last signal is given.

This Test Booklet contains procedures which are to be used to answer certain questions. These procedures are not necessarily those of the New York City Police Department. However, you are to answer these questions solely on the basis of the material given.

After the seventh signal is given, open this Test Booklet and begin work. You will have $4\frac{1}{2}$ hours to complete this test.

You may make notes in this booklet and use the scrap paper on your desk. If you need additional scrap paper, ask the monitor.

Remember, only your official Answer Sheet will be rated, so be sure to mark all your answers on the official Answer Sheet before the eighth signal. No additional time will be given for marking your answers after the test has ended.

DO NOT OPEN THIS BOOKLET UNTIL THE SEVENTH SIGNAL IS GIVEN!

HOOK
LINE
SINKER
FISHING
TACKLE
939-41
23 STREET
CLEANERS
INCOME TAX
937

SCENE 2

LIQUORS
Chelsea Music
945
8:21 51°
BANK
BAG6165

Answer questions 8 through 13 solely on the basis of sketch number 2.

8. The three people standing together are closest to the

(A) liquor store
(B) open manhole
(C) income tax office
(D) street light.

9. The license plate of the occupied auto is

(A) ARC 1211
(B) BAG 6165
(C) GAB 5616
(D) ABG 6165.

10. What is the total number of persons in the liquor store?

(A) 1
(B) 2
(C) 3
(D) 4.

11. The man dressed in the black outfit is standing in front of the

(A) Chelsea Music Store
(B) 23rd Street Cleaners
(C) Liquor Store
(D) Fishing-Tackle Store.

12. The temperature posted on the sign above the bank is

(A) 15°
(B) 25°
(C) 50°
(D) 51°.

13. The Income Tax Office is located between the

(A) liquor store and the bank
(B) 23rd Street Cleaners and the Fishing-Tackle Store
(C) Chelsea Music Store and the bank
(D) Fishing-Tackle Store and the liquor store.

Please check your Answer Sheet to make sure that you have written in and blackened your Social Security number correctly. If you have not yet written in and blackened your Social Security number, please do so immediately. If you have incorrectly written in or blackened your Social Security number, please correct the mistake immediately. Failure to correctly blacken your Social Security number may result in your Answer Sheet NOT being rated.

14. Police Officer Clay is giving a report to the news media regarding someone who has jumped from the Empire State Building. His report will include the following five sentences:

1. I responded to the 86th floor, where I found the person at the edge of the roof.
2. A security guard at the building had reported that a man was on the roof at the 86th floor.
3. At 5:30 P.M., the person jumped from the building.
4. I received a call from the radio dispatcher at 4:50 P.M. to respond to the Empire State Building.
5. I tried to talk to the person and convince him not to jump.

The most logical order for the above sentences to appear in the report is

(A) 1, 2, 4, 3, 5
(B) 3, 4, 1, 2, 5
(C) 2, 4, 1, 3, 5
(D) 4, 2, 1, 5, 3.

Answer question 15 solely on the basis of the following information.

Police Officers are required to notify the proper city agency of a street condition requiring corrective action. When a street condition requires corrective action, a Police Officer should follow these procedures, in the order given:

1. While on patrol, in the Memo Log, write an entry indicating what street condition requires correction.
2. The Memo Log entry must indicate the location of the street condition.
3. Inform the telephone switchboard operator of the street condition and location.
4. If a traffic signal light is not working properly, take all of the above actions and inform the Department of Traffic.

15. Police Officer Flanagan while on patrol observes that a traffic signal light on the corner of Second Avenue and 74th Street in Manhattan doesn't change from red. He takes all appropriate actions through indicating the location of the defective traffic signal light in his Memo Log. Police Officer Flanagan should next

(A) notify the Department of Traffic
(B) inform the telephone switchboard operator of the defective traffic signal light on Second Avenue and 74th Street in Manhattan
(C) write an entry in the Memo Log indicating that a street condition exists which requires corrective action
(D) write an entry in the Memo Log indicating that the telephone switchboard operator was notified.

Answer question <u>16</u> solely on the basis of the following information.

A Police Officer is trained in standard first aid techniques. Listed below are the techniques to stop severe bleeding:

1. Apply direct pressure by placing the hand directly over the wound, when possible.
2. Elevate a wound of the hand, neck, arm or leg unless there is evidence of a broken bone.
3. Apply pressure on the appropriate artery.
4. Use a tourniquet only as a last resort. Its use means sacrificing the injured leg or arm to save the person from bleeding to death.

16. While on foot patrol in Midtown Manhattan, Police Officer Charles is summoned by a passerby to aid an injured construction worker. The worker fell from a third-floor scaffold and injured his left leg, which is severely bleeding. An ambulance is on its way, but until its arrival, Police Officer Charles should

(A) apply direct pressure to the wound and elevate the leg, even if the leg is broken
(B) apply direct pressure to the wound and elevate the leg if it appears there are no broken bones
(C) elevate the leg immediately and apply pressure on the appropriate artery
(D) elevate the leg, apply pressure on the appropriate artery and automatically apply a tourniquet to save the leg.

17. The following five sentences are part of a report of a burglary written by Police Officer Reed:

1. When I arrived at 2400 1st Avenue, I noticed that the door was slightly open.
2. I yelled out, "Police, don't move!"
3. As I entered the apartment, I saw a man with a T.V. set passing it through a window to another man standing on a fire escape.
4. While on foot patrol, I was informed by the radio dispatcher that a burglary was in progress at 2400 1st Avenue.
5. However, the burglars quickly ran down the fire escape.

The most logical order for the above sentences to appear in the report is

(A) 1, 3, 4, 5, 2
(B) 4, 1, 3, 5, 2
(C) 4, 1, 3, 2, 5
(D) 1, 4, 3, 2, 5.

Answer questions 18 through 21 solely on the basis of the following passage.

At 11:55 A.M. Police Officer Benson was on foot patrol on 44th Street between 6th Avenue and Broadway. This post is known to be a high crime area with a large number of narcotics, robbery and prostitution arrests. Police Officer Benson approached a young woman he had previously arrested for prostitution. As he was about to question her, he heard a scream coming from the direction of a women's boutique on the opposite side of the street. A young black male was running up 44th Street towards Broadway, followed by a woman yelling "Stop that man!" Police Officer Benson ran after the woman but by the time he caught up with her, she had fallen after tripping on the badly cracked sidewalk. The woman was visibly shaken, and appeared to have broken her arm. Police Officer Benson decided that because the young black male had disappeared from sight, he should stay with the injured woman and call for an ambulance. While awaiting the arrival of the ambulance, the injured woman, Ms. Peever, told Police Officer Benson that she was the owner of the boutique and that the young black male had taken approximately $475 from the cash register while she went to check the price of an item. She also mentioned that the boutique was presently unattended because her two sales people had not come to work that morning.

Police Officer Benson called for back-up assistance at 12:35 P.M. and asked the dispatcher to send a Police Officer directly to the boutique located at 338 West 44th Street. Police Officers Maloney and Hernandez arrived at the boutique at 1:05 P.M. and saw that the store had been ransacked. Racks of clothing had been thrown down and the floor was littered with garments. The two Police Officers then conducted a search of the premises. When Police Officer Benson arrived at the premises at 1:20 P.M., the Police Officers told him that it would be impossible to determine what items had been taken since they had no listing of the store's merchandise.

A young woman then entered the store and identified herself as Ms. Peake, the part-time assistant whose shift started at 1:30 P.M. On seeing the condition of the store, she asked the Police Officers what had happened. They asked her where the merchandise list for the store was kept and she informed them that the stock clerks, Ms. Feldman and Mr. Austin, kept that information. Ms. Peake said that she would call Ms. Feldman in order to get a current listing of the store's merchandise.

Ms. Peake advised the Police Officers that several items were missing from the display case, including three fur jackets, seven leather handbags and four silk blouses, amounting to at least $985 in value.

18. At which one of the following addresses is the boutique located?

(A) 338 East 44th Street
(B) 44th Street and Broadway
(C) 338 West 44th Street
(D) 44th Street and 6th Avenue.

19. At what time did Police Officer Benson meet Police Officers Maloney and Hernandez at the boutique?

(A) 12:35 P.M.
(B) 12:55 P.M.
(C) 1:05 P.M.
(D) 1:20 P.M.

20. Which one of the following people owns the boutique?

(A) Ms. Peever
(B) Mr. Austin
(C) Ms. Feldman
(D) Ms. Peake.

21. What is Ms. Peake's starting time at the boutique?

(A) 12:35 P.M.
(B) 1:05 P.M.
(C) 1:20 P.M.
(D) 1:30 P.M.

Answer question 22 solely on the basis of the following information.

As a Police Officer in New York City you may have an occasion to deal with diplomats from other nations. You should be aware of the following definitions and procedure.

Definitions

1. Diplomats: Members of foreign missions, delegations, embassies and staff (I.D. cards are signed by United States Secretary of State and Chief of Protocol.)
2. Diplomatic immunity: Diplomats shall not be arrested or personally served with a summons. Uniformed members of the service will extend every courtesy and consideration to them. All reasonable assistance will be given to them.

Procedure

1. Take necessary action to protect life and property.
2. Obtain the name and the title of the diplomat and the name of the government he represents.
3. Notify the Operations Unit immediately by telephone that an incident involving a diplomat has occurred.
4. Do not detain a diplomat who has proper I.D.
5. Request a Patrol Supervisor to respond.
6. Telephone details to the desk officer.

22. Police Officers Rowan and Nieves are on patrol in the 44th Precinct when they respond to 1278 Sedgwick Avenue for a call of shots fired. They arrive and observe a male with a gun in his hand standing over a body. They order the man to drop the gun. He complies and states he is a member of the Soviet Mission to the U.N. and therefore cannot be arrested. He hands the Police Officers a State Department I.D. The Police Officers, after verifying the information, allow the man to leave. The actions of the Police Officers were

(A) proper, because once a diplomat is identified he must be released
(B) improper, because the man should have been arrested for shooting the other person
(C) improper, because they didn't let the Patrol Supervisor make the decision
(D) proper, because they weren't sure that he actually pulled the trigger.

Answer questions 23 and 24 solely on the basis of the following information.

A Police Officer may arrest a person for possession of an illegal gun. When the individual is arrested, in addition to following the normal arrest procedure, a Police Officer should follow these procedures in the order given:

1. Confiscate the illegal gun.
2. Charge the individual with a violation of the Penal Law or the Administrative Code.
3. Complete a Request for Laboratory Examination form.
4. Take the gun and the completed Request for Laboratory Examination form to the Ballistics Section.
5. Take the gun and Property Clerk's Invoice to the Property Clerk.

23. Police Officer Ritsik has made an arrest involving possession of an illegal gun. In addition to following the normal arrest procedure, after confiscating the illegal gun involved in the crime, he should

(A) take the illegal gun to the Ballistics Section
(B) complete the Request for Laboratory Examination form
(C) charge the individual with violation of the Penal Law or the Administrative Code
(D) take the illegal gun and the Property Clerk's Invoice to the Property Clerk.

24. Police Officer Ritsik has taken all appropriate actions through completing a Request for Laboratory Examination form. Police Officer Ritsik should next

(A) take the illegal gun and the Property Clerk's Invoice to the Property Clerk
(B) charge the individual with a violation of the Penal Law or the Administrative Code
(C) take the illegal gun and completed Request for Laboratory Examination form to the Property Clerk
(D) take the illegal gun and the completed Request for Laboratory Examination form to the Ballistics Section.

Answer question 25 solely on the basis of the following information.

When a Police Officer transports a prisoner to the hospital either in the patrol car or an ambulance, the Police Officer will remain with the prisoner at all times, and will not remove the handcuffs from the prisoner unless requested by the attending physician. Upon request, the Police Officer will remove the handcuffs only after informing the physician of the circumstances of the arrest. The handcuffs will be replaced at the completion of the medical exam.

25. According to the procedure, which one of the following police actions is appropriate?

(A) Handcuff a prisoner when transporting in a patrol car, and remove the handcuffs when riding in an ambulance.
(B) Remove the handcuffs automatically upon arrival of the ambulance at the hospital.
(C) Remove the handcuffs only after explaining the circumstances of the arrest to the requesting physician.
(D) Remove the handcuffs after completing the exam and before transporting to the hospital.

Answer question 26 solely on the basis of the following statement.

26. During an emergency a Police Officer may be required to go onto subway tracks.

In which one of the following cases would it be most appropriate for a Police Officer to go onto the tracks?

(A) A female passenger accidentally drops her handbag containing $2,000 in cash onto the tracks.
(B) A male passenger while leaning over the platform loses his balance and falls onto the tracks.
(C) A child is shouting at the top of his voice creating a crowd scene because he dropped a ball which rolled onto the tracks.
(D) A female passenger drops her last token and it rolls onto the tracks.

Answer question <u>27</u> solely on the basis of the following statement.

Police Officer Jones is told to notify his Command when he observes dangerous conditions.

27. For which one of the following should Police Officer Jones notify his Command?

(A) A motorist stalled in a bus stop preventing a bus from discharging passengers.
(B) A parking sign that has been painted over.
(C) A car's burglar alarm that has gone off late at night.
(D) Smoke coming from the first floor window of an apartment building.

Answer question <u>28</u> solely on the basis of the following information.

Police Officer Brooks has received three complaints from neighborhood storeowners over a two-week period concerning the theft of merchandise. In each case the perpetrator would run out of the store with an armful of designer jeans as soon as the owner's back was turned. The description of each suspect is as follows:

Incident No. 1 (November 14)—male, White, teenager 5′11″, 180 lbs., curly black hair, long sleeve shirt, blue jeans and black boots, tattoo on right hand.

Incident No. 2 (November 19)—male, White, 20–25, 5′10″, 175 lbs., curly black hair, tattoos on upper left arm and hand, tank top, brown pants and sneakers.

Incident No. 3 (November 23)—male, White, 17–21, 5′9½″, 183 lbs., short curly blond hair, tattoo on left forearm, sleeveless shirt, blue jeans and sneakers.

On November 29th, a fourth incident occurred, but this time the suspect was observed running from the store by a plainclothes Police Officer and was arrested. The description of this suspect is as follows:

Incident No. 4 (November 29)—male, White, 18, 5′10″, 180 lbs., short curly black hair, tattoo on chest, left forearm, and right hand, short sleeve shirt, blue jeans and sneakers.

28. Based on the descriptions given above of the suspects in the first three incidents, the suspect in Incident No. 4 should also be considered a suspect in

(A) Incident No. 1 and Incident No. 2, but not Incident No. 3
(B) Incident No. 1 and Incident No. 3, but not in Incident No. 2
(C) Incident No. 2, but not in Incident No. 1 or Incident No. 3
(D) None of the three incidents.

29. Police Officer Jenkins is preparing a report for Lost or Stolen Property. The report will include the following five sentences:

1. On the stairs, Mr. Harris slipped on a wet leaf and fell on the landing.
2. It wasn't until he got to the token booth that Mr. Harris realized his wallet was no longer in his back pants pocket.
3. A boy wearing a football jersey helped him up and brushed off the back of Mr. Harris' pants.
4. Mr. Harris states he was walking up the stairs to the elevated subway at Queensborough Plaza.
5. Before Mr. Harris could thank him, the boy was running down the stairs to the street.

The most logical order for the above sentences to appear in the report is

(A) 4, 3, 5, 1, 2
(B) 4, 1, 3, 5, 2
(C) 1, 4, 2, 3, 5
(D) 1, 2, 4, 3, 5.

Answer question 30 solely on the basis of the following information.

Reward for Official Misconduct—As a Police Officer, you are a public servant. There are many laws regarding your conduct. For example,

1. A public servant may not gain any benefit for violating or overlooking his duty.
2. A Police Officer may not ask for any such benefit.

However, a Police Officer has discretion regarding when to issue a traffic summons. This is the case when he believes a person did not realize that he was committing the violation, and did not intend to commit one. Nevertheless, the Police Officer must not benefit from using such discretion.

30. Police Officer Whyte on routine foot patrol observes a large group of double parked cars in front of Joe's Pizzeria. He opens his summons book and is about to issue summonses for the violations when Joe comes out to explain that it is Friday, his busiest night, and that the cars belong to his customers. Joe offers Police Officer Whyte a slice of pizza and a soda. Police Officer Whyte does not issue the summonses, but tells Joe to have the cars moved. He does not accept the pizza and soda. Police Officer Whyte's actions were

(A) proper, because he used his discretion but did not benefit from it.
(B) improper, because he should have contacted his Patrol Supervisor.
(C) proper, because summonses would have hurt Joe's business.
(D) improper, because when a Police Officer witnesses a violation he must write a summons.

Answer question 31 solely on the basis of the following statement.

A Police Officer may have to evacuate people from a dangerous area.

31. From which one of the following areas should a Police Officer evacuate people?

(A) A train delay at Grand Central Station
(B) An unconscious female on a crowded train
(C) A deranged male on a moving subway train
(D) An asbestos fire under a train in a tunnel.

32. Police Officer Hubbard is completing a report of a missing person. The report will contain the following five sentences:

1. I visited the store at 7:55 P.M. and asked the employees if they had seen a girl fitting the description I had been given.
2. She gave me a description and said she had gone into the local grocery store at about 6:15 P.M.
3. I asked the woman for a description of her daughter.
4. The distraught woman called the precinct to report that her daughter, aged 12, had not returned from an errand.
5. The storekeeper said a girl matching the description had been in the store earlier, but he could not give an exact time.

The most logical order for the above sentences to appear in the report is

(A) 1, 3, 2, 5, 4
(B) 4, 3, 2, 1, 5
(C) 5, 1, 2, 3, 4
(D) 3, 1, 2, 4, 5.

Answer question 33 solely on the basis of the following information.

The purpose of the Stop and Frisk procedure is to protect a Police Officer from injury while investigating a crime. When a Police Officer suspects a person has committed, is committing, or is about to commit a crime, the Police Officer should:

1. Stop the person and request identification and an explanation of his conduct.
2. Frisk if the Police Officer believes he may be physically injured or killed.
3. Search if the frisk reveals an object which may be a weapon.

33. While patrolling along Main Street about 10 P.M., Police Officer Jackson observes a man dressed in dark clothes walking slowly along the quiet street. Police Officer Jackson knows that during the past couple of weeks, a few burglaries have occurred in this area after business hours. Police Officer Jackson sees the man looking into the closed store windows, glancing up and down the street, and snaking the door knobs of various shops. Police Officer Jackson suspects this man is about to burglarize one of the stores on the block. According to the Stop and Frisk procedure, the Police Officer should:

(A) stop the man and frisk him even though the Police Officer does not feel endangered
(B) not stop the man because he hasn't committed any crime
(C) stop the man and search him because the man has already committed a crime
(D) stop the man and ask him to identify himself and explain his behavior.

Answer question 34 solely on the basis of the following information.

Police Officers are called upon to deliver a prisoner to court so that charges can be stated against the prisoner. When the Police Officer arrives at the court the following procedures should be followed, in the order given:

1. Escort the prisoner to the Detention Cell.
2. Write entries in the Detention Record Book.
3. Report to the Police Room.
4. Complete the Court Attendance Record Form.
5. Report to the Complaint Room.
6. Present one copy of the Arrest Report to the Assistant District Attorney.
7. Remove the prisoner from the Detention Cell to the Court Room when the Court Officer instructs you to do so.
8. Do not permit the prisoner to talk to any person or give anything to or accept anything from any person while the prisoner is being escorted to the Court Room.

9. If the prisoner is held without bail or cannot post the bail, escort the prisoner back to the Detention Cell.
10. If the prisoner is able to post the bail, escort the prisoner to the Court Clerk.

34. Police Officer Tanner has escorted a prisoner to court. If all appropriate steps are taken through completing a Court Attendance Record Form, Tanner should next

(A) report to the Police Room
(B) escort the prisoner to the Detention Cell
(C) report to the Complaint Room
(D) remove the prisoner from the Detention Cell to the Court Room when instructed to by the Court Officer.

Answer question <u>35</u> solely on the basis of the following information.

<u>Criminally Negligent Homicide</u>—The crime of criminally negligent homicide is committed when an individual behaves in such a way that his behavior creates a substantial risk for others, unintentionally causing the death of a person.

<u>Felony Murder</u>—A felony murder is committed when a person, acting alone or together with others, commits or attempts to commit robbery, burglary, kidnapping, arson, or rape, and in the course and furtherance of such crime or of immediate flight therefrom, he or another participant, if there be any, causes the death of a person other than one of the participants.

35. What is the difference between Criminally Negligent Homicide and Felony Murder?

(A) With Criminally Negligent Homicide the death that results is unintentional. With Felony Murder the criminal intends to kill another person.
(B) The victim of a Criminally Negligent Homicide is usually an acquaintence of the person committing the crime. The victim of a Felony Murder is usually someone who is trying to prevent the commission of a crime.
(C) With Criminally Negligent Homicide the death that results is unintentional. With a Felony Murder the criminal intends to commit a crime other than murder but someone dies in the commission of the crime.
(D) In Criminally Negligent Homicide the perpetrator has no control over his behavior and the death resulting from it. With Felony Murder the criminal is in complete control of his mental faculties and realizes that he may be called on to kill someone in order to successfully commit the crime.

Answer question 36 solely on the basis of the following information.

When a Police Officer arrests a taxicab driver, he should do the following in the order given:

1. Prepare a Report of Violation form.
2. Take the credentials of the taxicab driver only when they have been used as an instrument in, or as evidence of, the crime committed.
3. Prepare and deliver the form "Receipt for Credentials" to the prisoner, if the credentials are taken.
4. Prepare a Property Clerk's Invoice form when the credentials are taken.
5. Note under details on the Arrest Report that a "Report of Violation" has been prepared and, if applicable, the taking of the driver's credentials.

36. Police Officer Bunker has arrested a taxicab driver for robbery. The taxicab driver had not used his credentials while committing the crime. Police Officer Bunker has followed normal arrest procedures and prepared the "Report of Violation" form.

Which one of the following actions should Police Officer Bunker take next?

(A) Take the credentials of the driver.
(B) Prepare and deliver the form "Receipt for Credentials" to the driver.
(C) Prepare a Property Clerk's Invoice form.
(D) Note under details on the Arrest Report preparation of "Report of Violation".

Answer questions 37 and 38 solely on the basis of the following passage.

On July 10th, 1984, Police Officer William Jenkins, shield #815, of the Housing Authority Police Department, assigned to foot patrol in Sector (C) was dispatched at 4:00 P.M. to respond to 42-48 Colden Street, apartment #3C, on a past rape. Police Officer Jenkins arrived at the apartment at 4:15 P.M. Mrs. Julia Bookman, a black female, age 42, and her daughter Lucille live at that address.

Mrs. Bookman informs the Police Officer that her daughter Lucille, the rape victim, is in her bedroom. Police Officer Jenkins questions the victim, Lucille Bookman, a black female, age 17, date of birth 3/6/67, who states that she was returning home from school at 3:30 P.M. when an unknown male black entered the elevator with her and pressed the 11th floor button. The elevator door closed, the male pulled a knife from his waist, and informed the victim not to scream. The victim was pulled off the elevator on the 11th floor and into the staircase, where she was instructed to remove her skirt and undergarment. The male then raped her on the staircase landing.

Police Officer Jenkins informs the Police Radio Dispatcher at 4:26 P.M. to notify the Housing Sergeant to respond to the crime scene. Miss Bookman describes the suspect as a male black, 6 ft. 2 in., 170 pounds, 20 to 25 years old, dark complexion, missing right front tooth, who was wearing a brown leather jacket, brown pants, dark shoes, and spoke with an accent.

At 5:05 P.M. Police Officer Jenkins and Ambulance Attendant Hall, #1689, removed Miss Bookman to Jamaica Hospital where she was treated by Dr. Ling and released at 5:45 P.M.

Police Officer Jenkins noted the evidence obtained from Miss Bookman at the hospital. At 8:00 P.M. Police Officer Jenkins completed Police Complaint Report #4073, Aided Report #107, Evidence Report #B129075, and then returned to foot patrol.

37. What is Lucille Bookman's occupation?

(A) Secretary
(B) Student
(C) Housewife
(D) Waitress.

38. Which one of the following is Miss Bookman's correct home address?

(A) 42-48 Colden Street, apartment #3C
(B) 42-48 Golden Street, apartment #2C
(C) 44-48 Colden Street, apartment #2C
(D) 44-48 Golden Street, apartment #3C.

Answer question 39 solely on the basis of the following information.

Police Officers sometimes come upon unsafe street conditions. When such conditions exist, the Police Officers should do the following in the order given:

1. Make an Activity Log entry of the conditions and the location.
2. Notify the Telephone Switchboard Operator of the condition so that the Operator can notify the appropriate agency responsible for correcting the condition.
3. Direct traffic until the appropriate agency corrects the condition.

39. Police Officer Wright, while on patrol, noticed that the traffic lights at an intersection were not working. He noticed that the cars were slowing down at the intersection, causing traffic to back up. He also noticed that some cars were going through the intersection without stopping, creating a dangerous condition. Police Officer Wright took out his Activity Log and wrote down the location and conditions. Which one of the following should Police Officer Wright do next?

(A) Walk into the middle of the intersection and stop all traffic until the appropriate agency arrives to correct the condition.
(B) Notify the appropriate agency.
(C) Stop traffic from one direction for two minutes and then let traffic from the other direction go for two minutes.
(D) Notify the Telephone Switchboard Operator so that the Operator can notify the agency concerned.

Answer question 40 solely on the basis of the following statement.

A Police Officer is sometimes assigned to control the flow of traffic.

40. Police Officer Gaston is assigned to direct traffic at 15th Street and 17th Avenue. While directing traffic, Police Officer Gaston observes a man with dark glasses using a white cane with a red tip step off the curb and continue walking against the red light. What should Police Officer Gaston do?

(A) Allow the man to continue walking, then issue him a summons for jaywalking.
(B) Yell out to a bystander to bring the man back to the curb.
(C) Stop all traffic, because the man is blind.
(D) Call for an ambulance because the man is sick.

Answer questions 41 through 43 solely on the basis of the following passage.

On September 17, 1984 at approximately 11:05 A.M., Police Officers Jesse Harris, shield #115, and William Anderson, shield #110, assigned to Radio Patrol Car #9770, received a radio call to respond to a past burglary at 1428 Webster Avenue, apartment 21B. The Police Officers arrived at the apartment at 11:10 A.M. and were greeted by Mr. George Smith, a black male, age 61, date of birth 1/10/23. Mr. Smith informed the Police Officers that his apartment had been burglarized.

Mr. Smith told Police Officer Harris that he left his apartment at 9:30 A.M. that morning, 9/17/84, to shop for groceries. Upon his return at approximately 10:45 A.M., he noticed that the cylinder to his apartment lock was removed. Mr. Smith further stated that he did not enter his apartment but asked a neighbor to call the Police. Police Officer Harris and Anderson entered the apartment and found only the bedroom ransacked. Police Officer Harris asked Mr. Smith if he noticed any strange or suspicious person on his floor or in the lobby when leaving the building. Mr. Smith reported that he did not notice anyone unusual in the building.

Police Officer Anderson continued the investigation by questioning the tenants who resided on the 21st floor. The tenants questioned were Mrs. Vasques, an Hispanic female, age 40, who lives in apartment 21E, and Mr. John Fox, a white male, age 32, who lives in apartment 21F. Police Officer Anderson asked both tenants if they heard or saw anything unusual between the hours of 9:30 A.M. and 10:45 A.M.

At 12:20 P.M. Police Officer Harris notified Police Officer Bell, shield #169, at the Fingerprint Unit to respond to Mr. Smith's apartment for possible prints. Mr. Smith was informed not to touch anything in the bedroom until the Fingerprint Unit arrived to dust for prints. Police Officer Harris told Mr. Smith to wait until the Fingerprint Unit had completed its work before checking to see what property had been taken. Mr. Smith was told to prepare a list of the missing property and forward it to the precinct.

The Police Officers completed their Police Complaint Report #1010 at 12:40 P.M. and returned to patrol.

41. At what time was the call dispatched to Radio Patrol Car #9770?

(A) 9:30 A.M.
(B) 10:45 A.M.
(C) 11:05 A.M.
(D) 11:15 A.M.

42. Which one of the following is Mr. Smith's date of birth?

(A) 10/10/32
(B) 10/10/23
(C) 1/10/32
(D) 1/10/23.

43. How was the apartment entered?

(A) Door
(B) Window
(C) Roof
(D) Wall.

44. A Police Officer is completing an entry in his Daily Activity Log regarding traffic summonses which he issued. The following five sentences will be included in the entry:

1. I was on routine patrol parked 16 yards west of 170th Street and Clay Avenue.
2. The summonses were issued for unlicensed operator and disobeying a steady red light.

3. At 8 A.M. hours I observed an auto traveling westbound on 170th Street not stop for a steady red light at the intersection of Clay Avenue and 170th Street.
4. I stopped the driver of the auto and determined that he did not have a valid Driver's License.
5. After a brief conversation, I informed the motorist that he was receiving two summonses.

The most logical order for the above sentences to appear in the report is

(A) 1, 3, 4, 5, 2
(B) 3, 4, 2, 5, 1
(C) 5, 2, 1, 3, 4
(D) 4, 5, 2, 1, 3.

Answer question 45 solely on the basis of the following information.

The presence of a juvenile under 16 years of age in a bar that is licensed is unlawful. When a Police Officer observes a juvenile under 16 in a bar that is licensed, the Police Officer should do the following in the order given:

1. Determine the age of the juvenile.
2. Take the juvenile into protective custody if the presence is unlawful, and arrest the manager or person in charge.
3. Escort the juvenile home, if the home is located within the city.
4. Inform the juvenile's parents of the violation and request an explanation of the juvenile's conduct.
5. Advise the parents of their legal responsibilities.
6. Prepare a Juvenile Report to the Desk Officer.
7. Submit the Juvenile Report to the Desk Officer at the station house.

45. Police Officer Richards is part of an undercover team investigating violations involving a certain bar that is licensed in the Bronx. While on duty, Police Officer Richards and her partner enter a bar and notice a young girl inside who they suspect is underage. Police Officer Richards approaches the girl, identifies herself as a Police Officer, and requests identification. The girl produces a local high school identification card indicating that she is 14 years old. The next step the Police Officers should take is

(A) arrest the bar's manager and take the girl into protective custody
(B) locate the girl's parents and inform them of the violation
(C) arrest the girl and the bar's manager and take them to the station house
(D) escort the girl to her residence.

46. The following sentences appeared on an Incident Report:

1. Three teenagers who had been ejected from the theater were yelling at patrons who were now entering.
2. Police Officer Dixon told the teenagers to leave the area.
3. The teenagers said that they were told by the manager to leave the theatre because they were talking during the movie.
4. The theater manager called the Precinct at 10:20 P.M. to report a disturbance outside the theater.
5. A patrol car responded to the theater at 10:42 P.M. and two Police Officers went over to the teenagers.

The most logical for the above sentences to appear in the Incident Report is

(A) 1, 5, 4, 3, 2
(B) 4, 1, 5, 3, 2
(C) 4, 1, 3, 5, 2
(D) 4, 3, 1, 5, 2.

47. Activity Log entries are completed by Police Officers. Police Officer Samuels has written an entry concerning vandalism and part of it contains the following five sentences:

1. The man, in his early twenties, ran down the block and around the corner.
2. A man passing the store threw a brick through a window of the store.
3. I arrived on the scene and began to question the witnesses about the incident.
4. Malcolm Holmes, the owner of the Fast Service Shoe Repair Store, was working in the back of the store at approximately 3 P.M.
5. After the man fled, Mr. Holmes called the police.

The most logical order for the above sentences to appear in the Activity Log is

(A) 4, 2, 1, 5, 3
(B) 2, 4, 1, 3, 5
(C) 2, 1, 4, 3, 5
(D) 4, 2, 5, 3, 1.

Answer questions 48 and 49 solely on the basis of the following map. The flow of traffic is indicated by the arrows. If there is only one arrow shown, then traffic flows only in the direction indicted by the arrow. If there are two arrows shown, then traffic flows in both directions. You must follow the flow of traffic.

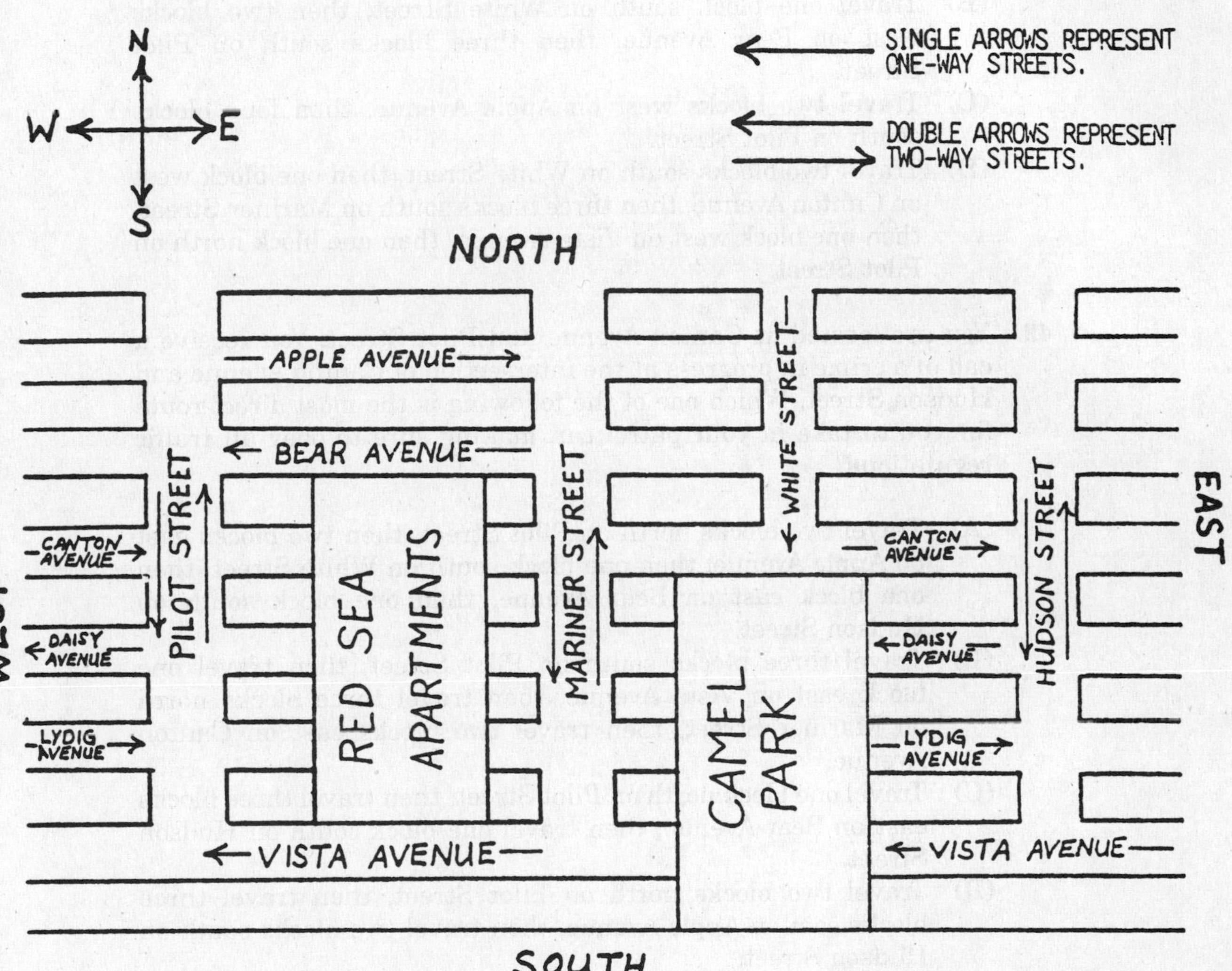

48. You are located at Apple Avenue and White Street. You receive a call to respond to the corner of Lydig Avenue and Pilot Street. Which one of the following is the most direct route for you to take in your patrol car, making sure to obey all traffic regulations?

(A) Travel two blocks south on White Street, then one block east on Canton Avenue, then one block north on Hudson Street, then three blocks west on Bear Avenue, then three blocks south on Pilot Street.
(B) Travel one block south on White Street, then two blocks west on Bear Avenue, then three blocks south on Pilot Street.
(C) Travel two blocks west on Apple Avenue, then four blocks south on Pilot Street.
(D) Travel two blocks south on White Street, then one block west on Canton Avenue, then three blocks south on Mariner Street, then one block west on Vista Avenue, then one block north on Pilot Street.

49. You are located at Canton Avenue and Pilot Street. You receive a call of a crime in progress at the intersection of Canton Avenue and Hudson Street. Which one of the following is the most direct route for you to take in your patrol car, making sure to obey all traffic regulations?

(A) Travel two blocks north on Pilot Street, then two blocks east on Apple Avenue, then one block south on White Street, then one block east on Bear Avenue, then one block south on Hudson Street.
(B) Travel three blocks south on Pilot Street, then travel one block east on Vista Avenue, then travel three blocks north on Mariner Street, then travel two blocks east on Canton Avenue.
(C) Travel one block north on Pilot Street, then travel three blocks east on Bear Avenue, then travel one block south on Hudson Street.
(D) Travel two blocks north on Pilot Street, then travel three blocks east on Apple Avenue, then travel two blocks south on Hudson Street.

Answer question 50 solely on the basis of the following information.

Police Officers must follow a set procedure when reporting sick. This is a very important procedure since Police Officers have unlimited sick time. The following steps must be followed in the order given:

1. Call your command at least two hours prior to your reporting time.
2. Contact your District Surgeon within 24 hours.
3. Follow the directions of your surgeon.

4. Remain in your residence while on sick report.
5. Notify your command if there is a change in residence.
6. Contact command when you are returned to duty.

50. Police Officer Jones becomes ill before going to work one day. He phones his command three hours before his scheduled time to report. What must he do next?

(A) Notify his command of a change in his residence.
(B) Follow the directions of the surgeon.
(C) Contact his surgeon within 24 hours.
(D) Remain in his residence while on sick report.

51. Police Officer Buckley is preparing a report concerning a dispute in a restaurant. The report will contain the following five sentences:

1. The manager, Charles Chin, and a customer, Edward Green, were standing near the register arguing over the bill.
2. The manager refused to press any charges providing Green pay the check and leave.
3. While on foot patrol, I was informed by a passerby of a disturbance in the Dragon Flame Restaurant.
4. Green paid the $7.50 check and left the restaurant.
5. According to witnesses, the customer punched the owner in the face when Chin asked him for the amount due.

The most logical order for the above sentences to appear in the report is

(A) 3, 1, 5, 2, 4
(B) 1, 2, 3, 4, 5
(C) 5, 1, 3, 2, 4
(D) 3, 5, 2, 4, 1.

Answer question 52 solely on the basis of the following information.

Police Officers in the course of a tour may be confronted with persons who need medical assistance. Police Officers know that in life-threatening situations in which they are the first on the scene, they must administer first aid until medical assistance arrives.

52. In which one of the following cases should a Police Officer administer first aid while waiting for medical assistance?

(A) A person bleeding profusely from the stomach area
(B) A person complaining of back pains
(C) A pregnant female in early labor
(D) A person complaining of sharp pains in his legs.

53. Police Officer Wilkins is preparing a report for leaving the scene of an accident. The report will include the following five sentences:

1. The Dodge struck the right rear fender of Mrs. Smith's 1980 Ford, and continued on its way.
2. Mrs. Smith stated she was making a left turn from 40th Street onto Third Avenue.
3. As the car passed, Mrs. Smith noticed the dangling rear license plate #412AEJ.
4. Mrs. Smith complained to police of back pains and was removed by ambulance to Bellevue Hospital.
5. An old green Dodge traveling up Third Avenue went through the red light at 40th Street and Third Avenue.

The most logical order for the above sentences to appear in the report is

(A) 5, 3, 1, 2, 4
(B) 1, 3, 2, 5, 4
(C) 4, 5, 1, 2, 3
(D) 2, 5, 1, 3, 4.

Answer question 54 solely on the basis of the following information.

When a person commits a traffic infraction, a Police Officer should:

1. Inform the violator of the offense committed.
2. Request the violator to show his or her driver's license, vehicle registration and insurance identification card.
   Failure to produce this required material may result in additional tickets. (Taxis, buses, and other rented vehicles do not require insurance identification cards.)
3. Enter only one infraction on each ticket.
4. Use a separate ticket for each additional infraction.

54. Police Officer Crane is assigned to a traffic post at Broadway and 34th Street to issue tickets for red light violations. Police Officer Crane stops a taxicab for going through a red light at this busy intersection. Police Officer Crane informs the cab driver of the violation, and asks for the required material. The driver hands the Police Officer his license and registration. Police Officer Crane should

(A) issue the cab driver a ticket for the red light violation and a separate ticket for no insurance card
(B) issue the cab driver one ticket for both the red light violation and no insurance card
(C) issue the cab driver a ticket only for the red light violation
(D) issue the cab driver a ticket only for not having an insurance card.

Answer question 55 solely on the basis of the following information.

Police Officer Fitzgerald notices that in his sector all of the burglaries took place on Newton Street. All of the auto thefts occurred on Franklin Street. Most of the rapes took place on Hamburg Avenue. All of the assaults happened on Sparta Place. All of the rapes occurred between 10 P.M. and 4 A.M. The auto thefts occurred between Midnight and 6 A.M. All of the burglaries occurred between 10 A.M. and 4 P.M. All of the assaults occurred between 6 P.M. and 10 P.M.

55. Police Officer Fitzgerald would most likely be able to reduce the incidence of rape by patrolling on

(A) Sparta Place from 10 A.M. to 4 P.M.
(B) Hamburg Avenue from 10 P.M. to 4 P.M.
(C) Sparta Place from 10 P.M. to 4 A.M.
(D) Hamburg Avenue from 6 P.M. to 10 P.M.

56. Detective Simon is completing a Crime Report. The report contains the following five sentences:

1. Police Officer Chin, while on foot patrol, heard the yelling and ran in the direction of the man.
2. The man, carrying a large hunting knife, left the High Sierra Sporting Goods Store at approximately 10:30 A.M.
3. When the man heard Police Officer Chin, he stopped, dropped the knife and began to cry.
4. As Police Officer Chin approached the man he drew his gun and yelled, "Police, freeze."
5. After the man left the store he began yelling, over and over, "I am going to kill myself!"

The most logical order for the above sentences to appear in the report is

(A) 5, 2, 1, 4, 3
(B) 2, 5, 1, 4, 3
(C) 2, 5, 4, 1, 3
(D) 2, 1, 5, 4, 3.

Answer question 57 solely on the basis of the following information.

Harassment occurs when a person annoys or alarms another person, but does not intend or cause physical injury.
Menacing occurs when a person threatens to cause serious physical injury to another person, but does not cause a serious physical injury.
Assault occurs when a person causes physical injury to another person.

After a softball game, team members from both the Tigers and Bombers go over to the local bar to drink a few beers. While there, Gardner, the third baseman for the losing Tigers, gets into a heated argument with Carter, the Bombers winning pitcher. Gardner threatens Carter, then picks up an empty beer bottle and smashes it over Carter's head, causing a serious head injury to Carter.

57. Based on the definitions above, Gardner should be charged with

(A) Harassment
(B) Menacing
(C) Assault
(D) no crime

Answer questions 58 through 61 solely on the basis of the following passage.

Housing Police Officer Jones, shield #691, assigned to foot patrol at Boringuen Plaza Housing Project and working a 4 P.M. to 12 P.M. tour on September 17th, 1984, received a call from the Police Radio Dispatcher at 6:10 P.M. to respond to 60 Moore Street, apartment 7E on a case involving an elderly woman in need of medical assistance.

Police Officer Jones stated to the dispatcher that he would respond but on two previous occasions he was called to that same location and the woman refused medical treatment.

Police Officer Jones arrived at 60 Moore St. at 6:15 P.M., took the elevator to the 7th floor and walked over to apartment 7E. The Police Officer found the apartment door open and inside he found the woman, her daughter and two paramedics. The paramedics had arrived five minutes before the Police Officer. Paramedics Smith #2634 and Hanson #1640 stated to Police Officer Jones that the woman identified as Maria Rivera, age 64, date of birth 5/29/20, who was lying on a dirty mattress in her bedroom, was in shock and in need of medical treatment, but she was refusing medical aid.

Police Officer Jones could not convince Mrs. Rivera to go to the hospital to receive medical treatment. Mrs. Aida Soto, age 32, daughter of Mrs. Rivera, who resides at 869 Flushing Avenue, apartment 11F, was also present, but she too was unable to convince her mother to go to the hospital.

Police Officer Jones called the Police Radio Dispatcher at 6:25 P.M. and requested the Housing Supervisor to respond to the location. The Housing Supervisor, Sergeant Cuevas, shield #664, arrived at 6:40 P.M. and Police Officer Jones informed him of the situation. Sergeant Cuevas spoke to Mrs. Rivera and her daughter in Spanish but could not get either to agree that Mrs. Rivera needed urgent medical treatment. Sergeant Cuevas directed paramedics Smith and Hanson to take Mrs. Rivera to the hospital.

Mrs. Rivera was removed from the apartment at 7:00 P.M. and was put in ambulance #1669 and taken to Greenwood Hospital. The ambulance arrived at the hospital at 7:10 P.M. and Mrs. Rivera received the medical treatment she so urgently needed.

Police Officer Jones and Sergeant Cuevas resumed normal patrol at 7:12 P.M. Police Officer Jones prepared Field Report #8964 before the end of his tour.

58. Which one of the following is the correct time that Police Officer Jones arrived at 60 Moore Street?

(A) 6:10 P.M.
(B) 6:15 P.M.
(C) 6:45 P.M.
(D) 7:15 P.M.

59. Which one of the following is the correct apartment to which Police Officer Jones responded?

(A) 11F
(B) 7F
(C) 11E
(D) 7E.

60. Which one of the following is the correct name of the sick woman's daughter?

(A) Aida Soto
(B) Aida Rivera
(C) Maria Rivera
(D) Anna Soto.

61. Which one of the following is the correct birthdate of Mrs. Rivera?

(A) 5/19/20
(B) 5/29/20
(C) 7/30/23
(D) 8/5/20.

Answer questions 62 and 63 solely on the basis of the following information.

Police Officers while on patrol may observe a recently vacated building which can create a safety hazard. In such situations, Police Officers should follow these procedures, in the order given:

1. Walk through the vacated building to determine if a safety hazard exists.
2. If a safety hazard exists, notify the supervisor on patrol.
3. Write an entry in the Activity Log.
4. Report the facts concerning the safety hazard in the vacant building to the Telephone Switchboard Operator.
5. Place barriers in front of the vacated building if directed by the Patrol Supervisor.

62. While on patrol, Police Officer Edwards observes a recently vacated building. What action should Police Officer Edwards take next?

(A) Report the safety hazard in the vacant building to the Telephone Switchboard Operator.
(B) Notify the supervisor on patrol.
(C) Write an entry in the Memo Log.
(D) Determine if a safety hazard exists in the vacated building.

63. Police Officer Henshaw, who has observed a safety hazard in a vacated building while on motor patrol, has already completed all appropriate actions through writing an entry in the Activity Log. Police Officer Henshaw should next

(A) determine if a safety hazard exists in other buildings on the block
(B) report the facts concerning the safety hazard to the Telephone Switchboard Operator
(C) notify the supervisor on patrol
(D) place barriers in front of the vacated building if directed by the Patrol Supervisor.

64. Police Officer Miller is preparing a Complaint Report which will include the following five sentences:

1. From across the lot, he yelled to the boys to get away from his car.
2. When he came out of the store, he noticed two teenage boys trying to break into his car.
3. The boys fled as Mr. Johnson ran to his car.
4. Mr. Johnson stated that he parked his car in the Municipal lot behind Tams Department Store.
5. Mr. Johnson saw that the door lock had been broken, but nothing was missing from inside the auto.

The most logical order for the above sentences to appear in the report is

(A) 4, 1, 2, 5, 3
(B) 2, 3, 1, 5, 4
(C) 4, 2, 1, 3, 5
(D) 1, 2, 3, 5, 4.

65. Police Officer O'Hara completes a Universal Summons for a motorist who has just passed a red traffic light. The Universal Summons includes the following five sentences:

1. As the car passed the light, I followed in the patrol car.
2. After the driver stopped the car, he stated that the light was yellow, not red.
3. A blue Cadillac sedan passed the red light on the corner of 79th Street and 3rd Avenue at 11:25 P.M.

4. As a result the driver was informed that he did pass a red light and that his brake lights were not working.
5. The driver in the Cadillac stopped his car as soon as he saw the patrol car and I noticed that the brake lights were not working.

The most logical order for the above sentences to appear in the Universal Summons is

(A) 1, 3, 5, 2, 4
(B) 3, 1, 5, 2, 4
(C) 3, 1, 5, 4, 2
(D) 1, 3, 4, 2, 5.

66. Detective Egan is preparing a follow-up report regarding a homicide on 170th Street and College Avenue. An unknown male was found at the scene. The report will contain the following five sentences:

1. Police Officer Gregory wrote down the names, addresses and phone numbers of the witnesses.
2. A 911 operator received a call of a man shot and dispatched Police Officers Worth and Gregory to the scene.
3. They discovered an unidentified male dead on the street.
4. Police Officer Worth notified the Precinct Detective Unit immediately.
5. At approximately 9:00 A.M., an unidentified male shot another male in the chest during an argument.

The most logical order for the above sentences to appear in the report is

(A) 5, 2, 3, 4, 1
(B) 2, 3, 5, 4, 1
(C) 4, 1, 5, 2, 3
(D) 5, 3, 2, 4, 1.

Answer question <u>67</u> solely on the basis of the following information.

A Police Officer normally does not issue summonses to cars with Diplomatic Credentials, that is, cars with "DPL" or "FC" license plates. However, when a car with "DPL" or "FC" license plates is observed creating a safety hazard, a Police Officer is allowed to issue a summons.

67. In which one of the following situations should a Police Officer issue a summons?

(A) A car with "FC" plates parked at a fire hydrant
(B) A car with "DPL" plates parked at an expired meter
(C) A car with "FC" plates parked in a school zone
(D) A car with "DPL" plates parked in a loading zone.

68. Police Officer Tracey is preparing a Robbery Report which will include the following five sentences.

1. I ran around the corner and observed a man pointing a gun at a taxi driver.
2. I informed the man I was a Police Officer and that he should not move.
3. I was on the corner of 125th Street and Park Avenue when I heard a scream coming from around the corner.
4. The man turned around and fired one shot at me.
5. I fired once, shooting him in the arm and causing him to fall to the ground.

The most logical order for the above sentences to appear on the report is

(A) 1, 3, 4, 2, 5
(B) 4, 5, 2, 1, 3
(C) 3, 1, 2, 4, 5
(D) 3, 1, 5, 2, 4.

Answer question 69 solely on the basis of the following information.

Police Officer Lee is told by her Patrol Supervisor that the sector to which she is assigned has a high incidence of drug dealing, homicides, assaults, robberies and burglaries. Police Officer Lee familiarizes herself with the crime statistics of the sector and finds that all the drug dealing takes place on Martin Street, all the homicides take place on Edward Street, all the assaults occur on Charles Street, all the robberies happen on Bruce Street, and all the burglaries are committed on Henry Street. The drug dealing occurs between 1 A.M. and 3 A.M.; the homicides take place between 2 A.M. and 4 P.M.; the assaults happen between 12 A.M. and 2 A.M.; the robberies occur between 3 A.M. and 7 A.M.; and the burglaries happen between 4 A.M. and 6 A.M. The drug dealing take place on Mondays, the homicides take place on Tuesdays, the assaults happen on Thursdays, the robberies happen on Mondays, and the burglaries happen on Tuesdays.

69. Police Officer Lee would most likely be able to reduce the incidence of assaults by patrolling

(A) Charles Street on Thursdays between 12 A.M. and 2 A.M.
(B) Bruce Street on Mondays between 3 A.M. and 7 A.M.
(C) Henry Street on Tuesdays between 4 A.M. and 6 A.M.
(D) Edward Street on Tuesdays between 2 A.M. and 4 A.M.

Answer question 70 solely on the basis of the following information.

According to New York City Police Department procedure, a notification will not be made to the relatives of a prisoner who dies in a Department of Correction facility unless a request is made by the Correction Supervisor in charge of the facility.

70. Prisoner Richard Jones dies at Rikers Island Correctional Facility where he had been serving a five-year prison term for robbery. Unable to notify the family of the deceased, Correction Supervisor Whitney requests the Police Department to make the notification. Police Officer Barry goes to the Jones residence to inform Mrs. Jones of her son's death. The action of Police Officer Barry in this case is

(A) proper, because it follows Police Department procedure regarding notifications
(B) improper, because the Department of Correction should have made its own notification
(C) proper, because the Police Department is required to make a notification whenever a prisoner dies
(D) improper, because the Sergeant should have made the notification by telephone.

Answer questions 71 through 75 solely on the basis of the following passage.

Police Officers Murphy, shield number 7348, and Dunkin, shield number 3329, were assigned to patrol sector E in the 90th Precinct at 3:30 A.M. in patrol car 1749 on October 2nd, 1984.

Sector E is a residential area of rundown dilapidated houses where most of the city's poor live. Police Officers Murphy and Dunkin were traveling south on Jersey Street having a fairly quiet tour when they heard a woman's scream coming from an alley about two blocks south on Jersey Street. Police Officer Dunkin looked at his watch and saw that it was 3:33 A.M. The Police Officers sped to the area where they believed the scream came from, and stopped in front of 998 Jersey Street, which was an abandoned building commonly frequented by junkies and derelicts. Police Officer Murphy called the Police Dispatcher at 3:35 A.M. to inform him that the Police Officers were investigating screams, and requested back-up assistance. The Police Officers then walked to the side of the building which forms an alleyway with 994 Jersey Street. Using flashlights, the Police Officers entered into an alley until they came upon a woman lying on her stomach. Police Officer Dunkin touched her arm, feeling for a pulse, when the woman started moaning. At 3:38 A.M. Police Officer Murphy radioed for an ambulance, while Police Officer Dunkin aided and gathered information from the victim. The woman told the Police Officer that her name is Gloria Vargas, age 21, born on 5/15/63 and that she lives at 1023 Jersey Avenue, apartment 3H, with her mother and father, Anna and Joseph Vargas, telephone number 784-3942. Ms. Vargas stated that she had been attending a birthday party for her friend, Jane Colon at 694 Jersey Street, apartment 6I, when she decided to leave at around 3:20 A.M. Since she didn't live far and the night was warm, she decided to walk home against the wishes of her friends.

She further stated to Police Officer Dunkin that she did not remember much after that. All she could recall was that she was four blocks from home when she was hit on the head and then woke up in the alley with two cops looking down on her and her purse missing. At 3:45 A.M. Police Officers Vasquez, shield number 473, and Booker, shield number 498, arrived in patrol car 1754 and were informed by Police Officer Dunkin to search the area for any suspicious person carrying a lady's purple purse. At 3:47 A.M. an ambulance arrived and Paramedics Anders, shield number 561, and Hargrove, shield number 623, administered first aid and prepared to take Ms. Vargas to Richmond County Hospital. Ms. Vargas refused to go to the hospital and stated that she wanted to go home so that her parents would not worry. After their attempts to convince Ms. Vargas to go to a hospital failed, Police Officers Murphy and Dunkin called the dispatcher at 4:02 A.M. to report they were escorting Ms. Vargas home. After a search of the area for suspects proved negative, Police Officers Vasquez and Booker reported to the dispatcher that they were resuming patrol at 4:05 A.M.

Police Officers Murphy and Dunkin arrived at the home of Ms. Vargas and saw that she was safely inside before calling the dispatcher at 4:10 A.M. to indicate that they were resuming patrol. The Police Officers completed Crime Report number 6395 and Aided Report number 523 at 4:30 A.M.

71. Of the following, what kind of area is Sector E described as?

(A) industrial
(B) suburban
(C) commercial
(D) residential

72. Of the following, what is the number of the radio car used by Police Officers Vasquez and Booker?

(A) 1745 **(B)** 1754 **(C)** 1574 **(D)** 5417.

73. What is the date of birth of Ms. Vargas?

(A) 5/11/63
(B) 5/15/63
(C) 5/11/65
(D) 5/15/65.

74. What other building helped form an alleyway with 998 Jersey Street?

(A) 994 Jersey Street
(B) 1023 Jersey Street
(C) 694 Jersey Street
(D) 949 Jersey Street.

75. In what direction were Police Officers Murphy and Dunkin traveling on Jersey Street?

(A) North **(B)** East **(C)** South **(D)** West.

Answer question 76 solely on the basis of the following information.

An extra Police Officer is assigned to guard prisoners being transported to detention facilities in each of the following situations:

1. More than two prisoners are being guarded and transport chains are not available, or
2. More than nine prisoners are being transported by transport chains, or
3. Several detention stops are involved, or
4. More than one prisoner is transported with different destinations.

76. In which one of the following cases should an additional escort Police Officer be assigned?

(A) Nine prisoners are being guarded and transport chains are available.
(B) Two prisoners are being guarded and transport chains are available.
(C) Nine prisoners are being transported by transport chains to the same destination.
(D) Five prisoners are being transported by transport chains to separate locations.

Answer question 77 solely on the basis of the following information.

During the month of November, three assualts occurred in the early evening near the Westville Movie Theatre on Concord Street. The description of each of the suspects is as follows:

Suspect No. 1 Male, Hispanic, early 30's, 5′6″, 130 lbs., short curly hair, 3 inch scar under left ear, black jacket, dark green pants, black boots

Suspect No. 2 Male, Hispanic, 30 to 35, 5′6″, 170 lbs., dark hair, dark green jacket, black pants, black boots

Suspect No. 3 Male, Hispanic, about 35, 5′6″, 132 lbs., short curly hair, black turtleneck sweater, green pants, running shoes.

On December 2nd, a fourth assault occurs. However, this time the suspect is arrested by a plainclothes Police Officer. The description of this suspect is as follows:

Suspect No. 4 Male, Hispanic, 30 to 35, 5′6″, 135lbs, short curly hair, scar on left side of neck, blue ski cap, black jacket, black denim pants, black boots.

77. Based upon the above descriptions of the suspects in the first three assaults, the suspect in the fourth assault should also be considered a suspect in

(A) Assault No. 1, but not assault No. 2 or assault No. 3
(B) Assault No. 1 and assault No. 3, but not assault No. 2
(C) Assault No. 2, but not assault No. 1 or assault No. 3
(D) Assault No. 1, assault No. 2, and assault No. 3.

Answer question 78 solely on the basis of the following statement.

Police Officer Dunn is patrolling his post and is told to report all hazardous conditions.

78. Which one of the following should the Police Officer report?

(A) Derelicts burning wood in a barrel in front of a vacant building to keep warm.
(B) Youths playing in a garbage-strewn lot.
(C) A large amount of oil spilled on a busy street.
(D) Cars double-parked on a one-way street.

Answer questions 79 and 80 solely on the basis of the following passage.

On Thursday, September 13th, 1984 at approximately 9:55 P.M. Detective George Smith, shield #796, was off-duty and visiting his mother at 415 East 106th Street. While looking out of the first floor window of his mother's apartment, he notices a suspicious black male sitting in a car with the motor running in front of Joe's Pharmacy, located at 430 East 106th Street between Third and Second Avenue. The car was a blue Chevy Vega with New York license plate number L-77985. Detective Smith leaves the apartment and approaches from the opposite side of the street where he observes two men, both Caucasian, in Joe's Pharmacy. One of the men was standing in front of the cash register, while the other man was pointing a gun at the proprietor, who was pinned against the wall. Detective Smith proceeds to a phone booth on the corner of 106th Street and Second Avenue and dials 911 at 10:00 P.M. He informs 911 operator number 372 of the robbery, gives the address of Joe's Pharmacy, and gives the following description of the perpetrators. The first is a male Caucasian, 5′9″, 155 lbs., blonde hair, wearing a brown jacket and black pants. The second is a male Caucasian, 6′3″, 175 lbs., bald head, wearing a blue navy coat, black pants and armed with a gun. The third is a black male, wearing dark clothing and sitting in a blue Chevy Vega, New York license plate number L-77985. Because Detective Smith is not in uniform he informs the 911 operator that he is wearing a black leather coat and gray pants. Detective Smith requests a back-up unit to respond without lights or siren. He then proceeds to position himself behind a green vehicle parked in front of a closed liquor store opposite Joe's Pharmacy.

Police Officers Brown and Simms respond in Radio Patrol Car #1186 at 10:03 P.M., and park their vehicle on the northwest side of 106th Street on Second Avenue. Approximately at 10:05 P.M. both perpetrators exit from Joe's Pharmacy and run directly to the waiting vehicle which was blocked by a gypsy cab whose owner entered a grocery store. Detective Smith approaches the suspects' vehicle from the rear, and Police Officers Brown and Simms position themselves in view of the suspects and their vehicle, blocking all means of escape. The perpetrators are apprehended, and the property recovered amounts to $1200 in cash and a hand gun. Police Officers Brown and Simms take the perpetrators to the 23rd Precinct for Detective Smith.

Detective Smith enters Joe's Pharmacy, questions Mr. Velez, the proprietor, informs him of the arrest procedure and explains to him that he is required to appear at the courthouse the following day to press charges.

Detective Smith, the arresting Police Officer, arrives at the 23rd Precinct at 10:55 P.M., finishes his Police Complaint Report at 11:09 P.M., and removes the perpetrators to Central Booking at 11:20 P.M.

79. Where did Police Officers Brown and Simms park their Radio Patrol Car?

(A) Southwest side of 105th Street on Second Avenue
(B) Southwest side of 105th Street on Third Avenue
(C) Northwest side of 106th Street on Second Avenue
(D) Northwest side of 106th Street on Third Avenue.

80. Which one of the following is the best description of the second perpetrator?

(A) 5′9″, 155 lbs. male, white, blond hair
(B) 5′9″, 175 lbs. male, white, bald head
(C) 6′3″, 155 lbs. male, white, blond hair
(D) 6′3″, 175 lbs. male, white, bald head.

81. Police Officer Ginzberg is told that she may have to decide when to help settle disputes. Which one of the following situations should Police Officer Ginzberg help settle?

(A) A group of young men talking about the score of a neighborhood softball game.
(B) Four men talking about the feature article in a popular magazine.
(C) Two women discussing the abilities of a national tennis star.
(D) A man demanding a refund for his ticket from a theater cashier.

82. Police Officer Peake is completing an entry in his Activity Log. The entry contains the following five sentences:

1. He went to his parked car only to find he was blocked in.
2. The owner of the vehicle refused to move the van until he had finished his lunch.
3. Approximately 30 minutes later, I arrived on the scene and ordered the owner of the van to remove the vehicle.
4. Mr. O'Neil had an appointment and was in a hurry to keep it.
5. Mr. O'Neil entered a nearby delicatessen and asked if anyone in there drove a dark blue van, license plate number BUS 265.

The most logical order for the above sentences to appear in the Activity Log is

(A) 2, 3, 1, 4, 5
(B) 4, 1, 5, 2, 3
(C) 5, 4, 1, 3, 2
(D) 2, 1, 3, 4, 5.

Answer question 83 solely on the basis of the following information.

Upon arrival at the scene of a person needing medical aid, a Police Officer should do the following in the order given:

1. Render reasonable aid to the sick or injured person.
2. Request an ambulance or doctor, if necessary.
3. Notify the Radio Dispatcher if the person is wearing a Medic-Alert emblem, indicating that the person suffers from diabetes, heart disease, or other serious medical problems.
4. Wait to direct the ambulance to the scene or have some responsible person do so.
5. Make a second call in 20 minutes if the ambulance does not arrive.
6. Make an Activity Log entry, including the name of the person notified regarding the Medic-Alert emblem.

83. While on foot patrol, Police Officer Grayson is approached by a woman who informs the Police Officer that an elderly man has just collapsed on the sidewalk around the corner. Police Officer Grayson, while offering aid, notices that the man is wearing a Medic-Alert emblem indicating heart disease. Police Officer Grayson now requests an ambulance to respond. The next step the Police Officer should take is

(A) wait for the ambulance to arrive
(B) have a responsible person direct the ambulance to the scene
(C) inform the Radio Dispatcher of the Medic-Alert emblem
(D) place a second call for the ambulance after 20 minutes.

84. Police Officer Harrison is preparing a report regarding a 10-year-old who was sexually abused at school. The report will include the following five sentences:

1. The child described the perpetrator as a white male with a mustache, six feet tall, wearing a green uniform.
2. On September 10, 1984, I responded to General Hospital to interview a child who was sexually abused.
3. He later confessed at the station house.
4. After I interviewed the child, I responded to the school and found a janitor who fit the description.
5. I interviewed the janitor and took him to the station house for further investigation.

The most logical order for the above sentences to appear in the report is

(A) 2, 4, 1, 5, 3 **(C)** 2, 1, 4, 5, 3
(B) 1, 4, 5, 2, 3 **(D)** 5, 3, 2, 1, 4.

85. Police Officer Madden is completing a report of a theft. The report will include the following five sentences:

1. I followed behind the suspect for two blocks.
2. I saw a man pass by the radio car, carrying a shopping bag.
3. I looked back in the direction he had just come from and noticed that the top of a parking meter was missing.
4. As he saw me, he started to walk faster and I noticed a red piece of metal with the word "violation" drop out of the shopping bag.
5. When I saw parking meter in the shopping bag, I apprehended the suspect and placed him under arrest.

The most logical order for the above sentences to appear in the report is

(A) 1, 4, 2, 3, 5 **(C)** 2, 4, 3, 1, 5
(B) 2, 1, 4, 5, 3 **(D)** 3, 2, 4, 1, 5.

Answer question 86 solely on the basis of the following information.

Transit Police Officer Crawford received a series of reports from several people who were mugged in the early evening as they were exiting from the Spruce Street subway station. The description of each suspect is as follows:

Report No. 1 (November 16)	Male, white, early 30's, 5′10″, 180 lbs., dark hair, moustache, one gold earring, blue jeans, black jacket, running shoes.

Report No. 2 (November 20) Male, white, 25–30, 5′6″, 120 lbs., dark hair, dark glasses, one gold earring, blue jeans, green sweat shirt, running shoes.

Report No. 3 (November 21) Male, white, 40–45, 5′10″, 130–140 lbs., dark hair, moustache, one gold earring, blue jeans, black jacket, running shoes.

On November 23rd, another person was mugged by a male who was loitering near the subway station exit. However, the token clerk witnessed the mugging, called 911, and the male was apprehended two blocks away. The description of the suspect is as follows:

Report No. 4 (November 23) Male, white, 25–30, 5′10″, 175 lbs., dark hair, moustache, blue jeans, black jacket, green ski cap, boots.

86. Based on the above description of the suspects in the first three reports, the suspect in Report No. 4 should also be considered a suspect in

(A) Report No. 1, but not in Report No. 2 and 3
(B) Report No. 1 and 2, but not in Report No. 3
(C) Report No. 2 and 3, but not in Report No. 1
(D) Report No. 1, 2, and 3.

87. Crime Reports are completed by Police Officers. One section of a report contains the following five sentences:

1. The man, seeing that the woman had the watch, pushed Mr. Lugano to the ground.
2. Frank Lugano was walking into the Flame Diner on Queens Boulevard when he was jostled by a man in front of him.
3. A few minutes later Mr. Lugano told a Police Officer on foot patrol about a man and a woman taking his watch.
4. As soon as he was jostled, a woman reached toward Mr. Lugano's wrist and removed his expensive watch.
5. The man and woman after taking Mr. Lugano's watch, ran around the corner.

The most logical order for the above sentences to appear in the report is

(A) 2, 4, 1, 3, 5 **(C)** 4, 1, 3, 2, 5
(B) 2, 4, 1, 5, 3 **(D)** 4, 2, 1, 5, 3.

Answer question 88 solely on the basis of the following information.

Murder—The crime of murder is committed when a person intends to cause the death of another person and he causes the person's death, or he causes a death because of a complete disregard for life by creating a great risk of immediate danger that someone may be killed. The person must be aware that such a risk exists.

88. Which one of the following situations is the best example of murder?

(A) A construction worker is operating a crane in midtown when the cable breaks. Three tons of steel fall to the sidewalk and kill three persons.
(B) Kevin Malloy is playing on the subway tracks with his friend John Wilson. Kevin is helping John off the tracks when he slips and lets go of his hand. A train comes and kills John.
(C) A nurse at Midtown Hospital gives a patient the wrong medication. The result is that the patient has an adverse reaction to the medication and dies.
(D) Billy Watson is a security guard at City Federal Bank. He goes out one afternoon and gets angry because his bus is late. He takes out a gun and starts firing wildly into a crowded bus stop. Billy Watson is fully aware of his actions but fires his gun anyway. One person dies as a result.

Answer question 89 solely on the basis of the following information.

When a Police Officer comes across an apparently lost child, the Police Officer should do the following in the order given:

1. Notify the Desk Officer and the Radio Dispatcher.
2. Ask the people in the vicinity of the place where the child was found what they might know concerning the child.
3. Bring the child to the station house if a relative of the child is not located.
4. Prepare an Aided Report.

89. Police Officer Dennis and his partner Police Officer Mills are patrolling a residential area of the precinct when they notice a young child wandering about the street. When approached by the Police Officers, the child begins crying and says she is lost. Police Officer Dennis telephones Lieutenant Bennett, the Desk Officer, while Police Officer Mills alerts the Radio Dispatcher. The next step the Police Officers should take is to

(A) take the child to the station house and explain the situation to the Desk Officer
(B) gather information and complete the Aided Report
(C) bring the relative to the station house when located
(D) question people in the area near where the child was found.

Answer question <u>90</u> solely on the basis of the following information.

When a Police Officer has an article of uniform or equipment that is lost or damaged, the Police Officer should do the following in the order given:

1. Prepare two copies of the proper report and address it to the Deputy Commissioner of Management and Budget, stating:
   a. How the damage or loss occurred.
   b. Date the article was purchased and the cost of the article.
2. Attach the statement of any witnesses.
3. Show the damaged article to the Commanding Officer.

90. Police Officer Gonder has ripped his pants while pursing a criminal. Two people witnessed the chase. He has prepared two copies of the proper report and sent it to the proper office. On the report he has stated the circumstances surrounding the cause of the damage and when it occurred. He has listed the date that the pants were purchased, and how much they cost. The next step Police Officer Gonder should take is to

(A) Attach the statement of witnesses.
(B) Address and send the report to the Deputy Commissioner of Management and Budget.
(C) List on the report the date the damage occurred.
(D) Show the damaged pants to the Commanding Officer.

91. Police Officer McCaslin is preparing a report of disorderly conduct which will include the following five sentences:

1. Police Officer Kenny and I were on patrol in a radio car when we received a dispatch to go to the Hard Rock Disco on Third Avenue.
2. We arrived at the scene and found three men arguing loudly and obviously intoxicated.
3. The dispatcher had received a call from a bartender regarding a dispute.
4. Two of the men left the disco shortly before we did.
5. We calmed the men down after managing to separate them.

The most logical order for the above sentences to appear in the report is

(A) 1, 2, 5, 3, 4
(B) 3, 1, 4, 2, 5
(C) 2, 1, 3, 4, 5
(D) 1, 3, 2, 5, 4.

92. Police Officer Langhorne is completing a report of a murder. The report will contain the following five statements made by a witness:

1. The noise created by the roar of a motorcycle caused me to look out of my window.
2. I ran out of the house and realized the man was dead, which is when I called the police.
3. I saw a man driving at high speed down the dead-end street on a motorcycle, closely followed by a green B.M.W.
4. The motorcyclist then parked the bike and approached the car, which was occupied by two males.
5. Two shots were fired and the cyclist fell to the ground, then the car made a U-turn and sped down the street.

The most logical order for the above sentences to appear in the report is

(A) 1, 2, 4, 3, 5
(B) 5, 2, 1, 4, 3
(C) 1, 3, 4, 5, 2
(D) 3, 4, 1, 2, 5.

93. Police Officer Murphy is preparing a report of a person who was assaulted. The report will include the following five sentences:

1. I responded to the scene, but Mr. Jones had already fled.
2. She was bleeding profusely from a cut above her right eye.
3. Mr. and Mrs. Jones apparently were fighting in the street when Mr. Jones punched his wife in the face.
4. I then applied pressure to the cut to control the bleeding.
5. I called the dispatcher on the radio to send an ambulance to respond to the scene.

The most logical order for the above sentences to appear in the report is

(A) 3, 2, 4, 1, 5
(B) 3, 1, 2, 4, 5
(C) 1, 5, 2, 3, 4
(D) 2, 5, 4, 3, 1.

Answer question 94 solely on the basis of the following information.

Within a seven-day period, a local precinct received three reports of stolen bicycles. All of the incidents occurred within a five block radius of Briarwood Park. In each incident, the bicycle rider, who was stopped at an intersection waiting for a red light to change, was forced to the ground by an adolescent male who was standing in the crosswalk. After wrestling the bicycle away from the rider, the adolescent then rode off. The description of each of the suspects is as follows:

Incident No. 1 Male, white, adolescent, blond curly hair, blue eyes, 5′4″, 120 lbs., sunglasses, white T-Shirt, scar on upper right arm, gray sweat pants, high-top sneakers.

Incident No. 2 Male, white, adolescent, light curly hair, blue eyes, 5′5″, 125 lbs., gray long-sleeved sweat shirt, running shorts, green socks, high-top sneakers.

Incident No. 3 Male, white, adolescent, brown curly hair, blue eyes, 5′4″, 120 to 130 lbs., tattoo on left arm, white tank top, blue sweat pants, running shoes.

In the following week, a fourth bicycle is stolen. However, this time the suspect is arrested by a Police Officer who observes the incident. The description of this suspect is as follows:

Incident No. 4 Male, white, adolescent, light curly hair, blue eyes, 5′5″, 124 lbs., scar on upper right arm, gray tank top, blue sweat pants, running shoes.

94. Based upon the descriptions of the suspects in the first three incidents, the suspect in the fourth incident should also be considered a suspect in

(A) Incident No. 1, but not in Incidents No. 2 and 3
(B) Incident No. 1 and 2, but not in Incident No. 3
(C) Incident No. 2 and 3 but not in Incident No. 1
(D) Incidents No. 1, 2, and 3.

Answer questions 95 through 98 solely on the basis of the following passage.

Police Officers Larson and Kelly were on patrol in their radio car in the area of the 13th Precinct when they received a dispatch to go to the scene of a robbery in progress. The dispatcher had received a call from a Mr. Morris, the owner of a liquor store located at 1341 3rd Avenue in Manhattan at 8 P.M.

As the Police Officers arrived at the scene approximately five minutes later, a red Buick was pulling away from the liquor store and Police Officer Kelly made a note of the license plate number, 346-BYI. They entered the store to find Mr. Morris standing beside an empty cash register. He said that one of the robbers was a white male about 5′10″ tall, approximately 180 lbs., blond hair, clean shaven, wearing a plaid shirt, blue dungarees and sunglasses. He described the other person as a black female about 5′6″ tall, about 140 lbs., black hair, also wearing dark glasses. She was dressed in a red T-Shirt and blue dungarees. The Police Officers asked Mr. Morris to describe what had happened. He stated that a female customer, someone he had never seen before, had just purchased some liquor. The woman asked him where the Peter Cooper apartment complex was located. Mr. Morris gave her directions and the woman left the store at approximately 7:50 P.M. Almost immediately, the robbers entered the store and the male drew a gun and demanded all the money in the cash register. Mr. Morris opened the register and the female took all the money, placed it in a large brown bag, and backed toward the door. The male followed closely while holding a light blue bag over the gun. It was then about 7:58 P.M. Mr. Morris ran to the door and saw the robbers get into a blue Chevy Vega, license plate number 574-KJL.

Police Officer Larson asked for a description of the female who had purchased the liquor immediately prior to the holdup and Mr. Morris said she was white, about 5′2″ tall, 120 lbs., wearing a straw hat, a smock type of dress and carrying a large black bag.

95. When did Mr. Morris report the robbery?

(A) 7:50 P.M. **(B)** 7:58 P.M. **(C)** 8:00 P.M. **(D)** 8:05 P.M.

96. The person who drew the gun on the store owner was a

(A) white male
(B) black female
(C) white female
(D) black male.

97. Which one of the following best describes the clothing worn by the female robber?

(A) plaid shirt, blue dungarees
(B) blue dungarees, blue T-Shirt
(C) smock type dress and straw hat
(D) red T-Shirt, blue dungarees.

98. Which one of the following is the correct license plate number of the car that the Police Officers saw pulling away from the liquor store?

(A) 346-BIY
(B) 574-KJL
(C) 346-BYI
(D) 574-KLJ.

99. Police Officer Carson is told to place barricades or signals on a roadway when it is necessary to warn motorists of hazardous conditions.

For which one of the following conditions should Police Officer Carson place a barricade on the roadway?

(A) A road with a broken overhead street lamp.
(B) A street with garbage piled four feet high on the sidewalk.
(C) A road with a tree fallen across one lane.
(D) A street with a filled-in pothole.

100. Police Officer Dunn is preparing a Complaint Report which will include the following five sentences:

1. Mrs. Field screamed and fought with the man.
2. A man wearing a blue ski mask grabbed Mrs. Field's purse.
3. Mrs. Fields was shopping on 34th Street and Broadway at 1 o'clock in the afternoon.
4. The man then ran around the corner.
5. The man was white, five feet six inches tall with a medium build.

The most logical order for the above sentences to appear in the report is

(A) 1, 5, 2, 4, 3
(B) 3, 2, 1, 4, 5
(C) 3, 4, 5, 1, 2
(D) 5, 4, 3, 1, 2.

101. Detective Adams completed a Crime Report which includes the following five sentences:

1. I arrived at the scene of the crime at 10:20 A.M. and began to question Mr. Sands about the security devices he had installed.
2. Several clearly identifiable fingerprints were found.
3. A Fingerprint Unit specialist arrived at the scene and immediately began to dust for fingerprints.
4. After questioning Mr. Sands, I called the Fingerprint Unit.
5. On Friday morning at 10 A.M., Mr. Sands, the owner of the High Fashion Fur Store on Fifth Avenue, called the Precinct to report that his safe had been broken into.

The most logical order for the above sentences to appear in the Crime Report is

(A) 1, 5, 4, 3, 2
(B) 1, 5, 3, 4, 2
(C) 5, 1, 4, 2, 3
(D) 5, 1, 4, 3, 2.

Answer questions 102 and 103 solely on the basis of the following information.

Police Officer Winter reads a report concerning robberies, burglaries, and assaults which occur in his sector. From the report, Police Officer Winter notices that all the robberies take place on Martin Street, all the burglaries take place on Adam Street and on William Street, and all the assaults take place on Eddy Street.

Most of the robberies occur on Thursdays and Fridays, most of the burglaries occur on Thursdays and most of the assaults occur on Saturdays.

Most of the robberies happen between 5 P.M. and 11 P.M., most of the burglaries happen between 7 P.M. and 12 A.M. and most of the assaults happen between 9 P.M. and 2 A.M.

102. Police Officer Winter would most likely be able to decrease the number of burglaries if he were to patrol

(A) Adam Street on Thursdays from 7 P.M. to 12 A.M.
(B) William Street on Fridays from 5 P.M. to 11 P.M.
(C) Eddy Street on Thursdays from 7 P.M. to 12 P.M.
(D) Martin Street on Fridays from 5 P.M. to 11 P.M.

103. Police Officer Winter would most likely be able to decrease the number of assaults if he were to patrol Eddy Street on

(A) Fridays from 5 P.M. to 11 P.M.
(B) Fridays from 9 A.M. to 2 A.M.
(C) Saturdays from 7 P.M. to 12 A.M.
(D) Saturdays from 9 P.M. to 2 A.M.

Answer questions 104 through 106 solely on the basis of the following information.

A Police Officer is told to notify the station house when he observes dangerous conditions.

104. For which one of the following should a Police Officer notify the station house?

(A) A male sleeping in the staircase of a building.
(B) A missing glass panel at the entrance of a building.
(C) An elevator door which has opened between floors.
(D) A broken bottle in the lobby of a building.

105. For which one of the following should a Police Officer notify the station house?

(A) A female dumping water out of a window.
(B) Smoke coming out of the fifth floor windows of a housing project.
(C) A fire hydrant opened in front of a building.
(D) A locked entrance door.

106. For which one of the following should a Police Officer notify the station house?

(A) Bricks falling from a tall building.
(B) A nude male in the lobby of a building.
(C) Two females arguing in front of a building entrance.
(D) An intoxicated male sleeping on the sidewalk.

Answer questions 107 and 108 solely on the basis of the following map. The flow of traffic is indicated by the arrows. If there is only one arrow shown, then traffic flows only in the direction indicated by the arrow. If there are two arrows shown, then traffic flows in both directions. You must follow the flow of traffic.

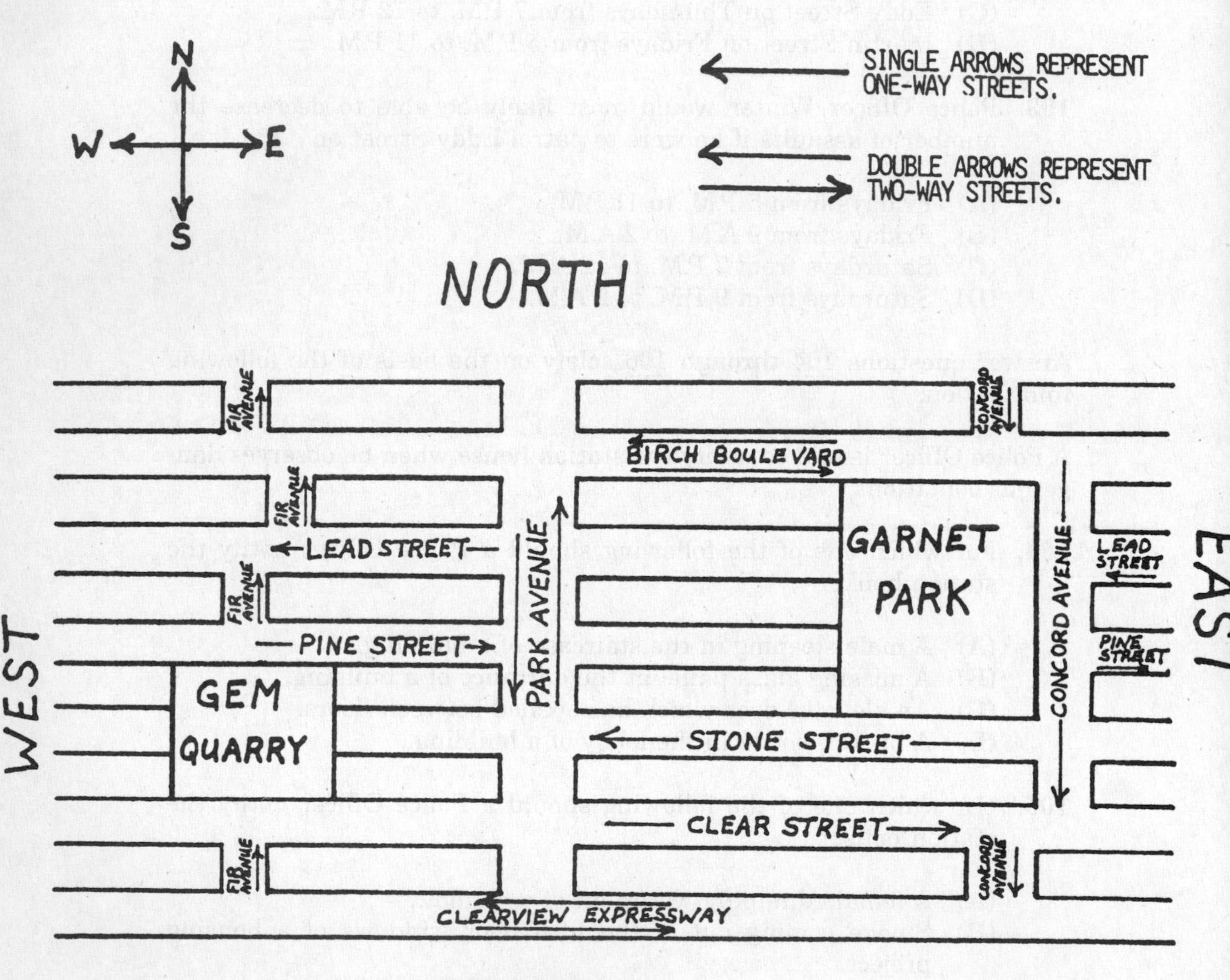

107. You are located at Fir Avenue and Birch Boulevard and receive a request to respond to a disturbance at Fir Avenue and Clear Street. Which one of the following is the most direct route for you to take in your patrol car, making sure to obey all traffic regulations?

(A) Travel one block east on Birch Boulevard, then four blocks south on Park Avenue, then one block east on Clear Street.
(B) Travel two blocks east on Birch Boulevard, then three blocks south on Concord Avenue, then two block west on Stone Street, then one block south on Park Avenue, then one block west on Clear Street.
(C) Travel one block east on Birch Boulevard, then five blocks south on Park Avenue, then one block west on the Clearview Expressway, then one block north on Fir Avenue.
(D) Travel two blocks south on Fir Avenue, then one block east on Pine Street, then three blocks south on Park Avenue, then one block east on the Clearview Expressway, then one block north on Fir Avenue.

108. You are located at the Clearview Expressway and Concord Avenue and receive a call to respond to a crime in progress at Concord Avenue and Pine Street. Which one of the following is the most direct route for you to take in your patrol car, making sure to obey all traffic regulations?

(A) Travel two blocks west on the Clearview Expressway, then one block north on Fir Avenue, then one block east on Clear Street, then four blocks north on Park Avenue, then one block east on Birch Boulevard, then two blocks south on Concord Avenue.
(B) Travel one block north on Concord Avenue, then one block west on Clear Street, then one block north on Park Avenue, then one block east on Stone Street, then one block north on Concord Avenue.
(C) Travel one block west on the Clearview Expressway, then four blocks north on Park Avenue, then one block west on Lead Street, then one block south on Fir Avenue.
(D) Travel one block west on the Clearview Expressway, then five blocks north on Park Avenue, then one block east on Birch Boulevard, then two blocks south on Concord Avenue.

109. Police Officer Ling is preparing a Complaint Report of a missing person. His report will contain the following five sentences:

1. I was greeted by Mrs. Miah Ali, who stated her daughter Lisa, age 17, did not return from school.
2. I questioned Mrs. Ali as to what time her daughter left for school, and what type of clothing she was wearing.
3. I notified the Patrol Sergeant, searched the building and area, and prepared a Missing Person Complaint Report.
4. I received a call from the Radio Dispatcher to respond to 9 Maple Street, apartment 1H, on a missing person complaint.
5. Mrs. Ali informed me that Lisa was wearing a gray suit and black shoes, and departed for school at 7:30 A.M.

The most logical order for the above sentences to appear in the report is

(A) 4, 1, 5, 2, 3
(B) 1, 4, 5, 3, 2
(C) 4, 1, 2, 5, 3
(D) 3, 1, 4, 2, 5.

110. Police Officer Jackson is told that he will sometimes be required to use his patrol car to transport seriously injured people to a hospital. However, the Police Officer should call an ambulance for people who are NOT seriously injured. For which one of the following people should Police Officer Jackson call an ambulance rather than use his patrol car?

(A) A person who is unconscious.
(B) A person who is bleeding from the chest.
(C) A person whose face is burned.
(D) A person who has a sprained wrist.

Answer question 111 solely on the basis of the following information.

When a Police Officer recovers a loaded gun, the Police Officer should do the following in the order given:

1. Unload the bullets from the gun.
2. Scratch an identifying mark on the side of the bullets.
3. Place the bullets in an envelope and seal the envelope.
4. Mark "Ammunition Removed from Firearm" across the face of the envelope and record the serial number of the gun.
5. Deliver the gun and the ammunition to the Desk Officer of the precinct.

111. Police Officer Parrish arrests a burglary suspect and discovers a loaded gun tucked in the jacket pocket of the suspect. At the precinct, the Police Officer unloads the gun and marks his initials on the side of each of the three bullets removed. The next step the Police Officer should take is to

(A) present the bullets to the precinct Desk Officer
(B) place the gun in an envelope and seal it
(C) mark the envelope across the face and record the serial number
(D) place the bullets in an envelope and seal it.

Answer question <u>112</u> solely on the basis of the following information.

Missing persons are often reported to the New York City Police Department. When the report involves people who are not able to fully care for themselves then a search of the area is required. A search is required when the missing person is a child under ten years of age; a possible drowning victim; a retarded or handicapped person; or an elderly person suffering from senility.

112. In which one of the following situations is a search required?

(A) Mrs. Johnson waits until 5:30 P.M. for John to come home from school. John is 11 years old and plays basketball after school every day, but today he didn't leave a note to that effect.
(B) Mrs. Smith waits until 3:45 P.M. but Bill, her 8-year-old son, hasn't come home from school. He has never been late before.
(C) Alexander Saunders is 25 years old and had a fight with his mother. He left and hasn't called in two days.
(D) Loraine Smith is a 17-year-old girl who wants to quit high school, but her mother won't let her. She left home and has not been heard from in three days.

Answer questions <u>113</u> through <u>115</u> solely on the basis of the following passage.

On Monday evening, February 6th, 1984 while I was on duty in the guard box outside the Liberian Embassy on Lexington Avenue and 38th Street, I noticed a gray Volvo, New York license plate No. 846 DSB, parked across the street on the northeast corner of 38th Street at approximately 5:15 P.M. There were two occupants in the car. One was a white male who had gray hair and was wearing a pale blue jacket; the other was a young male with a dark complexion who was wearing a hat, sunglasses and a dark gray jacket.

After about 20 minutes, the man wearing the dark gray jacket got out of the car and read the traffic sign which described the parking regulations. He then spoke to the driver of the car, the man wearing the blue jacket, and walked up 38th Street toward Park Avenue.

Because I know the parking rules of this area and since the car was not in violation, I ceased to observe it. However, approximately five minutes later, my attention was drawn to the sight of the male passenger who had previously left the car to walk up 38th Street. He now appeared on Lexington Avenue from the southeast corner of 39th Street and entered a high-rise building located directly opposite the Embassy. Almost simultaneously, a blue Ford bearing a New Jersey license plate No. 691 ASD, pulled up to the curb in front of the building, and the driver, a tall white male with blonde hair, who was wearing a dark blue suit and carrying a briefcase, got out and entered the lobby.

I walked across the street from the guard box and went into the lobby of the high-rise building where the doorman hurried over to ask if he could assist me. There was no sign of either of the men. After describing them, I asked the doorman if he knew whether they were tenants or visitors to the building. He said the tall blonde man was a tenant by the name of George Altman who lived in apartment 19G. The other young, dark complexioned man announced himself as Mr. Donabuto and entered the elevator with Mr. Altman, whom he had come to visit. The doorman also added that Mr. Donabuto had visited the building at least twice the previous week. On one occasion he visited Mr. Ehrenwald, a tenant who lives in apartment 19C. On the other occasion he visited Mr. Escobar, who lives in apartment 19D. In addition, the doorman said that he had observed Mr. Yepes, the driver of the gray Volvo, visit Mr. Altman the day before.

After investigating the layout of the building, I decided to make an entry in the Activity Log and report the incident as suspicious due to the fact that apartment 19G directly overlooks the room occupied by the Consul General in the Liberian Embassy.

113. Which one of the following best describes the driver of the Volvo?

(A) A dark-complexioned man
(B) A white, gray-haired man
(C) A tall blonde man
(D) A dark middle-aged man.

114. At approximately what time did the young male wearing a hat and sunglasses enter the building on Lexington Avenue?

(A) 5:15 P.M.
(B) 5:20 P.M.
(C) 5:40 P.M.
(D) 6:00 P.M.

115. At which one of the following locations was the gray Volvo parked?

(A) Southeast corner of 39th Street
(B) Northwest corner of 39th Street
(C) Southwest corner of 38th Street
(D) Northeast corner of 38th Street.

Answer question 116 based solely on the following statement:

According to New York State law, it is unlawful for a person to possess a loaded gun outside his home or place of business.

116. Based on this statement, which one of the following persons is violating the law?

(A) Joel Roberts manages a grocery store and keeps a loaded gun near the cash register of his store.
(B) Marcia Cohen works as a security guard and keeps her loaded gun in her apartment.
(C) Ken Caldwell owns a jewelry store and carries a loaded gun when he visits his brother's house in the Bronx.
(D) Steve Davis sells real estate and keeps his unloaded gun in his summer house upstate.

117. Police Officer Durant is completing a report of a robbery and assault. The report will contain the following five sentences:

1. I went to Mount Snow Hospital to interview a man who was attacked and robbed of his wallet earlier that night.
2. An ambulance arrived at 82nd Street and 3rd Avenue and took an intoxicated, wounded man to Mount Snow Hospital.
3. Two youths attacked the man and stole his wallet.
4. A well-dressed man left Hanratty's Bar very drunk, with his wallet hanging out of his back pocket.
5. A passerby dialed 911 and requested police and ambulance assistance.

The most logical order for the above sentences to appear in the report is

(A) 1, 2, 4, 3, 5
(B) 4, 3, 5, 2, 1
(C) 4, 5, 2, 3, 1
(D) 5, 4, 3, 2, 1.

118. Police Officer Boswell is preparing a report of an armed robbery and assault which will contain the following five sentences:

1. Both men approached the bartender and one of them drew a gun.
2. The bartender immediately went to grab the phone at the bar.
3. One of the men leaped over the counter and smashed a bottle over the bartender's head.
4. Two men in a blue Buick drove up to the bar and went inside.
5. I found the cash register empty and the bartender unconscious on the floor, with the phone still dangling off the hook.

The most logical order for the above sentences to appear in the report is

(A) 4, 1, 2, 3, 5
(B) 5, 4, 3, 1, 2
(C) 4, 3, 2, 5, 1
(D) 2, 1, 3, 4, 5.

119. Police Officer Mitzler is preparing a report of a bank robbery, which will contain the following five sentences:

1. The teller complied with the instructions on the note, but also hit the silent alarm.
2. The perpetrator then fled south on Broadway.
3. A suspicious male entered the bank at approximately 10:45 A.M.
4. At this time, an undetermined amount of money has been taken.
5. He approached the teller on the far right side and handed her a note.

The most logical order for the above sentences to appear in the report is

(A) 3, 5, 1, 2, 4
(B) 1, 3, 5, 2, 4
(C) 3, 5, 4, 1, 2
(D) 3, 5, 2, 4, 1.

120. A Police Officer is preparing an Accident Report for an accident which occurred at the intersection of East 119th Street and Lexington Avenue. The report will include the following five sentences:

1. On September 18th, 1984, while driving ten children to school, a school bus driver passed out.
2. Upon arriving at the scene I notified the dispatcher to send an ambulance.
3. I notified the parents of each child once I got to the Station House.
4. He said the school bus, while traveling west on East 119th Street, struck a parked Ford which was on the southwest corner of East 119th Street.
5. A witness by the name of John Ramos came up to me to described what happened.

The most logical order for the above sentences is

(A) 1, 2, 5, 3, 4
(B) 1, 2, 5, 4, 3
(C) 2, 5, 1, 3, 4
(D) 2, 5, 1, 4, 3.

121. A Police Officer is preparing a report concerning a dispute. The report will contain the following five sentences:

1. The passenger got out of the back of the taxi and leaned through the front window to complain to the driver about the fare.
2. The driver of the taxi caught up with the passenger and knocked him to the ground; the passenger then kicked the driver and a scuffle ensued.
3. The taxi drew up in front of the high-rise building and stopped.
4. The driver got out of the taxi and followed the passenger into the lobby of the apartment building.
5. The doorman tried but was unable to break up the fight, at which point he called the precinct.

The most logical order for the above sentences to appear in the report is

(A) 3, 1, 4, 2, 5
(B) 3, 4, 1, 2, 5
(C) 3, 4, 2, 5, 1
(D) 5, 1, 3, 4, 2.

Answer questions 122 and 123 solely on the basis of the following information.

Police Officer Forster notices that in his sector all the robberies take place on Eaton Street, all the traffic accidents occur on Country Club Road and all the assaults happen on Monmouth Street.

Most of the assaults take place between 8 A.M. and 11 A.M. and between 2 P.M. and 7 P.M. Most of the traffic accidents occur between 11 A.M. and 4 P.M. Most of the robberies take place between 7 P.M. and 11 P.M.

Most of the traffic accidents happen on Mondays, most of the robberies take place on Wednesdays and Saturdays, and most of the assaults occur on Thursdays.

122. Police Officer Forster would most likely be able to reduce the incidence of robberies by patrolling

(A) Monmouth Street on Thursdays from 8 P.M. to 11 P.M.
(B) Eaton Street on Wednesdays from 7 A.M. to 11 A.M.
(C) Eaton Street on Saturdays from 6 P.M. to 10 P.M.
(D) Eaton Street on Thursdays from noon to 4 P.M.

123. Due to his knowledge of the crime patterns in his sector, Police Officer Forster's superiors want him to work a steady tour each week that would allow him to concentrate on assaults and robberies within his sector. For this purpose it would be most appropriate for Police Officer Forster to work

(A) Monday through Friday, 4 P.M. to Midnight
(B) Tuesday through Saturday, 4 P.M. to Midnight
(C) Tuesday through Saturday, 2 P.M. to 10 P.M.
(D) Monday through Friday, 8 A.M. to 4 P.M.

124. Police Officer Morrow is writing an Incident Report. The report will include the following four sentences:

1. The man reached into his pocket and pulled out a gun.
2. While on foot patrol, I identified a suspect, who was wanted for six robberies in the area, from a wanted picture I was carrying.
3. I drew my weapon and fired six rounds at the suspect, killing him instantly.
4. I called for back-up assistance and told the man to put his hands up.

The most logical order for the above sentences to appear in the report is

(A) 2, 3, 4, 1
(B) 4, 1, 3, 2
(C) 4, 1, 2, 3
(D) 2, 4, 1, 3.

Answer questions <u>125</u> through <u>129</u> based solely on the basis of the following passage.

Police Officer Davies, shield number 3935, patrolling sector D in the 79th Precinct on scooter number 569, was dispatched at 9:26 A.M. on November 12, 1984, to Roosevelt Houses, 928 Dekalb Avenue, apartment 15J on a family dispute. Police Officer Davies requested back-up units to meet him in the front of the building.

Police Officer Davies arrived on the scene at 9:30 A.M. A back-up unit consisting of Police Officers Mark #2310 and Harris #1542, arrived at the same time in patrol car #9843. These Police Officers were assigned to the same precinct and sector. The Police Officers took the elevator to the 15th floor and proceeded to apartment 15J.

The Police Officers rang the apartment bell and were met by a black female who told them that she had a court Order of Protection against her husband. She further stated that her husband was trying to force his way into the apartment but fled the scene when she called the police. She gave the following description of her husband: male, black, age 38, date of birth 8/14/46, named Carl

Tyler, 6′1″ tall, about 185 pounds, clean shaven, wearing a dark blue long sleeve shirt, black pants and black shoes. She further stated that he resides at 89-27 Bellmore Avenue in Queens, apartment 2A.

At 9:35 A.M. Police Officers Mark and Harris searched the building and the surrounding area for Mr. Tyler or for someone fitting the description given by the woman, while Police Officer Davies obtained further information for his report.

The woman stated that her name is Betty Tyler, 37-years-old, born 4/10/47, home telephone number 387-3038. She gave Police Officer Davies her copy of the Order of Protection and he recorded the information in his Memo Book.

The Order of Protection was dated 11/5/84 issued at Brooklyn Criminal Court, 120 Schermerhorn Street, by Judge Harry Cohn, Docket number APG482/84, and in effect until 1/19/85.

Police Officers Mark and Harris returned to apartment 15J at 9:45 A.M. after a search for Mr. Tyler proved negative. The Police Officers advised Mrs. Tyler to call the police again if her husband returned.

Police Officers Mark and Harris notified the Radio Dispatcher that they were resuming patrol at 9:52 A.M. Police Officer Davies proceeded to the Station House to prepare two Complaint Reports and to refer the matter to the Detective Unit for follow-up.

125. In which precinct and sector do Police Officer Davies and the back-up Police Officers work?

(A) 79th Precinct, Sector D
(B) 79th Precinct, Sector B
(C) 97th Precinct, Sector D
(D) 97th Precinct, Sector B.

126. What is the total number of Police Officers who responded to assist Police Officer Davies on the family dispute?

(A) 1 **(B)** 2 **(C)** 3 **(D)** 4.

127. Which docket number did Police Officer Davies record in his Memo Book?

(A) AFG482/84
(B) APG428/84
(C) APG482/84
(D) AFG428/84.

128. Which one of the following is the approximate time that Police Officers Mark and Harris arrived at the location?

(A) 9:30 A.M.
(B) 9:35 A.M.
(C) 9:45 A.M.
(D) 9:52 A.M.

129. Which one of the following is the best description of Mr. Tyler?

(A) Black, 6 ft. 1 in. tall, 185 pounds
(B) Black, 6 ft. 1 in. tall, 160 pounds
(C) Black, 6 ft. 6 in. tall, 185 pounds
(D) Black, 6 ft. 6 in. tall, 160 pounds.

130. Sergeant Allen responds to a call at 16 Grove Street regarding a missing child. At the scene, the Sergeant is met by Police Officer Samuels, who gives a brief account of the incident consisting of the following five sentences:

1. I transmitted the description, and waited for you to arrive before I began searching the area.
2. Mrs. Banks, the mother, reports that she last saw her daughter Julie about 7:30 A.M. when she took her to school.
3. About 6 P.M., my partner and I arrived at this location to investigate a report of a missing 8-year-old girl.
4. When Mrs. Banks left her, Julie was wearing a red and white striped T-shirt, blue jeans, and white sneakers.
5. Mrs. Banks dropped her off in front of the playground of P.S. 11.

The most logical order for the above sentences to appear is

(A) 3, 5, 4, 2, 1
(B) 3, 2, 5, 4, 1
(C) 3, 4, 1, 2, 5
(D) 3, 2, 4, 1, 5.

131. Police Officer Franco is completing a report of an assault. The report will contain the following five sentences:

1. In the park I observed an elderly man lying on the ground, bleeding from a back wound.
2. I applied first aid to control the bleeding and radioed for an ambulance to respond.
3. The elderly man stated that he was sitting on the park bench when he was attacked from behind by two males.
4. I received a report of a man's scream coming from inside the park and I went to investigate.
5. The old man could not give a description of his attackers.

The most logical order for the above sentences to appear in the report is

(A) 4, 1, 2, 3, 5
(B) 5, 3, 1, 4, 2
(C) 4, 3, 5, 2, 1
(D) 2, 1, 5, 4, 3.

132. Police Officer Williams is completing a Crime Report. The report contains the following five sentences:

1. As Police Officer Hanson and I approached the store, we noticed that the front door was broken.
2. After determining that the burglars had fled, we notified the precinct of the burglary.
3. I walked through the front door as Police Officer Hanson walked around to the back.
4. At approximately midnight, an alarm was heard at the Apex Jewelry Store.
5. We searched the store and found no one.

The most logical order for the above sentences to appear in the report is

(A) 1, 4, 2, 3, 5
(B) 1, 4, 3, 5, 2
(C) 4, 1, 3, 2, 5
(D) 4, 1, 3, 5, 2.

Answer questions 133 through 140 on the basis of the following sketches. The first face, on the left, is a sketch of an alleged criminal based on witnesses' descriptions at the crime scene. One of the four sketches to the right is the way the suspect looked after changing appearance. Assume that NO surgery has been done on the suspect. Select the face which is most likely that of the suspect.

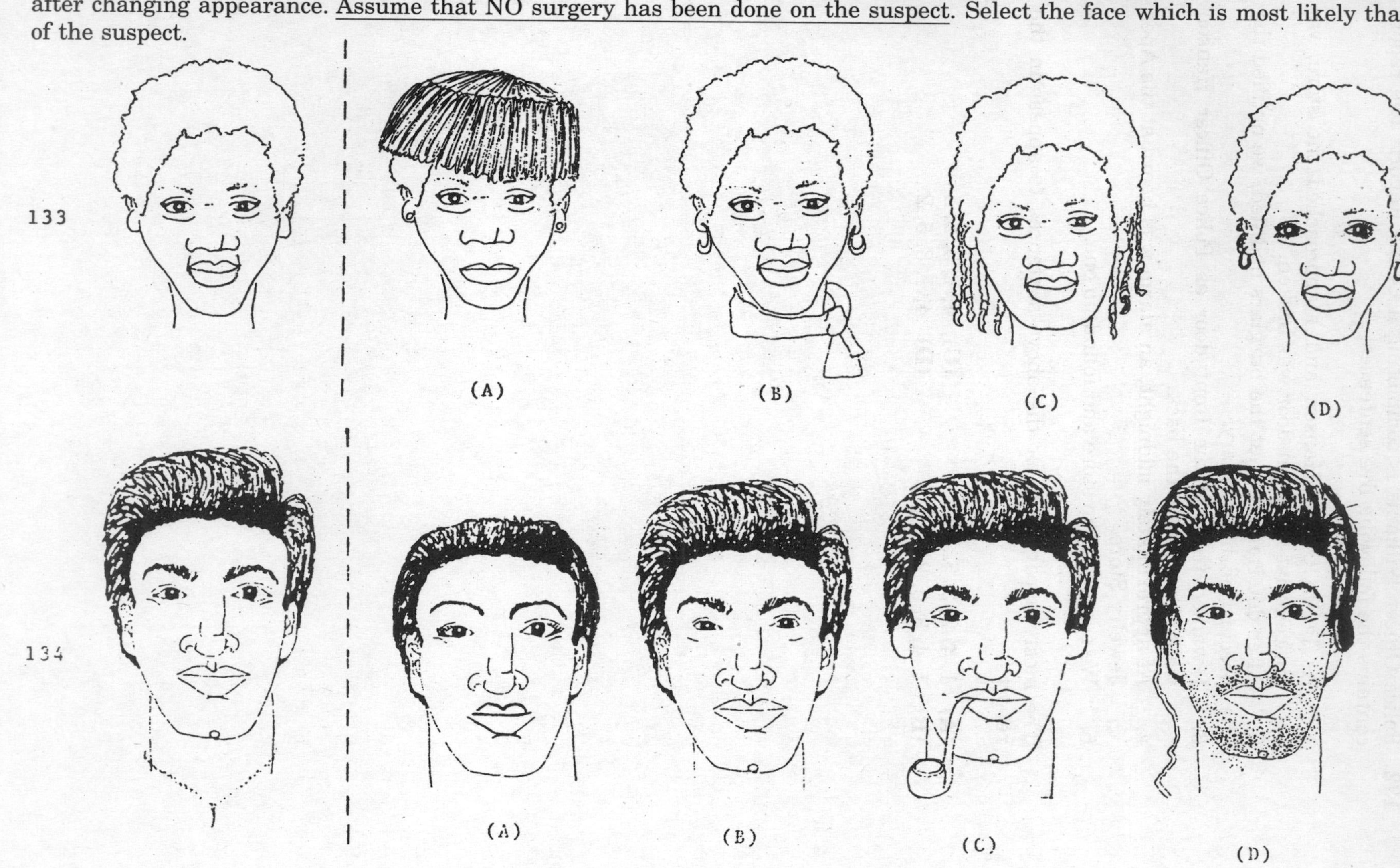

135
(A)
(B)
(C)
(D)
136
(A)
(B)
(C)
(D)

137
(A)
(B)
(C)
(D)
138
(A)
(B)
(C)
(D)

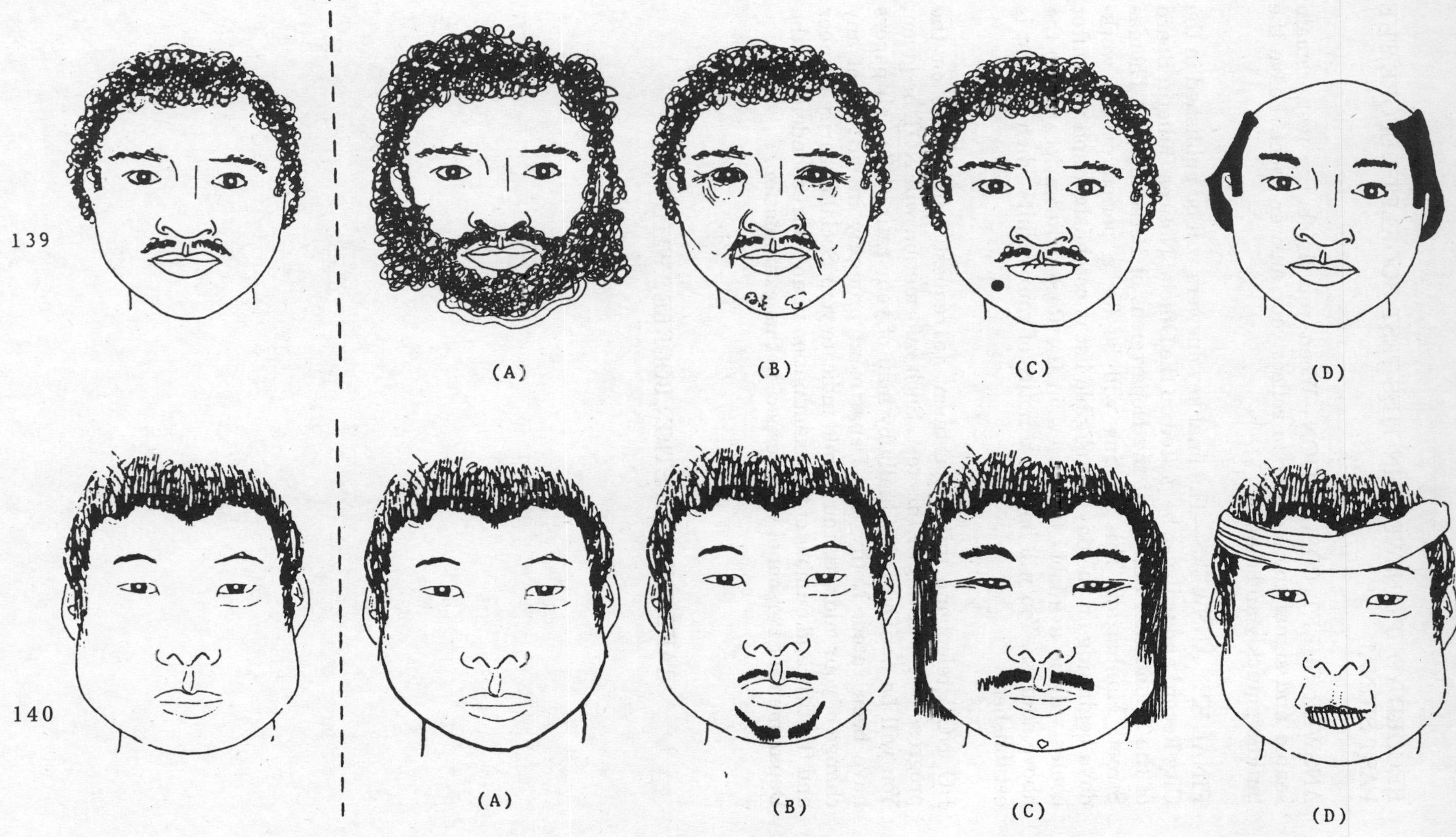
139
(A)
(B)
(C)
(D)
140
(A)
(B)
(C)
(D)

RECORD YOUR ANSWERS IN THIS TEST BOOKLET BEFORE THE LAST SIGNAL

ANSWER SHEET COLLECTION—When you finish the test, remain seated and signal the monitor to collect your answer sheet. Leave the building quickly and quietly.

FINAL KEY ANSWERS—The final key answers will be published in the City Record and will also be posted on the Official Notices Bulletin Board of the Application Section of the Department of Personnel, 49 Thomas Street, Manhattan. This posting will be for a period of ten workdays beginning on the day the eligible list is established and thereafter copies will be available for review in the Record Room located at the above address. You will be sent a notice of your results when the list is established.

DO NOT telephone this Department to request information on the progress of the rating of this test. Such information will NOT be given. You will be notified individually by mail of your rating after all papers have been rated. Notify this Department promptly in writing of any change of your address. You should indicate your Social Security number and the title and number of the examination in any correspondence to the Department of Personnel with respect to this examination.

TAKE THIS QUESTION BOOKLET WITH YOU

Answer Key, Diagnostic Procedure, and Explanations

Answer Key

1.	B	29.	B	57.	C	85.	C	113.	B
2.	B	30.	A	58.	B	86.	A	114.	C
3.	A	31.	D	59.	D	87.	B	115.	D
4.	D	32.	B	60.	A	88.	D	116.	C
5.	D	33.	D	61.	B	89.	D	117.	B
6.	A	34.	C	62.	D	90.	A	118.	A
7.	C	35.	C	63.	B	91.	D	119.	A
8.	D	36.	D	64.	C	92.	C	120.	B
9.	B	37.	B	65.	B	93.	B	121.	A
10.	B	38.	A	66.	A	94.	B	122.	C
11.	D	39.	D	67.	A	95.	C	123.	B and/or C
12.	D	40.	C	68.	C	96.	A	124.	D
13.	B	41.	C	69.	A	97.	D	125.	A
14.	D	42.	D	70.	A	98.	C	126.	B
15.	B	43.	A	71.	D	99.	C	127.	C
16.	B	44.	A	72.	B	100.	B	128.	A
17.	C	45.	A	73.	B	101.	D	129.	A
18.	C	46.	B	74.	A	102.	A	130.	B
19.	D	47.	A	75.	C	103.	D	131.	A
20.	A	48.	B	76.	D	104.	C	132.	D
21.	D	49.	D	77.	B	105.	B	133.	B
22.	A	50.	C	78.	C	106.	A	134.	D
23.	C	51.	A	79.	C	107.	C	135.	A
24.	D	52.	A	80.	D	108.	D	136.	B
25.	C	53.	D	81.	D	109.	C	137.	C
26.	B	54.	C	82.	B	110.	D	138.	D
27.	D	55.	B	83.	C	111.	D	139.	A
28.	B	56.	B	84.	C	112.	B	140.	B

Diagnostic Procedure

Insert the number of correct answers you obtained in the blank space for each section of the examination. The scale in the next column indicates how you did. The information at the bottom indicates how to correct your weaknesses.

SECTION	QUESTION NUMBER	AREA	YOUR NUMBER CORRECT	SCALE
1	1–13	Memory		13 right—excellent 11–12 right—good 9–10 right—fair under 9 right—poor
2	14, 17, 29, 32, 44, 46, 47, 51, 53, 56, 64–66, 68, 82, 84 85, 87, 91–93, 100, 101, 109, 117–121, 124, 130–132	Sentence Ordering		32 or 33 right—excellent 30 or 31 right—good 28 or 29 right—fair under 28 right—poor
3	15, 16, 22–27, 31 33, 34, 36, 39, 40, 45, 50, 52, 54, 62, 63, 67, 70, 76, 78, 81, 83, 89, 90, 99, 104–106, 110–112	Applying Police Procedures		34 or 35 right—excellent 32 or 33 right—good 30 or 31 right—fair under 30 right—poor
4	18–21, 28, 37, 38, 41–43, 55, 58–61, 69, 71–75, 77, 79, 80, 86, 94–98, 102, 103, 113–115, 122, 123, 125–129	Reading Comprehension		40–42 right—excellent 37–39 right—good 34–36 right—fair under 34 right—poor
5	30, 35, 57, 88, 116	Legal Definitions		5 right—excellent 4 right—fair under 4 right—poor
6	48, 49, 107, 108	Traffic Maps		4 right–excellent under 4 right—poor
7	133–140	Matching Sketches		8 right—excellent 7 right—good 6 right—fair under 6 right—poor

1. If you are weak in Section One, then concentrate on Chapters 5 and 6.

2. If you are weak in Section Two, then concentrate on Chapter 10, the section dealing with sentence ordering.

3. If you are weak in Section Three, then concentrate on Chapter 8.

4. If you are weak in Section Four, then concentrate on Chapters 4 and 5.

5. If you are weak in Section Five, then concentrate on Chapter 9.

6. If you are weak in Section Six, then concentrate on Chapter 10, the section dealing with traffic maps.

7. If you are weak in Section Seven, then concentrate on Chapter 10, the section dealing with matching sketches.

NOTE: Consider yourself weak in a section if your receive other than an excellent rating in it.

Answer Explanations

GENERAL COMMENT ON QUESTIONS 1 THROUGH 13:
Remember that one of the keys to taking memory questions is to maintain complete concentration. From the time you first look at the drawing or sketch until the time you answer the questions, you should concentrate exclusively on remembering what is included in the drawing or sketch. DON'T let your mind wander.

1. **B** Observing and remembering license plates is something police officers do on a daily basis. If there is a license plate number in the sketch on your examination, you can be sure you will be asked a question about it. The plate number on the truck was MAT-1. Were there any other license plate numbers in the sketch?

2. **B** What we said above about license plate numbers can also be said for addresses. Addresses are a prime area for questions. Remember that addresses help to answer the very important question, "Where did this happen?" If you develop associations to remember addresses, you can answer questions like this with no difficulty.

3. **A** The man with the sign is in front of the *pet* store and is walking towards the woman with a *pet*. This is the kind of association you should be making.

4. D A man's face appears on the truck. Underneath the man's face is the name "MAT'S" and the license plate on the truck is "MAT-1." These are the details that you must notice when studying the sketches. Once again we remind you that memory alone does not provide the answers to memory questions. You must learn to make associations that will help you remember details.

5. D The Con Ed man is working near an open manhole and the manhole cover is on the street next to him. An open manhole is a potentially dangerous condition and one that a police officer would be expected to notice.

6. A A dance school is located above the barber shop. A possible association could be, "Before going to *dance*, one should get a *haircut*." It doesn't matter how silly an association is if it helps you to remember.

7. C Don't forget what we told you in Chapter Six. *ALWAYS* count the number of people in the scene. In this case there were eight people.

8. D The three people in the scene are standing under a street light. Examiners frequently ask about the location of people in the scene; so always pay close attention to this when studying the sketch.

9. B As we said above, license plates are favorite question areas. The occupied auto's plate number is "BAG 6165."

10. B Once again we see a question about how many people were somewhere in the picture. One student of ours who took this examination told us he used the following association to remember this item—"No one should drink 'two' much"—since there are two people in the liquor store.

11. D The man in front of the fishing-tackle store is dressed all in black. No one else in the scene is similarly dressed. Learn to see and remember the unusual. It will help you not only on the official test but also when you become a police officer.

12. D If you had followed our advice from Chapter Six, then you would have been on the lookout for times, temperatures, and any other objective information that helps to describe the scene. The time on the clock above the bank is 8:2*1* and the temperature is 5*1*. Noticing that both the temperature and the time end in a *one* would be a helpful association to make.

13. B If you have a "clean" (the cleaning store) "income tax" return, you can relax and go "fishing." This is the order of the first three stores on the block. See if you can do this for the rest of the stores on the block.

14. D This is a "sentence ordering" question. The strategy for answering it is outlined in Chapter 10. If we apply that strategy to the question, we see that the sentences that the choices put first are:

Choice A—sentence one
Choice B—sentence three
Choice C—sentence two
Choice D—sentence four

— You can eliminate sentence five as the first sentence since it doesn't appear as a choice.
— Sentence one obviously doesn't come first, so Choice A can be eliminated. (Remember to mark an "X" through Choice A since it is a wrong choice.)
— Sentence two could possibly come first, so don't eliminate Choice C yet.
— Sentence three is obviously not the first thing that happened, so Choice B can be eliminated.
— Sentence four could be the first thing that happened, so don't eliminate Choice D.
— You are now left with Choices C and D as possible correct answers since they both contain sentences that could come first.
— Now concentrate on what happened last. Choice C puts sentence five last and Choice D puts sentence three last. In sentence five the officer is trying to convince the person not to jump from the building. In sentence three, the person jumped from the building. It is obvious that sentence three happened after sentence five. Therefore Choice D must be the answer.

Please notice that you arrived at the right answer without actually arranging all of the sentences in their correct order. This is where the savings in time comes in. With practice, these questions become quite simple.

15. B This is a question which tests your ability to apply written procedures to a specific situation as covered in Chapter Eight. In this question the officer already complied with Procedures 1 and 2 by making a log entry indicating the location of the defective signal light. He must now follow Procedure 3. Therefore, Choice B is the correct answer.

16. B Another "application of procedures" question. Choice B includes a combination of Procedures 1 and 2 and is the correct answer.

17. C Following the strategy for answering this "sentencing ordering" question which we outline above, we see that according to the choices only sentences one and four can come first (Choices A and D put sentence one first and Choices B and C put sentence four first). Upon examination, it is obvious that sentence four had to occur before sentence one, so Choices A and D can be eliminated.

Choice B puts sentence two last and Choice C puts sentence five last. Upon examination it is apparent that sentence five occurred last. This means that Choice C must be the correct answer.

Note that questions 18 through 21 are reading comprehension questions, the type discussed in Chapter Four.

18. C The third line of paragraph two clearly states the address of the boutique as being 338 West 44th Street. If you were following our recommended strategy, you would have known that one of the questions asked for the address of the boutique. When reading the passage, you should have used your pencil to highlight this address when you came across it.

19. D Line eight of the second paragraph states that Benson arrived at the premise at 1:20 P.M. Once again, reading the stem of the question before reading the paragraph would have helped a lot.

20. A By now it should be apparent that our code word "NEOTWY" should always be kept in mind. Question 18 asked a "where" question, number 19 asked a "when" question, and this is a "who" question. Line 16 of paragraph one states that Ms. Peever is the owner of the boutique. (See Chapter Five for a full explanation of the code word "NEOTWY")

21. D Another "when" question. Line two of paragraph three states that Ms. Peake starts her shift at 1:30 P.M.

22. A Item four of the procedure prohibits the police from detaining a properly identified diplomat. Therefore Choice A is correct. (A very similar question was asked as question 41 on a previous NYPD Police Officer Examination. Think you might see it again?)

Note that 23 and 24 ask for "Application of Procedures." If you are having difficulty with these questions, re-read Chapter Eight and make sure you are using the correct strategy. These questions are easy and should not be missed.

23. C After confiscating the illegal gun, Procedure 1, the police officer must charge the individual, Procedure 2, described in Choice C.

24. D According to the procedure, after completing the Request for Laboratory Examination form, the next step is to take the illegal gun and the form to the Ballistics Section.

25. C Lines three and four of the Procedure state that even upon request, the Officer shall remove the handcuffs *ONLY* after informing the physician of the circumstances of the arrest.

26. B Someone falling on the subway tracks is surely more of an emergency than the occurrences described in the other choices.

27. D Smoke coming from an apartment is an obviously dangerous condition. (Remember, you will not only be required to understand police procedures, you will also be asked to APPLY the procedures.)

28. B The suspect in Incident No. 2 had a tattoo on his left hand. The arrested individual had a tattoo on his right hand. Don't let the color of the hair confuse you. Remember that hair color and style are easily changed.

29. B Remember to consider only the orderings of the sentences that appear in the choices. Examine sentences one and four and it should be obvious that sentence four comes first. This leaves you with Choices A and B. Since both of these choices put sentence five last, you must consider the middle sentences. Upon examination, it should be obvious that Choice B is correct. The boy can't help Mr. Harris up until after Mr. Harris has fallen.

30. A This question tests your ability to understand legal definitions as explained in Chapter Nine and also tests your ability to understand police directives as covered in Chapter Eight. Choice A is correct because the Procedure allows the Officer to exercise discretion in a traffic case providing that the Officer does not benefit from using such discretion. Look up the word "discretion" if you are not exactly sure of its meaning. This question highlights the importance of your vocabulary.

31. D The question asks you to choose a situation which would require an evacuation of all of the people in an area. An asbestos fire in a tunnel under a train is certainly a dangerous situation which would require an evacuation.

32. B Sentence four is the only possible starting point for a report on this incident. You do not have to go any further since only Choice B puts sentence four first. You should clearly recognize at this point the unnecessary time and effort involved in attempting to arrange all of the sentences in their proper order.

33. D The passage indicates that the Officer suspects that the man is about to burglarize one of the stores, so the officer should stop the man. However, there is no suggestion that physical injury is a possibility or that a weapon is involved, so a frisk or a search is not required.

34. C Procedure 4 involves completing the Court Attendance Form. The next step, as indicated in Procedure 5, is to report to the Complaint Room.

35. C The difference between these two crimes lies in the intent of the criminal. Although in both cases the killing may be unintentional, in Felony Murder some other crime is intended.

36. D The cab driver did NOT use the credentials while committing the crime; therefore, Choices A, B, and C can be eliminated.

37. B Line four of the second paragraph states that Lucille was returning from school when she was accosted on the elevator. She could be a teacher, but that is not offered as a choice, and she is only 17. She must be a student.

38. A Lucille lives with her mother whose address, given in line three of paragraph one, is the same as Choice A.

39. D The officer has complied with Procedure 1 by making an Activity Log entry. His next responsibility, as listed in Procedure 2, is to notify the Telephone Switchboard Operator.

40. C Choice C is the only choice that deals with the control of the flow of traffic which is the subject of the statement. Choice C has to be the answer.

41. C Note that this is a "when" question. If you first read the choices, you spotted the answer right away. The time was stated in the first sentence of the first paragraph. A hanger!

42. D Another "when" question. Mr. Smith's date of birth, 1/10/23, is given in line seven of paragraph one. Look at the wrong choices to see how easy it would be to make a careless mistake. Each of the choices contains some combination of the numers 0-1-10-23 and 32. Concentrate!

43. A Lines three and four of the second paragraph tell you that the cylinder to his apartment lock was removed. Cylinder locks are found on doors, not on windows, roofs or walls.

44. A All you have to do to answer this question is decide which sentence should come first in a report. It should be fairly obvious that sentence one is the starting point. If you wanted more assurance, look at what happened last. Sentence two obviously occurred last. Choice A is the answer and it should only have taken you about thirty seconds to arrive at that conclusion.

45. A The girl is a juvenile under sixteen so her presence in a licensed bar is illegal. Therefore, the girl should be taken into protective custody and the bar's manager should be arrested, Procedure 2 and Choice A.

46. B Sentence four obviously comes before sentence one so Choice A can be eliminated. Since Choices B, C, and D all suggest that sentence two comes last, you must look at the middle sentences. Upon examination, it should be clear that the correct order is contained in Choice B. The location of sentence five in the sequence should have led you to the correct choice.

47. A This is an interesting question since both suggested first sentences could be correct. The key is what happened last. Examination of the choices shows that sentence three is the last thing that happened. Choice A must be the answer.

Questions 48 and 49 are a type of question that is known as the traffic map questions. A strategy for answering these questions is discussed in Chapter 10.

48. B In question 48, Choice A is wrong, not because it involves disobeying traffic rules, but because it is a less direct route than the one given in Choice B. Choice C is wrong because westbound traffic on Apple Avenue would be travelling the wrong way on a one-way street. Choice D is incorrect since westbound traffic on Canton Avenue would be travelling the wrong way on a one-way street. Please note that in addition to the correct answer, there is almost always a route that obeys traffic regulations but is a long way to go. This route will often appear as the first legal route, so consider all the choices before selecting an answer.

49. D Choice A is incorrect since it requires going the wrong way on Bear Avenue. Choice B is wrong since it requires going the wrong way on Vista Avenue. Choice C is wrong since it requires going the wrong way on Bear Avenue.

50. C The officer complied with Procedure one by calling his command within the allotted time frame. His next step is indicated in Procedure two and Choice C: he must contact his surgeon.

51. A After understanding that sentence three comes first, you can eliminate Choices B and C. Sentence four is the logical choice for the last sentence of the report, so you can eliminate Choice D.

52. A Of the four situations described, bleeding profusely is clearly the only life-threatening one. Therefore, Choice A is the case that would require first aid.

53. D This one is simple. Sentence two comes first. Only Choice D lists sentence two first, so without even reading the other suggested arrangements, you can pick Choice D.

54. C The Procedure states that taxis do not require insurance identification cards. Therefore, the only ticket that should be issued is one for going through the red light.

55. B Most of the rapes took place on Hamburg Avenue and all of them occurred between 10 P.M. and 4 A.M.

56. B Sentence two comes first, so Choice A can be eliminated. Since all of the remaining choices put sentence three last, we must consider the middle sentences. The key is to recognize that sentence one must come immediately after sentence five.

57. C Of the three crimes listed, only assault requires an actual physical injury. When Gardner struck Carter with the beer bottle, he caused physical injury. The correct charge is assault.

58. B As stated in line one of the third paragraph, the officer arrived at 60 Moore Street at 6:15 P.M.

59. D Line two of paragraph three states that the officer walked over to apartment 7E after getting off of the elevator. Also, line four of paragraph one states that the dispatcher directed the officer to apartment 7E.

60. A As stated in line two of paragraph four, Mrs. Aida Soto is the daughter of Mrs. Rivera, the sick woman.

61. B Mrs. Rivera's birthdate is given in line seven of paragraph three.

Please note how much easier questions 58–61 were if you remembered to read the stem of the questions before reading the paragraph.

62. D Procedure 1 requires the officer to walk through the vacated building to determine if a safety hazard exists.

63. B Writing an entry in the Activity Log is Procedure 3. The next step is Procedure 4, reporting the facts to the Telephone Switchboard Operator.

64. C Sentence four belongs first, so Choices B and D can be eliminated. Since sentence five is the logical choice for the last sentence, Choice C is the correct answer.

65. B Sentence three belongs first so Choices A and D can be eliminated. Sentence four belongs last, so Choice B is the correct answer. If you are having trouble with these sentence ordering questions, go back to the explained answer for question number 14 of this examination and re-read our recommended strategy for answering this type of question.

66. A Sentence five belongs first, and sentence one last. This leaves Choices A and D as possibly correct answers. Since sentence three must come after sentence two, Choice A is the correct one.

67. A Examiners quite correctly consider impediments to putting out fires as definite safety hazards. Therefore, parking by a fire hydrant is the correct answer.

68. C Sentence three should come first, so Choices A and B can be eliminated. Since sentence five occurs last, Choice C is correct.

69. A When answering questions like this, don't forget to take a quick look at the questions before starting a careful reading of the paragraph. In this way you will know what to look for when you are reading. In this question, all of the assaults occur on Charles Street between 12 A.M. and 2 A.M., as stated in Choice A.

70. A Since the Correction Supervisor requested the Police Department to make the notification, the Police Officer's actions were proper, although notifications are not always required. The key to the answer is that a request was made by the Corrections Supervisor. Choice A is correct.

71. D As stated in line one of paragraph two, Sector E is in a residential area.

72. B As stated in line six of paragraph three, Vasquez and Booker were using radio car number 1754. Car number 1749 was being used by two different officers. Be careful in cases like this to make certain you don't lose an easy point by getting the numbers in the wrong order.

73. B As stated in line 20 of paragraph two, Gloria Vargas was born on 5/15/63.

74. A As stated in lines eight and thirteen of paragraph two, an alleyway is formed by buildings 994 and 998 Jersey Street.

75. C As stated in lines two and three of paragraph two, the officers were travelling south on Jersey Street.

76. D According to Procedure four, any time more than one prisoner is being transported to different destinations an extra police officer must be assigned. Choice D describes a case involving five prisoners going to different destinations.

77. B There is a difference of about 40 pounds between suspect number two and suspect number four. For a person who is 5′6″, this is a considerable difference. Suspects one and three, however, could possibly be the same person as suspect four.

78. C The fact that the oil is spilled on a "busy" street is the key to this answer.

79. C As stated in line two of paragraph two, the officers parked their vehicle on the northwest side of 106th Street on Second Avenue.

80. D As stated in lines 18 and 19 of paragraph one, the second perpetrator is a male Caucasian (white), 6′3″, 175 lbs., with a bald head.

81. D The key that makes Choice D correct is the action verb "demanding." In the other choices the parties were either talking or discussing. The word "demanding" suggests a dispute.

82. B This is the easiest form of sentence ordering questions to answer since you do not have to do anything more than identify the first sentence. Since sentence four must come first and only Choice B lists sentence four first, Choice B must be the answer. Another hint to help you answer sentence ordering questions involves the use of pronouns and articles. When the pronouns "he," "she," "his," or "her" are used, they have to refer back to a noun which has already been used. For example, in this question, sentence one states, "He went to his parked car only to find he was blocked in." This could not be the first sentence in the report because a reader would not know who "he" was referring to in the story. However, once the person is named in the report, pronouns can be used appropriately.

83. C By requesting the ambulance, the officer complied with Procedure 2. He now has to comply with Procedure 3 which requires a notification to the Radio Dispatcher if the sick or injured person is wearing a Medic-Alert emblem, as the person in this question is. Therefore, Choice C is correct.

84. C Sentence two is obviously the first sentence in the report. This eliminates Choices B and D. Sentence three is last in both the remaining choices so we must look at the middle sentences to determine our answer. Since the interview described in sentence one must come before sentence four, Choice C is the correct answer.

85. C Sentence two should come first, so Choices A and D can be eliminated. Since sentence five describes the arrest, the final event in the report, Choice C is correct.

86. A Weight and age are the determining factors in answering this question. The suspect in report No. 2 is too short and too light, and the suspect in Report No. 3 is too old and too light.

87. B Sentence two should come first so Choices C and D can be eliminated. Since sentence three belongs after sentence five, Choice B is the answer.

88. D Firing wildly into a crowded bus stop clearly indicates a complete disregard for life.

89. D After notifying the Desk Officer and the Radio Dispatcher, the next step is to comply with Procedure two which requires asking people in the area about the child, Choice D.

90. A According to the question, the officer has already complied with Procedure 1, 1a, and 1b. The next step, required by Procedure 2, is to attach the statement of witnesses.

91. D Sentence one should come first, so Choices B and C can be eliminated. Both of the remaining choices put sentence four last so we have to go to the middle sentences. Since sentence three should immediately follow sentence one, Choice D is correct.

92. C Sentence one should come first, so Choices B and D can be eliminated. Since sentence two should come last, Choice C is the correct answer.

93. B Sentence three should come first, so Choices C and D can be eliminated. Both of the remaining choices put sentence five last, so we have to go to the middle sentences. Since sentence one must come before sentence four (the Officer must be at the scene before he can apply pressure to the wound), Choice B is the correct answer.

94. B The suspect in Incident No. 3 has a tattoo on his left arm while the suspect in Incident No. 4 has a scar on his upper right arm. This eliminates the suspect in Incident No. 3. Don't be fooled by the fact that there is no mention of a scar for the suspect in Incident No. 2. He had on a long-sleeved shirt, which would cover a scar on his upper arm.

95. C As stated in the last line of paragraph one, the dispatcher had received a call from Mr. Morris at 8 P.M.

96. A As stated in line 16 of paragraph two and in line five of the same paragraph, it was a white male who drew the gun. Notice that line five identifies the male as a white male and line sixteen states that the male drew a gun. Since there were only two robbers, and one of them was female, the male who drew the gun in line sixteen must be the white male described in line five.

97. D As stated in line ten of paragraph two, the female robber was dressed in a red T-shirt and blue dungarees.

98. C As stated in line four of paragraph two, the license plate of the car pulling away from the liquor store was 346-BYI.

99. C A fallen tree on a highway is a dangerous condition which could cause an accident. None of the other choices directly affects highway conditions.

100. B Sentence three should come first, so Choices A and D can be eliminated. Since sentence five belongs after sentence two, Choice B is correct.

101. D Sentence five should come first, so Choices A and B can be eliminated. Sentence two must come last, since the fingerprints cannot be found before the fingerprint unit specialist arrives and begins work. The correct answer is Choice D.

102. A All of the burglaries take place on Adam Street and on William Street so Choices C and D can be eliminated. Since most of the burglaries occur on Thursdays between 7 P.M. and 12 A.M., Choice A is the correct answer.

103. D Most of the assaults take place on Saturdays, between 9 P.M. and 2 A.M. Therefore Choice D is correct.

104. C An elevator door opened between floors is certainly more dangerous than any of the other conditions described in this question.

105. B Fires are always a danger.

106. A Falling bricks are obviously a danger.

107. C Remember the instructions we gave you earlier concerning these "map" questions. Use the "trace and erase" method, and be sure to consider all the choices. Choice A is wrong because going east on Clear Street after leaving Park Avenue would not bring you to your desired destination. Choice B is wrong because it requires travelling west on Clear Street, a one-way eastbound street. Choice D is wrong because it requires going south on Fir Avenue, a one-way northbound street.

108. D Make sure you use the "trace and erase" method on this one. Choice A takes a roundabout route, Choice B travels in the wrong direction on one-way streets, and Choice C lands you in the wrong place. Only Choice D takes you directly and legally to your destination.

109. C Sentence four belongs first, so Choices B and D can be eliminated. Both of the remaining choices put sentence three last, so we must look at the middle sentences. Since sentence two must come before sentence five, Choice C is correct.

110. D The injury in Choice D, a sprained wrist, is not as serious as those described in the other choices.

111. D By unloading the gun and marking the bullets, the officer complied with Procedures 1 and 2. His next step, required by Procedure 3, is to place the bullets in an envelope and seal it.

112. B Bill, the boy in Choice B, is under ten years of age and therefore a search would be required in this case.

113. B As stated in lines three and four of paragraph two, the driver of the car was wearing a blue jacket. Since lines six and seven of paragraph one state that the white male with gray hair was wearing the blue jacket, the driver of the car is a white, gray-haired man, Choice B.

114. C The incident began at 5:15 P.M. (paragraph one, line five), and twenty minutes later the male wearing the hat and sunglasses got out of the car (paragraph two, line one), and approximately five minutes later the man with the hat and sunglasses entered a building opposite the embassy (paragraph two, lines 6–11). We were told that the embassy was on Lexington Avenue in line two of paragraph one. Since 5:15 P.M. plus twenty minutes plus five minutes equals 5:40 P.M., the correct answer is Choice C.

115. D As stated in line four of paragraph one, the gray Volvo was parked on the northeast corner of 38th Street.

116. C Ken Caldwell is in violation of law because he has the loaded gun in his brother's house, not in his own home.

117. B Sentence four comes first since everything else happens after the well-dressed man leaves the bar. Therefore, Choices A and D can be eliminated. Both of the remaining choices put sentence one last so we must look at the middle sentences. Sentence three, the attack on the man, must come before sentence five, the request for the ambulance. Therefore, Choice B is the correct answer.

118. A Sentence four starts the action and must come first, so Choices B and D can be eliminated. The action described in sentence one cannot come last since it involves an approach to the bartender who later on gets knocked unconcious by a blow to the head. Sentence five, however, does represent the end of the action and should come last. Choice A is correct.

119. A Sentence three clearly begins the action, since everything happens after the male enters the bank. Sentence four comes last, since it follows all the action of the robbery. Choice A is the only one which puts sentence three first and sentence four last. Note that the words "at this time" often signal the last sentence in a report.

120. B Sentence one, which answers the "when" question, comes first, so Choices C and D can be eliminated. Sentence three comes last as the notifications can only be made after all of the information is obtained. Choice B puts sentence three last and is the correct answer.

121. A It should be clear to you that sentence three comes first since it starts the action. Choice D can be eliminated. Sentence five describes the end of the action and comes last, so Choice C can be eliminated. Sentence one describes the beginning of the dispute between the passenger and the taxi driver and must come immediately after sentence three. Therefore, Choice A is correct.

122. C All of the robberies occur on Eaton Street so Choice A can be eliminated. Most of the robberies take place on Wednesdays and Saturdays so Choice D can be eliminated. Most of the robberies take place between 7 P.M. and 11 P.M. so Choice B can be eliminated. Choice C is the best answer since it puts the patrol on the right street, on the right day of the week, at approximately the right times.

123. B/C This question had a double answer, according to the official key of the Department of Personnel. Choices A and D can be eliminated easily because they do not include any patrol on Saturdays and most of the robberies occur on Wednesdays and Saturdays. Since most of the assaults occur between 8 A.M. and 11 A.M. and between 2 P.M. and 7 P.M., and most of the robberies occur between 7 P.M. and 11 P.M. it was too difficult to determine which of the two remaining choices would be most likely to reduce the amount of assaults and robberies. Therefore, either answer was accepted.

124. D Once again, the sentence which tells "when" something happened comes first (sentence two), so Choices B and C can be eliminated. In sentence three the man is killed and he is alive in the other sentences, so sentence three must come last. The only answer with sentence two first and sentence three last is Choice D.

125. A As stated in lines one and two of paragraph one and lines three and four of paragraph two, both Officer Davies and Officers Mark and Harris are assigned to the 79th precinct, sector D. Note a favorite trick of examiners in Choices C and D. They switch the numbers from the 79th Precinct to the 97th Precinct.

126. B As stated in line two of paragraph two, two officers, Mark and Harris, responded to assist Officer Davies.

127. C As stated in lines two and three of paragraph six, the docket number is APG482/84.

128. A As stated in lines 1–3 of paragraph two, Officers Mark and Harris arrived at the scene at the same time as Officer Davies who arrived at 9:30 A.M.

129. A Carl Tyler's description is given in lines 6–8 of paragraph three.

130. B In this question, all of the choices put sentence three first. Please note that sentence three answers the "when" question. Note that sentence two must come before both sentence four and sentence five because sentence two explains that Mrs. Banks is the mother of the child. This eliminates Choices A and C. Since sentence one comes after the action is completed, it should be last as in Choice B.

131. A Sentence four starts the action and comes first, so Choices B and D can be eliminated. Remember that quite often in police work an account of how the police got involved in an incident begins a report. Sentence five marks the end of the action and comes last. Please note that sentence three must come after sentence one. Sentence three talks about "the" elderly man. This should tell you that the man must have been mentioned earlier in the report. "The" usually refers to something that has been previously mentioned. The words "a" or "an" are used when something is mentioned for the first time. For example, you would say, "There was *a* gun on the front seat of the car. *The* gun was loaded and within reach of the driver." If you reversed the words "a" and "the," the sentences would be confusing.

132. D The "when" sentence, number four, comes first, so Choices A and B can be eliminated. Sentence two must come after sentence five because sentence two mentions the results of the search made in sentence five. Therefore, Choice D is correct.

Questions 133–140 are a type known as matching sketches. They are covered in the chapter entitled "Handling Other Types of Questions."

133. B As for question 133, the correct answer is Choice B. The face in Choice A can be eliminated because the lines around the mouth are missing. Choice C can be eliminated because the shape of the jaw is different. Choice D can be eliminated because the eyes are different.

Please note that hair styles are NOT a factor in arriving at the correct answer.

134. D Eliminate Choice A because there is no cleft on the chin. Eliminate Choice B because the eyes are different. Eliminate Choice C because the ears are different.

135. A The noses are different in Choices B, C, and D.

136. B Eliminate Choices A and D because they are missing the cleft in the chin. Eliminate Choice C because of the ears.

137. C Eliminate Choice A because the mouth is wrong. Eliminate Choice B because the nose is wrong. Eliminate Choice D because the eyes are wrong.

138. D Eliminate Choice A because there is no line on the chin. Eliminate Choice B because of the shape of the ears. Eliminate Choice C because the eyes are not the same.

139. A Eliminate Choice B because the eyes are wrong. Eliminate Choice C because the mouth is wrong. Eliminate Choice D because the eyes are slightly different.

140. B Eliminate Choice A because of the shape of the jaw. Eliminate Choice C because of the cleft on the chin. Eliminate Choice D because of the different shaped mouth.

ractice Examination Three Answer Sheet

ANSWER SHEET — **THE CITY OF NEW YORK DEPARTMENT OF PERSONNEL**

DO NOT WRITE IN THIS BOX

DO NOT WRITE IN THIS BOX

T.P. NO.

YOUR SOCIAL SECURITY NO.	EXAM NO.
0 1 2 3 4 5 6 7 8 9 (each of 9 columns)	0 1 2 3 4 5 6 7 8 9 (each of 4 columns)

H	1	2
J	1	2
K	1	2
L	1	2
M	1	2
N	1	2
P	1	2
R	1	2
S	1	2
T	1	2

EXAM TITLE	TODAY'S DATE	
SCHOOL OR BUILDING	ROOM NO.	SEAT NO.

PRINT WITH SOFT PENCIL ONLY. Print, with pencil, your SOCIAL SECURITY NO. and the EXAM. NO. in the boxes at the tops of the columns. ONE NUMBER IN A BOX. In each column, darken (with pencil) the oval containing the number in the box at the top of the column. Only ONE OVAL in a COLUMN should be darkened. Then, using your pencil, print in the: Exam. Title, School or Building, Room No., Seat No., and Today's Date.

ollow the instructions given in the question booklet. Mark nothing but your answers in the ovals below.

AMPLE QUESTION: When we add 5 and 3 we get: (A) 11 (B) 9 (C) 8 (D) 2. Since the answer is 8, your answer should be marked like this: (A) (B) ● (D)

ARNING: Be sure that the oval you fill is in the row numbered the same as the question you are answering. Use a No. 2 pencil (soft pencil).

E SURE YOUR PENCIL MARKS ARE HEAVY AND BLACK. ERASE COMPLETELY ANY ANSWER YOU WISH TO CHANGE.

DO NOT make stray pencil dots, dashes or marks ANYPLACE on this SHEET.

START HERE

1 A B C D	2 A B C D	3 A B C D	4 A B C D	5 A B C D	6 A B C D
7 A B C D	8 A B C D	9 A B C D	10 A B C D	11 A B C D	12 A B C D
13 A B C D	14 A B C D	15 A B C D	16 A B C D	17 A B C D	18 A B C D
19 A B C D	20 A B C D	21 A B C D	22 A B C D	23 A B C D	24 A B C D
25 A B C D	26 A B C D	27 A B C D	28 A B C D	29 A B C D	30 A B C D
31 A B C D	32 A B C D	33 A B C D	34 A B C D	35 A B C D	36 A B C D
37 A B C D	38 A B C D	39 A B C D	40 A B C D	41 A B C D	42 A B C D
43 A B C D	44 A B C D	45 A B C D	46 A B C D	47 A B C D	48 A B C D
49 A B C D	50 A B C D	51 A B C D	52 A B C D	53 A B C D	54 A B C D
55 A B C D	56 A B C D	57 A B C D	58 A B C D	59 A B C D	60 A B C D
61 A B C D	62 A B C D	63 A B C D	64 A B C D	65 A B C D	66 A B C D
67 A B C D	68 A B C D	69 A B C D	70 A B C D	71 A B C D	72 A B C D
73 A B C D	74 A B C D	75 A B C D	76 A B C D	77 A B C D	78 A B C D
79 A B C D	80 A B C D	81 A B C D	82 A B C D	83 A B C D	84 A B C D
85 A B C D	86 A B C D	87 A B C D	88 A B C D	89 A B C D	90 A B C D
91 A B C D	92 A B C D	93 A B C D	94 A B C D	95 A B C D	96 A B C D
97 A B C D	98 A B C D	99 A B C D	100 A B C D	101 A B C D	102 A B C D
103 A B C D	104 A B C D	105 A B C D	106 A B C D	107 A B C D	108 A B C D
109 A B C D	110 A B C D	111 A B C D	112 A B C D	113 A B C D	114 A B C D
115 A B C D	116 A B C D	117 A B C D	118 A B C D	119 A B C D	120 A B C D
121 A B C D	122 A B C D	123 A B C D	124 A B C D	125 A B C D	126 A B C D
127 A B C D	128 A B C D	129 A B C D	130 A B C D	131 A B C D	132 A B C D
133 A B C D	134 A B C D	135 A B C D	136 A B C D	137 A B C D	138 A B C D
139 A B C D	140 A B C D	141 A B C D	142 A B C D	143 A B C D	144 A B C D
145 A B C D	146 A B C D	147 A B C D	148 A B C D	149 A B C D	150 A B C D

CONFIDENTIAL QUESTIONNAIRE: **Completion of this information is voluntary.** The Department of Personnel, pursuant to guidelines issued by the United States Equal Employment Opportunity Commission and provisions of the State Human Rights Law, requests that all candidates complete the section below. We request your cooperation in completing this Questionnaire section accurately. Answers to these questions will be used to conduct studies to identify and resolve possible problems in recruitment and testing for the purpose of insuring equal opportunity for employment in the Civil Service. Please darken one oval for each of the five items below.

ANSWER QUESTION 2 ON THE BASIS OF THE FOLLOWING INFORMATION: CHOOSING ONLY ONE GENERAL CATEGORY.
BLACK: African descent, Jamaican, Trinidadian, West Indian.
WHITE: Caucasian or white whose ancestors came from Europe or Western Asia, including Pakistan or East India.
SPANISH SURNAMED: Mexican, Puerto Rican, Cuban, Latin American, or Spanish descent.
AMERICAN INDIAN: American Indian or member of an Indian tribe.
ASIAN AMERICAN: Japanese, Chinese, Korean, or Filipino descent.
OTHER: Aleut, Eskimo, Malayan, Thai, or other not covered by above categories.

1. SEX — MALE / FEMALE

2. To which one of the following groups do you belong? — BLACK / WHITE / SPANISH SURNAMED / AMERICAN INDIAN / ASIAN AMERICAN / OTHER

3. MARK HIGHEST diploma or degree received. — HIGH SCHOOL DIPLOMA / ASSOCIATE DEGREE / BACCALAUREATE DEGREE / MASTERS DEGREE / DOCTORS DEGREE

4. If no diploma above, mark highest grade completed. — 6 / 7 / 8 / 9 / 10 / 11 / 12

5. If a diploma but no degree received, mark number of years of college completed. — 1 / 2 / 3 / 4

Misc. 1088N (3-81)

CHAPTER 15

Practice Examination Three

This chapter includes the last of three practice examinations that you will be taking. Like Practice Examination Two, this test is an official one previously administered by the NYCPD. By this time you should have taken the practice examinations in Chapters 13 and 14, and you should have seen steady improvement. If not, be sure to give a careful look at the Diagnostic Procedure for each of the previous examinations which you took and analyze your weaknesses. Then, spend time studying all those review chapters where you have gotten questions wrong. Only then should you take this last examination. *When you have taken this final examination, you should be prepared to take most major police officer examinations, including those for Transit and Housing Police administered in many cities.*

Be sure to take Practice Examination Three in one sitting. You will then become accustomed to concentrating for a period of 4½ hours, which is the length of time allowed for the examination. Be sure to review the test-taking strategy outlined in Chapter 2 before taking this practice examination.

Before You Take the Examination

When you begin this examination, look first at the material in the "Memory Booklet." After reading the material for the time specified, continue to the "Test Booklet" and do not look back at the material marked "Memory Booklet." Then continue with the rest of the test.

Remember to read each question and related material carefully before choosing your answers. Select the choice you believe to be the most correct, and mark your answer on the Answer Sheet provided at the beginning of this chapter. The Answer Key, Diagnostic Procedure, and Answer Explanations appear at the end of this chapter. (Be sure to gauge your time, averaging no more than 1½ to 2 minutes per question.)

Note that we have included a copy of the official Instruction Booklet on pages 521 to 525 so that you can become familiar with normal test procedures. We have not attempted to include all accompanying forms, as test instructions do change occasionally.

City of New York
Department of Personnel

EXAMINATION NO. 5114
POLICE OFFICER SERIES

Soc. Sec. No. ______
Seat No. ______
Room No. ______
School ______

Written Test: 70th Percentile Required, Weight 100

October 18, 1986

TEST INSTRUCTIONS FOR CANDIDATES—READ NOW

GENERAL INFORMATION Read these TEST INSTRUCTIONS FOR CANDIDATES and fill out the information requested at the top of this booklet. Following are explanations of the information requested.

The Soc. Sec. No. is your Social Security Number as shown on you admission card which you brought with you today. If your Social Security Number is not correct on your admission card, you must draw a line through the incorrect number, and write your correct Social Security Number on the card. Use your correct Social Security Number on the fingerprint card and the Answer Sheet. Be sure to fill out the pink correction form (DP-148) if your Social Security Number is incorrect, so that the correction can be taken care of after the test.

Your Seat No. is the number shown on the sheet of scrap paper on your desk.

Your Room No. and School are written on the blackboard.

THE FORMS: YOU MUST NOW FILL OUT YOUR FINGERPRINT CARD AND ANSWER SHEET AS EXPLAINED BELOW. Use pencil only.

Fingerprint Card: Print in pencil all information requested including your Social Security Number. Your fingerprints will be taken approximately 15 minutes after the seventh signal.

Answer Sheet: Print in pencil all the information requested on the Answer Sheet including your Social Security No., and the Exam. No. 5114 in the boxes at the top of the columns, ONE NUMBER IN A BOX. In each column, blacken (with pencil) the oval containing the number in the box at the top of the column; only ONE OVAL in a COLUMN should be blackened. Then, using your pencil, print the Exam. Title, School or Building, Room No., Seat No., and Today's Date in the appropriate spaces.

After filling in this information at the top of the Answer Sheet, please read the Confidential Questionnaire at the bottom of the Answer Sheet, and answer the questions accurately.

TEST INSTRUCTIONS (Continued)

After answering the Confidential Questionnaire, please complete the following survey questions.

LANGUAGE SURVEY The eligible list resulting from this examination may be selectively certified to fill vacancies which require a working knowledge of Spanish, Cantonese, or another language.

Only those candidates who possess the minimum requirements and are placed on the eligible list may be permitted to take a language proficiency test. Results of the language proficiency test will have no bearing on list standing.

In order to take a qualifying oral test to demonstrate your ability to speak and understand Spanish, blacken Item Number 148, option A.

In order to take a qualifying oral test to demonstrate your ability to speak and understand Cantonese, blacken Item Number 149, option A.

If you are interested in taking a qualifying oral test to demonstrate your ability to speak and understand any other language, blacken Item Number 150, option A.

RECRUITMENT SURVEY Please read the Recruitment Survey, and place your answers on the form attached to the questionnaire.

EIGHT SIGNALS WILL BE USED DURING THIS TEST. Following is an explanation of these signals.

FIRST SIGNAL: Memory Booklet is distributed. DO NOT OPEN THE BOOKLET.

SECOND SIGNAL: OPEN MEMORY BOOKLET. You will be given five minutes to try to remember as many details about the first scene as you can. You may not write or make any notes during this time. DO NOT TURN TO ANY OTHER PAGE DURING THIS TIME.

THIRD SIGNAL: TURN TO THE NEXT PAGE. DO NOT TURN TO ANY OTHER PAGE DURING THIS TIME.

FOURTH SIGNAL: TURN TO THE NEXT PAGE. Answer the seven questions on the Answer Sheet. You will have five minutes to complete this section. DO NOT TURN TO ANY OTHER PAGE DURING THIS TIME. You may wish to record your answers next to each question on the page.

TEST INSTRUCTIONS (Continued)

FIFTH SIGNAL: TURN TO THE NEXT SCENE. You will be given five minutes to try to remember as many details about the second scene as you can. You may not write or make any notes during this time. DO NOT TURN TO ANY OTHER PAGE DURING THIS TIME.

SIXTH SIGNAL: CLOSE THE MEMORY BOOKLET. It will be collected by the monitor. The Test Booklet will then be distributed. You may not write or make any notes during this time. DO NOT OPEN THE TEST BOOKLET.

SEVENTH SIGNAL: OPEN THE TEST BOOKLET and begin work. Finish the Memory questions first and then go on to the other questions. This test consists of 150 questions. After you finish the Memory questions check to make sure that the Test Booklet goes up to and includes question 140, and is not defective. You will have 4½ hours from this signal to complete all the questions. YOU WILL BE FINGERPRINTED DURING THIS PERIOD.

EIGHTH SIGNAL: END OF TEST. STOP ALL WORK. If you finish before this signal and wish to leave, raise you hand.

ANYONE DISOBEYING ANY OF THESE INSTRUCTIONS MAY BE DISQUALIFIED—THAT IS, YOU MAY RECEIVE A SCORE OF ZERO FOR THE ENTIRE TEST!

DIRECTIONS FOR ANSWERING QUESTIONS: Answer all the questions on the Answer Sheet before the Eighth Signal is given. ONLY YOUR ANSWER SHEET WILL BE MARKED. For future reference, you should also record your answers in your Test Booklet before the end of the test and in your Memory Booklet before the Fifth Signal. Use a soft pencil (No. 2) to mark your answers. If you want to change an answer, erase it and then mark your new answer. Do not make stray pencil dots, dashes or marks any place on the Answer Sheet. DO NOT fold, roll or tear the Answer Sheet.

Here is a sample of how to mark your answers:

SAMPLE O: When we add 5 and 3, we get

(A) 11 (B) 9 (C) 8 (D) 2

Since the answer is 8, your Answer Sheet is marked like this:

SAMPLE O: (A) (B) (■) (D)

WARNING: You are not allowed to copy answers from anyone, or to use books or notes. It is against the law to take the test for somebody else or to let somebody else take the test for you. There is to be NO SMOKING anywhere in the building.

LEAVING: After the test starts, candidates may not leave the building until after they are fingerprinted. No one may come in after 11:30 A.M. During the test, you may not leave the room unless accompanied by a monitor. If you want to drop out of the test and not have your answers marked, write "I withdraw" on your Answer Sheet and sign your name.

MEDICAL AND PHYSICAL STANDARDS: Eligibles must meet the medical and physical fitness standards to be established and posted on the Department of Personnel Bulletin Board at 49 Thomas Street, New York, N.Y., 10013. Candidates must pass a qualifying physical fitness test and a qualifying medical test. Eligibles will be rejected for any medical, psychiatric, or physical impairment which impairs their ability to perform the duties of Police Officer. Periodic reexaminations of employees in these titles will be required in accordance with Executive Order No. 31, dated October 10, 1966.

There are no height requirements.

Medical evidence to allow participation in the physical fitness test may be required, and the Department of Personnel reserves the right to exclude from the physical fitness test any eligibles who, upon examination of such evidence, are apparently medically unfit. Eligibles will take the physical fitness test at their own risk of injury, although every effort will be made to safeguard them.

CHARACTER: Proof of good character will be an absolute prerequisite to appointment.

The following are among the factors which would ordinarily be cause for disqualification: (a) conviction for an offense, the nature of which indicates lack of good moral character or disposition toward violence or disorder; (b) repeated convictions for offenses, where such convictions indicate a disrespect for the law; (c) repeated discharges from employment, where such discharges indicate poor performance or inability to adjust to discipline. In accordance with provisions of the law, persons convicted of a felony or receiving a dishonorable discharge from the Armed Forces are not eligible for appointment to this position. Persons convicted of petit larceny may be declared ineligible for appointment.

INVESTIGATION: At the time of appointment and at the time of investigation, candidates must present all the official documents and proof required to qualify. At the time of investigation, candidates will be required to present proof of date of birth by transcript of record from the Bureau of Vital Statistics or other satisfactory evidence. Proof of military service and similar documents may be required. Failure to present required documents, including proof of educational or license requirements, will result in disqualification for appointment or a direction to terminate services.

Any willful misstatement will be cause for disqualification.

Take This Booklet With You.

Certificate of Attendance
Department of Personnel
October 18, 1986

Soc. Sec. No. __________
Room No. ____________
Seat No. _____________
School _______________

This is to certify that ____________________________ took the examination for Police Officer Series, Exam No. 5114 on this date. The candidate was summoned for 10:30 A.M. and released by ___________.

____
Room Monitor

Date ____________

DEPARTMENT OF PERSONNEL

Social Security No. ______________
Room No. ______________
Seat No. ______________
School ______________

First Memory Booklet

POLICE OFFICER SERIES

October 18, 1986

EXAMINATION NO. 5114

DO NOT OPEN THIS BOOKLET UNTIL THE SECOND SIGNAL IS GIVEN!

Write your Social Security Number, Room Number, Seat Number and School in the appropriate spaces at the top of this page.

You must follow the instructions found on the TEST INSTRUCTION SHEET.

ANYONE DISOBEYING ANY OF THE INSTRUCTIONS FOUND ON THE TEST INSTRUCTION SHEET MAY BE DISQUALIFIED—RECEIVE A ZERO ON THE ENTIRE TEST.

This booklet contains one scene. Try to remember as many details in the scene as you can. You should pay equal attention both to objects and to people shown in the scene.

DO NOT WRITE OR MAKE ANY NOTES WHILE STUDYING THE SCENE.

DO NOT OPEN THIS BOOKLET UNTIL THE SECOND SIGNAL IS GIVEN!

The New York City Department of Personnel makes no commitment, and no implication is to be drawn, as to the content, style, or format of any future examination for the position of Police Officer.

ARMY RECRUITING CENTER
LAW OFFICE
LAWYER DAN COHAN
BIL LIAR DS
CLOSED
POOL
TANKER'S BAR
BODEGA 705
CHECKS CASHED
SHOES
NO-PARKING
LUNCH
Audio Shack
EATS
WAIK
SALE
25
31
BEER
B TRAIN DOWN TOWN

NO
TURN
VE. C
PARK
ITY BANK
33
12:00
DANCE STUDIO
SUPER MARKET
Deli – Fish
KATS
848
LOTTO-CANDY-NEWSPAPERS-
TUES. JUNE 22 LOTTO NUMBER
EAGLES
HERALD
U.S. MAIL
BILL
LAST PICK UP 5:30PM
MAIL

KEEP THIS BOOKLET CLOSED

DEPARTMENT OF PERSONNEL

Social Security No. ________________
Room No. ________________
Seat No. ________________
School ________________

Second Memory Booklet

POLICE OFFICER SERIES

October 18, 1986

EXAMINATION NO. 5114

DO NOT OPEN THIS BOOKLET UNTIL THE FOURTH SIGNAL IS GIVEN!

Write your Social Security Number, Room Number, Seat Number and School in the appropriate spaces at the top of this page.

You must follow the instructions found on the TEST INSTRUCTION SHEET.

ANYONE DISOBEYING ANY OF THE INSTRUCTIONS FOUND ON THE TEST INSTRUCTION SHEET MAY BE DISQUALIFIED—RECEIVE A ZERO ON THE ENTIRE TEST.

This booklet contains Questions 1 through 6, which are based on Scene 1 as shown in the First Memory Booklet. Answer Questions 1 through 6 after the fourth signal. At the FIFTH SIGNAL, you should turn to Scene 2. Try to remember as many details in the scene as you can. You should pay equal attention both to objects and to people shown in the scene.

DO NOT OPEN THIS BOOKLET UNTIL THE FOURTH SIGNAL IS GIVEN!

Answer questions 1 through 6 solely on the basis of sketch number 1.

1. What does the sign at the subway entrance say?

(A) Uptown 3
(B) Downtown 1
(C) Uptown A
(D) Downtown B.

2. At which one of the following times can a legal left turn be made from Avenue C onto Park?

(A) 8:30 A.M. Mondays
(B) 9:30 A.M. Tuesdays
(C) 12:00 P.M. Wednesdays
(D) 1:00 P.M. Thursdays.

3. Which one of the following persons is wearing glasses?

(A) The postal employee
(B) The woman pushing the stroller
(C) The newspaper vendor
(D) The man wearing baseball cap and sneakers.

4. What is the plate number on the bus?

(A) 313 **(B)** 530 **(C)** 731 **(D)** 848.

5. What is the last pick up time shown on the mailbox?

(A) 4:30 P.M. **(B)** 5:00 P.M. **(C)** 5:30 P.M. **(D)** 6:00 P.M.

6. What is the address of the bank?

(A) 33 Park
(B) 25 Avenue C
(C) 33 Avenue C
(D) 25 Park.

DO NOT TURN PAGE UNTIL NEXT SIGNAL

TURN TO NEXT PAGE FOR SECOND SCENE AFTER 5TH SIGNAL

VIDEO KING
RECORDS
Entrance Around The Corner 1032 Fulton St.
487
VARIETY STORE
MOE'S DISCOUNTS
SEAF
SALE
SALE
SALE
SALE
Phone
483-
CLOSED SATURDAY
MANY ITEMS UNDER $1.98
JETS
OPEN
Winston

MANNY'S
RESTAURANT
487
D
BAR
STEAKS
487
open
Ris
PHOTO
1 HOUR
ENLARGEMENTS
489
FRANKFURTERS
HOT SAUSAGE
15

KEEP THIS BOOKLET CLOSED

DEPARTMENT OF PERSONNEL

Social Security No. ____________________
Room No. ____________________
Seat No. ____________________

Question Booklet

October 18, 1986

POLICE OFFICER SERIES

EXAMINATION NO. 5114

Written Test: Weight 100

Time Allowed: 5 Hours

DO NOT OPEN THIS BOOKLET UNTIL THE SEVENTH SIGNAL IS GIVEN!

Record your answers on the official Answer Sheet before the last signal. If you wish, you may also record your answers in the Question Booklet before the last signal is given.

This Question Booklet contains procedures and definitions which are to be used to answer certain questions. These procedures and definitions are not necessarily those of the New York City Police Department. However, you are to answer these questions solely on the basis of the material given.

After the seventh signal is given, open this Question Booklet and begin work. You will have 5 hours to complete this test.

You may make notes in this booklet and use the scrap paper on your desk. If you need additional scrap paper, ask the monitor.

Remember, only your official Answer Sheet will be rated, so be sure to mark all your answers on the official Answer Sheet before the eighth signal. No additional time will be given for marking your answers after the test has ended.

DO NOT OPEN THIS BOOKLET UNTIL THE SEVENTH SIGNAL IS GIVEN!

Answer questions 7 through 12 solely on the basis of sketch number 2.

7. On what day is the Variety Store closed?

(A) Friday (B) Saturday (C) Sunday (D) Monday.

8. In front of which building is a crime taking place?

(A) 483 (B) 487 (C) 489 (D) 498.

9. Which one of the following best describes the perpetrator?

(A) White male, plaid jacket, black pants
(B) Black male, white jacket, white pants
(C) White male, black jacket, white pants
(D) Black male, plaid jacket, black pants.

10. Of the following, it appears that the victim of the crime is

(A) standing by the telephone booth
(B) buying a hot dog
(C) reading a newspaper
(D) lighting a cigarette.

11. Which one of the following best describes the victim?

(A) Male white, striped pants, white jacket, black shoes
(B) Male black, white pants, striped jacket, white shoes
(C) Male white, white pants, black jacket, black shoes
(D) Male black, black jacket, white pants, white shoes.

12. The woman who is closest to the crime is wearing

(A) a dress and carrying a pocketbook
(B) striped pants and eating a hot dog
(C) shorts and standing by the phone booth
(D) a skirt and holding a cigarette.

Please check your Answer Sheet to make sure that your have written in and blackened your Social Security number correctly. If you have not yet written in and blackened your Social Security number, please do so immediately. If you have incorrectly written in or blackened your Social Security number, please correct the mistake immediately. Failure to correctly blacken your Social Security number may result in your Answer Sheet NOT being rated.

13. Police Officer Daniels has just finished investigating a report of criminal mischief and has obtained the following information:

Place of Occurrence: In front of victim's residence
Time of Occurrence: Between 5:15 A.M. and 5:30 A.M.
Victim: Carl Burns, of 1856 Lenox Street, owner of vehicle
Crime: Criminal Mischief
Damage: Paint poured onto his vehicle.

Officer Daniels is preparing a report on the incident. Which one of the following expresses the above information most clearly and accurately?

(A) While parked in front of his residence, Carl Burns stated between 5:15 A.M. and 5:30 A.M., that paint was poured onto his vehicle at 1856 Lenox Street.
(B) Carl Burns, of 1865 Lenox Street, stated that between 5:15 A.M. and 5:30 A.M., paint was poured onto his vehicle while it was parked in front of his residence.
(C) Between 5:15 A.M. and 5:30 A.M., Carl Burns of 1865 Lenox Street stated, while parked in front of his residence, that paint was poured on his vehicle.
(D) Carl Burns between 5:15 A.M. and 5:30 A.M. while parked at 1865 Lenox Street, his residence, stated that paint was poured onto his vehicle.

14. Police Officer Johnson arrives at the National Savings Bank five minutes after it has been robbed at gunpoint. The following are details provided by eyewitnesses:

Suspect

Sex: Male
Ethnicity: White
Height: 5′10″ to 6′2″
Weight: 180 lbs. to 190 lbs.
Hair Color: blonde
Clothing: black jacket, blue dungarees
Weapon: .45 caliber revolver

Officer Johnson is completing a report on the incident. Which one of the following expresses the above information most clearly and accurately?

(A) A White male weighing 180–190 lbs. robbed the National Savings Bank. He was White with a black jacket with blonde hair, is 5′10″ to 6′2″, and blue dungarees. The robber was armed with a .45 caliber revolver.
(B) A White male weighing around 180 or 190 lbs. was wearing a black jacket and blue dungarees. He had blonde hair and had

a .45 caliber revolver, and was 5′10″ to 6′2″. He robbed the National Savings Bank.

(C) A White male who was 5′10″ to 6′2″ and was weighing 180 to 190 lbs., and has blonde hair and wearing blue dungarees and a black jacket with a revolver, robbed the National Savings Bank.

(D) A White male armed with a .45 caliber revolver robbed the National Savings Bank. The robber was described as being between 180–190 lbs., 5′10″ to 6′2″, with blonde hair. He was wearing a black jacket and blue dungarees.

15. Police Officers may have to close an area to traffic in certain situations, such as an accident, fire, or explosion. In which one of the following situations would it be most appropriate for an Officer to close off traffic?

(A) An airplane skids off the runway onto the air field, causing minor injuries to passengers.

(B) A car hits a tree late at night on a dead-end street, resulting in a broken headlight.

(C) A manhole cover explodes on a street in the afternoon, causing damage to nearby buildings.

(D) A fire breaks out on a boat while it is anchored in the middle of the harbor.

16. Police Officer Engle is completing a Complaint Report of a burglary which occurred at Monty's Bar. The following five sentences will be included in the Complaint Report:

1. The owner said that approximately $600 was taken along with eight bottles of expensive brandy.
2. The burglar apparently gained entry to the bar through the window and exited through the front door.
3. When Mr. Barrett returned to reopen the bar at 1:00 P.M., he found the front door open and items thrown all over the bar.
4. Mr. Barrett, the owner of Monty's Bar, said he closed the bar at 4:00 A.M. and locked all the doors.
5. After interviewing the owner, I conducted a search of the bar and found that a window in the back of the bar was broken.

The most logical order for the above sentences to appear in the report is

(A) 2, 4, 3, 5, 1 **(C)** 4, 2, 3, 1, 5
(B) 4, 3, 1, 5, 2 **(D)** 2, 5, 4, 3, 1.

Answer question 17 solely on the basis of the following information.

Reckless endangerment—the crime of reckless endangerment occurs when one engages in conduct which creates a substantial risk of serious physical injury to another person, in that one is aware of the risk of such conduct but continues anyway.

17. Which one of the following is the best example of reckless endangerment?

(A) Bill, a construction worker on a skyscraper, walks on a narrow beam hundreds of feet above the ground, even though if he falls he will probably die.
(B) Jason, a security guard in a warehouse, fires his revolver at an armed robber who is shooting at him, but misses and nearly hits a woman who has just walked in.
(C) George, who used to be an acrobat, walks on the ledge of a roof on his hands and does cartwheels in order to win a bet.
(D) John, while working on a scaffold, removes broken bricks from a building and throws them to the ground even though people on the street below are shouting that he could hurt someone.

Answer questions 18 through 20 solely on the basis of the following passage.

Police Officers Gillespie and Henderson, working an 8:00 A.M. to 4:00 P.M. shift in the 87th Precinct, receive a radio call to investigate a theft from an automobile at 870 Bayard Street. Officer Gillespie explains to his partner, who is new to the precinct, that the precinct receives a lot of calls around 9:30 A.M. regarding thefts from automobiles. This occurs because people come out at that time to move their cars due to the 10:30 A.M.—1:30 P.M. alternate side parking regulations.

Turning onto Bayard Street, the Officers notice that there are six automobiles parked on the south side of the street. Officer Gillespie pulls into a spot behind the last car, in front of 871 Bayard Street and is greeted by Mrs. Blount. She tells the Officers that at 9:15 A.M. she discovered that the right front vent window of her green 1982 Pontiac had been smashed and her car radio worth $500 had been stolen. She mentions that the cars of two of her neighbors, Mr. Abernathy and Pete Shaw, were also broken into.

Mr. Abernathy, who lives at 870 Bayard Street, comes out of his home and walks across the street to speak to the Officers. As Officer Henderson takes Mrs. Blount's report, Officer Gillespie walks with Mr. Abernathy to his car to fill out a report. Mr. Abernathy saw a white male trying to break into his silver-gray Le Sabre at 11:05 on the previous night. Mr. Abernathy called the police but the Officers who responded were unable to complete the report because they received a radio call to respond to an assault in progress. Officer Gillespie takes Mr. Abernathy's report and then rejoins his partner, who is already completing a report on Pete Shaw's automobile. Having been on the scene for an hour and ten minutes, they notice it is now 10:50 A.M. and all of the vehicles have been removed except those whose owners have just given reports.

18. Officer Henderson completed reports on

(A) Mrs. Blount and Mr. Abernathy
(B) Mr. Abernathy and Pete Shaw
(C) Mrs. Blount and Pete Shaw
(D) Mr. Abernathy, Pete Shaw, and Mrs. Blount.

19. Which side of Bayard Street did Mr. Abernathy live on?

(A) north **(B)** south **(C)** east **(D)** west.

20. When Officers Gillespie and Henderson file the reports, for which person will the date of the crime be different from the others?

(A) Mrs. Blount
(B) Mr. Abernathy
(C) Mr. Shaw
(D) Mr. Blount.

Answer question 21 solely on the basis of the following information.

Police Officers are required to handle calls regarding abused children. Officers handling cases of abused children should do the following in the order given:

1. Remove the child from the home with consent of the parents if continued presence may cause an immediate danger to the child's life or health.
2. Remove the child from home without the parents' consent if continued presence may cause an immediate danger to the child's life or health, and there is insufficient time to apply for a court order as directed by the Patrol Supervisor.
3. Bring child to precinct unless immediate hospitalization is necessary.
4. Prepare necessary reports.
5. Telephone facts to the Bureau of Child Welfare.
6. Obtain serial number and enter it on pertinent reports.
7. Telephone facts to the Society for the Prevention of Cruelty to Children.
8. Inform parents or guardian to contact the Department of Social Services caseworker.

21. Police Officers Gray and Turner are assigned to a radio patrol car. At approximately 3:30 P.M., they are dispatched to 305 Maplewood Terrace to handle an abused child case. Upon their arrival, the Officers are informed by Mrs. Smith that her husband continually beats her son for no apparent reason. She further states that her husband is extremely violent and is a heavy drinker. The Officers complete all steps up to and including the preparation of the necessary reports. Officers Gray and Turner should next

(A) inform the parents to contact the Department of Social Services caseworker
(B) apply for a court order after conferring with the Patrol Supervisor
(C) telephone the facts to the Society for the Prevention of Cruelty to Children
(D) telephone the facts to the Bureau of Child Welfare.

Answer question 22 solely on the basis of the following information.

Police Officers often have to handle emotionally disturbed persons who may be a danger to others.

22. At 10:30 P.M., while patrolling the Times Square area, Police Officer Larsen observes four emotionally disturbed persons within a three-block radius. Which one of the following would most likely present the greatest problem for Officer Larsen?

(A) An elderly woman is chanting loudly to people waiting in line for a movie.
(B) A youth is quickly pacing back and forth while cursing at people waiting for a bus.
(C) A woman is standing on a corner arguing loudly with herself about her son.
(D) A man is preaching to a crowd about the world coming to an end.

23. While on patrol Police Officer Rogers is approached by Terry Conyers, a young woman whose pocketbook has been stolen. Ms. Conyers tells Officer Rogers that the following items were in her pocketbook at the time it was taken:

–	4 Traveler's checks, each valued at	$20.00
–	3 Traveler's checks, each valued at	$25.00
–	Cash	$212.00
–	1 wedding band valued at	$450.00

Officer Rogers is preparing a Complaint Report on the robbery. Which one of the following is the total value of the property and cash taken from Ms. Conyers?

(A) $707.00 **(B)** $807.00 **(C)** $817.00 **(D)** $837.00.

24. While on patrol Police Officer Scott is dispatched to respond to a reported burglary. Two burglars entered the home of Mr. and Mrs. Walker and stole the following items:

–	3 watches valued at	$65.00 each
–	1 VCR valued at	$340.00
–	1 television set valued at	$420.00

Officer Scott is preparing a Complaint Report on the burglary. Which one of the following is the total value of the property stolen?

(A) $707.00 **(B)** $825.00 **(C)** $920.00 **(D)** $955.00.

25. While on patrol Police Officer Smith is dispatched to investigate a grand larceny. Deborah Paisley, a businesswoman, reports that her 1986 Porsche was broken into. The following items were taken:

–	1 car phone valued at	$2950.00
–	1 car stereo system valued at	$1060.00

Ms. Paisley's attache case valued at $200.00, was also taken from the car in the incident. The attache case contained two new solid gold pens valued at $970.00 each.

Officer Smith is completing a Complaint Report. Which one of the following is the total dollar value of the property stolen from Ms. Paisley's car?

(A) $5180.00 **(B)** $5980.00 **(C)** $6040.00 **(D)** $6150.00.

Answer questions 26 through 27 solely on the basis of the following map. The flow of traffic is indicated by the arrows. If there is only one arrow shown, then traffic flows only in the direction indicated by the arrow. If there are two arrows shown, then traffic flows in both directions. You must follow the flow of traffic.

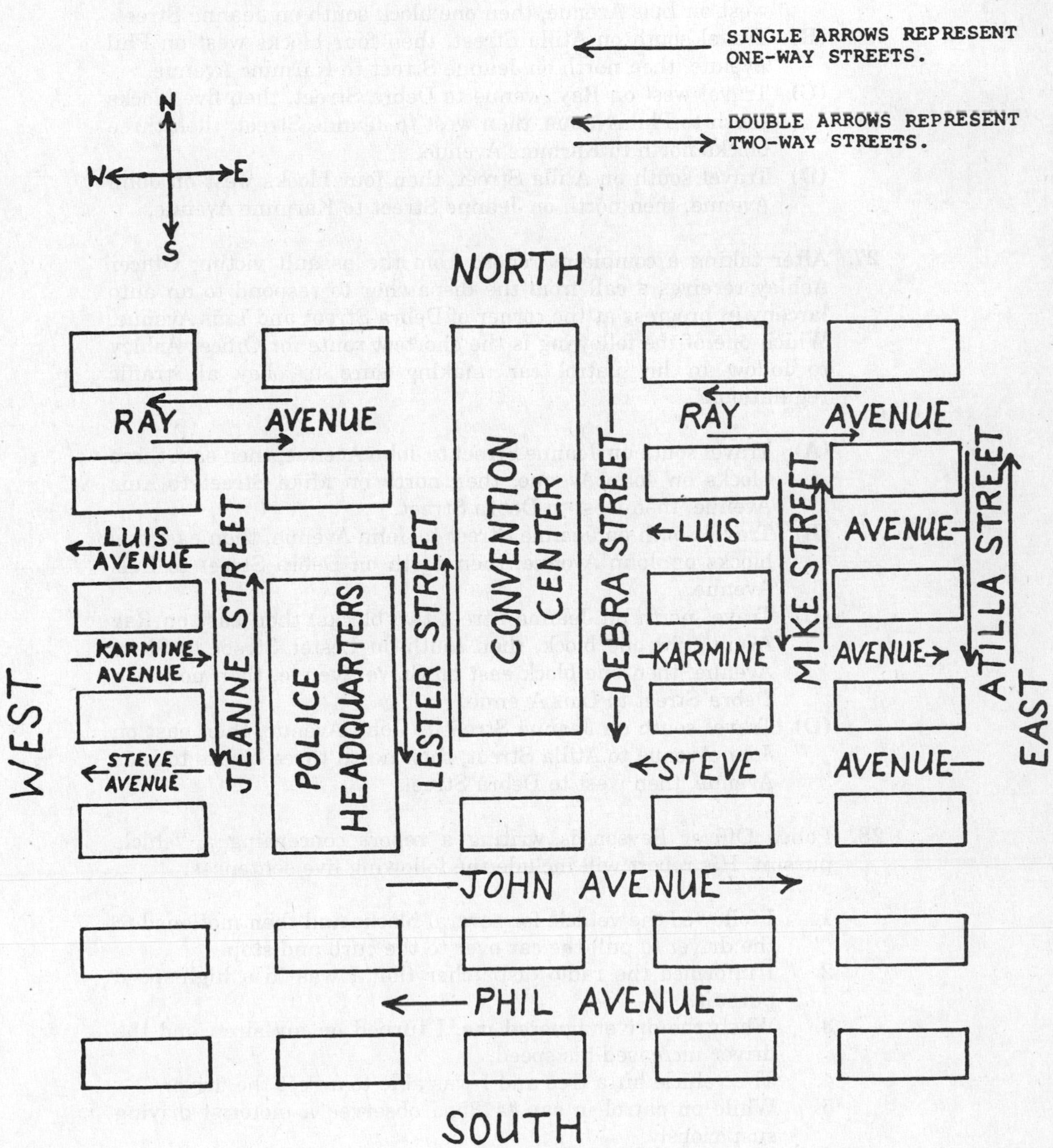

26. While in a patrol car located at Ray Avenue and Atilla Street, Police Officer Ashley receives a call from the dispatcher to respond to an assault at Jeanne Street and Karmine Avenue. Which one of the following is the shortest route for Officer Ashley to follow in his patrol car, making sure to obey all traffic regulations?

(A) Travel south on Atilla Street, west on Luis Avenue, south on Debra Street, west on Steve Avenue, north on Lester Street, west on Luis Avenue, then one block south on Jeanne Street.
(B) Travel south on Atilla Street, then four blocks west on Phil Avenue, then north on Jeanne Street to Karmine Avenue.
(C) Travel west on Ray Avenue to Debra Street, then five blocks south to Phil Avenue, then west to Jeanne Street, then three blocks north to Karmine Avenue.
(D) Travel south on Atilla Street, then four blocks west on John Avenue, then north on Jeanne Street to Karmine Avenue.

27. After taking a complaint report from the assault victim, Officer Ashley receives a call from the dispatcher to respond to an auto larceny in progress at the corner of Debra Street and Luis Avenue. Which one of the following is the shortest route for Officer Ashley to follow in his patrol car, making sure to obey all traffic regulations?

(A) Travel south on Jeanne Street to John Avenue, then east three blocks on John Avenue, then north on Mike Street to Luis Avenue, then west to Debra Street.
(B) Travel south on Jeanne Street to John Avenue, then east two blocks on John Avenue, then north on Debra Street to Luis Avenue.
(C) Travel north on Jeanne Street two blocks, then east on Ray Avenue for one block, then south on Lester Street to Steve Avenue, then one block east on Steve Avenue, then north on Debra Street to Luis Avenue.
(D) Travel south on Jeanne Street to John Avenue, then east on John Avenue to Atilla Street, then north three blocks to Luis Avenue, then west to Debra Street.

28. Police Officer Revson is writing a report concerning a vehicle pursuit. His report will include the following five sentences:

1. I followed the vehicle for several blocks and then motioned to the driver to pull the car over to the curb and stop.
2. I informed the radio dispatcher that I was in a high-speed pursuit.
3. When the driver ignored me, I turned on my siren and the driver increased his speed.
4. The vehicle hit a tree and I was able to arrest the driver.
5. While on patrol in car #4135, I observed a motorist driving suspiciously.

The most logical order for the above sentences to appear in the report is

(A) 5, 1, 3, 2, 4
(B) 2, 5, 3, 1, 4
(C) 5, 1, 2, 4, 3
(D) 2, 1, 5, 4, 3.

29. Police Officer Grundig is writing a Complaint Report regarding a burglary and assault case. Officer Grundig has obtained the following facts:

Place of Occurrence: 2244 Clark Street
Victim: Mrs. Willis
Suspect: Mr. Willis; Victim's ex-husband
Complaint: Unlawful entry, head injury inflicted with a bat.

Officer Grundig is completing a report on the incident. Which one of the following expresses the above information most clearly and accurately?

(A) He had no permission or authority to do so and it caused her head injuries, when Mr. Willis entered his ex-wife's premises. Mrs. Willis lives at 2244 Clark Street. He hit her with a bat.
(B) Mr. Willis entered 2244 Clark Street, the premises of his ex-wife. He hit her with a bat, without permission and authority to do so. It caused Mrs. Willis to have head injuries.
(C) After Mr. Willis hit his ex-wife, Mrs. Willis, at 2244 Clark Street, the bat caused her to have head injuries. He had no permission nor authority to do so.
(D) Mr. Willis entered his ex-wife's premises at 2244 Clark Street without her permission or authority. He then struck Mrs. Willis with a bat causing injuries to her head.

30. While on patrol, Police Officer York responds to a case of a missing child. The following information relating to this case was obtained by the Officer:

Name of Missing Child: Susan Spencer
Age: 7 years old
School: Mountainside School
Information Provided by: Mary Templeton, Principal
Disposition of Case: Child is all right; she arrived at school five minutes before Officer York arrived.

Officer York is completing a report on the incident. Which one of the following expresses the above information most clearly and accurately?

(A) Only five minutes before my arrival she was at the school and was all right. Mary Templeton, the Principal of Mountainside School said that the missing child, Susan Spencer was seven years old.

(B) I arrived at Mountainside School and spoke with Mary Templeton, the Principal. She informed me that the missing child, Susan Spencer, age seven, had arrived five minutes before I did and is fine.

(C) She arrived five minutes before I did. The Principal of Mountainside School, Mary Templeton, informed me that the missing child was seven years old, Susan Spencer, and was fine.

(D) Seven year old Susan Spencer was missing. Mary Templeton, Principal, Mountainside School said that only five minutes before my arrival she was at the school and was fine.

Answer question 31 solely on the basis of the following information.

Police Officers may be confronted with a situation involving a mentally ill or emotionally disturbed person who does not voluntarily seek medical assistance. When a Police Officer has reason to believe that an individual is mentally ill or emotionally disturbed, the Officer should do the following in the order given:

1. Request an ambulance if one has not already been dispatched and determine whether the Patrol Supervisor is responding; if not, request response.
2. Attempt to comfort the mentally ill or emotionally disturbed person.
3. Attempt to isolate and contain the mentally ill or emotionally disturbed person until the arrival of the Patrol Supervisor and the Emergency Service Unit.
4. Establish police lines.
5. After the person has been restrained, remove property that is dangerous to life or might help the person to escape.
6. Have person removed to hospital in ambulance.
7. Ride in the body of the ambulance with the person.
8. Safeguard the person at the hospital until examined by the psychiatrist.

31. Police Officer Emilio, while on foot patrol, is informed by Mr. Green, the superintendent of the building at 285 Jay Street, that there is a male tenant with a known history of mental illness in Apartment 3A yelling loudly that space aliens are controlling his thoughts and actions. The tenant is reported to have a violent temper and can be heard throwing things around the apartment. The building superintendent has already called an ambulance and Officer Emilio has requested that the Patrol Supervisor respond. The next step that Officer Emilio should take is to

(A) have the tenant taken to the hospital in the ambulance
(B) try to calm the tenant and comfort him
(C) establish police lines
(D) attempt to isolate and contain the tenant for his safety.

Answer question 32 solely on the basis of the following information.

Menacing—A person is guilty of menacing when, by physical means, he intentionally places or attempts to place another person in immediate fear of serious physical injury.

32. Which one of the following situations is the best example of menacing?

(A) Debbie walks up to Brain, says "I'm going to punch you", then punches Brian in the face, causing his jaw to ache for several hours.
(B) A terrorist secretly places a time bomb which could cause serious injury to many people in a busy shopping mall.
(C) During a heated argument Tom picks up a knife, holds it to Mike's throat, and tells Mike that he will cut his throat.
(D) Roy, who strongly dislikes his neighbor John, tells John that if he does not move out of his apartment within the next month, Roy will set it on fire when John is not around to stop him.

33. On occasion, Police Officers may require back-up assistance from other Officers. While on patrol Police Officer Casey observes a number of situations. For which one of the following would it be most appropriate for Officer Casey to request back-up assistance?

(A) A woman looking under the hood of the car while parked on the highway shoulder.
(B) A fight between two groups of teenage boys in a park concerning the use of a baseball field.
(C) A man who changes lanes as he drives without signaling.
(D) An argument between two women concerning who will park in a vacant space.

34. Police Officer Webster is preparing an Arrest Report which will include the following five sentences:

1. I noticed that the robber had a knife placed at the victim's neck.
2. I told the robber to drop the knife.
3. While on patrol I observed a robbery which was in progress.
4. I grabbed the robber, placed him in handcuffs, and took him to the precinct.
5. The robber dropped the knife and tried to flee.

The most logical order for the above sentences to appear in the report is

(A) 1, 2, 5, 4, 3
(B) 3, 1, 2, 5, 4
(C) 3, 2, 4, 1, 5
(D) 1, 3, 4, 5, 2.

Answer question <u>35</u> solely on the basis of the following information.

When a patrol car must be repaired, Police Officers should do the following in the order given:

1. Notify the Desk Officer.
2. Call for an appointment as follows:

   A. Make an appointment with the Borough Service Station for all repairs during normal business hours.
   B. Make an appointment with the Central Repair Shop for all repairs during other than normal business hours.
3. Prepare an Emergency Repair Requisition and drive the vehicle in for repairs at the appointed time.

35. Police Officer Visconti, while performing a night tour, checks her patrol car and notices a problem with the transmission. She calls the Desk Officer at 1:00 A.M. to report the problem. The next step the Police Officer should take is to

(A) call and make an appointment with the Borough Service Station
(B) prepare an Emergency Repair Requisition on her way to the repair shop
(C) arrange for an appointment with the Central Repair Shop
(D) drive the vehicle back to the precinct station house.

Answer question <u>36</u> solely on the basis of the following information.

Police Officers are sometimes required to provide emergency transportation for seriously injured persons.

36. Police Officer Phelan arrives at the 103rd Street subway station to provide assistance to a critically injured elderly man who fell from the stairs onto the platform. Which one of the following would be the <u>most serious</u> situation for the Officer to deal with?

(A) A crowd of onlookers has gathered ten feet away from the injured man.
(B) The ambulance dispatcher informs the Officer that an ambulance would not be available for twenty minutes.
(C) The injured man is unable to provide the Officer with the name of a relative to be contacted.
(D) Several onlookers start to complain about a delay in train service.

Answer questions 37 through 39 solely on the basis of the following passage.

At 2:00 P.M., while sitting in front of 215 Rover Street, Police Officers Casey and Rogers receive a radio call to investigate a suspected case of child abuse at 415 Dover Street, Apartment 12B. The radio dispatcher informs the Officers that the call came from Apartment 12A. The Officers arrive at the location and decide to go to the apartment the complaint came from to investigate. When the Officers knock, both Mr. and Mrs. Fine come to the door. Mrs. Fine states that she has heard a child crying since noon and asked her husband to call the police. The Officers thank Mr. and Mrs. Fine, go on to Apartment 12B, and knock on the door.

A male named John Brice opens the door and asks what seems to be the problem. After Officer Casey explains why they are at the apartment, Mr. Brice states that he works nights and often falls into a deep sleep. The crying of his child did not awaken him. Officer Casey asks to see the child and Mr. Brice complies. Officer Casey looks at the child and notices bruises and burn marks on the child's feet. The Officers then request a Patrol Supervisor and an ambulance. Sergeant Ramos arrives at the apartment at 2:30 P.M. and orders the child removed to a hospital. Fifteen minutes later, Mr. Brice is arrested. At 3:00 P.M. another patrol car is sent to notify Mrs. Brice at 725 Clover Street.

37. The police dispatcher received the call from

(A) 725 Clover Street, Apartment 12C
(B) 415 Dover Street, Apartment 12A
(C) 215 Rover Street, Apartment 12B
(D) 415 Dover Street, Apartment 12B.

38. Who called the police?

(A) Mrs. Fine
(B) Mr. Brice
(C) Mr. Fine
(D) Mrs. Brice.

39. From which of the following persons did the Officers receive initial information regarding this complaint?

(A) Mrs. Brice
(B) Mrs. Fine
(C) Mr. Brice
(D) Mr. Fine.

Answer question 40 solely on the basis of the following information.

Definitions:

Aided case: Any occurrence coming to the attention of a uniformed member of the service which requires that a person, other than a prisoner, receive medical aid or assistance because such person is

A. sick or injured (except vehicle accident)
B. dead (except vehicle accident)
C. a lost person
D. mentally ill
E. an abandoned, destitute, abused or neglected child.

Vehicle accident: One which occurs on a public highway or on a street between building lines and involves a vehicle, including a parked vehicle, attended or unattended, or vehicles on private property to which the public has access.

Procedures:

Upon arrival at the scene of a vehicle accident a Police Officer shall prepare a Police Accident Report.

Upon arrival at the scene of an aided incident a Police Officer shall render appropriate aid to the sick or injured person, request an ambulance or doctor if necessary, and prepare an aided report.

40. At about 6:00 P.M. on February 5, 1986, Police Officer Malone receives a radio call to respond to the scene of an accident. Witnesses inform him that a newspaper truck was struck in the rear by a garbage truck at the intersection of Mica and Gold Streets. The driver of the newspaper truck sustained a broken leg and a very bad facial cut. The driver of the garbage truck suffered a cut on his left arm. A female passerby, about 70 years old, observed the accident and had a heart attack. She was lying on the sidewalk, having trouble breathing.

In addition to making the necessary notifications, Police Officer Malone should prepare

(A) a Police Accident Report and an Aided Report for the victims of the vehicle accident
(B) an Aided Report and a Police Accident Report for the passerby
(C) a Police Accident Report for the vehicle accident only
(D) a Police Accident Report for the vehicle accident and an Aided Report for the passerby.

41. Police Officer Lee is preparing a report regarding someone who apparently attempted to commit suicide with a gun. The report will include the following five sentences:

1. At the location, the woman pointed to the open door of Apartment 7L.
2. I called for an ambulance to respond.

3. The male had a gun in his hand and a large head wound.
4. A call was received from the radio dispatcher regarding a woman who heard a gunshot at 936 45th Avenue.
5. Upon entering Apartment 7L, I saw the body of a male on the kitchen floor.

The most logical order for the above sentences to appear in the report is

(A) 4, 1, 5, 3, 2 **(C)** 1, 5, 3, 2, 4
(B) 1, 3, 5, 4, 2 **(D)** 4, 5, 3, 2, 1.

Answer question 42 solely on the basis of the following information.

Police Officers are sometimes required to arrest a person for whom a warrant has been issued. When making such an arrest, Officers should do the following in the order given:

1. Inform defendant of the warrant and the reason it was issued, unless physical resistance, escape or other factors make this impractical.
2. Show warrant, if requested.
3. Announce authority and purpose, if premises are involved and there is reasonable cause to believe that the defendant is inside, unless giving such notice may
   a. endanger the life or safety of the Officer or another person
   b. result in defendant attempting to escape
   c. result in material evidence being destroyed, damaged or hidden
4. Break into premises, if necessary.
5. Make arrest.
6. Take the prisoner to the station house.

42. Police Officers Haggerty and Adams are enroute to 2112 Jefferson Street, Apartment 2B, with a warrant to arrest Mark Johnson. The arrest warrant was issued when Mr. Johnson failed to appear in court on charges of bank robbery and rape. Upon arrival at Mr. Johnson's residence, Officer Haggerty knocks on the door and announces herself. Without hearing any acknowledgment from anyone, the Officers suddenly hear glass breaking inside the apartment. Officer Adams then forces the apartment door open, rushes inside, and stops a man who fits Mark Johnson's description from escaping through a bedroom window. The next step the Officers should take is to

(A) take Mr. Johnson to the station house for booking
(B) present the warrant to Mr. Johnson
(C) inform Mr. Johnson of the reason why a warrant was issued for his arrest
(D) arrest Mr. Johnson.

Answer questions 43 through 45 solely on the basis of the following passage.

Police Officers Wilson and Mylers had just begun their 4:00 P.M. to midnight tour of duty when they received a radio call to investigate a case of possible child abuse. Mrs. Margaret Volkman had called 911 and said she was going to hurt her two daughters. Mary Watson, Mrs. Volkman's mother, had urged her daughter to call the police after speaking with her over the phone. Mrs. Volkman had been drinking and her mother knew from past occasions that her daughter could become very aggressive after one or two beers. In fact, last year Mrs. Volkman's neighbor, Joyce Hill, had called the police to complain about Margaret's "drunken behavior." When the Officers arrived at 51 Broadway, Apartment 4C, they spoke briefly to Mrs. Volkman, who appeared to be very agitated. She stated that being a single parent of two young girls is very difficult and there are times when she feels she is at her wit's end. Officer Wilson asked if he could speak to the two children alone and she agreed to wait in the living room. She stated to Officer Mylers that she loved her girls and would never do anything to hurt them. Officer Wilson spoke to Gayle, the 13-year-old daughter, who told him that her mother "gets very worked up when she drinks and begins to scream at me and Mattie and cry at the same time, but has never tried to hurt us. After awhile she just falls asleep." After hearing this, Officer Wilson decided the children were not in any immediate danger. Before leaving, the Officers told Mrs. Volkman to call the precinct if she felt she might try to hurt her children again.

43. The call which prompted the Officers to respond to 51 Broadway was placed by

(A) Mary Watson
(B) Margaret Volkman
(C) Joyce Hill
(D) Gayle Mylers.

44. Officer Wilson decided that the children were not in any danger after speaking with

(A) Mattie Volkman
(B) Joyce Hill
(C) Gayle Volkman
(D) Mary Watson.

45. Which one of the following persons had made a complaint in the past concerning Margaret's drinking?

(A) Her mother
(B) Her daughter
(C) Her grandmother
(D) Her neighbor.

46. At 10:20 A.M. Police Officer Medina responds to a report of a robbery. The Officer obtains the following information regarding the incident:

Time of Occurrence: 10:15 A.M.
Place of Occurrence: Mike's Deli
1700 E. 9th Street
Victim: Chuck Baker, owner of Mike's Deli
Amount Stolen: $500.00
Suspects: 3 male Whites

Officer Medina is completing a report on the incident. Which one of the following expresses the above information most clearly and accurately?

(A) Chuck Baker, the owner of Mike's Deli, located at 1700 E. 9th Street, reported that at 10:15 A.M. three White males robbed his deli of $500.00.
(B) At 10:15 A.M., Chuck Baker, deli owner, reported that Mike's Deli, located at 1700 E. 9th Street was robbed of $500.00 by three White males.
(C) Chuck Baker reported that $500.00 had been taken from the owner of Mike's Deli, located at 1700 E. 9th Street at 10:15 A.M. by three White males.
(D) At 10:15 A.M. it was reported by the deli owner that three White males robbed $500.00 from Chuck Baker. Mike's Deli is located at 1700 E. 9th Street.

47. While on patrol, Police Officers Rydell and Francis receive a call to respond to a reported robbery. The following information related to the crime is obtained by the Officers:

Time of Occurrence: 10:00 A.M.
Place of Occurrence: 8012 Liberty Street
Victim: Leslie Reese, friend of witness
Witness: Lorraine Mitchell
Suspect: Bill Clark
Crime: Money and Jewelry stolen

Officer Francis is completing a report on the incident. Which one of the following expresses the above information most clearly and accurately?

(A) Lorraine Mitchell stated that while responding to a robbery, at 10:00 A.M., she was a witness at 8012 Liberty Street. Her friend, Leslie Reese, had her jewelry and money taken from her by Bill Clark.
(B) Lorraine Mitchell stated that at 10:00 A.M. she saw Bill Clark approach her friend, Leslie Reese, and take money and jewelry from her. The crime took place at 8012 Liberty Street.
(C) At 8012 Liberty Street, stolen money and jewelry were reported. This was witnessed by Lorraine Mitchell and her friend, Leslie Resse, who was also robbed of her money and

jewelry. The incident occurred at 10:00 A.M. The suspect is Bill Clark.

(D) At 10:00 A.M. Lorraine Mitchell saw Bill Clark enter 8012 Liberty Street. At that point Leslie Reese owned jewelry and money which were stolen.

Answer question 48 solely on the basis of the following information.

When assigned to safeguard a crime scene, a Police Officer should:

1. Request that a Patrol Supervisor respond to the scene.
2. Notify the Precinct Detective Unit.
3. Make sure that evidence found at scene is not disturbed.
4. Record in Memo Book any important observations, such as identity of suspects and witnesses.
5. Advise the Patrol Supervisor and Detectives of any witnesses detained and any other information regarding the crime.

48. Police Officer Best is assigned to a foot post on Rock Avenue between East Street and Pitt Street. While working an 8:00 A.M. to 4:00 P.M. shift, Officer Best hears what appears to be three gunshots coming from an apartment building located at 1400 Rock Avenue. After noting the time (10:00 A.M.) and address, Officer Best investigates and notices that the door of a first-floor apartment is open. She walks into the apartment and discovers a male, Black approximately 35 years old with three bullet holes in his chest lying on the floor. Officer Best checks for a pulse, but the man is dead. Next to the body there is a .38 caliber revolver. Officer Best checks the rest of the apartment. When satisfied that everything is secure, she, without touching anything, uses her radio to request that a Supervisor and the Detective Unit respond to the scene. Officer Best leaves the apartment and questions the people who have gathered outside the victim's apartment. She asks if anyone there knew the victim. Two people state that they did, and Officer Best records their names in her Memo Book.

The actions of Officer Best were

(A) improper, primarily because she should have picked up the revolver to see if there were three bullets missing from it
(B) proper, primarily because she was able to respond to the scene quickly
(C) improper, primarily because she should not have felt the man's pulse to determine if he was alive
(D) proper, primarily because she did not disturb any possible evidence at the scene.

Answer question 49 solely on the basis of the following information.

Police Officers are sometimes required to request transportation for seriously injured persons.

49. In which one of the following cases would it be most appropriate for a Police Officer to request emergency transportation?

(A) A man using an electric hedge trimmer accidentally scratches his finger.
(B) A nine-year-old girl falls off her bicycle, twists her ankle and suffers abrasions on her knees.
(C) An elderly man falls down a flight of stairs, and is knocked unconscious.
(D) A young mother complains of feeling faint.

Answer question 50 solely on the basis of the following information.

Upon arrival at the scene of a hit-and-run accident involving property damage, a Police Officer should do the following in the order given:

1. Prepare a Complaint Report.
2. If a New York license number is obtained for vehicle leaving the scene:
   A. Determine from the Stolen Property Inquiry Section if vehicle is reported stolen.
   B. Obtain the name and address of registered owner.
   C. Give the information to complainant.
3. If the vehicle leaving the scene is registered in another state:
   A. Request identity of registered owner from Inter-City Correspondence Unit.
   B. Inform complainant of identity of owner if obtained.

50. Police Officer Murphy responds to the scene of a hit-and-run accident involving damage to a black Chevrolet, with New York license plate number 315 ALV, owned by Mr. Mangione. He tells Officer Murphy that his car was hit by a blue Ford, bearing New Jersey license plate number 461 ESP. Mr. Mangione states that immediately after the collision, the unknown driver left the scene in his blue Ford. After preparing a Complaint Report, Officer Murphy's next step should be to

(A) determine from Stolen Property Inquiry Section if the hit-and-run vehicle is stolen
(B) provide operator of vehicle with name and address of hit-and-run driver
(C) try to learn identity of registered owner of hit-and-run vehicle from Inter-City Correspondence Unit
(D) request a computer check from the radio dispatcher to determine the identity of the hit-and-run driver.

51. Police Officer Modrak is completing a Memo Book entry which will include the following five sentences:

1. The victim, a male in his thirties, told me that the robbery occurred a few minutes ago.
2. My partner and I jumped out of the patrol car and arrested the suspect.
3. We responded to an armed robbery in progress at Billings Avenue and 59th Street.
4. On Chester Avenue and 68th Street, the victim spotted and identified the suspect.
5. I told the victim to get into the patrol car and that we would drive him around the area.

The most logical order for the above sentences to appear in the Memo Book is

(A) 3, 1, 5, 4, 2
(B) 1, 3, 5, 2, 4
(C) 1, 4, 3, 5, 2
(D) 3, 5, 1, 2, 4.

Answer question 52 solely on the basis of the following information.

Hazardous Material—any chemical, biological or radiological substance which a Police Officer believes to be dangerous to health. In a hazardous material incident, a Police Officer shall establish minimum "frozen areas" (where the public cannot enter) as follows:

A. Outdoors—At least 150 feet from hazardous material source or spillage.
B. Indoors—Evacuate room in which material is located.
C. Tanker Truck or Military Shipment—extend frozen area to at least 300 feet in radius.
D. Explosion or Fire—
   (1) Outdoors: at least 1000 feet in radius from explosive; at least 300 feet in radius from fire.
   (2) Indoors: extend frozen area to include all areas or rooms where a person might be exposed to material; include floors above and below the materials.
   (3) Tanker Truck or Military Shipment: extend frozen area to at least 1000 feet in radius.

52. While on patrol, Police Officers Hunt and Richardson were driving eastbound on the Soundview Highway, which was wet after heavy rains. At approximately 3:00 P.M. a tanker truck containing nuclear waste spun around and turned on its side approximately 300 feet in front of the patrol car. Officer Hunt immediately notified the radio dispatcher because there was liquid leaking from the tank which spread approximately 150 feet west of the truck. After about ten minutes, an explosion occurred which caused a fire. Officers Hunt and Richardson decided to block off the roadway and evacuate pedestrians in the area. In this situation, which of the following would be the most appropriate action for the Officers to take?

(A) Establish a frozen area 1000 feet west of the tanker truck.
(B) Establish a frozen area 300 feet in radius around the tanker truck.
(C) Establish a frozen area 1200 feet in radius from the tanker truck.
(D) Establish a frozen area 100 feet from the source of the leak.

53. Recently, there has been a significant increase in the number of drug sales at the Havenbrook High School. Police Officer Mair has been assigned to a special team to investigate this situation. He has been instructed to monitor closely any activities that appear to be suspicious.

Which one of the following should Officer Mair monitor?

(A) The school principal arriving one hour before the beginning of class every day
(B) Teachers who double park in front of the school every morning
(C) A hot dog vendor who arrives five minutes before the end of the lunch period every day
(D) Two students who are picked up at the school gate immediately after classes every Friday.

Answer questions 54 through 56 solely on the basis of the following passage.

Five minutes after the end of his noon to 1:00 P.M. lunch hour, Police Officer Miller is approached by two obviously frightened teenaged boys. The boys report being robbed by three men, while they were listening to music under the boardwalk about twenty minutes earlier.

Danny Brown, the older teenager, informs the Officer that the robbers took his large radio, silver watch and twenty dollars. His friend, Larry Jones, reports that they took a gold watch and ten dollars from him. The victims report that the perpetrators fled underneath the boardwalk towards the amusement area.

The Victims are able to describe the robbers. All three are White males in their late twenties. The first is about 5′6″, 160 lbs., wearing white jeans and a blue shirt. The second is about 5′10″, 145 lbs., and of dark complexion. The third is known to the younger victim as Redeye and is believed to be a resident of that neighborhood. During the robbery, Redeye was armed with a knife. He is described as being about the same height as the second perpetrator but at least ten pounds heavier than the first. Officer Miller gave the descriptions to the dispatcher.

Officer McMillan, working in the amusement park area, observes three men fitting the description of the robbers. One of the three is carrying a large radio while the other two are carrying baseball bats and wearing Walkman stereos. Officer McMillan quickly requests a police back-up unit to assist in the arrest.

Officers Smith and Campbell respond to provide back-up. Immediately after the three men are apprehended by Officer McMillan and the back-up officers, Officer Miller arrives on the scene accompanied by the victims. The victims identify the three men as the robbers and the Officers arrest them.

54. What weapon was used in the robbery?

(A) baseball bat
(B) knife
(C) hand gun
(D) sword.

55. Which one of the following best describes Redeye?

(A) Hispanic, 5′6″, dark complexion
(B) White, 5′10″, 170 lbs.
(C) Hispanic, 5′6″, 160 lbs.
(D) White, 5′10″, 155 lbs.

56. Which one of the following Officers was <u>not</u> present at the time the suspects were apprehended?

(A) McMillan
(B) Campbell
(C) Smith
(D) Miller.

Answer question <u>57</u> solely on the basis of the following information.

When a Police Officer receives a complaint concerning a crime that occurred in another precinct, the Officer should do the following in the order given:

1. Interview the complainant and obtain facts.
2. Prepare a Complaint Report.
3. Telephone complaint to the precinct of occurrence.
4. Record the name of the member of the department receiving the complaint at the precinct of occurrence under the "Details" section of the report.
5. Make Memo Book entries and forward all copies of the Complaint Report to the precinct of occurrence.

57. While walking his assigned foot post in the 99th Precinct, Police Officer Jones is approached by an elderly woman who states that her pocketbook had been snatched from her shoulder just four blocks away, in the 98th Precinct. Police Officer Jones speaks to the woman and records all the facts related to the incident. He then prepares a Complaint Report. At the Precinct, the next step Police Officer Jones should take is to

(A) make appropriate Memo Book entries and forward all copies of the Complaint Report
(B) telephone the complaint to the precinct of occurrence
(C) prepare a Complaint Report
(D) record the name of the member of the department receiving the complaint at the precinct of occurrence under the "Details" section of the report.

58. Police Officer Rodriguez is preparing a report concerning an incident in which she used her revolver. Her report will include the following five sentences:

1. Upon seeing my revolver, the robber dropped his gun to the ground.
2. At about 10:55 P.M., I was informed by a passerby that several people were being robbed at gunpoint on 174th Street and Walton Avenue.
3. I was assigned to patrol on 174th Street and Ghent Avenue during the evening shift.
4. I saw a man holding a gun on three people, took out my revolver and shouted, "Police, don't move!"
5. After calling for assistance, I went to 174th Street and Walton Avenue and took cover behind a car.

The most logical order for the above sentences to appear in the report is

(A) 2, 3, 4, 5, 1
(B) 4, 5, 1, 3, 2
(C) 3, 2, 5, 4, 1
(D) 2, 4, 1, 5, 3.

Answer question 59 solely on the basis of the following information.

Procedure for Safeguarding a Hospitalized Prisoner

Permit only the following persons on official business to interview the prisoner:

A. Ranking Officer of the Police Department
B. Detective
C. District Attorney or representative
D. Chief Medical Examiner or representative
E. Clergyman (if requested by prisoner)

59. Police Officer Roger Ziegler is guarding a prisoner at County Hospital. He is approached by Reverend Falter, a minister who wishes to speak with the prisoner, who is a member of his congregation. Reverend Falter feels that he might be able to persuade the prisoner to discuss his case. Also present at the hospital is Captain Lattimore of the Police Academy. The Captain, who is visiting a friend in the hospital while off duty, knows the minister from a previous assignment. The Captain tells Officer Ziegler that he can see no reason to keep Reverend Falter from talking with the prisoner. Officer Ziegler then permits Reverend Falter to see the prisoner.

This action by Officer Ziegler was

- **(A)** proper, primarily because Captain Lattimore gave his approval
- **(B)** improper, primarily because the prisoner did not ask to speak with Reverend Falter
- **(C)** proper primarily because Reverend Falter might be helpful in solving the case
- **(D)** improper, primarily because Captain Lattimore was off duty at the time.

Answer question <u>60</u> solely on the basis of the following information:

While on patrol, Police Officers routinely observe motorists and evaluate their capability to operate a motor vehicle. At times, it is necessary to pull someone over to the side of the road when the driver's capability is questionable.

60. In which one of the following cases would a Police Officer be <u>least</u> likely to pull the motorist over?

- **(A)** A man who weaves his car back and forth over the white dividing line
- **(B)** A woman in the car who suddenly swerves to avoid a dog
- **(C)** A man who changes lanes without looking behind him, cutting other motorists off
- **(D)** A woman who turns her head to reach for something in the back seat, and goes through a stop sign.

Answer questions <u>61</u> through <u>63</u> solely on the basis of the following passage.

On July 19, 1986, while walking home from the subway, Paul Carro was assaulted by three males on the corner of Evergreen Street and Appleseed Avenue. Mr. Carro suffered a slight concussion, a broken nose, and cuts or his face.

When Police Officers James and Blake arrived on the scene, Mr. Carro was lying on the ground in a semi-conscious state in front of the subway station. Just as the Officers arrived, a Mrs. Frankel of 1785 Appleseed Avenue, Mr. Jones of 1783 Appleseed Avenue, Ms. Brown of 851 Evergreen Street, and Mr. Peters of 1787 Appleseed Avenue came out of their apartments to see what had happened.

Officer James immediately radioed for an ambulance and then attempted to question Mr. Carro about the incident. Mr. Carro stated that "there were three young male Whites wearing dungarees, sneakers, and T-shirts." Mr. Carro also said that he hit one of the males in the face and kicked another before he was knocked to the ground.

In the meantime, Officer Blake interviewed the neighbors who were present. Mr. Jones gave the Officer Mr. Carro's address, and stated that he was Mr. Carro's roommate. He also stated that he heard a lot of noise on the street, but by the time he came outside, Mr. Carro was lying on the ground. Both Ms. Brown and Mr. Peters stated that they saw the three youths who attacked Mr. Carro because of a remark he made to them. Mr. Peters further stated that Mr. Carro did not fight back, and at one point said, "Please leave me alone." Mrs. Frankel stated that she rushed out of her apartment just in time to see the young men running off. She said that Mr. Carro pursued them for a half a block and then collapsed on the sidewalk. Mrs. Frankel further stated that this was not the first time that Mr. Carro had started trouble in the neighborhood.

61. Where did Mr. Carro live?

(A) 1783 Appleseed Avenue
(B) 1785 Appleseed Avenue
(C) 851 Evergreen Street
(D) 1787 Appleseed Avenue.

62. Whose statement to the police directly contradicted Mr. Carro's statement?

(A) Mr. Peters
(B) Mr. Jones
(C) Ms. Brown
(D) Mrs. Frankel.

63. Which one of the following witnesses was the first to be interviewed by Officer Blake?

(A) Mr. Peters
(B) Mr. Jones
(C) Ms. Brown
(D) Mrs. Frankel.

64. The following details were obtained by Police Officer Talbert at the scene of a shooting:

Place of Occurrence: 77 Greene Street, inside the Video Arcade
Victim: Mr. Gerald Jackson, Video Arcade customer
Suspect: Mr. Michael Benton, Video Arcade owner
Crime: Shooting
Action Taken: Suspect arrested.

Officer Talbert is completing a report on the incident. Which one of the following expresses the above information <u>most clearly</u> and <u>accurately</u>?

(A) Gerald Jackson was present in the Video Arcade when Michael Benton, the Arcade owner, was involved in a shooting. The shooting occurred at 77 Greene Street. An arrest was made.

(B) Michael Benton and Gerald Jackson were in a shooting at the Video Arcade located at 77 Greene Street. The person shot by the owner was a customer. An arrest was made.

(C) Gerald Jackson, a customer at the Video Arcade, located at 77 Greene Street, was shot by Michael Benton, the Arcade owner. Mr. Benton was arrested.

(D) Michael Benton, owner of the Video Arcade, located at 77 Greene Street and Gerald Jackson, an Arcade customer were involved in a shooting. An arrest was made.

65. While on patrol, Police Officers Cando and Poppy receive a call to respond to a reported burglary. The following information relating to the crime is obtained by the Police Officers:

Time of Occurrence: 4:00 A.M.
Place of Occurrence: 81-31 Mitts Street
Witness: Jennifer Wink
Victim: Bette Miller, neighbor
Suspect: John Haysport, neighbor
Crime: house burglarized; T.V. set stolen

The Officers are completing a report on the incident. Which one of the following expresses the above information most clearly and accurately?

(A) Jennifer Wink, while on patrol, stated to me that the house next to her house at 81-13 Mitts Street was burglarized. The crime was committed by John Haysport. The crime was the T.V. set was no longer there. Bette Miller, a neighbor could not find her T.V.

(B) At 4:00 A.M. Jennifer Wink, the witness, reported to me that before she had seen John Haysport, a neighbor, go into 81-13 Mitts Street and steal a T.V. set. The T.V. belonged to Bette Miller who also lives nearby.

(C) Jennifer Wink, the witness, states that John Haysport, burglarized her neighbor's house at 81-13 Mitts Street. She saw her neighbor leaving her neighbor's house at 4:00 A.M. with a T.V. set. The house was Bette Miller's house.

(D) Jennifer Wink, the witness, states that her neighbor's house located at 81-13 Mitts Street was burglarized. Mrs. Wink further states that at 4:00 A.M. she saw a neighbor, John Haysport, leave Mrs. Miller's house with a T.V. set.

Answer questions 66 through 68 solely on the basis of the following map. The flow of traffic is indicated by the arrows. If there is only one arrow shown, then traffic flows only in the direction indicated by the arrow. If there are two arrows, then traffic flows in both directions. You must follow the flow of traffic.

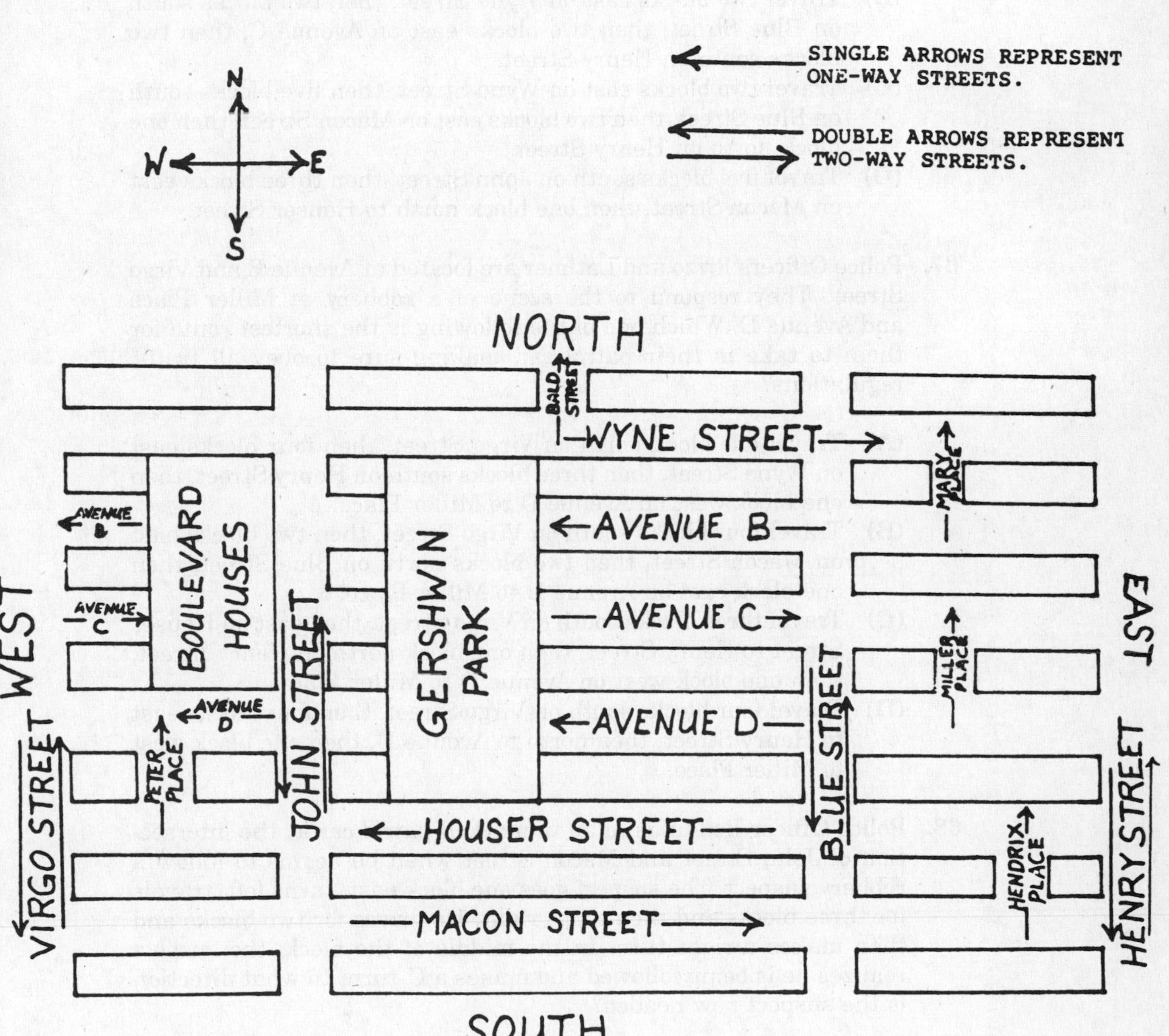

66. Police Officers Ranking and Fish are located at Wyne Street and John Street. The radio dispatcher has assigned them to investigate a motor vehicle accident at the corner of Henry Street and Houser Street. Which one of the following is the shortest route for them to take in their patrol car, making sure to obey all traffic regulations?

(A) Travel four blocks south on John Street, then three blocks east on Houser Street to Henry Street.
(B) Travel two blocks east on Wyne Street, then two blocks south on Blue Street, then two blocks east on Avenue C, then two blocks south on Henry Street.
(C) Travel two blocks east on Wyne Street, then five blocks south on Blue Street, then two blocks east on Macon Street, then one block north on Henry Street.
(D) Travel five blocks south on John Street, then three blocks east on Macon Street, then one block north to Houser Street.

67. Police Officers Rizzo and Latimer are located at Avenue B and Virgo Street. They respond to the scene of a robbery at Miller Place and Avenue D. Which one of the following is the shortest route for them to take in their patrol car, making sure to obey all traffic regulations?

(A) Travel one block north on Virgo Street, then four blocks east on Wyne Street, then three blocks south on Henry Street, then one block west on Avenue D to Miller Place.
(B) Travel four blocks south on Virgo Street, then two blocks east on Macon Street, then two blocks north on Blue Street, then one block east on Avenue D to Miller Place.
(C) Travel three blocks south on Virgo Street, then east on Houser Street to Henry Street, then one block north on Henry Street, then one block west on Avenue D to Miller Place.
(D) Travel four blocks south on Virgo Street, then four blocks east to Henry Street, then north to Avenue D, then one block west to Miller Place.

68. Police Officer Bendix is in an unmarked patrol car at the intersection of John Street and Macon Street when he begins to follow a robbery suspect. The suspect goes one block east, turns left, travels for three blocks and then turns right. He drives for two blocks and then makes a right turn. In the middle of the block, the suspect realizes he is being followed and makes a U-turn. In what direction is the suspect now headed?

(A) North (B) South (C) East (D) West.

Answer questions 69 and 70 solely on the basis of the following table.

CRIMES IN SECTOR C FOR JANUARY

Report #	Date	Day	Offense	Time	Location
1465	1/3	Friday	Robbery	2:00 A.M.	2300 Creston Avenue
1470	1/6	Monday	Burglary	3:20 P.M.	2650 Morris Avenue
1474	1/6	Monday	Assault	8:00 A.M.	2020 Davidson Avenue
1477	1/8	Wednesday	Assault	11:00 A.M.	2350 Creston Avenue
1478	1/10	Friday	Burglary	3:00 A.M.	2500 Creston Avenue
1480	1/10	Friday	Robbery	5:00 P.M.	2025 Morris Avenue
1484	1/10	Friday	Burglary	2:45 A.M.	2420 Cummings Street
1486	1/11	Saturday	Robbery	4:00 P.M.	2650 Morris Avenue
1488	1/15	Wednesday	Robbery	7:00 P.M.	2400 Morris Avenue
1490	1/17	Friday	Burglary	1:15 A.M.	2620 Creston Avenue
1494	1/20	Monday	Assault	7:00 A.M.	2515 Davidson Avenue
1498	1/21	Tuesday	Assault	11:45 A.M.	2614 Creston Avenue
1503	1/21	Tuesday	Burglary	5:00 A.M.	2230 Morris Avenue
1510	1/24	Friday	Burglary	7:00 A.M.	2719 Creston Avenue
1512	1/25	Saturday	Robbery	11:00 P.M.	2485 Davidson Avenue
1518	1/31	Friday	Robbery	4:00 P.M.	2355 Davidson Avenue

69. A Police Officer would most likely be able to reduce the number of burglaries by patrolling

(A) Creston Avenue between 7:00 A.M. and 3:00 P.M. on Mondays
(B) Morris Avenue between noon and 8:00 P.M. on Sundays
(C) Creston Avenue between midnight and 8:00 A.M. on Fridays
(D) Morris Avenue between midnight and 8:00 A.M. on Mondays.

70. A Police Officer would most likely be able to reduce the number of robberies by patrolling

(A) Davidson Avenue between 3:00 P.M. and 11:00 P.M., Tuesday through Saturday
(B) Morris Avenue between 2:00 P.M. and 10:00 P.M., Monday through Friday
(C) Morris Avenue between 3:00 P.M. and 11:00 P.M., Tuesday through Saturday
(D) Davidson Avenue between noon and 8 P.M., Monday through Friday.

Answer question 70 solely on the basis of the following information.

Police Officer Stacy has been directed to observe stopped vehicles if he believes the occupants' actions are suspicious.

71. Which one of the following should Officer Stacy consider most suspicious?

(A) A man and woman kissing in a parked van in front of a hospital

(B) Three men sitting in a parked car outside a closed liquor store
(C) Two women strolling down the street glancing in shop windows
(D) A man quickly running from a double-parked car into a pharmacy which is about to close.

Answer question <u>72</u> solely on the basis of the following information.

When assigned to investigate a rape, Police Officers should do the following in the order given:

1. Interview the victim and any witnesses, obtain the facts, and protect evidence.
2. Transmit a description of the suspect if it is known over the Police radio.
3. Detain witnesses if there are any.
4. Prepare a Complaint Report Worksheet.
5. Determine if the case should be closed or referred for further investigation.
6. Notify Precinct Detectives and Sex Crime Squad if further investigation is required.

72. Police Officer Johnson responds to a rape. She completes all appropriate actions through notifying the Precinct Detectives. The next step Officer Johnson should take is to

(A) interview the witnesses further
(B) prepare a Complaint Report Worksheet
(C) inform the Sex Crime Squad
(D) transmit a description of the suspect.

Answer question <u>73</u> solely on the basis of the following information.

Police Officer Roberts, a rookie, has been informed by some of the veteran Police Officers in his precinct that certain streets in his sector have unusually high rates of violent crime. All of the homicides take place on Locust Street between Ash Boulevard and Spruce Avenue. Most of the rapes take place on Ash Boulevard between Locust Street and Ennis Place. All of the assaults take place on Spruce Avenue between Ennis Place and Karna Drive. The rapes occur between 9:00 P.M. and 12:00 P.M., the assaults occur between 4:00 P.M. and 12:00 P.M., and most of the homicides occur between 7:00 P.M. and 11:00 P.M. The assaults usually occur on Wednesdays and Thursdays; the homicides occur on Mondays and Tuesdays; and the rapes occur on Fridays and Saturdays.

73. Officer Roberts would most likely be able to reduce the number of homicides by patrolling

(A) Ash Boulevard between Spruce Avenue and Ennis Place on Mondays and Tuesdays between 8:00 P.M. and 4:00 A.M.
(B) Locust Street between Ash Boulevard and Spruce Avenue on Fridays and Saturdays between 7:00 P.M. and 11:00 P.M.
(C) Spruce Avenue between Karna Drive and Ennis Place on Wednesdays and Thursdays between 4:00 P.M. and midnight
(D) Locust Street between Ash Boulevard and Spruce Avenue on Mondays and Tuesdays between 8:00 P.M. and midnight.

Answer questions 74 through 76 solely on the basis of the following passage.

Housing Police Officer Lewis is patrolling Woodrow Houses, a housing project consisting of ten 14-story apartment buildings. Officer Lewis is working a midnight to 8 A.M. tour of duty. Before going to his assigned post, Officer Lewis was told by Sergeant Smith that there has been an increase in the number of apartment burglaries on his post. Sergeant Smith also stated that the burglaries are occurring between 10 P.M. and 6 A.M. A male Hispanic, 5′5″ tall, dark complexion, tattoo of a cross on right forearm, large black mustache, and wearing dark sunglasses has been seen in the area just prior to a number of the burglaries. At 3:00 A.M. Officer Lewis is patrolling his post and notices a male Hispanic, 5′5″, dark complexion, no mustache, no sunglasses, a tattoo of a cross on his right forearm, exiting an apartment building carrying a portable TV and a Sony radio. Officer Lewis stops the man and asks him where he was coming from. The man says that he was just coming from his friend's 6th floor apartment and that he was going to have the TV and radio repaired in the morning. Officer Lewis asks the man to return to the apartment with him. The man then drops the TV and radio and starts to run. Officer Lewis pursues and apprehends the man and places him under arrest.

A short time later Officer Lewis learns that a burglary had occurred in a 6th floor apartment in the same building that the male Hispanic was seen leaving. Among the items stolen were a TV and radio.

74. What did the male Hispanic have in his possession when he was stopped by Officer Lewis?

(A) a portable radio and a Sony TV
(B) a portable TV and a Sony radio
(C) a Sony TV and a Zenith radio
(D) a Zenith TV and a Sony radio.

75. Sergeant Smith informed Officer Lewis of burglaries occurring on his post in the

(A) late evening and early morning
(B) early morning and early afternoon
(C) early afternoon and late afternoon
(D) late morning and early evening.

76. The man Officer Lewis stopped to question

(A) was about 5′5″ tall and wore dark sunglasses
(B) had a dark complexion and a large black mustache
(C) had a large black mustache and a tattoo on his forearm
(D) had a tattoo on his forearm and was about 5′5″ tall.

Answer question 77 solely on the basis of the following information.

The procedure that a Police Officer should follow when making an arrest is:

1. Inform the person in custody of the reason for his arrest.
2. Handcuff the person with hands behind his back.
3. Immediately search the person for weapons or evidence.
4. Advise the person of his legal rights.

77. Police Officer Jelko, while doing his regular 4:00 P.M. to midnight foot patrol, was approached by Sister Maria, who told him that she had just had her pocketbook stolen at gunpoint. Sister Maria further stated that the man who robbed her was standing across the street. Officer Jelko, after being assured by Sister Maria that the man did commit the crime, walked up to him and stated, "You are under arrest for robbery." Officer Jelko then proceeded to handcuff the man's hands behind his back, advise him of his legal rights, and take him to the precinct. The actions taken by officer Jelko were

(A) proper, primarily because the prisoner was handcuffed from behind
(B) improper, primarily because Sister Maria also should have gone to the precinct since she was the victim
(C) proper, primarily because the prisoner was positively identified by Sister Maria
(D) improper, primarily because the prisoner was not searched for any weapons or evidence.

78. Police Officer Davis is completing an Activity Log entry which will include the following five sentences:

1. A radio car was dispatched and the male was taken to Greenville Hospital.
2. Several people saw him and called the police.

3. A naked man was running down the street waving his arms above his head and screaming, "Insects are all over me!"
4. I arrived on the scene and requested an ambulance.
5. The dispatcher informed me that no ambulances were available.

The most logical order for the above sentences to appear in the Activity Log is:

(A) 3, 4, 5, 1, 2
(B) 2, 3, 5, 1, 4
(C) 3, 2, 4, 5, 1
(D) 2, 4, 3, 5, 1.

Answer question 79 solely on the basis of the following information.

Police Officers must sometimes rely on eyewitness accounts of incidents, even though eyewitnesses may make mistakes with regard to some details.

79. Police Officer Ballard responds to the report of a mugging. When she arrives at the scene, she interviews four witnesses who saw a man flee the scene in a white car. The following are license plate numbers provided by the four witnesses. Which one of these numbers should Officer Ballard consider most likely to be correct?

(A) L-41688 **(B)** L-41638 **(C)** L-41238 **(D)** L-31638.

Answer question 80 solely on the basis of the following information.

Upon arriving at the scene of a fire, a Police Officer should do the following in the order given:

1. Send an alarm to the Fire Department or make sure one has been sent.
2. Direct a responsible person to remain at the alarm box to direct fire apparatus (if the fire is not in view).
3. Park patrol car to prevent interference with fire-fighting operation.
4. Warn occupants of building and assist them in leaving.
5. Take other action required by the situation.
6. Establish police lines beyond the fire apparatus and hydrants in use.

80. While on patrol, Police Officers Kittle and Chiu are flagged down by a man running from an apartment building. The man tells the Officers that there is a fire on most of the fifth floor of the building located at 330 State Street. The man also tells the Officers that he has already notified the Fire Department by using the fire alarm box located at the corner of State Street and Bushwick Avenue. Officer Kittle tells the man to wait by the fire alarm box and to direct Fire Department personnel to the exact location of the fire when they arrive. The next step Officers Kittle and Chiu should take is to

(A) set up police lines beyond the fire apparatus and hydrants in use
(B) position their patrol car so it will prevent interference with fire-fighting operations
(C) warn occupants of the building and help them leave
(D) direct someone to remain at the alarm box to direct the fire apparatus.

Answer question <u>81</u> solely on the basis of the following information.

According to the Criminal Procedure Law of New York State, a Police Officer may temporarily stop a person in a public place for questioning when the Officer reasonably suspects a person is committing, has committed or is about to commit a crime. The grounds for reasonable suspicion may include any overheard conversations of the suspect, any information received from third parties, the time of day or night, the particular streets or area involved, or the actions of a suspect.

81. In which one of the following situations would it be <u>least</u> appropriate for the Officer to stop and question the other person?

(A) Officer Hicks sees Randy Jones, whom he arrested a year ago for shoplifting, walk into Lacy's Department Store.
(B) Officer Lance notices a person checking cars to see if the doors have been left open.
(C) Officer Blake is given a description of a man offering rides to little girls as they are leaving school.
(D) Officer Hines, while working in plain clothes, hears a man on a public phone discussing plans for a bank robbery.

82. Police Officer Jenner responds to the scene of a burglary at 2106 La Vista Boulevard. He is approached by an elderly man named Richard Jenkins whose account of the incident includes the following five sentences:

1. I saw that the lock on my apartment door had been smashed and the door was open.
2. My apartment was a shambles; my belongings were everywhere and my television set was missing.
3. As I walked down the hallway toward the bedroom, I heard someone opening a window.
4. I left work at 5:30 P.M. and took the bus home.
5. At that time, I called the police.

The most logical order for the above sentences to appear in the report is

(A) 1, 5, 4, 2, 3
(B) 4, 1, 2, 3, 5
(C) 1, 5, 2, 3, 4
(D) 4, 3, 2, 5, 1.

Answer questions 83 and 84 solely on the basis of the following information.

Police Officer Meadows is aware that in his sector all of the robberies take place on Edgewater Street; all of the homicides happen on Bay Street; and all of the assaults take place on Wentworth Avenue. Most of the homicides occur between midnight and 4:00 A.M.; most of the robberies take place between 8:00 P.M. and 11:00 P.M.; and most of the assaults happen from 7:00 P.M. to midnight. Most of the robberies occur on Saturdays, most of the assaults on Fridays, and most of the homicides on Wednesdays and Fridays.

83. Officer Meadows would be most able to reduce the number of assaults if he patrolled

(A) Edgewater Street on Wednesdays from 7:00 P.M. to midnight
(B) Bay Street on Thursdays from 8:00 P.M. to 11:00 P.M.
(C) Wentworth Avenue on Fridays from midnight to 4:00 A.M.
(D) Wentworth Avenue on Fridays from 7:00 P.M. to midnight.

84. In order to reduce the number of homicides in his sector, Officer Meadows' superiors ask him to work a steady tour that would allow him to concentrate on that crime. For this purpose it would be most appropriate for Officer Meadows to work

(A) Tuesday through Saturday, 4:00 P.M. to midnight
(B) Saturday through Wednesday, 8:00 P.M. to 4:00 A.M.
(C) Tuesday through Saturday, midnight to 8:00 A.M.
(D) Monday through Friday, 4:00 P.M. to midnight.

85. While on patrol, Police Officer Richardson receives a call to respond to a Grand Larceny. The following information relating to the crime is obtained by the Officer:

Time of Occurrence: Between 3:00 A.M. and 4:00 A.M.
Place of Occurrence: In front of 1122 Dumont Avenue
Victim: Bart Edwards
Crime: Car Theft
Type of Car: 1985 Monte Carlo

Officer Richardson is completing a report on the incident. Which one of the following expresses the above information most clearly and accurately?

(A) Reported stolen at 3:00 A.M. and 4:00 A.M. in front of 1122 Dumont Avenue was Bart Edwards' 1985 Monte Carlo.

(B) Bart Edwards reported that at some time between 3:00 A.M. and 4:00 A.M. his 1985 Monte Carlo was stolen from in front of 1122 Dumont Avenue.

(C) Between 3:00 A.M. and 4:00 A.M. Bart Edwards reported that his 1985 Monte Carlo was stolen in front of 1122 Dumont Avenue.

(D) In front of 1122 Dumont Avenue between 3:00 A.M. and 4:00 A.M., Bart Edwards reported that his 1985 Monte Carlo was stolen.

86. While on patrol, Police Officers Coates and Hall respond to a complaint about a stolen vehicle. The following information relating to the incident is obtained by the Officers:

Time of Occurrence: 3:00 A.M.
Stolen Vehicle: 1986 Corvette
Witness: Mark Wondon
Place: In front of 12-14 Diamond Street
Victim: John Silber
Suspect: James Frank

Officer Hall is completing a report on the incident. Which one of the following expresses the above information most clearly and accurately?

(A) Mark Wondon reports that at 3:00 A.M. he witnessed James Frank steal a 1986 Corvette from in front of 12-14 Diamond Street. Mr. Wondon states that the car belongs to John Silber.

(B) Mark Wondon reports that the 1986 Corvette taken was for John Silber. In front of 12-14 Diamond Street it was taken. The car was robbed by James Frank at 3:00 A.M.

(C) At 3:00 A.M. a 1986 Corvette stolen by James Frank was reported. Mark Wondon saw it in front of 12-14 Diamond Street. It was owned by John Silber.

(D) At 12-14 Diamond Street a 1986 Corvette was reported by Mark Wondon at 3:00 A.M. John Silber, the car owner, was the victim. It was done by James Frank.

Answer questions 87 through 90 solely on the basis of the following passage.

At 3:55 A.M., on August 3, 1986, Police Officer Snow observed four male Hispanics standing by the emergency exit at the 14th Street and Union Square subway station. After one of the males spotted Officer Snow, they all ran down the subway platform. Three of the males ran out the exit gate and up into the street, while the fourth male loitered on the platform, stuffing what appeared to be candy into a paper bag. At 3:57 A.M., Officer Snow stopped and questioned the male. While Officer Snow was questioning the male, a call came over her portable radio requesting her to search the station for unidentified vandals. Officer Snow decided to detain the male because of the radio call and proceeded to interview the railroad clerk who had called the police.

At 4:00 A.M., the railroad clerk, Mr. Wallace, stated that four male Hispanics had broken into the concession stand and removed several bars of candy, cigarettes, and some cash. Officer Snow arrested the male she had detained after the railroad clerk identified him as one of the thieves. Officer Snow read the suspect his constitutional rights at 4:02 A.M., and Sergeant Burns transported Officer Snow and the suspect to the District 4 office.

The suspect was identified as Louie Rodriguez, of 2948 W. 38th Street, New York, New York, age seventeen, 5′10″, 145 lbs., with brown eyes and black hair. Officer Snow described one of the other three suspects as a male Hispanic, approximately 17 to 20 years old, 5′10″, slim build, mustache, wearing a black leather jacket, blue jeans and white Puma sneakers.

The prisoner was searched by Officer Snow and drugs were found on his person. Lieutenant Nicholson classified the crime as Burglary and Unlawful Possession of a Controlled Substance. Officer Snow entered the crime classification on her arrest forms at 4:54 A.M., and fingerprinted and photographed the prisoner at 5:04 A.M. Officer Snow then called the Warrant Division by telephone to make sure the perpetrator did not have any outstanding warrants. In accordance with procedures, Officer Snow secured the drugs in a sealed envelope containing a serial number.

87. Who transported Officer Snow and the prisoner to the District 4 office?

(A) Lieutenant Nicholson
(B) Lieutenant Wallace
(C) Sergeant Burns
(D) Sergeant Rodriguez.

88. What time did Police Officer Snow fingerprint the prisoner?

(A) 3:57 A.M. **(B)** 4:02 A.M. **(C)** 4:54 A.M. **(D)** 5:04 A.M.

89. When Officer Snow first observed the four males, they were standing by the

(A) exit gate
(B) emergency exit
(C) concession stand
(D) token booth.

90. How did Officer Snow safeguard the drugs?

(A) Stored them in a locked safe
(B) Gave them to the supervisor
(C) Placed them in a sealed envelope
(D) Sent them to the lab for analysis.

Answer question 91 solely on the basis of the following information.

When Police Officers arrive at the scene of a serious crime, they should protect any evidence and detain witnesses for further investigation. The following steps should be taken in the order given:

1. Call for the Patrol Supervisor, Detectives and any other person that may be required.
2. Remove unauthorized persons from the area and secure the crime scene. Do not disturb any evidence found at the scene.
3. Detain witnesses and persons with information concerning the crime.
4. Record in Memo Book all observations, as well as the names, addresses and telephone numbers of witnesses, and relevant statements made by anyone, whether casually or as a formal statement.
5. Advise the Patrol Supervisor and Detectives of the identity of witnesses detained, and any other information regarding the crime.

91. Police Officer Hayward responds to a secluded area in Greenville Park after receiving an anonymous report that a dead body is at the location. When the Officer arrives, there is no one around, but the Officer sees what appears to be a body wrapped in plastic. Officer Hayward notifies the Patrol Supervisor and Detectives, and calls for an ambulance. After roping off the area, the Officer should next

(A) detain witnesses to the crime
(B) cut open the bag to determine if it actually contains a dead body
(C) write the appropriate entries in his Memo Book
(D) advise the Patrol Supervisor of all relevant details when the Supervisor arrives.

92. Police Officer LaJolla is writing an Incident Report in which back-up assistance was required. The report will contain the following five sentences:

1. The radio dispatcher asked what my location was and he then dispatched patrol cars for back-up assistance.
2. At approximately 9:30 P.M., while I was walking my assigned footpost, a gunman fired three shots at me.

3. I quickly turned around and saw a White male, approximately 5′10″, with black hair, wearing blue jeans, a yellow T-shirt and white sneakers, running across the avenue carrying a handgun.
4. When the back-up officers arrived, we searched the area but could not find the suspect.
5. I advised the radio dispatcher that a gunman had just fired a gun at me and then I gave the dispatcher a description of the man.

The most logical order for the above sentences to appear in the report is

(A) 3, 5, 2, 4, 1
(B) 2, 3, 5, 1, 4
(C) 3, 2, 4, 1, 5
(D) 2, 5, 1, 3, 4.

Answer question 93 solely on the basis of the following information.

Serious physical injury—injury which creates a substantial risk of death, or serious and protracted disfigurement, protracted impairment of health, or loss or impairment of function of any bodily organ.

Assault 2nd Degree—occurs when, with intent to cause physical injury to another, a person causes such injury to such person or to a third person by means of a deadly weapon or dangerous instrument.

Assault 1st Degree—occurs when, a person intends to cause serious physical injury to another, and causes such injury to that person or to a third person by means of a deadly weapon or dangerous instrument.

Manslaughter 1st Degree—occurs when, with intent to cause serious physical injury to another, a person causes death to that person or to a third person.

Murder 2nd Degree—occurs when, with intent to cause the death of another, a person causes the death of such person or third person.

93. Police Officers Hudson and Ellis are dispatched to the scene of a vehicle accident at 7th Avenue and Valentine Street. Upon their arrival they observe a man standing over a body lying in the gutter. The man, Ralph Vanderbilt, tells the Officers that he was stopped at a red light in his 1986 Lincoln Continental when he was struck from behind by a car driven by Richard Verde. Intending to break Verde's ribs, Vanderbilt took a baseball bat from his car and swung it at Mr. Verde. In trying to avoid the blow, Verde slipped and was struck in the head by the bat. Soon after, the Patrol Supervisor and an ambulance arrive at the scene. Officers Hudson and Ellis place

Mr. Vanderbilt under arrest. The Supervisor then informs the Officers that Mr. Verde is dead. In this situation it would be most appropriate for the Officers to charge Mr. Vanderbilt with

(A) Assault 1st Degree
(B) Murder 2nd Degree
(C) Manslaughter 1st Degree
(D) Assault 2nd Degree.

Answer question 94 solely on the basis of the following information.

Police Officers are required to observe locations where criminal activities may be taking place.

94. Which one of the following locations would most likely require further observation?

(A) Neighborhood residents complain that young people enter and quickly leave an abandoned building all day long.
(B) A diner which is open twenty-four hours a day and frequented by travelers from a nearby motel.
(C) A fast food outlet which has become a hangout for a young crowd.
(D) Numerous middle-aged and elderly women are observed entering office buildings in the late afternoon and leaving around midnight.

Answer questions 95 through 98 solely on the basis of the following passage.

Police Officers Ruden and Elliot were on routine patrol on the night of August 21, 1986 at 11 P.M. when they were dispatched to the scene of a shooting. They were told to respond to 228 West 64th Street. When they arrived at 11:03 P.M., they saw a man lying in the street in front of 226 West 64th Street. He was bleeding from a gunshot wound to the head. The injured man was identified as Raymond Lopez, a resident of 229 West 64th Street, Apartment 5C. A small crowd gathered along the sidewalk.

An ambulance arrived at 11:06 P.M. Police Officer Keyes helped to put Mr. Lopez into the ambulance, and then accompanied him in the ambulance to try to get more information on the shooting. Two paramedics, John Hayes and Robert Shelton, tried their best to save Mr. Lopez's life, but failed. He died at 11:12 P.M. on the way to the hospital. Officer Ruden remained at the scene to get a description of the man who shot Lopez, but witnesses were afraid to talk. Three persons were questioned: Ralph Ricardo, male Hispanic, business man, age 39, lives at 230 West 64th Street, Apartment 4C; John Fitzpatrick, male White, age 25, cab driver; and Jimmy Warren, male Black, age 13, who stated that he saw Arthur Gonzalez, the superintendent at 229 West 64th Street, shoot Lopez. Jimmy's mother agreed to let him testify against Gonzalez, who was arrested at 11:29 P.M. on November 25, when he returned to his apartment to get some clothes.

95. Which of the following persons claimed to have seen the shooting?

(A) Ricardo
(B) Warren
(C) Lopez
(D) Fitzpatrick.

96. When was Gonzalez arrested?

(A) 11:03 P.M., November 24
(B) 11:06 P.M., November 25
(C) 11:12 P.M., November 24
(D) 11:29 P.M., November 25.

97. The person who was arrested was

(A) a superintendent
(B) a cab driver
(C) a business man
(D) unemployed.

98. Where did the Police find Raymond Lopez?

(A) In Apartment 5C, 228 West 64th Street
(B) Opposite 229 West 64th Street
(C) In Apartment 4C, 230 West 64th Street
(D) In front of 226 West 64th Street.

Answer questions 99 and 100 solely on the basis of the following information.

Police Officer Quincy observes that all the cocaine sales in her sector take place on Bucket Avenue; all the heroin sales occur on Jones Road between Bucket Avenue and Wright Street; and all the "crack" sales happen on Albany Road between Hamilton Street and Jervis Avenue. Most of the heroin sales take place between 7:00 P.M. and midnight. Most of the "crack" sales occur between 6:00 P.M. and 10:00 P.M. and between 10:00 A.M. and 2:00 P.M. Most of the cocaine sales take place between 4:00 P.M. and 10:00 P.M. Most of the "crack" sales happen on Tuesdays, most of the heroin sales take place on Wednesdays and Fridays, and most of the cocaine sales take place on Fridays and Saturdays.

99. Officer Quincy would most likely be able to reduce the number of heroin sales by patrolling

(A) Bucket Avenue on Wednesday and Friday from 4:00 P.M. to 10:00 P.M.
(B) Jones Road on Wednesday and Thursday from 8:00 P.M. to midnight
(C) Jones Road on Wednesday and Friday from 7:00 P.M. to 11:00 P.M.
(D) Albany Road on Tuesday from 6:00 P.M. to 10:00 P.M.

100. Based on her knowledge of the drug sale patterns in her sector, Officer Quincy's supervisor wants her to work a steady tour each week that would allow her to concentrate on cocaine, heroin and "crack" sales within her sector. For this purpose it would be most appropriate for Officer Quincy to work

(A) Tuesday through Saturday, 4:00 P.M. to midnight
(B) Tuesday through Saturday, 2:00 P.M. to 10:00 P.M.
(C) Monday through Friday, 4:00 P.M. to midnight
(D) Wednesday through Sunday, 2:00 P.M. to 10:00 P.M.

101. Police Officer Davis is preparing a written report concerning child abuse. The report will include the following five sentences:

1. I responded to the scene and was met by an adult and a child who was approximately four years old.
2. I was notified by an unidentified pedestrian of a possible case of child abuse at 325 Belair Terrace.
3. The adult told me that the child fell and that the police were not needed.
4. I felt that this might be a case of child abuse and I requested that a Sergeant respond to the scene.
5. The child was bleeding from the head and had several bruises on the face.

The most logical order for the above sentences to appear in the report is

(A) 2, 1, 5, 3, 4
(B) 1, 2, 4, 3, 5
(C) 1, 3, 4, 2, 5
(D) 2, 4, 1, 5, 3.

102. While on patrol in the subway, Police Officer Conway is notified, via radio, to respond to the northbound platform to investigate a crime. The following information relating to the crime was obtained by the Officer:

Time of Occurrence: 5:30 P.M.
Place: Northbound "A" Train
Witness: Gertrude Stern
Victim: Matilda Jones
Crime: Chain Snatch

Officer Conway is completing a report on the incident. Which one of the following Memo Book entries expresses the above information <u>most clearly</u> and <u>accurately</u>?

(A) There was a chain snatching incident on the Northbound "A" train at 5:30 P.M. involving Matilda Jones and Gertrude Stern. There was a witness.

(B) Gertrude Stern, while traveling on the Northbound "A" train witnessed a chain snatching with Matilda Jones at 5:30 P.M.

(C) Matilda Jones and Gertrude Stern were on the Northbound "A" train at 5:30 P.M. when Gertrude witnessed a chain snatching.

(D) Matilda Jones informed me that her chain was snatched aboard a Northbound "A" train at 5:30 P.M. Gertrude Stern witnessed the chain snatching.

103. Police Officers Quinn and Dunn receive a call to respond to a reported robbery. The following information relating to the crime is obtained by the Officers:

Time of Occurrence: 10:00 P.M.
Place of Occurrence: 31-42 Maplewood Avenue, Liquor Store
Victim: Donna Miller, store owner
Witness: Thomas White, customer
Suspect: Michael Wall
Crime: Money stolen from cash register.

Officers Quinn and Dunn are completing a report on the incident. Which one of the following expresses the above information most clearly and accurately?

(A) The witness said that he got to the liquor store at 10:00 P.M. and when he got there the place was being held up. His name was Michael Wall. He took the money from Donna Miller, the owner of the liquor store on 31-42 Maplewood Avenue out of the store cash register. Thomas White reported these facts to us.

(B) At 10:00 P.M. Thomas White, the witness, states that after entering the liquor store at 31-42 Maplewood Avenue, he saw the suspect take money from the cash register which belongs to Donna Miller, the owner. Michael Wall is suspected.

(C) Thomas White reports that at 10:00 P.M. he went to the liquor store at 31-42 Maplewood Avenue and saw Michael Wall take money from the cash register. The store is owned by Donna Miller.

(D) Donna Miller, the owner, was robbed at 10:00 P.M. when the money from her cash register was taken at 31-42 Maplewood Avenue. Thomas White was in the liquor store at the time and saw Michael Wall do it.

Answer question 104 solely on the basis of the following information.

Police Officers may sometimes release persons charged with juvenile delinquency into the custody of a parent or guardian. In such cases the Officer should:

1. Determine if the person who would take custody is a parent, guardian, lawful custodian or responsible adult relative by checking the evidence of identity and relationship to the juvenile.
2. Call the Youth Records Unit to obtain information on the juvenile's prior police contacts.
3. Call the Central Warrants Unit to determine if juvenile is wanted by the police on a warrant.

NOTE: Juvenile will <u>not</u> be released if:

1. Person who would take custody is not capable of providing adequate supervision.
2. Juvenile is wanted on a warrant by the police.
3. Juvenile is not likely to appear in court on return date.
4. Juvenile's release would be dangerous to the community.

104. Police Officer Gardner arrested Roger Carter, a 15-year-old, for Grand Larceny. Carter gave Officer Gardner the phone number of his sister Ruth, who was then notified to come down to the station house. Officer Gardner checked the Central Warrants Unit and the Youth Records Unit and determined that Carter had no previous contacts with the police and could be released into a relative's custody. A half-hour later a young woman who appeared to be intoxicated entered the station house. There was a strong smell of alcohol on her breath. She had identification that proved she was Roger Carter's 21-year-old sister Ruth. Officer Gardner then released Roger Carter into Ruth's custody. In this situation, Officer Gardner's actions were

(A) proper, primarily because Ruth Carter could show that she was a relative who was old enough to take custody
(B) improper, primarily because Ruth Carter did not appear to be capable of providing adequate supervision
(C) proper, primarily because Roger Carter had no prior police contacts and was not wanted on any other charges
(D) improper, primarily because Roger Carter was unlikely to appear in court and would pose a threat to the community.

Answer questions <u>105</u> and <u>106</u> solely on the basis of the following information.

Police Officer Cruz is told by his supervisor that the sector he is assigned to has a high incidence of car accidents, assaults, burglaries, and robberies. Officer Cruz studies the crime statistics for his sector and notices that all of the assaults occur Tuesdays through Thursdays, car accidents on Fridays and Saturdays, burglaries on Fridays and Saturdays, and robberies on Fridays through Mondays. Most of the assaults occur on Maple Street, robberies on McDonald Street, car accidents on Merrick Street, and burglaries on Mason Street. Officer Cruz also noticed that all robberies occur between 7:00 P.M. and 11:00 P.M., burglaries between 1:00 P.M. and 5:00 P.M., car accidents between 10:00 P.M. and 3:00 A.M., and assaults between 7:00 P.M. and 11:00 P.M.

105. Officer Cruz would most likely be able to reduce the incidence of car accidents by patrolling

(A) Mason Street on Friday and Saturday between 10:00 P.M. and 4:00 A.M.
(B) Maple Street on Monday through Wednesday between 7:00 P.M. and 11:30 P.M.
(C) Merrick Street on Friday and Saturday between 10:00 P.M. and 4:00 A.M.
(D) McDonald Street on Tuesday and Thursday between 8:00 P.M. and 1:00 A.M.

106. Officer Cruz's superiors want him to work a steady tour each week that would allow him to concentrate on robberies within his sector. What would be the most appropriate tour for Officer Cruz to work?

(A) Monday through Friday, 4:00 P.M. to midnight
(B) Thursday through Monday, 1:00 P.M. to 9:00 P.M.
(C) Thursday through Monday, 4:00 P.M. to midnight
(D) Monday through Friday, 8:00 A.M. to 4:00 P.M.

107. The following five sentences will be part of a Memo Book entry concerning found property:

1. Mr. Gustav said that while cleaning the lobby he found six credit cards and a passport.
2. The credit cards and passport were issued to Manuel Gomez.
3. I went to the precinct to give the property to the Desk Officer.
4. I prepared a receipt listing the property, gave the receipt to Mr. Gustav, and had him sign my Memo Book.
5. While on foot patrol, I was approached by Mr. Gustav, the superintendent of 50-12 Maiden Parkway.

The most logical order for the above sentences to appear in the Memo Book is

(A) 5, 1, 2, 4, 3
(B) 1, 2, 4, 3, 5
(C) 5, 1, 3, 4, 2
(D) 1, 4, 3, 2, 5.

Answer question 108 solely on the basis of the following information.

When a juvenile is arrested and charged as a juvenile offender, a Police Officer should do the following in the order given:

1. Bring the juvenile to the area in the station house designated for interrogation of juveniles.

2. Notify parents or guardian that the juvenile is in custody and where the juvenile is located.
3. Do not question the juvenile until arrival of parents or guardian.
4. Advise juvenile and parents or guardian of constitutional rights prior to interrogation.
5. Prepare Arrest Report.

108. Police Officer Fernandez has made an arrest charging a juvenile as a juvenile offender. After the parents and juvenile have been read their rights before questioning, Officer Fernandez should next

(A) notify the detectives
(B) fill out an Arrest Report
(C) bring the juvenile to the area in the station house designated for questioning
(D) advise the juvenile and parents of their constitutional rights.

109. Police Officers Mains and Jacobs respond to a report of an assault and obtain the following information:

Time of Occurrence: 8:00 P.M.
Place of Occurrence: Lobby of 165 E. 210th Street
Victim: Charles Rayes, stabbed in chest
Witness: John McNam
Suspect: Lydon Syms
Weapon: Large kitchen knife

The Officers are completing a report on the incident. Which one of the following expresses the above information <u>most clearly</u> and <u>accurately</u>?

(A) Mr. John McNam states that at 8:00 P.M. he observed Lydon Syms stab Charles Rayes in the chest while entering the lobby of 165 E. 210th Street with a large kitchen knife.
(B) At 8:00 P.M. John McNam stated he saw Lydon Syms use a large kitchen knife on Charles Rayes in the chest in the lobby of 165 E. 210th Street.
(C) At 8:00 P.M. John McNam stated he observed Lydon Syms stab him in the chest with a kitchen knife while in the lobby of 165 E. 210th Street with Charles Rayes.
(D) Mr. John McNam stated that at 8:00 P.M. he observed Lydon Syms stab Charles Rayes in the chest with a large kitchen knife in the lobby of 165 E. 210th Street.

Answer question <u>110</u> solely on the basis of the following information.

Upon arriving at a location where a person is threatening to jump from a structure, a Police Officer should do the following in the order given:

1. Notify Communications Unit and request an Emergency Service Unit to respond.
2. Attempt to persuade or prevent the person from jumping.
3. Seek assistance from the person's relatives, friends or clergyman if available.
4. Confine the person to the side of the building facing the street.
5. Rope off area below and prevent persons from entering the area.
6. Prepare a Complaint Report and make appropriate Memo Book entries.

110. Police Officer Samuels is on a footpost when a woman runs up to him and states that her husband is on the roof of their twelve story apartment building and has threatened to jump. Officer Samuels and the woman go to the roof of the building. The man sees them and shouts, "You come any closer and I'll jump!" Officer Samuels radios the Communications Unit and requests an Emergency Service Unit to respond. While waiting for back-up assistance, Officer Samuels attempts to persuade the man not to jump. The next step Officer Samuels should take is to

(A) prepare a Complaint Report and make appropriate Memo Book entries
(B) rope off area below and prevent persons from entering the area
(C) ask the man's wife and any friends who may be present for assistance
(D) keep the man on the side of the building facing the street.

Answer question 111 solely on the basis of the following information.

A Police Officer may on occasion arrest a juvenile who is less than 16 years of age, take him into custody and charge him with a serious felony. When a juvenile is arrested and charged as a juvenile offender, the Officer should:

1. Put the juvenile in the forward compartment of the patrol wagon and adult prisoners in the rear compartment, if they are being transported at the same time.
2. Bring the juvenile to an appropriate area designated for questioning at the precinct of arrest.
3. Keep the juvenile separated from adult prisoners while in custody.

111. While on patrol Police Officer Morgan sees 15-year-old Mary Jarvis robbing a neighborhood candy store. Officer Morgan arrests Mary and calls for the patrol wagon to bring her to the local precinct. When the wagon arrives, a forty-year-old burglar named Harry Ryan is seated in the front compartment. Officer Morgan orders Ryan into the rear compartment and puts Mary in the front. The actions taken by Officer Morgan were

(A) proper, primarily because male and female prisoners should not be transported together
(B) improper, primarily because Ryan should have been left in the front compartment
(C) proper, primarily because Mary belonged in the front compartment
(D) improper, primarily because Mary should not be sent to the local precinct.

112. Police Officer Thomas is making a Memo Book entry that will include the following five sentences:

1. My partner obtained a brief description of the suspects and the direction they were heading when they left the store.
2. Edward Lemkin was asked to come with us to search the immediate area.
3. I transmitted this information over the radio.
4. At the corner of 72nd Street and Broadway our patrol car was stopped by Edward Lemkin, the owner of PJ Records.
5. He told us that a group of teenagers stole some merchandise from his record store.

The most logical order for the above sentences to appear in the report is

(A) 5, 4, 1, 3, 2
(B) 4, 5, 1, 3, 2
(C) 5, 1, 3, 2, 4
(D) 4, 1, 3, 2, 5.

Answer question 113 solely on the basis of the following information.

Police Officer Black has been informed by Police Officer Hunt that there have been three robberies of clothing shops on his assigned patrol post, during the month of June. All of the robberies occurred soon after the shops opened and the suspect escaped on foot. Officer Hunt is in charge of investigating this series of crimes. The description of each of the subjects is as follows:

Robbery No. 1—Male, White, about 18 years old, 5′6″, 120 lbs. Short hair with a tail on back. Blue dungarees, white short sleeve shirt, white sneakers, scar from his right wrist to elbow.

Robbery No. 2—Male, White, 20 to 23 years old, 5′5″, 140 lbs. Short curly black hair, blue dungarees, blue T-shirt, blue sneakers, tattoo on right arm, earring in right ear.

Robbery No. 3—Male, White, about 19 years old, 5′6″, 135 lbs. Short black hair. Wears an earring in left ear, black jogging pants, black jacket, white sneakers, scar on left hand.

On July 1, Police Officer Black arrested a suspect during an attempted robbery of another store. The description of this suspect is as follows:

Robbery No. 4—Male, White, 20 years old, 5′6″, 130 lbs., short straight black hair, white short sleeve shirt, blue dungarees, white sneakers, gold earring in left ear, tattoo on right arm, 4″ scar going from left hand to wrist.

113. Based on the above descriptions of the suspects in the first three robberies, Officer Black should tell Officer Hunt that the suspect in the fourth robbery should also be considered a suspect in

(A) Robbery No. 1, but not Robbery No. 2 or Robbery No. 3
(B) Robbery No. 3, but not Robbery No. 1 or Robbery No. 2
(C) Robbery No. 2 and Robbery No. 3, but not Robbery No. 1
(D) Robbery No. 1 and Robbery No. 2, but not Robbery No. 3.

114. While on patrol, Police Officers Murray and Crown receive a radio call to respond to a reported assault. The following information is given to them at the scene:

Time of Occurrence: 6:00 P.M.
Victim: Sarah Schwartz, wife
Witness: Cathy Morris, Sarah's sister
Suspect: Raymond Schwartz, husband
Crime: Assault with a knife.

The Officers are completing a report on the incident. Which one of the following expresses the above information most clearly and accurately?

(A) Cathy Morris stated that she was visiting her sister, Sarah Schwartz. They were cooking dinner when Raymond Schwartz, Sarah's husband, came home at 6:00 P.M. Raymond was drunk and started an argument with Sarah. During the argument, Raymond picked up a knife and cut Sarah.
(B) Sarah Schwartz stated that she was making dinner with her sister, Cathy Morris. Her husband Raymond came home real angry and was drunk at 6:00 P.M. They had an argument and Raymond cut her with a knife.
(C) According to Cathy Morris, her sister Sarah Schwartz was cooking dinner with her. Sarah's husband Raymond came home. They got into an argument. He was drunk and had a knife in his hand and cut her. This happened when he arrived at 6:00 P.M.
(D) Sarah Schwartz's sister reported to me that at 6:00 P.M. her husband Raymond came home drunk. Cathy Morris was with her making dinner. Raymond got mad at her, picked up a knife, and cut her.

115. Police Officer Halloway responds to a call for help inside the Municipal Parking Lot. The following information relating to an assault is obtained by the Officer.

Place of Occurrence: Municipal Parking Lot
Victim: Diane Gallagher
Suspect: Dominick DeLuca, victim's ex-boyfriend
Crime: Assault

Officer Halloway is completing a report on the incident. Which one of the following expresses the above information most clearly and accurately?

(A) The victim, Diane Gallagher, states that she was in the Municipal Parking Lot with her ex-boyfriend, Dominick DeLuca, when she was assaulted.
(B) Diane Gallagher states that she and her ex-boyfriend were in the Municipal Parking Lot when she was assaulted by Dominick DeLuca.
(C) Diane Gallagher, the victim, in the Municipal Parking Lot with Dominick DeLuca, states that she was assaulted by her ex-boyfriend.
(D) The victim, Diane Gallagher, states that she was assaulted by her ex-boyfriend, Dominick DeLuca, in the Municipal Parking Lot.

Answer question 116 solely on the basis of the following information.

Police Officer Fox, of the 62nd Precinct, notices that most of the assaults happen between 2:00 A.M. and 6:00 A.M.; most of the burglaries occur between 10:00 A.M. and 3:00 P.M.; and most of the purse snatches take place between 4:00 A.M. and 7:00 A.M.

Most of the burglaries occur on Wednesday; most of the assaults take place on Friday; and most of the purse snatches happen on Friday and Saturday.

116. Police Officer Fox's superiors instruct him to work a steady tour each week that would allow him to concentrate on purse snatches and burglaries within his patrol area. For this purpose it would be most appropriate for Officer Fox to work

(A) 4:00 A.M. to Noon, Tuesday through Saturday
(B) Noon to 8:00 P.M., Wednesday through Sunday
(C) Midnight to 8:00 A.M., Tuesday through Saturday
(D) 4:00 A.M. to Noon, Monday through Friday.

Answer question 117 solely on the basis of the following information.

A Police Officer may issue a Desk Appearance Ticket (DAT) instead of detaining a prisoner if the prisoner qualifies for one. When processing a prisoner charged with a misdemeanor or violation, in addition to following the normal arrest procedure, the arresting officer should do the following in the order given:

1. Inform the prisoner that he may be issued a DAT instead of detention if he qualifies.
2. Check the prisoner's name with the Central Warrant Unit to determine if the prisoner is wanted for another crime.
3. Issue the DAT after you determine that the prisoner is eligible.
4. Conduct an interview with the prisoner, using a Desk Appearance Ticket Investigation form.

117. Police Officer Perez has made an arrest involving a Petit Larceny. In addition to following the normal arrest procedure, Officer Perez has informed the prisoner that he may be eligible for a Desk Appearance Ticket. Officer Perez should next

(A) find out if the prisoner is wanted for committing another crime
(B) interview the prisoner
(C) inform the prisoner that he may be issued a Desk Appearance Ticket if he qualifies
(D) issue a Desk Appearance Ticket to the prisoner.

118. Police Officer Caldwell is completing a Complaint Report. The report will include the following five sentences:

1. When I yelled, "Don't move, Police," the taller man dropped the bat and ran.
2. I asked the girl for a description of the two men.
3. I called for an ambulance.
4. A young girl approached me and stated that a man with a baseball bat was beating another man in front of 1700 Grande Street.
5. Upon approaching the location, I observed the taller man hitting the other man with the bat.

The most logical order for the above sentences to appear in the report is

(A) 4, 5, 1, 2, 3 **(C)** 5, 1, 3, 4, 2
(B) 5, 4, 2, 3, 1 **(D)** 4, 2, 5, 1, 3.

Answer question 119 solely on the basis of the following information.

When a Police Officer is assigned to guard a hospitalized prisoner only the following persons are allowed to visit the prisoner:

1. Lawyer, if requested by the prisoner.
2. Member of the family, after written permission has been granted by the district Desk Officer of the district concerned or on official New York City Police Department letterhead of the precinct of arrest by the Station House Supervisor.

119. Agnes Smith who has recently committed a bank robbery is a prisoner at Bayview Hospital. In attempting to escape from the scene, Smith injured herself in an auto accident and has not been able to communicate since. Police Officer Cleon, who is guarding Ms. Smith, is approached by Betty Phillips, who requests permission to visit Ms. Smith. Officer Cleon explains to Ms. Phillips the rules for visiting a hospitalized prisoner. Ms. Phillips, who has documentation that shows she is a lawyer, also states that she is Ms. Smith's cousin. A nurse at the hospital, who knows them both, confirms this. In this situation, for Officer Cleon to allow Ms. Phillips to visit Ms. Smith would be

(A) proper, primarily because Ms. Phillips is a lawyer
(B) improper, primarily because only a doctor can determine who is allowed to see a patient who is seriously ill
(C) proper, primarily because Ms. Phillips is a member of Ms. Smith's family
(D) improper, primarily because Ms. Phillips lacks written permission to visit the patient.

Answer question 120 solely on the basis of the following information.

When a Police Officer stops a vehicle and discovers that the operator is driving with a suspended or revoked driver's license, the following should be done in the order given:

1. Confiscate driver's license.
2. Prepare Seized Driver's License Receipt/Report.
3. Give operator of the vehicle a receipt for the license.
4. If the driver has two or more unrelated suspensions or his license has been revoked for any reason, arrest him and take him to the precinct.
5. Do not mark or mutilate license in any manner.
6. Have violator's vehicle parked in a legal parking area until a registered owner can arrange to have the vehicle removed from the scene by a licensed operator.

120. Police Officer Winterman is directing traffic during rush hour at a very busy and dangerous intersection. After observing the driver of a green Volvo make an illegal U-turn at the intersection, Officer Winterman directs the driver to pull his car over to the curb. While inspecting the driver's license, Officer Winterman discovers that the license has been revoked. Officer Winterman should next

(A) arrest the driver
(B) take the driver's license
(C) give the operator of the vehicle a receipt for taking his license
(D) have the violator park his car in a legal parking area.

Answer question 121 solely on the basis of thc following information.

121. Police Officers Ortiz and Rinaldi patrol the harbor terminal area. Officer Ortiz works from 8:00 A.M. to 4:00 P.M., Monday through Friday. She takes her meal from noon to 1:00 P.M. each day. Officer Rinaldi works from 4:00 P.M. to midnight, Tuesday through Saturday. He takes his meal from 8:00 P.M. to 9:00 P.M. each day. Crime statistics for the terminal area show that most crimes in the daytime occur from 11:45 A.M. to 1:20 P.M. on Mondays, Tuesdays, and Thursdays, and from 12:05 P.M. to 1:20 P.M. on Wednesdays and Fridays. Most crimes at night are committed from 7:30 P.M. to 8:45 P.M. on Tuesdays and Thursdays, and from 8:30 P.M. to 9:15 P.M. on Wednesdays, Fridays, and Saturdays. In order to have an Officer on patrol during the periods when most crimes are committed, which of the following would be the most appropriate times for Officers Ortiz and Rinaldi to take their meals?

(A) Officer Ortiz: 1:30 P.M.–2:30 P.M.; Officer Rinaldi: 9:00 P.M.–10:00 P.M.
(B) Officer Ortiz: 12:30 P.M.–1:30 P.M.; Officer Rinaldi: 9:30 P.M.–10:30 P.M.
(C) Officer Ortiz: 1:30 P.M.–2:30 P.M.; Officer Rinaldi: 9:30 P.M.–10:30 P.M.
(D) Officer Ortiz: 1:00 P.M.–2:00 P.M.; Officer Rinaldi: 7:00 P.M.–8:00 P.M.

Answer question 122 solely on the basis of the following information.

Whenever a Police Officer responds to the scene of a family offense, the Officer should

1. obtain medical assistance for anyone who appears to need it
2. determine if an Order of Protection has been obtained by the complainant, which would mean that a violator would be subject to arrest
3. arrest the offender if a felony has been committed
4. not attempt to bring the parties together or mediate the dispute in felony cases—an arrest should be made

5. arrest the offender in a non-felony case when efforts to mediate are unsuccessful and the complainant wants the offender arrested.

122. Police Officer Berger responds to a family dispute. After investigating, he determines that a violent argument has occurred between Max Jansen and his wife, Maria. Max apparently slapped Maria in the face more than once. Although she does not need medical attention and does not have an Order of Protection, Mrs. Jansen wants her husband arrested. Officer Berger, who knows that this is a non-felony case, tells Mrs. Jansen that there are problems in many marriages, but she and her husband should be able to work things out. When Mrs. Jansen insists that she wants her husband arrested, Officer Berger tells her to think the matter over for a day or two and then call him at the precinct. In this situation, Officer Berger's actions were

(A) improper, primarily because Mrs. Jansen had been struck in the face and should have been taken to the hospital as a precaution
(B) proper, primarily because it was not a felony case and Mrs. Jansen did not need medical assistance
(C) improper, primarily because Mrs. Jansen insisted her husband be arrested
(D) proper, primarily because Mrs. Jansen had not obtained an Order of Protection.

123. In August, the number of robberies near Montgomery Avenue and Cedar Street sharply increased. Captain Jones decided to assign Police Officer Roberts to a post at that corner. He ordered the Officer to remain visible and observe anyone who looked suspicious.

Which one of the following situations should Officer Roberts observe most closely?

(A) A man standing near a bank cash machine watching people withdraw money
(B) A cab driver parked in the same spot for thirty minutes drinking a cup of coffee and smoking a cigar
(C) Two young men running down the block toward the park
(D) A young man walking with an elderly lady into a grocery store.

Answer question 124 solely on the basis of the following information.

Police Officers must sometimes rely on eyewitness accounts of incidents, even though eyewitnesses may make mistakes with regard to some details.

124. While walking his dog, Walter Twining is struck by a car at the corner of Bacon Avenue and Jersey Street. Police Officer Bond responds to the scene and questions four witnesses who saw the vehicle that struck Mr. Twining. The following are descriptions of the vehicle given by the witnesses. Which one of these descriptions should Officer Bond consider most likely to be correct?

(A) A blue Chevrolet, NY Plate 1736BOT.
(B) A black Chevrolet, NY Plate 1436BAT.
(C) A blue Oldsmobile, NY Plate 1736BAI.
(D) A blue Chevrolet, NY Plate 1736BAT.

Answer question 125 solely on the basis of the following information.

Robbery 2nd Degree—occurs when a person forcibly steals property and when:

1. He is aided by another person actually present; or
2. While committing the crime or immediately fleeing from it, he or another participant in the crime:
   (A) Causes physical injury to any person who is not a participant in the crime; or
   (B) Displays what appears to be a pistol, revolver, rifle, shotgun, machine gun or other firearm.

125. Which one of the following situations is the best example of Robbery in the Second Degree?

(A) Jim Jackson and Martin Hayes decide to rob a grocery store. Unknown to Jackson, Hayes decides to bring along his pistol. They walk into the store, push the owner against the counter, and tell him to hand over the money or they will hurt him. The owner gives them two hundred dollars and they flee the scene. Hayes never takes out his gun during the entire episode.
(B) Ben Tyler walks into a grocery store, tells the clerk that he has a gun, and demands money. Tyler has his finger extended in his pocket pretending he has a gun. The clerk becomes frightened and gives Tyler all the money in the cash register.
(C) Bill Jefferson and Warren Pierce plan to rob a liquor store. While entering the store, Pierce trips over a display and knocks over several bottles. This angers Jefferson, who punches Pierce in the face, causing a bloody nose. They then grab several bottles of liquor and run out of the store.
(D) John Harrison decides to rob a gas station. He drives up, gets out of his car, takes out a 12″ bowie knife and threatens the attendant with it. The attendant gives $500 to Harrison, who then drives away.

Answer question 126 solely on the basis of the following information.

When a crime has been committed and a Police Officer makes an arrest, he should do the following in the order given:

1. Inform the person in custody of the reason for the arrest unless the person arrested physically resists or attempts to flee, or if it would be impractical to do so.
2. Handcuff the person with hands behind the back.
3. Immediately search the person for weapons and evidence.
4. Advise the person of his legal rights before questioning.

126. Police Officers Darcy and Hayward were on patrol when they were approached by a woman on the corner of 236th Street and Katonah Avenue. The woman was very upset and said that an unidentified White male wearing a blue jacket was attempting to remove the stereo from her car, a green Oldsmobile, which was parked one block away on 237th Street. The Officers drove to 237th Street and saw a man fitting the description in the green Oldsmobile. When the Officers approached the auto, the man fled on foot, dropping the stereo as he left the vehicle. Officer Darcy caught the man about a block away, and after a brief struggle, placed the man under arrest. Officer Darcy should next

(A) search the man for possible weapons
(B) inform the man of the reason for the arrest
(C) advise the man of his rights before questioning
(D) handcuff the man with his hands behind his back.

127. Police Officer Moore is writing a Memo Book entry concerning a summons he issued. The entry will contain the following five sentences:

1. As I was walking down the platform, I heard music coming from a radio that a man was holding on his shoulder.
2. I asked the man for some identification.
3. I was walking in the subway when a passenger complained about a man playing a radio loudly at the opposite end of the station.
4. I then gave the man a summons for playing the radio.
5. As soon as the man saw me approaching, he turned the radio off.

The most logical order for the above sentences to appear in the Memo Book entry is

(A) 3, 5, 2, 1, 4
(B) 1, 2, 5, 4, 3
(C) 3, 1, 5, 2, 4
(D) 1, 5, 2, 4, 3.

Answer question <u>128</u> solely on the basis of the following information.

Police Officers Janson and Lorenz are assigned to cover sector C in a patrol car. They have been working together for over a year and know the sector well. They have noticed that all of the auto thefts occur on Diamond Avenue; all of the drug sales take place on Stag Street; most of the assaults occur on Beatle Street; and most of the burglaries occur on Bond Avenue. All of the drug sales occur between 2:00 P.M. and 11:00 P.M., and all of the auto thefts take place between midnight and 6:00 A.M. The assaults happen between 6:00 P.M. and 10:00 P.M. All of the burglaries take place between 8:00 P.M. and midnight.

128. Officers Janson and Lorenz will be working a steady 10:00 P.M. to 6:00 A.M. tour during the fourth week of October. During this tour they would most likely decrease the incidence of crime by patrolling on

(A) Bond Avenue
(B) Stag Street
(C) Diamond Avenue
(D) Beatle Street.

Answer question <u>129</u> solely on the basis of the following information.

A Police Officer may bring a suspect back to the crime scene for a prompt on-the-spot identification only

1. within a reasonable time after the crime was committed; and
2. the suspect was caught in an area reasonably near the scene of the crime; and
3. the suspect is shown to the witness as fairly as possible under the circumstances.

129. Police Officer Burke's patrol car is flagged down by Ed Weis, owner of Kay's Jewelry Store. Mr. Weis tells Officer Burke that just two minutes earlier his store was robbed. Mr. Weis gives the Officer a description of the robber, as well as the direction of his escape. About five minutes later Officer Burke sees a male who fits the description acting suspiciously. As soon as the male sees the police car he begins to run. After a brief chase, the male is apprehended by Officer Burke and brought back to the jewelry store, which is four blocks away. Mr. Weis identifies the male as the robber, and the Officer arrests him. In this situation, Officer Burke's actions were

(A) improper, primarily because the suspect was apprehended far away from the jewelry store
(B) proper, primarily because the Officer caught the suspect in an area near the scene of the crime and within a short period of time

(C) improper, primarily because the Officer deliberately brought the suspect back to the jewelry store to persuade the manager to identify him

(D) proper, primarily because the male began to run as soon as he saw the police car.

130. Police Officer Kashawahara is completing an Incident Report regarding fleeing suspects he had pursued earlier. The report will include the following five sentences:

1. I saw two males attempting to break into a store through the front window.
2. On Myrtle Avenue they ran into an alley between two abandoned buildings.
3. I yelled to them "Hey, what are you guys doing by that window?"
4. At that time I lost sight of the suspects and I returned to the station house.
5. They started to run south on Wycoff Avenue heading towards Myrtle Avenue.

The most logical order for the above sentences to appear in the report is

(A) 1, 5, 2, 4, 3
(B) 3, 5, 2, 4, 1
(C) 1, 3, 5, 2, 4
(D) 3, 1, 5, 2, 4.

Answer question <u>131</u> solely on the basis of the following information.

Police Officers who observe a person carrying a rifle or shotgun in public should do the following in the order given:

1. Determine if the person has a valid permit.
2. If there is no permit:
   A. Inform the person that he may surrender his firearm to the Officer at the scene or at the precinct.
   B. Serve a summons for violation or make an arrest.
   C. Prepare a receipt for the firearm and give a copy to the owner.
   D. Send the firearm to the gun lab if it is believed to have been used in a crime, or safeguard it at the precinct.
   E. Tell the owner to apply for a permit.

131. After stopping Mr. Jones for carrying a rifle on the street, Police Officer Scott determines that Mr. Jones does not have a valid permit. While holding Mr. Jones's rifle, Officer Scott writes a summons. After giving Mr. Jones a summons for not having a valid permit, Officer Scott should next

(A) tell Mr. Jones to apply for a permit
(B) send the rifle to the gun lab
(C) tell Mr. Jones to surrender his rifle
(D) make out a receipt for the firearm and give a copy to Mr. Jones.

Answer question 132 solely on the basis of the following information.

A Police Officer who attempts to arrest a person for whom a warrant has been issued must do the following:

1. Inform the person of the warrant and the reason it was issued unless he physically resists or attempts to flee.
2. Show the warrant if requested.
3. If premises are involved, do not announce authority and purpose if
   (A) the life and safety of the Officer or another person is endangered; or
   (B) an attempt to escape may result; or
   (C) material evidence might be destroyed, damaged or hidden
4. Break into the premises, if necessary.

132. Police Officer Ramos has a warrant for the arrest of Bill Jensen for failure to appear in court on a drug charge. As Officer Ramos approaches Mr. Jensen's apartment door, he hears a female in the apartment scream "Please don't shoot me!" Without announcing his identity or reason for being at the apartment, Officer Ramos kicks the door open, sees Mr. Jensen and arrests him. In this situation the action taken by Officer Ramos was

(A) proper, primarily because the life of the female in the apartment was in danger
(B) improper, primarily because Officer Ramos should have announced his authority before entering the apartment
(C) proper, primarily because Jensen had no opportunity to destroy drug-related evidence
(D) improper, primarily because Jensen had made no attempt to escape.

133. Police Officer Bloom is completing an entry in his Memo Book regarding a confession made by a perpetrator. The entry will include the following five sentences:

1. I went towards the dresser and took $400 in cash and a jewelry box with rings, watches, and other items in it.

2. There in the bedroom, lying on the bed, a woman was sleeping.
3. It was about 1:00 A.M. when I entered the apartment through an opened rear window.
4. I spun around, punched her in the face with my free hand, and then jumped out the window into the street.
5. I walked back to the window carrying the money and the jewelry box and was about to go out when all of a sudden I heard the woman scream.

The most logical order for the above sentences to appear in the Memo Book entry is

(A) 1, 3, 2, 5, 4
(B) 1, 5, 4, 3, 2
(C) 3, 2, 1, 5, 4
(D) 3, 5, 4, 1, 2.

Answer question 134 solely on the basis of the following information.

Resisting Arrest—a person is guilty of resisting arrest when he intentionally prevents or attempts to prevent a Police Officer from making an authorized arrest of himself or another person.

134. Tom Turbo is returning home from work when he sees Police Officer Bannon in the process of arresting his friend Dominick Foss for an assault that Foss has just committed. Turbo walks up to Officer Bannon and asks him what Foss has done. As Officer Bannon turns to answer Turbo's question, Foss begins to run down the street. Officer Bannon gives chase and recaptures Foss a few seconds later. In this situation

(A) Turbo should be charged with resisting arrest but Foss should not
(B) Foss should be charged with resisting arrest but Turbo should not
(C) Both Turbo and Foss should be charged with resisting arrest
(D) Neither Turbo nor Foss should be charged with resisting arrest.

Answer question 135 solely on the basis of the following information.

A Police Officer has discretion regarding when to issue a traffic summons. This is the case when the Officer believes a person did not realize that he was committing the violation, and did not intend to commit one. However, a Police Officer should never benefit from using such discretion.

135. Police Officer Gray is patrolling at the corner of Tull Street and Burke Avenue. The intersection is crowded with pedestrians and automobiles. The light on Tull Street is red but one man proceeds to cross the street against the light in view of Officer Gray. People standing on the corner waiting for the light to change tell Officer Gray to give the man a summons. Officer Gray questions the man and learns that he is a tourist from a foreign country. The man has just arrived in the United States and is unfamiliar with American traffic regulations. Officer Gray explains what a red light means, and tells the man that no summons will be issued this time. The man is extremely thankful and tells Officer Gray that if he ever visits the man's country Officer Gray will be treated to the best meal he has ever eaten. In this situation, the actions of Officer Gray were

(A) proper, primarily because the violation that was committed was not important
(B) improper, primarily because a summons should be issued whenever an Officer witnesses a violation
(C) proper, primarily because the violator was unfamiliar with the traffic regulations
(D) improper, primarily because the Officer would benefit by overlooking the violation.

136. Police Officer Allan responds to the scene of a robbery. The following information relating to the incident is obtained by the officer:

Time of Occurrence: 2:00 A.M.
Victim: Michael Harper
Perpetrator: Unknown
Description of Crime:—Victim was grabbed around neck from behind while walking home
—Money and Jewelry taken

Police Officer Allan is preparing a report on the robbery. Which of the following expresses the above information most clearly and accurately?

(A) At 2:00 A.M. while walking home, Michael Harper observed someone he could not identify. The victim was grabbed around the neck and his money and jewelry were stolen.
(B) At 2:00 A.M. while walking home, Michael Harper was grabbed around the neck from behind. His money and jewelry were stolen. Mr. Harper is unable to identify the perpetrator.
(C) Michael Harper is unable to identify the perpetrator because he grabbed him around the neck while walking home. The victim was robbed of money and jewelry at 2:00 A.M.
(D) Michael Harper was robbed of money and jewelry. The unknown perpetrator was not identified, however he grabbed him from behind while walking home.

137. While on patrol, Police Officer Silas responds to a report of a robbery. The following information is obtained by the Officer:

Time of Occurrence: 5:00 P.M.
Place of Occurrence: 40 Forman Street
Victim: Floyd Joy
Witness: Paul Clay
Suspect: Joe Lister
Crime: Robbery

Officer Silas is completing a report on the incident. Which one of the following expresses the above information <u>most clearly</u> and <u>accurately</u>?

(A) At 5:00 P.M., Paul Clay witnessed a robbery at 40 Forman Street. Floyd Joy was robbed by Joe Lister.
(B) At 5:00 P.M., Joe Lister was observed committing a robbery with Floyd Joy on 40 Forman Street by Paul Clay.
(C) At 40 Forman Street, Paul Clay stated to me that he had seen Floyd Joy getting robbed. The perpetrator, Joe Lister, committed the robbery at 5:00 P.M.
(D) Paul Clay stated that he witnessed a robbery taking place at 40 Forman Street at 5:00 P.M. with Joe Lister. The subject of the robbery was Floyd Joy.

Answer questions <u>138</u> and <u>139</u> solely on the basis of the following information.

Before engaging in a high-speed pursuit of a vehicle, Police Officers should do the following in the order given:

1. Determine whether a high-speed pursuit is necessary.
2. Notify radio dispatcher at start of pursuit and provide the following information:
   a. your location
   b. type of vehicle, color and direction of travel
   c. nature of offense
   d. state and number of license plate
   e. description of occupants
   f. any other pertinent information
3. Utilize patrol car's emergency signalling devices.
4. Inform radio dispatcher if vehicle changes direction, give last location of vehicle, as well as speed and direction of travel.
5. Notify radio dispatcher if pursued vehicle is lost or pursuit is terminated.

138. While on patrol, Police Officers Montalvo and Casadante observe a vehicle with two White males traveling at a very high speed go through a red light. Officer Montalvo decides to begin a high-speed pursuit. Officer Casadante informs the radio dispatcher that they are in a high-speed pursuit of a black Ford, NY license number UXY918, traveling east on the Grand Central Parkway in the vicinity of La Guardia Airport. Officer Casadante further advises that the vehicle ran a red light at the intersection of Northern Boulevard and 47th Avenue. Which one of the following should the Officers do next?

(A) Notify the radio dispatcher that back-up assistance is needed.
(B) Turn on the patrol car's emergency signalling lights and siren.
(C) Notify the radio dispatcher that the vehicle has changed direction.
(D) Give the radio dispatcher a description of the occupants in the Ford.

139. Assume that the Ford leaves the Grand Central Parkway and continues to travel east. After a mile or so the Officers lose sight of it. Officers Montalvo and Casadante should next inform the radio dispatcher

(A) that they are still in pursuit of the black Ford
(B) to advise the local precinct of the description of the vehicle
(C) that the Ford has changed its direction
(D) that they have lost the Ford.

140. Police Officer Sherman received the following information from a robbery victim:

Time of Occurrence: 8:00 P.M.
Place of Occurrence: Jack's Check Cashing Place
Victim: Frank Jackson, owner
Witness: Daryl Green
Description of Suspect: Unknown
Crime: Robbery of $1000

Police Officer Sherman is completing a report on the robbery. Which one of the following expresses the above information <u>most clearly</u> and <u>accurately</u>?

(A) Although Daryl Green, who reported the crime while in progress, was also a witness, the police arrived minutes after the robbery. Neither Mr. Green nor Mr. Jackson could describe the thief, and, he ran away with $1000. Frank Jackson, who owns Jack's Check Cashing Place, was robbed at 8:00 P.M.
(B) Jack's Check Cashing Place was robbed at 8:00 P.M. The owner, Frank Jackson could not give a description of the thief as the police arrived soon after. Daryl Green, a witness, reported the crime while it was in progress. He first entered the store next to the Check Cashing Place, but came out 10 minutes later. Mr. Jackson said the thief got away with $1000. Mr. Green could not describe the thief either.

(C) Frank Jackson, the owner of Jack's Check Cashing Place, was robbed there at 8:00 P.M. Daryl Green, a witness, reported the robbery while it was in progress. The police arrived minutes later. Mr. Jackson and Mr. Green could not provide a description of the thief, who escaped with $1000.

(D) The thief escaped with $1000, according to Frank Jackson, the owner. Daryl Green, who witnessed the robbery, could not describe the thief. He reported the incident while the thief was still there. Jack's Check Cashing Place was robbed at 8:00 P.M., however the owner could not describe him either.

141. While on patrol, Police Officer Wright receives a call to respond to a robbery. The following information relating to the crime is obtained by the Officer.

Place of Occurrence: Corner of Rockaway and New York Avenue.
Victim: Frank Holt
Suspect: Male White
Weapon: .357 Magnum

Officer Wright is completing a report on the incident. Which one of the following expresses the above information most clearly and accurately?

(A) On the corner of Rockaway and New York Avenues, Frank Holt reported that he was robbed with a .357 Magnum by a White male.

(B) Armed with a .357 Magnum on the corner of Rockaway and New York Avenues, Frank Holt reported that he was robbed by a White male.

(C) A White male on the corner of Rockaway and New York Avenues who was armed with a .357 Magnum committed a robbery, reported Frank Holt.

(D) Frank Holt reported that he was robbed on the corner of Rockaway and New York Avenues by a White male armed with a .357 Magnum.

Answer questions 142 through 150 on the basis of the following sketches. The first face on top, is a sketch of an alleged criminal based on witnesses' descriptions at the crime scene. One of the four sketches below that face is the way the suspect looked after changing appearance. Assume that NO surgery has been done on the suspect. Select the face which is most likely that of the suspect.

142.

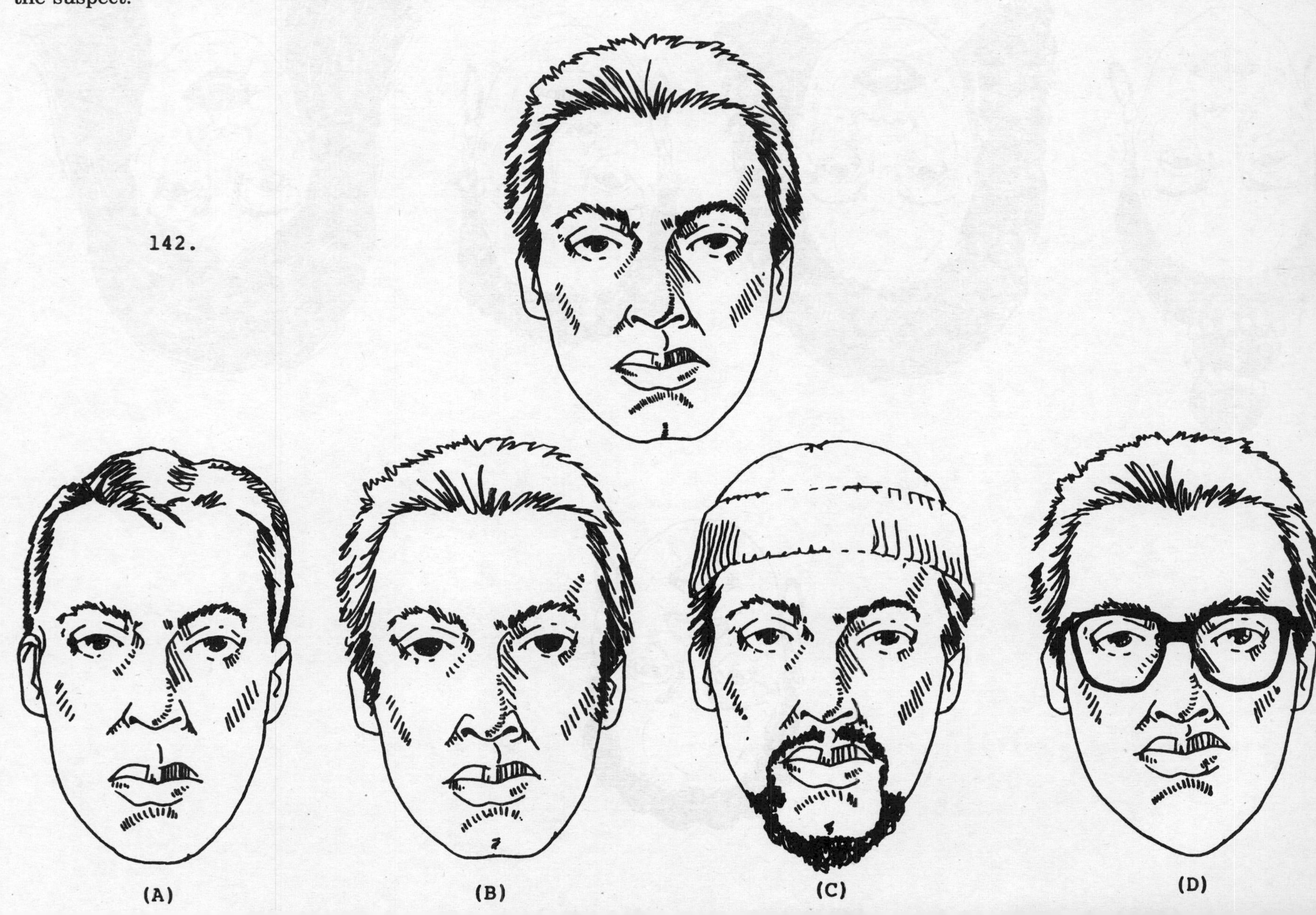

143.

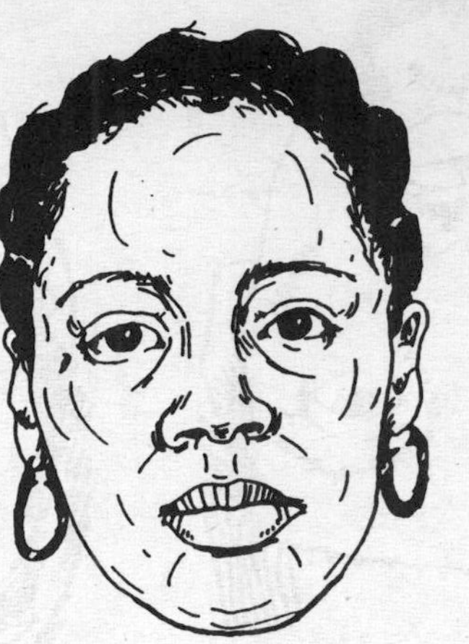

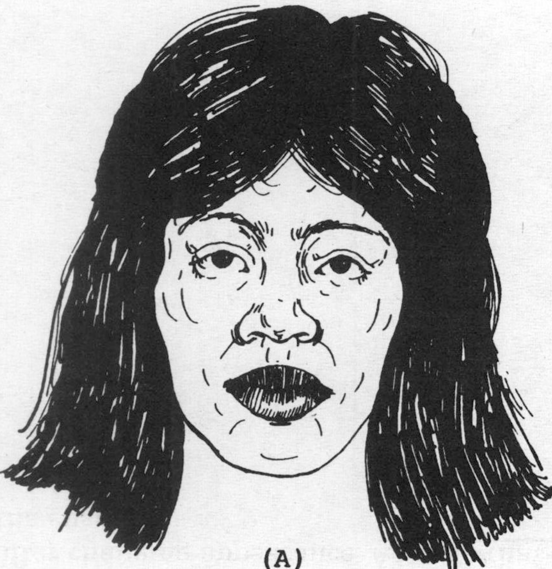

(A)

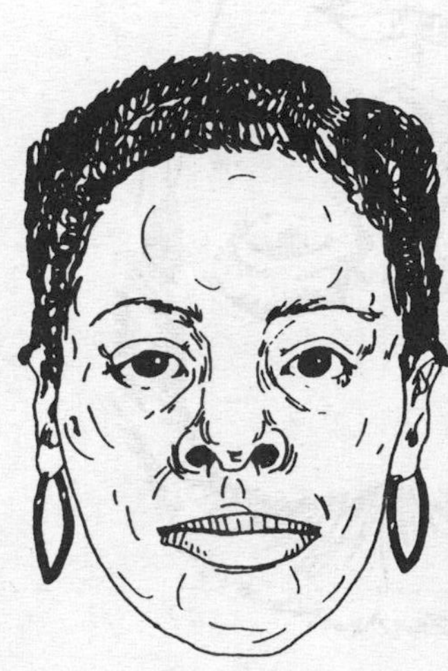

(B)

(C)

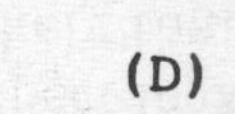

(D)

144.

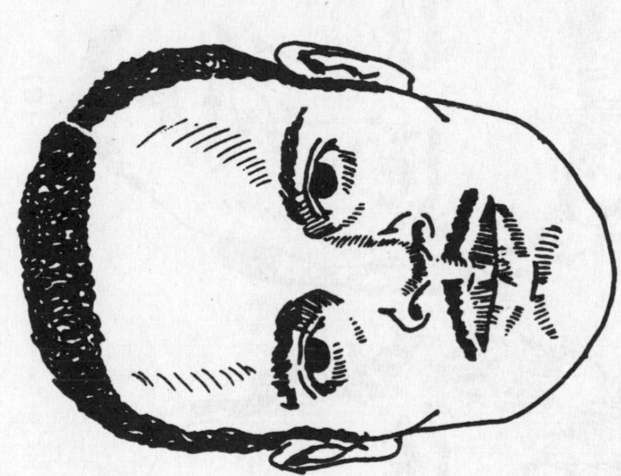

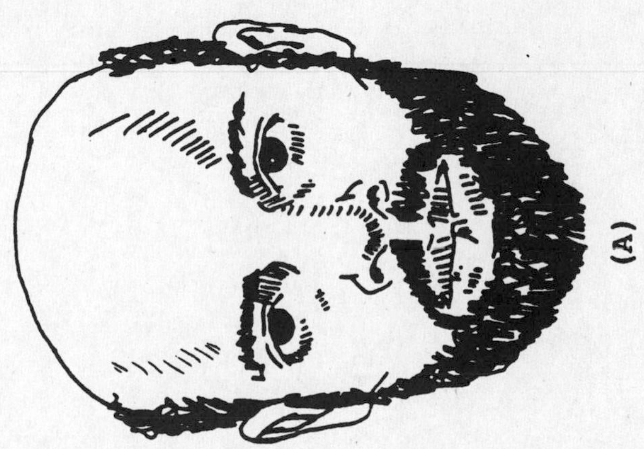

(A)

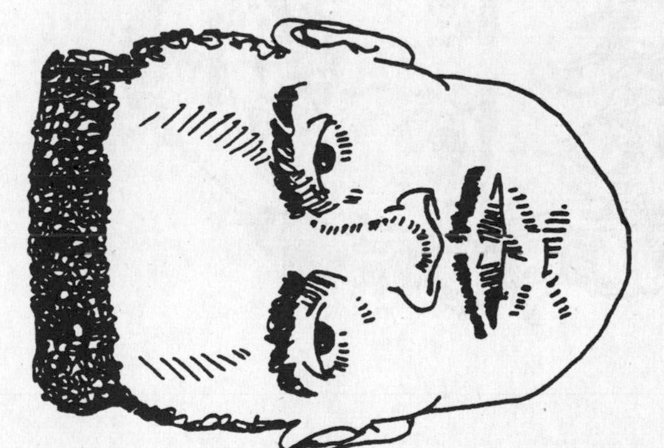

(B)

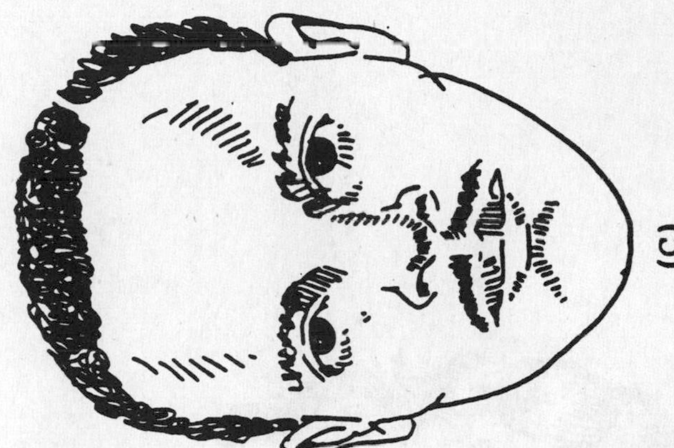

(C)

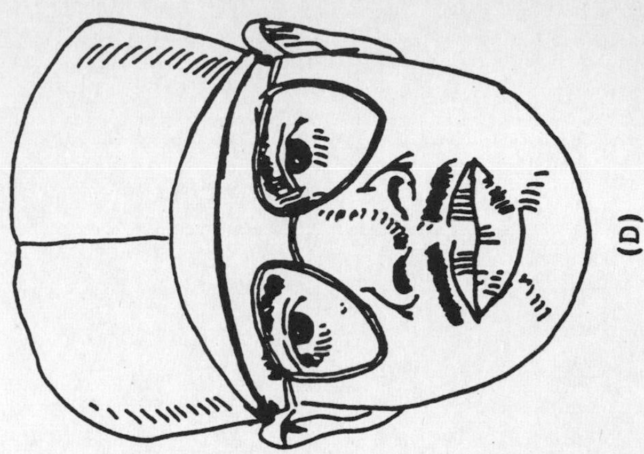

(D)

145.

146.

147.

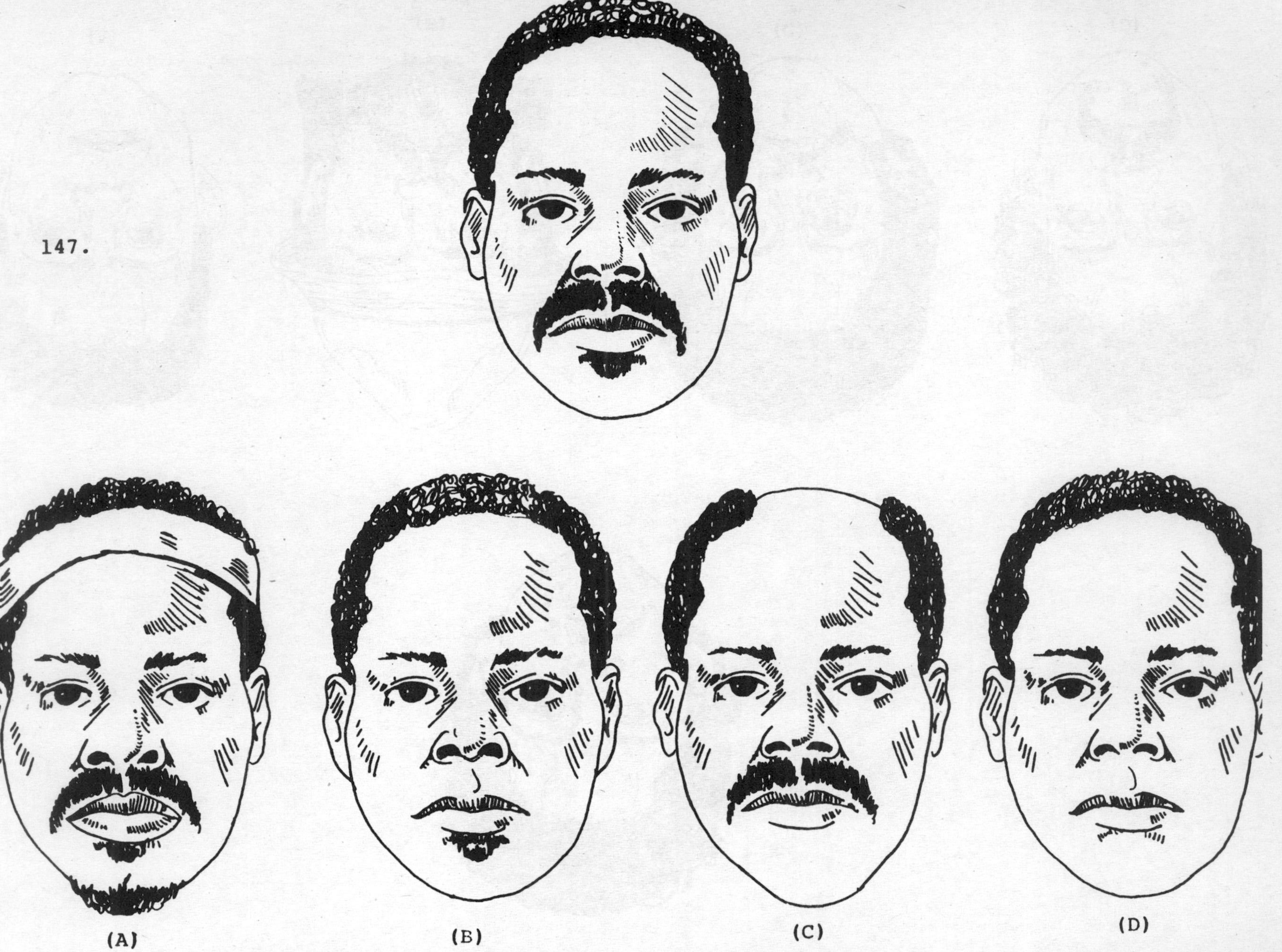

148.

(A)

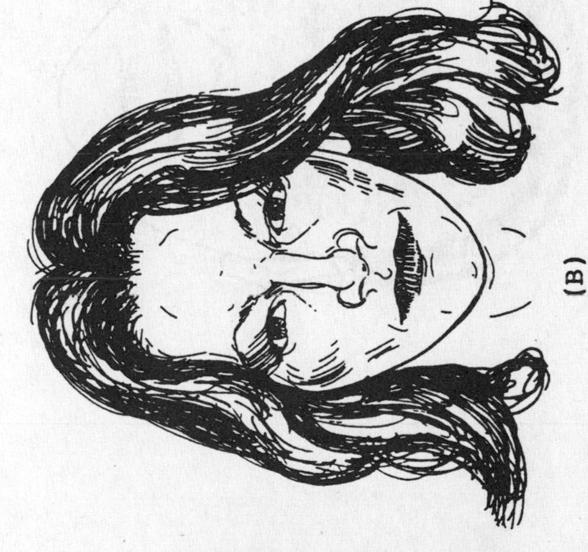

(B)

(C)

(D)

149.

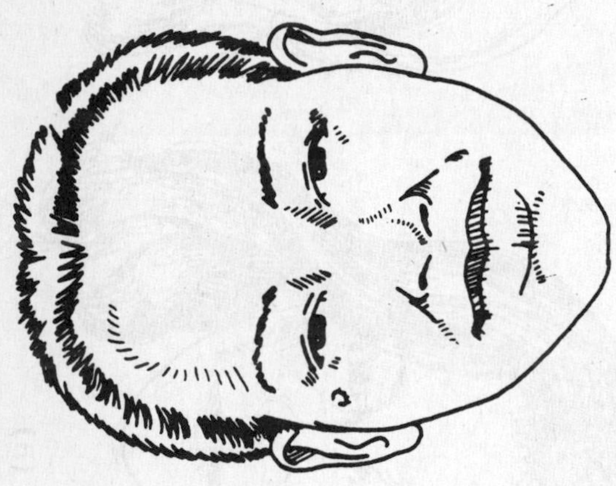

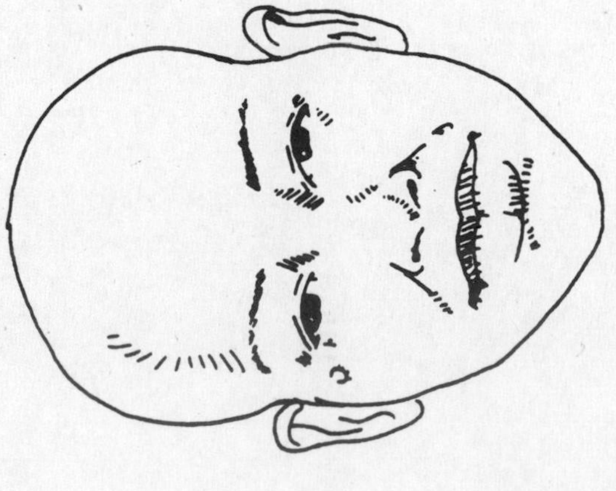

(A)

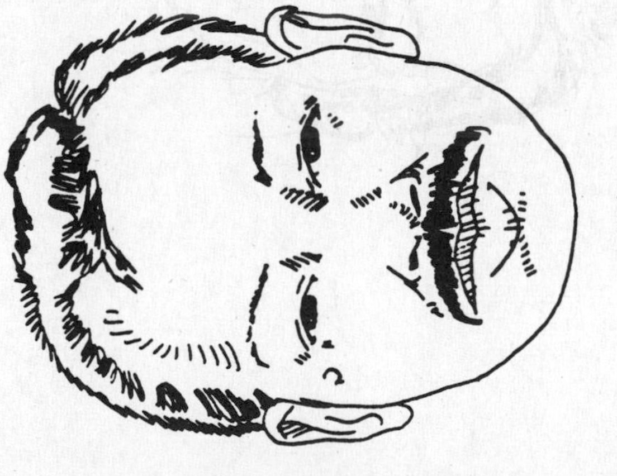

(B)

(C)

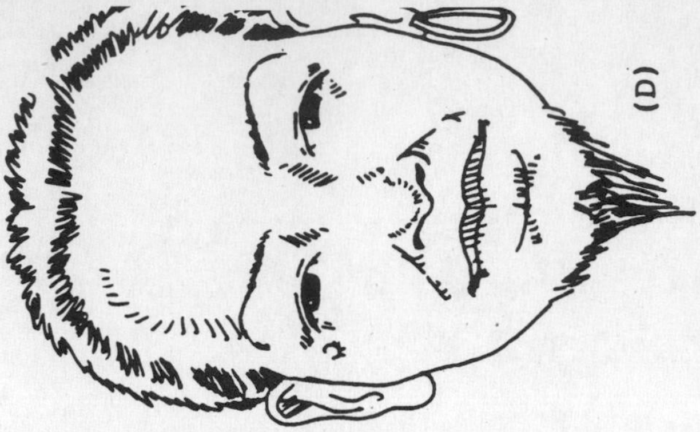

(D)

150.

(A)

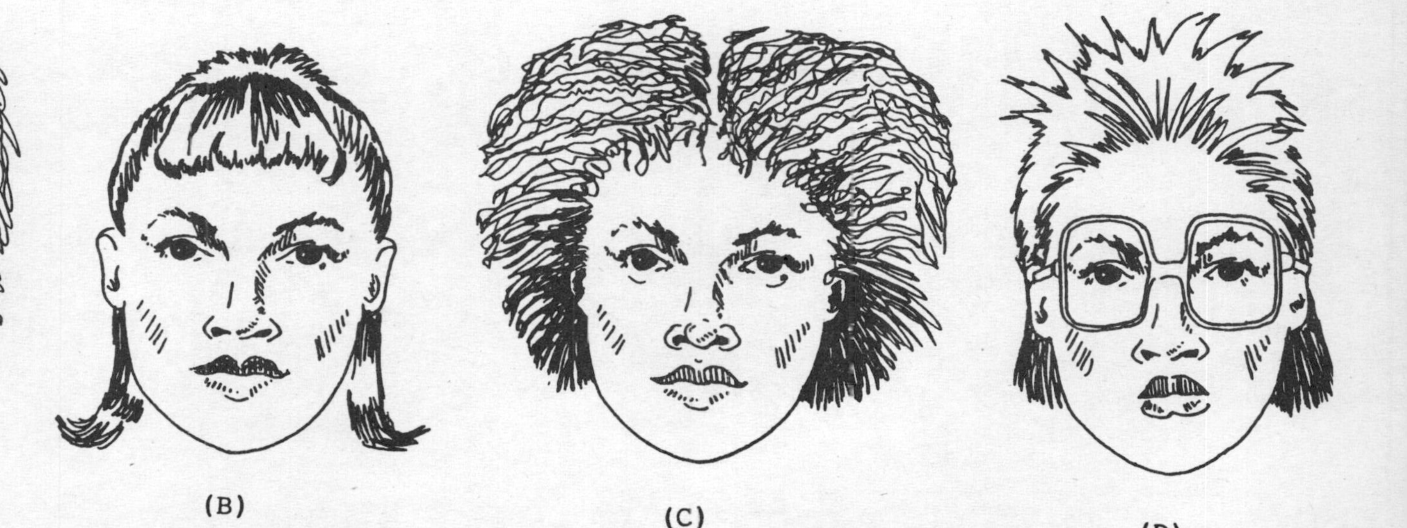

(B)

(C)

(D)

Answer Key, Diagnostic Procedure, and Explanations

Answer Key

1. D	31. B	61. A	91. C	121. C
2. A	32. C	62. A	92. B	122. C
3. C	33. B	63. B	93. C	123. A
4. D	34. B	64. C	94. A	124. D
5. C	35. C	65. D	95. B	125. A and/or B
6. A	36. B	66. B	96. D	126. D
7. B	37. B	67. A and/or D	97. A	127. C
8. B	38. C	68. A	98. D	128. C
9. A	39. B	69. C	99. C	129. B
10. D	40. D	70. C	100. A	130. C
11. C	41. A	71. B	101. A	131. D
12. D	42. D	72. C	102. D	132. A
13. B	43. B	73. D	103. C	133. C
14. D	44. C	74. B	104. B	134. B
15. C	45. D	75. A	105. C	135. C
16. B	46. A	76. D	106. C	136. B
17. D	47. B	77. D	107. A	137. A
18. C	48. D	78. C	108. B	138. D
19. A	49. C	79. B	109. D	139. D
20. B	50. C	80. B	110. C	140. C
21. D	51. A	81. A	111. C	141. D
22. B	52. C	82. B	112. B	142. C
23. C	53. C	83. D	113. B and/or C	143. C
24. D	54. B	84. C	114. A	144. A
25. D	55. B	85. B	115. D	145. A
26. A	56. D	86. A	116. A	146. B
27. A	57. B	87. C	117. A	147. D
28. A	58. C	88. B	118. D	148. C
29. D	59. B	89. B	119. D	149. A
30. B	60. B	90. C	120. B	150. B

Diagnostic Procedure

Insert the number of correct answers you obtained in the blank space for each section of the examination. The scale in the next column indicates how you did. The information at the bottom of the scale indicates how to correct your weaknesses.

SECTION	QUESTION NUMBER	AREA	YOUR NUMBER CORRECT	SCALE
1	1–12	MEMORY		12 Right—Excellent 10–11 Right—Good 8–9 Right—Fair Under 8 Right—Poor
2	16, 28, 34, 41, 51, 58, 78, 82, 92, 101, 107, 112, 118, 127, 130, 133	SENTENCE ORDERING		15–16 Right—Excellent 13–14 Right—Good 11–12 Right—Fair Under 11 Right—Poor
3	15, 21, 22, 31, 33, 35, 36, 40, 42, 48, 49, 50, 52, 53, 57, 59, 60, 71, 72, 77, 80, 91, 94, 104, 108, 110, 111, 117, 119, 120, 122, 126, 129, 131, 132, 135, 138 and 139	APPLYING POLICE PROCEDURES		37–38 Right—Excellent 35–36 Right—Good 33–34 Right—Fair Under 33 Right—Poor
4	18–20, 37–39, 43–45, 54–56, 61–63, 73–76, 79, 87–90, 95–100, 113, 123, 124	READING COMPRE-HENSION		32–33 Right—Excellent 30–31 Right—Good 28–29 Right—Fair Under 28 Right—Poor
5	17, 32, 81, 93 125, 134	LEGAL DEFINITIONS		6 Right—Excellent 5 Right—Good 4 Right—Fair Under 4 Right—Poor
6	26, 27, 66–68	TRAFFIC MAPS		5 Right—Excellent 4 Right—Good Under 4 Right—Poor
7	142–150	MATCHING SKETCHES		9 Right—Excellent 8 Right—Good 7 Right—Fair Under 7 Right—Poor
8	14, 29, 30, 46, 47, 64, 85, 86, 102, 103, 109, 114, 115, 136, 137, 140, 141	REPORT WRITING		18–19 Right—Excellent 16–17 Right—Good 14–15 Right—Fair Under 14 Right—Poor
9	69, 70, 83, 84, 105, 106, 116, 121, 128	DIRECTED PATROL		9 Right—Excellent 8 Right—Good 7 Right—Fair Under 7 Right—Poor
10	23–25	ARITHMETIC COMPUTATIONS		3 Right—Excellent Under 3 Right—Poor

1. If you are weak in Section One, then concentrate on Chapters 5 and 6.

2. If you are weak in Section Two, then concentrate on Chapter 10, the section dealing with Sentence Ordering.

3. If you are weak in Section Three, then concentrate on Chapter 8.

4. If you are weak in Section Four, then concentrate on Chapters 4 and 5.

5. If you are weak in Section Five, then concentrate on Chapter 9.

6. If you are weak in Section Six, then concentrate on Chapter 10, the section dealing with Traffic Maps.

7. If you are weak in Section Seven, then concentrate on Chapter 10, the section dealing with Matching Sketches.

8. If you are weak in Section Eight, then concentrate on Chapter 12, the section dealing with Report Writing.

9. If you are weak in Section Nine, then concentrate on Chapter 10, the section dealing with Directed Patrol.

10. If you are weak in Section Ten, then study the strategy outlined for questions 23–25 in the explained answers for this examination and also in Chapter 10.

NOTE: Consider yourself weak in a section if you receive other than an excellent rating in it.

Answer Explanations

1. **D** A police officer is often asked travel directions. Therefore, it is certainly reasonable for you to be expected to know transportation routes on your post.

2. **A** Here again, you must realize that a police officer is required to be familiar with any traffic regulations on his/her post.

3. **C** Developing some association would have been helpful here. The man wearing *Glasses* was next to *Gambling* information about Lotto.

4. **D** Remember, in almost every memory picture where license plate numbers are depicted, the plate numbers are the subject of a question.

5. **C** The examiner's fondness for numbers should begin to become quite clear to you now.

6. **A** Once again we have a question dealing with numbers. A suggested association might be that banks close at *3* P.M. (33 is the address) and there are four letters in the word *bank* as well as the word *park* (the street the bank is on).

7. **B** Remember to look for oddities. The unusual should always attract your attention. Unless a holiday, a variety store would not usually close its doors on a Saturday when the likelihood of an increased number of shoppers exists.

8. **B** Obviously, a police officer should be particularly observant of any crimes in progress on his/her post.

9. **A** After you noticed the crime in progress, an association should have been developed to remember the perpetrator, such as, the *pickpocket* was wearing a *plaid* jacket.

10. **D** The victim who is *lighting* a cigarette is about to *lose* his wallet.

11. **C** Remember to concentrate on oddities—that is, things that stand out. In the entire scene, the man having his pocket picked is the only person with a solid black top or jacket.

12. **D** The tip-off is that she was holding a cigarette. Remember, in number ten, the victim was lighting a cigarette.

13. *Delete* The official answer key lists Choice "B" as the answer. However, unless any additional information was given at the individual testing sites at the time of the examination, your authors think that none of the choices is correct. Choices B, C, and D all incorrectly indicate that Carl Burns resides at 1865 Lenox Avenue. Choice A indicates that Carl Burns made a statement to the police while he was parked in front of his residence. We just don't know that. Remember, do not assume information. Therefore, we are of the opinion that the question is defective and should be deleted.

14. **D** Choice A is incorrect because it repeats that the male is white. Choice B is incorrect since it begins to describe someone before explaining why the police are interested in the person being described. Choice C is incorrect since it fails to describe adequately the revolver as a .45 caliber weapon.

15. C It is appropriate to close off traffic on a street in the afternoon, as described in Choice C. It is not appropriate to close off traffic at an airport (Choice A), or on a dead-end street late at night (Choice B), or in the harbor (Choice D).

16. B Sentence 4 comes before sentence 2 since sentence 2 merely mentions "the bar" without explaining which bar it is, as is done in sentence 4. Therefore, choices A and D can be eliminated. Since sentence 2 ends the action it must be the last sentence. Therefore, choice C, which lists sentence 5 as coming last can be eliminated. Choice B is the answer.

17. D The key to answering this legal definition question correctly is to recognize that John is being advised by the people on the street that someone might be hurt by his actions but continues his reckless conduct anyway. This is actually the conduct that is described by the given definition of Reckless Endangerment.

18. C According to paragraph three of the passage, Officer Gillespie took Mr. Abernathy's report. Therefore, any choice which suggests that Officer Henderson took Mr. Abernathy's report is incorrect. Choice C is the answer.

19. A The officers parked their police car behind some cars which were parked on the south side of the street. Mr. Abernathy, who lives at 870 Bayard Street, came out of his home and walked across the street to speak to the officers. Mr. Abernathy has to live on the north side of the street.

20. B Mr. Abernathy reported that a white male was trying to break into his car "on the previous night." Therefore, the date of the crime will be different on his report.

21. D The next step after preparing the necessary reports, which is step 4, is to telephone the facts to the Bureau of Child Welfare, step 5.

22. B The key to answering this question is to recognize that the youth who is "cursing at people" is a greater potential problem than the chanting woman in Choice A, the woman arguing with herself in Choice C, or the preacher in Choice D.

23. C If you picked choice A you overlooked the fact that there were four traveler's checks worth twenty dollars each and three traveler's checks worth twenty-five dollars each. The overall value of the property and cash was $817.00. Please note that the examiners do not use these arithmetic computation questions to test your ability to do simple addition and subtraction. They also use them to test your powers of observation. For example, in this question they listed the value of one check, but told you that more than one had been stolen.

24. D Here again, the key was to recognize that there were *three* watches stolen valued at $65.00 *each*, or a total of $195.00. Therefore, the total value of the property stolen was $955.00 as suggested by choice D.

25. D When you add the value of the phone ($2950), the value of the stereo system ($1060), the value of the attache case ($200), and the value of two gold pens worth $970 each ($1940), you obtain a total dollar value of $6150.00, as suggested by choice D.

26. A Choice D is incorrect because it suggests that you travel west on John Avenue, which is a one-way eastbound street. Choices B and C suggest routes that will get you there but which are not as short as the route suggested in choice A.

27. A Choices B and C can be eliminated because they suggest you travel north on Debra Street which is a one-way southbound street. The route described in choice D follows the flow of traffic, but it is a longer route than the one described in choice A.

28. A Sentence 5 starts the action and indicates the reason for the pursuit so it must come before sentence 2. Thus we can eliminate choices B and D. Since sentence 4 ends the action and is the logical conclusion for the report, it must come last so we can eliminate choice C. Choice A is the answer.

29. D Choice A is wrong since it starts with the pronoun "He" without explaining whom "He" refers to. Besides Choice A is simply too awkward. Choice B is wrong since it conveys the idea that Mr. Willis hit his ex-wife without permission and authority to do so instead of conveying the correct notion that Mr. Willis entered his ex-wife's premises without permission or authority to do so. Choice C is wrong since it gives the impression that the bat acted on its own. Choice D is constructed properly. Note the chronological (time) arrangement. First he entered the premises and then he struck her.

30. B Choices A, C, and D are wrong for a number of reasons, one of which is that none of them clearly explain who "she" is.

31. B In the story, an ambulance is on the way and the patrol supervisor has been requested. Therefore, step one has been satisfied. The next action taken should be as outlined in step two, which is to comfort (calm) the mentally ill or emotionally disturbed person (the tenant).

32. C Choice A is wrong since an actual injury occurred, not just the creating of fear of an injury. Choice B is wrong because, among other reasons, it lacks immediacy in that it doesn't specify exactly when the bomb might go off. Choice D also lacks immediacy.

33. B Choice B involves two groups of teenage boys already fighting. When compared to the less serious situations described in the other three choices, it is the one which would most appropriately require back-up assistance.

34. B Sentence 3 starts the action so it comes first. Besides, before a robbery can be described, it must first be observed. Therefore, sentence 3 comes first and choices A and D can be eliminated. Sentence 5 has the robber attempting to flee while sentence 4 has the robber in custody. Therefore, sentence 4 must come last. Choice B is the answer.

35. C Step one is satisfied since the desk officer is notified. The key to answering the question correctly is recognizing that 1:00 A.M. is a time other than normal business hours. Therefore, an appointment must be made with the Central Repair Shop, as per Step 2B.

36. B Choice B is the only choice that deals with the providing of emergency transportation for seriously injured persons. Since the man is critically injured, and an ambulance is not available for at least 20 minutes, Choice B describes the most serious situation the officer has to deal with.

37. B Even though the suspected child abuse is occurring in apartment 12B of 415 Dover Street, the first paragraph clearly states that the call to the dispatcher came from apartment 12A of 415 Dover Street.

38. C Mr. Fine was asked by his wife to call the police.

39. B Although both Mr. and Mrs. Fine answered the door when the officers knocked on it, the first paragraph clearly states that it was Mrs. Fine who gave the police their initial information regarding the complaint.

40. D The described procedure does not require the preparation of an Aided Report for those involved in a vehicle accident. In addition, the definitions clearly exempt those injured in a vehicle accident from being considered as an "aided case." Therefore, what is needed is a Police Accident Report for the vehicle accident and an Aided Report for the passerby, as indicated in the correct answer, Choice D.

41. A Before the place of occurrence can be referred to as "the location," as in sentence 1, it must be specifically described, as in sentence 4. For that reason, and because it starts the action, sentence 4 must come first so choices B and C can be eliminated. Sentence 2 most logically concludes the action and must come last. Choice A is the correct answer.

42. D In the stem of the question it indicates that steps 1 through 4 have been satisfied. And, after breaking into the premises by forcing the apartment door open (step 4), the officers should make the arrest of Mr. Johnson (step 5).

43. B After being urged to do so by her mother, it was Mrs. Margaret Volkman who called 911. We hope that you were not "tricked" into selecting Joyce Hill (Choice C), who did call the police, but did so "last year."

44. C Officer Wilson made his decision that the children were not in any danger after speaking with Gayle Volkman, the 13-year-old daughter of the caller.

45. D It was the neighbor, Joyce Hill, who made a complaint in the past (last year) about Margaret's drinking.

46. A Choices B and D are incorrect since they suggest that the crime was reported at 10:15 A.M. when, in fact, that is the time the crime was committed. Choice C is not clear since it fails to state that Chuck Baker is the owner of Mike's Deli.

47. B Choice A is incorrect since it states that the witness, Lorraine Mitchell, was responding to a robbery. Choice C is incorrect since it gives the impression that two people were robbed. Choice D is incorrect since it gives the impression that Leslie Reese suddenly became the owner of the property which was then stolen.

48. D Remember, this type of question is answered solely on the basis of the procedure and not on the basis of logic, common sense or prior knowledge. Therefore, although Choice B sounds good, there is nothing to support it in the stated procedure. Picking up the revolver, as suggested in Choice A, is in violation of Procedure #3. Choice D is correct because it is supported in Step 3 of the procedure.

49. C The key words in the procedure are "seriously injured." An unconscious person (Choice C) is certainly more seriously injured than a person with a scratched finger (Choice A), or a girl with bruised knees (Choice B), or a mother who feels faint (Choice D).

50. C In the story, the officer already satisfied Step One by preparing the Complaint Report. The next step depends on whether the car involved is registered in New York or another state. Since the car involved was registered in another state (New Jersey), the next step is as indicated in Step Three A and Choice C: to try to learn the identity of the registered owner from the Inter-City Correspondence Unit.

51. A Before the words "the robbery" can be used as in sentence 1, the robbery must be more specifically described, as in sentence 3. For this reason, and because it starts the action, sentence 3 comes first. Therefore, Choices B and C can be eliminated. Since sentence 2 ends the action, it is the last sentence in the report. Choice D is therefore eliminated.

52. C When a tanker truck explodes, the procedure mandates a frozen area with a radius of at least 1000 feet. Choice A has the right dimension of 1000 feet but does not mention a radius. Choice C mentions a radius of 1200 feet and is correct since it meets the condition of being "at least 1000 feet in radius."

53. C We are looking in this question for an activity that appears to be suspicious. As the answer indicates, a vendor who arrives five minutes before the end of the lunch period (ostensibly a vendor wants maximum exposure to the lunch crowd) is more suspicious than the persons described in Choices A, B, or D.

54. B As indicated in paragraph three, the robber known as Redeye was armed with a knife.

55. B Paragraph three tells us that Redeye is the same height as the second perpetrator and at least ten pounds heavier than the first perpetrator. That makes Redeye 5′10″ and 170 pounds. And, remember, all three perpetrators are described as white, males.

56. D Officer Miller and the victims arrived at the scene immediately after the three suspects were apprehended.

57. B The stem of the question tells us that the officer satisfied Steps One and Two by speaking to the woman, recording all the facts, and preparing a complaint report. Therefore, the next step is as indicated in Step Three, to telephone the complaint to the precinct of occurrence.

58. C Police reports often begin with a statement as to how the police came to be involved in the incident which is the subject of the report. Since this is done in sentence 3, and since sentence 3 starts the action, it is the first sentence in the report. Only Choice C lists sentence 3 as coming first.

59. B According to Procedure E, the minister should be permitted to speak with the prisoner only upon the request of the prisoner.

60. B The necessity to pull someone over to the side of the road exists, according to the procedure, when the driver's capability is questionable. The question asks for the selection of the least likely situation when it would be necessary to pull someone over. Someone swerving to avoid a collision does not suggest questionable driving. There are two lessons to learn here. First, the examiner often asks that you select the least likely or the "wrong" situation. Second, your answer should be based solely on the given procedure.

61. A According to this passage, Mr. Jones lives at 1783 Appleseed Ave., and Mr. Jones is Mr. Carro's roommate. Therefore, 1783 Appleseed Ave. is also where Mr. Carro lives.

62. A Mr. Carro said he punched one of his attackers and kicked another. Mr. Peters, however, stated that Mr. Carro did not fight back.

63. B According to paragraph three of the passage, Officer Blake interviewed Mr. Jones first.

64. C Choice A is incorrect since it does not clearly indicate who shot whom. Choice B is incorrect since it does not clarify who is the suspect or who is the owner of the Arcade. Choice D is wrong since it does not clearly state who was arrested.

65. D Choice A is wrong for many reasons. Not only does it make it sound like the witness was on patrol; it doesn't specifically say the television was stolen. Choice B is incorrect since it lists 4:00 A.M. as the time of the reporting of the crime when it is actually the time of occurrence of the crime. Choice C is wrong since it doesn't identify John Haysport as a neighbor.

66. B Choice A is wrong since it suggests traveling east on Houser Street which is a one-way westbound street. Choices C and D both follow the flow of traffic but are not as short as the route described by Choice B.

67. A, D Choice B can be eliminated since it suggests going east on Avenue D which is a one-way westbound street. Choice C is wrong since it suggests you travel east on Houser Street which is a one-way westbound street. (Note: this is the same reason why choice A of question 66 was wrong. Check our strategy for a tip on how to save time when this happens.) While the routes described in choices A and D both follow the flow of traffic, the one in choice A is slightly shorter. However, the final key indicated that either choice A or D would be accepted as being correct. This is an example of how the appeal process works. After the examination you have a period of time within which to protest the tentative key. If you have a valid case, the Department of Personnel will accept two answers.

68. A The officer is at John Street and Macon Avenue when he begins to follow the suspect. After going one block east on Macon, they turn left and travel for three blocks, which would have them traveling north on Blue Street. A subsequent right turn would put them on Avenue C heading east. After two blocks, another right turn is made which would result in their heading south on Henry Street. In the middle of Henry Street, the suspect makes a U-turn which means he is now heading north, which is the answer. Remember, as we point out in our strategy for doing traffic map questions, always put yourself in the place of the driver of the vehicle when making left and right turns.

69. C Choices A, B, and D can be eliminated since no burglaries occurred on Sundays and only one occurred on Monday.

70. C The officer should focus his/her efforts in the area where most of the robberies are occurring, which is Morris Avenue. This eliminates choices A and D. Choice B ignores Saturday which is a day when two of the five reported robberies occurred. Choice C includes Morris Avenue and Saturdays and is the answer.

71. B The key here is what is most suspicious. A group in a parked car in front of a closed store should be suspicious to the police.

72. C As indicated in Step 6, after notifying the precinct detectives, the officer should inform the Sex Crime Squad.

73. D In this item type, you should first look at the stem of the question to see ahead of time what the question is asking. If you did this, you would have found out that the question was about homicides. Therefore, you could have ignored the other crime information and concentrated strictly on the homicide information. Choices A and C do not include high homicide locations and can be quickly eliminated. Choice B does not reflect high homicide days and can also be eliminated. This leaves Choice D which includes both the high homicide location and the high homicide days.

74. B We hope you read the choices carefully and did not confuse the Sony Radio with the portable TV. If you did, you probably incorrectly selected Choice A.

75. A The burglaries occurred between 10:00 P.M. (late evening) and 6:00 A.M. (early morning).

76. D The suspect stopped by the officer is described as having no mustache and no sunglasses. This eliminates choices A, B, and C, leaving choice D as the correct answer.

77. D According to Procedure #3, the officer should have immediately searched the prisoner for weapons or evidence. Such a search was not made. Remember to base your answers solely on the procedures.

78. C Remember our strategy. The first thing we do is look at the first sentence in the choices, then the last sentence. If the answer is still not clear, we go to the middle sentences, looking first at the second sentence. In this question, sentence 3 starts the action and comes first. Also note the reference in sentence 2 to "him." How could this sentence come first? Sentence 1 ends the action and comes last. Choice C is the answer.

79. B This type of question is actually a kind of reading comprehension question. It tests your ability to determine which of the descriptions given by various witnesses is most likely to be the most accurate. The strategy to follow is to ascertain what information is most common to the description given by each of the witnesses. For example, Choices A and B suggest license plate numbers which differ only in what the next to last number should be. Choice A states it is the number 8, while Choice B states that it is the number 3. However, the other two choices both suggest that the next to last number is number 3. Therefore, we can see that the description that is most common among all of the witnesses, and therefore most likely to be correct, is the one given in Choice B.

80. B After completing Step Two of the procedure, the officer is required to park the patrol car in a position which will prevent interference with fire-fighting operations, as indicated in Choice B.

81. A The officer has reasonable suspicion in Choice B due to the actions of the suspect, in Choice C due to information received from a third party, and in Choice D due to a conversation that the officer overheard. Note that all three of these choices list suspicious activities specifically mentioned in the text of the law upon which you are told to base your answer. There is no reasonable suspicion indicated in Choice A. It is the answer.

82. B Sentence 4 must come before sentence 1 since the victim must come home before he can discover that the door to his apartment is open. Therefore, sentence 4 comes first and Choices A and C can be eliminated. Sentence 5 ends the action and must come after sentence 1 so sentence 5 is the last sentence in the report. Choice B lists sentence 4 as coming first and sentence 5 as appearing last. It is the answer.

83. D Please note that reading the stems of questions 83 and 84 before reading the passage would have enabled you to concentrate only on information relating to assaults (question 83) and homicides question 84). In this question, Choices A and B suggest the wrong location to reduce assaults as all of the assaults take place on Wentworth Avenue. Choice C suggests the high assault location but the wrong times. Choice D is the best choice.

84. C Choices A and D are incorrect since the times of patrol do not correspond to the times when the homicides are occurring. Choice B is incorrect since it does not have the officer patrolling on the days when the homicides are occurring.

85. B Choice A is incorrect because it confuses the time of occurrence with the time of reporting. Choices C and D are incorrect for the same reason. As we indicated in our strategy in the chapter dealing with report writing questions, in the great majority of cases the correct answer to these questions begins with a person's name or a time.

86. A Once again the correct answer begins with a name. Choice B is incorrect because it does not clearly state who owns the vehicle. Choices C and D are incorrect because they confuse the time of reporting with the time of occurrence.

87. C As indicated in paragraph two of the passage, it was Sergeant Burns who transported the prisoner to the District Four Office.

88. D The prisoner was fingerprinted and photographed at 5:04 A.M.

89. B The answer to this question was in the first sentence of the first paragraph. If you followed our recommended strategy and read the stem of the question before the passage, you would have earned one quick point with ease and very quickly.

90. C This answer is in the very last sentence of the last paragraph. The drugs were secured in a sealed envelope.

91. C According to the information contained in the story, there is no one around. Therefore, after notifying the patrol supervisor and the detectives, and after calling for an ambulance and roping off the area, the next step for the officer is as outlined in Step 4, which is recording all observations in his Memo Book.

92. B Sentence 2 is a better sentence to begin the report than sentence 3. As we have often mentioned, police reports many times begin with a statement as to how the officer became involved in the incident and at what time his involvement began. We can therefore eliminate Choices A and C. As the next step we usually recommend finding which sentence should come last. But, in this case, both of the remaining choices suggest that sentence 4 is the last sentence. Therefore, we should seek to establish which sentence should come second. Examination reveals that sentence 3 should be second and ahead of sentence 5 since a description must be obtained before it can be transmitted to the radio dispatcher.

93. C As stated in the stem of the question, Mr. Vanderbilt intended to cause serious physical injury to Mr. Verde (he intended to break his ribs). Instead, however, Vanderbilt caused Verde's death. According to the definitions given, that is Manslaughter 1st degree.

94. A The procedure requires that officers observe locations where criminal activities may be taking place. Neighborhood residents complaining of youths coming and going from an abandoned building would require further observation.

95. B It was Jimmy Warren who stated that he saw Arthur Gonzalez, the superintendent, shoot Lopez.

96. D This answer is found in the last sentence of the passage.

97. A The arrested person, Arthur Gonzalez, was a superintendent.

98. D The police found Lopez lying in the street in front of 226 West 64th Street.

99. C All of the heroin sales occur on Jones Road. Therefore, we can eliminate Choices A and D. Choice B can be eliminated since Thursday is not a high heroin sale day. Choice C offers the best place, days, and times to combat heroin sales.

100. A Choice C does not offer any coverage on Saturdays, while Choice D disregards the need for coverage on Tuesdays. Both of these choices can be eliminated. Choice A offers better coverage than Choice B since it suggests more accurate times of the day for patrol to take place to combat drug sales.

101. A Sentence 1 must follow sentence 2 since, before a police officer can respond to "the scene," some notification must be made to the police about the incident. Therefore, sentence 2 must come first and Choices B and C can be eliminated. Sentence 4 should come after sentence 3 since the feeling that the case was one involving possible child abuse should be based on some information which has been obtained by the police. Therefore, sentence 4 must come last and Choice D can be eliminated, leaving us with Choice A as our answer.

102. D Choice A is incorrect because it does not clearly identify the witness. Choice B is incorrect because it fails to identify the victim. Choice C is incorrect because, while it names the witness, it is not clear concerning the identity of the victim.

103. C Choice A is incorrect because it gives the impression that Wall is the witness and not the suspect. Choice B is incorrect because it confuses the time of reporting of the crime with the time of occurrence of the crime. Choice D is incorrect because it gives the impression that the store owner, Donna Miller, was present at the time of the theft from the cash register even though there is no information to support that impression.

104. B In this questions, the officer acted improperly because Ruth Carter, the prisoner's sister, appeared to be intoxicated when she entered the station house. Therefore, it did not appear that she was capable of providing adequate supervision to her brother.

105. C According to the information given, the car accidents are occurring on Merrick Street.

106. C The robberies are occurring on Fridays through Mondays, between 7:00 P.M. and 11:00 P.M. Therefore, the most appropriate tour for Officer Cruz to work is as indicated in Choice C.

107. A Before any information from Mr. Gustav can be recorded in a police report, he should be identified. Thus, sentence 5 should precede sentence 1. Therefore, we can eliminate

Choices B and D. The most logical way to conclude the report is with a disposition of the property as in sentence 3. Choice A is the answer.

108. B After advising the juvenile and the parents of their rights, an arrest report should be prepared (see Steps 4 and 5).

109. D Choice A is incorrect because it is not clear if the witness observed the stabbing while entering the lobby, or if the suspect stabbed the victim while entering the lobby. Choice B is incorrect because it confuses the time of reporting of the crime with the time of occurrence of the crime (a very common error in this type of question). Choice C fails to clearly identify the victim.

110. C After attempting to persuade or prevent the man from jumping, the assistance of friends or relatives should be sought (see Steps 2 and 3).

111. C According to the procedure, when a juvenile offender is transported in a patrol wagon, the juvenile offender should ride in the front compartment and any adult prisoners should be transported in the rear compartment of the patrol wagon. Choice A may sound reasonable but it is not mentioned in the procedure. Remember to base your answer solely on the procedure given.

112. B Sentence 4 must come before sentence 5 since beginning a report with "he" without identifying who "he" is violates the principles of good report writing and is not logical. Thus, we can eliminate Choices A and C. Sentence 2 should come last and should be preceded by some explanation as to why the police would ask a citizen to search the immediate area with them. Choice B is the correct answer.

113. B, C The object of this type of question is to match the descriptions of the perpetrators of past crimes with the description of the suspect in a current investigation. The strategy we recommend to answer these questions is to first examine the description of the perpetrator of the current crime. You should note the gender, race, age, height, and weight given in the description of the current suspect. Then you should match that description with the other descriptions given of past perpetrators. Usually the descriptions should be considered similar if the ages are within five years, and the heights are within two inches, and the weights are within ten pounds. After eliminating as many suspects as possible, then eliminate any remaining suspects based on distinguishing marks such as scars, tattoos, and birthmarks. Remember, that just because a victim did not report a distinguishing mark, such as a scar, it doesn't mean that the descriptions do not match. Perhaps the scar was covered by a shirt, or eyeglasses, or any other article of clothing. In these cases the examiner will usually indicate that the suspect was wearing such clothing or glasses or the like. In this question, all of the suspects were male whites who were about the same age, height, and weight. The suspect in robbery number 4 was matched with the suspect in robbery number 2 through the tattoo on the right arm. The suspect in robbery number 4 was matched with the suspect in robbery number 3 by the scar on the left hand. However, the suspect in robbery number 1 was eliminated as a match for the suspect in robbery number 4 because of the scar on his right wrist. Bear in mind that, in these questions, clothing, hair color, and facial hair are not too significant since they can be easily changed by a suspect. Also note that the original key listed only Choice B as being correct, but the final key issued after the protests were considered included Choice C as a correct answer. Therefore, if you selected either B or C, take credit for a correct choice.

114. A Choice B is incorrect because it does not clearly indicate who is married to Raymond Schwartz. Choice C is incorrect because it does not explain exactly who was involved in the argument. Choice D is incorrect because it gives the impression that Cathy Morris was cut.

115. D The information given indicates that the victim was assaulted by her ex-boyfriend, Dominick DeLuca. Neither Choice A, nor B, nor C makes this clear to the reader. However, Choice D is very explicit in stating this.

116. A Choice A would allow the officer to patrol for three hours when purse snatchings are occurring and for two hours when burglaries are occurring. In addition, by working Tuesday through Saturday, the officer would be on patrol on the days of high incidence of both purse snatchings and burglaries.

117. A After informing the prisoner that he/she might be eligible for a Desk Appearance Ticket, the officer should check to see if the prisoner is wanted for any other crime by checking with the Central Warrant Unit (see Steps 1 and 2).

118. D The report should begin with sentence 4 since that sentence explains how the incident came to the attention of the police. Therefore, we can eliminate Choices B and C. Since both Choices A and D end with sentence 3, we must look at the middle sentences to determine our answer. And, when we go to the middle sentences, we first look at the second sentence. In this case, sentence 2 must come before sentence 1, otherwise, the officer would be asking the girl for a description of two men the officer had already encountered. Therefore, Choice A can be eliminated.

119. D Regardless of how reasonable and logical it may seem to allow the prisoner this visitor, you must follow the given procedure. Since the prisoner did not ask to see the visitor, who is a lawyer as well as being a relative, the visitor must first obtain written permission for the visit. The answer would have been different if the prisoner had requested to see his lawyer cousin.

120. B The procedure states that when an officer discovers that a driver's license is suspended or revoked, the officer should then confiscate (take) the driver's license from the driver (see Step 1).

121. C By taking their meals (going on a lunch break) during the times suggested in Choice C, both officers would be absent from their posts after the time periods in which the crimes seem to be occurring.

122. C In non-felony cases, as this one is, if attempts to mediate are unsuccessful and the complainant wants the offender arrested, the officer should arrest the offender (see Procedure 5).

123. A Someone standing near a bank cash machine watching people withdraw money is certainly acting in a suspicious manner. Notice how the examiner included in Choice C that the two young men were running toward a park. This was done to make their action of running not appear to be suspicious.

124. D Since two of the witnesses state that the vehicle is a blue Chevrolet, we focus on Choices A and D. Since two of the witnesses state that the license plate ends with the letters "BAT," we eliminate Choice A and select Choice D as our answer. Note that this is one question type when we use information from choices we have eliminated to arrive at the correct answer.

125. A, B Choice A describes Robbery in the second degree because there are two robbers and they forcibly stole property. Choice B describes Robbery in the second degree because the robber displayed what appeared to be a firearm of some sort (his extended finger in his pocket). The original key listed Choice A as the answer but the final key included Choice B. Take credit if you selected either choice.

126. D The first step in this procedure requires the officer to inform the person in custody of the reason for the arrest *unless* the person arrested physically resists or attempts to flee. In this question the person in custody attempted to flee so it is not necessary to follow Step 1. Therefore, the next thing for the officer to do is to follow the procedure in Step 2, which is to handcuff the prisoner with his hands behind his back.

127. C This report should begin with sentence 3 which explains how the incident came to the attention of the officer. Therefore, we can eliminate Choices B and D. Since both of the remaining choices end with sentence 4, we must move to the middle sentences. Since sentence 5 refers to "the man," and sentence 1 refers to "a man," sentence 1 must come before sentence 5. Therefore, sentence 1 is the second sentence and our answer should be Choice C.

128. C This question is slightly different from the usual directed patrol question. Here, you are told the tour the officers will work, which is 10:00 P.M. to 6:00 A.M. Given that fact you are asked to select the best area for them to work during 10:00 P.M. and 6:00 A.M. to reduce the incidence of crime. Since all of the auto thefts occur between midnight and 6:00 A.M., and they all occur on Diamond Avenue, the officers are most likely to reduce the incidence of crime by working their tour on Diamond Avenue.

129. B The officer's actions are correct for the reasons stated in Choice B which correspond with the requirements outlined in Steps 1 and 2 of the procedure. Note that although the reason given in Choice D sounds entirely logical, it was not stated in the procedure and cannot be the answer.

130. C Sentence 3 cannot come first since it indicates that the officer yelled to "them," and someone reading the report would have no way of knowing to whom "them" refers. Therefore, we can eliminate Choices B and D. Examining the remaining Choices A and C, we see that sentence 4 is the better ending sentence since it offers a conclusion to the report. In this kind of sentence ordering type questions, it should be apparent that in most cases it is *not* necessary to examine each of the sentences in each of the choices. To do so is a waste of valuable time.

131. D After serving the violator with a summons, the officer should prepare a receipt for the firearms and give a copy to the violator. See Steps 2b and 2c.

132. A Officer Ramos was correct in his actions because someone's life was endangered (see Step 3a of the procedure). Although Choice C is tempting, you should not have selected it because their was no mention in the story of drugs being in the apartment. Remember to base your answers solely on the basis of the information given.

133. C Sentence 3 places the perpetrator at the scene of the crime. It must come before sentence 1. Therefore, we can eliminate Choices A and B. Sentence 4 explains how the perpetrator left the scene and should conclude the report. We can eliminate Choice D and select Choice C.

134. B Only Foss attempted to prevent the officer from making the arrest.

135. C The officer believed that the violator did not intend to violate the law. Therefore, according to the procedure, it is appropriate for the officer to exercise discretion and not issue a summons.

136. B Choice A is incorrect because it does not identify the victim. Choice C is incorrect because it gives the impression that it was the perpetrator who was walking home when the crime occurred. Choice D is incorrect because it does not explain who grabbed whom.

137. A Choice B is incorrect because it gives the impression that the victim was involved in committing the robbery. Choice C is incorrect because it confuses the place of the report with the place of occurrence. Choice D is incorrect because it gives the impression that the suspect is a witness.

138. D After giving the information indicated in Step 2, subdivisions A through D, the officer should follow subdivision E and give the radio dispatcher a description of the occupants of the auto.

139. D Step 5 of the procedure indicates that the dispatcher should be notified if the pursued vehicle is lost. Since this is what occurred in the narrative, the answer is indicated in Choice D.

140. C Choices A and D are incorrect since they both give the impression that two separate robberies took place. Choice B is incorrect because it gives the impression that the owner could not give a description because the police arrived soon after the incident. In no way does this explain the facts. The answer is Choice C.

141. D Choice A is incorrect because it confuses the place of occurrence with the place of reporting. Choice B is incorrect because it gives the impression that the victim was armed with a gun. Choice C is incorrect because it does not clearly identify the victim.

142. C In "matching sketches" questions, you must eliminate each of the incorrect choices for a specific reason to consistently select the correct choice. Choices A and D can be eliminated by noting that they do not have chin clefts. Choice B can be eliminated because the pupils of the eyes are different from the subject's pupils.

143. C Choices A and B can be eliminated because of the shape of their nostrils. Choice D can be eliminated because of the chin structure.

144. A Choices B and D can be eliminated because of the shape of their noses. Choice C can be eliminated by an examination of his ears.

145. A Choice B can be eliminated by a comparison of the jaw and the chin structure. Choices C and D can be eliminated by examining their noses. Choice D also has different ears.

146. B Choices A and C can be eliminated because they have clefts in their chins. Choice D has different shaped eyes.

147. D Eliminate Choice A because of a fuller top lip, Choice B because of his nose, and Choice C because of his chin.

148. C Eliminate Choice A because of her nose, Choice B because of her chin, and Choice D because of her ears.

149. A Eliminate Choice B because of his chin structure, Choice C because of the lack of a mole under his right eye, and Choice D because of his ears.

150. B Eliminate Choice A because of the shape of her chin, Choice C because of her nose, and Choice D because of her mouth.

A FINAL WORD

CHAPTER 16

A Strategy for Final Preparation

The time draws near. What should be done in the days before the examination?

Do not be fearful. If you have prepared well, you should do well. Remember, while you may be taking the examination soon, you have helped yourself pass the examination every time you prepared with this text. In a sense, therefore, you will be collecting your reward when you take the examination.

But what actions should be taken on the days just before the examination, and, particularly, on the examination day?

The Countdown

SEVEN DAYS BEFORE THE EXAMINATION

Review the Diagnostic Examination in Chapter 3. Identify the areas in which you have the greatest difficulty.

Some time during this week, you should ensure that you know the exact location of the examination site and how to get there. If you are going on public transportation, take a "dry run." Get used to where the bus or train stops. Ask about the transportation schedule for the day of the examination.

Chances are that the examination will be given on a weekend. Do not be left standing waiting for a bus or train that does not run on the weekend. It has happened. You have greatly increased your chances of successfully competing in the examination by following the instructions given in this text. But, you have to get there.

The same applies if you are driving. Make sure the car you are using is in mechanical order. It is not a bad idea to have someone drive for you, if you can. In this way, should any difficulties with the vehicle arise, you can continue on your own. Be certain that you know the route to the examination, and be sure that you know where a safe, legal parking area exists. Taking the examination while you are preoccupied about your car is not a good idea. Give yourself every advantage.

SIX AND FIVE DAYS BEFORE THE EXAMINATION

Zero in on the chapter(s) which deal(s) with your greatest weakness. For example, if your taking of the Diagnostic Exam or the three practice examinations indicates a problem in understanding legal definitions, then you should be concentrating on Chapter 10. Spend these two days on this.

FOUR, THREE, AND TWO DAYS BEFORE THE EXAMINATION

On each of these three days, review one of the sample police officer examinations given in previous chapters. This will re-acquaint you with what to expect when you take the actual examination. Review the tests under simulated examination conditions, as follows.

Sit in a room at a desk or table. Time yourself. Make sure you stay within the time allotted. You will then be less uneasy about this during the actual examination. If you are a smoker, do not smoke during the practice examination. Chances are that you will not be able to smoke during the actual examination. Use the test techniques explained in Chapter 2.

Use the same kind of pencil you will use on examination day. Usually, you will be asked to bring a #2 lead pencil. Remember, the idea is to make everything as close to what you will be experiencing on examination day.

ONE DAY BEFORE THE EXAMINATION

Read Chapter 2 which deals with test taking. That's it. By now you should be prepared. Do not try to cram on this last day. Your test preparation is over. Begin to relax.

Eat a normal dinner on the evening before the examination. Take some good advice. Get your regular amount of sleep the night before. While you do not need more rest, you should not be getting less. Be very careful of taking sedatives to help you sleep. It may be harmful to you the next day.

The theme is to keep yourself as you would at any other time. Remember, tomorrow is just another day. You have taken good steps to pass the examination; nothing more need be done.

THE DAY OF THE EXAMINATION

On the day of the examination, wake up with enough time to dress, have a good breakfast, and check over whatever test-taking equipment you may be bringing with you. While an alarm clock may get you up, a call from a friend is sometimes helpful.

A word about test-taking equipment. Follow whatever instructions you may have received from the testing agency (for example, pencils, etc.). Bring an extra sweater. If it's not needed to keep warm, you can always take it off. (You may want to sit on it; a desk seat can become terribly uncomfortable after an hour or so.)

What else? Well, a pencil sharpener is helpful, as are a good eraser, and a working pen to sign in ink if required.

Some candidates have found that a chocolate candy bar is a source of quick energy during the examination. If you wear glasses, make sure you have an extra pair, if possible, and something with which to clean them.

THE EXAMINATION

When you arrive at the examination, follow the instructions of the proctors, and be sure to bring a watch with the correct time. Go to your assigned room and sit. Inspect your seat and report any problems to your proctor immediately. Follow instructions to the letter. You have been exposed to sample examinations in previous chapters. You are no stranger to the process. If you have done what we have outlined in this text, you should do well. Believe in your ability. Many others just like you have had to do it. You can too?

GOOD LUCK!

NOTES

NOTES

NOTES